The Java® Language Specification

Java SE 7 Edition

The Java® Language Specification

Java SE 7 Edition

James Gosling
Bill Joy
Guy Steele
Gilad Bracha
Alex Buckley

♦Addison-Wesley

Upper Saddle River, NJ • Boston • Indianapolis • San Francisco
New York • Toronto • Montreal • London • Munich • Paris • Madrid
Capetown • Sydney • Tokyo • Singapore • Mexico City

The publisher offers excellent discounts on this book when ordered in quantity for bulk purchases or special sales, which may include electronic versions and/or custom covers and content particular to your business, training goals, marketing focus, and branding interests. For more information, please contact U.S. Corporate and Government Sales, (800) 382-3419, corpsales@pearsontechgroup.com. For sales outside the United States, please contact International Sales, international@pearson.com.

Visit us on the Web: informit.com/aw

Library of Congress Control Number: 2012953694
ISBN-13: 978-0-13-326022-9
ISBN-10:   0-13-326022-4

Text printed in the United States on recycled paper at RR Donnelley in Crawfordsville, Indiana. First printing, January 2013.

Table of Contents

14 Blocks and Statements 365

15 Expressions 417

Preface to the Java SE 7 Edition

THE Java® SE 7 Edition of *The Java Language Specification* describes all the features that have been added to the Java programming language in Java SE 7. It also integrates changes made to the Java programming language under maintenance since the Third Edition in 2005.

Readers may send feedback about errors and ambiguities in *The Java Language Specification* to `jls-comments_ww@oracle.com`.

The majority of new features in this edition were specified by JSR 334, *Small Enhancements to the Java Programming Language*, led by Joe Darcy with an Expert Group of Joshua Bloch, Bruce Chapman, Alexey Kudravtsev, Mark Mahieu, Tim Peierls, and Olivier Thomann. The origins of these features lie in *Project Coin*, an OpenJDK project started in 2009 with the goal of "Making things programmers do every day easier". The project solicited proposals from the Java community for broadly useful language features that were, in comparison with "large" features like generics, relatively "small" in their specification, implementation, and testing.

Thousands of emails and six dozen proposals later, proposals were accepted from Joshua Bloch (the `try`-with-resources statement), Derek Foster/Bruce Chapman (improvements to literals), Neal Gafter (multi-`catch` and precise rethrow), Bob Lee (simplified variable arity method invocation), and Jeremy Manson (improved type inference for instance creation, a.k.a. the "diamond" syntax). The popular "strings in switch" feature was also accepted. Special thanks are due to Tom Ball, Stephen Colebourne, Rémi Forax, Shams Mahmood Imam, James Lowden, and all those who submitted interesting proposals and thoughtful comments to Project Coin. Over the course of the project, there were essential contributions from Mandy Chung, Jon Gibbons, Brian Goetz, David Holmes, and Dan Smith in areas ranging from library support to language specification. Stuart Marks led a "coinification" effort to apply the features to the Oracle JDK codebase, both to validate their utility and to develop conventions for wider use.

The "diamond" syntax and precise rethrow give type inference a new visibility in the Java programming language. To a great extent, inference is worthwhile only if it produces types no less specific than those in a manifestly-typed program prior to Java SE 7. Otherwise, new code may find inference insufficient, and migration from manifest to inferred types in existing code will be risky. To mitigate the risk, Joe Darcy and Maurizio Cimadamore measured the effectiveness of different inference schemes on a large corpus of open source Java code. Such "quantitative language design" greatly improves confidence in the suitability and safety of the final feature. The challenge of growing a mature language with millions of developers is partially offset by the ability of language designers to learn from developers' actual code.

The Java SE 7 platform adds features that cater for non-Java languages, effectively expanding the computational model of the platform. Without changes, the Java programming language would be unable to access or even express some of these features. Its static type system comes under particular stress when invoking code written in dynamically typed languages. Consequently, method invocation in the Java programming language has been modified to support method handle invocation as defined by JSR 292, *Dynamically Typed Languages on the Java Platform*.

The Java Compatibility Kit (JCK) team whose work helps validate this specification are due an enormous vote of thanks: Leonid Arbouzov, Alexey Gavrilov, Yulia Novozhilova, Sergey Reznick, and Victor Rudometov. Many other colleagues at Oracle (past or present) have also given valuable support to this specification: Uday Dhanikonda, Janet Koenig, Adam Messinger, Mark Reinhold, Georges Saab, Bill Shannon, and Bernard Traversat.

The following individuals have all provided many valuable comments which improved this specification: J. Stephen Adamczyk, Peter Ahé, Davide Ancona, Michael Bailey, Dmitry Batrak, Joshua Bloch, Kevin Bourrillion, Richard Bosworth, Martin Bravenboer, Martin Buchholz, Didier Cruette, Glenn Colman, Neal Gafter, Jim Holmlund, Ric Holt, Philippe Mulet, Bill Pugh, Vladimir Reshetnikov, John Spicer, Robert Stroud, and Mattias Ulbrich.

This edition is the first to be written in the DocBook XML format. Metadata in the XML markup forms a kind of static type system, classifying each paragraph by its role, such as a definition or an error. The reward is much crisper conformance testing. Many thanks go to Robert Stayton for sharing his considerable DocBook expertise and for helping to render DocBook in the traditional look and feel of *The Java Language Specification*.

Alex Buckley
Santa Clara, California

June, 2011

Preface to the Third Edition

THE Java SE 5.0 platform represents the largest set of changes in the history of the Java programming language. Generics, annotations, autoboxing and unboxing, enum types, foreach loops, variable arity methods, and static imports are all new to the language as of Autumn 2004.

This Third Edition of *The Java Language Specification* reflects these developments. It integrates all the changes made to the Java programming language since the publication of the Second Edition in 2000, including asserts from J2SE 1.4.

The Java programming language has grown a great deal in these past four years. Unfortunately, it is unrealistic to shrink a commercially successful programming language - only to grow it more and more. The challenge of managing this growth under the constraints of compatibility and the conflicting demands of a wide variety of uses and users is non-trivial. I can only hope that we have met this challenge successfully with this specification; time will tell.

This specification builds on the efforts of many people, both at Sun Microsystems and outside it.

The most crucial contribution is that of the people who actually turn the specification into real software. Chief among these are the maintainers of `javac`, the reference compiler for the Java programming language.

Neal Gafter was "Mr. `javac`" during the crucial period in which the large changes described here were integrated and productized. Neal's dedication and productivity can honestly be described as heroic. We literally could not have completed the task without him. In addition, his insight and skill made a huge contribution to the design of the new language features across the board. No one deserves more credit for this version of the Java programming language than he - but any blame for its deficiencies should be directed at myself and the members of the many JSR Expert Groups!

Neal has gone on in search of new challenges, and has been succeeded by Peter von der Ahé, who continues to improve and stengthen the implementation. Before Neal's involvement, Bill Maddox was in charge of `javac` when the previous edition was completed, and he nursed features such as generics and asserts through their early days.

Another individual who deserves to be singled out is Joshua Bloch. Josh participated in endless language design discussions, chaired several Expert Groups and was a key contributor to the Java platform. It is fair to say that Josh and Neal care more about this book than I do myself!

Many parts of the specification were developed by various Expert Groups in the framework of the Java Community Process.

The most pervasive set of language changes is the result of JSR 14, *Adding Generics to the Java Programming Language*. The members of the JSR 14 Expert Group were Norman Cohen, Christian Kemper, Martin Odersky, Kresten Krab Thorup, Philip Wadler, and myself. In the early stages, Sven-Eric Panitz and Steve Marx were members as well. All deserve thanks for their participation.

JSR 14 represents an unprecedented effort to fundamentally extend the type system of a widely used programming language under very stringent compatibility requirements. A prolonged and arduous process of design and implementation led us to the current language extension. Long before the JSR for generics was initiated, Martin Odersky and Philip Wadler had created an experimental language called Pizza to explore the ideas involved. In the spring of 1998, David Stoutamire and myself began a collaboration with Martin and Philip based on those ideas, that resulted in GJ. When the JSR 14 Expert Group was convened, GJ was chosen as the basis for extending the Java programming language. Martin Odersky implemented the GJ compiler, and his implementation became the basis for `javac` (starting with JDK 1.3, even though generics were disabled until 1.5).

The theoretical basis for the core of the generic type system owes a great debt to the expertise of Martin Odersky and Philip Wadler. Later, the system was extended with wildcards. These were based on the work of Atsushi Igarashi and Mirko Viroli, which itself built on earlier work by Kresten Thorup and Mads Torgersen. Wildcards were initially designed and implemented as part of a collaboration between Sun and Aarhus University. Neal Gafter and myself participated on Sun's behalf, and Erik Ernst and Mads Torgersen, together with Peter von der Ahé and Christian Plesner-Hansen, represented Aarhus. Thanks to Ole Lehrmann-Madsen for enabling and supporting that work.

Joe Darcy and Ken Russell implemented much of the specific support for reflection of generics. Neal Gafter, Josh Bloch and Mark Reinhold did a huge amount of work generifying the JDK libraries.

Honorable mention must go to individuals whose comments on the generics design made a significant difference. Alan Jeffrey made crucial contributions to JSR 14 by pointing out subtle flaws in the original type system. Bob Deen suggested the "? super T" syntax for lower bounded wildcards.

JSR 201 included a series of changes: autoboxing, enums, foreach loops, variable arity methods and static import. The members of the JSR 201 Expert Group were Cédric Beust, David Biesack, Joshua Bloch (co-chair), Corky Cartwright, Jim des Rivieres, David Flanagan, Christian Kemper, Doug Lea, Changshin Lee, Tim Peierls, Michel Trudeau, and myself (co-chair). Enums and the foreach loop were primarily designed by Josh Bloch and Neal Gafter. Variable arity methods would never have made it into the Java programming language without Neal's special efforts designing them (not to mention the small matter of implementing them).

Josh Bloch bravely took upon himself the responsibility for JSR 175, which added annotations to the Java programming language. The members of JSR 175 Expert Group were Cédric Beust, Joshua Bloch (chair), Ted Farrell, Mike French, Gregor Kiczales, Doug Lea, Deeptendu Majunder, Simon Nash, Ted Neward, Roly Perera, Manfred Schneider, Blake Stone, and Josh Street. Neal Gafter, as usual, was a major contributor on this front as well.

Another change in this edition is a complete revision of the Java memory model, undertaken by JSR 133. The members of the JSR 133 Expert Group were Hans Boehm, Doug Lea, Tim Lindholm (co-chair), Bill Pugh (co-chair), Martin Trotter, and Jerry Schwarz. The primary technical authors of the memory model are Sarita Adve, Jeremy Manson, and Bill Pugh. The Java memory model chapter in this book is in fact almost entirely their work, with only editorial revisions. Joseph Bowbeer, David Holmes, Victor Luchangco, and Jan-Willem Maessen made significant contributions as well. Key sections dealing with finalization in Chapter 12 owe much to this work as well, and especially to Doug Lea.

Many people have provided valuable comments on this edition.

I'd like to express my gratitude to Archibald Putt, who provided insight and encouragement. His writings are always an inspiration. Thanks once again to Joe Darcy for introducing us, as well as for many useful comments, and his specific contributions on numerical issues and the design of hexadecimal literals.

Many colleagues at Sun (past or present) have provided useful feedback and discussion, and helped produce this work in myriad ways: Andrew Bennett, Martin Buchholz, Jerry Driscoll, Robert Field, Jonathan Gibbons, Graham Hamilton, Mimi Hills, Jim Holmlund, Janet Koenig, Jeff Norton, Scott Seligman, Wei Tao, and David Ungar.

Special thanks to Laurie Tolson, my manager, for her support throughout the long process of deriving these specifications.

The following individuals all provided many valuable comments that have contributed to this specification: Scott Annanian, Martin Bravenboer, Bruce

Chapman, Lawrence Gonsalves, Tim Hanson, David Holmes, Angelika Langer, Pat Lavarre, Philippe Mulet, and Cal Varnson.

Ann Sellers, Greg Doench, and John Fuller at Addison-Wesley were exceedingly patient and ensured that the book materialized, despite the many missed deadlines for this text.

As always, I thank my wife Weihong and my son Teva for their support and cooperation.

Gilad Bracha
Los Altos, California

January, 2005

Preface to the Second Edition

OVER the past few years, the Java programming language has enjoyed unprecedented success. This success has brought a challenge: along with explosive growth in popularity, there has been explosive growth in the demands made on the language and its libraries. To meet this challenge, the language has grown as well (fortunately, not explosively) and so have the libraries.

This Second Edition of *The Java Language Specification* reflects these developments. It integrates all the changes made to the Java programming language since the publication of the First Edition in 1996. The bulk of these changes were made in the 1.1 release of the Java platform in 1997, and revolve around the addition of nested type declarations. Later modifications pertained to floating-point operations. In addition, this edition incorporates important clarifications and amendments involving method lookup and binary compatibility.

This specification defines the language as it exists today. The Java programming language is likely to continue to evolve. At this writing, there are ongoing initiatives through the Java Community Process to extend the language with generic types and assertions, refine the memory model, etc. However, it would be inappropriate to delay the publication of the Second Edition until these efforts are concluded.

The specifications of the libraries are now far too large to fit into this volume, and they continue to evolve. Consequently, API specifications have been removed from this book. The library specifications can be found on the Web; this specification now concentrates solely on the Java programming language proper.

Many people contributed to this book, directly and indirectly. Tim Lindholm brought extraordinary dedication to his role as technical editor of the Java Series. He also made invaluable technical contributions, especially on floating-point issues. The book would likely not see the light of day without him. Lisa Friendly, the Series editor, provided encouragement and advice for which I am very thankful.

David Bowen first suggested that I get involved in the specifications of the Java platform. I am grateful to him for introducing me to this uncommonly rich area.

John Rose, the father of nested types in the Java programming language, has been unfailingly gracious and supportive of my attempts to specify them accurately.

Many people have provided valuable comments on this edition. Special thanks go to Roly Perera at Ergnosis and to Leonid Arbouzov and his colleagues on the

Java platform conformance team in Novosibirsk: Konstantin Bobrovsky, Natalia Golovleva, Vladimir Ivanov, Alexei Kaigorodov, Serguei Katkov, Dmitri Khukhro, Eugene Latkin, Ilya Neverov, Pavel Ozhdikhin, Igor Pyankov, Viatcheslav Rybalov, Serguei Samoilidi, Maxim Sokolnikov, and Vitaly Tchaiko. Their thorough reading of earlier drafts has greatly improved the accuracy of this specification.

I am indebted to Martin Odersky and to Andrew Bennett and the members of the `javac` compiler team, past and present: Iris Garcia, Bill Maddox, David Stoutamire, and Todd Turnidge. They all worked hard to make sure the reference implementation conformed to the specification. For many enjoyable technical exchanges, I thank them and my other colleagues at Sun: Lars Bak, Joshua Bloch, Cliff Click, Robert Field, Mohammad Gharahgouzloo, Ben Gomes, Steffen Grarup, Robert Griesemer, Graham Hamilton, Gordon Hirsch, Peter Kessler, Sheng Liang, James McIlree, Philip Milne, Srdjan Mitrovic, Anand Palaniswamy, Mike Paleczny, Mark Reinhold, Kenneth Russell, Rene Schmidt, David Ungar, Chris Vick, and Hong Zhang.

Tricia Jordan, my manager, has been a model of patience, consideration and understanding. Thanks are also due to Larry Abrahams, director of Java 2 Standard Edition, for supporting this work.

The following individuals all provided useful comments that have contributed to this specification: Godmar Bak, Hans Boehm, Philippe Charles, David Chase, Joe Darcy, Jim des Rivieres, Sophia Drossopoulou, Susan Eisenbach, Paul Haahr, Urs Hoelzle, Bart Jacobs, Kent Johnson, Mark Lillibridge, Norbert Lindenberg, Phillipe Mulet, Kelly O'Hair, Bill Pugh, Cameron Purdy, Anthony Scian, Janice Shepherd, David Shields, John Spicer, Lee Worall, and David Wragg.

Suzette Pelouch provided invaluable assistance with the index and, together with Doug Kramer and Atul Dambalkar, assisted with FrameMaker expertise; Mike Hendrickson and Julie Dinicola at Addison-Wesley were gracious, helpful and ultimately made this book a reality.

On a personal note, I thank my wife Weihong for her love and support.

Finally, I'd like to thank my coauthors, James Gosling, Bill Joy, and Guy Steele for inviting me to participate in this work. It has been a pleasure and a privilege.

Gilad Bracha
Los Altos, California

April, 2000

Preface to the First Edition

T HE Java programming language was originally called Oak, and was designed for use in embedded consumer-electronic applications by James Gosling. After several years of experience with the language, and significant contributions by Ed Frank, Patrick Naughton, Jonathan Payne, and Chris Warth it was retargeted to the Internet, renamed, and substantially revised to be the language specified here. The final form of the language was defined by James Gosling, Bill Joy, Guy Steele, Richard Tuck, Frank Yellin, and Arthur van Hoff, with help from Graham Hamilton, Tim Lindholm, and many other friends and colleagues.

The Java programming language is a general-purpose concurrent class-based object-oriented programming language, specifically designed to have as few implementation dependencies as possible. It allows application developers to write a program once and then be able to run it everywhere on the Internet.

This book attempts a complete specification of the syntax and semantics of the language. We intend that the behavior of every language construct is specified here, so that all implementations will accept the same programs. Except for timing dependencies or other non-determinisms and given sufficient time and sufficient memory space, a program written in the Java programming language should compute the same result on all machines and in all implementations.

We believe that the Java programming language is a mature language, ready for widespread use. Nevertheless, we expect some evolution of the language in the years to come. We intend to manage this evolution in a way that is completely compatible with existing applications. To do this, we intend to make relatively few new versions of the language. Compilers and systems will be able to support the several versions simultaneously, with complete compatibility.

Much research and experimentation with the Java platform is already underway. We encourage this work, and will continue to cooperate with external groups to explore improvements to the language and platform. For example, we have already received several interesting proposals for parameterized types. In technically difficult areas, near the state of the art, this kind of research collaboration is essential.

We acknowledge and thank the many people who have contributed to this book through their excellent feedback, assistance and encouragement:

Particularly thorough, careful, and thoughtful reviews of drafts were provided by Tom Cargill, Peter Deutsch, Paul Hilfinger, Masayuki Ida, David Moon, Steven Muchnick, Charles L. Perkins, Chris Van Wyk, Steve Vinoski, Philip Wadler, Daniel Weinreb, and Kenneth Zadeck. We are very grateful for their extraordinary volunteer efforts.

We are also grateful for reviews, questions, comments, and suggestions from Stephen Adams, Bowen Alpern, Glenn Ammons, Leonid Arbouzov, Kim Bruce, Edwin Chan, David Chase, Pavel Curtis, Drew Dean, William Dietz, David Dill, Patrick Dussud, Ed Felten, John Giannandrea, John Gilmore, Charles Gust, Warren Harris, Lee Hasiuk, Mike Hendrickson, Mark Hill, Urs Hoelzle, Roger Hoover, Susan Flynn Hummel, Christopher Jang, Mick Jordan, Mukesh Kacker, Peter Kessler, James Larus, Derek Lieber, Bill McKeeman, Steve Naroff, Evi Nemeth, Robert O'Callahan, Dave Papay, Craig Partridge, Scott Pfeffer, Eric Raymond, Jim Roskind, Jim Russell, William Scherlis, Edith Schonberg, Anthony Scian, Matthew Self, Janice Shepherd, Kathy Stark, Barbara Steele, Rob Strom, William Waite, Greg Weeks, and Bob Wilson. (This list was generated semi-automatically from our E-mail records. We apologize if we have omitted anyone.)

The feedback from all these reviewers was invaluable to us in improving the definition of the language as well as the form of the presentation in this book. We thank them for their diligence. Any remaining errors in this book - we hope they are few - are our responsibility and not theirs.

We thank Francesca Freedman and Doug Kramer for assistance with matters of typography and layout. We thank Dan Mills of Adobe Systems Incorporated for assistance in exploring possible choices of typefaces.

Many of our colleagues at Sun Microsystems have helped us in one way or another. Lisa Friendly, our series editor, managed our relationship with Addison-Wesley. Susan Stambaugh managed the distribution of many hundreds of copies of drafts to reviewers. We received valuable assistance and technical advice from Ben Adida, Ole Agesen, Ken Arnold, Rick Cattell, Asmus Freytag, Norm Hardy, Steve Heller, David Hough, Doug Kramer, Nancy Lee, Marianne Mueller, Akira Tanaka, Greg Tarsy, David Ungar, Jim Waldo, Ann Wollrath, Geoff Wyant, and Derek White. We thank Alan Baratz, David Bowen, Mike Clary, John Doerr, Jon Kannegaard, Eric Schmidt, Bob Sproull, Bert Sutherland, and Scott McNealy for leadership and encouragement.

We are thankful for the tools and services we had at our disposal in writing this book: telephones, overnight delivery, desktop workstations, laser printers, photocopiers, text formatting and page layout software, fonts, electronic mail, the World Wide Web, and, of course, the Internet. We live in three different states, scattered across a continent, but collaboration with each other and with our reviewers has seemed almost effortless. Kudos to the thousands of people who have worked over the years to make these excellent tools and services work quickly and reliably.

Mike Hendrickson, Katie Duffy, Simone Payment, and Rosa Aimée González of Addison-Wesley were very helpful, encouraging, and patient during the long process of bringing this book to print. We also thank the copy editors.

Rosemary Simpson worked hard, on a very tight schedule, to create the index. We got into the act at the last minute, however; blame us and not her for any jokes you may find hidden therein.

Finally, we are grateful to our families and friends for their love and support during this last, crazy, year.

In their book *The C Programming Language*, Brian Kernighan and Dennis Ritchie said that they felt that the C language "wears well as one's experience with it grows." If you like C, we think you will like the Java programming language. We hope that it, too, wears well for you.

James Gosling
Cupertino, California

Bill Joy
Aspen, Colorado

Guy Steele
Chelmsford, Massachusetts

July, 1996

CHAPTER 1

Introduction

T HE Java® programming language is a general-purpose, concurrent, class-based, object-oriented language. It is designed to be simple enough that many programmers can achieve fluency in the language. The Java programming language is related to C and C++ but is organized rather differently, with a number of aspects of C and C++ omitted and a few ideas from other languages included. It is intended to be a production language, not a research language, and so, as C. A. R. Hoare suggested in his classic paper on language design, the design has avoided including new and untested features.

The Java programming language is strongly and statically typed. This specification clearly distinguishes between the *compile-time errors* that can and must be detected at compile time, and those that occur at run time. Compile time normally consists of translating programs into a machine-independent byte code representation. Run-time activities include loading and linking of the classes needed to execute a program, optional machine code generation and dynamic optimization of the program, and actual program execution.

The Java programming language is a relatively high-level language, in that details of the machine representation are not available through the language. It includes automatic storage management, typically using a garbage collector, to avoid the safety problems of explicit deallocation (as in C's `free` or C++'s `delete`). High-performance garbage-collected implementations can have bounded pauses to support systems programming and real-time applications. The language does not include any unsafe constructs, such as array accesses without index checking, since such unsafe constructs would cause a program to behave in an unspecified way.

The Java programming language is normally compiled to the bytecoded instruction set and binary format defined in *The Java Virtual Machine Specification, Java SE 7 Edition*.

1.1   Organization of the Specification

Chapter 2 describes grammars and the notation used to present the lexical and syntactic grammars for the language.

Chapter 3 describes the lexical structure of the Java programming language, which is based on C and C++. The language is written in the Unicode character set. It supports the writing of Unicode characters on systems that support only ASCII.

Chapter 4 describes types, values, and variables. Types are subdivided into primitive types and reference types.

The primitive types are defined to be the same on all machines and in all implementations, and are various sizes of two's-complement integers, single- and double-precision IEEE 754 standard floating-point numbers, a `boolean` type, and a Unicode character `char` type. Values of the primitive types do not share state.

Reference types are the class types, the interface types, and the array types. The reference types are implemented by dynamically created objects that are either instances of classes or arrays. Many references to each object can exist. All objects (including arrays) support the methods of the class `Object`, which is the (single) root of the class hierarchy. A predefined `String` class supports Unicode character strings. Classes exist for wrapping primitive values inside of objects. In many cases, wrapping and unwrapping is performed automatically by the compiler (in which case, wrapping is called boxing, and unwrapping is called unboxing). Class and interface declarations may be generic, that is, they may be parameterized by other reference types. Such declarations may then be invoked with specific type arguments.

Variables are typed storage locations. A variable of a primitive type holds a value of that exact primitive type. A variable of a class type can hold a null reference or a reference to an object whose type is that class type or any subclass of that class type. A variable of an interface type can hold a null reference or a reference to an instance of any class that implements the interface. A variable of an array type can hold a null reference or a reference to an array. A variable of class type `Object` can hold a null reference or a reference to any object, whether class instance or array.

Chapter 5 describes conversions and numeric promotions. Conversions change the compile-time type and, sometimes, the value of an expression. These conversions include the boxing and unboxing conversions between primitive types and reference types. Numeric promotions are used to convert the operands of a numeric operator to a common type where an operation can be performed. There are no loopholes in the language; casts on reference types are checked at run time to ensure type safety.

Chapter 6 describes declarations and names, and how to determine what names mean (denote). The language does not require types or their members to be declared before they are used. Declaration order is significant only for local variables, local classes, and the order of initializers of fields in a class or interface.

The Java programming language provides control over the scope of names and supports limitations on external access to members of packages, classes, and interfaces. This helps in writing large programs by distinguishing the implementation of a type from its users and those who extend it. Recommended naming conventions that make for more readable programs are described here.

Chapter 7 describes the structure of a program, which is organized into packages similar to the modules of Modula. The members of a package are classes, interfaces, and subpackages. Packages are divided into compilation units. Compilation units contain type declarations and can import types from other packages to give them short names. Packages have names in a hierarchical name space, and the Internet domain name system can usually be used to form unique package names.

Chapter 8 describes classes. The members of classes are classes, interfaces, fields (variables) and methods. Class variables exist once per class. Class methods operate without reference to a specific object. Instance variables are dynamically created in objects that are instances of classes. Instance methods are invoked on instances of classes; such instances become the current object `this` during their execution, supporting the object-oriented programming style.

Classes support single implementation inheritance, in which the implementation of each class is derived from that of a single superclass, and ultimately from the class `Object`. Variables of a class type can reference an instance of that class or of any subclass of that class, allowing new types to be used with existing methods, polymorphically.

Classes support concurrent programming with `synchronized` methods. Methods declare the checked exceptions that can arise from their execution, which allows compile-time checking to ensure that exceptional conditions are handled. Objects can declare a `finalize` method that will be invoked before the objects are discarded by the garbage collector, allowing the objects to clean up their state.

For simplicity, the language has neither declaration "headers" separate from the implementation of a class nor separate type and class hierarchies.

A special form of classes, enums, support the definition of small sets of values and their manipulation in a type safe manner. Unlike enumerations in other languages, enums are objects and may have their own methods.

Chapter 9 describes interface types, which declare a set of abstract methods, member types, and constants. Classes that are otherwise unrelated can implement the same interface type. A variable of an interface type can contain a reference to any object that implements the interface. Multiple interface inheritance is supported.

Annotation types are specialized interfaces used to annotate declarations. Such annotations are not permitted to affect the semantics of programs in the Java programming language in any way. However, they provide useful input to various tools.

Chapter 10 describes arrays. Array accesses include bounds checking. Arrays are dynamically created objects and may be assigned to variables of type `Object`. The language supports arrays of arrays, rather than multidimensional arrays.

Chapter 11 describes exceptions, which are nonresuming and fully integrated with the language semantics and concurrency mechanisms. There are three kinds of exceptions: checked exceptions, run-time exceptions, and errors. The compiler ensures that checked exceptions are properly handled by requiring that a method or constructor can result in a checked exception only if the method or constructor declares it. This provides compile-time checking that exception handlers exist, and aids programming in the large. Most user-defined exceptions should be checked exceptions. Invalid operations in the program detected by the Java Virtual Machine result in run-time exceptions, such as `NullPointerException`. Errors result from failures detected by the Java Virtual Machine, such as `OutOfMemoryError`. Most simple programs do not try to handle errors.

Chapter 12 describes activities that occur during execution of a program. A program is normally stored as binary files representing compiled classes and interfaces. These binary files can be loaded into a Java Virtual Machine, linked to other classes and interfaces, and initialized.

After initialization, class methods and class variables may be used. Some classes may be instantiated to create new objects of the class type. Objects that are class instances also contain an instance of each superclass of the class, and object creation involves recursive creation of these superclass instances.

When an object is no longer referenced, it may be reclaimed by the garbage collector. If an object declares a finalizer, the finalizer is executed before the object is reclaimed to give the object a last chance to clean up resources that would not otherwise be released. When a class is no longer needed, it may be unloaded.

Chapter 13 describes binary compatibility, specifying the impact of changes to types on other types that use the changed types but have not been recompiled. These considerations are of interest to developers of types that are to be widely distributed, in a continuing series of versions, often through the Internet. Good program development environments automatically recompile dependent code whenever a type is changed, so most programmers need not be concerned about these details.

Chapter 14 describes blocks and statements, which are based on C and C++. The language has no `goto` statement, but includes labeled `break` and `continue` statements. Unlike C, the Java programming language requires `boolean` (or `Boolean`) expressions in control-flow statements, and does not convert types to `boolean` implicitly (except through unboxing), in the hope of catching more errors at compile time. A `synchronized` statement provides basic object-level monitor locking. A `try` statement can include `catch` and `finally` clauses to protect against non-local control transfers.

Chapter 15 describes expressions. This document fully specifies the (apparent) order of evaluation of expressions, for increased determinism and portability. Overloaded methods and constructors are resolved at compile time by picking the most specific method or constructor from those which are applicable.

Chapter 16 describes the precise way in which the language ensures that local variables are definitely set before use. While all other variables are automatically initialized to a default value, the Java programming language does not automatically initialize local variables in order to avoid masking programming errors.

Chapter 17 describes the semantics of threads and locks, which are based on the monitor-based concurrency originally introduced with the Mesa programming language. The Java programming language specifies a memory model for shared-memory multiprocessors that supports high-performance implementations.

Chapter 18 presents a syntactic grammar for the language.

1.2 Example Programs

Most of the example programs given in the text are ready to be executed and are similar in form to:

```
class Test {
```

```
    public static void main(String[] args) {
        for (int i = 0; i < args.length; i++)
            System.out.print(i == 0 ? args[i] : " " + args[i]);
        System.out.println();
    }
}
```

On a machine with the Oracle JDK installed, this class, stored in the file `Test.java`, can be compiled and executed by giving the commands:

```
javac Test.java
java Test Hello, world.
```

producing the output:

```
Hello, world.
```

1.3   Notation

Throughout this specification we refer to classes and interfaces drawn from the Java SE platform API. Whenever we refer to a class or interface (other than those declared in an example) using a single identifier N, the intended reference is to the class or interface named N in the package `java.lang`. We use the canonical name (§6.7) for classes or interfaces from packages other than `java.lang`.

Non-normative information, designed to clarify the specification, is given in smaller, indented text.

> This is non-normative information. It provides intuition, rationale, advice, examples, etc.

1.4   Relationship to Predefined Classes and Interfaces

As noted above, this specification often refers to classes of the Java SE platform API. In particular, some classes have a special relationship with the Java programming language. Examples include classes such as `Object`, `Class`, `ClassLoader`, `String`, `Thread`, and the classes and interfaces in package `java.lang.reflect`, among others. This specification constrains the behavior of such classes and interfaces, but does not provide a complete specification for them. The reader is referred to the Java SE platform API documentation.

Consequently, this specification does not describe reflection in any detail. Many linguistic constructs have analogs in the reflection API, but these are generally not discussed here. For example, when we list the ways in which an object can be created, we generally do not include the ways in which the reflection API can accomplish this. Readers should be aware of these additional mechanisms even though they are not mentioned in the text.

1.5 References

Apple Computer. *Dylan Reference Manual*. Apple Computer Inc., Cupertino, California. September 29, 1995.

Bobrow, Daniel G., Linda G. DeMichiel, Richard P. Gabriel, Sonya E. Keene, Gregor Kiczales, and David A. Moon. *Common Lisp Object System Specification*, X3J13 Document 88-002R, June 1988; appears as Chapter 28 of Steele, Guy. *Common Lisp: The Language*, 2nd ed. Digital Press, 1990, ISBN 1-55558-041-6, 770-864.

Ellis, Margaret A., and Bjarne Stroustrup. *The Annotated C++ Reference Manual*. Addison-Wesley, Reading, Massachusetts, 1990, reprinted with corrections October 1992, ISBN 0-201-51459-1.

Goldberg, Adele and Robson, David. *Smalltalk-80: The Language*. Addison-Wesley, Reading, Massachusetts, 1989, ISBN 0-201-13688-0.

Harbison, Samuel. *Modula-3*. Prentice Hall, Englewood Cliffs, New Jersey, 1992, ISBN 0-13-596396.

Hoare, C. A. R. *Hints on Programming Language Design*. Stanford University Computer Science Department Technical Report No. CS-73-403, December 1973. Reprinted in SIGACT/SIGPLAN Symposium on Principles of Programming Languages. Association for Computing Machinery, New York, October 1973.

IEEE Standard for Binary Floating-Point Arithmetic. ANSI/IEEE Std. 754-1985. Available from Global Engineering Documents, 15 Inverness Way East, Englewood, Colorado 80112-5704 USA; 800-854-7179.

Kernighan, Brian W., and Dennis M. Ritchie. *The C Programming Language*, 2nd ed. Prentice Hall, Englewood Cliffs, New Jersey, 1988, ISBN 0-13-110362-8.

Madsen, Ole Lehrmann, Birger Møller-Pedersen, and Kristen Nygaard. *Object-Oriented Programming in the Beta Programming Language*. Addison-Wesley, Reading, Massachusetts, 1993, ISBN 0-201-62430-3.

Mitchell, James G., William Maybury, and Richard Sweet. *The Mesa Programming Language, Version 5.0*. Xerox PARC, Palo Alto, California, CSL 79-3, April 1979.

Stroustrup, Bjarne. *The C++ Progamming Language*, 2nd ed. Addison-Wesley, Reading, Massachusetts, 1991, reprinted with corrections January 1994, ISBN 0-201-53992-6.

Unicode Consortium, The. *The Unicode Standard, Version 6.0.0*. Mountain View, CA, 2011, ISBN 978-1-936213-01-6.

CHAPTER 2

Grammars

THIS chapter describes the context-free grammars used in this specification to define the lexical and syntactic structure of a program.

2.1 Context-Free Grammars

A *context-free grammar* consists of a number of *productions*. Each production has an abstract symbol called a *nonterminal* as its *left-hand side*, and a sequence of one or more nonterminal and *terminal* symbols as its *right-hand side*. For each grammar, the terminal symbols are drawn from a specified *alphabet*.

Starting from a sentence consisting of a single distinguished nonterminal, called the *goal symbol*, a given context-free grammar specifies a language, namely, the set of possible sequences of terminal symbols that can result from repeatedly replacing any nonterminal in the sequence with a right-hand side of a production for which the nonterminal is the left-hand side.

2.2 The Lexical Grammar

A *lexical grammar* for the Java programming language is given in §3. This grammar has as its terminal symbols the characters of the Unicode character set. It defines a set of productions, starting from the goal symbol *Input* (§3.5), that describe how sequences of Unicode characters (§3.1) are translated into a sequence of input elements (§3.5).

These input elements, with white space (§3.6) and comments (§3.7) discarded, form the terminal symbols for the syntactic grammar for the Java programming language and are called *tokens* (§3.5). These tokens are the identifiers (§3.8), keywords (§3.9), literals (§3.10), separators (§3.11), and operators (§3.12) of the Java programming language.

2.3   The Syntactic Grammar

A *syntactic grammar* for the Java programming language is given in Chapters 4, 6-10, 14, and 15. This grammar has tokens defined by the lexical grammar as its terminal symbols. It defines a set of productions, starting from the goal symbol *CompilationUnit* (§7.3), that describe how sequences of tokens can form syntactically correct programs.

Chapter 18 also gives a syntactic grammar for the Java programming language, better suited to implementation than exposition. The same language is accepted by both syntactic grammars.

2.4   Grammar Notation

Terminal symbols are shown in `fixed width` font in the productions of the lexical and syntactic grammars, and throughout this specification whenever the text is directly referring to such a terminal symbol. These are to appear in a program exactly as written.

Nonterminal symbols are shown in *italic* type. The definition of a nonterminal is introduced by the name of the nonterminal being defined followed by a colon. One or more alternative right-hand sides for the nonterminal then follow on succeeding lines.

For example, the syntactic definition:

IfThenStatement:
   `if` (*Expression*) *Statement*

states that the nonterminal *IfThenStatement* represents the token `if`, followed by a left parenthesis token, followed by an *Expression*, followed by a right parenthesis token, followed by a *Statement*.

As another example, the syntactic definition:

ArgumentList:
   Argument
   ArgumentList , Argument

states that an *ArgumentList* may represent either a single *Argument* or an *ArgumentList*, followed by a comma, followed by an *Argument*. This definition of *ArgumentList* is *recursive*, that is to say, it is defined in terms of itself. The result is that an *ArgumentList* may contain any positive number of arguments. Such recursive definitions of nonterminals are common.

The subscripted suffix "*opt*", which may appear after a terminal or nonterminal, indicates an *optional symbol*. The alternative containing the optional symbol actually specifies two right-hand sides, one that omits the optional element and one that includes it.

This means that:

BreakStatement:
   `break` *Identifier$_{opt}$* ;

is a convenient abbreviation for:

BreakStatement:
   `break` ;
   `break` *Identifier* ;

and that:

BasicForStatement:
   `for` (*ForInit$_{opt}$* ; *Expression$_{opt}$* ; *ForUpdate$_{opt}$*) *Statement*

is a convenient abbreviation for:

BasicForStatement:
   `for` (; *Expression$_{opt}$* ; *ForUpdate$_{opt}$*) *Statement*
   `for` (*ForInit* ; *Expression$_{opt}$* ; *ForUpdate$_{opt}$*) *Statement*

which in turn is an abbreviation for:

BasicForStatement:
   `for` (; ; *ForUpdate$_{opt}$*) *Statement*
   `for` (; *Expression* ; *ForUpdate$_{opt}$*) *Statement*
   `for` (*ForInit* ; ; *ForUpdate$_{opt}$*) *Statement*
   `for` (*ForInit* ; *Expression* ; *ForUpdate$_{opt}$*) *Statement*

which in turn is an abbreviation for:

BasicForStatement:
    `for` (; ;) *Statement*
    `for` (; ; *ForUpdate*) *Statement*
    `for` (; *Expression* ;) *Statement*
    `for` (; *Expression* ; *ForUpdate*) *Statement*
    `for` (*ForInit* ; ;) *Statement*
    `for` (*ForInit* ; ; *ForUpdate*) *Statement*
    `for` (*ForInit* ; *Expression* ;) *Statement*
    `for` (*ForInit* ; *Expression* ; *ForUpdate*) *Statement*

so the nonterminal *BasicForStatement* actually has eight alternative right-hand sides.

A very long right-hand side may be continued on a second line by substantially indenting this second line.

For example, the syntactic grammar contains this production:

ConstructorDeclaration:
    ConstructorModifiers$_{opt}$ ConstructorDeclarator
                  Throws$_{opt}$ ConstructorBody

which defines one right-hand side for the nonterminal *ConstructorDeclaration*.

When the words "one of" follow the colon in a grammar definition, they signify that each of the terminal symbols on the following line or lines is an alternative definition.

For example, the lexical grammar contains the production:

ZeroToThree: one of
    `0  1  2  3`

which is merely a convenient abbreviation for:

ZeroToThree:
    `0`
    `1`
    `2`
    `3`

When an alternative in a lexical production appears to be a token, it represents the sequence of characters that would make up such a token.

Thus, the definition:

BooleanLiteral: one of
```
true false
```

in a lexical grammar production is shorthand for:

BooleanLiteral:
```
t r u e
f a l s e
```

The right-hand side of a lexical production may specify that certain expansions are not permitted by using the phrase "but not" and then indicating the expansions to be excluded.

For example, this occurs in the productions for *InputCharacter* (§3.4) and *Identifier* (§3.8):

InputCharacter:
    UnicodeInputCharacter but not CR or LF

Identifier:
    IdentifierName but not a *Keyword* or *BooleanLiteral* or *NullLiteral*

Finally, a few nonterminal symbols are described by a descriptive phrase in roman type in cases where it would be impractical to list all the alternatives.

For example:

RawInputCharacter:
    any Unicode character

CHAPTER 3

Lexical Structure

THIS chapter specifies the lexical structure of the Java programming language.

Programs are written in Unicode (§3.1), but lexical translations are provided (§3.2) so that Unicode escapes (§3.3) can be used to include any Unicode character using only ASCII characters. Line terminators are defined (§3.4) to support the different conventions of existing host systems while maintaining consistent line numbers.

The Unicode characters resulting from the lexical translations are reduced to a sequence of input elements (§3.5), which are white space (§3.6), comments (§3.7), and tokens. The tokens are the identifiers (§3.8), keywords (§3.9), literals (§3.10), separators (§3.11), and operators (§3.12) of the syntactic grammar.

3.1 Unicode

Programs are written using the Unicode character set. Information about this character set and its associated character encodings may be found at `http://www.unicode.org/`.

The Java SE platform tracks the Unicode specification as it evolves. The precise version of Unicode used by a given release is specified in the documentation of the class `Character`.

> Versions of the Java programming language prior to 1.1 used Unicode version 1.1.5. Upgrades to newer versions of the Unicode Standard occurred in JDK 1.1 (to Unicode 2.0), JDK 1.1.7 (to Unicode 2.1), Java SE 1.4 (to Unicode 3.0), and Java SE 5.0 (to Unicode 4.0).

The Unicode standard was originally designed as a fixed-width 16-bit character encoding. It has since been changed to allow for characters whose representation requires more than 16 bits. The range of legal code points is now U+0000 to U+10FFFF, using the hexadecimal *U+n notation*. Characters whose code points are greater than U+FFFF are called supplementary characters. To represent the complete range of characters using only 16-bit units, the Unicode standard defines an encoding called UTF-16. In this encoding, supplementary characters are represented as pairs of 16-bit code units, the first from the high-surrogates range, (U+D800 to U+DBFF), the second from the low-surrogates range (U+DC00 to U +DFFF). For characters in the range U+0000 to U+FFFF, the values of code points and UTF-16 code units are the same.

The Java programming language represents text in sequences of 16-bit code units, using the UTF-16 encoding.

> Some APIs of the Java SE platform, primarily in the `Character` class, use 32-bit integers to represent code points as individual entities. The Java SE platform provides methods to convert between 16-bit and 32-bit representations.

This specification uses the terms *code point* and *UTF-16 code unit* where the representation is relevant, and the generic term *character* where the representation is irrelevant to the discussion.

Except for comments (§3.7), identifiers, and the contents of character and string literals (§3.10.4, §3.10.5), all input elements (§3.5) in a program are formed only from ASCII characters (or Unicode escapes (§3.3) which result in ASCII characters).

> ASCII (ANSI X3.4) is the American Standard Code for Information Interchange. The first 128 characters of the Unicode UTF-16 encoding are the ASCII characters.

3.2 Lexical Translations

A raw Unicode character stream is translated into a sequence of tokens, using the following three lexical translation steps, which are applied in turn:

1. A translation of Unicode escapes (§3.3) in the raw stream of Unicode characters to the corresponding Unicode character. A Unicode escape of the form \u*xxxx*, where *xxxx* is a hexadecimal value, represents the UTF-16 code unit whose encoding is *xxxx*. This translation step allows any program to be expressed using only ASCII characters.

2. A translation of the Unicode stream resulting from step 1 into a stream of input characters and line terminators (§3.4).

3. A translation of the stream of input characters and line terminators resulting from step 2 into a sequence of input elements (§3.5) which, after white space

(§3.6) and comments (§3.7) are discarded, comprise the tokens (§3.5) that are the terminal symbols of the syntactic grammar (§2.3).

The longest possible translation is used at each step, even if the result does not ultimately make a correct program while another lexical translation would.

Thus, the input characters a--b are tokenized (§3.5) as a, --, b, which is not part of any grammatically correct program, even though the tokenization a, -, -, b could be part of a grammatically correct program.

3.3 Unicode Escapes

A compiler for the Java programming language ("Java compiler") first recognizes Unicode escapes in its input, translating the ASCII characters \u followed by four hexadecimal digits to the UTF-16 code unit (§3.1) of the indicated hexadecimal value, and passing all other characters unchanged. Representing supplementary characters requires two consecutive Unicode escapes. This translation step results in a sequence of Unicode input characters.

UnicodeInputCharacter:
  UnicodeEscape
  RawInputCharacter

UnicodeEscape:
  \ *UnicodeMarker HexDigit HexDigit HexDigit HexDigit*

UnicodeMarker:
  u
  UnicodeMarker u

RawInputCharacter:
  any Unicode character

HexDigit: one of
  0 1 2 3 4 5 6 7 8 9 a b c d e f A B C D E F

The \, u, and hexadecimal digits here are all ASCII characters.

In addition to the processing implied by the grammar, for each raw input character that is a backslash \, input processing must consider how many other \ characters contiguously precede it, separating it from a non-\ character or the start of the input stream. If this number is even, then the \ is eligible to begin a Unicode escape; if the number is odd, then the \ is not eligible to begin a Unicode escape.

> For example, the raw input "\\u2126=\u2126" results in the eleven characters " \ \ u 2 1 2 6 = Ω " (\u2126 is the Unicode encoding of the character Ω).

If an eligible \ is not followed by u, then it is treated as a *RawInputCharacter* and remains part of the escaped Unicode stream.

If an eligible \ is followed by u, or more than one u, and the last u is not followed by four hexadecimal digits, then a compile-time error occurs.

The character produced by a Unicode escape does not participate in further Unicode escapes.

> For example, the raw input \u005cu005a results in the six characters \ u 0 0 5 a, because 005c is the Unicode value for \. It does not result in the character Z, which is Unicode character 005a, because the \ that resulted from the \u005c is not interpreted as the start of a further Unicode escape.

The Java programming language specifies a standard way of transforming a program written in Unicode into ASCII that changes a program into a form that can be processed by ASCII-based tools. The transformation involves converting any Unicode escapes in the source text of the program to ASCII by adding an extra u - for example, \uxxxx becomes \uuxxxx - while simultaneously converting non-ASCII characters in the source text to Unicode escapes containing a single u each.

This transformed version is equally acceptable to a Java compiler and represents the exact same program. The exact Unicode source can later be restored from this ASCII form by converting each escape sequence where multiple u's are present to a sequence of Unicode characters with one fewer u, while simultaneously converting each escape sequence with a single u to the corresponding single Unicode character.

> A Java compiler should use the \uxxxx notation as an output format to display Unicode characters when a suitable font is not available.

3.4   Line Terminators

A Java compiler next divides the sequence of Unicode input characters into lines by recognizing *line terminators*.

LineTerminator:
>   the ASCII LF character, also known as "newline"
>   the ASCII CR character, also known as "return"
>   the ASCII CR character followed by the ASCII LF character

InputCharacter:
>   *UnicodeInputCharacter* but not CR or LF

Lines are terminated by the ASCII characters CR, or LF, or CR LF. The two characters CR immediately followed by LF are counted as one line terminator, not two.

A line terminator specifies the termination of the `//` form of a comment (§3.7).

>   The lines defined by line terminators may determine the line numbers produced by a Java compiler.

The result is a sequence of line terminators and input characters, which are the terminal symbols for the third step in the tokenization process.

3.5   Input Elements and Tokens

The input characters and line terminators that result from escape processing (§3.3) and then input line recognition (§3.4) are reduced to a sequence of *input elements*.

Input:
  InputElements_{opt} Sub_{opt}

InputElements:
  InputElement
  InputElements InputElement

InputElement:
  WhiteSpace
  Comment
  Token

Token:
  Identifier
  Keyword
  Literal
  Separator
  Operator

Sub:
  the ASCII SUB character, also known as "control-Z"

Those input elements that are not white space (§3.6) or comments (§3.7) are *tokens*. The tokens are the terminal symbols of the syntactic grammar (§2.3).

White space (§3.6) and comments (§3.7) can serve to separate tokens that, if adjacent, might be tokenized in another manner. For example, the ASCII characters - and = in the input can form the operator token -= (§3.12) only if there is no intervening white space or comment.

As a special concession for compatibility with certain operating systems, the ASCII SUB character (\u001a, or control-Z) is ignored if it is the last character in the escaped input stream.

Consider two tokens x and y in the resulting input stream. If x precedes y, then we say that x is *to the left of* y and that y is *to the right of* x.

For example, in this simple piece of code:

```
class Empty {
}
```

we say that the } token is to the right of the { token, even though it appears, in this two-dimensional representation, downward and to the left of the { token. This convention about the use of the words left and right allows us to speak, for example, of the right-hand operand of a binary operator or of the left-hand side of an assignment.

3.6 White Space

White space is defined as the ASCII space character, horizontal tab character, form feed character, and line terminator characters (§3.4).

> *WhiteSpace:*
>   the ASCII SP character, also known as "space"
>   the ASCII HT character, also known as "horizontal tab"
>   the ASCII FF character, also known as "form feed"
>   *LineTerminator*

3.7 Comments

There are two kinds of comments.

- */* text */*

  A *traditional comment*: all the text from the ASCII characters /* to the ASCII characters */ is ignored (as in C and C++).

- *// text*

  An *end-of-line comment*: all the text from the ASCII characters // to the end of the line is ignored (as in C++).

Comment:
  TraditionalComment
  EndOfLineComment

TraditionalComment:
  / * CommentTail

EndOfLineComment:
  / / CharactersInLine$_{opt}$

CommentTail:
  * CommentTailStar
  NotStar CommentTail

CommentTailStar:
  /
  * CommentTailStar
  NotStarNotSlash CommentTail

NotStar:
  InputCharacter but not *
  LineTerminator

NotStarNotSlash:
  InputCharacter but not * or /
  LineTerminator

CharactersInLine:
  InputCharacter
  CharactersInLine InputCharacter

These productions imply all of the following properties:

- Comments do not nest.
- /* and */ have no special meaning in comments that begin with //.
- // has no special meaning in comments that begin with /* or /**.

  As a result, the text:

  ```
  /* this comment /* // /** ends here: */
  ```

is a single complete comment.

The lexical grammar implies that comments do not occur within character literals (§3.10.4) or string literals (§3.10.5).

3.8 Identifiers

An *identifier* is an unlimited-length sequence of *Java letters* and *Java digits*, the first of which must be a *Java letter*.

> *Identifier:*
>   *IdentifierChars* but not a *Keyword* or *BooleanLiteral* or *NullLiteral*
>
> *IdentifierChars:*
>   *JavaLetter*
>   *IdentifierChars JavaLetterOrDigit*
>
> *JavaLetter:*
>   any Unicode character that is a Java letter (see below)
>
> *JavaLetterOrDigit:*
>   any Unicode character that is a Java letter-or-digit (see below)

A "Java letter" is a character for which the method `Character.isJavaIdentifierStart(int)` returns true.

A "Java letter-or-digit" is a character for which the method `Character.isJavaIdentifierPart(int)` returns true.

The "Java letters" include uppercase and lowercase ASCII Latin letters `A-Z` (`\u0041-\u005a`), and `a-z` (`\u0061-\u007a`), and, for historical reasons, the ASCII underscore (`_`, or `\u005f`) and dollar sign (`$`, or `\u0024`). The `$` character should be used only in mechanically generated source code or, rarely, to access pre-existing names on legacy systems.

The "Java digits" include the ASCII digits `0-9` (`\u0030-\u0039`).

Letters and digits may be drawn from the entire Unicode character set, which supports most writing scripts in use in the world today, including the large sets for Chinese, Japanese, and Korean. This allows programmers to use identifiers in their programs that are written in their native languages.

An identifier cannot have the same spelling (Unicode character sequence) as a keyword (§3.9), boolean literal (§3.10.3), or the null literal (§3.10.7), or a compile-time error occurs.

Two identifiers are the same only if they are identical, that is, have the same Unicode character for each letter or digit. Identifiers that have the same external appearance may yet be different.

> For example, the identifiers consisting of the single letters LATIN CAPITAL LETTER A (A, \u0041), LATIN SMALL LETTER A (a, \u0061), GREEK CAPITAL LETTER ALPHA (A, \u0391), CYRILLIC SMALL LETTER A (a, \u0430) and MATHEMATICAL BOLD ITALIC SMALL A (a, \ud835\udc82) are all different.

> Unicode composite characters are different from their canonical equivalent decomposed characters. For example, a LATIN CAPITAL LETTER A ACUTE (Á, \u00c1) is different from a LATIN CAPITAL LETTER A (A, \u0041) immediately followed by a NON-SPACING ACUTE (´, \u0301) in identifiers. See The Unicode Standard, Section 3.11 "Normalization Forms".

> Examples of identifiers are:

> - `String`
> - `i3`
> - αρετη
> - `MAX_VALUE`
> - `isLetterOrDigit`

3.9 Keywords

50 character sequences, formed from ASCII letters, are reserved for use as keywords and cannot be used as identifiers (§3.8).

Keyword: one of

abstract	continue	for	new	switch
assert	default	if	package	synchronized
boolean	do	goto	private	this
break	double	implements	protected	throw
byte	else	import	public	throws
case	enum	instanceof	return	transient
catch	extends	int	short	try
char	final	interface	static	void
class	finally	long	strictfp	volatile
const	float	native	super	while

The keywords `const` and `goto` are reserved, even though they are not currently used. This may allow a Java compiler to produce better error messages if these C++ keywords incorrectly appear in programs.

While `true` and `false` might appear to be keywords, they are technically Boolean literals (§3.10.3). Similarly, while `null` might appear to be a keyword, it is technically the null literal (§3.10.7).

3.10 Literals

A *literal* is the source code representation of a value of a primitive type (§4.2), the `String` type (§4.3.3), or the null type (§4.1).

Literal:
  IntegerLiteral
  FloatingPointLiteral
  BooleanLiteral
  CharacterLiteral
  StringLiteral
  NullLiteral

3.10.1 Integer Literals

An *integer literal* may be expressed in decimal (base 10), hexadecimal (base 16), octal (base 8), or binary (base 2).

IntegerLiteral:
  DecimalIntegerLiteral
  HexIntegerLiteral
  OctalIntegerLiteral
  BinaryIntegerLiteral

DecimalIntegerLiteral:
  DecimalNumeral IntegerTypeSuffix$_{opt}$

HexIntegerLiteral:
  HexNumeral IntegerTypeSuffix$_{opt}$

OctalIntegerLiteral:
  OctalNumeral IntegerTypeSuffix$_{opt}$

BinaryIntegerLiteral:
  BinaryNumeral IntegerTypeSuffix$_{opt}$

IntegerTypeSuffix: one of
```
l L
```

An integer literal is of type `long` if it is suffixed with an ASCII letter `L` or `l` (ell); otherwise it is of type `int` (§4.2.1).

> The suffix `L` is preferred, because the letter `l` (ell) is often hard to distinguish from the digit `1` (one).

Underscores are allowed as separators between digits that denote the integer.

In a hexadecimal or binary literal, the integer is only denoted by the digits after the `0x` or `0b` characters and before any type suffix. Therefore, underscores may not appear immediately after `0x` or `0b`, or after the last digit in the numeral.

In a decimal or octal literal, the integer is denoted by *all* the digits in the literal before any type suffix. Therefore, underscores may not appear before the first digit or after the last digit in the numeral. Underscores may appear after the initial `0` in an octal numeral (since `0` is a digit that denotes part of the integer) and after the initial non-zero digit in a non-zero decimal literal.

A decimal numeral is either the single ASCII digit 0, representing the integer zero, or consists of an ASCII digit from 1 to 9 optionally followed by one or more ASCII digits from 0 to 9 interspersed with underscores, representing a positive integer.

DecimalNumeral:
  0
  NonZeroDigit Digits$_{opt}$
  NonZeroDigit Underscores Digits

Digits:
  Digit
  Digit DigitsAndUnderscores$_{opt}$ Digit

Digit:
  0
  NonZeroDigit

NonZeroDigit: one of
  1 2 3 4 5 6 7 8 9

DigitsAndUnderscores:
  DigitOrUnderscore
  DigitsAndUnderscores DigitOrUnderscore

DigitOrUnderscore:
  Digit

  _

Underscores:

  _
  Underscores _

A hexadecimal numeral consists of the leading ASCII characters 0x or 0X followed by one or more ASCII hexadecimal digits interspersed with underscores, and can represent a positive, zero, or negative integer.

Hexadecimal digits with values 10 through 15 are represented by the ASCII letters a through f or A through F, respectively; each letter used as a hexadecimal digit may be uppercase or lowercase.

HexNumeral:
   0 x *HexDigits*
   0 X *HexDigits*

HexDigits:
   HexDigit
   HexDigit HexDigitsAndUnderscores$_{opt}$ *HexDigit*

HexDigit: one of
   0 1 2 3 4 5 6 7 8 9 a b c d e f A B C D E F

HexDigitsAndUnderscores:
   HexDigitOrUnderscore
   HexDigitsAndUnderscores HexDigitOrUnderscore

HexDigitOrUnderscore:
   HexDigit

   _

The *HexDigit* production above comes from §3.3.

An octal numeral consists of an ASCII digit 0 followed by one or more of the ASCII digits 0 through 7 interspersed with underscores, and can represent a positive, zero, or negative integer.

OctalNumeral:
  0 *OctalDigits*
  0 *Underscores OctalDigits*

OctalDigits:
  OctalDigit
  OctalDigit OctalDigitsAndUnderscores$_{opt}$ OctalDigit

OctalDigit: one of
  0 1 2 3 4 5 6 7

OctalDigitsAndUnderscores:
  OctalDigitOrUnderscore
  OctalDigitsAndUnderscores OctalDigitOrUnderscore

OctalDigitOrUnderscore:
  OctalDigit

  _

Note that octal numerals always consist of two or more digits; 0 is always considered to be a decimal numeral - not that it matters much in practice, for the numerals 0, 00, and 0x0 all represent exactly the same integer value.

A binary numeral consists of the leading ASCII characters 0b or 0B followed by one or more of the ASCII digits 0 or 1 interspersed with underscores, and can represent a positive, zero, or negative integer.

BinaryNumeral:
  0 b *BinaryDigits*
  0 B *BinaryDigits*

BinaryDigits:
  BinaryDigit
  BinaryDigit BinaryDigitsAndUnderscores$_{opt}$ BinaryDigit

BinaryDigit: one of
  0 1

BinaryDigitsAndUnderscores:
  BinaryDigitOrUnderscore
  BinaryDigitsAndUnderscores BinaryDigitOrUnderscore

BinaryDigitOrUnderscore:
  BinaryDigit

  _

The largest decimal literal of type `int` is 2147483648 (2^{31}).

All decimal literals from 0 to 2147483647 may appear anywhere an `int` literal may appear.

It is a compile-time error if a decimal literal of type `int` is larger than 2147483648 (2^{31}), or if the decimal literal 2147483648 appears anywhere other than as the operand of the unary minus operator (§15.15.4).

The largest positive hexadecimal, octal, and binary literals of type `int` - each of which represents the decimal value 2147483647 (2^{31}-1) - are respectively:

- `0x7fff_ffff`,

- `0177_7777_7777`, and

- `0b0111_1111_1111_1111_1111_1111_1111_1111`

The most negative hexadecimal, octal, and binary literals of type `int` - each of which represents the decimal value -2147483648 (-2^{31}) - are respectively:

- `0x8000_0000`,

- `0200_0000_0000`, and

- `0b1000_0000_0000_0000_0000_0000_0000_0000`

The following hexadecimal, octal, and binary literals represent the decimal value -1:

- `0xffff_ffff`,

- `0377_7777_7777`, and

- `0b1111_1111_1111_1111_1111_1111_1111_1111`

It is a compile-time error if a hexadecimal, octal, or binary `int` literal does not fit in 32 bits.

The largest decimal literal of type `long` is `9223372036854775808L` (2^{63}).

All decimal literals from `0L` to `9223372036854775807L` may appear anywhere a `long` literal may appear.

It is a compile-time error if a decimal literal of type `long` is larger than `9223372036854775808L` (2^{63}), or if the decimal literal `9223372036854775808L` appears anywhere other than as the operand of the unary minus operator (§15.15.4).

The largest positive hexadecimal, octal, and binary literals of type `long` - each of which represents the decimal value `9223372036854775807L` (2^{63}-1) - are respectively:

- `0x7fff_ffff_ffff_ffffL`,

- `07_7777_7777_7777_7777_7777L`, and

- `0b0111_1111_1111_1111_1111_1111_1111_1111_1111_1111_1111_1111_1111_1111_1111_1111L`

The most negative hexadecimal, octal, and binary literals of type `long` - each of which represents the decimal value `-9223372036854775808L` (-2^{63}) - are respectively:

- `0x8000_0000_0000_0000L`, and

- `010_0000_0000_0000_0000_0000L`, and

- `0b1000_0000_0000_0000_0000_0000_0000_0000_0000_0000_0000_0000_0000_0000_0000_0000L`

The following hexadecimal, octal, and binary literals represent the decimal value `-1L`:

- `0xffff_ffff_ffff_ffffL`,

- `017_7777_7777_7777_7777_7777L`, and

- `0b1111_1111_1111_1111_1111_1111_1111_1111_1111_1111_1111_1111_1111_1111_1111_1111L`

It is a compile-time error if a hexadecimal, octal, or binary `long` literal does not fit in 64 bits.

Examples of `int` literals:

```
0    2    0372    0xDada_Cafe    1996    0x00_FF__00_FF
```

Examples of `long` literals:

```
01    0777L    0x100000000L    2_147_483_648L    0xC0B0L
```

3.10.2 Floating-Point Literals

A *floating-point literal* has the following parts: a whole-number part, a decimal or hexadecimal point (represented by an ASCII period character), a fraction part, an exponent, and a type suffix.

A floating-point literal may be expressed in decimal (base 10) or hexadecimal (base 16).

For decimal floating-point literals, at least one digit (in either the whole number or the fraction part) and either a decimal point, an exponent, or a float type suffix are required. All other parts are optional. The exponent, if present, is indicated by the ASCII letter `e` or `E` followed by an optionally signed integer.

For hexadecimal floating-point literals, at least one digit is required (in either the whole number or the fraction part), and the exponent is mandatory, and the float type suffix is optional. The exponent is indicated by the ASCII letter p or P followed by an optionally signed integer.

Underscores are allowed as separators between digits that denote the whole-number part, and between digits that denote the fraction part, and between digits that denote the exponent.

FloatingPointLiteral:
 DecimalFloatingPointLiteral
 HexadecimalFloatingPointLiteral

DecimalFloatingPointLiteral:
 Digits . *Digits*$_{opt}$ *ExponentPart*$_{opt}$ *FloatTypeSuffix*$_{opt}$
 . *Digits* *ExponentPart*$_{opt}$ *FloatTypeSuffix*$_{opt}$
 Digits *ExponentPart* *FloatTypeSuffix*$_{opt}$
 Digits *ExponentPart*$_{opt}$ *FloatTypeSuffix*

ExponentPart:
 ExponentIndicator SignedInteger

ExponentIndicator: one of
 e E

SignedInteger:
 Sign$_{opt}$ *Digits*

Sign: one of
 + -

FloatTypeSuffix: one of
 f F d D

33

HexadecimalFloatingPointLiteral:
  HexSignificand BinaryExponent FloatTypeSuffix$_{opt}$

HexSignificand:
  HexNumeral
  HexNumeral .
  0 x *HexDigits$_{opt}$. HexDigits*
  0 x *HexDigits$_{opt}$. HexDigits*

BinaryExponent:
  BinaryExponentIndicator SignedInteger

BinaryExponentIndicator:one of
  p P

A floating-point literal is of type `float` if it is suffixed with an ASCII letter F or f; otherwise its type is `double` and it can optionally be suffixed with an ASCII letter D or d (§4.2.3).

The elements of the types `float` and `double` are those values that can be represented using the IEEE 754 32-bit single-precision and 64-bit double-precision binary floating-point formats, respectively.

> The details of proper input conversion from a Unicode string representation of a floating-point number to the internal IEEE 754 binary floating-point representation are described for the methods `valueOf` of class `Float` and class `Double` of the package `java.lang`.

The largest positive finite literal of type `float` is 3.4028235e38f.

The smallest positive finite non-zero literal of type `float` is 1.40e-45f.

The largest positive finite literal of type `double` is 1.7976931348623157e308.

The smallest positive finite non-zero literal of type `double` is 4.9e-324.

It is a compile-time error if a non-zero floating-point literal is too large, so that on rounded conversion to its internal representation, it becomes an IEEE 754 infinity.

A program can represent infinities without producing a compile-time error by using constant expressions such as 1f/0f or -1d/0d or by using the predefined constants POSITIVE_INFINITY and NEGATIVE_INFINITY of the classes `Float` and `Double`.

It is a compile-time error if a non-zero floating-point literal is too small, so that, on rounded conversion to its internal representation, it becomes a zero.

A compile-time error does not occur if a non-zero floating-point literal has a small value that, on rounded conversion to its internal representation, becomes a non-zero denormalized number.

Predefined constants representing Not-a-Number values are defined in the classes `Float` and `Double` as `Float.NaN` and `Double.NaN`.

Examples of `float` literals:

```
1e1f    2.f    .3f    0f    3.14f    6.022137e+23f
```

Examples of `double` literals:

```
1e1    2.    .3    0.0    3.14    1e-9d    1e137
```

3.10.3 Boolean Literals

The `boolean` type has two values, represented by the *boolean literals* `true` and `false`, formed from ASCII letters.

BooleanLiteral: one of
    `true false`

A boolean literal is always of type `boolean` (§4.2.5).

3.10.4 Character Literals

A *character literal* is expressed as a character or an escape sequence (§3.10.6), enclosed in ASCII single quotes. (The single-quote, or apostrophe, character is \u0027.)

CharacterLiteral:
    ' SingleCharacter '
    ' EscapeSequence '

SingleCharacter:
    *InputCharacter but not ' or *

See §3.10.6 for the definition of *EscapeSequence*.

Character literals can only represent UTF-16 code units (§3.1), i.e., they are limited to values from \u0000 to \uffff. Supplementary characters must be represented either as a surrogate pair within a `char` sequence, or as an integer, depending on the API they are used with.

A character literal is always of type `char` (§4.2.1).

It is a compile-time error for the character following the *SingleCharacter* or *EscapeSequence* to be other than a `'`.

It is a compile-time error for a line terminator (§3.4) to appear after the opening `'` and before the closing `'`.

As specified in §3.4, the characters CR and LF are never an *InputCharacter*; each is recognized as constituting a *LineTerminator*.

The following are examples of `char` literals:

- `'a'`
- `'%'`
- `'\t'`
- `'\\'`
- `'\''`
- `'\u03a9'`
- `'\uFFFF'`
- `'\177'`
- `'Ω'`

Because Unicode escapes are processed very early, it is not correct to write `'\u000a'` for a character literal whose value is linefeed (LF); the Unicode escape `\u000a` is transformed into an actual linefeed in translation step 1 (§3.3) and the linefeed becomes a *LineTerminator* in step 2 (§3.4), and so the character literal is not valid in step 3. Instead, one should use the escape sequence `'\n'` (§3.10.6). Similarly, it is not correct to write `'\u000d'` for a character literal whose value is carriage return (CR). Instead, use `'\r'`.

In C and C++, a character literal may contain representations of more than one character, but the value of such a character literal is implementation-defined. In the Java programming language, a character literal always represents exactly one character.

3.10.5   String Literals

A *string literal* consists of zero or more characters enclosed in double quotes. Characters may be represented by escape sequences (§3.10.6) - one escape sequence for characters in the range U+0000 to U+FFFF, two escape sequences for the UTF-16 surrogate code units of characters in the range U+010000 to U+10FFFF.

StringLiteral:
   " *StringCharacters*$_{opt}$ "

StringCharacters:
   StringCharacter
   StringCharacters StringCharacter

StringCharacter:
   InputCharacter but not " or \
   EscapeSequence

See §3.10.6 for the definition of *EscapeSequence*.

A string literal is always of type `String` (§4.3.3).

It is a compile-time error for a line terminator to appear after the opening " and before the closing matching ".

As specified in §3.4, the characters CR and LF are never an *InputCharacter*; each is recognized as constituting a *LineTerminator*.

A long string literal can always be broken up into shorter pieces and written as a (possibly parenthesized) expression using the string concatenation operator + (§15.18.1).

The following are examples of string literals:

```
""                     // the empty string
"\""                   // a string containing " alone
"This is a string"     // a string containing 16 characters
"This is a " +         // actually a string-valued constant expression,
    "two-line string"   // formed from two string literals
```

Because Unicode escapes are processed very early, it is not correct to write `"\u000a"` for a string literal containing a single linefeed (LF); the Unicode escape \u000a is transformed into an actual linefeed in translation step 1 (§3.3) and the linefeed becomes a *LineTerminator* in step 2 (§3.4), and so the string literal is not valid in step 3. Instead, one should write `"\n"` (§3.10.6). Similarly, it is not correct to write `"\u000d"` for a string literal containing a single carriage return (CR). Instead, use `"\r"`. Finally, it is not possible to write `"\u0022"` for a string literal containing a double quotation mark (").

A string literal is a reference to an instance of class `String` (§4.3.1, §4.3.3).

Moreover, a string literal always refers to the *same* instance of class `String`. This is because string literals - or, more generally, strings that are the values of constant expressions (§15.28) - are "interned" so as to share unique instances, using the method `String.intern`.

Example 3.10.5-1. String Literals

The program consisting of the compilation unit (§7.3):

```
package testPackage;
class Test {
    public static void main(String[] args) {
        String hello = "Hello", lo = "lo";
        System.out.print((hello == "Hello") + " ");
        System.out.print((Other.hello == hello) + " ");
        System.out.print((other.Other.hello == hello) + " ");
        System.out.print((hello == ("Hel"+"lo")) + " ");
        System.out.print((hello == ("Hel"+lo)) + " ");
        System.out.println(hello == ("Hel"+lo).intern());
    }
}
class Other { static String hello = "Hello"; }
```

and the compilation unit:

```
package other;
public class Other { public static String hello = "Hello"; }
```

produces the output:

```
true true true true false true
```

This example illustrates six points:

- Literal strings within the same class (§8) in the same package (§7) represent references to the same String object (§4.3.1).

- Literal strings within different classes in the same package represent references to the same String object.

- Literal strings within different classes in different packages likewise represent references to the same String object.

- Strings computed by constant expressions (§15.28) are computed at compile time and then treated as if they were literals.

- Strings computed by concatenation at run time are newly created and therefore distinct.

- The result of explicitly interning a computed string is the same string as any pre-existing literal string with the same contents.

3.10.6   Escape Sequences for Character and String Literals

The character and string *escape sequences* allow for the representation of some nongraphic characters as well as the single quote, double quote, and backslash characters in character literals (§3.10.4) and string literals (§3.10.5).

EscapeSequence:
    \ b /* \u0008: backspace BS */
    \ t /* \u0009: horizontal tab HT */
    \ n /* \u000a: linefeed LF */
    \ f /* \u000c: form feed FF */
    \ r /* \u000d: carriage return CR */
    \ " /* \u0022: double quote " */
    \ ' /* \u0027: single quote ' */
    \ \   /* \u005c: backslash \ */
    OctalEscape   /* \u0000 to \u00ff: from octal value */

OctalEscape:
    \ *OctalDigit*
    \ *OctalDigit OctalDigit*
    \ *ZeroToThree OctalDigit OctalDigit*

OctalDigit: one of
    0 1 2 3 4 5 6 7

ZeroToThree: one of
    0 1 2 3

It is a compile-time error if the character following a backslash in an escape is not an ASCII b, t, n, f, r, ", ', \, 0, 1, 2, 3, 4, 5, 6, or 7. The Unicode escape \u is processed earlier (§3.3).

> Octal escapes are provided for compatibility with C, but can express only Unicode values \u0000 through \u00FF, so Unicode escapes are usually preferred.

3.10.7   The Null Literal

The null type has one value, the null reference, represented by the *null literal* null, which is formed from ASCII characters.

NullLiteral:
    null

A null literal is always of the null type (§4.1).

3.11   Separators

Nine ASCII characters are the *separators* (punctuators).

Separator: one of
   (   )   {   }   [   ]   ;   ,   .

3.12   Operators

37 tokens are the *operators*, formed from ASCII characters.

Operator: one of
   =   >   <   !   ~   ?   :
   ==   <=   >=   !=   && || ++   --
   +   -   *   /   & | ^   %   <<   >>   >>>
   +=   -=   *=   /=   &= |=   ^=   %=   <<=   >>=   >>>=

CHAPTER 4

Types, Values, and Variables

THE Java programming language is a *statically typed* language, which means that every variable and every expression has a type that is known at compile time.

The Java programming language is also a *strongly typed* language, because types limit the values that a variable (§4.12) can hold or that an expression can produce, limit the operations supported on those values, and determine the meaning of the operations. Strong static typing helps detect errors at compile time.

The types of the Java programming language are divided into two categories: primitive types and reference types. The primitive types (§4.2) are the `boolean` type and the numeric types. The numeric types are the integral types `byte`, `short`, `int`, `long`, and `char`, and the floating-point types `float` and `double`. The reference types (§4.3) are class types, interface types, and array types. There is also a special null type. An object (§4.3.1) is a dynamically created instance of a class type or a dynamically created array. The values of a reference type are references to objects. All objects, including arrays, support the methods of class `Object` (§4.3.2). String literals are represented by `String` objects (§4.3.3).

4.1 The Kinds of Types and Values

There are two kinds of types in the Java programming language: primitive types (§4.2) and reference types (§4.3). There are, correspondingly, two kinds of data values that can be stored in variables, passed as arguments, returned by methods, and operated on: primitive values (§4.2) and reference values (§4.3).

> *Type:*
> *PrimitiveType*
> *ReferenceType*

There is also a special *null type*, the type of the expression `null` (§3.10.7, §15.8.1), which has no name.

Because the null type has no name, it is impossible to declare a variable of the null type or to cast to the null type.

The null reference is the only possible value of an expression of null type.

The null reference can always undergo a widening reference conversion to any reference type.

> In practice, the programmer can ignore the null type and just pretend that null is merely a special literal that can be of any reference type.

4.2   Primitive Types and Values

A primitive type is predefined by the Java programming language and named by its reserved keyword (§3.9):

PrimitiveType:
  NumericType
  `boolean`

NumericType:
  IntegralType
  FloatingPointType

IntegralType: one of
  `byte short int long char`

FloatingPointType: one of
  `float double`

Primitive values do not share state with other primitive values.

The *numeric types* are the integral types and the floating-point types.

The *integral types* are `byte`, `short`, `int`, and `long`, whose values are 8-bit, 16-bit, 32-bit and 64-bit signed two's-complement integers, respectively, and `char`, whose values are 16-bit unsigned integers representing UTF-16 code units (§3.1).

The *floating-point types* are `float`, whose values include the 32-bit IEEE 754 floating-point numbers, and `double`, whose values include the 64-bit IEEE 754 floating-point numbers.

The `boolean` type has exactly two values: `true` and `false`.

4.2.1   Integral Types and Values

The values of the integral types are integers in the following ranges:

- For `byte`, from -128 to 127, inclusive

- For `short`, from -32768 to 32767, inclusive

- For `int`, from -2147483648 to 2147483647, inclusive

- For `long`, from -9223372036854775808 to 9223372036854775807, inclusive

- For `char`, from `'\u0000'` to `'\uffff'` inclusive, that is, from 0 to 65535

4.2.2   Integer Operations

The Java programming language provides a number of operators that act on integral values:

- The comparison operators, which result in a value of type `boolean`:
  - The numerical comparison operators `<`, `<=`, `>`, and `>=` (§15.20.1)
  - The numerical equality operators `==` and `!=` (§15.21.1)
- The numerical operators, which result in a value of type `int` or `long`:
  - The unary plus and minus operators `+` and `-` (§15.15.3, §15.15.4)
  - The multiplicative operators `*`, `/`, and `%` (§15.17)
  - The additive operators `+` and `-` (§15.18)
  - The increment operator `++`, both prefix (§15.15.1) and postfix (§15.14.2)
  - The decrement operator `--`, both prefix (§15.15.2) and postfix (§15.14.3)
  - The signed and unsigned shift operators `<<`, `>>`, and `>>>` (§15.19)
  - The bitwise complement operator `~` (§15.15.5)
  - The integer bitwise operators `&`, `^`, and `|` (§15.22.1)
- The conditional operator `?` `:` (§15.25)

- The cast operator (§15.16), which can convert from an integral value to a value of any specified numeric type

- The string concatenation operator + (§15.18.1), which, when given a `String` operand and an integral operand, will convert the integral operand to a `String` representing its value in decimal form, and then produce a newly created `String` that is the concatenation of the two strings

Other useful constructors, methods, and constants are predefined in the classes `Byte`, `Short`, `Integer`, `Long`, and `Character`.

If an integer operator other than a shift operator has at least one operand of type `long`, then the operation is carried out using 64-bit precision, and the result of the numerical operator is of type `long`. If the other operand is not `long`, it is first widened (§5.1.5) to type `long` by numeric promotion (§5.6).

Otherwise, the operation is carried out using 32-bit precision, and the result of the numerical operator is of type `int`. If either operand is not an `int`, it is first widened to type `int` by numeric promotion.

Any value of any integral type may be cast to or from any numeric type. There are no casts between integral types and the type `boolean`.

> See §4.2.5 for an idiom to convert integer expressions to `boolean`.

The integer operators do not indicate overflow or underflow in any way.

An integer operator can throw an exception (§11) for the following reasons:

- Any integer operator can throw a `NullPointerException` if unboxing conversion (§5.1.8) of a null reference is required.

- The integer divide operator / (§15.17.2) and the integer remainder operator % (§15.17.3) can throw an `ArithmeticException` if the right-hand operand is zero.

- The increment and decrement operators ++ (§15.14.2, §15.15.1) and -- (§15.14.3, §15.15.2) can throw an `OutOfMemoryError` if boxing conversion (§5.1.7) is required and there is not sufficient memory available to perform the conversion.

Example 4.2.2-1. Integer Operations

```
class Test {
    public static void main(String[] args) {
        int i = 1000000;
        System.out.println(i * i);
        long l = i;
        System.out.println(l * l);
        System.out.println(20296 / (l - i));
```

```
        }
    }
```

This program produces the output:

```
-727379968
1000000000000
```

and then encounters an `ArithmeticException` in the division by `1 - i`, because `1 - i` is zero. The first multiplication is performed in 32-bit precision, whereas the second multiplication is a `long` multiplication. The value `-727379968` is the decimal value of the low 32 bits of the mathematical result, `1000000000000`, which is a value too large for type `int`.

4.2.3   Floating-Point Types, Formats, and Values

The floating-point types are `float` and `double`, which are conceptually associated with the single-precision 32-bit and double-precision 64-bit format IEEE 754 values and operations as specified in *IEEE Standard for Binary Floating-Point Arithmetic*, ANSI/IEEE Standard 754-1985 (IEEE, New York).

The IEEE 754 standard includes not only positive and negative numbers that consist of a sign and magnitude, but also positive and negative zeros, positive and negative *infinities*, and special *Not-a-Number* values (hereafter abbreviated NaN). A NaN value is used to represent the result of certain invalid operations such as dividing zero by zero. NaN constants of both `float` and `double` type are predefined as `Float.NaN` and `Double.NaN`.

Every implementation of the Java programming language is required to support two standard sets of floating-point values, called the *float value set* and the *double value set*. In addition, an implementation of the Java programming language may support either or both of two extended-exponent floating-point value sets, called the *float-extended-exponent value set* and the *double-extended-exponent value set*. These extended-exponent value sets may, under certain circumstances, be used instead of the standard value sets to represent the values of expressions of type `float` or `double` (§5.1.13, §15.4).

The finite nonzero values of any floating-point value set can all be expressed in the form $s \cdot m \cdot 2^{(e - N + 1)}$, where s is +1 or -1, m is a positive integer less than 2^N, and e is an integer between $E_{min} = -(2^{K-1}-2)$ and $E_{max} = 2^{K-1}-1$, inclusive, and where N and K are parameters that depend on the value set. Some values can be represented in this form in more than one way; for example, supposing that a value v in a value set might be represented in this form using certain values for s, m, and e, then if it happened that m were even and e were less than 2^{K-1}, one could halve m and increase e by 1 to produce a second representation for the same value v. A representation in this form is called *normalized* if $m \geq 2^{N-1}$; otherwise the representation is said to be *denormalized*. If a value in a value set cannot be represented in such a way that $m \geq 2^{N-1}$, then the value is said to be a *denormalized value*, because it has no normalized representation.

The constraints on the parameters N and K (and on the derived parameters E_{min} and E_{max}) for the two required and two optional floating-point value sets are summarized in Table 4.1.

Table 4.1. Floating-point value set parameters

Parameter	float	float-extended-exponent	double	double-extended-exponent
N	24	24	53	53
K	8	≥ 11	11	≥ 15
E_{max}	+127	$\geq +1023$	+1023	$\geq +16383$
E_{min}	-126	≤ -1022	-1022	≤ -16382

Where one or both extended-exponent value sets are supported by an implementation, then for each supported extended-exponent value set there is a specific implementation-dependent constant K, whose value is constrained by Table 4.1; this value K in turn dictates the values for E_{min} and E_{max}.

Each of the four value sets includes not only the finite nonzero values that are ascribed to it above, but also NaN values and the four values positive zero, negative zero, positive infinity, and negative infinity.

Note that the constraints in Table 4.1 are designed so that every element of the float value set is necessarily also an element of the float-extended-exponent value set, the double value set, and the double-extended-exponent value set. Likewise, each element of the double value set is necessarily also an element of the double-extended-exponent value set. Each extended-exponent value set has a larger range of exponent values than the corresponding standard value set, but does not have more precision.

The elements of the float value set are exactly the values that can be represented using the single floating-point format defined in the IEEE 754 standard. The elements of the double value set are exactly the values that can be represented using the double floating-point format defined in the IEEE 754 standard. Note, however, that the elements of the float-extended-exponent and double-extended-exponent value sets defined here do *not* correspond to the values that can be represented using IEEE 754 single extended and double extended formats, respectively.

The float, float-extended-exponent, double, and double-extended-exponent value sets are not types. It is always correct for an implementation of the Java programming language to use an element of the float value set to represent a value of type `float`; however, it may be permissible in certain regions of code for an implementation to use an element of the float-extended-exponent value set instead. Similarly, it is always correct for an implementation to use an element of the double value set to represent a value of type `double`; however, it may be permissible in certain regions of code for an implementation to use an element of the double-extended-exponent value set instead.

Except for NaN, floating-point values are *ordered*; arranged from smallest to largest, they are negative infinity, negative finite nonzero values, positive and negative zero, positive finite nonzero values, and positive infinity.

IEEE 754 allows multiple distinct NaN values for each of its single and double floating-point formats. While each hardware architecture returns a particular bit pattern for NaN when a new NaN is generated, a programmer can also create NaNs with different bit patterns to encode, for example, retrospective diagnostic information.

For the most part, the Java SE platform treats NaN values of a given type as though collapsed into a single canonical value, and hence this specification normally refers to an arbitrary NaN as though to a canonical value.

> However, version 1.3 of the Java SE platform introduced methods enabling the programmer to distinguish between NaN values: the `Float.floatToRawIntBits` and `Double.doubleToRawLongBits` methods. The interested reader is referred to the specifications for the `Float` and `Double` classes for more information.

Positive zero and negative zero compare equal; thus the result of the expression `0.0==-0.0` is `true` and the result of `0.0>-0.0` is false. But other operations can distinguish positive and negative zero; for example, `1.0/0.0` has the value positive infinity, while the value of `1.0/-0.0` is negative infinity.

NaN is *unordered*, so:

- The numerical comparison operators `<`, `<=`, `>`, and `>=` return `false` if either or both operands are NaN (§15.20.1).

- The equality operator `==` returns `false` if either operand is NaN.

  In particular, `(x<y) == !(x>=y)` will be `false` if x or y is NaN.

- The inequality operator `!=` returns `true` if either operand is NaN (§15.21.1).

  In particular, `x!=x` is `true` if and only if x is NaN.

4.2.4 Floating-Point Operations

The Java programming language provides a number of operators that act on floating-point values:

- The comparison operators, which result in a value of type `boolean`:
  - The numerical comparison operators <, <=, >, and >= (§15.20.1)
  - The numerical equality operators == and != (§15.21.1)
- The numerical operators, which result in a value of type `float` or `double`:
  - The unary plus and minus operators + and - (§15.15.3, §15.15.4)
  - The multiplicative operators *, /, and % (§15.17)
  - The additive operators + and - (§15.18.2)
  - The increment operator ++, both prefix (§15.15.1) and postfix (§15.14.2)
  - The decrement operator --, both prefix (§15.15.2) and postfix (§15.14.3)
- The conditional operator ? : (§15.25)
- The cast operator (§15.16), which can convert from a floating-point value to a value of any specified numeric type
- The string concatenation operator + (§15.18.1), which, when given a `String` operand and a floating-point operand, will convert the floating-point operand to a `String` representing its value in decimal form (without information loss), and then produce a newly created `String` by concatenating the two strings

Other useful constructors, methods, and constants are predefined in the classes `Float`, `Double`, and `Math`.

If at least one of the operands to a binary operator is of floating-point type, then the operation is a floating-point operation, even if the other is integral.

If at least one of the operands to a numerical operator is of type `double`, then the operation is carried out using 64-bit floating-point arithmetic, and the result of the numerical operator is a value of type `double`. If the other operand is not a `double`, it is first widened (§5.1.5) to type `double` by numeric promotion (§5.6).

Otherwise, the operation is carried out using 32-bit floating-point arithmetic, and the result of the numerical operator is a value of type `float`. (If the other operand is not a `float`, it is first widened to type `float` by numeric promotion.)

Any value of a floating-point type may be cast to or from any numeric type. There are no casts between floating-point types and the type `boolean`.

See §4.2.5 for an idiom to convert floating-point expressions to `boolean`.

Operators on floating-point numbers behave as specified by IEEE 754 (with the exception of the remainder operator (§15.17.3)). In particular, the Java programming language requires support of IEEE 754 *denormalized* floating-point numbers and *gradual underflow*, which make it easier to prove desirable properties of particular numerical algorithms. Floating-point operations do not "flush to zero" if the calculated result is a denormalized number.

The Java programming language requires that floating-point arithmetic behave as if every floating-point operator rounded its floating-point result to the result precision. *Inexact* results must be rounded to the representable value nearest to the infinitely precise result; if the two nearest representable values are equally near, the one with its least significant bit zero is chosen. This is the IEEE 754 standard's default rounding mode known as *round to nearest*.

The Java programming language uses *round toward zero* when converting a floating value to an integer (§5.1.3), which acts, in this case, as though the number were truncated, discarding the mantissa bits. Rounding toward zero chooses at its result the format's value closest to and no greater in magnitude than the infinitely precise result.

A floating-point operation that overflows produces a signed infinity.

A floating-point operation that underflows produces a denormalized value or a signed zero.

A floating-point operation that has no mathematically definite result produces NaN.

All numeric operations with NaN as an operand produce NaN as a result.

A floating-point operator can throw an exception (§11) for the following reasons:

- Any floating-point operator can throw a `NullPointerException` if unboxing conversion (§5.1.8) of a null reference is required.

- The increment and decrement operators `++` (§15.14.2, §15.15.1) and `--` (§15.14.3, §15.15.2) can throw an `OutOfMemoryError` if boxing conversion (§5.1.7) is required and there is not sufficient memory available to perform the conversion.

Example 4.2.4-1. Floating-point Operations

```
class Test {
    public static void main(String[] args) {
        // An example of overflow:
        double d = 1e308;
        System.out.print("overflow produces infinity: ");
```

```
System.out.println(d + "*10==" + d*10);
// An example of gradual underflow:
d = 1e-305 * Math.PI;
System.out.print("gradual underflow: " + d + "\n   ");
for (int i = 0; i < 4; i++)
    System.out.print(" " + (d /= 100000));
System.out.println();
// An example of NaN:
System.out.print("0.0/0.0 is Not-a-Number: ");
d = 0.0/0.0;
System.out.println(d);
// An example of inexact results and rounding:
System.out.print("inexact results with float:");
for (int i = 0; i < 100; i++) {
    float z = 1.0f / i;
    if (z * i != 1.0f)
        System.out.print(" " + i);
}
System.out.println();
// Another example of inexact results and rounding:
System.out.print("inexact results with double:");
for (int i = 0; i < 100; i++) {
    double z = 1.0 / i;
    if (z * i != 1.0)
        System.out.print(" " + i);
}
System.out.println();
// An example of cast to integer rounding:
System.out.print("cast to int rounds toward 0: ");
d = 12345.6;
System.out.println((int)d + " " + (int)(-d));
    }
}
```

This program produces the output:

```
overflow produces infinity: 1.0e+308*10==Infinity
gradual underflow: 3.141592653589793E-305
3.1415926535898E-310 3.141592653E-315 3.142E-320 0.0
0.0/0.0 is Not-a-Number: NaN
inexact results with float: 0 41 47 55 61 82 83 94 97
inexact results with double: 0 49 98
cast to int rounds toward 0: 12345 -12345
```

This example demonstrates, among other things, that gradual underflow can result in a gradual loss of precision.

The results when i is 0 involve division by zero, so that z becomes positive infinity, and z * 0 is NaN, which is not equal to 1.0.

4.2.5   The `boolean` Type and boolean Values

The `boolean` type represents a logical quantity with two possible values, indicated by the literals `true` and `false` (§3.10.3).

The boolean operators are:

- The relational operators `==` and `!=` (§15.21.2)
- The logical complement operator `!` (§15.15.6)
- The logical operators `&`, `^`, and `|` (§15.22.2)
- The conditional-and and conditional-or operators `&&` (§15.23) and `||` (§15.24)
- The conditional operator `? :` (§15.25)
- The string concatenation operator `+` (§15.18.1), which, when given a `String` operand and a `boolean` operand, will convert the `boolean` operand to a `String` (either `"true"` or `"false"`), and then produce a newly created `String` that is the concatenation of the two strings

Boolean expressions determine the control flow in several kinds of statements:

- The `if` statement (§14.9)
- The `while` statement (§14.12)
- The `do` statement (§14.13)
- The `for` statement (§14.14)

A `boolean` expression also determines which subexpression is evaluated in the conditional `? :` operator (§15.25).

Only `boolean` and `Boolean` expressions can be used in control flow statements and as the first operand of the conditional operator `? :`.

An integer or floating-point expression `x` can be converted to a `boolean`, following the C language convention that any nonzero value is `true`, by the expression `x!=0`.

An object reference `obj` can be converted to a `boolean`, following the C language convention that any reference other than `null` is `true`, by the expression `obj!=null`.

A `boolean` can be converted to a `String` by string conversion (§5.4).

A cast of a `boolean` value to type `boolean` or `Boolean` is allowed (§5.1.1, §5.1.7). No other casts on type `boolean` are allowed.

4.3 Reference Types and Values

There are four kinds of *reference types*: class types (§8), interface types (§9), type variables (§4.4), and array types (§10).

ReferenceType:
  ClassOrInterfaceType
  TypeVariable
  ArrayType

ClassOrInterfaceType:
  ClassType
  InterfaceType

ClassType:
  TypeDeclSpecifier TypeArguments$_{opt}$

InterfaceType:
  TypeDeclSpecifier TypeArguments$_{opt}$

TypeDeclSpecifier:
  TypeName
  ClassOrInterfaceType . Identifier

TypeName:
  Identifier
  TypeName . Identifier

TypeVariable:
  Identifier

ArrayType:
  Type [ ]

The sample code:

```
class Point { int[] metrics; }
interface Move { void move(int deltax, int deltay); }
```

declares a class type `Point`, an interface type `Move`, and uses an array type `int[]` (an array of `int`) to declare the field `metrics` of the class `Point`.

A class or interface type consists of a *type declaration specifier*, optionally followed by type arguments (§4.5.1). If type arguments appear anywhere in a class or interface type, it is a parameterized type (§4.5).

A type declaration specifier may be either a type name (§6.5.5), or a class or interface type followed by "." and an identifier. In the latter case, the specifier has the form `T.id`, where `id` must be the simple name of an accessible (§6.6) member type (§8.5, §9.5) of `T`, or a compile-time error occurs. The specifier denotes that member type.

There are contexts in the Java programming language where a generic class or interface name is used without providing type arguments. Such contexts do not involve the use of raw types (§4.8). Rather, they are contexts where type arguments are unnecessary for, or irrelevant to, the meaning of the generic class or interface.

For example, a single-type-import declaration `import java.util.List;` puts the simple type name `List` in scope within a compilation unit so that parameterized types of the form `List<...>` may be used. As another example, invocation of a static method of a generic class needs only to give the (possibly qualified) name of the generic class without any type arguments, because such type arguments are irrelevant to a static method. (The method itself may be generic, and take its own type arguments, but the type parameters of a static method are necessarily unrelated to the type parameters of its enclosing generic class (§6.5.5).)

Because of the occasional need to use a generic class or interface name without type arguments, type names are distinct from type declaration specifiers. A type name is always qualified by means of another type name. In some cases, this is necessary to access an inner class that is a member of a parameterized type.

Here is an example of where a type declaration specifier is distinct from a type name:

```
class GenericOuter<T extends Number> {
    public class Inner<S extends Comparable<S>> {
        T getT() { return null; }
        S getS() { return null; }
    }
}

class Test {
    public static void main(String[] args) {
        GenericOuter<Integer>.Inner<Double> x1 = null;
        Integer i = x1.getT();
        Double d = x1.getS();
    }
}
```

If we accessed `Inner` by qualifying it with a type name, as in:

```
GenericOuter.Inner x2 = null;
```

we would force its use as a raw type, losing type information.

4.3.1 Objects

An *object* is a *class instance* or an *array*.

The reference values (often just *references*) are pointers to these objects, and a special null reference, which refers to no object.

A class instance is explicitly created by a class instance creation expression (§15.9).

An array is explicitly created by an array creation expression (§15.10).

A new class instance is implicitly created when the string concatenation operator + (§15.18.1) is used in a non-constant (§15.28) expression, resulting in a new object of type String (§4.3.3).

A new array object is implicitly created when an array initializer expression (§10.6) is evaluated; this can occur when a class or interface is initialized (§12.4), when a new instance of a class is created (§15.9), or when a local variable declaration statement is executed (§14.4).

New objects of the types Boolean, Byte, Short, Character, Integer, Long, Float, and Double may be implicitly created by boxing conversion (§5.1.7).

Example 4.3.1-1. Object Creation

```java
class Point {
    int x, y;
    Point() { System.out.println("default"); }
    Point(int x, int y) { this.x = x; this.y = y; }

    /* A Point instance is explicitly created at
       class initialization time: */
    static Point origin = new Point(0,0);

    /* A String can be implicitly created
       by a + operator: */
    public String toString() { return "(" + x + "," + y + ")"; }
}

class Test {
    public static void main(String[] args) {
        /* A Point is explicitly created
           using newInstance: */
        Point p = null;
        try {
            p = (Point)Class.forName("Point").newInstance();
        } catch (Exception e) {
            System.out.println(e);
```

```
            }

            /* An array is implicitly created
               by an array constructor: */
            Point a[] = { new Point(0,0), new Point(1,1) };

            /* Strings are implicitly created
               by + operators: */
            System.out.println("p: " + p);
            System.out.println("a: { " + a[0] + ", " + a[1] + " }");

            /* An array is explicitly created
               by an array creation expression: */
            String sa[] = new String[2];
            sa[0] = "he"; sa[1] = "llo";
            System.out.println(sa[0] + sa[1]);
        }
    }
```

This program produces the output:

```
default
p: (0,0)
a: { (0,0), (1,1) }
hello
```

The operators on references to objects are:

- Field access, using either a qualified name (§6.6) or a field access expression (§15.11)

- Method invocation (§15.12)

- The cast operator (§5.5, §15.16)

- The string concatenation operator + (§15.18.1), which, when given a String operand and a reference, will convert the reference to a String by invoking the toString method of the referenced object (using "null" if either the reference or the result of toString is a null reference), and then will produce a newly created String that is the concatenation of the two strings

- The instanceof operator (§15.20.2)

- The reference equality operators == and != (§15.21.3)

- The conditional operator ? : (§15.25).

There may be many references to the same object. Most objects have state, stored in the fields of objects that are instances of classes or in the variables that are the components of an array object. If two variables contain references to the same object, the state of the object can be modified using one variable's reference to the object, and then the altered state can be observed through the reference in the other variable.

Example 4.3.1-2. Primitive and Reference Identity

```
class Value { int val; }

class Test {
    public static void main(String[] args) {
        int i1 = 3;
        int i2 = i1;
        i2 = 4;
        System.out.print("i1==" + i1);
        System.out.println(" but i2==" + i2);
        Value v1 = new Value();
        v1.val = 5;
        Value v2 = v1;
        v2.val = 6;
        System.out.print("v1.val==" + v1.val);
        System.out.println(" and v2.val==" + v2.val);
    }
}
```

This program produces the output:

```
i1==3 but i2==4
v1.val==6 and v2.val==6
```

because `v1.val` and `v2.val` reference the same instance variable (§4.12.3) in the one `Value` object created by the only `new` expression, while `i1` and `i2` are different variables.

Each object is associated with a monitor (§17.1), which is used by `synchronized` methods (§8.4.3) and the `synchronized` statement (§14.19) to provide control over concurrent access to state by multiple threads (§17).

4.3.2 The Class `Object`

The class `Object` is a superclass (§8.1.4) of all other classes.

All class and array types inherit (§8.4.8) the methods of class `Object`, which are summarized as follows:

- The method `clone` is used to make a duplicate of an object.

- The method `equals` defines a notion of object equality, which is based on value, not reference, comparison.

- The method `finalize` is run just before an object is destroyed (§12.6).

- The method `getClass` returns the `Class` object that represents the class of the object.

  A `Class` object exists for each reference type. It can be used, for example, to discover the fully qualified name of a class, its members, its immediate superclass, and any interfaces that it implements.

  The type of a method invocation expression of `getClass` is `Class<? extends |T|>` where T is the class or interface searched (§15.12.1) for `getClass`.

  A class method that is declared `synchronized` (§8.4.3.6) synchronizes on the monitor associated with the `Class` object of the class.

- The method `hashCode` is very useful, together with the method `equals`, in hashtables such as `java.util.Hashmap`.

- The methods `wait`, `notify`, and `notifyAll` are used in concurrent programming using threads (§17.2).

- The method `toString` returns a `String` representation of the object.

4.3.3 The Class `String`

Instances of class `String` represent sequences of Unicode code points.

A `String` object has a constant (unchanging) value.

String literals (§3.10.5) are references to instances of class `String`.

The string concatenation operator + (§15.18.1) implicitly creates a new `String` object when the result is not a compile-time constant expression (§15.28).

4.3.4 When Reference Types Are the Same

Two reference types are the *same compile-time type* if they have the same binary name (§13.1) and their type arguments, if any, are the same, applying this definition recursively.

When two reference types are the same, they are sometimes said to be the *same class* or the *same interface*.

At run time, several reference types with the same binary name may be loaded simultaneously by different class loaders. These types may or may not represent the same type declaration. Even if two such types do represent the same type declaration, they are considered distinct.

Two reference types are the *same run-time type* if:

- They are both class or both interface types, are defined by the same class loader, and have the same binary name (§13.1), in which case they are sometimes said to be the *same run-time class* or the *same run-time interface*.

- They are both array types, and their component types are the same run-time type (§10).

4.4   Type Variables

A *type variable* is an unqualified identifier used as a type in class, interface, method, and constructor bodies.

A type variable is declared as a *type parameter* of a generic class declaration (§8.1.2), generic interface declaration (§9.1.2), generic method declaration (§8.4.4), or generic constructor declaration (§8.8.4).

> *TypeParameter:*
>   *TypeVariable TypeBound*$_{opt}$
>
> *TypeBound:*
>   extends *TypeVariable*
>   extends *ClassOrInterfaceType AdditionalBoundList*$_{opt}$
>
> *AdditionalBoundList:*
>   *AdditionalBound AdditionalBoundList*
>   *AdditionalBound*
>
> *AdditionalBound:*
>   & *InterfaceType*

The scope of a type variable declared as a type parameter is specified in §6.3.

Every type variable declared as a type parameter has a *bound*. If no bound is declared for a type variable, Object is assumed. If a bound is declared, it consists of either:

- a single type variable T, or

- a class or interface type T possibly followed by interface types I_1 & ... & I_n.

It is a compile-time error if any of the types $I_1 ... I_n$ is a class type or type variable.

The erasures (§4.6) of all constituent types of a bound must be pairwise different, or a compile-time error occurs.

A type variable must not at the same time be a subtype of two interface types which are different parameterizations of the same generic interface, or a compile-time error occurs.

The order of types in a bound is only significant in that the erasure of a type variable is determined by the first type in its bound, and that a class type or type variable may only appear in the first position.

The members of a type variable X with bound T & I_1 & ... & I_n are the members of the intersection type (§4.9) T & I_1 & ... & I_n appearing at the point where the type variable is declared.

Example 4.4-1. Members of a Type Variable

```
package TypeVarMembers;

class C {
    public      void mCPublic()     {}
    protected void mCProtected() {}
                void mCDefault()    {}
    private     void mCPrivate()    {}
}

interface I {
    void mI();
}

class CT extends C implements I {
    public void mI() {}
}

class Test {
    <T extends C & I> void test(T t) {
        t.mI();            // OK
        t.mCPublic();      // OK
        t.mCProtected();   // OK
        t.mCDefault();     // OK
        t.mCPrivate();     // Compile-time error
    }
}
```

The type variable T has the same members as the intersection type C & I, which in turn has the same members as the empty class CT, defined in the same scope with equivalent supertypes. The members of an interface are always `public`, and therefore always inherited (unless overridden). Hence mI is a member of CT and of T. Among the members of C, all but mCPrivate are inherited by CT, and are therefore members of both CT and T.

If C had been declared in a different package than T, then the call to mCDefault would give rise to a compile-time error, as that member would not be accessible at the point where T is declared.

4.5 Parameterized Types

A generic class or interface declaration C (§8.1.2, §9.1.2) with one or more type parameters $A_1,...,A_n$ which have corresponding bounds $B_1,...,B_n$ defines a set of parameterized types, one for each possible invocation of the type parameter section.

Each parameterized type in the set is of the form $C<T_1,...,T_n>$ where each type argument T_i ranges over all types that are subtypes of all types listed in the corresponding bound. That is, for each bound type S_i in B_i, T_i is a subtype of $S_i[F_1:=T_1, \ldots, F_n:=T_n]$.

A parameterized type is written as a *ClassType* or *InterfaceType* that contains at least one type declaration specifier immediately followed by a type argument list $<T_1,...,T_n>$. The type argument list denotes a particular invocation of the type parameters of the generic type indicated by the type declaration specifier.

Given a type declaration specifier immediately followed by a type argument list, let C be the final *Identifier* in the specifier.

It is a compile-time error if C is not the name of a generic class or interface, or if the number of type arguments in the type argument list differs from the number of type parameters of C.

Let $P = C<T_1,...,T_n>$ be a parameterized type. It must be the case that, after P is subjected to capture conversion (§5.1.10) resulting in the type $C<X_1,...,X_n>$, for each type argument X_i $(1 \leq i \leq n)$, $X_i <: B_i[A_1:=X_1, \ldots, A_n:=X_n]$ (§4.10), or a compile-time error occurs.

The notation $[A_i:=T_i]$ denotes substitution of the type variable A_i with the type T_i for $1 \leq i \leq n$, and is used throughout this specification.

In this specification, whenever we speak of a class or interface type, we include the generic version as well, unless explicitly excluded.

Examples of parameterized types:

- `Vector<String>`

- `Seq<Seq<A>>`

- `Seq<String>.Zipper<Integer>`

- `Collection<Integer>`

- `Pair<String,String>`

Examples of incorrect invocations of a generic type:

- `Vector<int>` is illegal, as primitive types cannot be type arguments.
- `Pair<String>` is illegal, as there are not enough type arguments.
- `Pair<String,String,String>` is illegal, as there are too many type arguments.

A parameterized type may be an invocation of a generic class or interface which is nested. For example, if a non-generic class `C` has a generic member class `D<T>`, then `C.D<Object>` is a parameterized type. And if a generic class `C<T>` has a non-generic member class `D`, then the member type `C<String>.D` is a parameterized type, even though the class `D` is not generic.

Two parameterized types are provably distinct if either of the following conditions hold:

- They are invocations of distinct generic type declarations.

- Any of their type arguments are provably distinct.

4.5.1 Type Arguments and Wildcards

Type arguments may be either reference types or wildcards. Wildcards are useful in situations where only partial knowledge about the type parameter is required.

TypeArguments:
  < TypeArgumentList >

TypeArgumentList:
  TypeArgument
  TypeArgumentList , TypeArgument

TypeArgument:
  ReferenceType
  Wildcard

Wildcard:
  ? WildcardBounds$_{opt}$

WildcardBounds:
  extends *ReferenceType*
  super *ReferenceType*

Example 4.5.1-1. Wildcards

```
import java.util.Collection;
import java.util.ArrayList;

class Test {
    static void printCollection(Collection<?> c) {
                                // a wildcard collection
        for (Object o : c) {
            System.out.println(o);
        }
    }

    public static void main(String[] args) {
        Collection<String> cs = new ArrayList<String>();
        cs.add("hello");
        cs.add("world");
        printCollection(cs);
    }
}
```

Note that using `Collection<Object>` as the type of the incoming parameter, `c`, would not be nearly as useful; the method could only be used with an argument expression that had type `Collection<Object>`, which would be quite rare. In contrast, the use of an unbounded wildcard allows any kind of collection to be used as a parameter.

Here is an example where the element type of an array is parameterized by a wildcard:

```
public Method getMethod(Class<?>[] parameterTypes) { ... }
```

Wildcards may be given explicit bounds, just like regular type variable declarations. An upper bound is signified by the following syntax, where *B* is the bound:

```
? extends B
```

Unlike ordinary type variables declared in a method signature, no type inference is required when using a wildcard. Consequently, it is permissible to declare lower bounds on a wildcard, using the following syntax, where *B* is a lower bound:

```
? super B
```

Example 4.5.1-2. Bounded Wildcards

```
boolean addAll(Collection<? extends E> c)
```

Here, the method is declared within the interface `Collection<E>`, and is designed to add all the elements of its incoming argument to the collection upon which it is invoked. A natural tendency would be to use `Collection<E>` as the type of c, but this is unnecessarily restrictive. An alternative would be to declare the method itself to be generic:

```
<T> boolean addAll(Collection<T> c)
```

This version is sufficiently flexible, but note that the type parameter is used only once in the signature. This reflects the fact that the type parameter is not being used to express any kind of interdependency between the type(s) of the argument(s), the return type and/or throws type. In the absence of such interdependency, generic methods are considered bad style, and wildcards are preferred.

```
Reference(T referent, ReferenceQueue<? super T> queue);
```

Here, the referent can be inserted into any queue whose element type is a supertype of the type T of the referent; T is the lower bound for the wildcard.

Two type arguments are provably distinct if one of the following is true:

- Neither argument is a type variable or wildcard, and the two arguments are not the same type.

- One type argument is a type variable or wildcard, with an upper bound (from capture conversion, if necessary) of S; and the other type argument T is not a type variable or wildcard; and neither $|S| <: |T|$ nor $|T| <: |S|$.

- Each type argument is a type variable or wildcard, with upper bounds (from capture conversion, if necessary) of S and T; and neither $|S| <: |T|$ nor $|T| <: |S|$.

A type argument T_1 is said to *contain* another type argument T_2, written $T_2 <= T_1$, if the set of types denoted by T_2 is provably a subset of the set of types denoted by T_1 under the reflexive and transitive closure of the following rules (where $<:$ denotes subtyping (§4.10)):

- `? extends` T `<= ? extends` S if $T <: S$

- `? super` T `<= ? super` S if $S <: T$

- T `<=` T

- T `<= ? extends` T

- T `<= ? super` T

The relationship of wildcards to established type theory is an interesting one, which we briefly allude to here. Wildcards are a restricted form of existential types. Given a generic type declaration G`<`T `extends` B`>`, G`<?>` is roughly analogous to `Some X <: B. G<X>`.

Historically, wildcards are a direct descendant of the work by Atsushi Igarashi and Mirko Viroli. Readers interested in a more comprehensive discussion should refer to *On Variance-Based Subtyping for Parametric Types* by Atsushi Igarashi and Mirko Viroli, in the *Proceedings of the 16th European Conference on Object Oriented Programming (ECOOP 2002)*. This work itself builds upon earlier work by Kresten Thorup and Mads Torgersen (*Unifying Genericity*, ECOOP 99), as well as a long tradition of work on declaration based variance that goes back to Pierre America's work on POOL (OOPSLA 89).

Wildcards differ in certain details from the constructs described in the aforementioned paper, in particular in the use of capture conversion (§5.1.10) rather than the `close` operation described by Igarashi and Viroli. For a formal account of wildcards, see *Wild FJ* by Mads Torgersen, Erik Ernst and Christian Plesner Hansen, in the 12th workshop on Foundations of Object Oriented Programming (FOOL 2005).

4.5.2 Members and Constructors of Parameterized Types

Let C be a generic class or interface declaration with type parameters $A_1,...,A_n$, and let C`<`$T_1,...,T_n$`>` be an invocation of C, where, for $1 \leq i \leq n$, T_i are types (rather than wildcards). Then:

- Let m be a member or constructor declaration (§8.2, §8.8.6) in C, whose type as declared is T.

  The type of m in C`<`$T_1,...,T_n$`>` is $T[A_1:=T_1, \ldots, A_n:=T_n]$.

- Let m be a member or constructor declaration in D, where D is a class extended by C or an interface implemented by C. Let D`<`$U_1,...,U_k$`>` be the supertype of C`<`$T_1,...,T_n$`>` that corresponds to D.

  The type of m in C`<`$T_1,...,T_n$`>` is the type of m in D`<`$U_1,...,U_k$`>`.

If any of the type arguments in the invocation of C are wildcards, then:

- The types of the fields, methods, and constructors in C`<`$T_1,...,T_n$`>` are the types of the fields, methods, and constructors in the capture conversion (§5.1.9) of C`<`$T_1,...,T_n$`>`.

• Let D be a (possibly generic) class or interface declaration in C. Then the type of D in $C<T_1,...,T_n>$ is D where, if D is generic, all type arguments are unbounded wildcards.

> This is of no consequence, as it is impossible to access a member of a parameterized type without performing capture conversion (§5.1.10), and it is impossible to use a wildcard type after the keyword `new` in a class instance creation expression.

> The sole exception to the previous paragraph is when a nested parameterized type is used as the expression in an `instanceof` operator (§15.20.2), where capture conversion is not applied.

4.6 Type Erasure

Type erasure is a mapping from types (possibly including parameterized types and type variables) to types (that are never parameterized types or type variables). We write $|T|$ for the erasure of type T. The erasure mapping is defined as follows:

• The erasure of a parameterized type (§4.5) $G<T_1,...,T_n>$ is $|G|$.

• The erasure of a nested type $T.C$ is $|T|.C$.

• The erasure of an array type $T[]$ is $|T|[]$.

• The erasure of a type variable (§4.4) is the erasure of its leftmost bound.

• The erasure of every other type is the type itself.

Type erasure also maps the signature (§8.4.2) of a constructor or method to a signature that has no parameterized types or type variables. The erasure of a constructor or method signature s is a signature consisting of the same name as s and the erasures of all the formal parameter types given in s.

The type parameters of a constructor or method (§8.4.4), and the return type (§8.4.5) of a method, also undergo erasure if the constructor or method's signature is erased.

The erasure of the signature of a generic method has no type parameters.

4.7 Reifiable Types

Because some type information is erased during compilation, not all types are available at run time. Types that are completely available at run time are known as *reifiable types*.

A type is *reifiable* if and only if one of the following holds:

- It refers to a non-generic class or interface type declaration.

- It is a parameterized type in which all type arguments are unbounded wildcards (§4.5.1).

- It is a raw type (§4.8).

- It is a primitive type (§4.2).

- It is an array type (§10.1) whose element type is reifiable.

- It is a nested type where, for each type T separated by a ".", T itself is reifiable.

> For example, if a generic class $X<T>$ has a generic member class $Y<U>$, then the type $X<?>.Y<?>$ is reifiable because $X<?>$ is reifiable and $Y<?>$ is reifiable. The type $X<?>.Y<Object>$ is not reifiable because $Y<Object>$ is not reifiable.

An intersection type is not reifiable.

> The decision not to make all generic types reifiable is one of the most crucial, and controversial design decisions involving the type system of the Java programming language.
>
> Ultimately, the most important motivation for this decision is compatibility with existing code. In a naive sense, the addition of new constructs such as generics has no implications for pre-existing code. The Java programming language, per se, is compatible with earlier versions as long as every program written in the previous versions retains its meaning in the new version. However, this notion, which may be termed language compatibility, is of purely theoretical interest. Real programs (even trivial ones, such as "Hello World") are composed of several compilation units, some of which are provided by the Java SE platform (such as elements of `java.lang` or `java.util`). In practice, then, the minimum requirement is platform compatibility - that any program written for the prior version of the Java SE platform continues to function unchanged in the new version.
>
> One way to provide platform compatibility is to leave existing platform functionality unchanged, only adding new functionality. For example, rather than modify the existing Collections hierarchy in `java.util`, one might introduce a new library utilizing generics.
>
> The disadvantages of such a scheme is that it is extremely difficult for pre-existing clients of the Collection library to migrate to the new library. Collections are used to exchange data between independently developed modules; if a vendor decides to switch to the new, generic, library, that vendor must also distribute two versions of their code, to be compatible

with their clients. Libraries that are dependent on other vendors code cannot be modified to use generics until the supplier's library is updated. If two modules are mutually dependent, the changes must be made simultaneously.

Clearly, platform compatibility, as outlined above, does not provide a realistic path for adoption of a pervasive new feature such as generics. Therefore, the design of the generic type system seeks to support migration compatibility. Migration compatibiliy allows the evolution of existing code to take advantage of generics without imposing dependencies between independently developed software modules.

The price of migration compatibility is that a full and sound reification of the generic type system is not possible, at least while the migration is taking place.

4.8 Raw Types

To facilitate interfacing with non-generic legacy code, it is possible to use as a type the erasure (§4.6) of a parameterized type (§4.5) or the erasure of an array type (§10.1) whose element type is a parameterized type. Such a type is called a *raw type*.

More precisely, a raw type is defined to be one of:

- The reference type that is formed by taking the name of a generic type declaration without an accompanying type argument list.

- An array type whose element type is a raw type.

- A non-static member type of a raw type R that is not inherited from a superclass or superinterface of R.

A non-generic class or interface type is not a raw type.

> To see why a non-static type member of a raw type is considered raw, consider the following example:

```
class Outer<T>{
    T t;
    class Inner {
        T setOuterT(T t1) { t = t1; return t; }
    }
}
```

> The type of the member(s) of Inner depends on the type parameter of Outer. If Outer is raw, Inner must be treated as raw as well, as there is no valid binding for T.

This rule applies only to type members that are not inherited. Inherited type members that depend on type variables will be inherited as raw types as a consequence of the rule that the supertypes of a raw type are erased, described later in this section.

Another implication of the rules above is that a generic inner class of a raw type can itself only be used as a raw type:

```
class Outer<T>{
    class Inner<S> {
        S s;
    }
}
```

It is not possible to access `Inner` as a partially raw type (a "rare" type):

```
Outer.Inner<Double> x = null;  // illegal
Double d = x.s;
```

because `Outer` itself is raw, hence so are all its inner classes including `Inner`, and so it is not possible to pass any type arguments to Inner.

The superclasses (respectively, superinterfaces) of a raw type are the erasures of the superclasses (superinterfaces) of any of its parameterized invocations.

The type of a constructor (§8.8), instance method (§8.4, §9.4), or non-static field (§8.3) M of a raw type C that is not inherited from its superclasses or superinterfaces is the raw type that corresponds to the erasure of its type in the generic declaration corresponding to C.

The type of a static method or static field of a raw type C is the same as its type in the generic declaration corresponding to C.

It is a compile-time error to pass type arguments to a non-`static` type member of a raw type that is not inherited from its superclasses or superinterfaces.

It is a compile-time error to attempt to use a type member of a parameterized type as a raw type.

This means that the ban on "rare" types extends to the case where the qualifying type is parameterized, but we attempt to use the inner class as a raw type:

```
Outer<Integer>.Inner x = null; // illegal
```

This is the opposite of the case discussed above. There is no practical justification for this half-baked type. In legacy code, no type arguments are used. In non-legacy code, we should use the generic types correctly and pass all the required type arguments.

The supertype of a class may be a raw type. Member accesses for the class are treated as normal, and member accesses for the supertype are treated as for raw types. In the constructor of the class, calls to `super` are treated as method calls on a raw type.

The use of raw types is allowed only as a concession to compatibility of legacy code. The use of raw types in code written after the introduction of generics into the Java programming language is strongly discouraged. It is possible that future versions of the Java programming language will disallow the use of raw types.

To make sure that potential violations of the typing rules are always flagged, some accesses to members of a raw type will result in compile-time unchecked warnings. The rules for compile-time unchecked warnings when accessing members or constructors of raw types are as follows:

- At an assignment to a field: if the type of the left-hand operand is a raw type, then a compile-time unchecked warning occurs if erasure changes the field's type.

- At an invocation of a method or constructor: if the type of the class or interface to search (§15.12.1) is a raw type, then a compile-time unchecked warning occurs if erasure changes any of the formal parameter types of the method or constructor.

- No compile-time unchecked warning occurs for a method call when the formal parameter types do not change under erasure (even if the result type and/or `throws` clause changes), for reading from a field, or for a class instance creation of a raw type.

> Note that the unchecked warnings above are distinct from the unchecked warnings possible from unchecked conversion (§5.1.9), casts (§5.5.2), method declarations (§8.4.1, §8.4.8.3, §8.4.8.4, §9.4.1.2), and variable arity method invocations (§15.12.4.2).
>
> The warnings here cover the case where a legacy consumer uses a generified library. For example, the library declares a generic class `Foo<T extends String>` that has a field `f` of type `Vector<T>`, but the consumer assigns a vector of integers to `e.f` where `e` has the raw type `Foo`. The legacy consumer receives a warning because it may have caused heap pollution (§4.12.2) for generified consumers of the generified library.
>
> (Note that the legacy consumer can assign a `Vector<String>` from the library to its own `Vector` variable without receiving a warning. That is, the subtyping rules (§4.10.2) of the Java programming language make it possible for a variable of a raw type to be assigned a value of any of the type's parameterized instances.)
>
> The warnings from unchecked conversion cover the dual case, where a generified consumer uses a legacy library. For example, a method of the library has the raw return type `Vector`, but the consumer assigns the result of the method invocation to a variable of type `Vector<String>`. This is unsafe, since the raw vector might have had a different element type than `String`, but is still permitted using unchecked conversion in order to enable interfacing with legacy code. The warning from unchecked conversion indicates that the

generified consumer may experience problems from heap pollution at other points in the program.

Example 4.8-1. Raw Types

```
class Cell<E> {
    E value;

    Cell(E v)      { value = v; }
    E get()        { return value; }
    void set(E v) { value = v; }

    public static void main(String[] args) {
        Cell x = new Cell<String>("abc");
        System.out.println(x.value);   // OK, has type Object
        System.out.println(x.get());   // OK, has type Object
        x.set("def");                  // unchecked warning
    }
}
```

Example 4.8-2. Raw Types and Inheritance

```
import java.util.*;
class NonGeneric {
    Collection<Number> myNumbers() { return null; }
}

abstract class RawMembers<T> extends NonGeneric
                            implements Collection<String> {
    static Collection<NonGeneric> cng =
        new ArrayList<NonGeneric>();

    public static void main(String[] args) {
        RawMembers rw = null;
        Collection<Number> cn = rw.myNumbers();
                        // OK
        Iterator<String> is = rw.iterator();
                        // Unchecked warning
        Collection<NonGeneric> cnn = rw.cng;
                            // OK, static member
    }
}
```

In this program, `RawMembers<T>` inherits the method:

```
Iterator<String> iterator()
```

from the `Collection<String>` superinterface. However, the type `RawMembers` inherits `iterator()` from the *erasure* of `Collection<String>`, which means that the return type of `iterator()` is the erasure of `Iterator<String>`, `Iterator`.

As a result, the attempt to assign to `rw.iterator()` requires an unchecked conversion (§5.1.9) from `Iterator` to `Iterator<String>`, causing an unchecked warning to be issued.

In contrast, the static member `cng` retains its full parameterized type even when accessed through a object of raw type. (Note that access to a static member through an instance is considered bad style and is to be discouraged.) The member `myNumbers` is inherited from the `NonGeneric` class (whose erasure is also `NonGeneric`) and so retains its full parameterized type.

Raw types are closely related to wildcards. Both are based on existential types. Raw types can be thought of as wildcards whose type rules are deliberately unsound, to accommodate interaction with legacy code. Historically, raw types preceded wildcards; they were first introduced in GJ, and described in the paper *Making the future safe for the past: Adding Genericity to the Java Programming Language* by Gilad Bracha, Martin Odersky, David Stoutamire, and Philip Wadler, in *Proceedings of the ACM Conference on Object-Oriented Programming, Systems, Languages and Applications (OOPSLA 98)*, October 1998.

4.9 Intersection Types

An intersection type takes the form T_1 & ... & T_n ($n > 0$), where T_i ($1 \leq i \leq n$) are type expressions.

Intersection types arise in the processes of capture conversion (§5.1.10) and type inference (§15.12.2.7). It is not possible to write an intersection type directly as part of a program; no syntax supports this.

The values of an intersection type are those objects that are values of all of the types T_i for $1 \leq i \leq n$.

The members of an intersection type T_1 & ... & T_n are determined as follows:

- For each T_i ($1 \leq i \leq n$), let C_i be the most specific class or array type such that $T_i <: C_i$. Then there must be some $T_k <: C_k$ such that $C_k <: C_i$ for any i ($1 \leq i \leq n$), or a compile-time error occurs.

- For $1 \leq j \leq n$, if T_j is a type variable, then let T_j' be an interface whose members are the same as the public members of T_j; otherwise, if T_j is an interface, then let T_j' be T_j.

- Then the intersection type has the same members as a class type (§8) with an empty body, direct superclass C_k and direct superinterfaces T_1', ..., T_n', declared in the same package in which the intersection type appears.

> It is worth dwelling upon the distinction between intersection types and the bounds of type variables. Every type variable bound induces an intersection type. This intersection type is often trivial (i.e., consists of a single type). The form of a bound is restricted (only the

first element may be a class or type variable, and only one type variable may appear in the bound) to preclude certain awkward situations coming into existence. However, capture conversion can lead to the creation of type variables whose bounds are more general (e.g., array types).

4.10   Subtyping

The subtype and supertype relations are binary relations on types.

The *supertypes* of a type are obtained by reflexive and transitive closure over the direct supertype relation, written $S >_1 T$, which is defined by rules given later in this section. We write $S :> T$ to indicate that the supertype relation holds between S and T.

S is a *proper supertype* of T, written $S > T$, if $S :> T$ and $S \neq T$.

The *subtypes* of a type T are all types U such that T is a supertype of U, and the null type. We write $T <: S$ to indicate that that the subtype relation holds between types T and S.

T is a *proper subtype* of S, written $T < S$, if $T <: S$ and $S \neq T$.

T is a *direct subtype* of S, written $T <_1 S$, if $S >_1 T$.

Subtyping does not extend through parameterized types: $T <: S$ does not imply that C<T> <: C<S>.

4.10.1   Subtyping among Primitive Types

The following rules define the direct supertype relation among the primitive types:

- `double` $>_1$ `float`

- `float` $>_1$ `long`

- `long` $>_1$ `int`

- `int` $>_1$ `char`

- `int` $>_1$ `short`

- `short` $>_1$ `byte`

4.10.2   Subtyping among Class and Interface Types

Given a generic type declaration $C<F_1,...,F_n>$, the direct supertypes of the parameterized type $C<T_1,...,T_n>$ are all of the following:

- The direct superclasses of C.

- The direct superinterfaces of C.

- The type `Object`, if C is an interface type with no direct superinterfaces.

- The raw type C.

The direct supertypes of the parameterized type $C<T_1,...,T_n>$, where T_i $(1 \leq i \leq n)$ is a type, are all of the following:

- $D<U_1 \theta,...,U_k \theta>$, where $D<U_1,...,U_k>$ is a direct supertype of $C<T_1,...,T_n>$ and θ is the substitution $[F_1:=T_1, ..., F_n:=T_n]$.

- $C<S_1,...,S_n>$, where S_i contains T_i $(1 \leq i \leq n)$ (§4.5.1).

The direct supertypes of the parameterized type $C<R_1,...,R_n>$, where at least one of the R_i $(1 \leq i \leq n)$ is a wildcard type argument, are the direct supertypes of $C<X_1,...,X_n>$ which is the result of applying capture conversion (§5.1.10) to $C<R_1,...,R_n>$.

The direct supertypes of an intersection type $T_1 \& ... \& T_n$ are T_i $(1 \leq i \leq n)$.

The direct supertypes of a type variable are the types listed in its bound.

A type variable is a direct supertype of its lower bound.

The direct supertypes of the null type are all reference types other than the null type itself.

4.10.3   Subtyping among Array Types

The following rules define the direct supertype relation among array types:

- If S and T are both reference types, then $S[] >_1 T[]$ iff $S >_1 T$.

- `Object` $>_1$ `Object[]`

- `Cloneable` $>_1$ `Object[]`

- `java.io.Serializable` $>_1$ `Object[]`

- If P is a primitive type, then:

  • `Object` $>_1$ $P[]$

  • `Cloneable` $>_1$ $P[]$

* `java.io.Serializable >`$_1$ `P[]`

4.11 Where Types Are Used

Types are used when they appear in declarations or in certain expressions.

Example 4.11-1. Usage of a Type˙

```
import java.util.Random;
import java.util.Collection;
import java.util.ArrayList;

class MiscMath<T extends Number> {
    int divisor;
    MiscMath(int divisor) { this.divisor = divisor; }
    float ratio(long l) {
        try {
            l /= divisor;
        } catch (Exception e) {
            if (e instanceof ArithmeticException)
                l = Long.MAX_VALUE;
            else
                l = 0;
        }
        return (float)l;
    }
    double gausser() {
        Random r = new Random();
        double[] val = new double[2];
        val[0] = r.nextGaussian();
        val[1] = r.nextGaussian();
        return (val[0] + val[1]) / 2;
    }
    Collection<Number> fromArray(Number[] na) {
        Collection<Number> cn = new ArrayList<Number>();
        for (Number n : na) cn.add(n);
        return cn;
    }
    <S> void loop(S s) { this.<S>loop(s); }
}
```

In this example, types are used in declarations of the following:

* Imported types (§7.5); here the type `Random`, imported from the type `java.util.Random` of the package `java.util`, is declared

* Fields, which are the class variables and instance variables of classes (§8.3), and constants of interfaces (§9.3); here the field `divisor` in the class `MiscMath` is declared to be of type `int`

- Method parameters (§8.4.1); here the parameter `l` of the method `ratio` is declared to be of type `long`

- Method results (§8.4); here the result of the method `ratio` is declared to be of type `float`, and the result of the method `gausser` is declared to be of type `double`

- Constructor parameters (§8.8.1); here the parameter of the constructor for `MiscMath` is declared to be of type `int`

- Local variables (§14.4, §14.14); the local variables `r` and `val` of the method `gausser` are declared to be of types `Random` and `double[]` (array of `double`)

- Exception parameters (§14.20); here the exception parameter `e` of the `catch` clause is declared to be of type `Exception`

- Type parameters (§4.4); here the type parameter of `MiscMath` is a type variable `T` with the type `Number` as its declared bound

- In any declaration that uses a parameterized type; here the type `Number` is used as a type argument (§4.5.1) in the parameterized type `Collection<Number>`.

and in expressions of the following kinds:

- Class instance creations (§15.9); here a local variable `r` of method `gausser` is initialized by a class instance creation expression that uses the type `Random`

- Generic class (§8.1.2) instance creations (§15.9); here `Number` is used as a type argument in the expression `new ArrayList<Number>()`

- Array creations (§15.10); here the local variable `val` of method `gausser` is initialized by an array creation expression that creates an array of `double` with size 2

- Generic method (§8.4.4) or constructor (§8.8.4) invocations (§15.12); here the method `loop` calls itself with an explicit type argument `S`

- Casts (§15.16); here the `return` statement of the method `ratio` uses the `float` type in a cast

- The `instanceof` operator (§15.20.2); here the `instanceof` operator tests whether `e` is assignment-compatible with the type `ArithmeticException`

4.12 Variables

A variable is a storage location and has an associated type, sometimes called its *compile-time type*, that is either a primitive type (§4.2) or a reference type (§4.3).

A variable's value is changed by an assignment (§15.26) or by a prefix or postfix ++ (increment) or -- (decrement) operator (§15.14.2, §15.14.3, §15.15.1, §15.15.2).

Compatibility of the value of a variable with its type is guaranteed by the design of the Java programming language, as long as a program does not give rise to compile-time unchecked warnings (§4.12.2). Default values (§4.12.5) are compatible and all assignments to a variable are checked for assignment compatibility (§5.2), usually at compile time, but, in a single case involving arrays, a run-time check is made (§10.5).

4.12.1   Variables of Primitive Type

A variable of a primitive type always holds a primitive value of that exact primitive type.

4.12.2   Variables of Reference Type

A variable of a class type T can hold a null reference or a reference to an instance of class T or of any class that is a subclass of T.

A variable of an interface type can hold a null reference or a reference to any instance of any class that implements the interface.

> Note that a variable is not guaranteed to always refer to a subtype of its declared type, but only to subclasses or subinterfaces of the declared type. This is due to the possibility of heap pollution discussed below.

If T is a primitive type, then a variable of type "array of T" can hold a null reference or a reference to any array of type "array of T".

If T is a reference type, then a variable of type "array of T" can hold a null reference or a reference to any array of type "array of S" such that type S is a subclass or subinterface of type T.

A variable of type `Object[]` can hold a reference to an array of any reference type.

A variable of type `Object` can hold a null reference or a reference to any object, whether it is an instance of a class or an array.

It is possible that a variable of a parameterized type will refer to an object that is not of that parameterized type. This situation is known as *heap pollution*.

Heap pollution can only occur if the program performed some operation involving a raw type that would give rise to a compile-time unchecked warning (§4.8, §5.1.9, §5.5.2, §8.4.1, §8.4.8.3, §8.4.8.4, §9.4.1.2, §15.12.4.2), or if the program aliases an array variable of non-reifiable element type through an array variable of a supertype which is either raw or non-generic.

> For example, the code:

```
List l = new ArrayList<Number>();
```

```
List<String> ls = l;   // Unchecked warning
```

gives rise to a compile-time unchecked warning, because it is not possible to ascertain, either at compile time (within the limits of the compile-time type checking rules) or at run time, whether the variable l does indeed refer to a List<String>.

If the code above is executed, heap pollution arises, as the variable ls, declared to be a List<String>, refers to a value that is not in fact a List<String>.

The problem cannot be identified at run time because type variables are not reified, and thus instances do not carry any information at run time regarding the type arguments used to create them.

In a simple example as given above, it may appear that it should be straightforward to identify the situation at compile time and give an error. However, in the general (and typical) case, the value of the variable l may be the result of an invocation of a separately compiled method, or its value may depend upon arbitrary control flow. The code above is therefore very atypical, and indeed very bad style.

Furthermore, the fact that Object[] is a supertype of all array types means that unsafe aliasing can occur which leads to heap pollution. For example, the following code compiles because it is statically type-correct:

```
static void m(List<String>... stringLists) {
    Object[] array = stringLists;
    List<Integer> tmpList = Arrays.asList(42);
    array[0] = tmpList;                // (1)
    String s = stringLists[0].get(0);  // (2)
}
```

Heap pollution occurs at (1) because a component in the stringLists array that should refer to a List<String> now refers to a List<Integer>. There is no way to detect this pollution in the presence of both a universal supertype (Object[]) and a non-reifiable type (the declared type of the formal parameter, List<String>[]). No unchecked warning is justified at (1); nevertheless, at run time, a ClassCastException will occur at (2).

A compile-time unchecked warning will be given at any invocation of the method above because an invocation is considered by the Java programming language's static type system to create an array whose element type, List<String>, is non-reifiable (§15.12.4.2). *If and only if* the body of the method was type-safe with respect to the variable arity parameter, then the programmer could use the SafeVarargs annotation to silence warnings at invocations (§9.6.3.7). Since the body of the method as written above causes heap pollution, it would be completely inappropriate to use the annotation to disable warnings for callers.

Finally, note that the stringLists array could be aliased through variables of types other than Object[], and heap pollution could still occur. For example, the type of the array variable could be java.util.Collection[] - a raw element type - and the body of the method above would compile without warnings or errors and still cause heap pollution. And if the Java SE platform defined, say, Sequence as a non-generic supertype of List<T>, then using Sequence as the type of array would also cause heap pollution.

The variable will always refer to an object that is an instance of a class that represents the parameterized type.

> The value of `ls` in the example above is always an instance of a class that provides a representation of a `List`.

> Assignment from an expression of a raw type to a variable of a parameterized type should only be used when combining legacy code which does not make use of parameterized types with more modern code that does.

> If no operation that requires a compile-time unchecked warning to be issued takes place, and no unsafe aliasing occurs of array variables with non-reifiable element types, then heap pollution cannot occur. Note that this does not imply that heap pollution only occurs if a compile-time unchecked warning actually occurred. It is possible to run a program where some of the binaries were produced by a compiler for an older version of the Java programming language, or from sources that explicitly suppressed unchecked warnings. This practice is unhealthy at best.

> Conversely, it is possible that despite executing code that could (and perhaps did) give rise to a compile-time unchecked warning, no heap pollution takes place. Indeed, good programming practice requires that the programmer satisfy herself that despite any unchecked warning, the code is correct and heap pollution will not occur.

4.12.3 Kinds of Variables

There are seven kinds of variables:

1. A *class variable* is a field declared using the keyword `static` within a class declaration (§8.3.1.1), or with or without the keyword `static` within an interface declaration (§9.3).

    A class variable is created when its class or interface is prepared (§12.3.2) and is initialized to a default value (§4.12.5). The class variable effectively ceases to exist when its class or interface is unloaded (§12.7).

2. An *instance variable* is a field declared within a class declaration without using the keyword `static` (§8.3.1.1).

    If a class *T* has a field `a` that is an instance variable, then a new instance variable `a` is created and initialized to a default value (§4.12.5) as part of each newly created object of class *T* or of any class that is a subclass of *T* (§8.1.4). The instance variable effectively ceases to exist when the object of which it is a field is no longer referenced, after any necessary finalization of the object (§12.6) has been completed.

3. *Array components* are unnamed variables that are created and initialized to default values (§4.12.5) whenever a new object that is an array is created (§10,

§15.10). The array components effectively cease to exist when the array is no longer referenced.

4. *Method parameters* (§8.4.1) name argument values passed to a method.

For every parameter declared in a method declaration, a new parameter variable is created each time that method is invoked (§15.12). The new variable is initialized with the corresponding argument value from the method invocation. The method parameter effectively ceases to exist when the execution of the body of the method is complete.

5. *Constructor parameters* (§8.8.1) name argument values passed to a constructor.

For every parameter declared in a constructor declaration, a new parameter variable is created each time a class instance creation expression (§15.9) or explicit constructor invocation (§8.8.7) invokes that constructor. The new variable is initialized with the corresponding argument value from the creation expression or constructor invocation. The constructor parameter effectively ceases to exist when the execution of the body of the constructor is complete.

6. An *exception parameter* is created each time an exception is caught by a `catch` clause of a `try` statement (§14.20).

The new variable is initialized with the actual object associated with the exception (§11.3, §14.18). The exception parameter effectively ceases to exist when execution of the block associated with the `catch` clause is complete.

7. *Local variables* are declared by local variable declaration statements (§14.4).

Whenever the flow of control enters a block (§14.2) or `for` statement (§14.14), a new variable is created for each local variable declared in a local variable declaration statement immediately contained within that block or `for` statement.

A local variable declaration statement may contain an expression which initializes the variable. The local variable with an initializing expression is not initialized, however, until the local variable declaration statement that declares it is executed. (The rules of definite assignment (§16) prevent the value of a local variable from being used before it has been initialized or otherwise assigned a value.) The local variable effectively ceases to exist when the execution of the block or for statement is complete.

Were it not for one exceptional situation, a local variable could always be regarded as being created when its local variable declaration statement is executed. The exceptional situation involves the `switch` statement (§14.11), where it is possible for control to enter a block but bypass execution of a local variable declaration statement. Because of the restrictions imposed by the rules of definite assignment (§16), however, the local variable declared by such a bypassed local variable declaration statement cannot be used before it has been definitely assigned a value by an assignment expression (§15.26).

Example 4.12.3-1. Different Kinds of Variables

```
class Point {
    static int numPoints;    // numPoints is a class variable
    int x, y;                // x and y are instance variables
    int[] w = new int[10];   // w[0] is an array component
    int setX(int x) {        // x is a method parameter
        int oldx = this.x;   // oldx is a local variable
        this.x = x;
        return oldx;
    }
}
```

4.12.4 `final` **Variables**

A variable can be declared `final`. A `final` variable may only be assigned to once. Declaring a variable `final` can serve as useful documentation that its value will not change and can help avoid programming errors.

It is a compile-time error if a `final` variable is assigned to unless it is definitely unassigned (§16) immediately prior to the assignment.

A *blank* `final` is a `final` variable whose declaration lacks an initializer.

Once a `final` variable has been assigned, it always contains the same value. If a `final` variable holds a reference to an object, then the state of the object may be changed by operations on the object, but the variable will always refer to the same object.

This applies also to arrays, because arrays are objects; if a `final` variable holds a reference to an array, then the components of the array may be changed by operations on the array, but the variable will always refer to the same array.

Example 4.12.4-1. Final Variables

```
class Point {
    int x, y;
    int useCount;
    Point(int x, int y) { this.x = x; this.y = y; }
    static final Point origin = new Point(0, 0);
}
```

In this program, the class `Point` declares a `final` class variable `origin`. The `origin` variable holds a reference to an object that is an instance of class `Point` whose coordinates are (0, 0). The value of the variable `Point.origin` can never change, so it always refers to the same `Point` object, the one created by its initializer. However, an operation on this `Point` object might change its state - for example, modifying its `useCount` or even, misleadingly, its `x` or `y` coordinate.

A variable of primitive type or type `String`, that is `final` and initialized with a compile-time constant expression (§15.28), is called a *constant variable*.

Whether a variable is a constant variable or not may have implications with respect to class initialization (§12.4.1), binary compatibility (§13.1, §13.4.9) and definite assignment (§16).

A resource of a `try`-with-resources statement (§14.20.3) and an exception parameter of a multi-`catch` clause (§14.20) are implicitly declared `final`.

An exception parameter of a uni-`catch` clause (§14.20) may be *effectively final* instead of being explicitly declared `final`. Such a parameter is never implicitly declared `final`.

4.12.5   Initial Values of Variables

Every variable in a program must have a value before its value is used:

- Each class variable, instance variable, or array component is initialized with a *default value* when it is created (§15.9, §15.10):

    - For type `byte`, the default value is zero, that is, the value of `(byte)0`.

    - For type `short`, the default value is zero, that is, the value of `(short)0`.

    - For type `int`, the default value is zero, that is, `0`.

    - For type `long`, the default value is zero, that is, `0L`.

    - For type `float`, the default value is positive zero, that is, `0.0f`.

    - For type `double`, the default value is positive zero, that is, `0.0d`.

    - For type `char`, the default value is the null character, that is, `'\u0000'`.

    - For type `boolean`, the default value is `false`.

    - For all reference types (§4.3), the default value is `null`.

- Each method parameter (§8.4.1) is initialized to the corresponding argument value provided by the invoker of the method (§15.12).

- Each constructor parameter (§8.8.1) is initialized to the corresponding argument value provided by a class instance creation expression (§15.9) or explicit constructor invocation (§8.8.7).

- An exception parameter (§14.20) is initialized to the thrown object representing the exception (§11.3, §14.18).

- A local variable (§14.4, §14.14) must be explicitly given a value before it is used, by either initialization (§14.4) or assignment (§15.26), in a way that can be verified using the rules for definite assignment (§16).

Example 4.12.5-1. Initial Values of Variables

```
class Point {
    static int npoints;
    int x, y;
    Point root;
}

class Test {
    public static void main(String[] args) {
        System.out.println("npoints=" + Point.npoints);
        Point p = new Point();
        System.out.println("p.x=" + p.x + ", p.y=" + p.y);
        System.out.println("p.root=" + p.root);
    }
}
```

This program prints:

```
npoints=0
p.x=0, p.y=0
p.root=null
```

illustrating the default initialization of npoints, which occurs when the class Point is prepared (§12.3.2), and the default initialization of x, y, and root, which occurs when a new Point is instantiated. See §12 for a full description of all aspects of loading, linking, and initialization of classes and interfaces, plus a description of the instantiation of classes to make new class instances.

4.12.6   Types, Classes, and Interfaces

In the Java programming language, every variable and every expression has a type that can be determined at compile time. The type may be a primitive type or a reference type. Reference types include class types and interface types. Reference types are introduced by *type declarations*, which include class declarations (§8.1) and interface declarations (§9.1). We often use the term *type* to refer to either a class or an interface.

In the Java Virtual Machine, every object belongs to some particular class: the class that was mentioned in the creation expression that produced the object (§15.9), or the class whose Class object was used to invoke a reflective method to produce the object, or the `String` class for objects implicitly created by the string concatenation operator + (§15.18.1). This class is called the *class of the object*. An object is said to be an *instance* of its class and of all superclasses of its class.

Every array also has a class. The method `getClass`, when invoked for an array object, will return a class object (of class `Class`) that represents the *class of the array* (§10.8).

The compile-time type of a variable is always declared, and the compile-time type of an expression can be deduced at compile time. The compile-time type limits the possible values that the variable can hold at run time or the expression can produce at run time. If a run-time value is a reference that is not `null`, it refers to an object or array that has a class, and that class will necessarily be compatible with the compile-time type.

Even though a variable or expression may have a compile-time type that is an interface type, there are no instances of interfaces. A variable or expression whose type is an interface type can reference any object whose class implements (§8.1.5) that interface.

Sometimes a variable or expression is said to have a "run-time type". This refers to the class of the object referred to by the value of the variable or expression at run time, assuming that the value is not `null`.

The correspondence between compile-time types and run-time types is incomplete for two reasons:

1. At run time, classes and interfaces are loaded by the Java Virtual Machine using class loaders. Each class loader defines its own set of classes and interfaces. As a result, it is possible for two loaders to load an identical class or interface definition but produce distinct classes or interfaces at run time. Consequently, code that compiled correctly may fail at link time if the class loaders that load it are inconsistent.

    > See the paper *Dynamic Class Loading in the Java Virtual Machine*, by Sheng Liang and Gilad Bracha, in *Proceedings of OOPSLA '98*, published as *ACM SIGPLAN Notices*, Volume 33, Number 10, October 1998, pages 36-44, and *The Java Virtual Machine Specification, Java SE 7 Edition* for more details.

2. Type variables (§4.4) and type arguments (§4.5.1) are not reified at run time. As a result, the same class or interface at run time represents multiple parameterized types (§4.5) from compile-time. Specifically, all compile-time invocations of a given generic type declaration (§8.1.2, §9.1.2) share a single run-time representation.

Under certain conditions, it is possible that a variable of a parameterized type refers to an object that is not of that parameterized type. This situation is known as *heap pollution* (§4.12.2). The variable will always refer to an object that is an instance of a class that represents the parameterized type.

Example 4.12.6-1. Type of a Variable versus Class of an Object

```
interface Colorable {
    void setColor(byte r, byte g, byte b);
}

class Point { int x, y; }

class ColoredPoint extends Point implements Colorable {
    byte r, g, b;
    public void setColor(byte rv, byte gv, byte bv) {
        r = rv; g = gv; b = bv;
    }
}

class Test {
    public static void main(String[] args) {
        Point p = new Point();
        ColoredPoint cp = new ColoredPoint();
        p = cp;
        Colorable c = cp;
    }
}
```

In this example:

- The local variable p of the method `main` of class `Test` has type `Point` and is initially assigned a reference to a new instance of class `Point`.

- The local variable cp similarly has as its type `ColoredPoint`, and is initially assigned a reference to a new instance of class `ColoredPoint`.

- The assignment of the value of cp to the variable p causes p to hold a reference to a `ColoredPoint` object. This is permitted because `ColoredPoint` is a subclass of `Point`, so the class `ColoredPoint` is assignment-compatible (§5.2) with the type `Point`. A `ColoredPoint` object includes support for all the methods of a `Point`. In addition to its particular fields r, g, and b, it has the fields of class `Point`, namely x and y.

- The local variable c has as its type the interface type `Colorable`, so it can hold a reference to any object whose class implements `Colorable`; specifically, it can hold a reference to a `ColoredPoint`.

Note that an expression such as `new Colorable()` is not valid because it is not possible to create an instance of an interface, only of a class. However, the expression `new Colorable() { public void setColor... }` is valid because it declares an anonymous class (§15.9.5) that implements the `Colorable` interface.

CHAPTER 5

Conversions and Promotions

EVERY expression written in the Java programming language has a type that can be deduced from the structure of the expression and the types of the literals, variables, and methods mentioned in the expression. It is possible, however, to write an expression in a context where the type of the expression is not appropriate. In some cases, this leads to an error at compile time. In other cases, the context may be able to accept a type that is related to the type of the expression; as a convenience, rather than requiring the programmer to indicate a type conversion explicitly, the Java programming language performs an implicit *conversion* from the type of the expression to a type acceptable for its surrounding context.

A specific conversion from type *s* to type *T* allows an expression of type *s* to be treated at compile time as if it had type *T* instead. In some cases this will require a corresponding action at run time to check the validity of the conversion or to translate the run-time value of the expression into a form appropriate for the new type *T*.

Example 5.0-1. Conversions at Compile Time and Run Time

- A conversion from type `Object` to type `Thread` requires a run-time check to make sure that the run-time value is actually an instance of class `Thread` or one of its subclasses; if it is not, an exception is thrown.

- A conversion from type `Thread` to type `Object` requires no run-time action; `Thread` is a subclass of `Object`, so any reference produced by an expression of type `Thread` is a valid reference value of type `Object`.

- A conversion from type `int` to type `long` requires run-time sign-extension of a 32-bit integer value to the 64-bit `long` representation. No information is lost.

- A conversion from type `double` to type `long` requires a nontrivial translation from a 64-bit floating-point value to the 64-bit integer representation. Depending on the actual run-time value, information may be lost.

In every conversion context, only certain specific conversions are permitted. For convenience of description, the specific conversions that are possible in the Java programming language are grouped into several broad categories:

- Identity conversions

- Widening primitive conversions

- Narrowing primitive conversions

- Widening reference conversions

- Narrowing reference conversions

- Boxing conversions

- Unboxing conversions

- Unchecked conversions

- Capture conversions

- String conversions

- Value set conversions

There are five *conversion contexts* in which conversion of expressions may occur. Each context allows conversions in some of the categories named above but not others. The term "conversion" is also used to describe the process of choosing a specific conversion for such a context. For example, we say that an expression that is an actual argument in a method invocation is subject to "method invocation conversion," meaning that a specific conversion will be implicitly chosen for that expression according to the rules for the method invocation argument context.

One conversion context is the operand of a numeric operator such as + or *. The conversion process for such operands is called *numeric promotion*. Promotion is special in that, in the case of binary operators, the conversion chosen for one operand may depend in part on the type of the other operand expression.

This chapter first describes the eleven categories of conversions (§5.1), including the special conversions to String allowed for the string concatenation operator + (§15.18.1). Then the five conversion contexts are described:

- Assignment conversion (§5.2, §15.26) converts the type of an expression to the type of a specified variable.

  Assignment conversion may cause an OutOfMemoryError (as a result of boxing conversion (§5.1.7)), a NullPointerException (as a result of unboxing conversion (§5.1.8)), or a `ClassCastException` (as a result of an unchecked conversion (§5.1.9)) to be thrown at run time.

- Method invocation conversion (§5.3, §15.9, §15.12) is applied to each argument in a method or constructor invocation and, except in one case, performs the same conversions that assignment conversion does.

  Method invocation conversion may cause an `OutOfMemoryError` (as a result of boxing conversion (§5.1.7)), a `NullPointerException` (as a result of unboxing conversion (§5.1.8)), or a `ClassCastException` (as a result of an unchecked conversion (§5.1.9)) to be thrown at run time.

- Casting conversion (§5.5) converts the type of an expression to a type explicitly specified by a cast operator (§15.16).

  It is more inclusive than assignment or method invocation conversion, allowing any specific conversion other than a string conversion, but certain casts to a reference type may cause an exception at run time.

- String conversion (§5.4) applies only to an operand of the binary + operator which is not a `String` when the other operand is a `String`.

  String conversion may cause an `OutOfMemoryError` (as a result of class instance creation (§12.5)) to be thrown at run time.

- Numeric promotion (§5.6) brings the operands of a numeric operator to a common type so that an operation can be performed.

Example 5.0-2. Conversion Contexts

```
class Test {
    public static void main(String[] args) {
        // Casting conversion (5.4) of a float literal to
        // type int. Without the cast operator, this would
        // be a compile-time error, because this is a
        // narrowing conversion (5.1.3):
        int i = (int)12.5f;
        // String conversion (5.4) of i's int value:
        System.out.println("(int)12.5f==" + i);
        // Assignment conversion (5.2) of i's value to type
        // float. This is a widening conversion (5.1.2):
        float f = i;
        // String conversion of f's float value:
        System.out.println("after float widening: " + f);
        // Numeric promotion (5.6) of i's value to type
        // float. This is a binary numeric promotion.
        // After promotion, the operation is float*float:
        System.out.print(f);
        f = f * i;
        // Two string conversions of i and f:
```

```
            System.out.println("*" + i + "==" + f);
            // Method invocation conversion (5.3) of f's value
            // to type double, needed because the method Math.sin
            // accepts only a double argument:
            double d = Math.sin(f);
            // Two string conversions of f and d:
            System.out.println("Math.sin(" + f + ")==" + d);
        }
    }
```

This program produces the output:

```
(int)12.5f==12
after float widening: 12.0
12.0*12==144.0
Math.sin(144.0)==-0.49102159389846934
```

5.1   Kinds of Conversion

Specific type conversions in the Java programming language are divided into 13 categories.

5.1.1   Identity Conversion

A conversion from a type to that same type is permitted for any type.

> This may seem trivial, but it has two practical consequences. First, it is always permitted for an expression to have the desired type to begin with, thus allowing the simply stated rule that every expression is subject to conversion, if only a trivial identity conversion. Second, it implies that it is permitted for a program to include redundant cast operators for the sake of clarity.

5.1.2   Widening Primitive Conversion

19 specific conversions on primitive types are called the *widening primitive conversions*:

- `byte` to `short`, `int`, `long`, `float`, or `double`

- `short` to `int`, `long`, `float`, or `double`

- `char` to `int`, `long`, `float`, or `double`

- `int` to `long`, `float`, or `double`

- `long` to `float` or `double`

- `float` to `double`

A widening primitive conversion does not lose information about the overall magnitude of a numeric value.

A widening primitive conversion from an integral type to another integral type, or from `float` to `double` in a `strictfp` expression (§15.4), does not lose any information at all; the numeric value is preserved exactly.

A widening primitive conversion from `float` to `double` that is not `strictfp` may lose information about the overall magnitude of the converted value.

A widening conversion of an `int` or a `long` value to `float`, or of a `long` value to `double`, may result in *loss of precision* - that is, the result may lose some of the least significant bits of the value. In this case, the resulting floating-point value will be a correctly rounded version of the integer value, using IEEE 754 round-to-nearest mode (§4.2.4).

A widening conversion of a signed integer value to an integral type *T* simply sign-extends the two's-complement representation of the integer value to fill the wider format.

A widening conversion of a `char` to an integral type *T* zero-extends the representation of the `char` value to fill the wider format.

Despite the fact that loss of precision may occur, a widening primitive conversion never results in a run-time exception (§11.1.1).

Example 5.1.2-1. Widening Primitive Conversion

```
class Test {
    public static void main(String[] args) {
        int big = 1234567890;
        float approx = big;
        System.out.println(big - (int)approx);
    }
}
```

This program prints:

```
-46
```

thus indicating that information was lost during the conversion from type `int` to type `float` because values of type `float` are not precise to nine significant digits.

5.1.3   Narrowing Primitive Conversion

22 specific conversions on primitive types are called the *narrowing primitive conversions*:

- `short` to `byte` or `char`

- `char` to `byte` or `short`

- `int` to `byte`, `short`, or `char`

- `long` to `byte`, `short`, `char`, or `int`

- `float` to `byte`, `short`, `char`, `int`, or `long`

- `double` to `byte`, `short`, `char`, `int`, `long`, or `float`

A narrowing primitive conversion may lose information about the overall magnitude of a numeric value and may also lose precision and range.

A narrowing primitive conversion from `double` to `float` is governed by the IEEE 754 rounding rules (§4.2.4). This conversion can lose precision, but also lose range, resulting in a `float` zero from a nonzero `double` and a `float` infinity from a finite `double`. A `double` NaN is converted to a `float` NaN and a `double` infinity is converted to the same-signed `float` infinity.

A narrowing conversion of a signed integer to an integral type T simply discards all but the n lowest order bits, where n is the number of bits used to represent type T. In addition to a possible loss of information about the magnitude of the numeric value, this may cause the sign of the resulting value to differ from the sign of the input value.

A narrowing conversion of a `char` to an integral type T likewise simply discards all but the n lowest order bits, where n is the number of bits used to represent type T. In addition to a possible loss of information about the magnitude of the numeric value, this may cause the resulting value to be a negative number, even though chars represent 16-bit unsigned integer values.

A narrowing conversion of a floating-point number to an integral type T takes two steps:

1. In the first step, the floating-point number is converted either to a `long`, if T is `long`, or to an `int`, if T is `byte`, `short`, `char`, or `int`, as follows:

   - If the floating-point number is NaN (§4.2.3), the result of the first step of the conversion is an `int` or `long` 0.

- Otherwise, if the floating-point number is not an infinity, the floating-point value is rounded to an integer value *v*, rounding toward zero using IEEE 754 round-toward-zero mode (§4.2.3). Then there are two cases:

  a. If *T* is `long`, and this integer value can be represented as a `long`, then the result of the first step is the `long` value *v*.

  b. Otherwise, if this integer value can be represented as an `int`, then the result of the first step is the `int` value *v*.

- Otherwise, one of the following two cases must be true:

  a. The value must be too small (a negative value of large magnitude or negative infinity), and the result of the first step is the smallest representable value of type `int` or `long`.

  b. The value must be too large (a positive value of large magnitude or positive infinity), and the result of the first step is the largest representable value of type `int` or `long`.

2. In the second step:

    - If *T* is `int` or `long`, the result of the conversion is the result of the first step.

    - If *T* is `byte`, `char`, or `short`, the result of the conversion is the result of a narrowing conversion to type *T* (§5.1.3) of the result of the first step.

Example 5.1.3-1. Narrowing Primitive Conversion

```
class Test {
    public static void main(String[] args) {
        float fmin = Float.NEGATIVE_INFINITY;
        float fmax = Float.POSITIVE_INFINITY;
        System.out.println("long: " + (long)fmin +
                           ".." + (long)fmax);
        System.out.println("int: " + (int)fmin +
                           ".." + (int)fmax);
        System.out.println("short: " + (short)fmin +
                           ".." + (short)fmax);
        System.out.println("char: " + (int)(char)fmin +
                           ".." + (int)(char)fmax);
        System.out.println("byte: " + (byte)fmin +
                           ".." + (byte)fmax);
    }
}
```

This program produces the output:

```
long: -9223372036854775808..9223372036854775807
int: -2147483648..2147483647
short: 0..-1
char: 0..65535
byte: 0..-1
```

The results for `char`, `int`, and `long` are unsurprising, producing the minimum and maximum representable values of the type.

The results for `byte` and `short` lose information about the sign and magnitude of the numeric values and also lose precision. The results can be understood by examining the low order bits of the minimum and maximum `int`. The minimum `int` is, in hexadecimal, `0x80000000`, and the maximum `int` is `0x7fffffff`. This explains the `short` results, which are the low 16 bits of these values, namely, `0x0000` and `0xffff`; it explains the char results, which also are the low 16 bits of these values, namely, `'\u0000'` and `'\uffff'`; and it explains the byte results, which are the low 8 bits of these values, namely, `0x00` and `0xff`.

Despite the fact that overflow, underflow, or other loss of information may occur, a narrowing primitive conversion never results in a run-time exception (§11.1.1).

Example 5.1.3-2. Narrowing Primitive Conversions that lose information

```
class Test {
    public static void main(String[] args) {
        // A narrowing of int to short loses high bits:
        System.out.println("(short)0x12345678==0x" +
                          Integer.toHexString((short)0x12345678));
        // An int value too big for byte changes sign and magnitude:
        System.out.println("(byte)255==" + (byte)255);
        // A float value too big to fit gives largest int value:
        System.out.println("(int)1e20f==" + (int)1e20f);
        // A NaN converted to int yields zero:
        System.out.println("(int)NaN==" + (int)Float.NaN);
        // A double value too large for float yields infinity:
        System.out.println("(float)-1e100==" + (float)-1e100);
        // A double value too small for float underflows to zero:
        System.out.println("(float)1e-50==" + (float)1e-50);
    }
}
```

This program produces the output:

```
(short)0x12345678==0x5678
(byte)255==-1
(int)1e20f==2147483647
(int)NaN==0
(float)-1e100==-Infinity
(float)1e-50==0.0
```

5.1.4   Widening and Narrowing Primitive Conversion

The following conversion combines both widening and narrowing primitive conversions:

- `byte` to `char`

First, the `byte` is converted to an `int` via widening primitive conversion (§5.1.2), and then the resulting `int` is converted to a `char` by narrowing primitive conversion (§5.1.3).

5.1.5   Widening Reference Conversion

A *widening reference* conversion exists from any reference type S to any reference type T, provided S is a subtype (§4.10) of T.

Widening reference conversions never require a special action at run time and therefore never throw an exception at run time. They consist simply in regarding a reference as having some other type in a manner that can be proved correct at compile time.

5.1.6   Narrowing Reference Conversion

Six kinds of conversions are called the *narrowing reference conversions*:

- From any reference type S to any reference type T, provided that S is a proper supertype of T (§4.10).

  An important special case is that there is a narrowing reference conversion from the class type `Object` to any other reference type (§4.12.4).

- From any class type C to any non-parameterized interface type K, provided that C is not `final` and does not implement K.

- From any interface type J to any non-parameterized class type C that is not `final`.

- From any interface type J to any non-parameterized interface type K, provided that J is not a subinterface of K.

- From the interface types `Cloneable` and `java.io.Serializable` to any array type T[].

- From any array type SC[] to any array type TC[], provided that SC and TC are reference types and there is a narrowing reference conversion from SC to TC.

Such conversions require a test at run time to find out whether the actual reference value is a legitimate value of the new type. If not, then a `ClassCastException` is thrown.

5.1.7   Boxing Conversion

Boxing conversion converts expressions of primitive type to corresponding expressions of reference type. Specifically, the following nine conversions are called the *boxing conversions*:

- From type `boolean` to type `Boolean`

- From type `byte` to type `Byte`

- From type `short` to type `Short`

- From type `char` to type `Character`

- From type `int` to type `Integer`

- From type `long` to type `Long`

- From type `float` to type `Float`

- From type `double` to type `Double`

- From the null type to the null type

> This rule is necessary because the conditional operator (§15.25) applies boxing conversion to the types of its operands, and uses the result in further calculations.

At run time, boxing conversion proceeds as follows:

- If p is a value of type `boolean`, then boxing conversion converts p into a reference r of class and type `Boolean`, such that r.`booleanValue()` $==$ p

- If p is a value of type `byte`, then boxing conversion converts p into a reference r of class and type `Byte`, such that r.`byteValue()` $==$ p

- If p is a value of type `char`, then boxing conversion converts p into a reference r of class and type `Character`, such that r.`charValue()` $==$ p

- If p is a value of type `short`, then boxing conversion converts p into a reference r of class and type `Short`, such that r.`shortValue()` $==$ p

- If p is a value of type `int`, then boxing conversion converts p into a reference r of class and type `Integer`, such that r.`intValue()` $==$ p

- If p is a value of type `long`, then boxing conversion converts p into a reference r of class and type `Long`, such that r.`longValue()` $==$ p

- If p is a value of type `float` then:

  - If p is not NaN, then boxing conversion converts p into a reference r of class and type `Float`, such that `r.floatValue()` evaluates to p

  - Otherwise, boxing conversion converts p into a reference r of class and type `Float` such that `r.isNaN()` evaluates to `true`

- If p is a value of type `double`, then:

  - If p is not NaN, boxing conversion converts p into a reference r of class and type `Double`, such that `r.doubleValue()` evaluates to p

  - Otherwise, boxing conversion converts p into a reference r of class and type `Double` such that `r.isNaN()` evaluates to `true`

- If p is a value of any other type, boxing conversion is equivalent to an identity conversion (§5.1.1).

If the value p being boxed is `true`, `false`, a `byte`, or a `char` in the range `\u0000` to `\u007f`, or an `int` or `short` number between -128 and `127` (inclusive), then let r_1 and r_2 be the results of any two boxing conversions of p. It is always the case that r_1 == r_2.

> Ideally, boxing a given primitive value p, would always yield an identical reference. In practice, this may not be feasible using existing implementation techniques. The rules above are a pragmatic compromise. The final clause above requires that certain common values always be boxed into indistinguishable objects. The implementation may cache these, lazily or eagerly. For other values, this formulation disallows any assumptions about the identity of the boxed values on the programmer's part. This would allow (but not require) sharing of some or all of these references.
>
> This ensures that in most common cases, the behavior will be the desired one, without imposing an undue performance penalty, especially on small devices. Less memory-limited implementations might, for example, cache all `char` and `short` values, as well as `int` and `long` values in the range of -32K to +32K.

A boxing conversion may result in an `OutOfMemoryError` if a new instance of one of the wrapper classes (`Boolean`, `Byte`, `Character`, `Short`, `Integer`, `Long`, `Float`, or `Double`) needs to be allocated and insufficient storage is available.

5.1.8 Unboxing Conversion

Unboxing conversion converts expressions of reference type to corresponding expressions of primitive type. Specifically, the following eight conversions are called the *unboxing conversions*:

- From type `Boolean` to type `boolean`

- From type `Byte` to type `byte`

- From type `Short` to type `short`

- From type `Character` to type `char`

- From type `Integer` to type `int`

- From type `Long` to type `long`

- From type `Float` to type `float`

- From type `Double` to type `double`

At run time, unboxing conversion proceeds as follows:

- If r is a reference of type `Boolean`, then unboxing conversion converts r into `r.booleanValue()`

- If r is a reference of type `Byte`, then unboxing conversion converts r into `r.byteValue()`

- If r is a reference of type `Character`, then unboxing conversion converts r into `r.charValue()`

- If r is a reference of type `Short`, then unboxing conversion converts r into `r.shortValue()`

- If r is a reference of type `Integer`, then unboxing conversion converts r into `r.intValue()`

- If r is a reference of type `Long`, then unboxing conversion converts r into `r.longValue()`

- If r is a reference of type `Float`, unboxing conversion converts r into `r.floatValue()`

- If r is a reference of type `Double`, then unboxing conversion converts r into `r.doubleValue()`

- If r is `null`, unboxing conversion throws a `NullPointerException`

A type is said to be *convertible to a numeric type* if it is a numeric type (§4.2), or it is a reference type that may be converted to a numeric type by unboxing conversion.

A type is said to be *convertible to an integral type* if it is an integral type, or it is a reference type that may be converted to an integral type by unboxing conversion.

5.1.9 Unchecked Conversion

Let G name a generic type declaration with *n* type parameters.

There is an *unchecked conversion* from the raw class or interface type (§4.8) G to any parameterized type of the form $G<T_1,...,T_n>$.

There is an *unchecked conversion* from the raw array type $G[]$ to any array type type of the form $G<T_1,...,T_n>[]$.

Use of an unchecked conversion causes a compile-time *unchecked warning* unless $G<...>$ is a parameterized type in which all type arguments are unbounded wildcards (§4.5.1), or the unchecked warning is suppressed by the `SuppressWarnings` annotation (§9.6.3.5).

> Unchecked conversion is used to enable a smooth interoperation of legacy code, written before the introduction of generic types, with libraries that have undergone a conversion to use genericity (a process we call generification). In such circumstances (most notably, clients of the Collections Framework in `java.util`), legacy code uses raw types (e.g. `Collection` instead of `Collection<String>`). Expressions of raw types are passed as arguments to library methods that use parameterized versions of those same types as the types of their corresponding formal parameters.

> Such calls cannot be shown to be statically safe under the type system using generics. Rejecting such calls would invalidate large bodies of existing code, and prevent them from using newer versions of the libraries. This in turn, would discourage library vendors from taking advantage of genericity. To prevent such an unwelcome turn of events, a raw type may be converted to an arbitrary invocation of the generic type declaration to which the raw type refers. While the conversion is unsound, it is tolerated as a concession to practicality. An unchecked warning is issued in such cases.

5.1.10 Capture Conversion

Let G name a generic type declaration (§8.1.2, §9.1.2) with *n* type parameters $A_1,...,A_n$ with corresponding bounds $U_1,...,U_n$.

There exists a *capture conversion* from a parameterized type $G<T_1,...,T_n>$ (§4.5) to a parameterized type $G<S_1,...,S_n>$, where, for $1 \leq i \leq n$:

- If T_i is a wildcard type argument (§4.5.1) of the form ?, then S_i is a fresh type variable whose upper bound is $U_i[A_1:=S_1, ..., A_n:=S_n]$ and whose lower bound is the null type (§4.1).

- If T_i is a wildcard type argument of the form ? `extends` B_i, then S_i is a fresh type variable whose upper bound is glb(B_i, $U_i[A_1:=S_1, ..., A_n:=S_n]$) and whose lower bound is the null type.

  glb($V_1,...,V_m$) is defined as V_1 & ... & V_m.

It is a compile-time error if, for any two classes (not interfaces) V_i and V_j, V_i is not a subclass of V_j or vice versa.

- If T_i is a wildcard type argument of the form ? super B_i, then S_i is a fresh type variable whose upper bound is $U_i[A_1:=S_1, \ldots, A_n:=S_n]$ and whose lower bound is B_i.

- Otherwise, $S_i = T_i$.

Capture conversion on any type other than a parameterized type (§4.5) acts as an identity conversion (§5.1.1).

Capture conversion is not applied recursively.

Capture conversion never requires a special action at run time and therefore never throws an exception at run time.

> Capture conversion is designed to make wildcards more useful. To understand the motivation, let's begin by looking at the method `java.util.Collections.reverse()`:
>
> ```
> public static void reverse(List<?> list);
> ```
>
> The method reverses the list provided as a parameter. It works for any type of list, and so the use of the wildcard type `List<?>` as the type of the formal parameter is entirely appropriate.
>
> Now consider how one would implement `reverse()`:
>
> ```
> public static void reverse(List<?> list) { rev(list); }
> private static <T> void rev(List<T> list) {
>     List<T> tmp = new ArrayList<T>(list);
>     for (int i = 0; i < list.size(); i++) {
>         list.set(i, tmp.get(list.size() - i - 1));
>     }
> }
> ```
>
> The implementation needs to copy the list, extract elements from the copy, and insert them into the original. To do this in a type-safe manner, we need to give a name, `T`, to the element type of the incoming list. We do this in the private service method `rev()`. This requires us to pass the incoming argument list, of type `List<?>`, as an argument to `rev()`. In general, `List<?>` is a list of unknown type. It is not a subtype of `List<T>`, for any type `T`. Allowing such a subtype relation would be unsound. Given the method:
>
> ```
> public static <T> void fill(List<T> l, T obj)
> ```
>
> the following code would undermine the type system:
>
> ```
> List<String> ls = new ArrayList<String>();
> List<?> l = ls;
> Collections.fill(l, new Object());  // not legal - but assume it was!
> ```

```
String s = ls.get(0); // ClassCastException - ls contains
                      // Objects, not Strings.
```

So, without some special dispensation, we can see that the call from `reverse()` to `rev()` would be disallowed. If this were the case, the author of `reverse()` would be forced to write its signature as:

```
public static <T> void reverse(List<T> list)
```

This is undesirable, as it exposes implementation information to the caller. Worse, the designer of an API might reason that the signature using a wildcard is what the callers of the API require, and only later realize that a type safe implementation was precluded.

The call from `reverse()` to `rev()` is in fact harmless, but it cannot be justified on the basis of a general subtyping relation between `List<?>` and `List<T>`. The call is harmless, because the incoming argument is doubtless a list of some type (albeit an unknown one). If we can capture this unknown type in a type variable `X`, we can infer `T` to be `X`. That is the essence of capture conversion. The specification of course must cope with complications, like non-trivial (and possibly recursively defined) upper or lower bounds, the presence of multiple arguments etc.

Mathematically sophisticated readers will want to relate capture conversion to established type theory. Readers unfamiliar with type theory can skip this discussion - or else study a suitable text, such as *Types and Programming Languages* by Benjamin Pierce, and then revisit this section.

Here then is a brief summary of the relationship of capture conversion to established type theoretical notions. Wildcard types are a restricted form of existential types. Capture conversion corresponds loosely to an opening of a value of existential type. A capture conversion of an expression *e* can be thought of as an `open` of *e* in a scope that comprises the top level expression that encloses *e*.

The classical `open` operation on existentials requires that the captured type variable must not escape the opened expression. The `open` that corresponds to capture conversion is always on a scope sufficiently large that the captured type variable can never be visible outside that scope. The advantage of this scheme is that there is no need for a `close` operation, as defined in the paper *On Variance-Based Subtyping for Parametric Types* by Atsushi Igarashi and Mirko Viroli, in the proceedings of the 16th European Conference on Object Oriented Programming (ECOOP 2002). For a formal account of wildcards, see *Wild FJ* by Mads Torgersen, Erik Ernst and Christian Plesner Hansen, in the 12th workshop on Foundations of Object Oriented Programming (FOOL 2005).

5.1.11   String Conversion

Any type may be converted to type `String` by *string conversion*.

A value *x* of primitive type *T* is first converted to a reference value as if by giving it as an argument to an appropriate class instance creation expression (§15.9):

- If *T* is `boolean`, then use `new Boolean(x)`.

- If *T* is char, then use new Character(*x*).

- If *T* is byte, short, or int, then use new Integer(*x*).

- If *T* is long, then use new Long(*x*).

- If *T* is float, then use new Float(*x*).

- If *T* is double, then use new Double(*x*).

This reference value is then converted to type String by string conversion.

Now only reference values need to be considered:

- If the reference is null, it is converted to the string "null" (four ASCII characters n, u, l, l).

- Otherwise, the conversion is performed as if by an invocation of the toString method of the referenced object with no arguments; but if the result of invoking the toString method is null, then the string "null" is used instead.

> The toString method is defined by the primordial class Object (§4.3.2). Many classes override it, notably Boolean, Character, Integer, Long, Float, Double, and String.

> See §5.4 for details of the string conversion context.

5.1.12   Forbidden Conversions

Any conversion that is not explicitly allowed is forbidden.

5.1.13   Value Set Conversion

Value set conversion is the process of mapping a floating-point value from one value set to another without changing its type.

Within an expression that is not FP-strict (§15.4), value set conversion provides choices to an implementation of the Java programming language:

- If the value is an element of the float-extended-exponent value set, then the implementation may, at its option, map the value to the nearest element of the float value set. This conversion may result in overflow (in which case the value is replaced by an infinity of the same sign) or underflow (in which case the value may lose precision because it is replaced by a denormalized number or zero of the same sign).

- If the value is an element of the double-extended-exponent value set, then the implementation may, at its option, map the value to the nearest element of the double value set. This conversion may result in overflow (in which case the value is replaced by an infinity of the same sign) or underflow (in which case the value may lose precision because it is replaced by a denormalized number or zero of the same sign).

Within an FP-strict expression (§15.4), value set conversion does not provide any choices; every implementation must behave in the same way:

- If the value is of type `float` and is not an element of the float value set, then the implementation must map the value to the nearest element of the float value set. This conversion may result in overflow or underflow.

- If the value is of type `double` and is not an element of the double value set, then the implementation must map the value to the nearest element of the double value set. This conversion may result in overflow or underflow.

Within an FP-strict expression, mapping values from the float-extended-exponent value set or double-extended-exponent value set is necessary only when a method is invoked whose declaration is not FP-strict and the implementation has chosen to represent the result of the method invocation as an element of an extended-exponent value set.

Whether in FP-strict code or code that is not FP-strict, value set conversion always leaves unchanged any value whose type is neither `float` nor `double`.

5.2 Assignment Conversion

Assignment conversion occurs when the value of an expression is assigned (§15.26) to a variable: the type of the expression must be converted to the type of the variable.

Assignment contexts allow the use of one of the following:

- an identity conversion (§5.1.1)

- a widening primitive conversion (§5.1.2)

- a widening reference conversion (§5.1.5)

- a boxing conversion (§5.1.7) optionally followed by a widening reference conversion

- an unboxing conversion (§5.1.8) optionally followed by a widening primitive conversion.

If, after the conversions listed above have been applied, the resulting type is a raw type (§4.8), unchecked conversion (§5.1.9) may then be applied.

It is a compile-time error if the chain of conversions contains two parameterized types that are not in the subtype relation.

> An example of such an illegal chain would be:
>
> ```
> Integer, Comparable<Integer>, Comparable, Comparable<String>
> ```
>
> The first three elements of the chain are related by widening reference conversion, while the last entry is derived from its predecessor by unchecked conversion. However, this is not a valid assignment conversion, because the chain contains two parameterized types, `Comparable<Integer>` and `Comparable<String>`, that are not subtypes.

In addition, if the expression is a constant expression (§15.28) of type `byte`, `short`, `char`, or `int`:

- A narrowing primitive conversion may be used if the type of the variable is `byte`, `short`, or `char`, and the value of the constant expression is representable in the type of the variable.

- A narrowing primitive conversion followed by a boxing conversion may be used if the type of the variable is:

  * `Byte` and the value of the constant expression is representable in the type `byte`.

  * `Short` and the value of the constant expression is representable in the type `short`.

  * `Character` and the value of the constant expression is representable in the type `char`.

> The compile-time narrowing of constants means that code such as:
>
> ```
> byte theAnswer = 42;
> ```
>
> is allowed. Without the narrowing, the fact that the integer literal `42` has type `int` would mean that a cast to `byte` would be required:
>
> ```
> byte theAnswer = (byte)42;   // cast is permitted but not required
> ```

A value of the null type (the null reference is the only such value) may be assigned to any reference type, resulting in a null reference of that type.

If the type of the expression cannot be converted to the type of the variable by a conversion permitted in an assignment context, then a compile-time error occurs.

If the type of an expression can be converted to the type of a variable by assignment conversion, we say the expression (or its value) is *assignable to* the variable or, equivalently, that the type of the expression is *assignment compatible with* the type of the variable.

If the type of the variable is `float` or `double`, then value set conversion (§5.1.13) is applied to the value *v* that is the result of the type conversion:

- If *v* is of type `float` and is an element of the float-extended-exponent value set, then the implementation must map *v* to the nearest element of the float value set. This conversion may result in overflow or underflow.

- If *v* is of type `double` and is an element of the double-extended-exponent value set, then the implementation must map *v* to the nearest element of the double value set. This conversion may result in overflow or underflow.

The only exceptions that an assignment conversion may cause are:

- A `ClassCastException` if, after the type conversions above have been applied, the resulting value is an object which is not an instance of a subclass or subinterface of the erasure (§4.6) of the type of the variable.

  > This circumstance can only arise as a result of heap pollution (§4.12.2). In practice, implementations need only perform casts when accessing a field or method of an object of parametized type, when the erased type of the field, or the erased result type of the method differ from their unerased type.

- An `OutOfMemoryError` as a result of a boxing conversion.

- A `NullPointerException` as a result of an unboxing conversion on a null reference.

- An `ArrayStoreException` in special cases involving array elements or field access (§10.5, §15.26.1).

Example 5.2-1. Assignment Conversion for Primitive Types

```java
class Test {
    public static void main(String[] args) {
        short s = 12;       // narrow 12 to short
        float f = s;        // widen short to float
        System.out.println("f=" + f);
        char c = '\u0123';
        long l = c;         // widen char to long
        System.out.println("l=0x" + Long.toString(l,16));
        f = 1.23f;
        double d = f;       // widen float to double
        System.out.println("d=" + d);
    }
```

```
    }
```

This program produces the output:

```
f=12.0
l=0x123
d=1.2300000190734863
```

The following program, however, produces compile-time errors:

```
class Test {
    public static void main(String[] args) {
        short s = 123;
        char c = s;     // error: would require cast
        s = c;          // error: would require cast
    }
}
```

because not all `short` values are `char` values, and neither are all `char` values `short` values.

Example 5.2-2. Assignment Conversion for Reference Types

```
class Point { int x, y; }
class Point3D extends Point { int z; }
interface Colorable { void setColor(int color); }

class ColoredPoint extends Point implements Colorable {
    int color;
    public void setColor(int color) { this.color = color; }
}

class Test {
    public static void main(String[] args) {
        // Assignments to variables of class type:
        Point p = new Point();
        p = new Point3D();
            // OK because Point3D is a subclass of Point
        Point3D p3d = p;
            // Error: will require a cast because a Point
            // might not be a Point3D (even though it is,
            // dynamically, in this example.)

        // Assignments to variables of type Object:
        Object o  = p;          // OK: any object to Object
        int[] a   = new int[3];
        Object o2 = a;          // OK: an array to Object

        // Assignments to variables of interface type:
        ColoredPoint cp = new ColoredPoint();
        Colorable c = cp;
            // OK: ColoredPoint implements Colorable
```

```
        // Assignments to variables of array type:
        byte[] b = new byte[4];
        a = b;
           // Error: these are not arrays of the same primitive type
        Point3D[] p3da = new Point3D[3];
        Point[] pa = p3da;
           // OK: since we can assign a Point3D to a Point
        p3da = pa;
           // Error: (cast needed) since a Point
           // can't be assigned to a Point3D
    }
}
```

The following test program illustrates assignment conversions on reference values, but fails to compile, as described in its comments. This example should be compared to the preceding one.

```
class Point { int x, y; }
interface Colorable { void setColor(int color); }
class ColoredPoint extends Point implements Colorable {
    int color;
    public void setColor(int color) { this.color = color; }
}

class Test {
    public static void main(String[] args) {
        Point p = new Point();
        ColoredPoint cp = new ColoredPoint();
        // Okay because ColoredPoint is a subclass of Point:
        p = cp;
        // Okay because ColoredPoint implements Colorable:
        Colorable c = cp;
        // The following cause compile-time errors because
        // we cannot be sure they will succeed, depending on
        // the run-time type of p; a run-time check will be
        // necessary for the needed narrowing conversion and
        // must be indicated by including a cast:
        cp = p;     // p might be neither a ColoredPoint
                    // nor a subclass of ColoredPoint
        c = p;      // p might not implement Colorable
    }
}
```

Example 5.2-3. Assignment Conversion for Array Types

```
class Point { int x, y; }
class ColoredPoint extends Point { int color; }

class Test {
    public static void main(String[] args) {
        long[] veclong = new long[100];
        Object o = veclong;          // okay
        Long l = veclong;            // compile-time error
```

```
        short[] vecshort = veclong;   // compile-time error
        Point[] pvec = new Point[100];
        ColoredPoint[] cpvec = new ColoredPoint[100];
        pvec = cpvec;                  // okay
        pvec[0] = new Point();         // okay at compile time,
                                       // but would throw an
                                       // exception at run time
        cpvec = pvec;                  // compile-time error
    }
}
```

In this example:

- The value of `veclong` cannot be assigned to a `Long` variable, because `Long` is a class type other than `Object`. An array can be assigned only to a variable of a compatible array type, or to a variable of type `Object`, `Cloneable` or `java.io.Serializable`.

- The value of `veclong` cannot be assigned to `vecshort`, because they are arrays of primitive type, and `short` and `long` are not the same primitive type.

- The value of `cpvec` can be assigned to `pvec`, because any reference that could be the value of an expression of type `ColoredPoint` can be the value of a variable of type `Point`. The subsequent assignment of the new `Point` to a component of `pvec` then would throw an `ArrayStoreException` (if the program were otherwise corrected so that it could be compiled), because a `ColoredPoint` array cannot have an instance of `Point` as the value of a component.

- The value of `pvec` cannot be assigned to `cpvec`, because not every reference that could be the value of an expression of type `ColoredPoint` can correctly be the value of a variable of type `Point`. If the value of `pvec` at run time were a reference to an instance of `Point[]`, and the assignment to `cpvec` were allowed, a simple reference to a component of `cpvec`, say, `cpvec[0]`, could return a `Point`, and a `Point` is not a `ColoredPoint`. Thus to allow such an assignment would allow a violation of the type system. A cast may be used (§5.5, §15.16) to ensure that `pvec` references a `ColoredPoint[]`:

```
        cpvec = (ColoredPoint[])pvec;  // OK, but may throw an
                                       // exception at run time
```

5.3   Method Invocation Conversion

Method invocation conversion is applied to each argument value in a method or constructor invocation (§8.8.7.1, §15.9, §15.12): the type of the argument expression must be converted to the type of the corresponding parameter.

Method invocation contexts allow the use of one of the following:

- an identity conversion (§5.1.1)

- a widening primitive conversion (§5.1.2)

- a widening reference conversion (§5.1.5)

- a boxing conversion (§5.1.7) optionally followed by widening reference conversion

- an unboxing conversion (§5.1.8) optionally followed by a widening primitive conversion.

If, after the conversions listed above have been applied, the resulting type is a raw type (§4.8), an unchecked conversion (§5.1.9) may then be applied.

It is a compile-time error if the chain of conversions contains two parameterized types that are not in the subtype relation.

A value of the null type (the null reference is the only such value) may be converted to any reference type.

If the type of the expression cannot be converted to the type of the parameter by a conversion permitted in a method invocation context, then a compile-time error occurs.

If the type of an argument expression is either `float` or `double`, then value set conversion (§5.1.13) is applied after the type conversion:

- If an argument value of type `float` is an element of the float-extended-exponent value set, then the implementation must map the value to the nearest element of the float value set. This conversion may result in overflow or underflow.

- If an argument value of type `double` is an element of the double-extended-exponent value set, then the implementation must map the value to the nearest element of the double value set. This conversion may result in overflow or underflow.

The only exceptions that an method invocation conversion may cause are:

- A `ClassCastException` if, after the type conversions above have been applied, the resulting value is an object which is not an instance of a subclass or subinterface of the erasure (§4.6) of the corresponding formal parameter type.

    This circumstance can only arise as a result of heap pollution (§4.12.2).

- An `OutOfMemoryError` as a result of a boxing conversion.

- A `NullPointerException` as a result of an unboxing conversion on a null reference.

    Method invocation conversions specifically do not include the implicit narrowing of integer constants which is part of assignment conversion (§5.2). The designers of the Java programming language felt that including these implicit narrowing conversions would add additional complexity to the overloaded method matching resolution process (§15.12.2).

Thus, the program:

```
class Test {
    static int m(byte a, int b) { return a+b; }
    static int m(short a, short b) { return a-b; }
    public static void main(String[] args) {
        System.out.println(m(12, 2));  // compile-time error
    }
}
```

causes a compile-time error because the integer literals 12 and 2 have type int, so neither method m matches under the rules of (§15.12.2). A language that included implicit narrowing of integer constants would need additional rules to resolve cases like this example.

5.4   String Conversion

String conversion applies only to an operand of the binary + operator which is not a String when the other operand is a String.

In this single special case, the non-String operand to the + is converted to a String (§5.1.11) and evaluation of the + operator proceeds as specified in §15.18.1.

5.5   Casting Conversion

Casting conversion is applied to the operand of a cast operator (§15.16): the type of the operand expression must be converted to the type explicitly named by the cast operator.

Casting contexts allow the use of one of:

- an identity conversion (§5.1.1)

- a widening primitive conversion (§5.1.2)

- a narrowing primitive conversion (§5.1.3)

- a widening and narrowing primitive conversion (§5.1.4)

- a widening reference conversion (§5.1.5) optionally followed by either an unboxing conversion (§5.1.8) or an unchecked conversion (§5.1.9)

- a narrowing reference conversion (§5.1.6) optionally followed by either an unboxing conversion (§5.1.8) or an unchecked conversion (§5.1.9)

- a boxing conversion (§5.1.7) optionally followed by a widening reference conversion (§5.1.5)

- an unboxing conversion (§5.1.8) optionally followed by a widening primitive conversion (§5.1.2).

Value set conversion (§5.1.13) is applied after the type conversion.

The compile-time legality of a casting conversion is as follows:

- An expression of a primitive type may undergo casting conversion to another primitive type, by an identity conversion (if the types are the same), or by a widening primitive conversion, or by a narrowing primitive conversion, or by a widening and narrowing primitive conversion.

- An expression of a primitive type may undergo casting conversion to a reference type without error, by boxing conversion.

- An expression of a reference type may undergo casting conversion to a primitive type without error, by unboxing conversion.

- An expression of a reference type may undergo casting conversion to another reference type if no compile-time error occurs given the rules in §5.5.1.

The following tables enumerate which conversions are used in certain casting conversions. Each conversion is signified by a symbol:

- - signifies no casting conversion allowed

- ≈ signifies identity conversion (§5.1.1)

- ω signifies widening primitive conversion (§5.1.2)

- η signifies narrowing primitive conversion (§5.1.3)

- ωη signifies widening and narrowing primitive conversion (§5.1.4)

- ⇑ signifies widening reference conversion (§5.1.5)

- ⇓ signifies narrowing reference conversion (§5.1.6)

- ⊡ signifies boxing conversion (§5.1.7)

- ⊔ signifies unboxing conversion (§5.1.8)

In the tables, a comma between symbols indicates that a casting conversion uses one conversion followed by another. The type `Object` means any reference type other than the eight wrapper classes `Boolean, Byte, Short, Character, Integer, Long, Float, Double`.

Table 5.1. Casting conversions to primitive types

To → From ↓	byte	short	char	int	long	float	double	boolean
byte	≈	ω	ωη	ω	ω	ω	ω	-
short	η	≈	η	ω	ω	ω	ω	-
char	η	η	≈	ω	ω	ω	ω	-
int	η	η	η	≈	ω	ω	ω	-
long	η	η	η	η	≈	ω	ω	-
float	η	η	η	η	η	≈	ω	-
double	η	η	η	η	η	η	≈	-
boolean	-	-	-	-	-	-	-	≈
Byte	⊔	⊔,ω	-	⊔,ω	⊔,ω	⊔,ω	⊔,ω	-
Short	-	⊔	-	⊔,ω	⊔,ω	⊔,ω	⊔,ω	-
Character	-	-	⊔	⊔,ω	⊔,ω	⊔,ω	⊔,ω	-
Integer	-	-	-	⊔	⊔,ω	⊔,ω	⊔,ω	-
Long	-	-	-	-	⊔	⊔,ω	⊔,ω	-
Float	-	-	-	-	-	⊔	⊔,ω	-
Double	-	-	-	-	-	-	⊔	-
Boolean	-	-	-	-	-	-	-	⊔
Object	⇓,⊔	⇓,⊔	⇓,⊔	⇓,⊔	⇓,⊔	⇓,⊔	⇓,⊔	⇓,⊔

Table 5.2. Casting conversions to reference types

To → From ↓	Byte	Short	Character	Integer	Long	Float	Double	Boolean	Object
byte	⊡	-	-	-	-	-	-	-	⊡, ⇑
short	-	⊡	-	-	-	-	-	-	⊡, ⇑
char	-	-	⊡	-	-	-	-	-	⊡, ⇑
int	-	-	-	⊡	-	-	-	-	⊡, ⇑
long	-	-	-	-	⊡	-	-	-	⊡, ⇑
float	-	-	-	-	-	⊡	-	-	⊡, ⇑
double	-	-	-	-	-	-	⊡	-	⊡, ⇑
boolean	-	-	-	-	-	-	-	⊡	⊡, ⇑
Byte	≈	-	-	-	-	-	-	-	⇑
Short	-	≈	-	-	-	-	-	-	⇑
Character	-	-	≈	-	-	-	-	-	⇑
Integer	-	-	-	≈	-	-	-	-	⇑
Long	-	-	-	-	≈	-	-	-	⇑
Float	-	-	-	-	-	≈	-	-	⇑
Double	-	-	-	-	-	-	≈	-	⇑
Boolean	-	-	-	-	-	-	-	≈	⇑
Object	⇓	⇓	⇓	⇓	⇓	⇓	⇓	⇓	≈

5.5.1 Reference Type Casting

Given a compile-time reference type s (source) and a compile-time reference type T (target), a casting conversion exists from s to T if no compile-time errors occur due to the following rules.

If s is a class type:

- If T is a class type, then either $|s| <: |T|$, or $|T| <: |s|$. Otherwise, a compile-time error occurs.

  Furthermore, if there exists a supertype x of T, and a supertype y of s, such that both x and y are provably distinct parameterized types (§4.5), and that the erasures of x and y are the same, a compile-time error occurs.

- If T is an interface type:

  - If S is not a `final` class (§8.1.1), then, if there exists a supertype X of T, and a supertype Y of S, such that both X and Y are provably distinct parameterized types, and that the erasures of X and Y are the same, a compile-time error occurs.

    Otherwise, the cast is always legal at compile time (because even if S does not implement T, a subclass of S might).

  - If S is a `final` class (§8.1.1), then S must implement T, or a compile-time error occurs.

- If T is a type variable, then this algorithm is applied recursively, using the upper bound of T in place of T.

- If T is an array type, then S must be the class `Object`, or a compile-time error occurs.

If S is an interface type:

- If T is an array type, then S must be the type `java.io.Serializable` or `Cloneable` (the only interfaces implemented by arrays), or a compile-time error occurs.

- If T is a type that is not `final` (§8.1.1), then if there exists a supertype X of T, and a supertype Y of S, such that both X and Y are provably distinct parameterized types, and that the erasures of X and Y are the same, a compile-time error occurs.

  Otherwise, the cast is always legal at compile time (because even if T does not implement S, a subclass of T might).

- If T is a type that is `final`, then:

  - If S is not a parameterized type or a raw type, then T must implement S, or a compile-time error occurs.

  - Otherwise, S is either a parameterized type that is an invocation of some generic type declaration G, or a raw type corresponding to a generic type declaration G. Then there must exist a supertype X of T, such that X is an invocation of G, or a compile-time error occurs.

    Furthermore, if S and X are provably distinct parameterized types then a compile-time error occurs.

If S is a type variable, then this algorithm is applied recursively, using the upper bound of S in place of S.

If S is an intersection type A_1 & ... & A_n, then it is a compile-time error if there exists an A_i ($1 \leq i \leq n$) such that S cannot be cast to A_i by this algorithm. That is, the success of the cast is determined by the most restrictive component of the intersection type.

If S is an array type $SC[\,]$, that is, an array of components of type SC:

- If T is a class type, then if T is not `Object`, then a compile-time error occurs (because `Object` is the only class type to which arrays can be assigned).

- If T is an interface type, then a compile-time error occurs unless T is the type `java.io.Serializable` or the type `Cloneable` (the only interfaces implemented by arrays).

- If T is a type variable, then:

  - If the upper bound of T is `Object` or `java.io.Serializable` or `Cloneable`, or a type variable that S could undergo casting conversion to, then the cast is legal (though unchecked).

  - If the upper bound of T is an array type $TC[\,]$, then a compile-time error occurs unless the type $SC[\,]$ can undergo casting conversion to $TC[\,]$.

  - Otherwise, a compile-time error occurs.

- If T is an array type $TC[\,]$, that is, an array of components of type TC, then a compile-time error occurs unless one of the following is true:

  - TC and SC are the same primitive type.

  - TC and SC are reference types and type SC can undergo casting conversion to TC.

Example 5.5.1-1. Casting Conversion for Reference Types

```
class Point { int x, y; }
interface Colorable { void setColor(int color); }
class ColoredPoint extends Point implements Colorable {
    int color;
    public void setColor(int color) { this.color = color; }
}
final class EndPoint extends Point {}

class Test {
    public static void main(String[] args) {
        Point p = new Point();
        ColoredPoint cp = new ColoredPoint();
        Colorable c;
        // The following may cause errors at run time because
        // we cannot be sure they will succeed; this possibility
        // is suggested by the casts:
        cp = (ColoredPoint)p;  // p might not reference an
                               // object which is a ColoredPoint
```

```
                                   // or a subclass of ColoredPoint
        c = (Colorable)p;          // p might not be Colorable
        // The following are incorrect at compile time because
        // they can never succeed as explained in the text:
        Long l = (Long)p;                  // compile-time error #1
        EndPoint e = new EndPoint();
        c = (Colorable)e;                  // compile-time error #2
    }
}
```

Here, the first compile-time error occurs because the class types `Long` and `Point` are unrelated (that is, they are not the same, and neither is a subclass of the other), so a cast between them will always fail.

The second compile-time error occurs because a variable of type `EndPoint` can never reference a value that implements the interface `Colorable`. This is because `EndPoint` is a `final` type, and a variable of a `final` type always holds a value of the same run-time type as its compile-time type. Therefore, the run-time type of variable e must be exactly the type `EndPoint`, and type `EndPoint` does not implement `Colorable`.

Example 5.5.1-2. Casting Conversion for Array Types

```
class Point {
    int x, y;
    Point(int x, int y) { this.x = x; this.y = y; }
    public String toString() { return "("+x+","+y+")"; }
}
interface Colorable { void setColor(int color); }
class ColoredPoint extends Point implements Colorable {
    int color;
    ColoredPoint(int x, int y, int color) {
        super(x, y); setColor(color);
    }
    public void setColor(int color) { this.color = color; }
    public String toString() {
        return super.toString() + "@" + color;
    }
}

class Test {
    public static void main(String[] args) {
        Point[] pa = new ColoredPoint[4];
        pa[0] = new ColoredPoint(2, 2, 12);
        pa[1] = new ColoredPoint(4, 5, 24);
        ColoredPoint[] cpa = (ColoredPoint[])pa;
        System.out.print("cpa: {");
        for (int i = 0; i < cpa.length; i++)
            System.out.print((i == 0 ? " " : ", ") + cpa[i]);
        System.out.println(" }");
    }
}
```

This program compiles without errors and produces the output:

```
cpa: { (2,2)@12, (4,5)@24, null, null }
```

5.5.2   Checked Casts and Unchecked Casts

A cast from a type S to a type T is *statically known to be correct* if and only if S <: T (§4.10).

A cast from a type S to a parameterized type (§4.5) T is *unchecked* unless at least one of the following conditions holds:

* S <: T

* All of the type arguments (§4.5.1) of T are unbounded wildcards

* T <: S and S has no subtype X other than T where the type arguments of X are not contained in the type arguments of T.

A cast from a type S to a type variable T is unchecked unless S <: T.

An unchecked cast from S to T is *completely unchecked* if the cast from $|S|$ to $|T|$ is statically known to be correct. Otherwise, it is *partially unchecked*.

An unchecked cast causes a compile-time unchecked warning, unless suppressed by the `SuppressWarnings` annotation (§9.6.3.5).

A cast is *checked* if it is not statically known to be correct and it is not unchecked.

If a cast to a reference type is not a compile-time error, there are several cases:

* The cast is statically known to be correct.

  No run-time action is performed for such a cast.

* The cast is a completely unchecked cast.

  No run-time action is performed for such a cast.

* The cast is a partially unchecked cast.

  Such a cast requires a run-time validity check. The check is performed as if the cast had been a checked cast between $|S|$ and $|T|$, as described below.

* The cast is a checked cast.

  Such a cast requires a run-time validity check. If the value at run time is `null`, then the cast is allowed. Otherwise, let R be the class of the object referred to by the run-time reference value, and let T be the erasure (§4.6) of the type named in the cast operator. A cast conversion must check, at run time, that the class R is assignment compatible with the type T, via the algorithm in §5.5.3.

Note that R cannot be an interface when these rules are first applied for any given cast, but R may be an interface if the rules are applied recursively because the run-time reference value may refer to an array whose element type is an interface type.

5.5.3   Checked Casts at Run Time

Here is the algorithm to check whether the run-time type R of an object is assignment compatible with the type T which is the erasure (§4.6) of the type named in the cast operator. If a run-time exception is thrown, it is a `ClassCastException`.

If R is an ordinary class (not an array class):

- If T is a class type, then R must be either the same class (§4.3.4) as T or a subclass of T, or a run-time exception is thrown.

- If T is an interface type, then R must implement (§8.1.5) interface T, or a run-time exception is thrown.

- If T is an array type, then a run-time exception is thrown.

If R is an interface:

- If T is a class type, then T must be `Object` (§4.3.2), or a run-time exception is thrown.

- If T is an interface type, then R must be either the same interface as T or a subinterface of T, or a run-time exception is thrown.

- If T is an array type, then a run-time exception is thrown.

If R is a class representing an array type $RC[]$, that is, an array of components of type RC:

- If T is a class type, then T must be `Object` (§4.3.2), or a run-time exception is thrown.

- If T is an interface type, then a run-time exception is thrown unless T is the type `java.io.Serializable` or the type `Cloneable` (the only interfaces implemented by arrays).

> This case could slip past the compile-time checking if, for example, a reference to an array were stored in a variable of type `Object`.

- If *T* is an array type *TC*[], that is, an array of components of type *TC*, then a runtime exception is thrown unless one of the following is true:

  - *TC* and *RC* are the same primitive type.

  - *TC* and *RC* are reference types and type *RC* can be cast to *TC* by a recursive application of these run-time rules for casting.

Example 5.5.3-1. Incompatible Types at Run Time

```
class Point { int x, y; }
interface Colorable { void setColor(int color); }
class ColoredPoint extends Point implements Colorable {
    int color;
    public void setColor(int color) { this.color = color; }
}

class Test {
    public static void main(String[] args) {
        Point[] pa = new Point[100];

        // The following line will throw a ClassCastException:
        ColoredPoint[] cpa = (ColoredPoint[])pa;
        System.out.println(cpa[0]);
        int[] shortvec = new int[2];
        Object o = shortvec;

        // The following line will throw a ClassCastException:
        Colorable c = (Colorable)o;
        c.setColor(0);
    }
}
```

This program uses casts to compile, but it throws exceptions at run time, because the types are incompatible.

5.6   Numeric Promotions

Numeric promotion is applied to the operands of an arithmetic operator.

Numeric promotion contexts allow the use of:

- an identity conversion (§5.1.1)
- a widening primitive conversion (§5.1.2)
- an unboxing conversion (§5.1.8)

117

Numeric promotions are used to convert the operands of a numeric operator to a common type so that an operation can be performed. The two kinds of numeric promotion are unary numeric promotion (§5.6.1) and binary numeric promotion (§5.6.2).

5.6.1   Unary Numeric Promotion

Some operators apply *unary numeric promotion* to a single operand, which must produce a value of a numeric type:

- If the operand is of compile-time type `Byte`, `Short`, `Character`, or `Integer`, it is subjected to unboxing conversion (§5.1.8). The result is then promoted to a value of type `int` by a widening primitive conversion (§5.1.2) or an identity conversion (§5.1.1).

- Otherwise, if the operand is of compile-time type `Long`, `Float`, or `Double`, it is subjected to unboxing conversion (§5.1.8).

- Otherwise, if the operand is of compile-time type `byte`, `short`, or `char`, it is promoted to a value of type `int` by a widening primitive conversion (§5.1.2).

- Otherwise, a unary numeric operand remains as is and is not converted.

In any case, value set conversion (§5.1.13) is then applied.

Unary numeric promotion is performed on expressions in the following situations:

- Each dimension expression in an array creation expression (§15.10)

- The index expression in an array access expression (§15.13)

- The operand of a unary plus operator + (§15.15.3)

- The operand of a unary minus operator – (§15.15.4)

- The operand of a bitwise complement operator ~ (§15.15.5)

- Each operand, separately, of a shift operator >>, >>>, or << (§15.19).

  A `long` shift distance (right operand) does not promote the value being shifted (left operand) to `long`.

Example 5.6.1-1. Unary Numeric Promotion

```
class Test {
    public static void main(String[] args) {
        byte b = 2;
        int a[] = new int[b];   // dimension expression promotion
        char c = '\u0001';
        a[c] = 1;               // index expression promotion
```

```
a[0] = -c;                    // unary - promotion
System.out.println("a: " + a[0] + "," + a[1]);
b = -1;
int i = ~b;                   // bitwise complement promotion
System.out.println("~0x" + Integer.toHexString(b)
                + "==0x" + Integer.toHexString(i));
i = b << 4L;                  // shift promotion (left operand)
System.out.println("0x" + Integer.toHexString(b)
                + "<<4L==0x" + Integer.toHexString(i));
    }
}
```

This program produces the output:

```
a: -1,1
~0xffffffff==0x0
0xffffffff<<4L==0xfffffff0
```

5.6.2   Binary Numeric Promotion

When an operator applies *binary numeric promotion* to a pair of operands, each of which must denote a value that is convertible to a numeric type, the following rules apply, in order:

1. If any operand is of a reference type, it is subjected to unboxing conversion (§5.1.8).

2. Widening primitive conversion (§5.1.2) is applied to convert either or both operands as specified by the following rules:

    *   If either operand is of type `double`, the other is converted to `double`.

    *   Otherwise, if either operand is of type `float`, the other is converted to `float`.

    *   Otherwise, if either operand is of type `long`, the other is converted to `long`.

    *   Otherwise, both operands are converted to type `int`.

After the type conversion, if any, value set conversion (§5.1.13) is applied to each operand.

Binary numeric promotion is performed on the operands of certain operators:

*   The multiplicative operators `*`, `/` and `%` (§15.17)

*   The addition and subtraction operators for numeric types `+` and `-` (§15.18.2)

*   The numerical comparison operators `<`, `<=`, `>`, and `>=` (§15.20.1)

*   The numerical equality operators `==` and `!=` (§15.21.1)

- The integer bitwise operators &, ^, and | (§15.22.1)

- In certain cases, the conditional operator ? : (§15.25)

Example 5.6.2-1. Binary Numeric Promotion

```
class Test {
    public static void main(String[] args) {
        int i    = 0;
        float f  = 1.0f;
        double d = 2.0;
        // First int*float is promoted to float*float, then
        // float==double is promoted to double==double:
        if (i * f == d) System.out.println("oops");

        // A char&byte is promoted to int&int:
        byte b = 0x1f;
        char c = 'G';
        int control = c & b;
        System.out.println(Integer.toHexString(control));

        // Here int:float is promoted to float:float:
        f = (b==0) ? i : 4.0f;
        System.out.println(1.0/f);
    }
}
```

This program produces the output:

```
7
0.25
```

The example converts the ASCII character G to the ASCII control-G (BEL), by masking off all but the low 5 bits of the character. The 7 is the numeric value of this control character.

CHAPTER 6

Names

NAMES are used to refer to entities declared in a program.

A declared entity (§6.1) is a package, class type (normal or enum), interface type (normal or annotation type), member (class, interface, field, or method) of a reference type, type parameter (of a class, interface, method or constructor), parameter (to a method, constructor, or exception handler), or local variable.

Names in programs are either *simple*, consisting of a single identifier, or *qualified*, consisting of a sequence of identifiers separated by "." tokens (§6.2).

Every declaration that introduces a name has a *scope* (§6.3), which is the part of the program text within which the declared entity can be referred to by a simple name.

A qualified name *N.x* may be used to refer to a *member* of a package or reference type, where *N* is a simple or qualified name and *x* is an identifier. If *N* names a package, then *x* is a member of that package, which is either a class or interface type or a subpackage. If *N* names a reference type or a variable of a reference type, then *x* names a member of that type, which is either a class, an interface, a field, or a method.

In determining the meaning of a name (§6.5), the context of the occurrence is used to disambiguate among packages, types, variables, and methods with the same name.

Access control (§6.6) can be specified in a class, interface, method, or field declaration to control when *access* to a member is allowed. Access is a different concept from scope. Access specifies the part of the program text within which the declared entity can be referred to by a qualified name, a field access expression (§15.11), or a method invocation expression (§15.12) in which the method is not specified by a simple name. The default access is that a member can be accessed anywhere within the package that contains its declaration; other possibilities are `public`, `protected`, and `private`.

Fully qualified and canonical names (§6.7) are also discussed in this chapter.

6.1 Declarations

A *declaration* introduces an entity into a program and includes an identifier (§3.8) that can be used in a name to refer to this entity.

A declared entity is one of the following:

- A package, declared in a `package` declaration (§7.4)
- An imported type, declared in a single-type-import declaration (§7.5.1) or a type-import-on-demand declaration (§7.5.2)
- A class, declared in a class type declaration (§8.1)
- An interface, declared in an interface type declaration (§9.1)
- A type variable (§4.4), declared as a type parameter of a generic class (§8.1.2), interface (§9.1.2), method (§8.4.4), or constructor (§8.8.1).
- A member of a reference type (§8.2, §9.2, §10.7), one of the following:
  - A member class (§8.5, §9.5)
  - A member interface (§8.5, §9.5)
  - An enum constant (§8.9)
  - A field, one of the following:
    - A field declared in a class type (§8.3)
    - A field declared in an interface type (§9.3)
    - The field `length`, which is implicitly a member of every array type (§10.7)
  - A method, one of the following:
    - A method (`abstract` or otherwise) declared in a class type (§8.4)
    - A method (always `abstract`) declared in an interface type (§9.4)
- A parameter, one of the following:
  - A parameter of a method or constructor of a class (§8.4.1, §8.8.1)
  - A parameter of an abstract method of an interface (§9.4)

- A parameter of an exception handler declared in a `catch` clause of a `try` statement (§14.20)
- A local variable, one of the following:
  - A local variable declared in a block (§14.4)
  - A local variable declared in a `for` statement (§14.14)

Constructors (§8.8) are also introduced by declarations, but use the name of the class in which they are declared rather than introducing a new name.

The class libraries of the Java SE platform attempt to use, whenever possible, names chosen according to the conventions presented below. These conventions help to make code more readable and avoid certain kinds of name conflicts.

We recommend these conventions for use in all programs written in the Java programming language. However, these conventions should not be followed slavishly if long-held conventional usage dictates otherwise. So, for example, the `sin` and `cos` methods of the class `java.lang.Math` have mathematically conventional names, even though these method names flout the convention suggested here because they are short and are not verbs.

Package Names

Developers should take steps to avoid the possibility of two published packages having the same name by choosing *unique package names* for packages that are widely distributed. This allows packages to be easily and automatically installed and catalogued. This section specifies a suggested convention for generating such unique package names. Implementations of the Java SE platform are encouraged to provide automatic support for converting a set of packages from local and casual package names to the unique name format described here.

If unique package names are not used, then package name conflicts may arise far from the point of creation of either of the conflicting packages. This may create a situation that is difficult or impossible for the user or programmer to resolve. The class `ClassLoader` can be used to isolate packages with the same name from each other in those cases where the packages will have constrained interactions, but not in a way that is transparent to a naïve program.

You form a unique package name by first having (or belonging to an organization that has) an Internet domain name, such as `oracle.com`. You then reverse this name, component by component, to obtain, in this example, `com.oracle`, and use this as a prefix for your package names, using a convention developed within your organization to further administer package names. Such a convention might specify that certain package name components be division, department, project, machine, or login names.

Example 6.1-1. Unique Package Names

```
com.nighthacks.java.jag.scrabble
org.openjdk.tools.compiler
net.jcip.annotations
edu.cmu.cs.bovik.cheese
gov.whitehouse.socks.mousefinder
```

The first component of a unique package name is always written in all-lowercase ASCII letters and should be one of the top level domain names, such as `com`, `edu`, `gov`, `mil`, `net`, or `org`, or one of the English two-letter codes identifying countries as specified in *ISO Standard 3166*.

The name of a package is not meant to imply where the package is stored on the Internet. The suggested convention for generating unique package names is merely a way to piggyback a package naming convention on top of an existing, widely known unique name registry instead of having to create a separate registry for package names.

For example, a package named `edu.cmu.cs.bovik.cheese` is not necessarily obtainable from Internet address `cmu.edu` or `cs.cmu.edu` or `bovik.cs.cmu.edu`.

In some cases, the Internet domain name may not be a valid package name. Here are some suggested conventions for dealing with these situations:

- If the domain name contains a hyphen, or any other special character not allowed in an identifier (§3.8), convert it into an underscore.
- If any of the resulting package name components are keywords (§3.9), append an underscore to them.
- If any of the resulting package name components start with a digit, or any other character that is not allowed as an initial character of an identifier, have an underscore prefixed to the component.

Names of packages intended only for local use should have a first identifier that begins with a lowercase letter, but that first identifier specifically should not be the identifier `java`; package names that start with the identifier `java` are reserved for package of the Java SE platform.

Class and Interface Type Names

Names of class types should be descriptive nouns or noun phrases, not overly long, in mixed case with the first letter of each word capitalized.

Example 6.1-2. Descriptive Class Names

```
ClassLoader
SecurityManager
Thread
Dictionary
BufferedInputStream
```

Likewise, names of interface types should be short and descriptive, not overly long, in mixed case with the first letter of each word capitalized. The name may be a descriptive noun or noun phrase, which is appropriate when an interface is used as if it were an abstract superclass, such as interfaces `java.io.DataInput` and `java.io.DataOutput`; or it may be an adjective describing a behavior, as for the interfaces `Runnable` and `Cloneable`.

Type Variable Names

Type variable names should be pithy (single character if possible) yet evocative, and should not include lower case letters. This makes it easy to distinguish type parameters from ordinary classes and interfaces.

Container types should use the name `E` for their element type. Maps should use `K` for the type of their keys and `V` for the type of their values. The name `X` should be used for arbitrary exception types. We use `T` for type, whenever there is not anything more specific about the type to distinguish it. (This is often the case in generic methods.)

If there are multiple type parameters that denote arbitrary types, one should use letters that neighbor `T` in the alphabet, such as `S`. Alternately, it is acceptable to use numeric subscripts (e.g., `T1`, `T2`) to distinguish among the different type variables. In such cases, all the variables with the same prefix should be subscripted.

If a generic method appears inside a generic class, it is a good idea to avoid using the same names for the type parameters of the method and class, to avoid confusion. The same applies to nested generic classes.

Example 6.1-3. Conventional Type Variable Names

```
public class HashSet<E> extends AbstractSet<E> { ... }
public class HashMap<K,V> extends AbstractMap<K,V> { ... }
public class ThreadLocal<T> { ... }
public interface Functor<T, X extends Throwable> {
    T eval() throws X;
}
```

When type parameters do not fall conveniently into one of the categories mentioned, names should be chosen to be as meaningful as possible within the confines of a single letter. The names mentioned above (`E`, `K`, `V`, `X`, `T`) should not be used for type parameters that do not fall into the designated categories.

Method Names

Method names should be verbs or verb phrases, in mixed case, with the first letter lowercase and the first letter of any subsequent words capitalized. Here are some additional specific conventions for method names:

- Methods to get and set an attribute that might be thought of as a variable *V* should be named `getV` and `setV`. An example is the methods `getPriority` and `setPriority` of class `Thread`.

- A method that returns the length of something should be named `length`, as in class `String`.

- A method that tests a boolean condition *V* about an object should be named is*V*. An example is the method `isInterrupted` of class `Thread`.

- A method that converts its object to a particular format *F* should be named to*F*. Examples are the method `toString` of class `Object` and the methods `toLocaleString` and `toGMTString` of class `java.util.Date`.

Whenever possible and appropriate, basing the names of methods in a new class on names in an existing class that is similar, especially a class from the Java SE platform API, will make it easier to use.

Field Names

Names of fields that are not `final` should be in mixed case with a lowercase first letter and the first letters of subsequent words capitalized. Note that well-designed classes have very few `public` or `protected` fields, except for fields that are constants (`static final` fields).

Fields should have names that are nouns, noun phrases, or abbreviations for nouns.

Examples of this convention are the fields `buf`, `pos`, and `count` of the class `java.io.ByteArrayInputStream` and the field `bytesTransferred` of the class `java.io.InterruptedIOException`.

Constant Names

The names of constants in interface types should be, and `final` variables of class types may conventionally be, a sequence of one or more words, acronyms, or abbreviations, all uppercase, with components separated by underscore "_" characters. Constant names should be descriptive and not unnecessarily abbreviated. Conventionally they may be any appropriate part of speech.

Examples of names for constants include `MIN_VALUE`, `MAX_VALUE`, `MIN_RADIX`, and `MAX_RADIX` of the class `Character`.

A group of constants that represent alternative values of a set, or, less frequently, masking bits in an integer value, are sometimes usefully specified with a common acronym as a name prefix.

For example:

```
interface ProcessStates {
    int PS_RUNNING   = 0;
    int PS_SUSPENDED = 1;
}
```

Local Variable and Parameter Names

Local variable and parameter names should be short, yet meaningful. They are often short sequences of lowercase letters that are not words, such as:

- Acronyms, that is the first letter of a series of words, as in `cp` for a variable holding a reference to a `ColoredPoint`

- Abbreviations, as in `buf` holding a pointer to a buffer of some kind

- Mnemonic terms, organized in some way to aid memory and understanding, typically by using a set of local variables with conventional names patterned after the names of parameters to widely used classes. For example:

  - `in` and `out`, whenever some kind of input and output are involved, patterned after the fields of `System`

  - `off` and `len`, whenever an offset and length are involved, patterned after the parameters to the `read` and `write` methods of the interfaces `DataInput` and `DataOutput` of `java.io`

One-character local variable or parameter names should be avoided, except for temporary and looping variables, or where a variable holds an undistinguished value of a type. Conventional one-character names are:

- b for a `byte`
- c for a `char`
- d for a `double`
- e for an `Exception`
- f for a `float`
- i, j, and k for `int`s
- l for a `long`
- o for an `Object`
- s for a `String`
- v for an arbitrary value of some type

Local variable or parameter names that consist of only two or three lowercase letters should not conflict with the initial country codes and domain names that are the first component of unique package names.

6.2 Names and Identifiers

A *name* is used to refer to an entity declared in a program.

There are two forms of names: simple names and qualified names.

A *simple name* is a single identifier.

A *qualified name* consists of a name, a "." token, and an identifier.

In determining the meaning of a name (§6.5), the context in which the name appears is taken into account. The rules of §6.5 distinguish among contexts where a name must denote (refer to) a package (§6.5.3), a type (§6.5.5), a variable or value in an expression (§6.5.6), or a method (§6.5.7).

> Packages and reference types have *members* which may be accessed by qualified names. As background for the discussion of qualified names and the determination of the meaning of names, see the descriptions of membership in §4.4, §4.5.2, §4.8, §4.9, §7.1, §8.2, §9.2, and §10.7.

Not all identifiers in a program are a part of a name. Identifiers are also used in the following situations:

- In declarations (§6.1), where an identifier may occur to specify the name by which the declared entity will be known.

- As labels in labeled statements (§14.7) and in `break` and `continue` statements (§14.15, §14.16) that refer to statement labels.

- In field access expressions (§15.11), where an identifier occurs after a "." token to indicate a member of an object that is the value of an expression or the keyword `super` that appears before the "." token

- In some method invocation expressions (§15.12), where an identifier may occur after a "." token and before a "(" token to indicate a method to be invoked for an object that is the value of an expression or the keyword `super` that appears before the "." token

- In qualified class instance creation expressions (§15.9), where an identifier occurs immediately to the right of the leftmost `new` token to indicate a type that must be a member of the compile-time type of the primary expression preceding the "." preceding the leftmost `new` token.

> In this program:

```
class Test {
    public static void main(String[] args) {
        Class c = System.out.getClass();
        System.out.println(c.toString().length() +
                           args[0].length() + args.length);
    }
}
```

> the identifiers `Test`, `main`, and the first occurrences of `args` and `c` are not names. Rather, they are used in declarations to specify the names of the declared entities. The names `String`, `Class`, `System.out.getClass`, `System.out.println`, `c.toString`,

args, and `args.length` appear in the example. The occurrence of `length` in `args[0].length()` is not a name, but rather an identifier appearing in a method invocation expression (§15.12). The occurrence of `length` in `args.length` is a name because `args.length` is a qualified name (§6.5.6.2) and not a field access expression (§15.11). (A field access expression, like a method invocation expression, uses an identifier rather than a name to denote the member of interest.)

One might wonder why these kinds of expression use an identifier rather than a simple name, which is after all just an identifier. The reason is that a simple expression name is defined in terms of the lexical environment; that is, a simple expression name must be in the scope of a variable declaration. But field access, and method invocation qualified by a *Primary*, and qualified class instance creation all denote members whose names are not in the lexical environment. By definition, such names are bound only in the context provided by the *Primary* of the field access expression, method invocation expression, or class instance creation expression. Therefore, we denote such members with identifiers rather than simple names.

To complicate things further, a field access expression is not the only way to denote a field of an object. For parsing reasons, a qualified name is used to denote a field of an in-scope variable. (The variable itself is denoted with a simple name, alluded to above.) It is necessary for access control (§6.6) to capture both mechanisms for denoting a field.

The identifiers used in labeled statements (§14.7) and their associated `break` and `continue` statements (§14.15, §14.16) are completely separate from those used in declarations.

Example 6.2-1. Identifiers and Obscuring

The following code was taken from a version of the class `String` and its method `indexOf`, where the label was originally called `test`. Changing the label to have the same name as the local variable `i` does not obscure (§6.4.2) the label in the scope of the declaration of `i`. Thus, the code is valid.

```
class Test {
    char[] value;
    int offset, count;
    int indexOf(TestString str, int fromIndex) {
        char[] v1 = value, v2 = str.value;
        int max = offset + (count - str.count);
        int start = offset + ((fromIndex < 0) ? 0 : fromIndex);
    i:
        for (int i = start; i <= max; i++) {
            int n = str.count, j = i, k = str.offset;
            while (n-- != 0) {
                if (v1[j++] != v2[k++])
                    continue i;
            }
            return i - offset;
        }
        return -1;
    }
}
```

```
}
```

The identifier max could also have been used as the statement label; the label would not obscure the local variable max within the labeled statement.

6.3 Scope of a Declaration

The *scope* of a declaration is the region of the program within which the entity declared by the declaration can be referred to using a simple name, provided it is visible (§6.4.1).

A declaration is said to be *in scope* at a particular point in a program if and only if the declaration's scope includes that point.

The scope of the declaration of an observable (§7.4.3) top level package is all observable compilation units (§7.3).

The declaration of a package that is not observable is never in scope.

The declaration of a subpackage is never in scope.

The package java is always in scope.

The scope of a type imported by a single-type-import declaration (§7.5.1) or a type-import-on-demand declaration (§7.5.2) is all the class and interface type declarations (§7.6) in the compilation unit in which the import declaration appears, as well as any annotations on the package declaration (if any) of the compilation unit .

The scope of a member imported by a single-static-import declaration (§7.5.3) or a static-import-on-demand declaration (§7.5.4) is all the class and interface type declarations (§7.6) in the compilation unit in which the import declaration appears, as well as any annotations on the package declaration (if any) of the compilation unit .

The scope of a top level type (§7.6) is all type declarations in the package in which the top level type is declared.

The scope of a declaration of a member m declared in or inherited by a class type c (§8.1.6) is the entire body of c, including any nested type declarations.

The scope of a declaration of a member m declared in or inherited by an interface type I (§9.1.4) is the entire body of I, including any nested type declarations.

The scope of an enum constant c declared in an enum type T is the body of T, and any case label of a switch statement whose expression is of enum type T.

The scope of a formal parameter of a method (§8.4.1) or constructor (§8.8.1) is the entire body of the method or constructor.

The scope of a class's type parameter (§8.1.2) is the type parameter section of the class declaration, the type parameter section of any superclass or superinterface of the class declaration, and the class body.

The scope of an interface's type parameter (§9.1.2) is the type parameter section of the interface declaration, the type parameter section of any superinterface of the interface declaration, and the interface body.

The scope of a method's type parameter (§8.4.4) is the entire declaration of the method, including the type parameter section, but excluding the method modifiers.

The scope of a constructor's type parameter (§8.8.4) is the entire declaration of the constructor, including the type parameter section, but excluding the constructor modifiers.

The scope of a local class declaration immediately enclosed by a block (§14.2) is the rest of the immediately enclosing block, including its own class declaration.

The scope of a local class declaration immediately enclosed by a switch block statement group (§14.11) is the rest of the immediately enclosing switch block statement group, including its own class declaration.

The scope of a local variable declaration in a block (§14.4) is the rest of the block in which the declaration appears, starting with its own initializer and including any further declarators to the right in the local variable declaration statement.

The scope of a local variable declared in the *ForInit* part of a basic `for` statement (§14.14.1) includes all of the following:

- Its own initializer

- Any further declarators to the right in the *ForInit* part of the `for` statement

- The *Expression* and *ForUpdate* parts of the `for` statement

- The contained *Statement*

The scope of a local variable declared in the *FormalParameter* part of an enhanced `for` statement (§14.14.2) is the contained *Statement*.

The scope of a parameter of an exception handler that is declared in a `catch` clause of a `try` statement (§14.20) is the entire block associated with the `catch`.

The scope of a variable declared in the *ResourceSpecification* of a `try`-with-resources statement (§14.20.3) is from the declaration rightward over the remainder of the *ResourceSpecification* and the entire `try` block associated with the `try`-with-resources statement.

The translation of a `try`-with-resources statement implies the rule above.

Example 6.3-1. Scope and Type Declarations

These rules imply that declarations of class and interface types need not appear before uses of the types. In the following program, the use of `PointList` in class `Point` is valid, because the scope of the class declaration `PointList` includes both class `Point` and class `PointList`, as well as any other type declarations in other compilation units of package points.

```
package points;
class Point {
    int x, y;
    PointList list;
    Point next;
}

class PointList {
    Point first;
}
```

Example 6.3-2. Scope of Local Variable Declarations

```
class Test1 {
    static int x;
    public static void main(String[] args) {
        int x = x;
    }
}
```

This program causes a compile-time error because the initialization of x is within the scope of the declaration of x as a local variable, and the local variable x does not yet have a value and cannot be used.

The following program does compile:

```
class Test2 {
    static int x;
    public static void main(String[] args) {
        int x = (x=2)*2;
        System.out.println(x);
    }
}
```

because the local variable x is definitely assigned (§16) before it is used. It prints:

```
4
```

In the following program, the initializer for `three` can correctly refer to the variable `two` declared in an earlier declarator, and the method invocation in the next line can correctly refer to the variable `three` declared earlier in the block.

```
class Test3 {
    public static void main(String[] args) {
        System.out.print("2+1=");
        int two = 2, three = two + 1;
        System.out.println(three);
    }
}
```

This program produces the output:

```
2+1=3
```

6.4 Shadowing and Obscuring

A local variable (§14.4), formal parameter (§8.4.1), exception parameter (§14.20), and local class (§14.3) can only be referred to using a simple name (§6.2), not a qualified name (§6.6).

Some declarations are not permitted within the scope of a local variable, formal parameter, exception parameter, or local class declaration because it would be impossible to distinguish between the declared entities using only simple names.

> For example, if the name of a formal parameter of a method could be redeclared as the name of a local variable in the method body, then the local variable would shadow the formal parameter and the formal parameter would no longer be visible - an undesirable outcome.

It is a compile-time error if the name of a formal parameter is redeclared as a local variable of the method or constructor; or as an exception parameter of a `catch` clause in a `try` statement in the body of the method or constructor; or as a resource in a `try`-with-resources statement in the body of the method or constructor.

It is a compile-time error if the name of a local variable v is redeclared as a local variable of the directly enclosing method, constructor, or initializer block within the scope of v; or as an exception parameter of a `catch` clause in a `try` statement of the directly enclosing method, constructor or initializer block within the scope of v; or as a resource in a `try`-with-resources statement of the directly enclosing method, constructor or initializer block within the scope of v.

It is a compile-time error if the name of a local class *c* is redeclared as a local class of the directly enclosing method, constructor, or initializer block within the scope of *c*.

It is a compile-time error if the name of an exception parameter is redeclared within the *Block* of the `catch` clause as a local variable of the directly enclosing method, constructor, or initializer block; or as an exception parameter of a `catch` clause in a `try` statement of the directly enclosing method, constructor or initializer block; or as a resource in a `try`-with-resources statement of the directly enclosing method, constructor or initializer block.

It is a compile-time error if the name of a variable declared in a *ResourceSpecification* of a `try`-with-resources statement (§14.20.3) is redeclared within the `try` *Block* as a local variable of the directly enclosing method, constructor, or initializer block, or as an exception parameter of a `catch` clause in a `try` statement of the directly enclosing method or initializer block.

The translation of a `try`-with-resources statement implies the rule above.

Despite the above rules against redeclaration of variables, the rules of shadowing (§6.4.1) allow redeclaration in certain nested class declarations (i.e. local classes (§14.3) and anonymous classes (§15.9)) as follows:

- A formal parameter of a method or constructor may be shadowed anywhere inside a class declaration nested within that method or constructor.

- A local variable of a method, constructor, or initializer may be shadowed anywhere inside a class declaration nested within the scope of the local variable.

- A local class declaration may be shadowed anywhere inside a class declaration nested within the local class declaration's scope.

- An exception parameter may be shadowed anywhere inside a class declaration nested within the *Block* of the `catch` clause.

- A variable declared in a *ResourceSpecification* may be shadowed anywhere inside a class declaration nested within the `try` *Block*.

Example 6.4-1. Attempted Shadowing Of A Local Variable

Because a declaration of an identifier as a local variable of a method, constructor, or initializer block must not appear within the scope of a parameter or local variable of the same name, a compile-time error occurs for the following program:

```
class Test1 {
    public static void main(String[] args) {
        int i;
        for (int i = 0; i < 10; i++)
            System.out.println(i);
    }
```

```
        }
```

This restriction helps to detect some otherwise very obscure bugs. A similar restriction on shadowing of members by local variables was judged impractical, because the addition of a member in a superclass could cause subclasses to have to rename local variables. Related considerations make restrictions on shadowing of local variables by members of nested classes, or on shadowing of local variables by local variables declared within nested classes unattractive as well.

Hence, the following program compiles without error:

```
class Test2 {
    public static void main(String[] args) {
        int i;
        class Local {
            {
                for (int i = 0; i < 10; i++)
                    System.out.println(i);
            }
        }
        new Local();
    }
}
```

On the other hand, local variables with the same name may be declared in two separate blocks or `for` statements, neither of which contains the other:

```
class Test3 {
    public static void main(String[] args) {
        for (int i = 0; i < 10; i++)
            System.out.print(i + " ");
        for (int i = 10; i > 0; i--)
            System.out.print(i + " ");
        System.out.println();
    }
}
```

This program compiles without error and, when executed, produces the output:

```
0 1 2 3 4 5 6 7 8 9 10 9 8 7 6 5 4 3 2 1
```

6.4.1   Shadowing

Some declarations may be *shadowed* in part of their scope by another declaration of the same name, in which case a simple name cannot be used to refer to the declared entity.

Shadowing is distinct from hiding (§8.3, §8.4.8.2, §8.5, §9.3, §9.5), which applies only to members which would otherwise be inherited but are not because of a declaration in a subclass. Shadowing is also distinct from obscuring (§6.4.2).

A declaration d is said to be *visible at point p in a program* if the scope of d includes p, and d is not shadowed by any other declaration at p.

When the program point we are discussing is clear from context, we will often simply say that a declaration is *visible*.

A declaration d of a type named n shadows the declarations of any other types named n that are in scope at the point where d occurs throughout the scope of d.

A declaration d of a field or formal parameter named n shadows, throughout the scope of d, the declarations of any other variables named n that are in scope at the point where d occurs.

A declaration d of a local variable or exception parameter named n shadows, throughout the scope of d, (a) the declarations of any other fields named n that are in scope at the point where d occurs, and (b) the declarations of any other variables named n that are in scope at the point where d occurs but are *not* declared in the innermost class in which d is declared.

A declaration d of a method named n shadows the declarations of any other methods named n that are in an enclosing scope at the point where d occurs throughout the scope of d.

A package declaration never shadows any other declaration.

A type-import-on-demand declaration never causes any other declaration to be shadowed.

A static-import-on-demand declaration never causes any other declaration to be shadowed.

A single-type-import declaration d in a compilation unit c of package p that imports a type named n shadows, throughout c, the declarations of:

- any top level type named n declared in another compilation unit of p
- any type named n imported by a type-import-on-demand declaration in c
- any type named n imported by a static-import-on-demand declaration in c

A single-static-import declaration d in a compilation unit c of package p that imports a field named n shadows the declaration of any static field named n imported by a static-import-on-demand declaration in c, throughout c.

A single-static-import declaration d in a compilation unit c of package p that imports a method named n with signature s shadows the declaration of any static method named n with signature s imported by a static-import-on-demand declaration in c, throughout c.

A single-static-import declaration d in a compilation unit c of package p that imports a type named n shadows, throughout c, the declarations of:

- any static type named n imported by a static-import-on-demand declaration in c;

- any top level type (§7.6) named n declared in another compilation unit (§7.3) of p;

- any type named n imported by a type-import-on-demand declaration (§7.5.2) in c.

Example 6.4.1-1. Shadowing of a Field Declaration by a Local Variable Declaration

```
class Test {
    static int x = 1;
    public static void main(String[] args) {
        int x = 0;
        System.out.print("x=" + x);
        System.out.println(", Test.x=" + Test.x);
    }
}
```

This program produces the output:

```
x=0, Test.x=1
```

This program declares:

- a class `Test`

- a class (`static`) variable `x` that is a member of the class `Test`

- a class method `main` that is a member of the class `Test`

- a parameter `args` of the `main` method

- a local variable `x` of the `main` method

Since the scope of a class variable includes the entire body of the class (§8.2), the class variable `x` would normally be available throughout the entire body of the method `main`. In this example, however, the class variable `x` is shadowed within the body of the method `main` by the declaration of the local variable `x`.

A local variable has as its scope the rest of the block in which it is declared (§6.4); in this case this is the rest of the body of the `main` method, namely its initializer "0" and the invocations of `System.out.print` and `System.out.println`.

This means that:

- The expression x in the invocation of `print` refers to (denotes) the value of the local variable x.

- The invocation of `println` uses a qualified name (§6.6) `Test.x`, which uses the class type name `Test` to access the class variable x, because the declaration of `Test.x` is shadowed at this point and cannot be referred to by its simple name.

The keyword `this` can also be used to access a shadowed field x, using the form `this.x`. Indeed, this idiom typically appears in constructors (§8.8):

```
class Pair {
    Object first, second;
    public Pair(Object first, Object second) {
        this.first = first;
        this.second = second;
    }
}
```

Here, the constructor takes parameters having the same names as the fields to be initialized. This is simpler than having to invent different names for the parameters and is not too confusing in this stylized context. In general, however, it is considered poor style to have local variables with the same names as fields.

Example 6.4.1-2. Shadowing of a Type Declaration by Another Type Declaration

```
import java.util.*;
class Vector {
    int val[] = { 1 , 2 };
}

class Test {
    public static void main(String[] args) {
        Vector v = new Vector();
        System.out.println(v.val[0]);
    }
}
```

The program compiles and prints:

```
1
```

using the class `Vector` declared here in preference to the generic class `java.util.Vector` (§8.1.2) that might be imported on demand.

6.4.2   Obscuring

A simple name may occur in contexts where it may potentially be interpreted as the name of a variable, a type, or a package. In these situations, the rules of §6.5

specify that a variable will be chosen in preference to a type, and that a type will be chosen in preference to a package. Thus, it is may sometimes be impossible to refer to a visible type or package declaration via its simple name. We say that such a declaration is *obscured*.

Obscuring is distinct from shadowing (§6.4.1) and hiding (§8.3, §8.4.8.2, §8.5, §9.3, §9.5).

The naming conventions of §6.1 help reduce obscuring, but if it does occur, here are some notes about what you can do to avoid it.

When package names occur in expressions:

- If a package name is obscured by a field declaration, then `import` declarations (§7.5) can usually be used to make available the type names declared in that package.
- If a package name is obscured by a declaration of a parameter or local variable, then the name of the parameter or local variable can be changed without affecting other code.

The first component of a package name is normally not easily mistaken for a type name, as a type name normally begins with a single uppercase letter. (The Java programming language does not actually rely on case distinctions to determine whether a name is a package name or a type name.)

Obscuring involving class and interface type names is rare. Names of fields, parameters, and local variables normally do not obscure type names because they conventionally begin with a lowercase letter whereas type names conventionally begin with an uppercase letter.

Method names cannot obscure or be obscured by other names (§6.5.7).

Obscuring involving field names is rare; however:

- If a field name obscures a package name, then an `import` declaration (§7.5) can usually be used to make available the type names declared in that package.
- If a field name obscures a type name, then a fully qualified name for the type can be used unless the type name denotes a local class (§14.3).
- Field names cannot obscure method names.
- If a field name is shadowed by a declaration of a parameter or local variable, then the name of the parameter or local variable can be changed without affecting other code.

Obscuring involving constant names is rare:

- Constant names normally have no lowercase letters, so they will not normally obscure names of packages or types, nor will they normally shadow fields, whose names typically contain at least one lowercase letter.
- Constant names cannot obscure method names, because they are distinguished syntactically.

6.5   Determining the Meaning of a Name

The meaning of a name depends on the context in which it is used. The determination of the meaning of a name requires three steps:

- First, context causes a name syntactically to fall into one of six categories: *PackageName*, *TypeName*, *ExpressionName*, *MethodName*, *PackageOrTypeName*, or *AmbiguousName*.

- Second, a name that is initially classified by its context as an *AmbiguousName* or as a *PackageOrTypeName* is then reclassified to be a *PackageName*, *TypeName*, or *ExpressionName*.

- Third, the resulting category then dictates the final determination of the meaning of the name (or a compile-time error if the name has no meaning).

> *PackageName:*
>   *Identifier*
>   *PackageName . Identifier*
>
> *TypeName:*
>   *Identifier*
>   *PackageOrTypeName . Identifier*
>
> *ExpressionName:*
>   *Identifier*
>   *AmbiguousName . Identifier*
>
> *MethodName:*
>   *Identifier*
>   *AmbiguousName . Identifier*
>
> *PackageOrTypeName:*
>   *Identifier*
>   *PackageOrTypeName . Identifier*
>
> *AmbiguousName:*
>   *Identifier*
>   *AmbiguousName . Identifier*

The use of context helps to minimize name conflicts between entities of different kinds. Such conflicts will be rare if the naming conventions described in §6.1 are followed. Nevertheless, conflicts may arise unintentionally as types developed by different programmers or different organizations evolve. For example, types, methods, and fields may have the same name. It is always possible to distinguish between a method and a field with the same name, since the context of a use always tells whether a method is intended.

6.5.1 Syntactic Classification of a Name According to Context

A name is syntactically classified as a *PackageName* in these contexts:

- In a package declaration (§7.4)

- To the left of the "." in a qualified *PackageName*

A name is syntactically classified as a *TypeName* in these contexts:

- In a single-type-import declaration (§7.5.1)

- To the left of the "." in a single-static-import declaration (§7.5.3)

- To the left of the "." in a static-import-on-demand declaration (§7.5.4)

- To the left of the "<" in a parameterized type (§4.5)

- In a type argument list (§4.5.1) of a parameterized type

- In an explicit type argument list in a method or constructor invocation

- In an `extends` clause in a type variable declaration (§8.1.2)

- In an `extends` clause of a wildcard type argument (§4.5.1)

- In a `super` clause of a wildcard type argument (§4.5.1)

- In an `extends` clause in a class declaration (§8.1.4)

- In an `implements` clause in a class declaration (§8.1.5)

- In an `extends` clause in an interface declaration (§9.1.3)

- After the "@" sign in an annotation (§9.7)

- As a *Type* (or the part of a *Type* that remains after all brackets are deleted) in any of the following contexts:

  - In a field declaration (§8.3, §9.3)

  - As the result type of a method (§8.4, §9.4)

  - As the type of a formal parameter of a method or constructor (§8.4.1, §8.8.1, §9.4)

  - As the type of an exception that can be thrown by a method or constructor (§8.4.6, §8.8.5, §9.4)

- As the type of a local variable (§14.4)

- As the type of an exception parameter in a `catch` clause of a `try` statement (§14.20)

- As the type in a class literal (§15.8.2)

- As the qualifying type of a qualified `this` expression (§15.8.4).

- As the class type which is to be instantiated in an unqualified class instance creation expression (§15.9)

- As the direct superclass or direct superinterface of an anonymous class (§15.9.5) which is to be instantiated in an unqualified class instance creation expression (§15.9)

- As the element type of an array to be created in an array creation expression (§15.10)

- As the qualifying type of field access using the keyword `super` (§15.11.2)

- As the qualifying type of a method invocation using the keyword `super` (§15.12)

- As the type mentioned in the cast operator of a cast expression (§15.16)

- As the type that follows the `instanceof` relational operator (§15.20.2)

A name is syntactically classified as an *ExpressionName* in these contexts:

- As the qualifying expression in a qualified superclass constructor invocation (§8.8.7.1)

- As the qualifying expression in a qualified class instance creation expression (§15.9)

- As the array reference expression in an array access expression (§15.13)

- As a *PostfixExpression* (§15.14)

- As the left-hand operand of an assignment operator (§15.26)

A name is syntactically classified as a *MethodName* in these contexts:

- Before the "(" in a method invocation expression (§15.12)

- To the left of the "=" sign in an annotation's element value pair (§9.7)

A name is syntactically classified as a *PackageOrTypeName* in these contexts:

- To the left of the "." in a qualified *TypeName*

- In a type-import-on-demand declaration (§7.5.2)

A name is syntactically classified as an *AmbiguousName* in these contexts:

- To the left of the "." in a qualified *ExpressionName*

- To the left of the "." in a qualified *MethodName*

- To the left of the "." in a qualified *AmbiguousName*

- In the default value clause of an annotation type element declaration (§9.6)

- To the right of an "=" in an an element value pair (§9.7)

> The effect of syntactic classification is to restrict certain kinds of entities to certain parts of expressions:
>
> - The name of a field, parameter, or local variable may be used as an expression (§15.14.1).
>
> - The name of a method may appear in an expression only as part of a method invocation expression (§15.12).
>
> - The name of a class or interface type may appear in an expression only as part of a class literal (§15.8.2), a qualified `this` expression (§15.8.4), a class instance creation expression (§15.9), an array creation expression (§15.10), a cast expression (§15.16), an `instanceof` expression (§15.20.2), an enum constant (§8.9), or as part of a qualified name for a field or method.
>
> - The name of a package may appear in an expression only as part of a qualified name for a class or interface type.

6.5.2 Reclassification of Contextually Ambiguous Names

An *AmbiguousName* is then reclassified as follows.

If the *AmbiguousName* is a simple name, consisting of a single *Identifier*:

- If the *Identifier* appears within the scope (§6.3) of a local variable declaration (§14.4) or parameter declaration (§8.4.1, §8.8.1, §14.20) or field declaration (§8.3) with that name, then the *AmbiguousName* is reclassified as an *ExpressionName*.

- Otherwise, if a field of that name is declared in the compilation unit (§7.3) containing the *Identifier* by a single-static-import declaration (§7.5.3), or by a static-import-on-demand declaration (§7.5.4) then the *AmbiguousName* is reclassified as an *ExpressionName*.

- Otherwise, if the *Identifier* appears within the scope (§6.3) of a top level class (§8) or interface type declaration (§9), a local class declaration (§14.3) or member type declaration (§8.5, §9.5) with that name, then the *AmbiguousName* is reclassified as a *TypeName*.

- Otherwise, if a type of that name is declared in the compilation unit (§7.3) containing the *Identifier*, either by a single-type-import declaration (§7.5.1), or by a type-import-on-demand declaration (§7.5.2), or by a single-static-import declaration (§7.5.3), or by a static-import-on-demand declaration (§7.5.4), then the *AmbiguousName* is reclassified as a *TypeName*.

- Otherwise, the *AmbiguousName* is reclassified as a *PackageName*. A later step determines whether or not a package of that name actually exists.

If the *AmbiguousName* is a qualified name, consisting of a name, a ".", and an *Identifier*, then the name to the left of the "." is first reclassified, for it is itself an *AmbiguousName*. There is then a choice:

- If the name to the left of the "." is reclassified as a *PackageName*, then:

  - If there is a package whose name is the name to the left of the "." and that package contains a declaration of a type whose name is the same as the *Identifier*, then this *AmbiguousName* is reclassified as a *TypeName*.

  - Otherwise, this *AmbiguousName* is reclassified as a *PackageName*. A later step determines whether or not a package of that name actually exists.

- If the name to the left of the "." is reclassified as a *TypeName*, then:

  - If the *Identifier* is the name of a method or field of the type denoted by *TypeName*, this *AmbiguousName* is reclassified as an *ExpressionName*.

  - Otherwise, if the *Identifier* is the name of a member type of the type denoted by *TypeName*, this *AmbiguousName* is reclassified as a *TypeName*.

  - Otherwise, a compile-time error occurs.

- If the name to the left of the "." is reclassified as an *ExpressionName*, then let T be the type of the expression denoted by *ExpressionName*.

  - If the *Identifier* is the name of a method or field of the type denoted by T, this *AmbiguousName* is reclassified as an *ExpressionName*.

  - Otherwise, if the *Identifier* is the name of a member type (§8.5, §9.5) of the type denoted by T, then this *AmbiguousName* is reclassified as a *TypeName*.

  - Otherwise, a compile-time error occurs.

Example 6.5.2-1. Reclassification of Contextually Ambiguous Names

Consider the following contrived "library code":

```
package org.rpgpoet;
import java.util.Random;
public interface Music { Random[] wizards = new Random[4]; }
```

and then consider this example code in another package:

```
package bazola;
class Gabriel {
    static int n = org.rpgpoet.Music.wizards.length;
}
```

First of all, the name `org.rpgpoet.Music.wizards.length` is classified as an *ExpressionName* because it functions as a *PostfixExpression*. Therefore, each of the names:

```
org.rpgpoet.Music.wizards
org.rpgpoet.Music
org.rpgpoet
org
```

is initially classified as an *AmbiguousName*. These are then reclassified:

- The simple name `org` is reclassified as a *PackageName* (since there is no variable or type named org in scope).

- Next, assuming that there is no class or interface named `rpgpoet` in any compilation unit of package `org` (and we know that there is no such class or interface because package `org` has a subpackage named `rpgpoet`), the qualified name `org.rpgpoet` is reclassified as a *PackageName*.

- Next, because package `org.rpgpoet` has an accessible (§6.6) interface type named `Music`, the qualified name `org.rpgpoet.Music` is reclassified as a *TypeName*.

- Finally, because the name `org.rpgpoet.Music` is a *TypeName*, the qualified name `org.rpgpoet.Music.wizards` is reclassified as an *ExpressionName*.

6.5.3   Meaning of Package Names

The meaning of a name classified as a *PackageName* is determined as follows.

6.5.3.1   *Simple Package Names*

If a package name consists of a single *Identifier*, then this identifier denotes a top level package named by that identifier.

If no top level package of that name is in scope (§6.3), then a compile-time error occurs.

6.5.3.2   *Qualified Package Names*

If a package name is of the form $Q.Id$, then Q must also be a package name. The package name $Q.Id$ names a package that is the member named Id within the package named by Q.

If Q does not name an observable package (§7.4.3), or Id is not the simple name of an observable subpackage of that package, then a compile-time error occurs.

6.5.4   Meaning of *PackageOrTypeNames*

6.5.4.1   *Simple PackageOrTypeNames*

If the *PackageOrTypeName*, Q, occurs in the scope of a type named Q, then the *PackageOrTypeName* is reclassified as a *TypeName*.

Otherwise, the *PackageOrTypeName* is reclassified as a *PackageName*. The meaning of the *PackageOrTypeName* is the meaning of the reclassified name.

6.5.4.2   *Qualified PackageOrTypeNames*

Given a qualified *PackageOrTypeName* of the form $Q.Id$, if the type or package denoted by Q has a member type named Id, then the qualified *PackageOrTypeName* name is reclassified as a *TypeName*.

Otherwise, it is reclassified as a *PackageName*. The meaning of the qualified *PackageOrTypeName* is the meaning of the reclassified name.

6.5.5   Meaning of Type Names

The meaning of a name classified as a *TypeName* is determined as follows.

6.5.5.1   *Simple Type Names*

If a type name consists of a single *Identifier*, then the identifier must occur in the scope of exactly one visible declaration of a type with this name, or a compile-time error occurs. The meaning of the type name is that type.

6.5.5.2   *Qualified Type Names*

If a type name is of the form $Q.Id$, then Q must be either a type name or a package name.

If *Id* names exactly one accessible type (§6.6) that is a member of the type or package denoted by ϱ, then the qualified type name denotes that type.

If *Id* does not name a member type (§8.5, §9.5) within ϱ, or there is not exactly one accessible (§6.6) member type named *Id* within ϱ, or *Id* names a static member type (§8.5.1) within ϱ and ϱ is parameterized, then a compile-time error occurs.

Example 6.5.5.2-1. Qualified Type Names

```
class Test {
    public static void main(String[] args) {
        java.util.Date date =
            new java.util.Date(System.currentTimeMillis());
        System.out.println(date.toLocaleString());
    }
}
```

This program produced the following output the first time it was run:

```
Sun Jan 21 22:56:29 1996
```

In this example, the name `java.util.Date` must denote a type, so we first use the procedure recursively to determine if `java.util` is an accessible type or a package, which it is, and then look to see if the type `Date` is accessible in this package.

6.5.6   Meaning of Expression Names

The meaning of a name classified as an *ExpressionName* is determined as follows.

6.5.6.1   *Simple Expression Names*

If an expression name consists of a single *Identifier*, then there must be exactly one declaration denoting either a local variable, parameter, or field visible (§6.4.1) at the point at which the *Identifier* occurs. Otherwise, a compile-time error occurs.

If the declaration denotes an instance variable (§8.3), the expression name must appear within the declaration of an instance method (§8.4), constructor (§8.8), instance initializer (§8.6), or instance variable initializer (§8.3.2.2). If the expression name appears within a static method (§8.4.3.2), static initializer (§8.7), or initializer for a static variable (§8.3.2.1, §12.4.2), then a compile-time error occurs.

If the declaration declares a `final` variable which is definitely assigned before the simple expression, the meaning of the name is the value of that variable. Otherwise, the meaning of the expression name is the variable declared by the declaration.

If the expression name appears in a context where it is subject to assignment conversion or method invocation conversion or casting conversion, then the type of the expression name is the declared type of the field, local variable, or parameter after capture conversion (§5.1.10).

Otherwise, the type of the expression name is the declared type of the field, local variable or parameter.

That is, if the expression name appears "on the right hand side", its type is subject to capture conversion. If the expression name is a variable that appears "on the left hand side", its type is not subject to capture conversion.

Example 6.5.6.1-1. Simple Expression Names

```
class Test {
    static int v;
    static final int f = 3;
    public static void main(String[] args) {
        int i;
        i = 1;
        v = 2;
        f = 33;   // compile-time error
        System.out.println(i + " " + v + " " + f);
    }
}
```

In this program, the names used as the left-hand-sides in the assignments to i, v, and f denote the local variable i, the field v, and the value of f (not the variable f, because f is a `final` variable). The example therefore produces an error at compile time because the last assignment does not have a variable as its left-hand side. If the erroneous assignment is removed, the modified code can be compiled and it will produce the output:

```
1 2 3
```

6.5.6.2   Qualified Expression Names

If an expression name is of the form Q.Id, then Q has already been classified as a package name, a type name, or an expression name.

If Q is a package name, then a compile-time error occurs.

If Q is a type name that names a class type (§8), then:

• If there is not exactly one accessible (§6.6) member of the class type that is a field named Id, then a compile-time error occurs.

• Otherwise, if the single accessible member field is not a class variable (that is, it is not declared `static`), then a compile-time error occurs.

- Otherwise, if the class variable is declared `final`, then *Q.Id* denotes the value of the class variable.

  The type of the expression *Q.Id* is the declared type of the class variable after capture conversion (§5.1.10).

  If *Q.Id* appears in a context that requires a variable and not a value, then a compile-time error occurs.

- Otherwise, *Q.Id* denotes the class variable.

  The type of the expression *Q.Id* is the declared type of the class variable after capture conversion (§5.1.10).

  > Note that this clause covers the use of `enum` constants (§8.9), since these always have a corresponding `final` class variable.

If *Q* is a type name that names an interface type (§9), then:

- If there is not exactly one accessible (§6.6) member of the interface type that is a field named *Id*, then a compile-time error occurs.

- Otherwise, *Q.Id* denotes the value of the field.

  The type of the expression *Q.Id* is the declared type of the field after capture conversion (§5.1.10).

  If *Q.Id* appears in a context that requires a variable and not a value, then a compile-time error occurs.

If *Q* is an expression name, let *T* be the type of the expression *Q*:

- If *T* is not a reference type, a compile-time error occurs.

- If there is not exactly one accessible (§6.6) member of the type *T* that is a field named *Id*, then a compile-time error occurs.

- Otherwise, if this field is any of the following:

  - A field of an interface type

  - A `final` field of a class type (which may be either a class variable or an instance variable)

  - The `final` field `length` of an array type

  then *Q.Id* denotes the value of the field, unless it appears in a context that requires a variable and the field is a definitely unassigned blank `final` field, in which case it yields a variable.

The type of the expression $Q.Id$ is the declared type of the field after capture conversion (§5.1.10).

If $Q.Id$ appears in a context that requires a variable and not a value, and the field denoted by $Q.Id$ is definitely assigned, then a compile-time error occurs.

- Otherwise, $Q.Id$ denotes a variable, the field Id of class T, which may be either a class variable or an instance variable.

The type of the expression $Q.Id$ is the type of the field member after capture conversion (§5.1.10).

Example 6.5.6.2-1. Qualified Expression Names

```
class Point {
    int x, y;
    static int nPoints;
}

class Test {
    public static void main(String[] args) {
        int i = 0;
        i.x++;          // compile-time error
        Point p = new Point();
        p.nPoints();  // compile-time error
    }
}
```

This program encounters two compile-time errors, because the `int` variable `i` has no members, and because `nPoints` is not a method of class `Point`.

Example 6.5.6.2-2. Qualifying an Expression with a Type Name

Note that expression names may be qualified by type names, but not by types in general. A consequence is that it is not possible to access a class variable through a parameterized type.

For example, given the code:

```
class Foo<T> {
    public static int classVar = 42;
}
```

the following assignment is illegal:

```
Foo<String>.classVar = 91; // illegal
```

Instead, one writes

```
Foo.classVar = 91;
```

This does not restrict the Java programming language in any meaningful way. Type parameters may not be used in the types of static variables, and so the type arguments of a parameterized type can never influence the type of a static variable. Therefore, no expressive power is lost. Technically, the type name `Foo` above is a raw type, but this use of raw types is harmless, and does not give rise to warnings

6.5.7   Meaning of Method Names

The meaning of a name classified as a *MethodName* is determined as follows.

6.5.7.1   *Simple Method Names*

A simple method name may appear as the element name in an element-value pair.

In that case, the *Identifier* in an *ElementValuePair* must be the simple name of one of the elements of the annotation type identified by *TypeName* in the containing annotation, or a compile-time error occurs.

> In other words, the identifier in an element-value pair must also be a method name in the interface identified by *TypeName*.

Otherwise, a simple method name necessarily appears in the context of a method invocation expression. In that case, if a method name consists of a single *Identifier*, then *Identifier* is the method name to be used for method invocation.

The *Identifier* must name at least one method that is visible at the point where the *Identifier* appears (§6.4.1), or a method imported by a single-static-import declaration (§7.5.3) or static-import-on-demand declaration (§7.5.4) within the compilation unit within which the *Identifier* appears, or else a compile-time error occurs *by the rules of §15.12*.

6.5.7.2   *Qualified Method Names*

A qualified method name can only appear in the context of a method invocation expression.

If a method name is of the form $Q.Id$, then Q has already been classified as a package name, a type name, or an expression name:

- If Q is a package name, then a compile-time error occurs.

- Otherwise, Q is a type name or an expression name.

  Id is the method name to be used for method invocation.

  If Q is a type name, then Id must name at least one `static` method of the type Q, or a compile-time error occurs *by the rules of §15.12*.

If Q is an expression name, then let T be the type of the expression Q. Id must name at least one method of the type T, or a compile-time error occurs *by the rules of §15.12.*

Like expression names, method names may be qualified by type names, but not by types in general. The implications are similar to those for expression names as discussed in §6.5.6.2.

6.6 Access Control

The Java programming language provides mechanisms for *access control*, to prevent the users of a package or class from depending on unnecessary details of the implementation of that package or class. If access is permitted, then the accessed entity is said to be *accessible*.

Note that accessibility is a static property that can be determined at compile time; it depends only on types and declaration modifiers.

Qualified names are a means of access to members of packages and reference types. When the name of such a member is classified from its context (§6.5.1) as a qualified type name (denoting a member of a package or reference type, §6.5.5.2) or a qualified expression name (denoting a member of a reference type, §6.5.6.2), access control is applied.

For example, a single-type-import statement (§7.5.1) must use a qualified type name, so the type name being imported must be accessible from the compilation unit containing the import statement. As another example, a class declaration may use a qualified type name for a superclass (§8.1.5), and again the qualified type name must be accessible.

Some obvious expressions are "missing" from context classification in §6.5.1: field access on a *Primary* (§15.11.1), method invocation on a *Primary* (§15.12), and the instantiated class in a qualified class instance creation (§15.9). Each of these expressions uses identifiers, rather than names, for the reason given in §6.2. Consequently, access control to members (whether fields, methods, types) is applied *explicitly* by field access expressions, method invocation expressions, and qualified class instance creation expressions. (Note that access to a field may also be denoted by a qualified name occuring as a postfix expression.)

Note that qualified names, field access expressions, method invocation expressions, and qualified class instance creation expressions are syntactically similar in that a "." token appears, preceded by some indication of a package, type, or expression having a type, and followed by an *Identifier* that names a member of the package or type. (A `new` token intercedes between the . and the *Identifier* in a qualified class instance creation expression.)

Many statements and expressions allow the use of types rather than type names. For example, a class declaration may use a parameterized type (§4.5) to denote a superclass. Because a parameterized type is not a qualified type name, it is necessary for the class declaration to explicitly perform access control for the denoted superclass. Consequently, most of the statements and expressions that provide contexts in §6.5.1 to classify a *TypeName* must also perform their own access control checks.

Beyond access to members of a package or reference type, there is the matter of access to constructors of a reference type. Access control must be checked when a constructor is invoked explicitly or implicitly. Consequently, access control is checked by an explicit constructor invocation statement (§8.8.7.1) and by a class instance creation expression (§15.9.3). These "manual" checks are necessary because §6.5.1 ignores explicit constructor invocation statements (because they reference constructor names indirectly) and is unaware of the distinction between the class type denoted by an unqualified class instance creation expression and a constructor of that class type. Also, constructors do not have qualified names, so we cannot rely on access control being checked during classification of qualified type names.

Accessibility affects inheritance of class members (§8.2), including hiding and method overriding (§8.4.8.1).

6.6.1 Determining Accessibility

- A package is always accessible.

- If a class or interface type is declared `public`, then it may be accessed by any code, provided that the compilation unit (§7.3) in which it is declared is observable.

  If a top level class or interface type is not declared `public`, then it may be accessed only from within the package in which it is declared.

- An array type is accessible if and only if its element type is accessible.

- A member (class, interface, field, or method) of a reference (class, interface, or array) type or a constructor of a class type is accessible only if the type is accessible and the member or constructor is declared to permit access:

  - If the member or constructor is declared `public`, then access is permitted.

    All members of interfaces are implicitly `public`.

  - Otherwise, if the member or constructor is declared `protected`, then access is permitted only when one of the following is true:

    - Access to the member or constructor occurs from within the package containing the class in which the protected member or constructor is declared.

    - Access is correct as described in §6.6.2.

- Otherwise, if the member or constructor is declared `private`, then access is permitted if and only if it occurs within the body of the top level class (§7.6) that encloses the declaration of the member or constructor.

- Otherwise, we say there is *default access*, which is permitted only when the access occurs from within the package in which the type is declared.

Example 6.6-1. Access Control

Consider the two compilation units:

```
package points;
class PointVec { Point[] vec; }
```

and:

```
package points;
public class Point {
    protected int x, y;
    public void move(int dx, int dy) { x += dx; y += dy; }
    public int getX() { return x; }
    public int getY() { return y; }
}
```

which declare two class types in the package `points`:

- The class type `PointVec` is not `public` and not part of the `public` interface of the package `points`, but rather can be used only by other classes in the package.

- The class type `Point` is declared `public` and is available to other packages. It is part of the `public` interface of the package `points`.

- The methods `move`, `getX`, and `getY` of the class `Point` are declared `public` and so are available to any code that uses an object of type `Point`.

- The fields `x` and `y` are declared `protected` and are accessible outside the package `points` only in subclasses of class `Point`, and only when they are fields of objects that are being implemented by the code that is accessing them.

See §6.6.2 for an example of how the `protected` access modifier limits access.

Example 6.6-2. Access to `public` Fields, Methods, and Constructors

A `public` class member or constructor is accessible throughout the package where it is declared and from any other package, provided the package in which it is declared is observable (§7.4.3). For example, in the compilation unit:

```
package points;
public class Point {
    int x, y;
```

```
    public void move(int dx, int dy) {
        x += dx; y += dy;
        moves++;
    }
    public static int moves = 0;
}
```

the public class Point has as public members the move method and the moves field. These `public` members are accessible to any other package that has access to package points. The fields x and y are not `public` and therefore are accessible only from within the package `points`.

Example 6.6-3. Access to `public` **and Non-**`public` **Classes**

If a class lacks the `public` modifier, access to the class declaration is limited to the package in which it is declared (§6.6). In the example:

```
package points;
public class Point {
    public int x, y;
    public void move(int dx, int dy) { x += dx; y += dy; }
}
class PointList {
    Point next, prev;
}
```

two classes are declared in the compilation unit. The class `Point` is available outside the package `points`, while the class `PointList` is available for access only within the package. Thus a compilation unit in another package can access `points.Point`, either by using its fully qualified name:

```
package pointsUser;
class Test1 {
    public static void main(String[] args) {
        points.Point p = new points.Point();
        System.out.println(p.x + " " + p.y);
    }
}
```

or by using a single-type-import declaration (§7.5.1) that mentions the fully qualified name, so that the simple name may be used thereafter:

```
package pointsUser;
import points.Point;
class Test2 {
    public static void main(String[] args) {
        Point p = new Point();
        System.out.println(p.x + " " + p.y);
    }
}
```

155

However, this compilation unit cannot use or import `points.PointList`, which is not declared `public` and is therefore inaccessible outside package `points`.

Example 6.6-4. Access to Default-Access Fields, Methods, and Constructors

If none of the access modifiers `public`, `protected`, or `private` are specified, a class member or constructor is accessible throughout the package that contains the declaration of the class in which the class member is declared, but the class member or constructor is not accessible in any other package.

If a `public` class has a method or constructor with default access, then this method or constructor is not accessible to or inherited by a subclass declared outside this package.

For example, if we have:

```
package points;
public class Point {
    public int x, y;
    void move(int dx, int dy) { x += dx; y += dy; }
    public void moveAlso(int dx, int dy) { move(dx, dy); }
}
```

then a subclass in another package may declare an unrelated `move` method, with the same signature (§8.4.2) and return type. Because the original `move` method is not accessible from package `morepoints`, `super` may not be used:

```
package morepoints;
public class PlusPoint extends points.Point {
    public void move(int dx, int dy) {
        super.move(dx, dy);  // compile-time error
        moveAlso(dx, dy);
    }
}
```

Because `move` of `Point` is not overridden by `move` in `PlusPoint`, the method `moveAlso` in `Point` never calls the method `move` in `PlusPoint`. Thus if you delete the `super.move` call from `PlusPoint` and execute the test program:

```
import points.Point;
import morepoints.PlusPoint;
class Test {
    public static void main(String[] args) {
        PlusPoint pp = new PlusPoint();
        pp.move(1, 1);
    }
}
```

it terminates normally. If `move` of `Point` were overridden by `move` in `PlusPoint`, then this program would recurse infinitely, until a `StackOverflowError` occurred.

Example 6.6-5. Access to `private` **Fields, Methods, and Constructors**

A `private` class member or constructor is accessible only within the body of the top level class (§7.6) that encloses the declaration of the member or constructor. It is not inherited by subclasses. In the example:

```
class Point {
    Point() { setMasterID(); }
    int x, y;
    private int ID;
    private static int masterID = 0;
    private void setMasterID() { ID = masterID++; }
}
```

the private members `ID`, `masterID`, and `setMasterID` may be used only within the body of class `Point`. They may not be accessed by qualified names, field access expressions, or method invocation expressions outside the body of the declaration of `Point`.

See §8.8.8 for an example that uses a `private` constructor.

6.6.2 Details on protected Access

A `protected` member or constructor of an object may be accessed from outside the package in which it is declared only by code that is responsible for the implementation of that object.

6.6.2.1 *Access to a* `protected` *Member*

Let *c* be the class in which a `protected` member is declared. Access is permitted only within the body of a subclass *s* of *c*.

In addition, if *Id* denotes an instance field or instance method, then:

- If the access is by a qualified name *Q*.*Id*, where *Q* is an *ExpressionName*, then the access is permitted if and only if the type of the expression *Q* is *s* or a subclass of *s*.

- If the access is by a field access expression *E*.*Id*, where *E* is a *Primary* expression, or by a method invocation expression *E*.*Id*(. . .), where *E* is a *Primary* expression, then the access is permitted if and only if the type of *E* is *s* or a subclass of *s*.

> More information about access to `protected` members can be found in *Checking Access to Protected Members in the Java Virtual Machine* by Alessandro Coglio, in the *Journal of Object Technology*, October 2005.

6.6.2.2   *Qualified Access to a* `protected` *Constructor*

Let `C` be the class in which a `protected` constructor is declared and let `S` be the innermost class in whose declaration the use of the `protected` constructor occurs. Then:

- If the access is by a superclass constructor invocation `super(. . .)` or by a qualified superclass constructor invocation of the form `E.super(. . .)`, where `E` is a *Primary* expression, then the access is permitted.

- If the access is by an anonymous class instance creation expression of the form `new C(. . .){...}` or by a qualified class instance creation expression of the form `E.new C(. . .){...}`, where `E` is a *Primary* expression, then the access is permitted.

- Otherwise, if the access is by a simple class instance creation expression of the form `new C(. . .)` or by a qualified class instance creation expression of the form `E.new C(. . .)`, where `E` is a *Primary* expression, then the access is not permitted.

A `protected` constructor can be accessed by a class instance creation expression (that does not declare an anonymous class) only from within the package in which it is defined.

Example 6.6.2-1. Access to `protected` **Fields, Methods, and Constructors**

Consider this example, where the `points` package declares:

```
package points;
public class Point {
    protected int x, y;
    void warp(threePoint.Point3d a) {
        if (a.z > 0)  // compile-time error: cannot access a.z
            a.delta(this);
    }
}
```

and the `threePoint` package declares:

```
package threePoint;
import points.Point;
public class Point3d extends Point {
    protected int z;
    public void delta(Point p) {
        p.x += this.x;  // compile-time error: cannot access p.x
        p.y += this.y;  // compile-time error: cannot access p.y
    }
    public void delta3d(Point3d q) {
        q.x += this.x;
```

```
            q.y += this.y;
            q.z += this.z;
        }
    }
```

A compile-time error occurs in the method `delta` here: it cannot access the `protected` members `x` and `y` of its parameter `p`, because while `Point3d` (the class in which the references to fields `x` and `y` occur) is a subclass of `Point` (the class in which `x` and `y` are declared), it is not involved in the implementation of a `Point` (the type of the parameter `p`). The method `delta3d` can access the `protected` members of its parameter `q`, because the class `Point3d` is a subclass of `Point` and is involved in the implementation of a `Point3d`.

The method `delta` could try to cast (§5.5, §15.16) its parameter to be a `Point3d`, but this cast would fail, causing an exception, if the class of `p` at run time were not `Point3d`.

A compile-time error also occurs in the method `warp`: it cannot access the `protected` member `z` of its parameter `a`, because while the class `Point` (the class in which the reference to field `z` occurs) is involved in the implementation of a `Point3d` (the type of the parameter `a`), it is not a subclass of `Point3d` (the class in which `z` is declared).

6.7 Fully Qualified Names and Canonical Names

Every primitive type, named package, top level class, and top level interface has a *fully qualified name*:

- The fully qualified name of a primitive type is the keyword for that primitive type, namely `byte`, `short`, `char`, `int`, `long`, `float`, `double`, or `boolean`.

- The fully qualified name of a named package that is not a subpackage of a named package is its simple name.

- The fully qualified name of a named package that is a subpackage of another named package consists of the fully qualified name of the containing package, followed by ".", followed by the simple (member) name of the subpackage.

- The fully qualified name of a top level class or top level interface that is declared in an unnamed package is the simple name of the class or interface.

- The fully qualified name of a top level class or top level interface that is declared in a named package consists of the fully qualified name of the package, followed by ".", followed by the simple name of the class or interface.

Each member class, member interface, and array type *may* have a fully qualified name:

- A member class or member interface *M* of another class or interface *C* has a fully qualified name if and only if *C* has a fully qualified name.

In that case, the fully qualified name of *M* consists of the fully qualified name of *C*, followed by ".", followed by the simple name of *M*.

- An array type has a fully qualified name if and only if its element type has a fully qualified name.

  In that case, the fully qualified name of an array type consists of the fully qualified name of the component type of the array type followed by "[ ]".

A local class does not have a fully qualified name.

Example 6.7-1. Fully Qualified Names

- The fully qualified name of the type `long` is "`long`".
- The fully qualified name of the package `java.lang` is "`java.lang`" because it is subpackage `lang` of package `java`.
- The fully qualified name of the class `Object`, which is defined in the package `java.lang`, is "`java.lang.Object`".
- The fully qualified name of the interface `Enumeration`, which is defined in the package `java.util`, is "`java.util.Enumeration`".
- The fully qualified name of the type "array of `double`" is "`double[]`".
- The fully qualified name of the type "array of array of array of array of `String`" is "`java.lang.String[][][][]`".

In the code:

```
package points;
class Point     { int x, y; }
class PointVec { Point[] vec; }
```

the fully qualified name of the type `Point` is "`points.Point`"; the fully qualified name of the type `PointVec` is "`points.PointVec`"; and the fully qualified name of the type of the field `vec` of class `PointVec` is "`points.Point[]`".

Every primitive type, named package, top level class, and top level interface has a *canonical name*:

- For every primitive type, named package, top level class, and top level interface, the canonical name is the same as the fully qualified name.

Each member class, member interface, and array type *may* have a canonical name:

- A member class or member interface *M* declared in another class *C* has a canonical name if and only if *C* has a canonical name.

In that case, the canonical name of *M* consists of the canonical name of *C*, followed by ".", followed by the simple name of *M*.

- An array type has a canonical name if and only if its component type has a canonical name.

  In that case, the canonical name of the array type consists of the canonical name of the component type of the array type followed by "[]".

A local class does not have a canonical name.

Example 6.7-2. Fully Qualified Names v. Canonical Name

The difference between a fully qualified name and a canonical name can be seen in code such as:

```
package p;
class O1 { class I {} }
class O2 extends O1 {}
```

Both p.O1.I and p.O2.I are fully qualified names that denote the member class I, but only p.O1.I is its canonical name.

CHAPTER 7

Packages

PROGRAMS are organized as sets of packages. Each package has its own set of names for types, which helps to prevent name conflicts.

A top level type is accessible (§6.6) outside the package that declares it only if the type is declared `public`.

The naming structure for packages is hierarchical (§7.1). The members of a package are class and interface types (§7.6), which are declared in compilation units of the package, and subpackages, which may contain compilation units and subpackages of their own.

A package can be stored in a file system or in a database (§7.2). Packages that are stored in a file system may have certain constraints on the organization of their compilation units to allow a simple implementation to find classes easily.

A package consists of a number of compilation units (§7.3). A compilation unit automatically has access to all types declared in its package and also automatically imports all of the `public` types declared in the predefined package `java.lang`.

For small programs and casual development, a package can be unnamed (§7.4.2) or have a simple name, but if code is to be widely distributed, unique package names should be chosen using qualified names. This can prevent the conflicts that would otherwise occur if two development groups happened to pick the same package name and these packages were later to be used in a single program.

7.1 Package Members

The members of a package are its subpackages and all the top level class types (§7.6, §8) and top level interface types (§9) declared in all the compilation units (§7.3) of the package.

For example, in the Java SE platform API:

- The package `java` has subpackages `awt`, `applet`, `io`, `lang`, `net`, and `util`, but no compilation units.

- The package `java.awt` has a subpackage named `image`, as well as a number of compilation units containing declarations of class and interface types.

If the fully qualified name (§6.7) of a package is P, and Q is a subpackage of P, then $P.Q$ is the fully qualified name of the subpackage, and furthermore denotes a package.

A package may not contain two members of the same name, or a compile-time error results.

Here are some examples:

- Because the package `java.awt` has a subpackage `image`, it cannot (and does not) contain a declaration of a class or interface type named `image`.

- If there is a package named `mouse` and a member type `Button` in that package (which then might be referred to as `mouse.Button`), then there cannot be any package with the fully qualified name `mouse.Button` or `mouse.Button.Click`.

- If `com.nighthacks.java.jag` is the fully qualified name of a type, then there cannot be any package whose fully qualified name is either `com.nighthacks.java.jag` or `com.nighthacks.java.jag.scrabble`.

It is however possible for members of different packages to have the same simple name. For example, it is possible to declare a package:

```
package vector;
public class Vector { Object[] vec; }
```

that has as a member a `public` class named `Vector`, even though the package `java.util` also declares a class named `Vector`. These two class types are different, reflected by the fact that they have different fully qualified names (§6.7). The fully qualified name of this example `Vector` is `vector.Vector`, whereas `java.util.Vector` is the fully qualified name of the `Vector` class included in the Java SE platform. Because the package `vector` contains a class named `Vector`, it cannot also have a subpackage named `Vector`.

The hierarchical naming structure for packages is intended to be convenient for organizing related packages in a conventional manner, but has no significance in itself other than the prohibition against a package having a subpackage with the same simple name as a top level type (§7.6) declared in that package.

For example, there is no special access relationship between a package named `oliver` and another package named `oliver.twist`, or between packages named `evelyn.wood` and `evelyn.waugh`. That is, the code in a package named `oliver.twist` has no better access to the types declared within package `oliver` than code in any other package.

7.2 Host Support for Packages

Each host system determines how packages and compilation units are created and stored.

Each host system also determines which compilation units are observable (§7.3) in a particular compilation. The observability of compilation units in turn determines which packages are observable, and which packages are in scope.

In simple implementations of the Java SE platform, packages and compilation units may be stored in a local file system. Other implementations may store them using a distributed file system or some form of database.

If a host system stores packages and compilation units in a database, then the database must not impose the optional restrictions (§7.6) on compilation units permissible in file-based implementations.

> For example, a system that uses a database to store packages may not enforce a maximum of one public class or interface per compilation unit.

Systems that use a database must, however, provide an option to convert a program to a form that obeys the restrictions, for purposes of export to file-based implementations.

> As an extremely simple example of storing packages in a file system, all the packages and source and binary code in a project might be stored in a single directory and its subdirectories. Each immediate subdirectory of this directory would represent a top level package, that is, one whose fully qualified name consists of a single simple name. Each further level of subdirectory would represent a subpackage of the package represented by the containing directory, and so on.
>
> The directory might contain the following immediate subdirectories:
>
> ```
> com
> gls
> jag
> java
> wnj
> ```
>
> where directory `java` would contain the Java SE platform packages; the directories `jag`, `gls`, and `wnj` might contain packages that three of the authors of this specification created for their personal use and to share with each other within this small group; and the directory `com` would contain packages procured from companies that used the conventions described in §6.1 to generate unique names for their packages.
>
> Continuing the example, the directory `java` would contain, among others, the following subdirectories:

```
applet
awt
io
lang
net
util
```

corresponding to the packages `java.applet`, `java.awt`, `java.io`, `java.lang`, `java.net`, and `java.util` that are defined as part of the Java SE platform API.

Still continuing the example, if we were to look inside the directory `util`, we might see the following files:

```
BitSet.java        Observable.java
BitSet.class       Observable.class
Date.java          Observer.java
Date.class         Observer.class
...
```

where each of the `.java` files contains the source for a compilation unit (§7.3) that contains the definition of a class or interface whose binary compiled form is contained in the corresponding `.class` file.

Under this simple organization of packages, an implementation of the Java SE platform would transform a package name into a pathname by concatenating the components of the package name, placing a file name separator (directory indicator) between adjacent components.

For example, if this simple organization were used on an operating system where the file name separator is /, the package name:

```
jag.scrabble.board
```

would be transformed into the directory name:

```
jag/scrabble/board
```

A package name component or class name might contain a character that cannot correctly appear in a host file system's ordinary directory name, such as a Unicode character on a system that allows only ASCII characters in file names. As a convention, the character can be escaped by using, say, the @ character followed by four hexadecimal digits giving the numeric value of the character, as in the \u*xxxx* escape (§3.3).

Under this convention, the package name:

```
children.activities.crafts.papierM\u00e2ch\u00e9
```

which can also be written using full Unicode as:

```
children.activities.crafts.papierMâché
```

might be mapped to the directory name:

```
children/activities/crafts/papierM@00e2ch@00e9
```

If the @ character is not a valid character in a file name for some given host file system, then some other character that is not valid in a identifier could be used instead.

7.3 Compilation Units

CompilationUnit is the goal symbol (§2.1) for the syntactic grammar (§2.3) of Java programs. It is defined by the following productions:

> *CompilationUnit:*
>   *PackageDeclaration_{opt} ImportDeclarations_{opt} TypeDeclarations_{opt}*

> *ImportDeclarations:*
>   *ImportDeclaration*
>   *ImportDeclarations ImportDeclaration*

> *TypeDeclarations:*
>   *TypeDeclaration*
>   *TypeDeclarations TypeDeclaration*

A *compilation unit* consists of three parts, each of which is optional:

- A `package` declaration (§7.4), giving the fully qualified name (§6.7) of the package to which the compilation unit belongs.

  A compilation unit that has no `package` declaration is part of an unnamed package (§7.4.2).

- `import` declarations (§7.5) that allow types from other packages and `static` members of types to be referred to using their simple names.

- Top level type declarations (§7.6) of class and interface types.

Every compilation unit implicitly imports every `public` type name declared in the predefined package `java.lang`, as if the declaration `import java.lang.*;` appeared at the beginning of each compilation unit immediately after any `package` statement. As a result, the names of all those types are available as simple names in every compilation unit.

All the compilation units of the predefined package `java` and its subpackages `lang` and `io` are always *observable*.

For all other packages, the host system determines which compilation units are observable.

The observability of a compilation unit influences the observability of its package (§7.4.3).

Types declared in different compilation units can depend on each other, circularly. A Java compiler must arrange to compile all such types at the same time.

7.4   Package Declarations

A `package` declaration appears within a compilation unit to indicate the package to which the compilation unit belongs.

7.4.1   Named Packages

A *package declaration* in a compilation unit specifies the name (§6.2) of the package to which the compilation unit belongs.

> *PackageDeclaration:*
>   *Annotations$_{opt}$* `package` *PackageName* `;`

The package name mentioned in a `package` declaration must be the fully qualified name (§6.7) of the package.

The *PackageName* in a package declaration ensures there is an observable package with the supplied canonical name, and that it is not subject to the rules in §6.5.3 for determining the meaning of a package name.

The scope and shadowing of a package declaration is specified in §6.3 and §6.4.

The keyword `package` may optionally be preceded by annotation modifiers. If an annotation *a* (§9.7) on a package declaration corresponds to an annotation type *T* (§9.6), and *T* has a (meta-)annotation *m* that corresponds to `java.lang.annotation.Target`, then *m* must have an element whose value is `java.lang.annotation.ElementType.PACKAGE`, or a compile-time error occurs.

At most one annotated `package` declaration is permitted for a given package.

The manner in which this restriction is enforced must, of necessity, vary from implementation to implementation. The following scheme is strongly recommended for file-system-based implementations: The sole annotated `package` declaration, if it exists, is placed in a source file called `package-info.java` in the directory containing the source files for the package. This file does not contain the source for a class called `package-`

info.java; indeed it would be illegal for it to do so, as package-info is not a legal identifier. Typically package-info.java contains only a package declaration, preceded immediately by the annotations on the package. While the file could technically contain the source code for one or more package-private (default-access) classes, it would be very bad form.

It is recommended that package-info.java, if it is present, take the place of package.html for javadoc and other similar documentation generation systems. If this file is present, the documentation generation tool should look for the package documentation comment immediately preceding the (possibly annotated) package declaration in package-info.java. In this way, package-info.java becomes the sole repository for package-level annotations and documentation. If, in future, it becomes desirable to add any other package-level information, this file should prove a convenient home for this information.

7.4.2 Unnamed Packages

A compilation unit that has no package declaration is part of an *unnamed package*.

Unnamed packages are provided by the Java SE platform principally for convenience when developing small or temporary applications or when just beginning development.

Note that an unnamed package cannot have subpackages, since the syntax of a package declaration always includes a reference to a named top level package.

As an example, the compilation unit:

```
class FirstCall {
    public static void main(String[] args) {
        System.out.println("Mr. Watson, come here. "
                            + "I want you.");
    }
}
```

defines a very simple compilation unit as part of an unnamed package.

An implementation of the Java SE platform must support at least one unnamed package; it may support more than one unnamed package but is not required to do so. Which compilation units are in each unnamed package is determined by the host system.

In implementations of the Java SE platform that use a hierarchical file system for storing packages, one typical strategy is to associate an unnamed package with each directory; only one unnamed package is observable at a time, namely the one that is associated with the "current working directory". The precise meaning of "current working directory" depends on the host system.

169

7.4.3   Observability of a Package

A package is *observable* if and only if either:

- A compilation unit containing a declaration of the package is observable (§7.3).

- A subpackage of the package is observable.

The packages `java`, `java.lang`, and `java.io` are always observable.

> One can conclude this from the rule above and from the rules of observable compilation units, as follows. The predefined package `java.lang` declares the class `Object`, so the compilation unit for `Object` is always observable (§7.3). Hence, the `java.lang` package is observable (§7.4.3), and the `java` package also. Furthermore, since `Object` is observable, the array type `Object[]` implicitly exists. Its superinterface `java.io.Serializable` (§10.1) also exists, hence the `java.io` package is observable.

7.5   Import Declarations

An *import declaration* allows a named type or a `static` member to be referred to by a simple name (§6.2) that consists of a single identifier.

Without the use of an appropriate `import` declaration, the only way to refer to a type declared in another package, or a `static` member of another type, is to use a fully qualified name (§6.7).

> *ImportDeclaration:*
>   *SingleTypeImportDeclaration*
>   *TypeImportOnDemandDeclaration*
>   *SingleStaticImportDeclaration*
>   *StaticImportOnDemandDeclaration*

- A single-type-import declaration (§7.5.1) imports a single named type, by mentioning its canonical name (§6.7).

- A type-import-on-demand declaration (§7.5.2) imports all the accessible types (§6.6) of a named type or named package as needed, by mentioning the canonical name of a type or package.

- A single-static-import declaration (§7.5.3) imports all accessible `static` members with a given name from a type, by giving its canonical name.

- A static-import-on-demand declaration (§7.5.4) imports all accessible `static` members of a named type as needed, by mentioning the canonical name of a type.

The scope and shadowing of a type or member imported by these declarations is specified in §6.3 and §6.4.

> An `import` declaration makes types or members available by their simple names only within the compilation unit that actually contains the `import` declaration. The scope of the type(s) or member(s) introduced by an `import` declaration specifically does not include the *PackageName* of a package declaration, other `import` declarations in the current compilation unit, or other compilation units in the same package.
>
> A type in an unnamed package (§7.4.2) has no canonical name, so the requirement for a canonical name in every kind of import declaration implies that (a) types in an unnamed package cannot be imported, and (b) `static` members of types in an unnamed package cannot be imported. As such, §7.5.1, §7.5.2, §7.5.3, and §7.5.4 all require a compile-time error on any attempt to import a type (or `static` member thereof) in an unnamed package.

7.5.1 Single-Type-Import Declarations

A *single-type-import declaration* imports a single type by giving its canonical name, making it available under a simple name in the class and interface declarations of the compilation unit in which the single-type-import declaration appears.

> *SingleTypeImportDeclaration:*
>   `import` *TypeName* ;

The *TypeName* must be the canonical name (§6.7) of a class type, interface type, enum type, or annotation type.

It is a compile-time error if the named type is not accessible (§6.6).

> **Example 7.5.1-1. Single-Type-Import**
>
> ```
> import java.util.Vector;
> ```
>
> causes the simple name `Vector` to be available within the class and interface declarations in a compilation unit. Thus, the simple name `Vector` refers to the type declaration `Vector` in the package `java.util` in all places where it is not shadowed (§6.4.1) or obscured (§6.4.2) by a declaration of a field, parameter, local variable, or nested type declaration with the same name.
>
> Note that `java.util.Vector` is declared as a generic type (§8.1.2). Once imported, the name `Vector` can be used without qualification in a parameterized type such as `Vector<String>`, or as the raw type `Vector`. This highlights a limitation of the `import` declaration: a type nested inside a generic type declaration can be imported, but its outer type is always erased.

If two single-type-import declarations in the same compilation unit attempt to import types with the same simple name, then a compile-time error occurs, unless the two types are the same type, in which case the duplicate declaration is ignored.

If the type imported by the single-type-import declaration is declared in the compilation unit that contains the `import` declaration, the `import` declaration is ignored.

If a single-type-import declaration imports a type whose simple name is n, and the compilation unit also declares a top level type (§7.6) whose simple name is n, a compile-time error occurs.

If a compilation unit contains both a single-type-import declaration that imports a type whose simple name is n, and a single-static-import declaration (§7.5.3) that imports a type whose simple name is n, a compile-time error occurs.

Example 7.5.1-2. Duplicate Type Declarations

This program:

```
import java.util.Vector;
class Vector { Object[] vec; }
```

causes a compile-time error because of the duplicate declaration of `Vector`, as does:

```
import java.util.Vector;
import myVector.Vector;
```

where `myVector` is a package containing the compilation unit:

```
package myVector;
public class Vector { Object[] vec; }
```

Example 7.5.1-3. No Import of a Subpackage

Note that an `import` statement cannot import a subpackage, only a type.

For example, it does not work to try to import `java.util` and then use the name `util.Random` to refer to the type `java.util.Random`:

```
import java.util;
class Test { util.Random generator; }
    // incorrect: compile-time error
```

Example 7.5.1-4. Importing a Type Name that is also a Package Name

Package names and type names are usually different under the naming conventions described in §6.1. Nevertheless, in a contrived example where there is an unconventionally-named package `Vector`, which declares a public class whose name is `Mosquito`:

```
package Vector;
public class Mosquito { int capacity; }
```

and then the compilation unit:

```
package strange;
import java.util.Vector;
import Vector.Mosquito;
class Test {
    public static void main(String[] args) {
        System.out.println(new Vector().getClass());
        System.out.println(new Mosquito().getClass());
    }
}
```

the single-type-import declaration importing class `Vector` from package `java.util` does not prevent the package name `Vector` from appearing and being correctly recognized in subsequent `import` declarations. The example compiles and produces the output:

```
class java.util.Vector
class Vector.Mosquito
```

7.5.2   Type-Import-on-Demand Declarations

A *type-import-on-demand declaration* allows all accessible types of a named package or type to be imported as needed.

> *TypeImportOnDemandDeclaration:*
>   `import` *PackageOrTypeName* `.` `*` `;`

The *PackageOrTypeName* must be the canonical name (§6.7) of a package, a class type, an interface type, an enum type, or an annotation type.

It is a compile-time error if the named package or type is not accessible (§6.6).

It is not a compile-time error to name the current package or `java.lang` in a type-import-on-demand declaration. The type-import-on-demand declaration is ignored in such cases.

Example 7.5.2-1. Type-Import-on-Demand

```
import java.util.*;
```

causes the simple names of all `public` types declared in the package `java.util` to be available within the class and interface declarations of the compilation unit. Thus, the simple name `Vector` refers to the type `Vector` in the package `java.util` in all places in the compilation unit where that type declaration is not shadowed (§6.4.1) or obscured (§6.4.2).

173

The declaration might be shadowed by a single-type-import declaration of a type whose simple name is `Vector`; by a type named `Vector` and declared in the package to which the compilation unit belongs; or any nested classes or interfaces.

The declaration might be obscured by a declaration of a field, parameter, or local variable named `Vector`.

(It would be unusual for any of these conditions to occur.)

Two or more type-import-on-demand declarations in the same compilation unit may name the same type or package. All but one of these declarations are considered redundant; the effect is as if that type was imported only once.

If a compilation unit contains both a type-import-on-demand declaration and a static-import-on-demand declaration (§7.5.4) that name the same type, the effect is as if the `static` member types of that type (§8.5, §9.5) were imported only once.

7.5.3 Single-Static-Import Declarations

A *single-static-import declaration* imports all accessible `static` members with a given simple name from a type. This makes these `static` members available under their simple name in the class and interface declarations of the compilation unit in which the single-static-import declaration appears.

> *SingleStaticImportDeclaration:*
>   `import static` *TypeName* . *Identifier* ;

The *TypeName* must be the canonical name (§6.7) of a class type, interface type, enum type, or annotation type.

It is a compile-time error if the named type is not accessible (§6.6).

The *Identifier* must name at least one `static` member of the named type. It is a compile-time error if there is no `static` member of that name, or if all of the named members are not accessible.

It is permissible for one single-static-import declaration to import several fields or types with the same name, or several methods with the same name and signature.

If a single-static-import declaration imports a type whose simple name is n, and the compilation unit also declares a top level type (§7.6) whose simple name is n, a compile-time error occurs.

If a compilation unit contains both a single-static-import declaration that imports a type whose simple name is n, and a single-type-import declaration (§7.5.1) that imports a type whose simple name is n, a compile-time error occurs.

7.5.4 Static-Import-on-Demand Declarations

A *static-import-on-demand declaration* allows all accessible `static` members of a named type to be imported as needed.

StaticImportOnDemandDeclaration:
> `import static` *TypeName* `. * ;`

The *TypeName* must be the canonical name (§6.7) of a class type, interface type, enum type, or annotation type.

It is a compile-time error if the named type is not accessible (§6.6).

Two or more static-import-on-demand declarations in the same compilation unit may name the same type; the effect is as if there was exactly one such declaration.

Two or more static-import-on-demand declarations in the same compilation unit may name the same member; the effect is as if the member was imported exactly once.

It is permissible for one static-import-on-demand declaration to import several fields or types with the same name, or several methods with the same name and signature.

If a compilation unit contains both a static-import-on-demand declaration and a type-import-on-demand declaration (§7.5.2) that name the same type, the effect is as if the `static` member types of that type (§8.5, §9.5) were imported only once.

7.6 Top Level Type Declarations

A *top level type declaration* declares a top level class type (§8) or a top level interface type (§9).

TypeDeclaration:
> *ClassDeclaration*
> *InterfaceDeclaration*
> `;`

By default, the top level types declared in a package are accessible only within the compilation units of that package, but a type may be declared to be `public` to grant access to the type from code in other packages (§6.6, §8.1.1, §9.1.1).

It is a compile-time error if a top level type declaration contains any one of the following access modifiers: `protected`, `private`, or `static`.

It is a compile-time error if the name of a top level type appears as the name of any other top level class or interface type declared in the same package.

It is a compile-time error if the name of a top level type is also declared as a type by a single-type-import declaration (§7.5.1) in the compilation unit containing the type declaration.

Example 7.6-1. Conflicting Top Level Type Declarations

```
package test;
import java.util.Vector;
class Point {
    int x, y;
}
interface Point {  // compile-time error #1
    int getR();
    int getTheta();
}
class Vector { Point[] pts; }  // compile-time error #2
```

Here, the first compile-time error is caused by the duplicate declaration of the name `Point` as both a class and an interface in the same package. A second compile-time error is the attempt to declare the name `Vector` both by a class type declaration and by a single-type-import declaration.

Note, however, that it is not an error for the name of a class to also name a type that otherwise might be imported by a type-import-on-demand declaration (§7.5.2) in the compilation unit (§7.3) containing the class declaration. Thus, in this program:

```
package test;
import java.util.*;
class Vector {}  // not a compile-time error
```

the declaration of the class `Vector` is permitted even though there is also a class `java.util.Vector`. Within this compilation unit, the simple name `Vector` refers to the class `test.Vector`, not to `java.util.Vector` (which can still be referred to by code within the compilation unit, but only by its fully qualified name).

Example 7.6-2. Scope of Top Level Types

```
package points;
class Point {
    int x, y;           // coordinates
    PointColor color;   // color of this point
    Point next;         // next point with this color
    static int nPoints;
}
class PointColor {
    Point first;        // first point with this color
    PointColor(int color) { this.color = color; }
```

```
          private int color;  // color components
     }
```

This program defines two classes that use each other in the declarations of their class members. Because the class types `Point` and `PointColor` have all the type declarations in package `points`, including all those in the current compilation unit, as their scope, this program compiles correctly. That is, forward reference is not a problem.

The scope and shadowing of a top level type is specified in §6.3 and §6.4.

The fully qualified name of a top level type is specified in §6.7.

Example 7.6-3. Fully Qualified Names

```
     class Point { int x, y; }
```

In this code, the class `Point` is declared in a compilation unit with no `package` statement, and thus `Point` is its fully qualified name, whereas in the code:

```
     package vista;
     class Point { int x, y; }
```

the fully qualified name of the class `Point` is `vista.Point`. (The package name `vista` is suitable for local or personal use; if the package were intended to be widely distributed, it would be better to give it a unique package name (§6.1).)

An implementation of the Java SE platform must keep track of types within packages by their binary names (§13.1). Multiple ways of naming a type must be expanded to binary names to make sure that such names are understood as referring to the same type.

For example, if a compilation unit contains the single-type-import declaration (§7.5.1):

```
import java.util.Vector;
```

then within that compilation unit the simple name `Vector` and the fully qualified name `java.util.Vector` refer to the same type.

If and only if packages are stored in a file system (§7.2), the host system may choose to enforce the restriction that it is a compile-time error if a type is not found in a file under a name composed of the type name plus an extension (such as `.java` or `.jav`) if either of the following is true:

- The type is referred to by code in other compilation units of the package in which the type is declared.

- The type is declared `public` (and therefore is potentially accessible from code in other packages).

This restriction implies that there must be at most one such type per compilation unit. This restriction makes it easy for a Java compiler to find a named class within a package. In practice, many programmers choose to put each class or interface type in its own compilation unit, whether or not it is `public` or is referred to by code in other compilation units.

For example, the source code for a `public` type `wet.sprocket.Toad` would be found in a file `Toad.java` in the directory `wet/sprocket`, and the corresponding object code would be found in the file `Toad.class` in the same directory.

CHAPTER 8

Classes

CLASS declarations define new reference types and describe how they are implemented (§8.1).

A *top level class* is a class that is not a nested class.

A *nested class* is any class whose declaration occurs within the body of another class or interface.

This chapter discusses the common semantics of all classes - top level (§7.6) and nested (including member classes (§8.5, §9.5), local classes (§14.3) and anonymous classes (§15.9.5)). Details that are specific to particular kinds of classes are discussed in the sections dedicated to these constructs.

A named class may be declared `abstract` (§8.1.1.1) and must be declared abstract if it is incompletely implemented; such a class cannot be instantiated, but can be extended by subclasses. A class may be declared `final` (§8.1.1.2), in which case it cannot have subclasses. If a class is declared `public`, then it can be referred to from other packages. Each class except `Object` is an extension of (that is, a subclass of) a single existing class (§8.1.4) and may implement interfaces (§8.1.5). Classes may be *generic* (§8.1.2), that is, they may declare type variables whose bindings may differ among different instances of the class.

Classes may be decorated with annotations (§9.7) just like any other kind of declaration.

The body of a class declares members (fields and methods and nested classes and interfaces), instance and static initializers, and constructors (§8.1.6). The scope (§6.3) of a member (§8.2) is the entire body of the declaration of the class to which the member belongs. Field, method, member class, member interface, and constructor declarations may include the access modifiers (§6.6) `public`, `protected`, or `private`. The members of a class include both declared and inherited members (§8.2). Newly declared fields can hide fields declared in a superclass or superinterface. Newly declared class members and interface members can hide class or interface members declared in a superclass or superinterface. Newly declared methods can hide, implement, or override methods declared in a superclass or superinterface.

Field declarations (§8.3) describe class variables, which are incarnated once, and instance variables, which are freshly incarnated for each instance of the class. A field may be declared `final` (§8.3.1.2), in which case it can be assigned to only once. Any field declaration may include an initializer.

Member class declarations (§8.5) describe nested classes that are members of the surrounding class. Member classes may be `static`, in which case they have no access to the instance variables of the surrounding class; or they may be inner classes (§8.1.3).

Member interface declarations (§8.5) describe nested interfaces that are members of the surrounding class.

Method declarations (§8.4) describe code that may be invoked by method invocation expressions (§15.12). A class method is invoked relative to the class type; an instance method is invoked with respect to some particular object that is an instance of a class type. A method whose declaration does not indicate how it is implemented must be declared `abstract`. A method may be declared `final` (§8.4.3.3), in which case it cannot be hidden or overridden. A method may be implemented by platform-dependent `native` code (§8.4.3.4). A `synchronized` method (§8.4.3.6) automatically locks an object before executing its body and automatically unlocks the object on return, as if by use of a `synchronized` statement (§14.19), thus allowing its activities to be synchronized with those of other threads (§17).

Method names may be overloaded (§8.4.9).

Instance initializers (§8.6) are blocks of executable code that may be used to help initialize an instance when it is created (§15.9).

Static initializers (§8.7) are blocks of executable code that may be used to help initialize a class.

Constructors (§8.8) are similar to methods, but cannot be invoked directly by a method call; they are used to initialize new class instances. Like methods, they may be overloaded (§8.8.8).

8.1 Class Declarations

A class declaration specifies a new named reference type.

There are two kinds of class declarations: *normal class declarations* and *enum declarations*.

> *ClassDeclaration:*
>   *NormalClassDeclaration*
>   *EnumDeclaration*
>
> *NormalClassDeclaration:*
>   *ClassModifiers*$_{opt}$ `class` *Identifier TypeParameters*$_{opt}$
>   *Super*$_{opt}$ *Interfaces*$_{opt}$ *ClassBody*

The rules in this section apply to all class declarations unless this specification explicitly states otherwise. In many cases, special restrictions apply to enum declarations (§8.9).

The *Identifier* in a class declaration specifies the name of the class.

It is a compile-time error if a class has the same simple name as any of its enclosing classes or interfaces.

The scope and shadowing of a class declaration is specified in §6.3 and §6.4.

8.1.1 Class Modifiers

A class declaration may include *class modifiers*.

> *ClassModifiers:*
>   *ClassModifier*
>   *ClassModifiers ClassModifier*
>
> *ClassModifier: one of*
>   *Annotation* `public` `protected` `private`
>   `abstract static final strictfp`

If an annotation `a` (§9.7) on a class declaration corresponds to an annotation type `T` (§9.6), and `T` has a (meta-)annotation `m` that corresponds to `java.lang.annotation.Target`, then `m` must have an element whose value is `java.lang.annotation.ElementType.TYPE`, or a compile-time error occurs.

The access modifier `public` (§6.6) pertains only to top level classes (§7.6) and to member classes (§8.5), not to local classes (§14.3) or anonymous classes (§15.9.5).

The access modifiers `protected` and `private` (§6.6) pertain only to member classes within a directly enclosing class or enum declaration (§8.5).

The modifier `static` pertains only to member classes (§8.5.1), not to top level or local or anonymous classes.

It is a compile-time error if the same modifier appears more than once in a class declaration.

> If two or more (distinct) class modifiers appear in a class declaration, then it is customary, though not required, that they appear in the order consistent with that shown above in the production for *ClassModifier*.

8.1.1.1   `abstract` *Classes*

An `abstract` class is a class that is incomplete, or to be considered incomplete.

Normal classes may have `abstract` methods (§8.4.3.1, §9.4), that is, methods that are declared but not yet implemented, only if they are `abstract` classes.

If a normal class that is not `abstract` contains an `abstract` method, then a compile-time error occurs.

An enum type (§8.9) must not be declared `abstract`, or a compile-time error occurs.

It is a compile-time error for an enum type E to have an `abstract` method m as a member unless E has one or more enum constants, and all of E's enum constants have class bodies that provide concrete implementations of m.

It is a compile-time error for the class body of an enum constant to declare an `abstract` method.

A class C has `abstract` methods if any of the following is true:

- C explicitly contains a declaration of an `abstract` method (§8.4.3).

- Any of C's superclasses has an `abstract` method and C neither declares nor inherits a method that implements (§8.4.8.1) it.

- A direct superinterface (§8.1.5) of C declares or inherits a method (which is therefore necessarily `abstract`) and C neither declares nor inherits a method that implements it.

It is a compile-time error if an attempt is made to create an instance of an `abstract` class using a class instance creation expression (§15.9).

A subclass of an `abstract` class that is not itself `abstract` may be instantiated, resulting in the execution of a constructor for the `abstract` class and, therefore, the execution of the field initializers for instance variables of that class.

It is a compile-time error to declare an `abstract` class type such that it is not possible to create a subclass that implements all of its `abstract` methods. This situation can occur if the class would have as members two abstract methods that have the same method signature (§8.4.2) but return types for which there is no type which is return-type-substitutable (§8.4.5) with both.

Example 8.1.1.1-1. Abstract Class Declaration

```
abstract class Point {
    int x = 1, y = 1;
    void move(int dx, int dy) {
        x += dx;
        y += dy;
        alert();
    }
    abstract void alert();
}
abstract class ColoredPoint extends Point {
    int color;
}
class SimplePoint extends Point {
    void alert() { }
}
```

Here, a class `Point` is declared that must be declared `abstract`, because it contains a declaration of an `abstract` method named `alert`. The subclass of `Point` named `ColoredPoint` inherits the `abstract` method `alert`, so it must also be declared `abstract`. On the other hand, the subclass of `Point` named `SimplePoint` provides an implementation of `alert`, so it need not be `abstract`.

The statement:

```
Point p = new Point();
```

would result in a compile-time error; the class `Point` cannot be instantiated because it is `abstract`. However, a `Point` variable could correctly be initialized with a reference to any subclass of `Point`, and the class `SimplePoint` is not `abstract`, so the statement:

```
Point p = new SimplePoint();
```

would be correct. Instantiation of a `SimplePoint` causes the default constructor and field initializers for x and y of `Point` to be executed.

Example 8.1.1.1-2. Abstract Class Declaration that Prohibits Subclasses

```
interface Colorable {
```

```
        void setColor(int color);
    }
    abstract class Colored implements Colorable {
        public abstract int setColor(int color);
    }
```

These declarations result in a compile-time error: it would be impossible for any subclass of class `Colored` to provide an implementation of a method named `setColor`, taking one argument of type `int`, that can satisfy both abstract method specifications, because the one in interface `Colorable` requires the same method to return no value, while the one in class `Colored` requires the same method to return a value of type `int` (§8.4).

A class type should be declared `abstract` only if the intent is that subclasses can be created to complete the implementation. If the intent is simply to prevent instantiation of a class, the proper way to express this is to declare a constructor (§8.8.10) of no arguments, make it `private`, never invoke it, and declare no other constructors. A class of this form usually contains class methods and variables.

The class `Math` is an example of a class that cannot be instantiated; its declaration looks like this:

```
public final class Math {
    private Math() { }  // never instantiate this class
    . . . declarations of class variables and methods . . .
}
```

8.1.1.2   `final` *Classes*

A class can be declared `final` if its definition is complete and no subclasses are desired or required.

It is a compile-time error if the name of a `final` class appears in the `extends` clause (§8.1.4) of another class declaration; this implies that a `final` class cannot have any subclasses.

It is a compile-time error if a class is declared both `final` and `abstract`, because the implementation of such a class could never be completed (§8.1.1.1).

Because a `final` class never has any subclasses, the methods of a `final` class are never overridden (§8.4.8.1).

8.1.1.3   `strictfp` *Classes*

The effect of the `strictfp` modifier is to make all `float` or `double` expressions within the class declaration (including within variable initializers, instance initializers, static initializers, and constructors) be explicitly FP-strict (§15.4).

This implies that all methods declared in the class, and all nested types declared in the class, are implicitly `strictfp`.

8.1.2 Generic Classes and Type Parameters

A class is *generic* if it declares one or more type variables (§4.4).

These type variables are known as the *type parameters* of the class. The type parameter section follows the class name and is delimited by angle brackets.

> *TypeParameters:*
>   < *TypeParameterList* >
>
> *TypeParameterList:*
>   *TypeParameterList , TypeParameter*
>   *TypeParameter*

In a class's type parameter section, a type variable T *directly depends* on a type variable S if S is the bound of T, while T *depends* on S if either T directly depends on S or T directly depends on a type variable U that depends on S (using this definition recursively).

It is a compile-time error if a type variable in a class's type parameter section depends on itself.

The scope and shadowing of a class's type parameter is specified in §6.3 and §6.4.

Example 8.1.2-1. Mutually Recursive Type Variable Bounds

```
interface ConvertibleTo<T> {
    T convert();
}
class ReprChange<T extends ConvertibleTo<S>,
                 S extends ConvertibleTo<T>> {
    T t;
    void set(S s) { t = s.convert();   }
    S get()       { return t.convert(); }
}
```

A generic class declaration defines a set of parameterized types (§4.5), one for each possible invocation of the type parameter section by type arguments. All of these parameterized types share the same class at run time.

For instance, executing the code:

```
Vector<String>  x = new Vector<String>();
Vector<Integer> y = new Vector<Integer>();
boolean b = x.getClass() == y.getClass();
```

will result in the variable b holding the value true.

It is a compile-time error if a generic class is a direct or indirect subclass of Throwable (§11.1.1).

> This restriction is needed since the catch mechanism of the Java Virtual Machine works only with non-generic classes.

It is a compile-time error to refer to a type parameter of a generic class *c* anywhere in:

- the declaration of a static member of *c* (§8.3.1.1, §8.4.3.2, §8.5.1), or

- the declaration of a static member of any type declaration nested within *c*, or

- a static initializer of *c* (§8.7), or

- a static initializer of any class declaration nested within *c*.

Generic class declarations can be nested inside other declarations.

Example 8.1.2-2. Nested Generic Classes

```
class Seq<T> {
    T       head;
    Seq<T> tail;

    Seq() { this(null, null); }
    Seq(T head, Seq<T> tail) {
        this.head = head;
        this.tail = tail;
    }
    boolean isEmpty() { return tail == null; }

    class Zipper<S> {
        Seq<Pair<T,S>> zip(Seq<S> that) {
            if (isEmpty() || that.isEmpty()) {
                return new Seq<Pair<T,S>>();
            } else {
                Seq<T>.Zipper<S> tailZipper =
                    tail.new Zipper<S>();
                return new Seq<Pair<T,S>>(
                    new Pair<T,S>(head, that.head),
                    tailZipper.zip(that.tail));
            }
        }
    }
}
class Pair<T, S> {
    T fst; S snd;
    Pair(T f, S s) { fst = f; snd = s; }
}
class Test {
    public static void main(String[] args) {
```

```
        Seq<String> strs =
            new Seq<String>(
                "a",
                new Seq<String>("b",
                            new Seq<String>()));
        Seq<Number> nums =
            new Seq<Number>(
                new Integer(1),
                new Seq<Number>(new Double(1.5),
                            new Seq<Number>()));

        Seq<String>.Zipper<Number> zipper =
            strs.new Zipper<Number>();

        Seq<Pair<String,Number>> combined =
            zipper.zip(nums);
    }
}
```

8.1.3   Inner Classes and Enclosing Instances

An *inner class* is a nested class that is not explicitly or implicitly declared `static`.

Inner classes include local (§14.3), anonymous (§15.9.5) and non-static member classes (§8.5).

Inner classes may not declare static initializers (§8.7) or member interfaces, or a compile-time error occurs.

Inner classes may not declare static members, unless they are constant variables (§4.12.4), or a compile-time error occurs.

Inner classes may inherit static members that are not constant variables even though they may not declare them.

Nested classes that are not inner classes may declare static members freely, in accordance with the usual rules of the Java programming language. Member interfaces (§8.5) are implicitly `static` so they are never considered to be inner classes.

Example 8.1.3-1. Inner Class Declarations and Static Members

```
class HasStatic {
    static int j = 100;
}
class Outer {
    class Inner extends HasStatic {
        static final int x = 3;  // OK: compile-time constant
        static int y = 4;  // Compile-time error: an inner class
    }
    static class NestedButNotInner{
```

```
            static int z = 5;    // OK: not an inner class
        }
        interface NeverInner {}  // Interfaces are never inner
    }
```

A statement or expression *occurs in a static context* if and only if the innermost method, constructor, instance initializer, static initializer, field initializer, or explicit constructor invocation statement enclosing the statement or expression is a static method, a static initializer, the variable initializer of a static variable, or an explicit constructor invocation statement (§8.8.7).

An inner class c is a *direct inner class of a class* o if o is the immediately lexically enclosing class of c and the declaration of c does not occur in a static context.

A class c is an *inner class of class* o if it is either a direct inner class of o or an inner class of an inner class of o.

A class o is the *zeroth lexically enclosing class of itself.*

A class o is the *n'th lexically enclosing class of a class* c if it is the immediately enclosing class of the *n-1*'th lexically enclosing class of c.

An instance i of a direct inner class c of a class o is associated with an instance of o, known as the *immediately enclosing instance* of i. The immediately enclosing instance of an object, if any, is determined when the object is created (§15.9.2).

An object o is the *zeroth lexically enclosing instance of itself.*

An object o is the *n'th lexically enclosing instance of an instance* i if it is the immediately enclosing instance of the *n-1*'th lexically enclosing instance of i.

An instance of an inner class I whose declaration occurs in a static context has no lexically enclosing instances. However, if I is immediately declared within a static method or static initializer then I does have an *enclosing block*, which is the innermost block statement lexically enclosing the declaration of I.

For every superclass s of c which is itself a direct inner class of a class so, there is an instance of so associated with i, known as the *immediately enclosing instance of i with respect to s*. The immediately enclosing instance of an object with respect to its class' direct superclass, if any, is determined when the superclass constructor is invoked via an explicit constructor invocation statement.

When an inner class (whose declaration does not occur in a static context) refers to an instance variable that is a member of a lexically enclosing class, the variable of the corresponding lexically enclosing instance is used.

Any local variable, formal parameter, or exception parameter used but not declared in an inner class must be declared `final`.

Any local variable used but not declared in an inner class must be definitely assigned (§16) before the body of the inner class.

A blank `final` (§4.12.4) field of a lexically enclosing class may not be assigned within an inner class, or a compile-time error occurs.

Example 8.1.3-2. Inner Class Declarations

```
class Outer {
    int i = 100;
    static void classMethod() {
        final int l = 200;
        class LocalInStaticContext {
            int k = i;   // Compile-time error
            int m = l;   // OK
        }
    }
    void foo() {
        class Local {   // A local class
            int j = i;
        }
    }
}
```

The declaration of class `LocalInStaticContext` occurs in a static context due to being within the static method `classMethod`. Instance variables of class `Outer` are not available within the body of a static method. In particular, instance variables of `Outer` are not available inside the body of `LocalInStaticContext`. However, local variables from the surrounding method may be referred to without error (provided they are marked `final`).

Inner classes whose declarations do not occur in a static context may freely refer to the instance variables of their enclosing class. An instance variable is always defined with respect to an instance. In the case of instance variables of an enclosing class, the instance variable must be defined with respect to an enclosing instance of that class. For example, the class `Local` above has an enclosing instance of class `Outer`. As a further example:

```
class WithDeepNesting {
    boolean toBe;
    WithDeepNesting(boolean b) { toBe = b; }

    class Nested {
        boolean theQuestion;
        class DeeplyNested {
            DeeplyNested(){
                theQuestion = toBe || !toBe;
            }
        }
    }
}
```

Here, every instance of `WithDeepNesting.Nested.DeeplyNested` has an enclosing instance of class `WithDeepNesting.Nested` (its immediately enclosing instance) and an enclosing instance of class `WithDeepNesting` (its 2nd lexically enclosing instance).

8.1.4 Superclasses and Subclasses

The optional `extends` clause in a normal class declaration specifies the *direct superclass* of the current class.

Super:
> `extends` *ClassType*

The following is repeated from §4.3 to make the presentation here clearer:

ClassType:
> *TypeDeclSpecifier TypeArguments$_{opt}$*

The `extends` clause must not appear in the definition of the class `Object`, or a compile-time error occurs, because it is the primordial class and has no direct superclass.

The *ClassType* must name an accessible (§6.6) class type, or a compile-time error occurs.

If the specified *ClassType* names a class that is `final` (§8.1.1.2), then a compile-time error occurs, as `final` classes are not allowed to have subclasses.

It is a compile-time error if the *ClassType* names the class `Enum` or any invocation of it.

If the *TypeDeclSpecifier* is followed by any type arguments, it must be a correct invocation of the type declaration denoted by *TypeDeclSpecifier*, and none of the type arguments may be wildcard type arguments, or a compile-time error occurs.

Given a (possibly generic) class declaration for $C\!<\!F_1,...,F_n\!>$ ($n \geq 0$, $C \neq$ `Object`), the direct superclass of the class type $C\!<\!F_1,...,F_n\!>$ is the type given in the `extends` clause of the declaration of C if an `extends` clause is present, or `Object` otherwise.

Let $C\!<\!F_1,...,F_n\!>$ ($n > 0$) be a generic class declaration. The direct superclass of the parameterized class type $C\!<\!T_1,...,T_n\!>$, where T_i ($1 \leq i \leq n$) is a type, is $D\!<\!U_1\,\theta,...,U_k\,\theta\!>$, where $D\!<\!U_1,...,U_k\!>$ is the direct superclass of $C\!<\!F_1,...,F_n\!>$, and θ is the substitution $[F_1\!:=\!T_1,\,...,\,F_n\!:=\!T_n]$.

The direct superclass of an enum type E is `Enum<E>`.

A class is said to be a *direct subclass* of its direct superclass. The direct superclass is the class from whose implementation the implementation of the current class is derived.

Example 8.1.4-1. Direct Superclasses and Subclasses

```
class Point { int x, y; }
final class ColoredPoint extends Point { int color; }
class Colored3DPoint extends ColoredPoint { int z; }  // error
```

Here, the relationships are as follows:

- The class `Point` is a direct subclass of `Object`.
- The class `Object` is the direct superclass of the class `Point`.
- The class `ColoredPoint` is a direct subclass of class `Point`.
- The class `Point` is the direct superclass of class `ColoredPoint`.

The declaration of class `Colored3dPoint` causes a compile-time error because it attempts to extend the final class `ColoredPoint`.

The *subclass* relationship is the transitive closure of the direct subclass relationship. A class A is a subclass of class C if either of the following is true:

- A is the direct subclass of C
- There exists a class B such that A is a subclass of B, and B is a subclass of C, applying this definition recursively.

Class C is said to be a *superclass* of class A whenever A is a subclass of C.

Example 8.1.4-2. Superclasses and Subclasses

```
class Point { int x, y; }
class ColoredPoint extends Point { int color; }
final class Colored3dPoint extends ColoredPoint { int z; }
```

Here, the relationships are as follows:

- The class `Point` is a superclass of class `ColoredPoint`.
- The class `Point` is a superclass of class `Colored3dPoint`.
- The class `ColoredPoint` is a subclass of class `Point`.
- The class `ColoredPoint` is a superclass of class `Colored3dPoint`.
- The class `Colored3dPoint` is a subclass of class `ColoredPoint`.
- The class `Colored3dPoint` is a subclass of class `Point`.

A class *C directly depends* on a type *T* if *T* is mentioned in the extends or implements clause of *C* either as a superclass or superinterface, or as a qualifier of a superclass or superinterface name.

A class *C depends* on a reference type *T* if any of the following conditions hold:

- *C* directly depends on *T*.

- *C* directly depends on an interface *I* that depends (§9.1.3) on *T*.

- *C* directly depends on a class *D* that depends on *T* (using this definition recursively).

It is a compile-time error if a class depends on itself.

If circularly declared classes are detected at run time, as classes are loaded (§12.2), then a ClassCircularityError is thrown.

Example 8.1.4-3. Class Depends on Itself

```
class Point extends ColoredPoint { int x, y; }
class ColoredPoint extends Point { int color; }
```

This program causes a compile-time error.

8.1.5   Superinterfaces

The optional implements clause in a class declaration lists the names of interfaces that are direct superinterfaces of the class being declared.

Interfaces:
    implements *InterfaceTypeList*

InterfaceTypeList:
    InterfaceType
    InterfaceTypeList , *InterfaceType*

The following is repeated from §4.3 to make the presentation here clearer:

ClassType:
    TypeDeclSpecifier TypeArguments$_{opt}$

Each *InterfaceType* must name an accessible (§6.6) interface type, or a compile-time error occurs.

If the *TypeName* is followed by any type arguments, it must be a correct invocation of the type declaration denoted by *TypeName*, and none of the type arguments may be wildcard type arguments, or a compile-time error occurs.

It is a compile-time error if the same interface is mentioned as a direct superinterface two or more times in a single `implements` clause's names. This is true even if the interface is named in different ways.

Given a (possibly generic) class declaration for $C<F_1,...,F_n>$ ($n \geq 0$, $C \neq$ `Object`), the *direct superinterfaces* of the class type $C<F_1,...,F_n>$ are the types given in the `implements` clause of the declaration of C, if an `implements` clause is present.

Let $C<F_1,...,F_n>$ ($n > 0$) be a generic class declaration. The direct superinterfaces of the parameterized class type $C<T_1,...,T_n>$, where T_i ($1 \leq i \leq n$) is a type, are all types $I<U_1\theta,...,U_k\theta>$, where $I<U_1,...,U_k>$ is a direct superinterface of $C<F_1,...,F_n>$, and θ is the substitution $[F_1:=T_1, \ldots, F_n:=T_n]$.

Example 8.1.5-1. Illegal Superinterfaces

```
class Redundant implements java.lang.Cloneable, Cloneable {
    int x;
}
```

This program results in a compile-time error because the names `java.lang.Cloneable` and `Cloneable` refer to the same interface.

An interface type I is a superinterface of class type C if any of the following is true:

- I is a direct superinterface of C.

- C has some direct superinterface J for which I is a superinterface, using the definition of "superinterface of an interface" given in §9.1.3.

- I is a superinterface of the direct superclass of C.

A class can have a superinterface in more than one way.

A class is said to *implement* all its superinterfaces.

Example 8.1.5-2. Superinterfaces

```
interface Colorable {
    void setColor(int color);
    int getColor();
}
enum Finish { MATTE, GLOSSY }
interface Paintable extends Colorable {
    void setFinish(Finish finish);
    Finish getFinish();
}
```

```
class Point { int x, y; }
class ColoredPoint extends Point implements Colorable {
    int color;
    public void setColor(int color) { this.color = color; }
    public int getColor() { return color; }
}
class PaintedPoint extends ColoredPoint implements Paintable {
    Finish finish;
    public void setFinish(Finish finish) {
        this.finish = finish;
    }
    public Finish getFinish() { return finish; }
}
```

Here, the relationships are as follows:

- The interface Paintable is a superinterface of class PaintedPoint.

- The interface Colorable is a superinterface of class ColoredPoint and of class PaintedPoint.

- The interface Paintable is a subinterface of the interface Colorable, and Colorable is a superinterface of Paintable, as defined in §9.1.3.

The class PaintedPoint has Colorable as a superinterface both because it is a superinterface of ColoredPoint and because it is a superinterface of Paintable.

Unless the class being declared is abstract, the declarations of all the method members of each direct superinterface must be implemented either by a declaration in this class or by an existing method declaration inherited from the direct superclass, because a class that is not abstract is not permitted to have abstract methods (§8.1.1.1).

It is permitted for a single method declaration in a class to implement methods of more than one superinterface.

Example 8.1.5-3. Implementing Methods of a Superinterface

```
interface Colorable {
    void setColor(int color);
    int getColor();
}
class Point { int x, y; };
class ColoredPoint extends Point implements Colorable {
    int color;
}
```

This program causes a compile-time error, because ColoredPoint is not an abstract class but fails to provide an implementation of methods setColor and getColor of the interface Colorable.

In the following program:

```
interface Fish  { int getNumberOfScales(); }
interface Piano { int getNumberOfScales(); }
class Tuna implements Fish, Piano {
    // You can tune a piano, but can you tuna fish?
    public int getNumberOfScales() { return 91; }
}
```

the method `getNumberOfScales` in class `Tuna` has a name, signature, and return type that matches the method declared in interface `Fish` and also matches the method declared in interface `Piano`; it is considered to implement both.

On the other hand, in a situation such as this:

```
interface Fish       { int    getNumberOfScales(); }
interface StringBass { double getNumberOfScales(); }
class Bass implements Fish, StringBass {
    // This declaration cannot be correct,
    // no matter what type is used.
    public ?? getNumberOfScales() { return 91; }
}
```

it is impossible to declare a method named `getNumberOfScales` whose signature and return type are compatible with those of both the methods declared in interface `Fish` and in interface `StringBass`, because a class cannot have multiple methods with the same signature and different primitive return types (§8.4). Therefore, it is impossible for a single class to implement both interface `Fish` and interface `StringBass` (§8.4.8).

A class may not at the same time be a subtype of two interface types which are different invocations of the same generic interface (§9.1.2), or a subtype of an invocation of a generic interface and a raw type naming that same generic interface, or a compile-time error occurs.

This requirement was introduced in order to support translation by type erasure (§4.6).

Example 8.1.5-4. Illegal Multiple Inheritance of an Interface

```
interface I<T> {}
class B implements I<Integer> {}
class C extends B implements I<String> {}
```

8.1.6   Class Body and Member Declarations

A *class body* may contain declarations of members of the class, that is, fields (§8.3), methods (§8.4), classes (§8.5), and interfaces (§8.5).

A class body may also contain instance initializers (§8.6), static initializers (§8.7), and declarations of constructors (§8.8) for the class.

ClassBody:
   { ClassBodyDeclarations$_{opt}$ }

ClassBodyDeclarations:
   ClassBodyDeclaration
   ClassBodyDeclarations ClassBodyDeclaration

ClassBodyDeclaration:
   ClassMemberDeclaration
   InstanceInitializer
   StaticInitializer
   ConstructorDeclaration

ClassMemberDeclaration:
   FieldDeclaration
   MethodDeclaration
   ClassDeclaration
   InterfaceDeclaration
   ;

The scope and shadowing of a declaration of a member m declared in or inherited by a class type c is specified in §6.3 and §6.4.

> If c itself is a nested class, there may be definitions of the same kind (variable, method, or type) and name as m in enclosing scopes. (The scopes may be blocks, classes, or packages.) In all such cases, the member m declared in or inherited by c shadows (§6.4.1) the other definitions of the same kind and name.

8.2   Class Members

The members of a class type are all of the following:

- Members inherited from its direct superclass (§8.1.4), except in class `Object`, which has no direct superclass

- Members inherited from any direct superinterfaces (§8.1.5)

- Members declared in the body of the class (§8.1.6)

Members of a class that are declared `private` are not inherited by subclasses of that class.

Only members of a class that are declared `protected` or `public` are inherited by subclasses declared in a package other than the one in which the class is declared.

Constructors, static initializers, and instance initializers are not members and therefore are not inherited.

We use the phrase *the type of a member* to denote:

- For a field, its type.

- For a method, an ordered 3-tuple consisting of:

  - argument types: a list of the types of the arguments to the method member.

  - return type: the return type of the method member.

  - throws clause: exception types declared in the throws clause of the method member.

Fields, methods, and member types of a class type may have the same name, since they are used in different contexts and are disambiguated by different lookup procedures (§6.5). However, this is discouraged as a matter of style.

Example 8.2-1. Use of Class Members

```
class Point {
    int x, y;
    private Point() { reset(); }
    Point(int x, int y) { this.x = x; this.y = y; }
    private void reset() { this.x = 0; this.y = 0; }
}
class ColoredPoint extends Point {
    int color;
    void clear() { reset(); }  // error
}
class Test {
    public static void main(String[] args) {
        ColoredPoint c = new ColoredPoint(0, 0);  // error
        c.reset();  // error
    }
}
```

This program causes four compile-time errors.

One error occurs because `ColoredPoint` has no constructor declared with two `int` parameters, as requested by the use in `main`. This illustrates the fact that `ColoredPoint` does not inherit the constructors of its superclass `Point`.

Another error occurs because ColoredPoint declares no constructors, and therefore a default constructor for it is automatically created (§8.8.9), and this default constructor is equivalent to:

```
ColoredPoint() { super(); }
```

which invokes the constructor, with no arguments, for the direct superclass of the class ColoredPoint. The error is that the constructor for Point that takes no arguments is private, and therefore is not accessible outside the class Point, even through a superclass constructor invocation (§8.8.7).

Two more errors occur because the method reset of class Point is private, and therefore is not inherited by class ColoredPoint. The method invocations in method clear of class ColoredPoint and in method main of class Test are therefore not correct.

Example 8.2-2. Inheritance of Class Members with Default Access

Consider the example where the points package declares two compilation units:

```
package points;
public class Point {
    int x, y;
    public void move(int dx, int dy) { x += dx; y += dy; }
}
```

and:

```
package points;
public class Point3d extends Point {
    int z;
    public void move(int dx, int dy, int dz) {
        x += dx; y += dy; z += dz;
    }
}
```

and a third compilation unit, in another package, is:

```
import points.Point3d;
class Point4d extends Point3d {
    int w;
    public void move(int dx, int dy, int dz, int dw) {
        x += dx; y += dy; z += dz; w += dw; // compile-time errors
    }
}
```

Here both classes in the points package compile. The class Point3d inherits the fields x and y of class Point, because it is in the same package as Point. The class Point4d, which is in a different package, does not inherit the fields x and y of class Point or the field z of class Point3d, and so fails to compile.

A better way to write the third compilation unit would be:

```
import points.Point3d;
class Point4d extends Point3d {
    int w;
    public void move(int dx, int dy, int dz, int dw) {
        super.move(dx, dy, dz); w += dw;
    }
}
```

using the move method of the superclass Point3d to process dx, dy, and dz. If Point4d is written in this way, it will compile without errors.

Example 8.2-3. Inheritance of public and protected Class Members

Given the class Point:

```
package points;
public class Point {
    public int x, y;
    protected int useCount = 0;
    static protected int totalUseCount = 0;
    public void move(int dx, int dy) {
        x += dx; y += dy; useCount++; totalUseCount++;
    }
}
```

the public and protected fields x, y, useCount, and totalUseCount are inherited in all subclasses of Point.

Therefore, this test program, in another package, can be compiled successfully:

```
class Test extends points.Point {
    public void moveBack(int dx, int dy) {
        x -= dx; y -= dy; useCount++; totalUseCount++;
    }
}
```

Example 8.2-4. Inheritance of private Class Members

```
class Point {
    int x, y;
    void move(int dx, int dy) {
        x += dx; y += dy; totalMoves++;
    }
    private static int totalMoves;
    void printMoves() { System.out.println(totalMoves); }
}
class Point3d extends Point {
    int z;
    void move(int dx, int dy, int dz) {
        super.move(dx, dy); z += dz; totalMoves++; // error
```

```
    }
  }
```

Here, the class variable `totalMoves` can be used only within the class `Point`; it is not inherited by the subclass `Point3d`. A compile-time error occurs because method move of class `Point3d` tries to increment `totalMoves`.

Example 8.2-5. Accessing Members of Inaccessible Classes

Even though a class might not be declared `public`, instances of the class might be available at run time to code outside the package in which it is declared by means a `public` superclass or superinterface. An instance of the class can be assigned to a variable of such a `public` type. An invocation of a `public` method of the object referred to by such a variable may invoke a method of the class if it implements or overrides a method of the `public` superclass or superinterface. (In this situation, the method is necessarily declared `public`, even though it is declared in a class that is not `public`.)

Consider the compilation unit:

```
package points;
public class Point {
    public int x, y;
    public void move(int dx, int dy) {
        x += dx; y += dy;
    }
}
```

and another compilation unit of another package:

```
package morePoints;
class Point3d extends points.Point {
    public int z;
    public void move(int dx, int dy, int dz) {
        super.move(dx, dy); z += dz;
    }
    public void move(int dx, int dy) {
        move(dx, dy, 0);
    }
}
public class OnePoint {
    public static points.Point getOne() {
        return new Point3d();
    }
}
```

An invocation `morePoints.OnePoint.getOne()` in yet a third package would return a `Point3d` that can be used as a `Point`, even though the type `Point3d` is not available outside the package `morePoints`. The two-argument version of method move could then be invoked for that object, which is permissible because method move of `Point3d` is `public` (as it must be, for any method that overrides a `public` method must itself be `public`, precisely so that situations such as this will work out correctly). The fields x and y of that object could also be accessed from such a third package.

While the field z of class Point3d is public, it is not possible to access this field from code outside the package morePoints, given only a reference to an instance of class Point3d in a variable p of type Point. This is because the expression p.z is not correct, as p has type Point and class Point has no field named z; also, the expression ((Point3d)p).z is not correct, because the class type Point3d cannot be referred to outside package morePoints.

The declaration of the field z as public is not useless, however. If there were to be, in package morePoints, a public subclass Point4d of the class Point3d:

```
package morePoints;
public class Point4d extends Point3d {
    public int w;
    public void move(int dx, int dy, int dz, int dw) {
        super.move(dx, dy, dz); w += dw;
    }
}
```

then class Point4d would inherit the field z, which, being public, could then be accessed by code in packages other than morePoints, through variables and expressions of the public type Point4d.

8.3 Field Declarations

The variables of a class type are introduced by *field declarations*.

FieldDeclaration:
  FieldModifiers$_{opt}$ Type VariableDeclarators ;

VariableDeclarators:
  VariableDeclarator
  VariableDeclarators , VariableDeclarator

VariableDeclarator:
  VariableDeclaratorId
  VariableDeclaratorId = VariableInitializer

VariableDeclaratorId:
  Identifier
  VariableDeclaratorId [ ]

VariableInitializer:
  Expression
  ArrayInitializer

The *FieldModifiers* are described in §8.3.1.

The *Identifier* in a *FieldDeclarator* may be used in a name to refer to the field.

More than one field may be declared in a single field declaration by using more than one declarator; the *FieldModifiers* and *Type* apply to all the declarators in the declaration.

The declared type of a field is denoted by the *Type* that appears in the field declaration, followed by any bracket pairs that follow the *Identifier* in the declarator.

It is a compile-time error for the body of a class declaration to declare two fields with the same name.

The scope and shadowing of a field declaration is specified in §6.3 and §6.4.

If the class declares a field with a certain name, then the declaration of that field is said to *hide* any and all accessible declarations of fields with the same name in superclasses, and superinterfaces of the class.

In this respect, hiding of fields differs from hiding of methods (§8.4.8.3), for there is no distinction drawn between static and non-static fields in field hiding whereas a distinction is drawn between static and non-static methods in method hiding.

A hidden field can be accessed by using a qualified name (§6.5.6.2) if it is `static`, or by using a field access expression that contains the keyword `super` (§15.11.2) or a cast to a superclass type.

> In this respect, hiding of fields is similar to hiding of methods.

If a field declaration hides the declaration of another field, the two fields need not have the same type.

A class inherits from its direct superclass and direct superinterfaces all the non-private fields of the superclass and superinterfaces that are both accessible to code in the class and not hidden by a declaration in the class.

A `private` field of a superclass might be accessible to a subclass - for example, if both classes are members of the same class. Nevertheless, a `private` field is never inherited by a subclass.

It is possible for a class to inherit more than one field with the same name. Such a situation does not in itself cause a compile-time error. However, any attempt within the body of the class to refer to any such field by its simple name will result in a compile-time error, because such a reference is ambiguous.

There might be several paths by which the same field declaration might be inherited from an interface. In such a situation, the field is considered to be inherited only once, and it may be referred to by its simple name without ambiguity.

A value stored in a field of type `float` is always an element of the float value set (§4.2.3); similarly, a value stored in a field of type `double` is always an element of the double value set. It is not permitted for a field of type `float` to contain an element of the float-extended-exponent value set that is not also an element of the float value set, nor for a field of type `double` to contain an element of the double-extended-exponent value set that is not also an element of the double value set.

Example 8.3-1. Multiply Inherited Fields

A class may inherit two or more fields with the same name, either from two interfaces or from its superclass and an interface. A compile-time error occurs on any attempt to refer to any ambiguously inherited field by its simple name. A qualified name or a field access expression that contains the keyword `super` (§15.11.2) may be used to access such fields unambiguously. In the program:

```
interface Frob   { float v = 2.0f; }
class SuperTest { int   v = 3; }
class Test extends SuperTest implements Frob {
    public static void main(String[] args) {
        new Test().printV();
    }
```

```
    void printV() { System.out.println(v); }
}
```

the class Test inherits two fields named v, one from its superclass SuperTest and one from its superinterface Frob. This in itself is permitted, but a compile-time error occurs because of the use of the simple name v in method printV: it cannot be determined which v is intended.

The following variation uses the field access expression super.v to refer to the field named v declared in class SuperTest and uses the qualified name Frob.v to refer to the field named v declared in interface Frob:

```
interface Frob  { float v = 2.0f; }
class SuperTest { int   v = 3; }
class Test extends SuperTest implements Frob {
    public static void main(String[] args) {
        new Test().printV();
    }
    void printV() {
        System.out.println((super.v + Frob.v)/2);
    }
}
```

It compiles and prints:

```
2.5
```

Even if two distinct inherited fields have the same type, the same value, and are both final, any reference to either field by simple name is considered ambiguous and results in a compile-time error. In the program:

```
interface Color        { int RED=0, GREEN=1,  BLUE=2;  }
interface TrafficLight { int RED=0, YELLOW=1, GREEN=2; }
class Test implements Color, TrafficLight {
    public static void main(String[] args) {
        System.out.println(GREEN);  // compile-time error
        System.out.println(RED);    // compile-time error
    }
}
```

it is not astonishing that the reference to GREEN should be considered ambiguous, because class Test inherits two different declarations for GREEN with different values. The point of this example is that the reference to RED is also considered ambiguous, because two distinct declarations are inherited. The fact that the two fields named RED happen to have the same type and the same unchanging value does not affect this judgment.

Example 8.3-2. Re-inheritance of Fields

If the same field declaration is inherited from an interface by multiple paths, the field is considered to be inherited only once. It may be referred to by its simple name without ambiguity. For example, in the code:

```
interface Colorable {
    int RED = 0xff0000, GREEN = 0x00ff00, BLUE = 0x0000ff;
}
interface Paintable extends Colorable {
    int MATTE = 0, GLOSSY = 1;
}
class Point { int x, y; }
class ColoredPoint extends Point implements Colorable {}
class PaintedPoint extends ColoredPoint implements Paintable {
    int p = RED;
}
```

the fields RED, GREEN, and BLUE are inherited by the class PaintedPoint both through its direct superclass ColoredPoint and through its direct superinterface Paintable. The simple names RED, GREEN, and BLUE may nevertheless be used without ambiguity within the class PaintedPoint to refer to the fields declared in interface Colorable.

8.3.1 Field Modifiers

FieldModifiers:
    FieldModifier
    FieldModifiers FieldModifier

FieldModifier: one of
    Annotation public protected private
    static final transient volatile

If an annotation `a` (§9.7) on a field declaration corresponds to an annotation type `T` (§9.6), and `T` has a (meta-)annotation `m` that corresponds to java.lang.annotation.Target, then `m` must have an element whose value is java.lang.annotation.ElementType.FIELD, or a compile-time error occurs.

The access modifiers public, protected, and private are discussed in §6.6.

It is a compile-time error if the same modifier appears more than once in a field declaration, or if a field declaration has more than one of the access modifiers public, protected, and private.

If two or more (distinct) field modifiers appear in a field declaration, it is customary, though not required, that they appear in the order consistent with that shown above in the production for *FieldModifier*.

8.3.1.1 static *Fields*

If a field is declared static, there exists exactly one incarnation of the field, no matter how many instances (possibly zero) of the class may eventually be created.

A static field, sometimes called a class variable, is incarnated when the class is initialized (§12.4).

A field that is not declared `static` (sometimes called a non-`static` field) is called an *instance variable*. Whenever a new instance of a class is created (§12.5), a new variable associated with that instance is created for every instance variable declared in that class or any of its superclasses.

Example 8.3.1.1-1. `static` **Fields**

```
class Point {
    int x, y, useCount;
    Point(int x, int y) { this.x = x; this.y = y; }
    static final Point origin = new Point(0, 0);
}
class Test {
    public static void main(String[] args) {
        Point p = new Point(1,1);
        Point q = new Point(2,2);
        p.x = 3;
        p.y = 3;
        p.useCount++;
        p.origin.useCount++;
        System.out.println("(" + q.x + "," + q.y + ")");
        System.out.println(q.useCount);
        System.out.println(q.origin == Point.origin);
        System.out.println(q.origin.useCount);
    }
}
```

This program prints:

```
(2,2)
0
true
1
```

showing that changing the fields x, y, and useCount of p does not affect the fields of q, because these fields are instance variables in distinct objects. In this example, the class variable origin of the class Point is referenced both using the class name as a qualifier, in Point.origin, and using variables of the class type in field access expressions (§15.11), as in p.origin and q.origin. These two ways of accessing the origin class variable access the same object, evidenced by the fact that the value of the reference equality expression (§15.21.3):

```
q.origin==Point.origin
```

is true. Further evidence is that the incrementation:

```
p.origin.useCount++;
```

causes the value of `q.origin.useCount` to be 1; this is so because `p.origin` and `q.origin` refer to the same variable.

Example 8.3.1.1-2. Hiding of Class Variables

```
class Point {
    static int x = 2;
}
class Test extends Point {
    static double x = 4.7;
    public static void main(String[] args) {
        new Test().printX();
    }
    void printX() {
        System.out.println(x + " " + super.x);
    }
}
```

This program produces the output:

```
4.7 2
```

because the declaration of x in class `Test` hides the definition of x in class `Point`, so class `Test` does not inherit the field x from its superclass `Point`. Within the declaration of class `Test`, the simple name x refers to the field declared within class `Test`. Code in class `Test` may refer to the field x of class `Point` as `super.x` (or, because x is `static`, as `Point.x`). If the declaration of `Toot.x` is deleted:

```
class Point {
    static int x = 2;
}
class Test extends Point {
    public static void main(String[] args) {
        new Test().printX();
    }
    void printX() {
        System.out.println(x + " " + super.x);
    }
}
```

then the field x of class `Point` is no longer hidden within class `Test`; instead, the simple name x now refers to the field `Point.x`. Code in class `Test` may still refer to that same field as `super.x`. Therefore, the output from this variant program is:

```
2 2
```

Example 8.3.1.1-3. Hiding of Instance Variables

```
class Point {
    int x = 2;
}
class Test extends Point {
```

```
        double x = 4.7;
        void printBoth() {
            System.out.println(x + " " + super.x);
        }
        public static void main(String[] args) {
            Test sample = new Test();
            sample.printBoth();
            System.out.println(sample.x + " " + ((Point)sample).x);
        }
    }
```

This program produces the output:

```
4.7 2
4.7 2
```

because the declaration of x in class Test hides the definition of x in class Point, so class Test does not inherit the field x from its superclass Point. It must be noted, however, that while the field x of class Point is not inherited by class Test, it is nevertheless *implemented* by instances of class Test. In other words, every instance of class Test contains two fields, one of type int and one of type double. Both fields bear the name x, but within the declaration of class Test, the simple name x always refers to the field declared within class Test. Code in instance methods of class Test may refer to the instance variable x of class Point as super.x.

Code that uses a field access expression to access field x will access the field named x in the class indicated by the type of reference expression. Thus, the expression sample.x accesses a double value, the instance variable declared in class Test, because the type of the variable sample is Test, but the expression ((Point)sample).x accesses an int value, the instance variable declared in class Point, because of the cast to type Point.

If the declaration of x is deleted from class Test, as in the program:

```
class Point {
    static int x = 2;
}
class Test extends Point {
    void printBoth() {
        System.out.println(x + " " + super.x);
    }
    public static void main(String[] args) {
        Test sample = new Test();
        sample.printBoth();
        System.out.println(sample.x + " " + ((Point)sample).x);
    }
}
```

then the field x of class Point is no longer hidden within class Test. Within instance methods in the declaration of class Test, the simple name x now refers to the field declared within class Point. Code in class Test may still refer to that same field as super.x. The expression sample.x still refers to the field x within type Test, but that field is now an inherited field, and so refers to the field x declared in class Point. The output from this variant program is:

```
2 2
2 2
```

8.3.1.2 final *Fields*

A field can be declared final (§4.12.4). Both class and instance variables (static and non-static fields) may be declared final.

It is a compile-time error if a blank final (§4.12.4) class variable is not definitely assigned (§16.8) by a static initializer (§8.7) of the class in which it is declared.

A blank final instance variable must be definitely assigned (§16.9) at the end of every constructor (§8.8) of the class in which it is declared; otherwise a compile-time error occurs.

8.3.1.3 transient *Fields*

Variables may be marked transient to indicate that they are not part of the persistent state of an object.

> **Example 8.3.1.3-1. Persistence of transient Fields**
>
> If an instance of the class Point:
>
> ```
> class Point {
>     int x, y;
>     transient float rho, theta;
> }
> ```
>
> were saved to persistent storage by a system service, then only the fields x and y would be saved. This specification does not specify details of such services; see the specification of java.io.Serializable for an example of such a service.

8.3.1.4 volatile *Fields*

The Java programming language allows threads to access shared variables (§17.1). As a rule, to ensure that shared variables are consistently and reliably updated, a thread should ensure that it has exclusive use of such variables by obtaining a lock that, conventionally, enforces mutual exclusion for those shared variables.

The Java programming language provides a second mechanism, volatile fields, that is more convenient than locking for some purposes.

A field may be declared volatile, in which case the Java Memory Model ensures that all threads see a consistent value for the variable (§17.4).

It is a compile-time error if a `final` variable is also declared `volatile`.

Example 8.3.1.4-1. `volatile` **Fields**

If, in the following example, one thread repeatedly calls the method `one` (but no more than `Integer.MAX_VALUE` times in all), and another thread repeatedly calls the method `two`:

```
class Test {
    static int i = 0, j = 0;
    static void one() { i++; j++; }
    static void two() {
        System.out.println("i=" + i + " j=" + j);
    }
}
```

then method `two` could occasionally print a value for `j` that is greater than the value of `i`, because the example includes no synchronization and, under the rules explained in §17.4, the shared values of `i` and `j` might be updated out of order.

One way to prevent this out-or-order behavior would be to declare methods `one` and `two` to be `synchronized` (§8.4.3.6):

```
class Test {
    static int i = 0, j = 0;
    static synchronized void one() { i++; j++; }
    static synchronized void two() {
        System.out.println("i=" + i + " j=" + j);
    }
}
```

This prevents method `one` and method `two` from being executed concurrently, and furthermore guarantees that the shared values of `i` and `j` are both updated before method `one` returns. Therefore method `two` never observes a value for `j` greater than that for `i`; indeed, it always observes the same value for `i` and `j`.

Another approach would be to declare `i` and `j` to be `volatile`:

```
class Test {
    static volatile int i = 0, j = 0;
    static void one() { i++; j++; }
    static void two() {
        System.out.println("i=" + i + " j=" + j);
    }
}
```

This allows method `one` and method `two` to be executed concurrently, but guarantees that accesses to the shared values for `i` and `j` occur exactly as many times, and in exactly the same order, as they appear to occur during execution of the program text by each thread. Therefore, the shared value for `j` is never greater than that for `i`, because each update to `i` must be reflected in the shared value for `i` before the update to `j` occurs. It is possible, however, that any given invocation of method `two` might observe a value for `j` that is much greater than the value observed for i, because method one might be executed many times between the moment when method two fetches the value of i and the moment when method two fetches the value of j.

See §17.4 for more discussion and examples.

8.3.2   Initialization of Fields

If a field declarator contains a *variable initializer*, then it has the semantics of an assignment (§15.26) to the declared variable, and:

- If the declarator is for a class variable (that is, a static field), then the variable initializer is evaluated and the assignment performed exactly once, when the class is initialized (§12.4.2).

- If the declarator is for an instance variable (that is, a field that is not static), then the variable initializer is evaluated and the assignment performed each time an instance of the class is created (§12.5).

Example 8.3.2-1. Field Initialization

```
class Point {
    int x = 1, y = 5;
}
class Test {
    public static void main(String[] args) {
        Point p = new Point();
        System.out.println(p.x + ", " + p.y);
    }
}
```

This program produces the output:

```
1, 5
```

because the assignments to x and y occur whenever a new Point is created.

Exception checking for a variable initializer in a field declaration is specified in §11.2.3.

Variable initializers are also used in local variable declaration statements (§14.4), where the initializer is evaluated and the assignment performed each time the local variable declaration statement is executed.

8.3.2.1   *Initializers for Class Variables*

If a reference by simple name to any instance variable occurs in an initialization expression for a class variable, then a compile-time error occurs.

If the keyword `this` (§15.8.3) or the keyword `super` (§15.11.2, §15.12) occurs in an initialization expression for a class variable, then a compile-time error occurs.

At run time, `static` fields that are `final` and that are initialized with constant expressions (§15.28) are initialized first (§12.4.2). This also applies to such fields in interfaces (§9.3.1). These fields are "constants" that will never be observed to have their default initial values (§4.12.5), even by devious programs (§13.4.9).

> Use of class variables whose declarations appear textually after the use is sometimes restricted, even though these class variables are in scope. See §8.3.2.3 for the precise rules governing forward reference to class variables.

8.3.2.2 *Initializers for Instance Variables*

Initialization expressions for instance variables may use the simple name of any static variable declared in or inherited by the class, even one whose declaration occurs textually later.

Example 8.3.2.2-1. Out-of-order Field Initialization

```
class Test {
    float f = j;
    static int j = 1;
}
```

> This program compiles without error; it initializes j to 1 when class Test is initialized, and initializes f to the current value of j every time an instance of class Test is created.

Initialization expressions for instance variables are permitted to refer to the current object `this` (§15.8.3) and to use the keyword `super` (§15.11.2, §15.12).

> Use of instance variables whose declarations appear textually after the use is sometimes restricted, even though these instance variables are in scope. See §8.3.2.3 for the precise rules governing forward reference to instance variables.

8.3.2.3 *Restrictions on the use of Fields during Initialization*

The declaration of a member needs to appear textually before it is used only if the member is an instance (respectively `static`) field of a class or interface *c* and all of the following conditions hold:

- The usage occurs in an instance (respectively `static`) variable initializer of *c* or in an instance (respectively `static`) initializer of *c*.

- The usage is not on the left hand side of an assignment.

- The usage is via a simple name.

- *c* is the innermost class or interface enclosing the usage.

It is a compile-time error if any of the four requirements above are not met.

Example 8.3.2.3-1. Restrictions on Field Initialization

A compile-time error occurs for this program:

```
class Test1 {
    int i = j;   // compile-time error:
                 // incorrect forward reference
    int j = 1;
}
```

whereas the following program compiles without error:

```
class Test2 {
    Test2() { k = 2; }
    int j = 1;
    int i = j;
    int k;
}
```

even though the constructor (§8.8) for Test refers to the field k that is declared three lines later.

The restrictions above are designed to catch, at compile time, circular or otherwise malformed initializations. Thus, both:

```
class Z {
    static int i = j + 2;
    static int j = 4;
}
```

and:

```
class Z {
    static { i = j + 2; }
    static int i, j;
    static { j = 4; }
}
```

result in compile-time errors. Accesses by methods are not checked in this way, so:

```
class Z {
    static int peek() { return j; }
    static int i = peek();
    static int j = 1;
}
class Test {
    public static void main(String[] args) {
```

```
                    System.out.println(Z.i);
            }
        }
```

produces the output:

```
        0
```

because the variable initializer for i uses the class method peek to access the value of the variable j before j has been initialized by its variable initializer, at which point it still has its default value (§4.12.5).

A more elaborate example is:

```
class UseBeforeDeclaration {
    static {
        x = 100;
          // ok - assignment
        int y = x + 1;
          // error - read before declaration
        int v = x = 3;
          // ok - x at left hand side of assignment
        int z = UseBeforeDeclaration.x * 2;
          // ok - not accessed via simple name

        Object o = new Object() {
            void foo() { x++; }
              // ok - occurs in a different class
            { x++; }
              // ok - occurs in a different class
        };
    }

    {
        j = 200;
          // ok - assignment
        j = j + 1;
          // error - right hand side reads before declaration
        int k = j = j + 1;
          // error - illegal forward reference to j
        int n = j = 300;
          // ok - j at left hand side of assignment
        int h = j++;
          // error - read before declaration
        int l = this.j * 3;
          // ok - not accessed via simple name

        Object o = new Object() {
            void foo(){ j++; }
              // ok - occurs in a different class
            { j = j + 1; }
              // ok - occurs in a different class
```

```
        };
    }

    int w = x = 3;
      // ok - x at left hand side of assignment
    int p = x;
      // ok - instance initializers may access static fields

    static int u =
        (new Object() { int bar() { return x; } }).bar();
     // ok - occurs in a different class

    static int x;

    int m = j = 4;
      // ok - j at left hand side of assignment
    int o =
        (new Object() { int bar() { return j; } }).bar();
        // ok - occurs in a different class
    int j;
}
```

8.4 Method Declarations

A *method* declares executable code that can be invoked, passing a fixed number of values as arguments.

> *MethodDeclaration:*
>   *MethodHeader MethodBody*

> *MethodHeader:*
>   *MethodModifiers$_{opt}$ TypeParameters$_{opt}$ Result MethodDeclarator Throws$_{opt}$*

> *MethodDeclarator:*
>   *Identifier* (*FormalParameterList$_{opt}$*)

The *FormalParameterList* is described in §8.4.1, the *MethodModifiers* clause in §8.4.3, the *TypeParameters* clause in §8.4.4, the *Result* clause in §8.4.5, the *Throws* clause in §8.4.6, and the *MethodBody* in §8.4.7.

The *Identifier* in a *MethodDeclarator* may be used in a name to refer to the method.

It is a compile-time error for the body of a class to declare as members two methods with override-equivalent signatures (§8.4.2).

The scope and shadowing of a method declaration is specified in §6.3 and §6.4.

For compatibility with older versions of the Java SE platform, the declaration of a method that returns an array is allowed to place (some or all of) the empty bracket pairs that form the declaration of the array type after the formal parameter list. This is supported by the following obsolescent production, but should not be used in new code.

> *MethodDeclarator:*
>   *MethodDeclarator* [ ]

8.4.1   Formal Parameters

The *formal parameters* of a method or constructor, if any, are specified by a list of comma-separated parameter specifiers. Each parameter specifier consists of a type (optionally preceded by the `final` modifier and/or one or more annotations) and an identifier (optionally followed by brackets) that specifies the name of the parameter.

The last formal parameter of a method or constructor is special: it may be a *variable arity parameter*, indicated by an ellipsis following the type.

If the last formal parameter is a variable arity parameter, the method is a *variable arity method*. Otherwise, it is a *fixed arity method*.

If a method or constructor has no formal parameters, only an empty pair of parentheses appears in the declaration of the method or constructor.

FormalParameterList:
  LastFormalParameter
  FormalParameters , LastFormalParameter

FormalParameters:
  FormalParameter
  FormalParameters , FormalParameter

FormalParameter:
  VariableModifiers$_{opt}$ *Type VariableDeclaratorId*

VariableModifiers:
  VariableModifier
  VariableModifiers VariableModifier

VariableModifier: one of
  Annotation final

LastFormalParameter:
  VariableModifiers$_{opt}$ *Type . . . VariableDeclaratorId*
  FormalParameter

The following is repeated from §8.3 to make the presentation here clearer:

VariableDeclaratorId:
  Identifier
  VariableDeclaratorId [ ]

If an annotation *a* (§9.7) on a formal parameter corresponds to an annotation type *T* (§9.6), and *T* has a (meta-)annotation *m* that corresponds to java.lang.annotation.Target, then *m* must have an element whose value is java.lang.annotation.ElementType.PARAMETER, or a compile-time error occurs.

The scope and shadowing of a formal parameter is specified in §6.3 and §6.4.

It is a compile-time error for a method or constructor to declare two formal parameters with the same name. (That is, their declarations mention the same *Identifier*.)

It is a compile-time error if a formal parameter that is declared final is assigned to within the body of the method or constructor.

It is a compile-time error to use mixed array notation (§10.2) for a variable arity parameter.

The declared type of a formal parameter is denoted by the *Type* that appears in its parameter specifier, followed by any bracket pairs that follow the *Identifier* in the declarator, except for a variable arity parameter, whose declared type is an array type whose component type is the *Type* that appears in its parameter specifier.

If the declared type of a variable arity parameter has a non-reifiable element type (§4.7), then a compile-time unchecked warning occurs for the declaration of the variable arity method, unless the method is annotated with the `SafeVarargs` annotation (§9.6.3.7) or the unchecked warning is suppressed by the `SuppressWarnings` annotation (§9.6.3.5).

When the method or constructor is invoked (§15.12), the values of the actual argument expressions initialize newly created parameter variables, each of the declared type, before execution of the body of the method or constructor. The *Identifier* that appears in the *DeclaratorId* may be used as a simple name in the body of the method or constructor to refer to the formal parameter.

Invocations of a variable arity method may contain more actual argument expressions than formal parameters. All the actual argument expressions that do not correspond to the formal parameters preceding the variable arity parameter will be evaluated and the results stored into an array that will be passed to the method invocation (§15.12.4.2).

A method or constructor parameter of type `float` always contains an element of the float value set (§4.2.3); similarly, a method or constructor parameter of type `double` always contains an element of the double value set. It is not permitted for a method or constructor parameter of type `float` to contain an element of the float-extended-exponent value set that is not also an element of the float value set, nor for a method parameter of type `double` to contain an element of the double-extended-exponent value set that is not also an element of the double value set.

Where an actual argument expression corresponding to a parameter variable is not FP-strict (§15.4), evaluation of that actual argument expression is permitted to use intermediate values drawn from the appropriate extended-exponent value sets. Prior to being stored in the parameter variable, the result of such an expression is mapped to the nearest value in the corresponding standard value set by method invocation conversion (§5.3).

8.4.2   Method Signature

Two methods have the *same signature* if they have the same name and argument types.

Two method or constructor declarations M and N have the *same argument types* if all of the following conditions hold:

- They have the same number of formal parameters (possibly zero)

- They have the same number of type parameters (possibly zero)

- Let $A_1, ..., A_n$ be the type parameters of M and let $B_1, ..., B_n$ be the type parameters of N. After renaming each occurrence of a B_i in N's type to A_i, the bounds of corresponding type variables are the same, and the formal parameter types of M and N are the same.

The signature of a method m_1 is a *subsignature* of the signature of a method m_2 if either:

- m_2 has the same signature as m_1, or

- the signature of m_1 is the same as the erasure (§4.6) of the signature of m_2.

Two method signatures m_1 and m_2 are *override-equivalent* iff either m_1 is a subsignature of m_2 or m_2 is a subsignature of m_1.

It is a compile-time error to declare two methods with override-equivalent signatures in a class.

> **Example 8.4.2-1. Override-Equivalent Signatures**
>
> ```
> class Point {
>     int x, y;
>     abstract void move(int dx, int dy);
>     void move(int dx, int dy) { x += dx; y += dy; }
> }
> ```
>
> This program causes a compile-time error because it declares two `move` methods with the same (and hence, override-equivalent) signature. This is an error even though one of the declarations is `abstract`.
>
> The notion of subsignature is designed to express a relationship between two methods whose signatures are not identical, but in which one may override the other. Specifically, it allows a method whose signature does not use generic types to override any generified version of that method. This is important so that library designers may freely generify methods independently of clients that define subclasses or subinterfaces of the library.
>
> Consider the example:
>
> ```
> class CollectionConverter {
> ```

```
        List toList(Collection c) {...}
    }
class Overrider extends CollectionConverter {
        List toList(Collection c) {...}
    }
```

Now, assume this code was written before the introduction of generics, and now the author of class `CollectionConverter` decides to generify the code, thus:

```
class CollectionConverter {
    <T> List<T> toList(Collection<T> c) {...}
}
```

Without special dispensation, `Overrider.toList` would no longer override `CollectionConverter.toList`. Instead, the code would be illegal. This would significantly inhibit the use of generics, since library writers would hesitate to migrate existing code.

8.4.3 Method Modifiers

MethodModifiers:
  MethodModifier
  MethodModifiers MethodModifier

MethodModifier: one of
  Annotation `public protected private abstract`
  `static final synchronized native strictfp`

If an annotation a (§9.7) on a method declaration corresponds to an annotation type T (§9.6), and T has a (meta-)annotation m that corresponds to `java.lang.annotation.Target`, then m must have an element whose value is `java.lang.annotation.ElementType.METHOD`, or a compile-time error occurs.

It is a compile-time error if the same modifier appears more than once in a method declaration, or if a method declaration has more than one of the access modifiers `public`, `protected`, and `private` (§6.6).

It is a compile-time error if a method declaration that contains the keyword `abstract` also contains any one of the keywords `private`, `static`, `final`, `native`, `strictfp`, or `synchronized`.

It is a compile-time error if a method declaration that contains the keyword `native` also contains `strictfp`.

> If two or more (distinct) method modifiers appear in a method declaration, it is customary, though not required, that they appear in the order consistent with that shown above in the production for *MethodModifier*.

8.4.3.1 `abstract` *Methods*

An `abstract` method declaration introduces the method as a member, providing its signature (§8.4.2), return type, and `throws` clause (if any), but does not provide an implementation.

The declaration of an `abstract` method *m* must appear directly within an `abstract` class (call it *A*) unless it occurs within an enum (§8.9); otherwise a compile-time error occurs.

Every subclass of *A* that is not `abstract` (§8.1.1.1) must provide an implementation for *m*, or a compile-time error occurs.

> It would be impossible for a subclass to implement a `private abstract` method, because `private` methods are not inherited by subclasses; therefore such a method could never be used.

An `abstract` class can override an `abstract` method by providing another `abstract` method declaration.

> This can provide a place to put a documentation comment, to refine the return type, or to declare that the set of checked exceptions (§11.2) that can be thrown by that method, when it is implemented by its subclasses, is to be more limited.

An instance method that is not `abstract` can be overridden by an `abstract` method.

Example 8.4.3.1-1. Abstract/Abstract Method Overriding

```
class BufferEmpty extends Exception {
    BufferEmpty() { super(); }
    BufferEmpty(String s) { super(s); }
}
class BufferError extends Exception {
    BufferError() { super(); }
    BufferError(String s) { super(s); }
}
interface Buffer {
    char get() throws BufferEmpty, BufferError;
}
abstract class InfiniteBuffer implements Buffer {
    public abstract char get() throws BufferError;
}
```

The overriding declaration of method `get` in class `InfiniteBuffer` states that method `get` in any subclass of `InfiniteBuffer` never throws a `BufferEmpty` exception, putatively because it generates the data in the buffer, and thus can never run out of data.

Example 8.4.3.1-2. Abstract/Non-Abstract Overriding

We can declare an abstract class Point that requires its subclasses to implement toString if they are to be complete, instantiable classes:

```
abstract class Point {
    int x, y;
    public abstract String toString();
}
```

This abstract declaration of toString overrides the non-abstract toString method of class Object. (Class Object is the implicit direct superclass of class Point.) Adding the code:

```
class ColoredPoint extends Point {
    int color;
    public String toString() {
        return super.toString() + ": color " + color;   // error
    }
}
```

results in a compile-time error because the invocation super.toString() refers to method toString in class Point, which is abstract and therefore cannot be invoked. Method toString of class Object can be made available to class ColoredPoint only if class Point explicitly makes it available through some other method, as in:

```
abstract class Point {
    int x, y;
    public abstract String toString();
    protected String objString() { return super.toString(); }
}
class ColoredPoint extends Point {
    int color;
    public String toString() {
        return objString() + ": color " + color;   // correct
    }
}
```

8.4.3.2   static *Methods*

A method that is declared static is called a *class method*.

It is a compile-time error to use the name of a type parameter of any surrounding declaration in the header or body of a class method.

A class method is always invoked without reference to a particular object. It is a compile-time error to attempt to reference the current object using the keyword this (§15.8.3) or the keyword super (§15.11.2).

A method that is not declared `static` is called an *instance method*, and sometimes called a non-`static` method.

An instance method is always invoked with respect to an object, which becomes the current object to which the keywords `this` and `super` refer during execution of the method body.

8.4.3.3 `final` *Methods*

A method can be declared `final` to prevent subclasses from overriding or hiding it.

It is a compile-time error to attempt to override or hide a `final` method.

A `private` method and all methods declared immediately within a `final` class (§8.1.1.2) behave as if they are `final`, since it is impossible to override them.

> At run time, a machine-code generator or optimizer can "inline" the body of a `final` method, replacing an invocation of the method with the code in its body. The inlining process must preserve the semantics of the method invocation. In particular, if the target of an instance method invocation is `null`, then a `NullPointerException` must be thrown even if the method is inlined. A Java compiler must ensure that the exception will be thrown at the correct point, so that the actual arguments to the method will be seen to have been evaluated in the correct order prior to the method invocation.
>
> Consider the example:
>
> ```
> final class Point {
>     int x, y;
>     void move(int dx, int dy) { x += dx; y += dy; }
> }
> class Test {
>     public static void main(String[] args) {
>         Point[] p = new Point[100];
>         for (int i = 0; i < p.length; i++) {
>             p[i] = new Point();
>             p[i].move(i, p.length-1-i);
>         }
>     }
> }
> ```
>
> Inlining the method `move` of class `Point` in method `main` would transform the `for` loop to the form:
>
> ```
> for (int i = 0; i < p.length; i++) {
>         p[i] = new Point();
>         Point pi = p[i];
>         int j = p.length-1-i;
>         pi.x += i;
>         pi.y += j;
> }
> ```

The loop might then be subject to further optimizations.

Such inlining cannot be done at compile time unless it can be guaranteed that `Test` and `Point` will always be recompiled together, so that whenever `Point` - and specifically its `move` method - changes, the code for `Test.main` will also be updated.

8.4.3.4   `native` *Methods*

A method that is `native` is implemented in platform-dependent code, typically written in another programming language such as C. The body of a `native` method is given as a semicolon only, indicating that the implementation is omitted, instead of a block.

For example, the class `RandomAccessFile` of the package `java.io` might declare the following `native` methods:

```
package java.io;
public class RandomAccessFile
    implements DataOutput, DataInput {
    . . .
    public native void open(String name, boolean writeable)
        throws IOException;
    public native int readBytes(byte[] b, int off, int len)
        throws IOException;
    public native void writeBytes(byte[] b, int off, int len)
        throws IOException;
    public native long getFilePointer() throws IOException;
    public native void seek(long pos) throws IOException;
    public native long length() throws IOException;
    public native void close() throws IOException;
}
```

8.4.3.5   `strictfp` *Methods*

The effect of the `strictfp` modifier is to make all `float` or `double` expressions within the method body be explicitly FP-strict (§15.4).

8.4.3.6   `synchronized` *Methods*

A `synchronized` method acquires a monitor (§17.1) before it executes.

For a class (`static`) method, the monitor associated with the `Class` object for the method's class is used.

For an instance method, the monitor associated with `this` (the object for which the method was invoked) is used.

Example 8.4.3.6-1. synchronized **Monitors**

These are the same monitors that can be used by the synchronized statement (§14.19).

Thus, the code:

```
class Test {
    int count;
    synchronized void bump() {
        count++;
    }
    static int classCount;
    static synchronized void classBump() {
        classCount++;
    }
}
```

has exactly the same effect as:

```
class BumpTest {
    int count;
    void bump() {
        synchronized (this) { count++; }
    }
    static int classCount;
    static void classBump() {
        try {
            synchronized (Class.forName("BumpTest")) {
                classCount++;
            }
        } catch (ClassNotFoundException e) {}
    }
}
```

Example 8.4.3.6-2. synchronized **Methods**

```
public class Box {
    private Object boxContents;
    public synchronized Object get() {
        Object contents = boxContents;
        boxContents = null;
        return contents;
    }
    public synchronized boolean put(Object contents) {
        if (boxContents != null) return false;
        boxContents = contents;
        return true;
    }
}
```

This program defines a class which is designed for concurrent use. Each instance of the class Box has an instance variable boxContents that can hold a reference to any object.

You can put an object in a `Box` by invoking `put`, which returns `false` if the box is already full. You can get something out of a `Box` by invoking `get`, which returns a null reference if the box is empty.

If `put` and `get` were not `synchronized`, and two threads were executing methods for the same instance of `Box` at the same time, then the code could misbehave. It might, for example, lose track of an object because two invocations to put occurred at the same time.

8.4.4   Generic Methods

A method is *generic* if it declares one or more type variables (§4.4).

These type variables are known as the *type parameters* of the method. The form of the type parameter section of a generic method is identical to the type parameter section of a generic class (§8.1.2).

A generic method declaration defines a set of methods, one for each possible invocation of the type parameter section by type arguments. Type arguments may not need to be provided explicitly when a generic method is invoked, as they can often be inferred (§15.12.2.7).

The scope and shadowing of a method's type parameter is specified in §6.3.

8.4.5   Method Return Type

The *result* of a method declaration either declares the type of value that the method returns (the *return type*), or uses the keyword `void` to indicate that the method does not return a value.

> *Result:*
>   *Type*
>   `void`

Return types may vary among methods that override each other if the return types are reference types. The notion of return-type-substitutability supports *covariant returns*, that is, the specialization of the return type to a subtype.

A method declaration d_1 with return type R_1 is *return-type-substitutable* for another method d_2 with return type R_2, if and only if the following conditions hold:

- If R_1 is `void` then R_2 is `void`.

- If R_1 is a primitive type, then R_2 is identical to R_1.

- If R_1 is a reference type then:

* R_1 is either a subtype of R_2 or R_1 can be converted to a subtype of R_2 by unchecked conversion (§5.1.9), or

* $R_1 = |R_2|$

An unchecked conversion is allowed in the definition, despite being unsound, as a special allowance to allow smooth migration from non-generic to generic code. If an unchecked conversion is used to determine that R_1 is return-type-substitutable for R_2, then R_1 is necessarily not a subtype of R_2 and the rules for overriding (§8.4.8.3, §9.4.1) will require a compile-time unchecked warning.

8.4.6 Method Throws

A `throws` clause is used to declare any checked exception classes (§11.1.1) that the statements in a method or constructor body can throw (§11.2.2).

Throws:
　　throws *ExceptionTypeList*

ExceptionTypeList:
　ExceptionType
　ExceptionTypeList , *ExceptionType*

ExceptionType:
　TypeName
　TypeVariable

It is a compile-time error if any *ExceptionType* mentioned in a `throws` clause is not a subtype (§4.10) of `Throwable`.

Type variables are allowed in a `throws` clause even though they are not allowed in a `catch` clause.

Example 8.4.6-1. Type Variables as Thrown Exception Types

```
import java.io.FileNotFoundException;
interface PrivilegedExceptionAction<E extends Exception> {
    void run() throws E;
}
class AccessController {
    public static <E extends Exception>
    Object doPrivileged(PrivilegedExceptionAction<E> action) throws E {
        action.run();
        return "success";
    }
}
```

```
class Test {
    public static void main(String[] args) {
        try {
            AccessController.doPrivileged(
                new PrivilegedExceptionAction<FileNotFoundException>() {
                    public void run() throws FileNotFoundException {
                        // ... delete a file ...
                    }
                });
        } catch (FileNotFoundException f) { /* Do something */ }
    }
}
```

It is permitted but not required to mention unchecked exception classes (§11.1.1) in a `throws` clause.

The relationship between a `throws` clause and the exception checking for a method or constructor body is specified in §11.2.3.

> Essentially, for each checked exception that can result from execution of the body of a method or constructor, a compile-time error occurs unless its exception type or a supertype of its exception type is mentioned in a `throws` clause in the declaration of the method or constructor.
>
> The requirement to declare checked exceptions allows a Java compiler to ensure that code for handling such error conditions has been included. Methods or constructors that fail to handle exceptional conditions thrown as checked exceptions in their bodies will normally cause compile-time errors if they lack proper exception types in their `throws` clauses. The Java programming language thus encourages a programming style where rare and otherwise truly exceptional conditions are documented in this way.

The relationship between the `throws` clause of a method and the `throws` clauses of overridden or hidden methods is specified in §8.4.8.3.

8.4.7   Method Body

A *method body* is either a block of code that implements the method or simply a semicolon, indicating the lack of an implementation.

> *MethodBody:*
>   *Block*
>   *;*

It is a compile-time error if a method declaration is either `abstract` or `native` and has a block for its body.

It is a compile-time error if a method declaration is neither `abstract` nor `native` and has a semicolon for its body.

If an implementation is to be provided for a method declared `void`, but the implementation requires no executable code, the method body should be written as a block that contains no statements: "`{ }`".

If a method is declared `void`, then its body must not contain any `return` statement (§14.17) that has an *Expression*, or a compile-time error occurs.

If a method is declared to have a return type, then every `return` statement (§14.17) in its body must have an *Expression*, or a compile-time error occurs.

If a method is declared to have a return type, then a compile-time error occurs if the body of the method can complete normally (§14.1).

In other words, a method with a return type must return only by using a `return` statement that provides a value return; it is not allowed to "drop off the end of its body".

Note that it is possible for a method to have a declared return type and yet contain no `return` statements. Here is one example:

```
class DizzyDean {
    int pitch() { throw new RuntimeException("90 mph?!"); }
}
```

8.4.8 Inheritance, Overriding, and Hiding

A class c *inherits* from its direct superclass and direct superinterfaces all `abstract` and non-`abstract` methods of the superclass and superinterfaces that are `public`, `protected`, or declared with default access in the same package as c, and are neither overridden (§8.4.8.1) nor hidden (§8.4.8.2) by a declaration in the class.

Methods are overridden or hidden on a signature-by-signature basis.

If, for example, a class declares two `public` methods with the same name (§8.4.9), and a subclass overrides one of them, the subclass still inherits the other method.

If the method not inherited is declared in a class, or the method not inherited is declared in an interface and the new declaration is `abstract`, then the new declaration is said to *override* it.

If the method not inherited is `abstract` and the new declaration is not `abstract`, then the new declaration is said to *implement* it.

8.4.8.1 *Overriding (by Instance Methods)*

An instance method m_1, declared in class c, overrides another instance method m_2, declared in class A iff all of the following are true:

- C is a subclass of A.

- The signature of m_1 is a subsignature (§8.4.2) of the signature of m_2.

- Either:

  • m_2 is public, protected, or declared with default access in the same package as C, or

  • m_1 overrides a method m_3 (m_3 distinct from m_1, m_3 distinct from m_2), such that m_3 overrides m_2.

Moreover, if m_1 is not abstract, then m_1 is said to *implement* any and all declarations of abstract methods that it overrides.

> The signature of an overriding method may differ from the overridden one if a formal parameter in one of the methods has a raw type, while the corresponding parameter in the other has a parameterized type.

> The rules allow the signature of the overriding method to differ from the overridden one, to accommodate migration of pre-existing code to take advantage of generics. See §8.4.2 for further analysis.

It is a compile-time error if an instance method overrides a static method.

> In this respect, overriding of methods differs from hiding of fields (§8.3), for it is permissible for an instance variable to hide a static variable.

An overridden method can be accessed by using a method invocation expression (§15.12) that contains the keyword super.

A qualified name or a cast to a superclass type is not effective in attempting to access an overridden method; in this respect, overriding of methods differs from hiding of fields (§15.12.4.4).

The presence or absence of the strictfp modifier has absolutely no effect on the rules for overriding methods and implementing abstract methods. For example, it is permitted for a method that is not FP-strict to override an FP-strict method and it is permitted for an FP-strict method to override a method that is not FP-strict.

Example 8.4.8.1-1. Overriding

```
class Point {
    int x = 0, y = 0;
    void move(int dx, int dy) { x += dx; y += dy; }
}
class SlowPoint extends Point {
    int xLimit, yLimit;
    void move(int dx, int dy) {
        super.move(limit(dx, xLimit), limit(dy, yLimit));
```

```
        }
        static int limit(int d, int limit) {
            return d > limit ? limit : d < -limit ? -limit : d;
        }
    }
```

Here, the class `SlowPoint` overrides the declarations of method `move` of class `Point` with its own `move` method, which limits the distance that the point can move on each invocation of the method. When the `move` method is invoked for an instance of class `SlowPoint`, the overriding definition in class `SlowPoint` will always be called, even if the reference to the `SlowPoint` object is taken from a variable whose type is `Point`.

Example 8.4.8.1-2. Overriding

Overriding makes it easy for subclasses to extend the behavior of an existing class, as shown in this example:

```
import java.io.OutputStream;
import java.io.IOException;

class BufferOutput {
    private OutputStream o;
    BufferOutput(OutputStream o) { this.o = o; }
    protected byte[] buf = new byte[512];
    protected int pos = 0;
    public void putchar(char c) throws IOException {
        if (pos == buf.length) flush();
        buf[pos++] = (byte)c;
    }
    public void putstr(String s) throws IOException {
        for (int i = 0; i < s.length(); i++)
            putchar(s.charAt(i));
    }
    public void flush() throws IOException {
        o.write(buf, 0, pos);
        pos = 0;
    }
}
class LineBufferOutput extends BufferOutput {
    LineBufferOutput(OutputStream o) { super(o); }
    public void putchar(char c) throws IOException {
        super.putchar(c);
        if (c == '\n') flush();
    }
}
class Test {
    public static void main(String[] args) throws IOException {
        LineBufferOutput lbo = new LineBufferOutput(System.out);
        lbo.putstr("lbo\nlbo");
        System.out.print("print\n");
        lbo.putstr("\n");
    }
```

```
}
```

This program produces the output:

```
lbo
print
lbo
```

The class `BufferOutput` implements a very simple buffered version of an `OutputStream`, flushing the output when the buffer is full or `flush` is invoked. The subclass `LineBufferOutput` declares only a constructor and a single method `putchar`, which overrides the method `putchar` of `BufferOutput`. It inherits the methods `putstr` and `flush` from class `BufferOutput`.

In the `putchar` method of a `LineBufferOutput` object, if the character argument is a newline, then it invokes the `flush` method. The critical point about overriding in this example is that the method `putstr`, which is declared in class `BufferOutput`, invokes the `putchar` method defined by the current object `this`, which is not necessarily the `putchar` method declared in class `BufferOutput`.

Thus, when `putstr` is invoked in `main` using the `LineBufferOutput` object `lbo`, the invocation of `putchar` in the body of the `putstr` method is an invocation of the `putchar` of the object `lbo`, the overriding declaration of `putchar` that checks for a newline. This allows a subclass of `BufferOutput` to change the behavior of the `putstr` method without redefining it.

Documentation for a class such as `BufferOutput`, which is designed to be extended, should clearly indicate what is the contract between the class and its subclasses, and should clearly indicate that subclasses may override the `putchar` method in this way. The implementor of the `BufferOutput` class would not, therefore, want to change the implementation of `putstr` in a future implementation of `BufferOutput` not to use the method `putchar`, because this would break the pre-existing contract with subclasses. See the discussion of binary compatibility in §13, especially §13.2.

8.4.8.2 *Hiding (by Class Methods)*

If a class declares a `static` method *m*, then the declaration *m* is said to *hide* any method *m'*, where the signature of *m* is a subsignature (§8.4.2) of the signature of *m'*, in the superclasses and superinterfaces of the class that would otherwise be accessible to code in the class.

It is a compile-time error if a `static` method hides an instance method.

In this respect, hiding of methods differs from hiding of fields (§8.3), for it is permissible for a `static` variable to hide an instance variable. Hiding is also distinct from shadowing (§6.4.1) and obscuring (§6.4.2).

A hidden method can be accessed by using a qualified name or by using a method invocation expression (§15.12) that contains the keyword `super` or a cast to a superclass type.

In this respect, hiding of methods is similar to hiding of fields.

Example 8.4.8.2-1. Invocation of Hidden Class Methods

A class (`static`) method that is hidden can be invoked by using a reference whose type is the class that actually contains the declaration of the method. In this respect, hiding of `static` methods is different from overriding of instance methods. The example:

```
class Super {
    static String greeting() { return "Goodnight"; }
    String name() { return "Richard"; }
}
class Sub extends Super {
    static String greeting() { return "Hello"; }
    String name() { return "Dick"; }
}
class Test {
    public static void main(String[] args) {
        Super s = new Sub();
        System.out.println(s.greeting() + ", " + s.name());
    }
}
```

produces the output:

```
Goodnight, Dick
```

because the invocation of `greeting` uses the type of `s`, namely `Super`, to figure out, at compile time, which class method to invoke, whereas the invocation of `name` uses the class of `s`, namely `Sub`, to figure out, at run time, which instance method to invoke.

8.4.8.3 *Requirements in Overriding and Hiding*

If a method declaration d_1 with return type R_1 overrides or hides the declaration of another method d_2 with return type R_2, then d_1 must be return-type-substitutable (§8.4.5) for d_2, or a compile-time error occurs.

This rule allows for covariant return types - refining the return type of a method when overriding it.

If R_1 is not a subtype of R_2, a compile-time unchecked warning occurs unless suppressed by the `SuppressWarnings` annotation (§9.6.3.5).

A method that overrides or hides another method, including methods that implement `abstract` methods defined in interfaces, may not be declared to throw more checked exceptions than the overridden or hidden method.

> In this respect, overriding of methods differs from hiding of fields (§8.3), for it is permissible for a field to hide a field of another type.

More precisely, suppose that B is a class or interface, and A is a superclass or superinterface of B, and a method declaration n in B overrides or hides a method declaration m in A. Then:

- If n has a `throws` clause that mentions any checked exception types, then m must have a `throws` clause, or a compile-time error occurs.

- For every checked exception type listed in the `throws` clause of n, that same exception class or one of its supertypes must occur in the erasure (§4.6) of the `throws` clause of m; otherwise, a compile-time error occurs.

- If the unerased `throws` clause of m does not contain a supertype of each exception type in the `throws` clause of n, a compile-time unchecked warning occurs.

It is a compile-time error if a type declaration T has a member method m_1 and there exists a method m_2 declared in T or a supertype of T such that all of the following conditions hold:

- m_1 and m_2 have the same name.

- m_2 is accessible from T.

- The signature of m_1 is not a subsignature (§8.4.2) of the signature of m_2.

- The signature of m_1 or some method m_1 overrides (directly or indirectly) has the same erasure as the signature of m_2 or some method m_2 overrides (directly or indirectly).

> These restrictions are necessary because generics are implemented via erasure. The rule above implies that methods declared in the same class with the same name must have different erasures. It also implies that a type declaration cannot implement or extend two distinct invocations of the same generic interface.

The access modifier (§6.6) of an overriding or hiding method must provide at least as much access as the overridden or hidden method, as follows:

- If the overridden or hidden method is `public`, then the overriding or hiding method must be `public`; otherwise, a compile-time error occurs.

- If the overridden or hidden method is `protected`, then the overriding or hiding method must be `protected` or `public`; otherwise, a compile-time error occurs.

- If the overridden or hidden method has default (package) access, then the overriding or hiding method must *not* be `private`; otherwise, a compile-time error occurs.

  Note that a `private` method cannot be hidden or overridden in the technical sense of those terms. This means that a subclass can declare a method with the same signature as a `private` method in one of its superclasses, and there is no requirement that the return type or `throws` clause of such a method bear any relationship to those of the `private` method in the superclass.

Example 8.4.8.3-1. Covariant Return Types

The following declarations are legal in the Java programming language from Java SE 5.0 onwards:

```
class C implements Cloneable {
    C copy() throws CloneNotSupportedException {
        return (C)clone();
    }
}
class D extends C implements Cloneable {
    D copy() throws CloneNotSupportedException {
        return (D)clone();
    }
}
```

The relaxed rule for overriding also allows one to relax the conditions on abstract classes implementing interfaces.

Example 8.4.8.3-2. Unchecked Warning from Return Type

Consider:

```
class StringSorter {
    // turns a collection of strings into a sorted list
    List toList(Collection c) {...}
}
```

and assume that someone subclasses `StringSorter`:

```
class Overrider extends StringSorter {
    List toList(Collection c) {...}
}
```

Now, at some point the author of `StringSorter` decides to generify the code:

```
class StringSorter {
    // turns a collection of strings into a sorted list
    List<String> toList(Collection<String> c) {...}
```

235

```
    }
```

An unchecked warning would be given when compiling `Overrider` against the new definition of `StringSorter` because the return type of `Overrider.toList` is `List`, which is not a subtype of the return type of the overridden method, `List<String>`.

Example 8.4.8.3-3. Incorrect Overriding because of `throws`

This program uses the usual and conventional form for declaring a new exception type, in its declaration of the class `BadPointException`:

```
class BadPointException extends Exception {
    BadPointException() { super(); }
    BadPointException(String s) { super(s); }
}
class Point {
    int x, y;
    void move(int dx, int dy) { x += dx; y += dy; }
}
class CheckedPoint extends Point {
    void move(int dx, int dy) throws BadPointException {
        if ((x + dx) < 0 || (y + dy) < 0)
            throw new BadPointException();
        x += dx; y += dy;
    }
}
```

The program results in a compile-time error, because the override of method `move` in class `CheckedPoint` declares that it will throw a checked exception that the `move` in class `Point` has not declared. If this were not considered an error, an invoker of the method `move` on a reference of type `Point` could find the contract between it and `Point` broken if this exception were thrown.

Removing the `throws` clause does not help:

```
class CheckedPoint extends Point {
    void move(int dx, int dy) {
        if ((x + dx) < 0 || (y + dy) < 0)
            throw new BadPointException();
        x += dx; y += dy;
    }
}
```

A different compile-time error now occurs, because the body of the method `move` cannot throw a checked exception, namely `BadPointException`, that does not appear in the `throws` clause for `move`.

Example 8.4.8.3-4. Erasure Affects Overriding

A class cannot have two member methods with the same name and type erasure:

```
class C<T> {
    T id (T x) {...}
}
class D extends C<String> {
    Object id(Object x) {...}
}
```

This is illegal since `D.id(Object)` is a member of `D`, `C<String>.id(String)` is declared in a supertype of `D`, and:

- The two methods have the same name, `id`

- `C<String>.id(String)` is accessible to `D`

- The signature of `D.id(Object)` is not a subsignature of that of `C<String>.id(String)`

- The two methods have the same erasure

Two different methods of a class may not override methods with the same erasure:

```
class C<T> {
    T id(T x) {...}
}
interface I<T> {
    T id(T x);
}
class D extends C<String> implements I<Integer> {
    public String  id(String x)  {...}
    public Integer id(Integer x) {...}
}
```

This is also illegal, since `D.id(String)` is a member of `D`, `D.id(Integer)` is declared in `D`, and:

- The two methods have the same name, `id`

- `D.id(Integer)` is accessible to `D`

- The two methods have different signatures (and neither is a subsignature of the other)

- `D.id(String)` overrides `C<String>.id(String)` and `D.id(Integer)` overrides `I.id(Integer)` yet the two overridden methods have the same erasure

8.4.8.4 *Inheriting Methods with Override-Equivalent Signatures*

It is possible for a class to inherit multiple methods with override-equivalent signatures (§8.4.2).

It is a compile-time error if a class *c* inherits a concrete method whose signature is a subsignature of another concrete method inherited by *c*. This can happen if a superclass is generic, and it has two methods that were distinct in the generic declaration, but have the same signature in the particular invocation used.

Otherwise, there are two possible cases:

- If one of the inherited methods is not `abstract`, then there are two subcases:

  - If the method that is not `abstract` is `static`, a compile-time error occurs.

  - Otherwise, the method that is not `abstract` is considered to override, and therefore to implement, all the other methods on behalf of the class that inherits it.

    If the signature of the non-`abstract` method is not a subsignature of each of the other inherited methods, a compile-time unchecked warning occurs unless suppressed by the `SuppressWarnings` annotation (§9.6.3.5).

    If the return type of the non-`abstract` method is not a subtype of the return type of any of the other inherited methods, a compile-time unchecked warning occurs unless suppressed by the `SuppressWarnings` annotation (§9.6.3.5).

    A compile-time error occurs if the return type of the non-`abstract` method is not return-type-substitutable (§8.4.5) for each of the other inherited methods.

    A compile-time error occurs if the inherited method that is not `abstract` has a `throws` clause that conflicts (§8.4.6) with that of any other of the inherited methods.

- If all the inherited methods are `abstract`, then the class is necessarily an `abstract` class and is considered to inherit all the `abstract` methods.

  One of the inherited methods must be return-type-substitutable for every other inherited method; otherwise, a compile-time error occurs. (The `throws` clauses do not cause errors in this case.)

There might be several paths by which the same method declaration might be inherited from an interface. This fact causes no difficulty and never, of itself, results in a compile-time error.

8.4.9   Overloading

If two methods of a class (whether both declared in the same class, or both inherited by a class, or one declared and one inherited) have the same name but signatures that are not override-equivalent, then the method name is said to be *overloaded*.

This fact causes no difficulty and never of itself results in a compile-time error. There is no required relationship between the return types or between the `throws` clauses of two methods with the same name, unless their signatures are override-equivalent.

When a method is invoked (§15.12), the number of actual arguments (and any explicit type arguments) and the compile-time types of the arguments are used, at compile time, to determine the signature of the method that will be invoked (§15.12.2). If the method that is to be invoked is an instance method, the actual method to be invoked will be determined at run time, using dynamic method lookup (§15.12.4).

Example 8.4.9-1. Overloading

```
class Point {
    float x, y;
    void move(int dx, int dy) { x += dx; y += dy; }
    void move(float dx, float dy) { x += dx; y += dy; }
    public String toString() { return "("+x+","+y+")"; }
}
```

Here, the class `Point` has two members that are methods with the same name, `move`. The overloaded `move` method of class `Point` chosen for any particular method invocation is determined at compile time by the overloading resolution procedure given in §15.12.

In total, the members of the class `Point` are the `float` instance variables x and y declared in `Point`, the two declared `move` methods, the declared `toString` method, and the members that `Point` inherits from its implicit direct superclass `Object` (§4.3.2), such as the method `hashCode`. Note that `Point` does not inherit the `toString` method of class `Object` because that method is overridden by the declaration of the `toString` method in class `Point`.

Example 8.4.9-2. Overloading, Overriding, and Hiding

```
class Point {
    int x = 0, y = 0;
    void move(int dx, int dy) { x += dx; y += dy; }
    int color;
}
class RealPoint extends Point {
    float x = 0.0f, y = 0.0f;
    void move(int dx, int dy) { move((float)dx, (float)dy); }
    void move(float dx, float dy) { x += dx; y += dy; }
}
```

Here, the class `RealPoint` hides the declarations of the `int` instance variables x and y of class `Point` with its own `float` instance variables x and y, and overrides the method `move` of class `Point` with its own `move` method. It also overloads the name `move` with another method with a different signature (§8.4.2).

In this example, the members of the class `RealPoint` include the instance variable `color` inherited from the class `Point`, the `float` instance variables x and y declared in `RealPoint`, and the two `move` methods declared in `RealPoint`.

Which of these overloaded `move` methods of class `RealPoint` will be chosen for any particular method invocation will be determined at compile time by the overloading resolution procedure described in §15.12.

This following program is an extended variation of the preceding program:

```
class Point {
    int x = 0, y = 0, color;
    void move(int dx, int dy) { x += dx; y += dy; }
    int getX() { return x; }
    int getY() { return y; }
}
class RealPoint extends Point {
    float x - 0.0f, y = 0.0f;
    void move(int dx, int dy) { move((float)dx, (float)dy); }
    void move(float dx, float dy) { x += dx; y += dy; }
    float getX() { return x; }
    float getY() { return y; }
}
```

Here, the class `Point` provides methods `getX` and `getY` that return the values of its fields x and y; the class `RealPoint` then overrides these methods by declaring methods with the same signature. The result is two errors at compile time, one for each method, because the return types do not match; the methods in class `Point` return values of type `int`, but the wanna-be overriding methods in class `RealPoint` return values of type `float`.

This program corrects the errors of the preceding program:

```
class Point {
    int x = 0, y = 0;
    void move(int dx, int dy) { x += dx; y += dy; }
    int getX() { return x; }
    int getY() { return y; }
    int color;
}
class RealPoint extends Point {
    float x = 0.0f, y = 0.0f;
    void move(int dx, int dy) { move((float)dx, (float)dy); }
    void move(float dx, float dy) { x += dx; y += dy; }
    int getX() { return (int)Math.floor(x); }
    int getY() { return (int)Math.floor(y); }
}
```

Here, the overriding methods `getX` and `getY` in class `RealPoint` have the same return types as the methods of class `Point` that they override, so this code can be successfully compiled.

Consider, then, this test program:

```
class Test {
    public static void main(String[] args) {
        RealPoint rp = new RealPoint();
        Point p = rp;
        rp.move(1.71828f, 4.14159f);
        p.move(1, -1);
        show(p.x, p.y);
        show(rp.x, rp.y);
        show(p.getX(), p.getY());
        show(rp.getX(), rp.getY());
    }
    static void show(int x, int y) {
        System.out.println("(" + x + ", " + y + ")");
    }
    static void show(float x, float y) {
        System.out.println("(" + x + ", " + y + ")");
    }
}
```

The output from this program is:

```
(0, 0)
(2.7182798, 3.14159)
(2, 3)
(2, 3)
```

The first line of output illustrates the fact that an instance of RealPoint actually contains the two integer fields declared in class Point; it is just that their names are hidden from code that occurs within the declaration of class RealPoint (and those of any subclasses it might have). When a reference to an instance of class RealPoint in a variable of type Point is used to access the field x, the integer field x declared in class Point is accessed. The fact that its value is zero indicates that the method invocation p.move(1, -1) did not invoke the method move of class Point; instead, it invoked the overriding method move of class RealPoint.

The second line of output shows that the field access rp.x refers to the field x declared in class RealPoint. This field is of type float, and this second line of output accordingly displays floating-point values. Incidentally, this also illustrates the fact that the method name show is overloaded; the types of the arguments in the method invocation dictate which of the two definitions will be invoked.

The last two lines of output show that the method invocations p.getX() and rp.getX() each invoke the getX method declared in class RealPoint. Indeed, there is no way to invoke the getX method of class Point for an instance of class RealPoint from outside the body of RealPoint, no matter what the type of the variable we may use to hold the reference to the object. Thus, we see that fields and methods behave differently: hiding is different from overriding.

8.5   Member Type Declarations

A *member class* is a class whose declaration is directly enclosed in another class or interface declaration.

A *member interface* is an interface whose declaration is directly enclosed in another class or interface declaration.

The accessibility of a member type in a class declaration is specified in §6.6.

It is a compile-time error if a member type declaration has more than one of the access modifiers `public`, `protected`, and `private`.

Member type declarations may have annotation modifiers (§9.7) like any other type or member declaration.

The scope and shadowing of a member type is specified in §6.3 and §6.4.

If a class declares a member type with a certain name, then the declaration of that type is said to *hide* any and all accessible declarations of member types with the same name in superclasses and superinterfaces of the class.

> In this respect, hiding of member types is similar to hiding of fields (§8.3).

A class inherits from its direct superclass and direct superinterfaces all the non-`private` member types of the superclass and superinterfaces that are both accessible to code in the class and not hidden by a declaration in the class.

A class may inherit two or more type declarations with the same name, either from two interfaces or from its superclass and an interface. It is a compile-time error to attempt to refer to any ambiguously inherited class or interface by its simple name.

If the same type declaration is inherited from an interface by multiple paths, the class or interface is considered to be inherited only once. It may be referred to by its simple name without ambiguity.

8.5.1   Static Member Type Declarations

The `static` keyword may modify the declaration of a member type C within the body of a non-inner class or interface T. Its effect is to declare that C is not an inner class. Just as a `static` method of T has no current instance of T in its body, C also has no current instance of T, nor does it have any lexically enclosing instances.

It is a compile-time error if a `static` class contains a usage of a non-`static` member of an enclosing class.

A member interface is implicitly `static` (§9.1.1). It is permitted for the declaration of a member interface to redundantly specify the `static` modifier.

8.6 Instance Initializers

An *instance initializer* declared in a class is executed when an instance of the class is created (§12.5, §15.9, §8.8.7.1).

> *InstanceInitializer:*
>   *Block*

It is a compile-time error if an instance initializer cannot complete normally (§14.21).

It is a compile-time error if a `return` statement (§14.17) appears anywhere within an instance initializer.

Instance initializers are permitted to refer to the current object via the keyword `this` (§15.8.3), to use the keyword `super` (§15.11.2, §15.12), and to use any type variables in scope.

> Use of instance variables whose declarations appear textually after the use is sometimes restricted, even though these instance variables are in scope. See §8.3.2.3 for the precise rules governing forward reference to instance variables.

Exception checking for an instance initializer is specified in §11.2.3.

8.7 Static Initializers

A *static initializer* declared in a class is executed when the class is initialized (§12.4.2). Together with any field initializers for class variables (§8.3.2), static initializers may be used to initialize the class variables of the class.

> *StaticInitializer:*
>   `static` *Block*

It is a compile-time error if a static initializer cannot complete normally (§14.21).

It is a compile-time error if a `return` statement (§14.17) appears anywhere within a static initializer.

It is a compile-time error if the keyword `this` (§15.8.3) or the keyword `super` (§15.11, §15.12) or any type variable declared outside the static initializer, appears anywhere within a static initializer.

> Use of class variables whose declarations appear textually after the use is sometimes restricted, even though these class variables are in scope. See §8.3.2.3 for the precise rules governing forward reference to class variables.

Exception checking for a static initializer is specified in §11.2.3.

8.8   Constructor Declarations

A *constructor* is used in the creation of an object that is an instance of a class (§12.5, §15.9).

> *ConstructorDeclaration:*
>   *ConstructorModifiers$_{opt}$ ConstructorDeclarator*
>   *Throws$_{opt}$ ConstructorBody*
>
> *ConstructorDeclarator:*
>   *TypeParameters$_{opt}$ SimpleTypeName (FormalParameterList$_{opt}$)*

The *SimpleTypeName* in the *ConstructorDeclarator* must be the simple name of the class that contains the constructor declaration; otherwise a compile-time error occurs.

In all other respects, the constructor declaration looks just like a method declaration that has no result type.

Constructor declarations are not members. They are never inherited and therefore are not subject to hiding or overriding.

Example 8.8-1. Constructor Declarations

```
class Point {
    int x, y;
    Point(int x, int y) { this.x = x; this.y = y; }
}
```

Constructors are invoked by class instance creation expressions (§15.9), by the conversions and concatenations caused by the string concatenation operator + (§15.18.1), and by explicit constructor invocations from other constructors (§8.8.7).

Constructors are never invoked by method invocation expressions (§15.12).

Access to constructors is governed by access modifiers (§6.6).

> This is useful, for example, in preventing instantiation by declaring an inaccessible constructor (§8.8.10).

8.8.1   Formal Parameters and Type Parameters

The formal parameters and type parameters of a constructor are identical in syntax and semantics to those of a method (§8.4.1).

8.8.2   Constructor Signature

It is a compile-time error to declare two constructors with override-equivalent signatures (§8.4.2) in a class.

It is a compile-time error to declare two constructors whose signatures have the same erasure (§4.6) in a class.

8.8.3   Constructor Modifiers

> *ConstructorModifiers:*
>   *ConstructorModifier*
>   *ConstructorModifiers ConstructorModifier*
>
> *ConstructorModifier: one of*
>   *Annotation* `public` `protected` `private`

If an annotation `a` (§9.7) on a constructor corresponds to an annotation type `T` (§9.6), and `T` has a (meta-)annotation `m` that corresponds to `java.lang.annotation.Target`, then `m` must have an element whose value is `java.lang.annotation.ElementType.CONSTRUCTOR`, or a compile-time error occurs.

> The access modifiers `public`, `protected`, and `private` are discussed in §6.6.

It is a compile-time error if the same modifier appears more than once in a constructor declaration, or if a constructor declaration has more than one of the access modifiers `public`, `protected`, and `private`.

It is a compile-time error if the constructor of an enum type (§8.9) is declared `public` or `protected`.

If no access modifier is specified for the constructor of a normal class, the constructor has default access.

If no access modifier is specified for the constructor of an enum type, the constructor is `private`.

> If two or more (distinct) method modifiers appear in a method declaration, it is customary, though not required, that they appear in the order consistent with that shown above in the production for *MethodModifier*.
>
> Unlike methods, a constructor cannot be `abstract`, `static`, `final`, `native`, `strictfp`, or `synchronized`:
>
> - A constructor is not inherited, so there is no need to declare it `final`.
> - An `abstract` constructor could never be implemented.
> - A constructor is always invoked with respect to an object, so it makes no sense for a constructor to be `static`.
> - There is no practical need for a constructor to be `synchronized`, because it would lock the object under construction, which is normally not made available to other threads until all constructors for the object have completed their work.
> - The lack of `native` constructors is an arbitrary language design choice that makes it easy for an implementation of the Java Virtual Machine to verify that superclass constructors are always properly invoked during object creation.
> - The inability to declare a constructor as `strictfp` (in contrast to a method (§8.4.3)) is an intentional language design choice; it effectively ensures that a constructor is FP-strict if and only if its class is FP-strict (§15.4).

8.8.4   Generic Constructors

It is possible for a constructor to be declared generic, independently of whether the class the constructor is declared in is itself generic.

A constructor is *generic* if it declares one or more type variables (§4.4).

These type variables are known as the *type parameters* of the constructor. The form of the type parameter section of a generic constructor is identical to the type parameter section of a generic class (§8.1.2).

A generic constructor declaration defines a set of constructors, one for each possible invocation of the type parameter section by type arguments. Type arguments may not need to be provided explicitly when a generic constructor is invoked, as they can often by inferred (§15.12.2.7).

The scope and shadowing of a constructor's type parameter is specified in §6.3 and §6.4.

8.8.5 Constructor Throws

The `throws` clause for a constructor is identical in structure and behavior to the `throws` clause for a method (§8.4.6).

8.8.6 The Type of a Constructor

The type of a constructor consists of its signature and the exception types given its `throws` clause.

8.8.7 Constructor Body

The first statement of a constructor body may be an explicit invocation of another constructor of the same class or of the direct superclass (§8.8.7.1).

> *ConstructorBody:*
>   { *ExplicitConstructorInvocation*$_{opt}$ *BlockStatements*$_{opt}$ }

It is a compile-time error for a constructor to directly or indirectly invoke itself through a series of one or more explicit constructor invocations involving `this`.

If the constructor is a constructor for an enum type (§8.9), it is a compile-time error for it to invoke the superclass constructor explicitly.

If a constructor body does not begin with an explicit constructor invocation and the constructor being declared is not part of the primordial class `Object`, then the constructor body implicitly begins with a superclass constructor invocation `"super();"`, an invocation of the constructor of its direct superclass that takes no arguments.

Except for the possibility of explicit constructor invocations, the body of a constructor is like the body of a method (§8.4.7).

A `return` statement (§14.17) may be used in the body of a constructor if it does not include an expression.

Example 8.8.7-1. Constructor Bodies

```
class Point {
    int x, y;
    Point(int x, int y) { this.x = x; this.y = y; }
}
class ColoredPoint extends Point {
    static final int WHITE = 0, BLACK = 1;
    int color;
```

```
ColoredPoint(int x, int y) {
    this(x, y, WHITE);
}
ColoredPoint(int x, int y, int color) {
    super(x, y);
    this.color = color;
}
}
```

Here, the first constructor of `ColoredPoint` invokes the second, providing an additional argument; the second constructor of `ColoredPoint` invokes the constructor of its superclass `Point`, passing along the coordinates.

8.8.7.1   *Explicit Constructor Invocations*

ExplicitConstructorInvocation:
  NonWildTypeArguments$_{opt}$ this (*ArgumentList$_{opt}$*) ;
  NonWildTypeArguments$_{opt}$ super (*ArgumentList$_{opt}$*) ;
  Primary . NonWildTypeArguments$_{opt}$ super (*ArgumentList$_{opt}$*) ;

NonWildTypeArguments:
  < ReferenceTypeList >

ReferenceTypeList:
  ReferenceType
  ReferenceTypeList , ReferenceType

Explicit constructor invocation statements can be divided into two kinds:

- *Alternate constructor invocations* begin with the keyword `this` (possibly prefaced with explicit type arguments). They are used to invoke an alternate constructor of the same class.

- *Superclass constructor invocations* begin with either the keyword `super` (possibly prefaced with explicit type arguments) or a *Primary* expression. They are used to invoke a constructor of the direct superclass.

Superclass constructor invocations may be subdivided:

  - *Unqualified superclass constructor invocations* begin with the keyword `super` (possibly prefaced with explicit type arguments).

  - *Qualified superclass constructor invocations* begin with a *Primary* expression.

    They allow a subclass constructor to explicitly specify the newly created object's immediately enclosing instance with respect to the direct superclass (§8.1.3). This may be necessary when the superclass is an inner class.

An explicit constructor invocation statement in a constructor body may not refer to any instance variables or instance methods or inner classes declared in this class or any superclass, or use `this` or `super` in any expression; otherwise, a compile-time error occurs.

The exception types that an explicit constructor invocation statement can throw are specified in §11.2.2.

Example 8.8.7.1-1. Qualified Superclass Constructor Invocation

```
class Outer {
    class Inner {}
}
class ChildOfInner extends Outer.Inner {
    ChildOfInner() { (new Outer()).super(); }
}
```

Example 8.8.7.1-2. Restrictions on Explicit Constructor Invocation Statements

If the first constructor of `ColoredPoint` in the example from §8.8.7 were changed as follows:

```
class Point {
    int x, y;
    Point(int x, int y) { this.x = x; this.y = y; }
}
class ColoredPoint extends Point {
    static final int WHITE = 0, BLACK = 1;
    int color;
    ColoredPoint(int x, int y) {
        this(x, y, color);   // Changed to color from WHITE
    }
    ColoredPoint(int x, int y, int color) {
        super(x, y);
        this.color = color;
    }
}
```

then a compile-time error would occur, because the instance variable `color` cannot be used by a explicit constructor invocation statement.

Let c be the class being instantiated, and let s be the direct superclass of c.

It is a compile-time error if s is not accessible (§6.6).

If a superclass constructor invocation statement is qualified, then:

- If s is not an inner class, or if the declaration of s occurs in a static context, then a compile-time error occurs.

- Otherwise, let p be the *Primary* expression immediately preceding ".super". Let o be the innermost lexically enclosing class of s.

  It is a compile-time error if the type of p is not o or a subclass of o, or if the type of p is not accessible (§6.6).

If a superclass constructor invocation statement is unqualified, and if s is an inner member class, then it is a compile-time error if s is not a member of a lexically enclosing class of c by declaration or inheritance.

Evaluation of an alternate constructor invocation statement proceeds by first evaluating the arguments to the constructor, left-to-right, as in an ordinary method invocation; and then invoking the constructor.

Evaluation of a superclass constructor invocation statement is more complicated, as follows:

1. Let c be the class being instantiated, let s be the direct superclass of c, and let i be the instance being created.

2. The immediately enclosing instance of i with respect to s (if any) must be determined:

   - If s is not an inner class, or if the declaration of s occurs in a static context, no immediately enclosing instance of i with respect to s exists.

   - If the superclass constructor invocation is qualified, then the *Primary* expression p immediately preceding ".super" is evaluated.

     If p evaluates to null, a NullPointerException is raised, and the superclass constructor invocation completes abruptly.

     Otherwise, the result of this evaluation is the immediately enclosing instance of i with respect to s.

   - If the superclass constructor invocation is not qualified, then:

     - If s is a local class (§14.3), then let o be the innermost lexically enclosing class of s. Let n be an integer such that o is the n'th lexically enclosing class of c.

       The immediately enclosing instance of i with respect to s is the n'th lexically enclosing instance of this.

     - Otherwise, s is an inner member class (§8.5).

       Let o be the innermost lexically enclosing class of s, and let n be an integer such that o is the n'th lexically enclosing class of c.

The immediately enclosing instance of `i` with respect to `s` is the *n*'th lexically enclosing instance of `this`.

3. After determining the immediately enclosing instance of `i` with respect to `s` (if any), evaluation of the superclass constructor invocation statement proceeds by evaluating the arguments to the constructor, left-to-right, as in an ordinary method invocation; and then invoking the constructor.

4. Finally, if the superclass constructor invocation statement completes normally, then all instance variable initializers of `c` and all instance initializers of `c` are executed. If an instance initializer or instance variable initializer `I` textually precedes another instance initializer or instance variable initializer `J`, then `I` is executed before `J`.

   Execution of instance variable initializers and instance initializers is performed regardless of whether the superclass constructor invocation actually appears as an explicit constructor invocation statement or is provided automatically. (An alternate constructor invocation does not perform this additional implicit execution.)

8.8.8   Constructor Overloading

Overloading of constructors is identical in behavior to overloading of methods (§8.4.9). The overloading is resolved at compile time by each class instance creation expression (§15.9).

8.8.9   Default Constructor

If a class contains no constructor declarations, then a default constructor with no formal parameters and no `throws` clause is implicitly declared.

If the class being declared is the primordial class `Object`, then the default constructor has an empty body. Otherwise, the default constructor simply invokes the superclass constructor with no arguments.

It is a compile-time error if a default constructor is implicitly declared but the superclass does not have an accessible constructor (§6.6) that takes no arguments and has no `throws` clause.

In a class type, if the class is declared `public`, then the default constructor is implicitly given the access modifier `public` (§6.6); if the class is declared `protected`, then the default constructor is implicitly given the access modifier `protected` (§6.6); if the class is declared `private`, then the default constructor is implicitly given the access modifier `private` (§6.6); otherwise, the default constructor has the default access implied by no access modifier.

In an enum type, the default constructor is implicitly `private` (§8.9.2).

Example 8.8.9-1. Default Constructors

The declaration:

```
public class Point {
    int x, y;
}
```

is equivalent to the declaration:

```
public class Point {
    int x, y;
    public Point() { super(); }
}
```

where the default constructor is `public` because the class `Point` is `public`.

Example 8.8.9-2. Accessibility of Constructors v. Classes

The rule that the default constructor of a class has the same access modifier as the class itself is simple and intuitive. Note, however, that this does not imply that the constructor is accessible whenever the class is accessible. Consider:

```
package p1;
public class Outer {
    protected class Inner {}
}
package p2;
class SonOfOuter extends p1.Outer {
    void foo() {
        new Inner();  // compile-time access error
    }
}
```

The constructor for `Inner` is `protected`. However, the constructor is `protected` relative to `Inner`, while `Inner` is `protected` relative to `Outer`. So, `Inner` is accessible in `SonOfOuter`, since it is a subclass of `Outer`. `Inner`'s constructor is not accessible in `SonOfOuter`, because the class `SonOfOuter` is not a subclass of `Inner`! Hence, even though `Inner` is accessible, its default constructor is not.

8.8.10 Preventing Instantiation of a Class

A class can be designed to prevent code outside the class declaration from creating instances of the class by declaring at least one constructor, to prevent the creation of an implicit constructor, and by declaring all constructors to be `private`.

A `public` class can likewise prevent the creation of instances outside its package by declaring at least one constructor, to prevent creation of a default constructor with public access, and by declaring no constructor that is `public`.

> **Example 8.8.10-1. Preventing Instantiation via Constructor Accessibility**
>
> ```
> class ClassOnly {
>     private ClassOnly() { }
>     static String just = "only the lonely";
> }
> ```

Here, the class `ClassOnly` cannot be instantiated, while in the following code:

```
package just;
public class PackageOnly {
    PackageOnly() { }
    String[] justDesserts = { "cheesecake", "ice cream" };
}
```

the class `PackageOnly` can be instantiated only within the package `just`, in which it is declared.

8.9 Enums

An *enum declaration* specifies a new enum type.

> *EnumDeclaration:*
>   *ClassModifiers$_{opt}$* enum *Identifier Interfaces$_{opt}$ EnumBody*

> *EnumBody:*
>   { *EnumConstants$_{opt}$* ,$_{opt}$ *EnumBodyDeclarations$_{opt}$* }

Enum types (§8.9) must not be declared `abstract`; doing so will result in a compile-time error.

An enum type is implicitly `final` unless it contains at least one enum constant that has a class body.

It is a compile-time error to explicitly declare an enum type to be `final`.

Nested enum types are implicitly `static`. It is permissible to explicitly declare a nested enum type to be `static`.

> This implies that it is impossible to define a local (§14.3) enum, or to define an enum in an inner class (§8.1.3).

The direct superclass of an enum type named E is `Enum<E>` (§8.1.4).

An enum type has no instances other than those defined by its enum constants. It is a compile-time error to attempt to explicitly instantiate an enum type (§15.9.1).

> The `final clone` method in `Enum` ensures that enum constants can never be cloned, and the special treatment by the serialization mechanism ensures that duplicate instances are never created as a result of deserialization. Reflective instantiation of enum types is prohibited. Together, these four things ensure that no instances of an enum type exist beyond those defined by the enum constants.

8.9.1   Enum Constants

The body of an enum type may contain *enum constants*. An enum constant defines an instance of the enum type.

> *EnumConstants:*
>   *EnumConstant*
>   *EnumConstants* , *EnumConstant*
>
> *EnumConstant:*
>   *Annotations$_{opt}$ Identifier Arguments$_{opt}$ ClassBody$_{opt}$*
>
> *Arguments:*
>   (*ArgumentList$_{opt}$*)
>
> *EnumBodyDeclarations:*
>   ; *ClassBodyDeclarations$_{opt}$*

An enum constant may optionally be preceded by annotation modifiers. If an annotation a (§9.7) on an enum constant corresponds to an annotation type T (§9.6), and T has a (meta-)annotation m that corresponds to `java.lang.annotation.Target`, then m must have an element whose value is `java.lang.annotation.ElementType.FIELD`, or a compile-time error occurs.

The *Identifier* in a *EnumConstant* may be used in a name to refer to the enum constant.

The scope and shadowing of an enum constant is specified in §6.3 and §6.4.

An enum constant may be followed by arguments, which are passed to the constructor of the enum type when the constant is created during class initialization as described later in this section. The constructor to be invoked is chosen using the normal overloading rules (§15.12.2). If the arguments are omitted, an empty argument list is assumed.

The optional class body of an enum constant implicitly defines an anonymous class declaration (§15.9.5) that extends the immediately enclosing enum type. The class body is governed by the usual rules of anonymous classes; in particular it cannot contain any constructors.

Instance methods declared in these class bodies may be invoked outside the enclosing enum type only if they override accessible methods in the enclosing enum type.

It is a compile-time error for the class body of an enum constant to declare an abstract method.

Because there is only one instance of each enum constant, it is permissible to use the == operator in place of the `equals` method when comparing two object references if it is known that at least one of them refers to an enum constant.

> The `equals` method in `Enum` is a `final` method that merely invokes `super.equals` on its argument and returns the result, thus performing an identity comparison.

Example 8.9.1-1. Iterating Over Enum Constants With An Enhanced `for` **Loop**

```
public class Test {
    enum Season { WINTER, SPRING, SUMMER, FALL }

    public static void main(String[] args) {
        for (Season s : Season.values())
            System.out.println(s);
    }
}
```

This program produces the output:

```
WINTER
SPRING
SUMMER
FALL
```

Example 8.9.1-2. Use Of `java.util.EnumSet` **For Subranges**

```
import java.util.EnumSet;

public class Test {
    enum Day { MONDAY, TUESDAY, WEDNESDAY,
```

```
                    THURSDAY, FRIDAY, SATURDAY, SUNDAY }

    public static void main(String[] args) {
        System.out.print("Weekdays: ");
        for (Day d : EnumSet.range(Day.MONDAY, Day.FRIDAY))
            System.out.print(d + " ");
    }
}
```

This program produces the output:

```
Weekdays: MONDAY TUESDAY WEDNESDAY THURSDAY FRIDAY
```

`java.util.EnumSet` contains a rich family of static factories, so this technique can be generalized to work with non-contiguous subsets as well as subranges. At first glance, it might appear wasteful to generate a `java.util.EnumSet` object for a single iteration, but they are so cheap that this is the recommended idiom for iteration over a subrange. Internally, a `java.util.EnumSet` is represented with a single `long` assuming the enum type has 64 or fewer elements.

8.9.2   Enum Body Declarations

Any constructor or member declarations within an enum declaration apply to the enum type exactly as if they had been present in the class body of a normal class declaration, unless explicitly stated otherwise.

It is a compile-time error if a constructor declaration of an enum type is `public` or `protected`.

If an enum type has no constructor declarations, then a `private` constructor that takes no parameters (to match the implicit empty argument list) is automatically provided.

It is a compile-time error for an enum declaration to declare a finalizer. An instance of an enum type may never be finalized.

It is a compile-time error for an enum type E to have an abstract method m as a member unless E has one or more enum constants, and all of E's enum constants have class bodies that provide concrete implementations of m.

In addition to the members that an enum type E inherits from `Enum<E>`, for each declared enum constant with the name n, the enum type has an implicitly declared `public static final` field named n of type E. These fields are considered to be declared in the same order as the corresponding enum constants, before any `static` fields explicitly declared in the enum type. Each such field is initialized to the enum constant that corresponds to it. Each such field is also considered to be annotated by the same annotations as the corresponding enum constant. The enum constant is said to be *created* when the corresponding field is initialized.

In addition, if E is the name of an enum type, then that type has the following implicitly declared static methods:

```
/**
 * Returns an array containing the constants of this enum
 * type, in the order they're declared.  This method may be
 * used to iterate over the constants as follows:
 *
 *     for(E c : E.values())
 *         System.out.println(c);
 *
 * @return an array containing the constants of this enum
 * type, in the order they're declared
 */
public static E[] values();

/**
 * Returns the enum constant of this type with the specified
 * name.
 * The string must match exactly an identifier used to declare
 * an enum constant in this type.  (Extraneous whitespace
 * characters are not permitted.)
 *
 * @return the enum constant with the specified name
 * @throws IllegalArgumentException if this enum type has no
 * constant with the specified name
 */
public static E valueOf(String name);
```

It follows that enum type declarations cannot contain fields that conflict with the enum constants, and cannot contain methods that conflict with the automatically generated methods (values() and valueOf(String)) or methods that override the final methods in Enum (equals(Object), hashCode(), clone(), compareTo(Object), name(), ordinal(), and getDeclaringClass()).

It is a compile-time error to reference a static field of an enum type that is not a constant variable (§4.12.4) from constructors, instance initializer blocks, or instance variable initializer expressions of that type.

It is a compile-time error for the constructors, instance initializer blocks, or instance variable initializer expressions of an enum constant e to refer to e or to an enum constant of the same type that is declared to the right of e.

Example 8.9.2-1. Restriction On Enum Constant Self-Reference

Without this rule, apparently reasonable code would fail at run time due to the initialization circularity inherent in enum types. (A circularity exists in any class with a "self-typed" static field.) Here is an example of the sort of code that would fail:

```
import java.util.Map;
import java.util.HashMap;
enum Color {
    RED, GREEN, BLUE;

    static final Map<String,Color> colorMap =
        new HashMap<String,Color>();
    Color() { colorMap.put(toString(), this); }
}
```

Static initialization of this enum type would throw a `NullPointerException` because the `static` variable `colorMap` is uninitialized when the constructors for the enum constants run. The restriction above ensures that such code won't compile.

Note that the example can easily be refactored to work properly:

```
import java.util.Map;
import java.util.HashMap;

enum Color {
    RED, GREEN, BLUE;

    static final Map<String,Color> colorMap =
        new HashMap<String,Color>();
    static {
        for (Color c : Color.values())
            colorMap.put(c.toString(), c);
    }
}
```

The refactored version is clearly correct, as static initialization occurs top to bottom.

Example 8.9.2-2. Enum Type With Members

```
enum Coin {
    PENNY(1), NICKEL(5), DIME(10), QUARTER(25);
    Coin(int value) { this.value = value; }
    private final int value;
    public int value() { return value; }
}
```

Each enum constant arranges for a different value in the field `value`, passed in via a constructor. The field represents the value, in cents, of an American coin. Note that there are no restrictions on the type or number of parameters that may be declared by an enum type's constructor.

A `switch` statement is useful for simulating the addition of a method to an enum type from outside the type. This example "adds" a `color` method to the `Coin` type, and prints a table of coins, their values, and their colors.

```
class Test {
```

```
        public static void main(String[] args) {
            for (Coin c : Coin.values())
                System.out.println(c + "\t\t" +
                                     c.value() + "\t" + color(c));
        }

        private enum CoinColor { COPPER, NICKEL, SILVER }
        private static CoinColor color(Coin c) {
            switch(c) {
                case PENNY:
                    return CoinColor.COPPER;
                case NICKEL:
                    return CoinColor.NICKEL;
                case DIME: case QUARTER:
                    return CoinColor.SILVER;
                default:
                    throw new AssertionError("Unknown coin: " + c);
            }
        }
    }
```

This program produces the output:

```
PENNY          1        COPPER
NICKEL         5        NICKEL
DIME           10       SILVER
QUARTER        25       SILVER
```

Example 8.9.2-3. Multiple Enum Types

In the following program, a playing card class is built atop two simple enum types. Note that each enum type would be as long as the entire example in the absence of the enum facility:

```
import java.util.List;
import java.util.ArrayList;
class Card implements Comparable<Card>,
                      java.io.Serializable {
    public enum Rank { DEUCE, THREE, FOUR, FIVE, SIX, SEVEN,
                       EIGHT, NINE, TEN,JACK, QUEEN, KING, ACE }

    public enum Suit { CLUBS, DIAMONDS, HEARTS, SPADES }

    private final Rank rank;
    private final Suit suit;
    public Rank rank() { return rank; }
    public Suit suit() { return suit; }

    private Card(Rank rank, Suit suit) {
        if (rank == null || suit == null)
            throw new NullPointerException(rank + ", " + suit);
        this.rank = rank;
        this.suit = suit;
```

```
        }

        public String toString() { return rank + " of " + suit; }

        // Primary sort on suit, secondary sort on rank
        public int compareTo(Card c) {
            int suitCompare = suit.compareTo(c.suit);
            return (suitCompare != 0 ?
                        suitCompare :
                        rank.compareTo(c.rank));
        }

        private static final List<Card> prototypeDeck =
            new ArrayList<Card>(52);

        static {
            for (Suit suit : Suit.values())
                for (Rank rank : Rank.values())
                    prototypeDeck.add(new Card(rank, suit));
        }

        // Returns a new deck
        public static List<Card> newDeck() {
            return new ArrayList<Card>(prototypeDeck);
        }
    }
```

The following program exercises the Card class. It takes two integer parameters on the command line, representing the number of hands to deal and the number of cards in each hand:

```
import java.util.List;
import java.util.ArrayList;
import java.util.Collections;
class Deal {
    public static void main(String args[]) {
        int numHands     = Integer.parseInt(args[0]);
        int cardsPerHand = Integer.parseInt(args[1]);
        List<Card> deck  = Card.newDeck();
        Collections.shuffle(deck);
        for (int i=0; i < numHands; i++)
            System.out.println(dealHand(deck, cardsPerHand));
    }

    /**
     * Returns a new ArrayList consisting of the last n
     * elements of deck, which are removed from deck.
     * The returned list is sorted using the elements'
     * natural ordering.
     */
    public static <E extends Comparable<E>>
    ArrayList<E> dealHand(List<E> deck, int n) {
        int deckSize = deck.size();
```

```
            List<E> handView = deck.subList(deckSize - n, deckSize);
            ArrayList<E> hand = new ArrayList<E>(handView);
            handView.clear();
            Collections.sort(hand);
            return hand;
        }
    }
```

The program produces the output:

```
java Deal 4 3
[DEUCE of CLUBS, SEVEN of CLUBS, QUEEN of DIAMONDS]
[NINE of HEARTS, FIVE of SPADES, ACE of SPADES]
[THREE of HEARTS, SIX of HEARTS, TEN of SPADES]
[TEN of CLUBS, NINE of DIAMONDS, THREE of SPADES]
```

Example 8.9.2-4. Enum Constants with Class Bodies

```
enum Operation {
    PLUS {
        double eval(double x, double y) { return x + y; }
    },
    MINUS {
        double eval(double x, double y) { return x - y; }
    },
    TIMES {
        double eval(double x, double y) { return x * y; }
    },
    DIVIDED_BY {
        double eval(double x, double y) { return x / y; }
    };

    // Each constant supports an arithmetic operation
    abstract double eval(double x, double y);

    public static void main(String args[]) {
        double x = Double.parseDouble(args[0]);
        double y = Double.parseDouble(args[1]);
        for (Operation op : Operation.values())
            System.out.println(x + " " + op + " " + y +
                                " = " + op.eval(x, y));
    }
}
```

Constant-specific class bodies attach behaviors to the constants. The program produces the output:

```
java Operation 2.0 4.0
2.0 PLUS 4.0 = 6.0
2.0 MINUS 4.0 = -2.0
2.0 TIMES 4.0 = 8.0
2.0 DIVIDED_BY 4.0 = 0.5
```

The above pattern is much safer than using a `switch` statement in the base type (`Operation`), as the pattern precludes the possibility of forgetting to add a behavior for a new constant (since the enum declaration would cause a compile-time error).

CHAPTER 9

Interfaces

$\mathbf{A}$N interface declaration introduces a new reference type whose members are classes, interfaces, constants, and abstract methods. This type has no implementation, but otherwise unrelated classes can implement it by providing implementations for its abstract methods.

A *nested interface* is any interface whose declaration occurs within the body of another class or interface.

A *top level interface* is an interface that is not a nested interface.

We distinguish between two kinds of interfaces - normal interfaces and annotation types.

This chapter discusses the common semantics of all interfaces - normal interfaces, both top level (§7.6) and nested (§8.5, §9.5), and annotation types (§9.6). Details that are specific to particular kinds of interfaces are discussed in the sections dedicated to these constructs.

Programs can use interfaces to make it unnecessary for related classes to share a common `abstract` superclass or to add methods to `Object`.

An interface may be declared to be a *direct extension* of one or more other interfaces, meaning that it implicitly specifies all the member types, abstract methods, and constants of the interfaces it extends, except for any member types and constants that it may hide.

A class may be declared to *directly implement* one or more interfaces, meaning that any instance of the class implements all the `abstract` methods specified by the interface or interfaces. A class necessarily implements all the interfaces that its direct superclasses and direct superinterfaces do. This (multiple) interface inheritance allows objects to support (multiple) common behaviors without sharing any implementation.

A variable whose declared type is an interface type may have as its value a reference to any instance of a class which implements the specified interface. It is not sufficient that the class happen to implement all the `abstract` methods of the interface; the class or one of its superclasses must actually be declared to implement the interface, or else the class is not considered to implement the interface.

9.1   Interface Declarations

An *interface declaration* specifies a new named reference type. There are two kinds of interface declarations - *normal interface declarations* and *annotation type declarations* (§9.6).

> *InterfaceDeclaration:*
>   *NormalInterfaceDeclaration*
>   *AnnotationTypeDeclaration*

> *NormalInterfaceDeclaration:*
>   *InterfaceModifiers$_{opt}$* interface *Identifier*
>   *TypeParameters$_{opt}$ ExtendsInterfaces$_{opt}$ InterfaceBody*

The *Identifier* in an interface declaration specifies the name of the interface.

It is a compile-time error if an interface has the same simple name as any of its enclosing classes or interfaces.

The scope and shadowing of an interface declaration is specified in §6.3 and §6.4.

9.1.1   Interface Modifiers

An interface declaration may include *interface modifiers*.

> *InterfaceModifiers:*
>   *InterfaceModifier*
>   *InterfaceModifiers InterfaceModifier*

> *InterfaceModifier: one of*
>   *Annotation* public protected private
>   abstract static strictfp

If an annotation a (§9.7) on an interface declaration corresponds to an annotation type T (§9.6), and T has a (meta-)annotation m that corresponds to `java.lang.annotation.Target`, then *m* must have an element whose value is `java.lang.annotation.ElementType.TYPE`, or a compile-time error occurs.

The access modifier `public` (§6.6) pertains to every kind of interface declaration.

The access modifiers `protected` and `private` pertain only to member interfaces within a directly enclosing class or enum declaration (§8.5.1).

The modifier `static` pertains only to member interfaces (§8.5.1, §9.5), not to top level interfaces (§7.6).

It is a compile-time error if the same modifier appears more than once in an interface declaration.

If two or more (distinct) interface modifiers appear in an interface declaration, then it is customary, though not required, that they appear in the order consistent with that shown above in the production for *InterfaceModifier*.

9.1.1.1 `abstract` *Interfaces*

Every interface is implicitly `abstract`.

This modifier is obsolete and should not be used in new programs.

9.1.1.2 `strictfp` *Interfaces*

The effect of the `strictfp` modifier is to make all `float` or `double` expressions within the interface declaration be explicitly FP-strict (§15.4).

This implies that all nested types declared in the interface are implicitly `strictfp`.

9.1.2   Generic Interfaces and Type Parameters

An interface is *generic* if it declares one or more type variables (§4.4).

These type variables are known as the *type parameters* of the interface. The type parameter section follows the interface name and is delimited by angle brackets.

In an interface's type parameter section, a type variable *T directly depends* on a type variable *S* if *S* is the bound of *T*, while *T depends* on *S* if either *T* directly depends on *S* or *T* directly depends on a type variable *U* that depends on *S* (using this definition recursively).

It is a compile-time error if a type variable in a interface's type parameter section depends on itself.

The scope of an interface's type parameter is specified in §6.3.

It is a compile-time error to refer to a type parameter of an interface I anywhere in the declaration of a field or type member of I.

A generic interface declaration defines a set of parameterized types (§4.5), one for each possible invocation of the type parameter section by type arguments. All of these parameterized types share the same interface at run time.

9.1.3   Superinterfaces and Subinterfaces

If an `extends` clause is provided, then the interface being declared extends each of the other named interfaces and therefore inherits the member types, methods, and constants of each of the other named interfaces.

These other named interfaces are the *direct superinterfaces* of the interface being declared.

Any class that `implements` the declared interface is also considered to implement all the interfaces that this interface `extends`.

> *ExtendsInterfaces:*
>   `extends` *InterfaceTypeList*

The following is repeated from §4.3 and §8.1.5 to make the presentation here clearer:

> *InterfaceTypeList:*
>   *InterfaceType*
>   *InterfaceTypeList , InterfaceType*

> *InterfaceType:*
>   *TypeDeclSpecifier TypeArguments$_{opt}$*

Given a (possibly generic) interface declaration for $I<F_1,...,F_n>$ $(n \geq 0)$, the *direct superinterfaces* of the interface type $I<F_1,...,F_n>$ are the types given in the `extends` clause of the declaration of I if an `extends` clause is present.

Let $I<F_1,...,F_n>$ $(n > 0)$, be a generic interface declaration. The direct superinterfaces of the parameterized interface type $I<T_1,...,T_n>$, where T_i $(1 \leq i \leq n)$ is a type, are all types $J<U_1 \theta,...,U_k \theta>$, where $J<U_1,...,U_k>$ is a direct superinterface of $I<F_1,...,F_n>$, and θ is the substitution $[F_1:=T_1, \ldots, F_n:=T_n]$.

Each *InterfaceType* in the `extends` clause of an interface declaration must name an accessible (§6.6) interface type; otherwise a compile-time error occurs.

The *superinterface* relationship is the transitive closure of the direct superinterface relationship. An interface K is a superinterface of interface I if either of the following is true:

- K is a direct superinterface of I.

- There exists an interface J such that K is a superinterface of J, and J is a superinterface of I, applying this definition recursively.

Interface I is said to be a *subinterface* of interface K whenever K is a superinterface of I.

While every class is an extension of class Object, there is no single interface of which all interfaces are extensions.

An interface I *directly depends* on a type T if T is mentioned in the extends clause of I either as a superinterface or as a qualifier within a superinterface name.

An interface I *depends* on a reference type T if any of the following conditions hold:

- I directly depends on T.

- I directly depends on a class C that depends (§8.1.5) on T.

- I directly depends on an interface J that depends on T (using this definition recursively).

It is a compile-time error if an interface depends on itself.

If circularly declared interfaces are detected at run time, as interfaces are loaded (§12.2), then a ClassCircularityError is thrown.

9.1.4   Interface Body and Member Declarations

The body of an interface may declare members of the interface, that is, fields (§9.3), methods (§9.4), classes (§9.5), and interfaces (§9.5).

InterfaceBody:
   { *InterfaceMemberDeclarations$_{opt}$* }

InterfaceMemberDeclarations:
   InterfaceMemberDeclaration
   InterfaceMemberDeclarations InterfaceMemberDeclaration

InterfaceMemberDeclaration:
   ConstantDeclaration
   AbstractMethodDeclaration
   ClassDeclaration
   InterfaceDeclaration
   ;

The scope of a declaration of a member *m* declared in or inherited by an interface type *I* is specified in §6.3.

9.2   Interface Members

The members of an interface are:

- Those members declared in the interface.

- Those members inherited from direct superinterfaces.

- If an interface has no direct superinterfaces, then the interface implicitly declares a `public abstract` member method *m* with signature *s*, return type *r*, and `throws` clause *t* corresponding to each `public` instance method *m* with signature *s*, return type *r*, and `throws` clause *t* declared in `Object`, unless a method with the same signature, same return type, and a compatible `throws` clause is explicitly declared by the interface.

  It is a compile-time error if the interface explicitly declares such a method *m* in the case where *m* is declared to be `final` in `Object`.

  It follows that is a compile-time error if the interface declares a method with a signature that is override-equivalent (§8.4.2) to a `public` method of `Object`, but has a different return type or incompatible `throws` clause.

The interface inherits, from the interfaces it extends, all members of those interfaces, except for (a) fields, classes, and interfaces that it hides and (b) methods that it overrides (§9.4.1).

Fields, methods, and member types of an interface type may have the same name, since they are used in different contexts and are disambiguated by different lookup procedures (§6.5). However, this is discouraged as a matter of style.

9.3   Field (Constant) Declarations

ConstantDeclaration:
   ConstantModifiers_{opt} Type VariableDeclarators ;

ConstantModifiers:
   ConstantModifier
   ConstantModifier ConstantModifers

ConstantModifier: one of
   Annotation `public static final`

If an annotation `a` (§9.7) on a field declaration corresponds to an annotation type `T` (§9.6), and `T` has a (meta-)annotation `m` that corresponds to `java.lang.annotation.Target`, then `m` must have an element whose value is `java.lang.annotation.ElementType.FIELD`, or a compile-time error occurs.

Every field declaration in the body of an interface is implicitly `public`, `static`, and `final`. It is permitted to redundantly specify any or all of these modifiers for such fields.

> If two or more (distinct) field modifiers appear in a field declaration, it is customary, though not required, that they appear in the order consistent with that shown above in the production for *ConstantModifier*.

It is a compile-time error if the same modifier appears more than once in a field declaration.

It is a compile-time error for the body of an interface declaration to declare two fields with the same name.

The declared type of a field is denoted by the *Type* that appears in the field declaration, followed by any bracket pairs that follow the *Identifier* in the declarator.

If the interface declares a field with a certain name, then the declaration of that field is said to *hide* any and all accessible declarations of fields with the same name in superinterfaces of the interface.

It is possible for an interface to inherit more than one field with the same name. Such a situation does not in itself cause a compile-time error. However, any attempt within the body of the interface to refer to any such field by its simple name will result in a compile-time error, because such a reference is ambiguous.

There might be several paths by which the same field declaration might be inherited from an interface. In such a situation, the field is considered to be inherited only once, and it may be referred to by its simple name without ambiguity.

Example 9.3-1. Ambiguous Inherited Fields

If two fields with the same name are inherited by an interface because, for example, two of its direct superinterfaces declare fields with that name, then a single ambiguous member results. Any use of this ambiguous member will result in a compile-time error. In the program:

```
interface BaseColors {
    int RED = 1, GREEN = 2, BLUE = 4;
}
interface RainbowColors extends BaseColors {
    int YELLOW = 3, ORANGE = 5, INDIGO = 6, VIOLET = 7;
}
interface PrintColors extends BaseColors {
    int YELLOW = 8, CYAN = 16, MAGENTA = 32;
}
interface LotsOfColors extends RainbowColors, PrintColors {
    int FUCHSIA = 17, VERMILION = 43, CHARTREUSE = RED+90;
}
```

the interface `LotsOfColors` inherits two fields named `YELLOW`. This is all right as long as the interface does not contain any reference by simple name to the field `YELLOW`. (Such a reference could occur within a variable initializer for a field.)

Even if interface `PrintColors` were to give the value 3 to `YELLOW` rather than the value 8, a reference to field `YELLOW` within interface `LotsOfColors` would still be considered ambiguous.

Example 9.3-2. Multiply Inherited Fields

If a single field is inherited multiple times from the same interface because, for example, both this interface and one of this interface's direct superinterfaces extend the interface that declares the field, then only a single member results. This situation does not in itself cause a compile-time error.

In the previous example, the fields `RED`, `GREEN`, and `BLUE` are inherited by interface `LotsOfColors` in more than one way, through interface `RainbowColors` and also through interface `PrintColors`, but the reference to field `RED` in interface `LotsOfColors` is not considered ambiguous because only one actual declaration of the field `RED` is involved.

9.3.1 Initialization of Fields in Interfaces

Every field in the body of an interface must have an initialization expression, which need not be a constant expression (§15.28), or a compile-time error occurs.

It is a compile-time error if an initialization expression for an interface field contains a reference by simple name to the same field or to another field whose declaration occurs textually later in the same interface.

> **Example 9.3.1-1. Forward Reference to a Field**
>
> ```
> interface Test {
>     float f = j;
>     int   j = 1;
>     int   k = k + 1;
> }
> ```
>
> This program causes two compile-time errors, because j is referred to in the initialization of f before j is declared, and because the initialization of k refers to k itself.

If the keyword `this` (§15.8.3) or the keyword `super` (§15.11.2, §15.12) occurs in an initialization expression for a field of an interface, then unless the occurrence is within the body of an anonymous class (§15.9.5), a compile-time error occurs.

The variable initializer is evaluated and the assignment performed exactly once, when the interface is initialized (§12.4.2).

At run time, interface fields that are initialized with constant expressions (§15.28) are initialized first (§12.4.2). This also applies to `static final` fields in classes (§8.3.2.1). These fields are "constants" that will never be observed to have their default initial values (§4.12.5), even by devious programs (§13.4.9).

9.4 Abstract Method Declarations

AbstractMethodDeclaration:
    AbstractMethodModifiers$_{opt}$ TypeParameters$_{opt}$ Result
                 MethodDeclarator Throws$_{opt}$;

AbstractMethodModifiers:
    AbstractMethodModifier
    AbstractMethodModifiers AbstractMethodModifier

AbstractMethodModifier: one of
    Annotation `public abstract`

If an annotation *a* (§9.7) on a method declaration corresponds to an annotation type *T* (§9.6), and *T* has a (meta-)annotation *m* that corresponds to `java.lang.annotation.Target`, then *m* must have an element whose value is `java.lang.annotation.ElementType.METHOD`, or a compile-time error occurs.

Every method declaration in the body of an interface is implicitly `public` (§6.6).

Every method declaration in the body of an interface is implicitly `abstract`, so its body is always represented by a semicolon, not a block.

It is permitted, but discouraged as a matter of style, to redundantly specify the `public` and/or `abstract` modifier for a method declared in an interface.

It is a compile-time error if the same modifier appears more than once on a method declared in an interface.

It is a compile-time error if a method declared in an interface is declared `static`, because `static` methods cannot be `abstract`.

It is a compile-time error if a method declared in an interface is `strictfp` or `native` or `synchronized`, because those keywords describe implementation properties rather than interface properties.

However, a method declared in an interface may be implemented by a method that is declared `strictfp` or `native` or `synchronized` in a class that implements the interface.

It is a compile-time error if a method declared in an interface is declared `final`.

However, a method declared in an interface may be implemented by a method that is declared `final` in a class that implements the interface.

It is a compile-time error for the body of an interface to declare, explicitly or implicitly, two methods with override-equivalent signatures (§8.4.2).

However, an interface may inherit several methods with such signatures (§9.4.1).

A method in an interface may be generic. The rules for type parameters of a generic method in an interface are the same as for a generic method in a class (§8.4.4).

9.4.1 Inheritance and Overriding

An interface inherits from its direct superinterfaces all methods of the superinterfaces that are not overridden by a declaration in the interface.

Methods are overridden on a signature-by-signature basis.

If, for example, an interface declares two `public` methods with the same name (§9.4.2), and a subinterface overrides one of them, the subinterface still inherits the other method.

9.4.1.1   *Overriding (by Instance Methods)*

An instance method m_1 declared in an interface I overrides another instance method, m_2, declared in interface J iff both of the following are true:

- I is a subinterface of J.

- The signature of m_1 is a subsignature (§8.4.2) of the signature of m_2.

> **Example 9.4.1.1-1. Overriding an** `abstract` **Method Declaration**
>
> Methods declared in interfaces are `abstract` and thus contain no implementation. About all that can be accomplished by an overriding method declaration, other than to affirm a method signature, is to refine the return type or to restrict the exceptions that might be thrown by an implementation of the method. Here is a variation of the example shown in (§8.4.3.1):
>
> ```
> class BufferEmpty     extends Exception {}
> class BufferException extends Exception {}
>
> interface Buffer {
>     char get() throws BufferEmpty, BufferException;
> }
> interface InfiniteBuffer extends Buffer {
>     char get() throws BufferException;  // override
> }
> ```

9.4.1.2   *Requirements in Overriding*

The relationship between the return type of an interface method and the return types of any overridden interface methods is specified in §8.4.8.3.

The relationship between the `throws` clause of an interface method and the `throws` clauses of any overridden interface methods are specified in §8.4.8.3.

The relationship between the signature of an interface method and the signatures of overridden interface methods are specified in §8.4.8.3.

9.4.1.3   *Inheriting Methods with Override-Equivalent Signatures*

It is possible for an interface to inherit several methods with override-equivalent signatures (§8.4.2). Such a situation does not in itself cause a compile-time error. The interface is considered to inherit all the methods.

However, one of the inherited methods must be return-type-substitutable for every other inherited method; otherwise, a compile-time error occurs. (The `throws` clauses do not cause errors in this case.)

There might be several paths by which the same method declaration is inherited from an interface. This fact causes no difficulty and never, of itself, results in a compile-time error.

9.4.2   Overloading

If two methods of an interface (whether both declared in the same interface, or both inherited by an interface, or one declared and one inherited) have the same name but different signatures that are not override-equivalent (§8.4.2), then the method name is said to be *overloaded*.

This fact causes no difficulty and never of itself results in a compile-time error. There is no required relationship between the return types or between the `throws` clauses of two methods with the same name but different signatures that are not override-equivalent.

Example 9.4.2-1. Overloading an `abstract` Method Declaration

```
interface PointInterface {
    void move(int dx, int dy);
}
interface RealPointInterface extends PointInterface {
    void move(float dx, float dy);
    void move(double dx, double dy);
}
```

Here, the method named `move` is overloaded in interface `RealPointInterface` with three different signatures, two of them declared and one inherited. Any non-`abstract` class that implements interface `RealPointInterface` must provide implementations of all three method signatures.

9.5   Member Type Declarations

Interfaces may contain member type declarations (§8.5).

A member type declaration in an interface is implicitly `static` and `public`. It is permitted to redundantly specify either or both of these modifiers.

It is a compile-time error if the same modifier appears more than once in a member type declaration in an interface.

If an interface declares a member type with a certain name, then the declaration of that type is said to *hide* any and all accessible declarations of member types with the same name in superinterfaces of the interface.

An interface inherits from its direct superinterfaces all the non-`private` member types of the superinterfaces that are both accessible to code in the interface and not hidden by a declaration in the interface.

An interface may inherit two or more type declarations with the same name. It is a compile-time error to attempt to refer to any ambiguously inherited class or interface by its simple name.

If the same type declaration is inherited from an interface by multiple paths, the class or interface is considered to be inherited only once; it may be referred to by its simple name without ambiguity.

9.6 Annotation Types

An *annotation type declaration* is a special kind of interface declaration. To distinguish an annotation type declaration from an ordinary interface declaration, the keyword `interface` is preceded by an at-sign (`@`).

> Note that the at-sign (`@`) and the keyword `interface` are two distinct tokens. Technically it is possible to separate them with whitespace, but this is discouraged as a matter of style.

AnnotationTypeDeclaration:
    InterfaceModifiers$_{opt}$ `@ interface` *Identifier AnnotationTypeBody*

AnnotationTypeBody:
    { *AnnotationTypeElementDeclarations*$_{opt}$ }

AnnotationTypeElementDeclarations:
    AnnotationTypeElementDeclaration
    AnnotationTypeElementDeclarations AnnotationTypeElementDeclaration

If an annotation *a* (§9.7) on an annotation type declaration corresponds to an annotation type *T*, and *T* has a (meta-)annotation *m* that corresponds to `java.lang.annotation.Target`, then *m* must have either an element whose value is `java.lang.annotation.ElementType.ANNOTATION_TYPE`, or an element whose value is `java.lang.annotation.ElementType.TYPE`, or a compile-time error occurs.

The *Identifier* in an annotation type declaration specifies the name of the annotation type.

It is a compile-time error if an annotation type has the same simple name as any of its enclosing classes or interfaces.

The direct superinterface of an annotation type is always `java.lang.annotation.Annotation`.

> By virtue of the *AnnotationTypeDeclaration* syntax, an annotation type declaration cannot be generic, and no `extends` clause is permitted.

> A consequence of the fact that an annotation type cannot explicitly declare a superclass or superinterface is that a subclass or subinterface of an annotation type is never itself an annotation type. Similarly, `java.lang.annotation.Annotation` is not itself an annotation type.

An annotation type declaration inherits several members from `java.lang.annotation.Annotation`, including the implicitly declared methods corresponding to the instance methods in `Object`, yet these methods do not define elements (§9.6.1) of the annotation type and it is illegal to use them in annotations.

> Without this rule, we could not ensure that the elements were of the types representable in annotations, or that accessor methods for them would be available.

Unless explicitly modified herein, all of the rules that apply to ordinary interface declarations apply to annotation type declarations.

> For example, annotation types share the same namespace as ordinary class and interface types; and annotation type declarations are legal wherever interface declarations are legal, and have the same scope and accessibility.

9.6.1   Annotation Type Elements

Each method declaration in an annotation type declaration defines an *element* of the annotation type.

Annotation types can have zero or more elements. An annotation type has no elements other than those defined by the methods it explicitly declares.

AnnotationTypeElementDeclaration:
  AbstractMethodModifiers$_{opt}$ *Type Identifier* ( ) *Dims*$_{opt}$ *DefaultValue*$_{opt}$;
  ConstantDeclaration
  ClassDeclaration
  InterfaceDeclaration
  EnumDeclaration
  AnnotationTypeDeclaration
  ;

DefaultValue:
  default *ElementValue*

By virtue of the *AnnotationTypeElementDeclaration* syntax, a method declaration in an annotation type declaration cannot have any formal parameters or type parameters, or a throws clause.

By convention, no *AbstractMethodModifiers* should be present on an annotation type element except for annotations.

Example 9.6.1-1. Annotation Type Declarations

The following annotation type declaration defines an annotation type with several elements:

```
/**
 * Describes the "request-for-enhancement" (RFE)
 * that led to the presence of the annotated API element.
 */
@interface RequestForEnhancement {
    int     id();       // Unique ID number associated with RFE
    String synopsis();  // Synopsis of RFE
    String engineer();  // Name of engineer who implemented RFE
    String date();      // Date RFE was implemented
}
```

The following annotation type declaration defines an annotation type with no elements, termed a *marker annotation type*:

```
/**
 * An annotation with this type indicates that the
 * specification of the annotated API element is
 * preliminary and subject to change.
 */
@interface Preliminary {}
```

It is a compile-time error if the return type of a method declared in an annotation type is not one of the following: a primitive type, String, Class, any parameterized invocation of `Class`, an enum type (§8.9), an annotation type, or an array type (§10) whose element type is one of the preceding types.

> This specification precludes elements whose types are nested arrays. For example, this annotation type declaration is illegal:
>
> ```
> @interface Verboten {
>     String[][] value();
> }
> ```

It is a compile-time error if any method declared in an annotation type has a signature that is override-equivalent to that of any `public` or `protected` method declared in class `Object` or in the interface `java.lang.annotation.Annotation`.

It is a compile-time error if an annotation type declaration *T* contains an element of type *T*, either directly or indirectly.

> For example, this is illegal:
>
> ```
> @interface SelfRef { SelfRef value(); }
> ```
>
> and so is this:
>
> ```
> @interface Ping { Pong value(); }
> @interface Pong { Ping value(); }
> ```

By convention, the name of the sole element in a single-element annotation type is `value`. Linguistic support for this convention is provided by the single element annotation construct (§9.7.3); one must obey the convention in order to take advantage of the construct.

Example 9.6.1-2. Single-Element Annotation Type Declarations

The convention is illustrated in the following annotation type declaration:

```
/**
 * Associates a copyright notice with the annotated API element.
 */
@interface Copyright {
    String value();
}
```

The following annotation type declaration defines a single-element annotation type whose sole element has an array type:

```
/**
 * Associates a list of endorsers with the annotated class.
 */
```

```
@interface Endorsers {
    String[] value();
}
```

The following annotation type declaration shows a `Class` annotation whose value is restricted by a bounded wildcard:

```
interface Formatter {}

// Designates a formatter to pretty-print the annotated class
@interface PrettyPrinter {
    Class<? extends Formatter> value();
}
```

Note that the grammar for annotation type declarations permits other element declarations besides method declarations. For example, one might choose to declare a nested enum for use in conjunction with an annotation type:

```
@interface Quality {
    enum Level { BAD, INDIFFERENT, GOOD }
    Level value();
}
```

Example 9.6.2-3. Complex Annotation Type Declaration

Here is an example of a complex annotation type, that is, an annotation type that contains one or more elements whose types are also annotation types.

```
/**
 * A person's name.  This annotation type is not designed
 * to be used directly to annotate program elements, but to
 * define elements of other annotation types.
 */
@interface Name {
    String first();
    String last();
}
/**
 * Indicates the author of the annotated program element.
 */
@interface Author {
    Name value();
}
/**
 * Indicates the reviewer of the annotated program element.
 */
@interface Reviewer {
    Name value();
}
```

9.6.2   Defaults for Annotation Type Elements

An annotation type element may have a default value specified for it. This is done by following its (empty) parameter list with the keyword `default` and the default value of the element.

Defaults are applied dynamically at the time annotations are read; default values are not compiled into annotations. Thus, changing a default value affects annotations even in classes that were compiled before the change was made (presuming these annotations lack an explicit value for the defaulted element).

An *ElementValue* (§9.7) is used to specify a default value.

It is a compile-time error if the type of the element is not commensurate (§9.7) with the default value specified.

Example 9.6.2-1. Annotation Type Declaration With Default Values

```
@interface RequestForEnhancementDefault {
    int     id();           // No default - must be specified in
                            // each annotation
    String synopsis();      // No default - must be specified in
                            // each annotation
    String engineer()   default "[unassigned]";
    String date()       default "[unimplemented]";
}
```

9.6.3   Predefined Annotation Types

Several annotation types are predefined in the libraries of the Java SE platform. Some of these predefined annotation types have special semantics. These semantics are specified in this section. This section does not provide a complete specification for the predefined annotations contained here in; that is the role of the appropriate API specifications. Only those semantics that require special behavior on the part of a Java compiler or Java Virtual Machine implementation are specified here.

9.6.3.1   `@Target`

The annotation type `java.lang.annotation.Target` is intended to be used in meta-annotations that indicate the kind of program element that an annotation type is applicable to.

`java.lang.annotation.Target` has one element, of type `java.lang.annotation.ElementType[]`.

It is a compile-time error if a given enum constant appears more than once in an annotation whose corresponding type is `java.lang.annotation.Target`.

See §7.4.1, §8.1.1, §8.3.1, §8.4.1, §8.4.3, §8.8.3, §8.9, §9.1.1, §9.3, §9.4, §9.6 and §14.4 for the other effects of `java.lang.annotation.Target` annotations.

9.6.3.2 `@Retention`

Annotations may be present only in source code, or they may be present in the binary form of a class or interface. An annotation that is present in the binary form may or may not be available at run time via the reflection libraries of the Java SE platform. The annotation type `java.lang.annotation.Retention` is used to choose among these possibilities.

If an annotation *a* corresponds to a type *T*, and *T* has a (meta-)annotation *m* that corresponds to `java.lang.annotation.Retention`, then:

- If   *m*   has   an   element   whose   value   is `java.lang.annotation.RetentionPolicy.SOURCE`, then a Java compiler must ensure that *a* is not present in the binary representation of the class or interface in which *a* appears.

- If   *m*   has   an   element   whose   value   is `java.lang.annotation.RetentionPolicy.CLASS`   or `java.lang.annotation.RetentionPolicy.RUNTIME`, then a Java compiler must ensure that *a* is represented in the binary representation of the class or interface in which *a* appears, unless *m* annotates a local variable declaration.

  An annotation on a local variable declaration is never retained in the binary representation.

  In   addition,   if   *m*   has   an   element   whose   value   is `java.lang.annotation.RetentionPolicy.RUNTIME`, the reflection libraries of the Java SE platform must make *a* available at run time.

If   *T*   does   not   have   a   (meta-)annotation   *m*   that   corresponds   to `java.lang.annotation.Retention`, then a Java compiler must treat *T* as if it does have such a meta-annotation *m* with an element whose value is `java.lang.annotation.RetentionPolicy.CLASS`.

9.6.3.3 `@Inherited`

The annotation type `java.lang.annotation.Inherited` is used to indicate that annotations on a class *C* corresponding to a given annotation type are inherited by subclasses of *C*.

9.6.3.4   `@Override`

Programmers occasionally overload a method declaration when they mean to override it, leading to subtle problems. The annotation type `Override` supports early detection of such problems.

> The classic example concerns the `equals` method. Programmers write the following in class `Foo`:
>
> ```
> public boolean equals(Foo that) { ... }
> ```
>
> when they mean to write:
>
> ```
> public boolean equals(Object that) { ... }
> ```
>
> This is perfectly legal, but class `Foo` inherits the `equals` implementation from `Object`, which can cause some very subtle bugs.

If a method declaration is annotated with the annotation `@Override`, but the method does not override or implement a method declared in a supertype, or is not override-equivalent to a `public` method of `Object`, a compile-time error occurs.

> This behavior differs from Java SE 5.0, where `@Override` only caused a compile-time error if applied to a method that implemented a method from a superinterface that was not also present in a superclass.
>
> The clause about overriding a `public` method is motivated by use of `@Override` in an interface. Consider the following type declarations:
>
> ```
> class Foo    { @Override public int hashCode() {..} }
> interface Bar { @Override int hashCode(); }
> ```
>
> The use of `@Override` in the class declaration is legal by the first clause, because `Foo.hashCode` overrides `Object.hashCode` (§8.4.8).
>
> For the interface declaration, consider that while an interface does not have `Object` as a supertype, an interface does have `public abstract` members that correspond to the `public` members of `Object` (§9.2). If an interface chooses to declare them explicitly (i.e. to declare members that are override-equivalent to `public` methods of `Object`), then the interface is deemed to override them (§8.4.8), and use of `@Override` is allowed.
>
> However, consider an interface that attempts to use `@Override` on a `clone` method: (`finalize` could also be used in this example)
>
> ```
> interface Quux { @Override Object clone(); }
> ```
>
> Because `Object.clone` is not `public`, there is no member called `clone` implicitly declared in `Quux`. Therefore, the explicit declaration of `clone` in `Quux` is not deemed

to "implement" any other method, and it is erroneous to use `@Override`. (The fact that `Quux.clone` is `public` is not relevant.)

In contrast, a class declaration that declares `clone` is simply overriding `Object.clone`, so is able to use `@Override`:

```
class Beep { @Override protected Object clone() {..} }
```

9.6.3.5 `@SuppressWarnings`

Java compilers are increasingly capable of issuing helpful "lint-like" warnings. To encourage the use of such warnings, there should be some way to disable a warning in a part of the program when the programmer knows that the warning is inappropriate.

The annotation type `SuppressWarnings` supports programmer control over warnings otherwise issued by a Java compiler. It contains a single element that is an array of `String`.

If a program declaration is annotated with the annotation `@SuppressWarnings(value = {`S_1`, ..., `S_k`})`, then a Java compiler must not report any warning identified by one of S_1 ... S_k if that warning would have been generated as a result of the annotated declaration or any of its parts.

Unchecked warnings are identified by the string `"unchecked"`.

> Compiler vendors should document the warning names they support in conjunction with this annotation type. Vendors are encouraged to cooperate to ensure that the same names work across multiple compilers.

9.6.3.6 `@Deprecated`

A program element annotated `@Deprecated` is one that programmers are discouraged from using, typically because it is dangerous, or because a better alternative exists.

A Java compiler must produce a deprecation warning when a type, method, field, or constructor whose declaration is annotated with the annotation `@Deprecated` is used (i.e. overridden, invoked, or referenced by name), unless:

- The use is within an entity that is itself annotated with the annotation `@Deprecated`; or

- The use is within an entity that is annotated to suppress the warning with the annotation `@SuppressWarnings("deprecation")`; or

- The use and declaration are both within the same outermost class.

Use of the `@Deprecated` annotation on a local variable declaration or on a parameter declaration has no effect.

9.6.3.7   `@SafeVarargs`

A variable arity parameter with a non-reifiable element type (§4.7) can cause heap pollution (§4.12.2) and give rise to compile-time unchecked warnings (§5.1.9). Such warnings are uninformative if the body of the variable arity method is well-behaved with respect to the variable arity parameter.

The annotation type `SafeVarargs`, when used to annotate a method or constructor declaration, makes a programmer assertion that prevents a Java compiler from reporting unchecked warnings for the declaration or invocation of a variable arity method or constructor where the compiler would otherwise do so due to the variable arity parameter having a non-reifiable element type.

> The `SafeVarargs` annotation has non-local effects because it suppresses unchecked warnings at method invocation expressions in addition to an unchecked warning pertaining to the declaration of the variable arity method itself (§8.4.1). In contrast, the `@SuppressWarnings("unchecked")` annotation has local effects because it only suppresses unchecked warnings pertaining to the declaration of a method.
>
> The canonical target for a `SafeVarargs` annotation is a method like `java.util.Collections.addAll`, whose declaration starts with:
>
> ```
> public static <T> boolean
>   addAll(Collection<? super T> c, T... elements)
> ```
>
> The variable arity parameter has declared type `T[]`, which is non-reifiable. However, the method fundamentally just reads from the input array and adds the elements to a collection, both of which are safe operations with respect to the array. Therefore, any compile-time unchecked warnings at method invocation expressions for `java.util.Collections.addAll` are arguably spurious and uninformative. Applying a `SafeVarargs` annotation to the method declaration prevents generation of these unchecked warnings at the method invocation expressions.

It is a compile-time error if a fixed arity method or constructor declaration is annotated with the `SafeVarargs` annotation.

It is a compile-time error if a variable arity method declaration that is neither `static` nor `final` is annotated with the `SafeVarargs` annotation.

> Since a `SafeVarargs` annotation is only applicable to `static` methods, `final` instance methods, and constructors, the annotation is not usable where method overriding occurs. Annotation inheritance only works on classes (not methods, interfaces, or constructors), so a `SafeVarargs`-style annotation cannot be passed through instance methods in classes or through interfaces.

9.7 Annotations

An *annotation* is a modifier consisting of the name of an annotation type (§9.6) and zero or more element-value pairs, each of which associates a value with a different element of the annotation type.

The purpose of an annotation is simply to associate information with the annotated program element.

Annotations must contain an element-value pair for every element of the corresponding annotation type, except for those elements with default values, or a compile-time error occurs.

Annotations may, but are not required to, contain element-value pairs for elements with default values.

Annotations may be used as modifiers in any declaration, whether package (§7.4.1), class (§8.1.1) (including enums (§8.9)), interface (§9.1.1) (including annotation types (§9.6)), field (§8.3.1, §9.3), method (§8.4.3, §9.4), formal parameter (§8.4.1), constructor (§8.8.3), or local variable (§14.4.1).

Annotations may also be used on enum constants. Such annotations are placed immediately before the enum constant they annotate.

It is a compile-time error if a declaration is annotated with more than one annotation for a given annotation type.

> Annotations are conventionally placed before all other modifiers, but this is not a requirement; they may be freely intermixed with other modifiers.

Annotations:
  Annotation
  Annotations Annotation

Annotation:
  NormalAnnotation
  MarkerAnnotation
  SingleElementAnnotation

There are three kinds of annotations. The first (normal annotation) is fully general. The others (marker annotation and single-element annotation) are merely shorthands.

9.7.1   Normal Annotations

A *normal annotation* is used to annotate a program element.

> *NormalAnnotation:*
>   @ *TypeName* (*ElementValuePairs*$_{opt}$)

> *ElementValuePairs:*
>   *ElementValuePair*
>   *ElementValuePairs* , *ElementValuePair*

> *ElementValuePair:*
>   *Identifier* = *ElementValue*

> *ElementValue:*
>   *ConditionalExpression*
>   *Annotation*
>   *ElementValueArrayInitializer*

> *ElementValueArrayInitializer:*
>   { *ElementValues*$_{opt}$,$_{opt}$ }

> *ElementValues:*
>   *ElementValue*
>   *ElementValues* , *ElementValue*

The *TypeName* names the annotation type corresponding to the annotation.

> Note that the at-sign (@) is a token unto itself. Technically it is possible to put whitespace between it and the *TypeName*, but this is discouraged as a matter of style.

It is a compile-time error if *TypeName* does not name an annotation type that is accessible (§6.6) at the point where the annotation is used.

The *Identifier* in an *ElementValuePair* must be the simple name of one of the elements (i.e. methods) of the annotation type identified by *TypeName*; otherwise, a compile-time error occurs.

The return type of this method defines the element type of the element-value pair.

An *ElementValueArrayInitializer* is similar to a normal array initializer (§10.6), except that annotations are permitted in place of expressions.

An element type *T* is *commensurate* with an element value *v* if and only if one of the following conditions is true:

- *T* is an array type *E[]* and either:

  - *v* is an *ElementValueArrayInitializer* and each *ElementValue* (analogous to a *VariableInitializer* in an array initializer) in *v* is commensurate with *E*; or

  - *v* is an *ElementValue* that is commensurate with *E*.

- The type of *v* is assignment compatible (§5.2) with *T*, and furthermore:

  - If *T* is a primitive type or `String`, and *v* is a constant expression (§15.28).

  - *v* is not `null`.

  - If *T* is `Class`, or an invocation of `Class`, and *v* is a class literal (§15.8.2).

  - If *T* is an enum type, and *v* is an enum constant.

  > Note that `null` is not a legal element value for any element type.

It is a compile-time error if the element type is not commensurate with the *ElementValue*.

If the element type is not an annotation type or an array type, *ElementValue* must be a *ConditionalExpression* (§15.25).

> A *ConditionalExpression* is simply an expression without assignments, and not necessarily an expression involving the conditional operator (? :). *ConditionalExpression* is preferred over *Expression* in *ElementValue* because an element value has a simple structure (constant expression or class literal or enum constant) that may easily be represented in binary form.

If the element type is an array type and the corresponding *ElementValue* is not an *ElementValueArrayInitializer*, then an array value whose sole element is the value represented by the *ElementValue* is associated with the element. Otherwise, if the corresponding *ElementValue* is an *ElementValueArrayInitializer*, then the array value represented by the *ElementValueArrayInitializer* is associated with the element.

> In other words, it is permissible to omit the curly braces when a single-element array is to be associated with an array-valued annotation type element.

> Note that the array's element type cannot be an array type. That is, nested array types are not permitted as element types. (While the annotation syntax would permit this, the annotation type declaration syntax would not.)

An *ElementValue* is always FP-strict (§15.4).

An annotation on an annotation type declaration is known as a *meta-annotation*.

An annotation type may be used to annotate its own declaration. More generally, circularities in the transitive closure of the "annotates" relation are permitted.

For example, it is legal to annotate an annotation type declaration with another annotation type, and to annotate the latter type's declaration with the former type. (The pre-defined meta-annotation types contain several such circularities.)

Example 9.7.1-1. Normal Annotations

Here is an example of a normal annotation.

```
@RequestForEnhancement(
    id       = 2868724,
    synopsis = "Provide time-travel functionality",
    engineer = "Mr. Peabody",
    date     = "4/1/2004"
)
public static void travelThroughTime(Date destination) { ... }
```

Here is an example of a normal annotation that takes advantage of default values.

```
@RequestForEnhancement(
    id       = 4561414,
    synopsis = "Balance the federal budget"
)
public static void balanceFederalBudget() {
    throw new UnsupportedOperationException("Not implemented");
}
```

Note that the types of the annotations in the examples in this section are the annotation types defined in the examples in §9.6. Note also that the elements are in the above annotation are in the same order as in the corresponding annotation type declaration. This is not required, but unless specific circumstances dictate otherwise, it is a reasonable convention to follow.

9.7.2   Marker Annotations

The second form of annotation, *marker annotation*, is a shorthand designed for use with marker annotation types.

MarkerAnnotation:
   @ *Identifier*

It is shorthand for the normal annotation:

```
@Identifier()
```

It is legal to use the marker annotation form for annotation types with elements, so long as all the elements have default values.

Example 9.7.2-1. Marker Annotations

Here is an example using the `Preliminary` marker annotation type from §9.6.1:

```
@Preliminary public class TimeTravel { ... }
```

9.7.3   Single-Element Annotations

The third form of annotation, *single-element annotation*, is a shorthand designed for use with single-element annotation types.

> *SingleElementAnnotation:*
>   @ *Identifier* (*ElementValue*)

It is shorthand for the normal annotation:

```
@Identifier(value = ElementValue)
```

It is legal to use single-element annotations for annotation types with multiple elements, so long as one element is named `value`, and all other elements have default values.

Example 9.7.3-1. Single-Element Annotations

Here is an example of a single-element annotation.

```
@Copyright("2002 Yoyodyne Propulsion Systems, Inc.")
public class OscillationOverthruster { ... }
```

Here is an example of an array-valued single-element annotation.

```
@Endorsers({"Children", "Unscrupulous dentists"})
public class Lollipop { ... }
```

Here is an example of a single-element array-valued single-element annotation. Note that the curly braces are omitted.

```
@Endorsers("Epicurus")
public class Pleasure { ... }
```

Here is an example with of a single-element annotation that contains a normal annotation.

```
@Author(@Name(first = "Joe", last = "Hacker"))
```

```
public class BitTwiddle { ... }
```

Here is an example of a single-element annotation with a `Class` element whose value is restricted by the use of a bounded wildcard.

```
class GorgeousFormatter implements Formatter { ... }

@PrettyPrinter(GorgeousFormatter.class)
public class Petunia { ... }

// Illegal; String is not a subtype of Formatter
@PrettyPrinter(String.class)
public class Begonia { ... }
```

Here is an example of a single-element annotation using an enum type defined inside the annotation type.

```
@Quality(Quality.Level.GOOD)
public class Karma { ... }
```

CHAPTER 10

Arrays

IN the Java programming language, *arrays* are objects (§4.3.1), are dynamically created, and may be assigned to variables of type `Object` (§4.3.2). All methods of class `Object` may be invoked on an array.

An array object contains a number of variables. The number of variables may be zero, in which case the array is said to be *empty*. The variables contained in an array have no names; instead they are referenced by array access expressions that use non-negative integer index values. These variables are called the *components* of the array. If an array has *n* components, we say *n* is the length of the array; the components of the array are referenced using integer indices from 0 to *n* - 1, inclusive.

All the components of an array have the same type, called the *component type* of the array. If the component type of an array is *T*, then the type of the array itself is written *T*[].

The value of an array component of type `float` is always an element of the float value set (§4.2.3); similarly, the value of an array component of type `double` is always an element of the double value set. It is not permitted for the value of an array component of type `float` to be an element of the float-extended-exponent value set that is not also an element of the float value set, nor for the value of an array component of type `double` to be an element of the double-extended-exponent value set that is not also an element of the double value set.

The component type of an array may itself be an array type. The components of such an array may contain references to subarrays. If, starting from any array type, one considers its component type, and then (if that is also an array type) the component type of that type, and so on, eventually one must reach a component type that is not an array type; this is called the *element type* of the original array, and the components at this level of the data structure are called the *elements* of the original array.

There are some situations in which an element of an array can be an array: if the element type is `Object` or `Cloneable` or `java.io.Serializable`, then some or all of the elements may be arrays, because any array object can be assigned to any variable of these types.

10.1 Array Types

Array types are used in declarations and in cast expressions (§15.16).

An array type is written as the name of an element type followed by some number of empty pairs of square brackets `[]`. The number of bracket pairs indicates the depth of array nesting.

An array's length is not part of its type.

The element type of an array may be any type, whether primitive or reference. In particular:

• Arrays with an interface type as the element type are allowed.

  An element of such an array may have as its value a null reference or an instance of any type that implements the interface.

• Arrays with an `abstract` class type as the element type are allowed.

  An element of such an array may have as its value a null reference or an instance of any subclass of the `abstract` class that is not itself `abstract`.

The supertypes of an array type are specified in §4.10.3.

The direct superclass of an array type is `Object`.

Every   array   type   implements   the   interfaces   `Cloneable`   and `java.io.Serializable`.

10.2 Array Variables

A variable of array type holds a reference to an object. Declaring a variable of array type does not create an array object or allocate any space for array components. It creates only the variable itself, which can contain a reference to an array.

However, the initializer part of a declarator (§8.3, §9.3, §14.4.1) may create an array, a reference to which then becomes the initial value of the variable.

Example 10.2-1. Declarations of Array Variables

```
int[]      ai;        // array of int
short[][] as;         // array of array of short
short      s,         // scalar short
           aas[][];   // array of array of short
Object[] ao,          // array of Object
           otherAo;   // array of Object
Collection<?>[] ca;   // array of Collection of unknown type
```

The declarations above do not create array objects. The following are examples of declarations of array variables that do create array objects:

```
Exception ae[]  = new Exception[3];
Object aao[][]  = new Exception[2][3];
int[] factorial = { 1, 1, 2, 6, 24, 120, 720, 5040 };
char ac[]       = { 'n', 'o', 't', ' ', 'a', ' ',
                    'S', 't', 'r', 'i', 'n', 'g' };
String[] aas    = { "array", "of", "String", };
```

The [] may appear as part of the type at the beginning of the declaration, or as part of the declarator for a particular variable, or both.

For example:

```
byte[] rowvector, colvector, matrix[];
```

This declaration is equivalent to:

```
byte rowvector[], colvector[], matrix[][];
```

In a variable declaration (§8.3, §8.4.1, §9.3, §14.14, §14.20) except for a variable arity parameter, the array type of a variable is denoted by the array type that appears at the beginning of the declaration, followed by any bracket pairs that follow the variable's *Identifier* in the declarator.

For example, the local variable declaration:

```
int a, b[], c[][];
```

is equivalent to the series of declarations:

```
int a;
int[] b;
int[][] c;
```

Brackets are allowed in declarators as a nod to the tradition of C and C++. The general rules for variable declaration, however, permit brackets to appear on both the type and in declarators, so that the local variable declaration:

```
float[][] f[][], g[][][], h[];  // Yechh!
```

is equivalent to the series of declarations:

```
float[][][][] f;
float[][][][][] g;
float[][][] h;
```

We do not recommend "mixed notation" in an array variable declaration, where brackets appear on both the type and in declarators.

Once an array object is created, its length never changes. To make an array variable refer to an array of different length, a reference to a different array must be assigned to the variable.

A single variable of array type may contain references to arrays of different lengths, because an array's length is not part of its type.

If an array variable v has type $A[]$, where A is a reference type, then v can hold a reference to an instance of any array type $B[]$, provided B can be assigned to A (§5.2). This may result in a run-time exception on a *later* assignment; see §10.5 for a discussion.

10.3   Array Creation

An array is created by an array creation expression (§15.10) or an array initializer (§10.6).

An array creation expression specifies the element type, the number of levels of nested arrays, and the length of the array for at least one of the levels of nesting. The array's length is available as a `final` instance variable `length`.

An array initializer creates an array and provides initial values for all its components.

10.4   Array Access

A component of an array is accessed by an array access expression (§15.13) that consists of an expression whose value is an array reference followed by an indexing expression enclosed by `[` and `]`, as in `A[i]`.

All arrays are 0-origin. An array with length *n* can be indexed by the integers 0 to *n*-1.

Example 10.4-1. Array Access

```
class Gauss {
    public static void main(String[] args) {
        int[] ia = new int[101];
        for (int i = 0; i < ia.length; i++) ia[i] = i;
        int sum = 0;
        for (int e : ia) sum += e;
        System.out.println(sum);
    }
}
```

This program produces the output:

```
5050
```

The program declares a variable ia that has type array of int, that is, int[]. The variable ia is initialized to reference a newly created array object, created by an array creation expression (§15.10). The array creation expression specifies that the array should have 101 components. The length of the array is available using the field length, as shown. The program fills the array with the integers from 0 to 100, sums these integers, and prints the result.

Arrays must be indexed by int values; short, byte, or char values may also be used as index values because they are subjected to unary numeric promotion (§5.6.1) and become int values.

An attempt to access an array component with a long index value results in a compile-time error.

All array accesses are checked at run time; an attempt to use an index that is less than zero or greater than or equal to the length of the array causes an ArrayIndexOutOfBoundsException to be thrown.

10.5 Array Store Exception

For an array whose type is A[], where A is a reference type, an assignment to a component of the array is checked at run time to ensure that the value being assigned is assignable to the component.

If the type of the value being assigned is not assignment-compatible (§5.2) with the component type, an ArrayStoreException is thrown.

If the component type of an array were not reifiable (§4.7), the Java Virtual Machine could not perform the store check described in the preceding paragraph. This is why an array creation expression with a non-reifiable element type is forbidden (§15.10). One may declare a variable of an array type whose element type is non-reifiable, but assignment of the result of an array creation expression to the variable will necessarily cause an unchecked warning (§5.1.9).

Example 10.5-1. `ArrayStoreException`

```
class Point { int x, y; }
class ColoredPoint extends Point { int color; }
class Test {
    public static void main(String[] args) {
        ColoredPoint[] cpa = new ColoredPoint[10];
        Point[] pa = cpa;
        System.out.println(pa[1] == null);
        try {
            pa[0] = new Point();
        } catch (ArrayStoreException e) {
            System.out.println(e);
        }
    }
}
```

This program produces the output:

```
true
java.lang.ArrayStoreException: Point
```

The variable `pa` has type `Point[]` and the variable `cpa` has as its value a reference to an object of type `ColoredPoint[]`. A `ColoredPoint` can be assigned to a `Point`; therefore, the value of `cpa` can be assigned to `pa`.

A reference to this array `pa`, for example, testing whether `pa[1]` is `null`, will not result in a run-time type error. This is because the element of the array of type `ColoredPoint[]` is a `ColoredPoint`, and every `ColoredPoint` can stand in for a `Point`, since `Point` is the superclass of `ColoredPoint`.

On the other hand, an assignment to the array `pa` can result in a run-time error. At compile time, an assignment to an element of `pa` is checked to make sure that the value assigned is a `Point`. But since `pa` holds a reference to an array of `ColoredPoint`, the assignment is valid only if the type of the value assigned at run time is, more specifically, a `ColoredPoint`.

The Java Virtual Machine checks for such a situation at run time to ensure that the assignment is valid; if not, an `ArrayStoreException` is thrown.

10.6 Array Initializers

An *array initializer* may be specified in a declaration (§8.3, §9.3, §14.4), or as part of an array creation expression (§15.10), to create an array and provide some initial values.

> *ArrayInitializer:*
>   { *VariableInitializers*$_{opt}$ *,*$_{opt}$ }

> *VariableInitializers:*
>   *VariableInitializer*
>   *VariableInitializers* , *VariableInitializer*

The following is repeated from §8.3 to make the presentation here clearer:

> *VariableInitializer:*
>   *Expression*
>   *ArrayInitializer*

An array initializer is written as a comma-separated list of expressions, enclosed by braces { and }.

A trailing comma may appear after the last expression in an array initializer and is ignored.

Each variable initializer must be assignment-compatible (§5.2) with the array's component type, or a compile-time error occurs.

It is a compile-time error if the component type of the array being initialized is not reifiable (§4.7).

The length of the array to be constructed is equal to the number of variable initializers immediately enclosed by the braces of the array initializer. Space is allocated for a new array of that length. If there is insufficient space to allocate the array, evaluation of the array initializer completes abruptly by throwing an OutOfMemoryError. Otherwise, a one-dimensional array is created of the specified length, and each component of the array is initialized to its default value (§4.12.5).

The variable initializers immediately enclosed by the braces of the array initializer are then executed from left to right in the textual order they occur in the source code. The *n*'th variable initializer specifies the value of the *n*-1'th array component. If execution of a variable initializer completes abruptly, then execution of the array initializer completes abruptly for the same reason. If all the variable initializer expressions complete normally, the array initializer completes normally, with the value of the newly initialized array.

If the component type is an array type, then the variable initializer specifying a component may itself be an array initializer; that is, array initializers may be nested. In this case, execution of the nested array initializer constructs and initializes an array object by recursive application of the algorithm above, and assigns it to the component.

Example 10.6-1. Array Initializers

```
class Test {
    public static void main(String[] args) {
        int ia[][] = { {1, 2}, null };
        for (int[] ea : ia) {
            for (int e: ea) {
                System.out.println(e);
            }
        }
    }
}
```

This program produces the output:

```
1
2
```

before causing a `NullPointerException` in trying to index the second component of the array `ia`, which is a null reference.

10.7   Array Members

The members of an array type are all of the following:

- The `public final` field `length`, which contains the number of components of the array. `length` may be positive or zero.

- The `public` method `clone`, which overrides the method of the same name in class `Object` and throws no checked exceptions. The return type of the `clone` method of an array type `T[]` is `T[]`.

  A clone of a multidimensional array is shallow, which is to say that it creates only a single new array. Subarrays are shared.

- All the members inherited from class `Object`; the only method of `Object` that is not inherited is its `clone` method.

An array thus has the same public fields and methods as the following class:

```
class A<T> implements Cloneable, java.io.Serializable {
    public final int length = X ;
    public T[] clone() {
        try {
            return (T[])super.clone(); // unchecked warning
        } catch (CloneNotSupportedException e) {
            throw new InternalError(e.getMessage());
        }
    }
}
```

Note that the cast in the example above would generate an unchecked warning (§5.1.9) if arrays were really implemented this way.

See §9.6.3.4 for another situation where the difference between public and non-public methods of Object requires special care.

Example 10.7-1. Arrays Are Cloneable

```
class Test1 {
    public static void main(String[] args) {
        int ia1[] = { 1, 2 };
        int ia2[] = ia1.clone();
        System.out.print((ia1 == ia2) + " ");
        ia1[1]++;
        System.out.println(ia2[1]);
    }
}
```

This program produces the output:

```
false 2
```

showing that the components of the arrays referenced by ia1 and ia2 are different variables.

Example 10.7-2. Shared Subarrays After A Clone

The fact that subarrays are shared when a multidimensional array is cloned is shown by this program:

```
class Test2 {
    public static void main(String[] args) throws Throwable {
        int ia[][] = { {1,2}, null };
        int ja[][] = ia.clone();
        System.out.print((ia == ja) + " ");
        System.out.println(ia[0] == ja[0] && ia[1] == ja[1]);
    }
}
```

This program produces the output:

```
false true
```

showing that the int[] array that is ia[0] and the int[] array that is ja[0] are the same array.

10.8 Class **Objects for Arrays**

Every array has an associated Class object, shared with all other arrays with the same component type.

Example 10.8-1. Class **Object Of Array**

```
class Test {
    public static void main(String[] args) {
        int[] ia = new int[3];
        System.out.println(ia.getClass());
        System.out.println(ia.getClass().getSuperclass());
    }
}
```

This program produces the output:

```
class [I
class java.lang.Object
```

where the string "[I" is the run-time type signature for the class object "array with component type int".

Example 10.8-2. Array Class **Objects Are Shared**

```
class Test {
    public static void main(String[] args) {
        int[] ia = new int[3];
        int[] ib = new int[6];
        System.out.println(ia.getClass() == ib.getClass());
        System.out.println("ia has length=" + ia.length);
    }
}
```

This program produces the output:

```
true
ia has length=3
```

The program uses the method getClass inherited from class Object, and the field length. The result of the comparison of the Class objects in the first println demonstrates that all arrays whose components are of type int are instances of the same array type, which is int[].

10.9 An Array of Characters is Not a String

In the Java programming language, unlike C, an array of char is not a String, and neither a String nor an array of char is terminated by '\u0000' (the NUL character).

A String object is immutable, that is, its contents never change, while an array of char has mutable elements.

> The method toCharArray in class String returns an array of characters containing the same character sequence as a String. The class StringBuffer implements useful methods on mutable arrays of characters.

Exceptions

WHEN a program violates the semantic constraints of the Java programming language, the Java Virtual Machine signals this error to the program as an *exception*.

An example of such a violation is an attempt to index outside the bounds of an array. Some programming languages and their implementations react to such errors by peremptorily terminating the program; other programming languages allow an implementation to react in an arbitrary or unpredictable way. Neither of these approaches is compatible with the design goals of the Java SE platform: to provide portability and robustness.

Instead, the Java programming language specifies that an exception will be thrown when semantic constraints are violated and will cause a non-local transfer of control from the point where the exception occurred to a point that can be specified by the programmer.

An exception is said to be *thrown* from the point where it occurred and is said to be *caught* at the point to which control is transferred.

Programs can also throw exceptions explicitly, using throw statements (§14.18).

Explicit use of throw statements provides an alternative to the old-fashioned style of handling error conditions by returning funny values, such as the integer value −1 where a negative value would not normally be expected. Experience shows that too often such funny values are ignored or not checked for by callers, leading to programs that are not robust, exhibit undesirable behavior, or both.

Every exception is represented by an instance of the class Throwable or one of its subclasses (§11.1). Such an object can be used to carry information from the point at which an exception occurs to the handler that catches it. Handlers are established by catch clauses of try statements (§14.20).

During the process of throwing an exception, the Java Virtual Machine abruptly completes, one by one, any expressions, statements, method and constructor invocations, initializers, and field initialization expressions that have begun but not completed execution in the current thread. This process continues until a handler is found that indicates that it handles that particular exception by naming the class of the exception or a superclass of the class of the exception (§11.2). If no such handler is found, then the exception may be handled by one of a hierarchy of uncaught exception handlers (§11.3) - thus every effort is made to avoid letting an exception go unhandled.

The exception mechanism of the Java SE platform is integrated with its synchronization model (§17.1), so that monitors are unlocked as `synchronized` statements (§14.19) and invocations of `synchronized` methods (§8.4.3.6, §15.12) complete abruptly.

11.1   The Kinds and Causes of Exceptions

11.1.1   The Kinds of Exceptions

An exception is represented by an instance of the class `Throwable` (a direct subclass of `Object`) or one of its subclasses.

`Throwable` and all its subclasses are, collectively, the *exception classes*.

> Note that a subclass of `Throwable` must not be generic (§8.1.2).

The classes `Exception` and `Error` are direct subclasses of `Throwable`.

`Exception` is the superclass of all the exceptions from which ordinary programs may wish to recover.

`Error` is the superclass of all the exceptions from which ordinary programs are not ordinarily expected to recover.

`Error` and all its subclasses are, collectively, the *error classes*.

> The class `Error` is a separate subclass of `Throwable`, distinct from `Exception` in the class hierarchy, to allow programs to use the idiom `"} catch (Exception e) {"` (§11.2.3) to catch all exceptions from which recovery may be possible without catching errors from which recovery is typically not possible.

The class `RuntimeException` is a direct subclass of `Exception`. `RuntimeException` is the superclass of all the exceptions which may be thrown for many reasons during expression evaluation, but from which recovery may still be possible.

`RuntimeException` and all its subclasses are, collectively, the *run-time exception classes*.

The *unchecked exception classes* are the run-time exception classes and the error classes.

The *checked exception classes* are all exception classes other than the unchecked exception classes. That is, the checked exception classes are all subclasses of `Throwable` other than `RuntimeException` and its subclasses and `Error` and its subclasses.

> Programs can use the pre-existing exception classes of the Java SE platform API in `throw` statements, or define additional exception classes as subclasses of `Throwable` or of any of its subclasses, as appropriate. To take advantage of compile-time checking for exception handlers (§11.2), it is typical to define most new exception classes as checked exception classes, that is, as subclasses of `Exception` that are not subclasses of `RuntimeException`.

11.1.2   The Causes of Exceptions

An exception is thrown for one of three reasons:

- A `throw` statement (§14.18) was executed.

- An abnormal execution condition was synchronously detected by the Java Virtual Machine, namely:

  - evaluation of an expression violates the normal semantics of the Java programming language (§15.6), such as an integer divide by zero.

  - an error occurs while loading, linking, or initializing part of the program (§12.2, §12.3, §12.4); in this case, an instance of a subclass of `LinkageError` is thrown.

  - an internal error or resource limitation prevents the Java Virtual Machine from implementing the semantics of the Java programming language; in this case, an instance of a subclass of `VirtualMethodError` is thrown.

  These exceptions are not thrown at an arbitrary point in the program, but rather at a point where they are specified as a possible result of an expression evaluation or statement execution.

- An asynchronous exception occurred (§11.1.3).

11.1.3   Asynchronous Exceptions

Most exceptions occur synchronously as a result of an action by the thread in which they occur, and at a point in the program that is specified to possibly result in such an exception. An *asynchronous exception* is, by contrast, an exception that can potentially occur at any point in the execution of a program.

Asynchronous exceptions occur only as a result of:

- An invocation of the (deprecated) `stop` method of class `Thread` or `ThreadGroup`.

  The (deprecated) `stop` methods may be invoked by one thread to affect another thread or all the threads in a specified thread group. They are asynchronous because they may occur at any point in the execution of the other thread or threads.

- An internal error or resource limitation in the Java Virtual Machine that prevents it from implementing the semantics of the Java programming language. In this case, the asynchronous exception that is thrown is an instance of a subclass of `VirtualMethodError`.

  > Note that `StackOverflowError`, a subclass of `VirtualMethodError`, may be thrown synchronously by method invocation (§15.12.4.5) as well as asynchronously due to `native` method execution or Java Virtual Machine resource limitations. Similarly, `OutOfMemoryError`, another subclass of `VirtualMethodError`, may be thrown synchronously during object creation (§12.5), array creation (§15.10.1, §10.6), class initialization (§12.4.2), and boxing conversion (§5.1.7), as well as asynchronously.

The Java SE platform permits a small but bounded amount of execution to occur before an asynchronous exception is thrown.

> Asynchronous exceptions are rare, but proper understanding of their semantics is necessary if high-quality machine code is to be generated.

> The delay noted above is permitted to allow optimized code to detect and throw these exceptions at points where it is practical to handle them while obeying the semantics of the Java programming language. A simple implementation might poll for asynchronous exceptions at the point of each control transfer instruction. Since a program has a finite size, this provides a bound on the total delay in detecting an asynchronous exception. Since no asynchronous exception will occur between control transfers, the code generator has some flexibility to reorder computation between control transfers for greater performance. The paper *Polling Efficiently on Stock Hardware* by Marc Feeley, *Proc. 1993 Conference on Functional Programming and Computer Architecture*, Copenhagen, Denmark, pp. 179-187, is recommended as further reading.

11.2   Compile-Time Checking of Exceptions

The Java programming language requires that a program contains handlers for *checked exceptions* which can result from execution of a method or constructor. For each checked exception which is a possible result, the `throws` clause for the method (§8.4.6) or constructor (§8.8.5) must mention the class of that exception or one of the superclasses of the class of that exception (§11.2.3).

This compile-time checking for the presence of exception handlers is designed to reduce the number of exceptions which are not properly handled. The checked exception classes (§11.1.1) named in the `throws` clause are part of the contract between the implementor and user of the method or constructor. The `throws` clause of an overriding method may not specify that this method will result in throwing any checked exception which the overridden method is not permitted, by its `throws` clause, to throw (§8.4.8.3).

When interfaces are involved, more than one method declaration may be overridden by a single overriding declaration. In this case, the overriding declaration must have a `throws` clause that is compatible with all the overridden declarations (§9.4.1).

The unchecked exception classes (§11.1.1) are exempted from compile-time checking.

> Of the unchecked exception classes, error classes are exempted because they can occur at many points in the program and recovery from them is difficult or impossible. A program declaring such exceptions would be cluttered, pointlessly. Sophisticated programs may yet wish to catch and attempt to recover from some of these conditions.

> Of the unchecked exception classes, run-time exception classes are exempted because, in the judgment of the designers of the Java programming language, having to declare such exceptions would not aid significantly in establishing the correctness of programs. Many of the operations and constructs of the Java programming language can result in exceptions at run time. The information available to a Java compiler, and the level of analysis a compiler performs, are usually not sufficient to establish that such run-time exceptions cannot occur, even though this may be obvious to the programmer. Requiring such exception classes to be declared would simply be an irritation to programmers.

> For example, certain code might implement a circular data structure that, by construction, can never involve null references; the programmer can then be certain that a `NullPointerException` cannot occur, but it would be difficult for a Java compiler to prove it. The theorem-proving technology that is needed to establish such global properties of data structures is beyond the scope of this specification.

We say that a statement or expression *can throw* a checked exception class *E* if, according to the rules in §11.2.1 and §11.2.2, the execution of the statement or expression can result in an exception of class *E* being thrown.

We say that a `catch` clause *can catch* its catchable exception class(es).

The *catchable exception class* of a uni-`catch` clause is the declared type of its exception parameter (§14.20).

The *catchable exception classes* of a multi-`catch` clause are the alternatives in the union that denotes the type of its exception parameter (§14.20).

11.2.1   Exception Analysis of Expressions

A class instance creation expression (§15.9) can throw an exception class E iff either:

- The expression is a qualified class instance creation expression and the qualifying expression can throw E; or

- Some expression of the argument list can throw E; or

- E is determined to be an exception class of the `throws` clause of the constructor that is invoked (§15.12.2.6); or

- The class instance creation expression includes a *ClassBody*, and some instance initializer block or instance variable initializer expression in the *ClassBody* can throw E.

A method invocation expression (§15.12) can throw an exception class E iff either:

- The method to be invoked is of the form *Primary.Identifier* and the *Primary* expression can throw E; or

- Some expression of the argument list can throw E; or

- E is determined to be an exception class of the `throws` clause of the method that is invoked (§15.12.2.6).

For every other kind of expression, the expression can throw an exception class E iff one of its immediate subexpressions can throw E.

11.2.2   Exception Analysis of Statements

A `throw` statement (§14.18) whose thrown expression has static type E and is not a final or effectively final exception parameter can throw E or any exception class that the thrown expression can throw.

> For example, the statement `throw new java.io.FileNotFoundException();` can throw `java.io.FileNotFoundException` only. Formally, it is not the case that it "can throw" a subclass or superclass of `java.io.FileNotFoundException`.

A `throw` statement whose thrown expression is a final or effectively final exception parameter of a `catch` clause C can throw an exception class E iff:

- E is an exception class that the `try` block of the `try` statement which declares C can throw; and

- E is assignment compatible with any of C's catchable exception classes; and

- E is not assignment compatible with any of the catchable exception classes of the `catch` clauses declared to the left of C in the same `try` statement.

A `try` statement (§14.20) can throw an exception class E iff either:

- The `try` block can throw E, or an expression used to initialize a resource (in a `try`-with-resources statement) can throw E, or the automatic invocation of the `close()` method of a resource (in a `try`-with-resources statement) can throw E, and E is not assignment compatible with any catchable exception class of any `catch` clause of the `try` statement, and either no `finally` block is present or the `finally` block can complete normally; or

- Some `catch` block of the `try` statement can throw E and either no `finally` block is present or the `finally` block can complete normally; or

- A `finally` block is present and can throw E.

An explicit constructor invocation statement (§8.8.7.1) can throw an exception class E iff either:

- Some expression of the constructor invocation's parameter list can throw E; or

- E is determined to be an exception class of the `throws` clause of the constructor that is invoked (§15.12.2.6).

Any other statement S can throw an exception class E iff an expression or statement immediately contained in S can throw E.

11.2.3   Exception Checking

It is a compile-time error if a method or constructor body *can throw* some exception class E when E is a checked exception class and E is not a subclass of some class declared in the `throws` clause of the method or constructor.

It is a compile-time error if a class variable initializer (§8.3.2) or static initializer (§8.7) of a named class or interface *can throw* a checked exception class.

It is a compile-time error if an instance variable initializer or instance initializer of a named class *can throw* a checked exception class unless that exception class or one of its superclasses is explicitly declared in the `throws` clause of each constructor of its class and the class has at least one explicitly declared constructor.

Note that no compile-time error is due if an instance variable initializer or instance initializer of an anonymous class (§15.9.5) can throw an exception class. In a named class, it is the responsibility of the programmer to propagate information about which exception classes can be thrown by initializers, by declaring a suitable `throws` clause on any explicit constructor declaration. This relationship between the checked exception classes thrown by a class's initializers and the checked exception classes declared by a class's constructors is assured implicitly for an anonymous class declaration, because no explicit constructor declarations are possible and a Java compiler always generates a constructor with a suitable `throws` clause for that anonymous class declaration based on the checked exception classes that its initializers can throw.

It is a compile-time error if a `catch` clause *can catch* checked exception class E_1 and it is not the case that the `try` block corresponding to the `catch` clause *can throw* a checked exception class that is a subclass or superclass of E_1, unless E_1 is `Exception` or a superclass of `Exception`.

It is a compile-time error if a `catch` clause *can catch* (§11.2) checked exception class E_1 and a preceding `catch` clause of the immediately enclosing `try` statement *can catch* E_1 or a superclass of E_1.

A Java compiler is encouraged to issue a warning if a `catch` clause *can catch* (§11.2) checked exception class E_1 and the `try` block corresponding to the `catch` clause *can throw* checked exception class E_2, a subclass of E_1, and a preceding `catch` clause of the immediately enclosing `try` statement *can catch* checked exception class E_3 where $E_2 <: E_3 <: E_1$.

Example 11.2.3-1. Catching Checked Exceptions

```
import java.io.*;

class StaticallyThrownExceptionsIncludeSubtypes {
    public static void main(String[] args) {
        try {
            throw new FileNotFoundException();
        } catch (IOException ioe) {
            // Legal in Java SE 6 and 7. "catch IOException"
            // catches IOException and any subtype.
        }

        try {
            throw new FileNotFoundException();
                // Statement "can throw" FileNotFoundException.
                // It is not the case that statement "can throw"
                // a subtype or supertype of FileNotFoundException.
        } catch (FileNotFoundException fnfe) {
            // Legal in Java SE 6 and 7.
        } catch (IOException ioe) {
            // Legal in Java SE 6 and 7, but compilers are
            // encouraged to throw warnings as of Java SE 7.
            // All subtypes of IOException that the try block
            // can throw have already been caught.
```

```
        }

        try {
            m();
                // Method m's declaration says "throws IOException".
                // m "can throw" IOException. It is not the case
                // that m "can throw" a subtype or supertype of
                // IOException, e.g. Exception, though Exception or
                // a supertype of Exception can always be caught.
        } catch (FileNotFoundException fnfe) {
                // Legal in Java SE 6 and 7, because the dynamic type
                // of the IOException might be FileNotFoundException.
        } catch (IOException ioe) {
                // Legal in Java SE 6 and 7.
        } catch (Throwable t) {
                // Legal in Java SE 6 and 7.
        }
    }

    static void m() throws IOException {
        throw new FileNotFoundException();
    }
}
```

By the rules above, each alternative in a multi-`catch` clause (§14.20) must be able to catch some exception class thrown by the `try` block and uncaught by previous `catch` clauses. For example, the second `catch` clause below would cause a compile-time error because exception analysis determines that `SubclassOfFoo` is already caught by the first `catch` clause:

```
try { ... }
catch (Foo f) { ... }
catch (Bar | SubclassOfFoo e) { ... }
```

11.3 Run-Time Handling of an Exception

When an exception is thrown (§14.18), control is transferred from the code that caused the exception to the nearest dynamically enclosing `catch` clause, if any, of a `try` statement (§14.20) that can handle the exception.

A statement or expression is *dynamically enclosed* by a `catch` clause if it appears within the `try` block of the `try` statement of which the `catch` clause is a part, or if the caller of the statement or expression is dynamically enclosed by the `catch` clause.

The caller of a statement or expression depends on where it occurs:

- If within a method, then the caller is the method invocation expression (§15.12) that was executed to cause the method to be invoked.

- If within a constructor or an instance initializer or the initializer for an instance variable, then the caller is the class instance creation expression (§15.9) or the method invocation of `newInstance` that was executed to cause an object to be created.

- If within a static initializer or an initializer for a `static` variable, then the caller is the expression that used the class or interface so as to cause it to be initialized (§12.4).

Whether a particular `catch` clause *can handle* an exception is determined by comparing the class of the object that was thrown to the catchable exception classes of the `catch` clause. The `catch` clause can handle the exception if one of its catchable exception classes is the class of the exception or a superclass of the class of the exception.

> Equivalently, a `catch` clause will catch any exception object that is an `instanceof` (§15.20.2) one of its catchable exception classes.

The control transfer that occurs when an exception is thrown causes abrupt completion of expressions (§15.6) and statements (§14.1) until a `catch` clause is encountered that can handle the exception; execution then continues by executing the block of that `catch` clause. The code that caused the exception is never resumed.

All exceptions (synchronous and asynchronous) are *precise*: when the transfer of control takes place, all effects of the statements executed and expressions evaluated before the point from which the exception is thrown must appear to have taken place. No expressions, statements, or parts thereof that occur after the point from which the exception is thrown may appear to have been evaluated.

> If optimized code has speculatively executed some of the expressions or statements which follow the point at which the exception occurs, such code must be prepared to hide this speculative execution from the user-visible state of the program.

If no `catch` clause that can handle an exception can be found, then the current thread (the thread that encountered the exception) is terminated. Before termination, all `finally` clauses are executed and the uncaught exception is handled according to the following rules:

- If the current thread has an uncaught exception handler set, then that handler is executed.

- Otherwise, the method `uncaughtException` is invoked for the `ThreadGroup` that is the parent of the current thread. If the `ThreadGroup` and its parent `ThreadGroup`s do not override `uncaughtException`, then the default handler's `uncaughtException` method is invoked.

In situations where it is desirable to ensure that one block of code is always executed after another, even if that other block of code completes abruptly, a `try` statement with a `finally` clause (§14.20.2) may be used.

If a `try` or `catch` block in a `try-finally` or `try-catch-finally` statement completes abruptly, then the `finally` clause is executed during propagation of the exception, even if no matching `catch` clause is ultimately found.

If a `finally` clause is executed because of abrupt completion of a `try` block and the `finally` clause itself completes abruptly, then the reason for the abrupt completion of the `try` block is discarded and the new reason for abrupt completion is propagated from there.

The exact rules for abrupt completion and for the catching of exceptions are specified in detail with the specification of each statement in §14 and for expressions in §15 (especially §15.6).

Example 11.3-1. Throwing and Catching Exceptions

The following program declares an exception class `TestException`. The `main` method of class `Test` invokes the `thrower` method four times, causing exceptions to be thrown three of the four times. The `try` statement in method `main` catches each exception that the thrower throws. Whether the invocation of `thrower` completes normally or abruptly, a message is printed describing what happened.

```
class TestException extends Exception {
    TestException()          { super(); }
    TestException(String s) { super(s); }
}

class Test {
    public static void main(String[] args) {
        for (String arg : args) {
            try {
                thrower(arg);
                System.out.println("Test \"" + arg +
                                   "\" didn't throw an exception");
            } catch (Exception e) {
                System.out.println("Test \"" + arg +
                                   "\" threw a " + e.getClass() +
                                   "\n     with message: " +
                                   e.getMessage());
            }
        }
    }
    static int thrower(String s) throws TestException {
```

```
            try {
                if (s.equals("divide")) {
                    int i = 0;
                    return i/i;
                }
                if (s.equals("null")) {
                    s = null;
                    return s.length();
                }
                if (s.equals("test")) {
                    throw new TestException("Test message");
                }
                return 0;
            } finally {
                System.out.println("[thrower(\"" + s + "\") done]");
            }
        }
    }
```

If we execute the program, passing it the arguments:

```
divide null not test
```

it produces the output:

```
[thrower("divide") done]
Test "divide" threw a class java.lang.ArithmeticException
    with message: / by zero
[thrower("null") done]
Test "null" threw a class java.lang.NullPointerException
    with message: null
[thrower("not") done]
Test "not" didn't throw an exception
[thrower("test") done]
Test "test" threw a class TestException
    with message: Test message
```

The declaration of the method `thrower` must have a `throws` clause because it can throw instances of `TestException`, which is a checked exception class (§11.1.1). A compile-time error would occur if the `throws` clause were omitted.

Notice that the `finally` clause is executed on every invocation of `thrower`, whether or not an exception occurs, as shown by the "`[thrower(...) done]`" output that occurs for each invocation.

CHAPTER **12**

Execution

THIS chapter specifies activities that occur during execution of a program. It is organized around the life cycle of the Java Virtual Machine and of the classes, interfaces, and objects that form a program.

The Java Virtual Machine starts up by loading a specified class and then invoking the method main in this specified class. Section §12.1 outlines the loading, linking, and initialization steps involved in executing main, as an introduction to the concepts in this chapter. Further sections specify the details of loading (§12.2), linking (§12.3), and initialization (§12.4).

The chapter continues with a specification of the procedures for creation of new class instances (§12.5); and finalization of class instances (§12.6). It concludes by describing the unloading of classes (§12.7) and the procedure followed when a program exits (§12.8).

12.1 Java Virtual Machine Startup

The Java Virtual Machine starts execution by invoking the method main of some specified class, passing it a single argument, which is an array of strings. In the examples in this specification, this first class is typically called Test.

The precise semantics of Java Virtual Machine startup are given in Chapter 5 of *The Java Virtual Machine Specification, Java SE 7 Edition*. Here we present an overview of the process from the viewpoint of the Java programming language.

The manner in which the initial class is specified to the Java Virtual Machine is beyond the scope of this specification, but it is typical, in host environments that use command lines, for the fully-qualified name of the class to be specified as a command-line argument and for following command-line arguments to be used as strings to be provided as the argument to the method main.

For example, in a UNIX implementation, the command line:

```
java Test reboot Bob Dot Enzo
```

will typically start a Java Virtual Machine by invoking method `main` of class `Test` (a class in an unnamed package), passing it an array containing the four strings "`reboot`", "`Bob`", "`Dot`", and "`Enzo`".

We now outline the steps the Java Virtual Machine may take to execute `Test`, as an example of the loading, linking, and initialization processes that are described further in later sections.

12.1.1   Load the Class `Test`

The initial attempt to execute the method `main` of class `Test` discovers that the class `Test` is not loaded - that is, that the Java Virtual Machine does not currently contain a binary representation for this class. The Java Virtual Machine then uses a class loader to attempt to find such a binary representation. If this process fails, then an error is thrown. This loading process is described further in §12.2.

12.1.2   Link `Test`: **Verify, Prepare, (Optionally) Resolve**

After `Test` is loaded, it must be initialized before `main` can be invoked. And `Test`, like all (class or interface) types, must be linked before it is initialized. Linking involves verification, preparation, and (optionally) resolution. Linking is described further in §12.3.

Verification checks that the loaded representation of `Test` is well-formed, with a proper symbol table. Verification also checks that the code that implements `Test` obeys the semantic requirements of the Java programming language and the Java Virtual Machine. If a problem is detected during verification, then an error is thrown. Verification is described further in §12.3.1.

Preparation involves allocation of static storage and any data structures that are used internally by the implementation of the Java Virtual Machine, such as method tables. Preparation is described further in §12.3.2.

Resolution is the process of checking symbolic references from `Test` to other classes and interfaces, by loading the other classes and interfaces that are mentioned and checking that the references are correct.

The resolution step is optional at the time of initial linkage. An implementation may resolve symbolic references from a class or interface that is being linked very early, even to the point of resolving all symbolic references from the classes and interfaces that are further referenced, recursively. (This resolution may result in errors from these further loading and linking steps.) This implementation choice represents one extreme and is similar to the kind of "static" linkage that has been done for many years in simple implementations of the C language. (In these implementations, a compiled program is typically represented as an "a.out" file that contains a fully-linked version of the program, including completely resolved links to library routines used by the program. Copies of these library routines are included in the "a.out" file.)

An implementation may instead choose to resolve a symbolic reference only when it is actively used; consistent use of this strategy for all symbolic references would represent the "laziest" form of resolution. In this case, if Test had several symbolic references to another class, then the references might be resolved one at a time, as they are used, or perhaps not at all, if these references were never used during execution of the program.

The only requirement on when resolution is performed is that any errors detected during resolution must be thrown at a point in the program where some action is taken by the program that might, directly or indirectly, require linkage to the class or interface involved in the error. Using the "static" example implementation choice described above, loading and linkage errors could occur before the program is executed if they involved a class or interface mentioned in the class Test or any of the further, recursively referenced, classes and interfaces. In a system that implemented the "laziest" resolution, these errors would be thrown only when an incorrect symbolic reference is actively used.

The resolution process is described further in §12.3.3.

12.1.3   Initialize Test: Execute Initializers

In our continuing example, the Java Virtual Machine is still trying to execute the method main of class Test. This is permitted only if the class has been initialized (§12.4.1).

Initialization consists of execution of any class variable initializers and static initializers of the class Test, in textual order. But before Test can be initialized, its direct superclass must be initialized, as well as the direct superclass of its direct superclass, and so on, recursively. In the simplest case, Test has Object as its implicit direct superclass; if class Object has not yet been initialized, then it must be initialized before Test is initialized. Class Object has no superclass, so the recursion terminates here.

If class `Test` has another class `Super` as its superclass, then `Super` must be initialized before `Test`. This requires loading, verifying, and preparing `Super` if this has not already been done and, depending on the implementation, may also involve resolving the symbolic references from `Super` and so on, recursively.

Initialization may thus cause loading, linking, and initialization errors, including such errors involving other types.

The initialization process is described further in §12.4.

12.1.4   Invoke `Test.main`

Finally, after completion of the initialization for class `Test` (during which other consequential loading, linking, and initializing may have occurred), the method `main` of `Test` is invoked.

The method `main` must be declared `public`, `static`, and `void`. It must specify a formal parameter (§8.4.1) whose declared type is array of `String`. Therefore, either of the following declarations is acceptable:

```
public static void main(String[] args)

public static void main(String... args)
```

12.2   Loading of Classes and Interfaces

Loading refers to the process of finding the binary form of a class or interface type with a particular name, perhaps by computing it on the fly, but more typically by retrieving a binary representation previously computed from source code by a Java compiler, and constructing, from that binary form, a `Class` object to represent the class or interface.

The precise semantics of loading are given in Chapter 5 of *The Java Virtual Machine Specification, Java SE 7 Edition*. Here we present an overview of the process from the viewpoint of the Java programming language.

The binary format of a class or interface is normally the `class` file format described in *The Java Virtual Machine Specification, Java SE 7 Edition* cited above, but other formats are possible, provided they meet the requirements specified in §13.1. The method `defineClass` of class `ClassLoader` may be used to construct `Class` objects from binary representations in the `class` file format.

Well-behaved class loaders maintain these properties:

- Given the same name, a good class loader should always return the same class object.

- If a class loader $L1$ delegates loading of a class C to another loader $L2$, then for any type T that occurs as the direct superclass or a direct superinterface of C, or as the type of a field in C, or as the type of a formal parameter of a method or constructor in C, or as a return type of a method in C, $L1$ and $L2$ should return the same Class object.

A malicious class loader could violate these properties. However, it could not undermine the security of the type system, because the Java Virtual Machine guards against this.

> For further discussion of these issues, see *The Java Virtual Machine Specification, Java SE 7 Edition* and the paper *Dynamic Class Loading in the Java Virtual Machine*, by Sheng Liang and Gilad Bracha, in *Proceedings of OOPSLA '98*, published as *ACM SIGPLAN Notices*, Volume 33, Number 10, October 1998, pages 36-44. A basic principle of the design of the Java programming language is that the run-time type system cannot be subverted by code written in the Java programming language, not even by implementations of such otherwise sensitive system classes as ClassLoader and SecurityManager.

12.2.1   The Loading Process

The loading process is implemented by the class ClassLoader and its subclasses.

Different subclasses of ClassLoader may implement different loading policies. In particular, a class loader may cache binary representations of classes and interfaces, prefetch them based on expected usage, or load a group of related classes together. These activities may not be completely transparent to a running application if, for example, a newly compiled version of a class is not found because an older version is cached by a class loader. It is the responsibility of a class loader, however, to reflect loading errors only at points in the program where they could have arisen without prefetching or group loading.

If an error occurs during class loading, then an instance of one of the following subclasses of class LinkageError will be thrown at any point in the program that (directly or indirectly) uses the type:

- ClassCircularityError: A class or interface could not be loaded because it would be its own superclass or superinterface (§8.1.4, §9.1.3, §13.4.4).

- ClassFormatError: The binary data that purports to specify a requested compiled class or interface is malformed.

- NoClassDefFoundError: No definition for a requested class or interface could be found by the relevant class loader.

Because loading involves the allocation of new data structures, it may fail with an OutOfMemoryError.

12.3   Linking of Classes and Interfaces

Linking is the process of taking a binary form of a class or interface type and combining it into the run-time state of the Java Virtual Machine, so that it can be executed. A class or interface type is always loaded before it is linked.

Three different activities are involved in linking: verification, preparation, and resolution of symbolic references.

The precise semantics of linking are given in Chapter 5 of *The Java Virtual Machine Specification, Java SE 7 Edition*. Here we present an overview of the process from the viewpoint of the Java programming language.

This specification allows an implementation flexibility as to when linking activities (and, because of recursion, loading) take place, provided that the semantics of the Java programming language are respected, that a class or interface is completely verified and prepared before it is initialized, and that errors detected during linkage are thrown at a point in the program where some action is taken by the program that might require linkage to the class or interface involved in the error.

For example, an implementation may choose to resolve each symbolic reference in a class or interface individually, only when it is used (lazy or late resolution), or to resolve them all at once while the class is being verified (static resolution). This means that the resolution process may continue, in some implementations, after a class or interface has been initialized.

Because linking involves the allocation of new data structures, it may fail with an OutOfMemoryError.

12.3.1   Verification of the Binary Representation

Verification ensures that the binary representation of a class or interface is structurally correct. For example, it checks that every instruction has a valid operation code; that every branch instruction branches to the start of some other instruction, rather than into the middle of an instruction; that every method is provided with a structurally correct signature; and that every instruction obeys the type discipline of the Java Virtual Machine language.

If an error occurs during verification, then an instance of the following subclass of class `LinkageError` will be thrown at the point in the program that caused the class to be verified:

- `VerifyError`: The binary definition for a class or interface failed to pass a set of required checks to verify that it obeys the semantics of the Java Virtual Machine language and that it cannot violate the integrity of the Java Virtual Machine. (See §13.4.2, §13.4.4, §13.4.9, and §13.4.17 for some examples.)

12.3.2   Preparation of a Class or Interface Type

Preparation involves creating the `static` fields (class variables and constants) for a class or interface and initializing such fields to the default values (§4.12.5). This does not require the execution of any source code; explicit initializers for static fields are executed as part of initialization (§12.4), not preparation.

> Implementations of the Java Virtual Machine may precompute additional data structures at preparation time in order to make later operations on a class or interface more efficient. One particularly useful data structure is a "method table" or other data structure that allows any method to be invoked on instances of a class without requiring a search of superclasses at invocation time.

12.3.3   Resolution of Symbolic References

The binary representation of a class or interface references other classes and interfaces and their fields, methods, and constructors symbolically, using the binary names (§13.1) of the other classes and interfaces (§13.1). For fields and methods, these symbolic references include the name of the class or interface type of which the field or method is a member, as well as the name of the field or method itself, together with appropriate type information.

Before a symbolic reference can be used it must undergo resolution, wherein a symbolic reference is checked to be correct and, typically, replaced with a direct reference that can be more efficiently processed if the reference is used repeatedly.

If an error occurs during resolution, then an error will be thrown. Most typically, this will be an instance of one of the following subclasses of the class `IncompatibleClassChangeError`, but it may also be an instance of some other subclass of `IncompatibleClassChangeError` or even an instance of the class `IncompatibleClassChangeError` itself. This error may be thrown at any point in the program that uses a symbolic reference to the type, directly or indirectly:

- `IllegalAccessError`: A symbolic reference has been encountered that specifies a use or assignment of a field, or invocation of a method, or creation of an instance of a class, to which the code containing the reference does not have access because the field or method was declared with `private`, `protected`, or default access (not `public`), or because the class was not declared `public`.

This can occur, for example, if a field that is originally declared `public` is changed to be `private` after another class that refers to the field has been compiled (§13.4.7).

- `InstantiationError`: A symbolic reference has been encountered that is used in class instance creation expression, but an instance cannot be created because the reference turns out to refer to an interface or to an abstract class.

  This can occur, for example, if a class that is originally not `abstract` is changed to be `abstract` after another class that refers to the class in question has been compiled (§13.4.1).

- `NoSuchFieldError`: A symbolic reference has been encountered that refers to a specific field of a specific class or interface, but the class or interface does not contain a field of that name.

  This can occur, for example, if a field declaration was deleted from a class after another class that refers to the field was compiled (§13.4.8).

- `NoSuchMethodError`: A symbolic reference has been encountered that refers to a specific method of a specific class or interface, but the class or interface does not contain a method of that signature.

  This can occur, for example, if a method declaration was deleted from a class after another class that refers to the method was compiled (§13.4.12).

Additionally, an `UnsatisfiedLinkError`, a subclass of `LinkageError`, may be thrown if a class declares a `native` method for which no implementation can be found. The error will occur if the method is used, or earlier, depending on what kind of resolution strategy is being used by an implementation of the Java Virtual Machine (§12.3).

12.4   Initialization of Classes and Interfaces

Initialization of a class consists of executing its static initializers and the initializers for `static` fields (class variables) declared in the class.

Initialization of an interface consists of executing the initializers for fields (constants) declared in the interface.

Before a class is initialized, its direct superclass must be initialized, but interfaces implemented by the class are not initialized. Similarly, the superinterfaces of an interface are not initialized before the interface is initialized.

12.4.1 When Initialization Occurs

A class or interface type T will be initialized immediately before the first occurrence of any one of the following:

- T is a class and an instance of T is created.

- T is a class and a static method declared by T is invoked.

- A static field declared by T is assigned.

- A static field declared by T is used and the field is not a constant variable (§4.12.4).

- T is a top level class (§7.6), and an assert statement (§14.10) lexically nested within T (§8.1.3) is executed.

A reference to a static field (§8.3.1.1) causes initialization of only the class or interface that actually declares it, even though it might be referred to through the name of a subclass, a subinterface, or a class that implements an interface.

Invocation of certain reflective methods in class Class and in package java.lang.reflect also causes class or interface initialization.

A class or interface will not be initialized under any other circumstance.

The intent is that a class or interface type has a set of initializers that put it in a consistent state, and that this state is the first state that is observed by other classes. The static initializers and class variable initializers are executed in textual order, and may not refer to class variables declared in the class whose declarations appear textually after the use, even though these class variables are in scope (§8.3.2.3). This restriction is designed to detect, at compile time, most circular or otherwise malformed initializations.

The fact that initialization code is unrestricted allows examples to be constructed (§8.3.2.3) where the value of a class variable can be observed when it still has its initial default value, before its initializing expression is evaluated, but such examples are rare in practice. (Such examples can be also constructed for instance variable initialization (§12.5).) The full power of the Java programming language is available in these initializers; programmers must exercise some care. This power places an extra burden on code generators, but this burden would arise in any case because the Java programming language is concurrent (§12.4.2).

Example 12.4.1-1. Superclasses Are Initialized Before Subclasses

```
class Super {
    static { System.out.print("Super "); }
}
class One {
    static { System.out.print("One "); }
}
class Two extends Super {
    static { System.out.print("Two "); }
}
class Test {
    public static void main(String[] args) {
        One o = null;
        Two t = new Two();
        System.out.println((Object)o == (Object)t);
    }
}
```

This program produces the output:

```
Super Two false
```

The class `One` is never initialized, because it not used actively and therefore is never linked to. The class `Two` is initialized only after its superclass `Super` has been initialized.

Example 12.4.1-2. Only The Class That Declares `static` Field Is Initialized

```
class Super {
    static int taxi = 1729;
}
class Sub extends Super {
    static { System.out.print("Sub "); }
}
class Test {
    public static void main(String[] args) {
        System.out.println(Sub.taxi);
    }
}
```

This program prints only:

```
1729
```

because the class `Sub` is never initialized; the reference to `Sub.taxi` is a reference to a field actually declared in class `Super` and does not trigger initialization of the class `Sub`.

Example 12.4.1-3. Interface Initialization Does Not Initialize Superinterfaces

```
interface I {
    int i = 1, ii = Test.out("ii", 2);
```

```
    }
interface J extends I {
    int j = Test.out("j", 3), jj = Test.out("jj", 4);
}
interface K extends J {
    int k = Test.out("k", 5);
}
class Test {
    public static void main(String[] args) {
        System.out.println(J.i);
        System.out.println(K.j);
    }
    static int out(String s, int i) {
        System.out.println(s + "=" + i);
        return i;
    }
}
```

This program produces the output:

```
1
j=3
jj=4
3
```

The reference to J.i is to a field that is a constant variable (§4.12.4); therefore, it does not cause I to be initialized (§13.4.9).

The reference to K.j is a reference to a field actually declared in interface J that is not a constant variable; this causes initialization of the fields of interface J, but not those of its superinterface I, nor those of interface K.

Despite the fact that the name K is used to refer to field j of interface J, interface K is not initialized.

12.4.2   Detailed Initialization Procedure

Because the Java programming language is multithreaded, initialization of a class or interface requires careful synchronization, since some other thread may be trying to initialize the same class or interface at the same time. There is also the possibility that initialization of a class or interface may be requested recursively as part of the initialization of that class or interface; for example, a variable initializer in class A might invoke a method of an unrelated class B, which might in turn invoke a method of class A. The implementation of the Java Virtual Machine is responsible for taking care of synchronization and recursive initialization by using the following procedure.

The procedure assumes that the `Class` object has already been verified and prepared, and that the `Class` object contains state that indicates one of four situations:

- This `Class` object is verified and prepared but not initialized.

- This `Class` object is being initialized by some particular thread T.

- This `Class` object is fully initialized and ready for use.

- This `Class` object is in an erroneous state, perhaps because initialization was attempted and failed.

For each class or interface C, there is a unique initialization lock LC. The mapping from C to LC is left to the discretion of the Java Virtual Machine implementation. The procedure for initializing C is then as follows:

1. Synchronize on the initialization lock, LC, for C. This involves waiting until the current thread can acquire LC.

2. If the `Class` object for C indicates that initialization is in progress for C by some other thread, then release LC and block the current thread until informed that the in-progress initialization has completed, at which time repeat this step.

3. If the `Class` object for C indicates that initialization is in progress for C by the current thread, then this must be a recursive request for initialization. Release LC and complete normally.

4. If the `Class` object for C indicates that C has already been initialized, then no further action is required. Release LC and complete normally.

5. If the `Class` object for C is in an erroneous state, then initialization is not possible. Release LC and throw a `NoClassDefFoundError`.

6. Otherwise, record the fact that initialization of the `Class` object for C is in progress by the current thread, and release LC.

   Then, initialize the `final` class variables and fields of interfaces whose values are compile-time constant expressions (§8.3.2.1, §9.3.1, §13.4.9, §15.28).

7. Next, if C is a class rather than an interface, and its superclass SC has not yet been initialized, then recursively perform this entire procedure for SC. If necessary, verify and prepare SC first. If the initialization of SC completes abruptly because of a thrown exception, then acquire LC, label the `Class` object for C as erroneous, notify all waiting threads, release LC, and complete abruptly, throwing the same exception that resulted from initializing SC.

8. Next, determine whether assertions are enabled (§14.10) for c by querying its defining class loader.

9. Next, execute either the class variable initializers and static initializers of the class, or the field initializers of the interface, in textual order, as though they were a single block.

10. If the execution of the initializers completes normally, then acquire LC, label the `Class` object for c as fully initialized, notify all waiting threads, release LC, and complete this procedure normally.

11. Otherwise, the initializers must have completed abruptly by throwing some exception E. If the class of E is not `Error` or one of its subclasses, then create a new instance of the class `ExceptionInInitializerError`, with E as the argument, and use this object in place of E in the following step. But if a new instance of `ExceptionInInitializerError` cannot be created because an `OutOfMemoryError` occurs, then instead use an `OutOfMemoryError` object in place of E in the following step.

12. Acquire LC, label the `Class` object for c as erroneous, notify all waiting threads, release LC, and complete this procedure abruptly with reason E or its replacement as determined in the previous step.

An implementation may optimize this procedure by eliding the lock acquisition in step 1 (and release in step 4/5) when it can determine that the initialization of the class has already completed, provided that, in terms of the memory model, all happens-before orderings that would exist if the lock were acquired, still exist when the optimization is performed.

Code generators need to preserve the points of possible initialization of a class or interface, inserting an invocation of the initialization procedure just described. If this initialization procedure completes normally and the `Class` object is fully initialized and ready for use, then the invocation of the initialization procedure is no longer necessary and it may be eliminated from the code - for example, by patching it out or otherwise regenerating the code.

Compile-time analysis may, in some cases, be able to eliminate many of the checks that a type has been initialized from the generated code, if an initialization order for a group of related types can be determined. Such analysis must, however, fully account for concurrency and for the fact that initialization code is unrestricted.

12.5 Creation of New Class Instances

A new class instance is explicitly created when evaluation of a class instance creation expression (§15.9) causes a class to be instantiated.

A new class instance may be implicitly created in the following situations:

- Loading of a class or interface that contains a `String` literal (§3.10.5) may create a new `String` object to represent that literal. (This might not occur if the same `String` has previously been interned (§3.10.5).)

- Execution of an operation that causes boxing conversion (§5.1.7). Boxing conversion may create a new object of a wrapper class associated with one of the primitive types.

- Execution of a string concatenation operator (§15.18.1) that is not part of a constant expression (§15.28) sometimes creates a new `String` object to represent the result. String concatenation operators may also create temporary wrapper objects for a value of a primitive type.

Each of these situations identifies a particular constructor (§8.8) to be called with specified arguments (possibly none) as part of the class instance creation process.

Whenever a new class instance is created, memory space is allocated for it with room for all the instance variables declared in the class type and all the instance variables declared in each superclass of the class type, including all the instance variables that may be hidden (§8.3).

If there is not sufficient space available to allocate memory for the object, then creation of the class instance completes abruptly with an `OutOfMemoryError`. Otherwise, all the instance variables in the new object, including those declared in superclasses, are initialized to their default values (§4.12.5).

Just before a reference to the newly created object is returned as the result, the indicated constructor is processed to initialize the new object using the following procedure:

1. Assign the arguments for the constructor to newly created parameter variables for this constructor invocation.

2. If this constructor begins with an explicit constructor invocation (§8.8.7.1) of another constructor in the same class (using `this`), then evaluate the arguments and process that constructor invocation recursively using these same five steps. If that constructor invocation completes abruptly, then this procedure completes abruptly for the same reason; otherwise, continue with step 5.

3. This constructor does not begin with an explicit constructor invocation of another constructor in the same class (using `this`). If this constructor is for a class other than `Object`, then this constructor will begin with an explicit or implicit invocation of a superclass constructor (using `super`). Evaluate the arguments and process that superclass constructor invocation recursively using

these same five steps. If that constructor invocation completes abruptly, then this procedure completes abruptly for the same reason. Otherwise, continue with step 4.

4. Execute the instance initializers and instance variable initializers for this class, assigning the values of instance variable initializers to the corresponding instance variables, in the left-to-right order in which they appear textually in the source code for the class. If execution of any of these initializers results in an exception, then no further initializers are processed and this procedure completes abruptly with that same exception. Otherwise, continue with step 5.

5. Execute the rest of the body of this constructor. If that execution completes abruptly, then this procedure completes abruptly for the same reason. Otherwise, this procedure completes normally.

Unlike C++, the Java programming language does not specify altered rules for method dispatch during the creation of a new class instance. If methods are invoked that are overridden in subclasses in the object being initialized, then these overriding methods are used, even before the new object is completely initialized.

Example 12.5-1. Evaluation of Instance Creation

```
class Point {
    int x, y;
    Point() { x = 1; y = 1; }
}
class ColoredPoint extends Point {
    int color = 0xFF00FF;
}
class Test {
    public static void main(String[] args) {
        ColoredPoint cp = new ColoredPoint();
        System.out.println(cp.color);
    }
}
```

Here, a new instance of `ColoredPoint` is created. First, space is allocated for the new `ColoredPoint`, to hold the fields x, y, and `color`. All these fields are then initialized to their default values (in this case, 0 for each field). Next, the `ColoredPoint` constructor with no arguments is first invoked. Since `ColoredPoint` declares no constructors, a default constructor of the form:

```
ColoredPoint() { super(); }
```

is provided for it automatically by the Java compiler.

This constructor then invokes the `Point` constructor with no arguments. The `Point` constructor does not begin with an invocation of a constructor, so the Java compiler provides

329

an implicit invocation of its superclass constructor of no arguments, as though it had been written:

```
Point() { super(); x = 1; y = 1; }
```

Therefore, the constructor for `Object` which takes no arguments is invoked.

The class `Object` has no superclass, so the recursion terminates here. Next, any instance initializers and instance variable initializers of `Object` are invoked. Next, the body of the constructor of `Object` that takes no arguments is executed. No such constructor is declared in `Object`, so the Java compiler supplies a default one, which in this special case is:

```
Object() { }
```

This constructor executes without effect and returns.

Next, all initializers for the instance variables of class `Point` are executed. As it happens, the declarations of x and y do not provide any initialization expressions, so no action is required for this step of the example. Then the body of the `Point` constructor is executed, setting x to 1 and y to 1.

Next, the initializers for the instance variables of class `ColoredPoint` are executed. This step assigns the value `0xFF00FF` to `color`. Finally, the rest of the body of the `ColoredPoint` constructor is executed (the part after the invocation of `super`); there happen to be no statements in the rest of the body, so no further action is required and initialization is complete.

Example 12.5-2. Dynamic Dispatch During Instance Creation

```
class Super {
    Super() { printThree(); }
    void printThree() { System.out.println("three"); }
}
class Test extends Super {
    int three = (int)Math.PI;  // That is, 3
    void printThree() { System.out.println(three); }

    public static void main(String[] args) {
        Test t = new Test();
        t.printThree();
    }
}
```

This program produces the output:

```
0
3
```

This shows that the invocation of `printThree` in the constructor for class `Super` does not invoke the definition of `printThree` in class `Super`, but rather invokes the overriding definition of `printThree` in class `Test`. This method therefore runs before the field initializers of `Test` have been executed, which is why the first value output is `0`, the default value to which the field `three` of `Test` is initialized. The later invocation of `printThree` in method `main` invokes the same definition of `printThree`, but by that point the initializer for instance variable `three` has been executed, and so the value `3` is printed.

12.6 Finalization of Class Instances

The class `Object` has a `protected` method called `finalize`; this method can be overridden by other classes. The particular definition of `finalize` that can be invoked for an object is called the *finalizer* of that object. Before the storage for an object is reclaimed by the garbage collector, the Java Virtual Machine will invoke the finalizer of that object.

Finalizers provide a chance to free up resources that cannot be freed automatically by an automatic storage manager. In such situations, simply reclaiming the memory used by an object would not guarantee that the resources it held would be reclaimed.

The Java programming language does not specify how soon a finalizer will be invoked, except to say that it will happen before the storage for the object is reused.

The Java programming language does not specify which thread will invoke the finalizer for any given object.

It is important to note that many finalizer threads may be active (this is sometimes needed on large shared memory multiprocessors), and that if a large connected data structure becomes garbage, all of the `finalize` methods for every object in that data structure could be invoked at the same time, each finalizer invocation running in a different thread.

The Java programming language imposes no ordering on `finalize` method calls. Finalizers may be called in any order, or even concurrently.

As an example, if a circularly linked group of unfinalized objects becomes unreachable (or finalizer-reachable), then all the objects may become finalizable together. Eventually, the finalizers for these objects may be invoked, in any order, or even concurrently using multiple threads. If the automatic storage manager later finds that the objects are unreachable, then their storage can be reclaimed.

It is straightforward to implement a class that will cause a set of finalizer-like methods to be invoked in a specified order for a set of objects when all the objects become unreachable. Defining such a class is left as an exercise for the reader.

It is guaranteed that the thread that invokes the finalizer will not be holding any user-visible synchronization locks when the finalizer is invoked.

If an uncaught exception is thrown during the finalization, the exception is ignored and finalization of that object terminates.

The completion of an object's constructor happens-before (§17.4.5) the execution of its `finalize` method (in the formal sense of happens-before).

The `finalize` method declared in class `Object` takes no action. The fact that class `Object` declares a `finalize` method means that the `finalize` method for any class can always invoke the `finalize` method for its superclass. This should always be done, unless it is the programmer's intent to nullify the actions of the finalizer in the superclass. (Unlike constructors, finalizers do not automatically invoke the finalizer for the superclass; such an invocation must be coded explicitly.)

> For efficiency, an implementation may keep track of classes that do not override the `finalize` method of class `Object`, or override it in a trivial way.
>
> For example:

```
protected void finalize() throws Throwable {
    super.finalize();
}
```

> We encourage implementations to treat such objects as having a finalizer that is not overridden, and to finalize them more efficiently, as described in §12.6.1.

A finalizer may be invoked explicitly, just like any other method.

The package `java.lang.ref` describes weak references, which interact with garbage collection and finalization. As with any API that has special interactions with the Java programming language, implementors must be cognizant of any requirements imposed by the `java.lang.ref` API. This specification does not discuss weak references in any way. Readers are referred to the API documentation for details.

12.6.1 Implementing Finalization

Every object can be characterized by two attributes: it may be *reachable*, *finalizer-reachable*, or *unreachable*, and it may also be *unfinalized*, *finalizable*, or *finalized*.

A *reachable* object is any object that can be accessed in any potential continuing computation from any live thread.

A *finalizer-reachable* object can be reached from some finalizable object through some chain of references, but not from any live thread.

An *unreachable* object cannot be reached by either means.

An *unfinalized* object has never had its finalizer automatically invoked.

A *finalized* object has had its finalizer automatically invoked.

A *finalizable* object has never had its finalizer automatically invoked, but the Java Virtual Machine may eventually automatically invoke its finalizer.

An object `o` is not finalizable until its constructor has invoked the constructor for `Object` on `o` and that invocation has completed successfully (that is, without throwing an exception). Every pre-finalization write to a field of an object must be visible to the finalization of that object. Furthermore, none of the pre-finalization reads of fields of that object may see writes that occur after finalization of that object is initiated.

Optimizing transformations of a program can be designed that reduce the number of objects that are reachable to be less than those which would naively be considered reachable. For example, a Java compiler or code generator may choose to set a variable or parameter that will no longer be used to `null` to cause the storage for such an object to be potentially reclaimable sooner.

Another example of this occurs if the values in an object's fields are stored in registers. The program may then access the registers instead of the object, and never access the object again. This would imply that the object is garbage. Note that this sort of optimization is only allowed if references are on the stack, not stored in the heap.

For example, consider the *Finalizer Guardian* pattern:

```
class Foo {
    private final Object finalizerGuardian = new Object() {
        protected void finalize() throws Throwable {
            /* finalize outer Foo object */
        }
    }
}
```

The finalizer guardian forces `super.finalize` to be called if a subclass overrides `finalize` and does not explicitly call `super.finalize`.

If these optimizations are allowed for references that are stored on the heap, then a Java compiler can detect that the `finalizerGuardian` field is never read, null it out, collect the object immediately, and call the finalizer early. This runs counter to the intent: the programmer probably wanted to call the `Foo` finalizer when the `Foo` instance became unreachable. This sort of transformation is therefore not legal: the inner class object should be reachable for as long as the outer class object is reachable.

Transformations of this sort may result in invocations of the `finalize` method occurring earlier than might be otherwise expected. In order to allow the user to prevent this, we enforce the notion that synchronization may keep the object alive. *If an object's finalizer can result in synchronization on that object, then that object must be alive and considered reachable whenever a lock is held on it.*

Note that this does not prevent synchronization elimination: synchronization only keeps an object alive if a finalizer might synchronize on it. Since the finalizer occurs in another thread, in many cases the synchronization could not be removed anyway.

12.6.2   Interaction with the Memory Model

It must be possible for the memory model (§17.4) to decide when it can commit actions that take place in a finalizer. This section describes the interaction of finalization with the memory model.

Each execution has a number of *reachability decision points*, labeled *di*. Each action either *comes-before di* or *comes-after di*. Other than as explicitly mentioned, the comes-before ordering described in this section is unrelated to all other orderings in the memory model.

If *r* is a read that sees a write *w* and *r* comes-before *di*, then *w* must come-before *di*.

If *x* and *y* are synchronization actions on the same variable or monitor such that *so(x, y)* (§17.4.4) and *y* comes-before *di*, then *x* must come-before *di*.

At each reachability decision point, some set of objects are marked as unreachable, and some subset of those objects are marked as finalizable. These reachability decision points are also the points at which references are checked, enqueued, and cleared according to the rules provided in the API documentation for the package `java.lang.ref`.

The only objects that are considered definitely reachable at a point *di* are those that can be shown to be reachable by the application of these rules:

- An object B is definitely reachable at *di* from `static` fields if there exists a write *w1* to a `static` field *v* of a class C such that the value written by *w1* is a reference to B, the class C is loaded by a reachable classloader, and there does not exist a write *w2* to *v* such that *hb(w2, w1)* is not true and both *w1* and *w2* come-before *di*.

- An object B is definitely reachable from A at *di* if there is a write *w1* to an element *v* of A such that the value written by *w1* is a reference to B and there does not exist a write *w2* to *v* such that *hb(w2, w1)* is not true and both *w1* and *w2* come-before *di*.

- If an object C is definitely reachable from an object B, and object B is definitely reachable from an object A, then C is definitely reachable from A.

If an object X is marked as unreachable at *di*, then:

- x must not be definitely reachable at *di* from `static` fields; and

- All *active uses* of x in thread `t` that come-after *di* must occur in the finalizer invocation for x or as a result of thread `t` performing a read that comes-after *di* of a reference to x; and

- All reads that come after *di* that see a reference to x must see writes to elements of objects that were unreachable at *di*, or see writes that came-after *di*.

An action *a* is an active use of x if and only if at least one of the following conditions holds:

- *a* reads or writes an element of x

- *a* locks or unlocks x and there is a lock action on x that happens-after the invocation of the finalizer for x

- *a* writes a reference to x

- *a* is an active use of an object Y, and x is definitely reachable from Y

If an object x is marked as finalizable at *di*, then:

- x must be marked as unreachable at *di*; and

- *di* must be the only place where x is marked as finalizable; and

- actions that happen-after the finalizer invocation must come-after *di*.

12.7 Unloading of Classes and Interfaces

An implementation of the Java programming language may *unload* classes.

A class or interface may be unloaded if and only if its defining class loader may be reclaimed by the garbage collector as discussed in §12.6.

Classes and interfaces loaded by the bootstrap loader may not be unloaded.

> Class unloading is an optimization that helps reduce memory use. Obviously, the semantics of a program should not depend on whether and how a system chooses to implement an optimization such as class unloading. To do otherwise would compromise the portability of programs. Consequently, whether a class or interface has been unloaded or not should be transparent to a program.
>
> However, if a class or interface *c* was unloaded while its defining loader was potentially reachable, then *c* might be reloaded. One could never ensure that this would not happen. Even if the class was not referenced by any other currently loaded class, it might be

referenced by some class or interface, *D*, that had not yet been loaded. When *D* is loaded by *C*'s defining loader, its execution might cause reloading of *C*.

Reloading may not be transparent if, for example, the class has `static` variables (whose state would be lost), static initializers (which may have side effects), or `native` methods (which may retain static state). Furthermore, the hash value of the `Class` object is dependent on its identity. Therefore it is, in general, impossible to reload a class or interface in a completely transparent manner.

Since we can never guarantee that unloading a class or interface whose loader is potentially reachable will not cause reloading, and reloading is never transparent, but unloading must be transparent, it follows that one must not unload a class or interface while its loader is potentially reachable. A similar line of reasoning can be used to deduce that classes and interfaces loaded by the bootstrap loader can never be unloaded.

One must also argue why it is safe to unload a class *C* if its defining class loader can be reclaimed. If the defining loader can be reclaimed, then there can never be any live references to it (this includes references that are not live, but might be resurrected by finalizers). This, in turn, can only be true if there are can never be any live references to any of the classes defined by that loader, including *C*, either from their instances or from code.

Class unloading is an optimization that is only significant for applications that load large numbers of classes and that stop using most of those classes after some time. A prime example of such an application is a web browser, but there are others. A characteristic of such applications is that they manage classes through explicit use of class loaders. As a result, the policy outlined above works well for them.

Strictly speaking, it is not essential that the issue of class unloading be discussed by this specification, as class unloading is merely an optimization. However, the issue is very subtle, and so it is mentioned here by way of clarification.

12.8   Program Exit

A program terminates all its activity and *exits* when one of two things happens:

- All the threads that are not daemon threads terminate.

- Some thread invokes the `exit` method of class `Runtime` or class `System`, and the `exit` operation is not forbidden by the security manager.

CHAPTER 13

Binary Compatibility

DEVELOPMENT tools for the Java programming language should support automatic recompilation as necessary whenever source code is available. Particular implementations may also store the source and binary of types in a versioning database and implement a `ClassLoader` that uses integrity mechanisms of the database to prevent linkage errors by providing binary-compatible versions of types to clients.

Developers of packages and classes that are to be widely distributed face a different set of problems. In the Internet, which is our favorite example of a widely distributed system, it is often impractical or impossible to automatically recompile the pre-existing binaries that directly or indirectly depend on a type that is to be changed. Instead, this specification defines a set of changes that developers are permitted to make to a package or to a class or interface type while preserving (not breaking) compatibility with pre-existing binaries.

Within the framework of *Release-to-Release Binary Compatibility in SOM* (Forman, Conner, Danforth, and Raper, *Proceedings of OOPSLA '95*), Java programming language binaries are binary compatible under all relevant transformations that the authors identify (with some caveats with respect to the addition of instance variables). Using their scheme, here is a list of some important binary compatible changes that the Java programming language supports:

- Reimplementing existing methods, constructors, and initializers to improve performance.

- Changing methods or constructors to return values on inputs for which they previously either threw exceptions that normally should not occur or failed by going into an infinite loop or causing a deadlock.

- Adding new fields, methods, or constructors to an existing class or interface.

- Deleting `private` fields, methods, or constructors of a class.

- When an entire package is updated, deleting default (package-only) access fields, methods, or constructors of classes and interfaces in the package.

- Reordering the fields, methods, or constructors in an existing type declaration.

- Moving a method upward in the class hierarchy.

- Reordering the list of direct superinterfaces of a class or interface.

- Inserting new class or interface types in the type hierarchy.

This chapter specifies minimum standards for binary compatibility guaranteed by all implementations. The Java programming language guarantees compatibility when binaries of classes and interfaces are mixed that are not known to be from compatible sources, but whose sources have been modified in the compatible ways described here. Note that we are discussing compatibility between releases of an application. A discussion of compatibility among releases of the Java SE platform is beyond the scope of this chapter.

We encourage development systems to provide facilities that alert developers to the impact of changes on pre-existing binaries that cannot be recompiled.

This chapter first specifies some properties that any binary format for the Java programming language must have (§13.1). It next defines binary compatibility, explaining what it is and what it is not (§13.2). It finally enumerates a large set of possible changes to packages (§13.3), classes (§13.4), and interfaces (§13.5), specifying which of these changes are guaranteed to preserve binary compatibility and which are not.

13.1   The Form of a Binary

Programs must be compiled either into the `class` file format specified by *The Java Virtual Machine Specification, Java SE 7 Edition*, or into a representation that can be mapped into that format by a class loader written in the Java programming language.

Furthermore, the resulting `class` file must have certain properties. A number of these properties are specifically chosen to support source code transformations that preserve binary compatibility. The required properties are:

1. The class or interface must be named by its *binary name*, which must meet the following constraints:

    - The binary name of a top level type (§7.6) is its canonical name (§6.7).

- The binary name of a member type (§8.5, §9.5) consists of the binary name of its immediately enclosing type, followed by $, followed by the simple name of the member.

- The binary name of a local class (§14.3) consists of the binary name of its immediately enclosing type, followed by $, followed by a non-empty sequence of digits, followed by the simple name of the local class.

- The binary name of an anonymous class (§15.9.5) consists of the binary name of its immediately enclosing type, followed by $, followed by a non-empty sequence of digits.

- The binary name of a type variable declared by a generic class or interface (§8.1.2, §9.1.2) is the binary name of its immediately enclosing type, followed by $, followed by the simple name of the type variable.

- The binary name of a type variable declared by a generic method (§8.4.4) is the binary name of the type declaring the method, followed by $, followed by the descriptor of the method as defined in *The Java Virtual Machine Specification, Java SE 7 Edition*, followed by $, followed by the simple name of the type variable.

- The binary name of a type variable declared by a generic constructor (§8.8.4) is the binary name of the type declaring the constructor, followed by $, followed by the descriptor of the constructor as defined in *The Java Virtual Machine Specification, Java SE 7 Edition*, followed by $, followed by the simple name of the type variable.

2. A reference to another class or interface type must be symbolic, using the binary name of the type.

3. References to fields that are constant variables (§4.12.4) are resolved at compile time to the constant value that is denoted. No reference to such a field should be present in the code in a binary file (except in the class or interface containing the field, which will have code to initialize it). Such a field must always appear to have been initialized (§12.4.2); the default initial value for the type of such a field must never be observed. See §13.4.9 for a discussion.

4. Given a legal expression denoting a field access in a class *c*, referencing a non-constant (§13.4.9) field named *f* declared in a (possibly distinct) class or interface *D*, we define the *qualifying type of the field reference* as follows:

   - If the expression is of the form *Primary*. *f* then:

- If the compile-time type of *Primary* is an intersection type (§4.9) V_1 & ... & V_n, then the qualifying type of the reference is V_1.

- Otherwise, the compile-time type of *Primary* is the qualifying type of the reference.

- If the expression is of the form `super.f` then the superclass of `C` is the qualifying type of the reference.

- If the expression is of the form `X.super.f` then the superclass of `X` is the qualifying type of the reference.

- If the reference is of the form `X.f`, where `X` denotes a class or interface, then the class or interface denoted by `X` is the qualifying type of the reference.

- If the expression is referenced by a simple name, then if `f` is a member of the current class or interface, `C`, then let `T` be `C`. Otherwise, let `T` be the innermost lexically enclosing class of which `f` is a member. In either case, `T` is the qualifying type of the reference.

The reference to `f` must be compiled into a symbolic reference to the erasure (§4.6) of the qualifying type of the reference, plus the simple name of the field, `f`. The reference must also include a symbolic reference to the erasure of the declared type of the field so that the verifier can check that the type is as expected.

5. Given a method invocation expression in a class or interface `C` referencing a method named `m` declared (or implicitly declared (§9.2)) in a (possibly distinct) class or interface `D`, we define the *qualifying type of the method invocation* as follows:

- If `D` is `Object` then the qualifying type of the expression is `Object`.

- Otherwise:

  - If the expression is of the form *Primary*.`m` then:

    - If the compile-time type of *Primary* is an intersection type (§4.9) V_1 & ... & V_n, then the qualifying type of the method invocation is V_1.

    - Otherwise, the compile-time type of *Primary* is the qualifying type of the method invocation.

  - If the expression is of the form `super.m` then the superclass of `C` is the qualifying type of the method invocation.

  - If the expression is of the form `X.super.m` then the superclass of `X` is the qualifying type of the method invocation.

- If the reference is of the form $x.m$, where x denotes a class or interface, then the class or interface denoted by x is the qualifying type of the method invocation.

- If the method is referenced by a simple name, then if m is a member of the current class or interface, c, then let T be c. Otherwise, let T be the innermost lexically enclosing class of which m is a member. In either case, T is the qualifying type of the method invocation.

A reference to a method must be resolved at compile time to a symbolic reference to the erasure (§4.6) of the qualifying type of the invocation, plus the erasure of the signature (§8.4.2) of the method. The signature of a method must include all of the following as determined by §15.12.3:

- The simple name of the method

- The number of parameters to the method

- A symbolic reference to the type of each parameter

A reference to a method must also include either a symbolic reference to the erasure of the return type of the denoted method or an indication that the denoted method is declared `void` and does not return a value.

6. Given a class instance creation expression (§15.9) or a constructor invocation statement (§8.8.7.1) in a class or interface c referencing a constructor m declared in a (possibly distinct) class or interface D, we define the qualifying type of the constructor invocation as follows:

- If the expression is of the form `new D(...)` or `X.new D(...)`, then the qualifying type of the invocation is D.

- If the expression is of the form `new D(...){...}` or `X.new D(...){...}`, then the qualifying type of the expression is the compile-time type of the expression.

- If the expression is of the form `super(...)` or *Primary*.`super(...)` then the qualifying type of the expression is the direct superclass of c.

- If the expression is of the form `this(...)`, then the qualifying type of the expression is c.

A reference to a constructor must be resolved at compile time to a symbolic reference to the erasure (§4.6) of the qualifying type of the invocation, plus the signature of the constructor (§8.8.2). The signature of a constructor must include both:

- The number of parameters of the constructor

- A symbolic reference to the type of each formal parameter

In addition, the constructor of a non-`private` inner member class must be compiled such that it has as its first parameter, an additional implicit parameter representing the immediately enclosing instance (§8.1.3).

7. Any constructs introduced by a Java compiler that do not have a corresponding construct in the source code must be marked as synthetic, except for default constructors, the class initialization method, and the `values` and `valueOf` methods of the `Enum` class.

A binary representation for a class or interface must also contain all of the following:

1. If it is a class and is not class `Object`, then a symbolic reference to the erasure (§4.6) of the direct superclass of this class.

2. A symbolic reference to the erasure of each direct superinterface, if any.

3. A specification of each field declared in the class or interface, given as the simple name of the field and a symbolic reference to the erasure of the type of the field.

4. If it is a class, then the erased signature of each constructor, as described above.

5. For each method declared in the class or interface (excluding, for an interface, its implicitly declared methods (§9.2)), its erased signature and return type, as described above.

6. The code needed to implement the class or interface:

   - For an interface, code for the field initializers

   - For a class, code for the field initializers, the instance and static initializers, and the implementation of each method or constructor

7. Every type must contain sufficient information to recover its canonical name (§6.7).

8. Every member type must have sufficient information to recover its source level access modifier.

9. Every nested class must have a symbolic reference to its immediately enclosing class.

10. Every class that contains a nested class must contain symbolic references to all of its member classes, and to all local and anonymous classes that appear in its methods, constructors, and static or instance initializers.

The following sections discuss changes that may be made to class and interface type declarations without breaking compatibility with pre-existing binaries. Under the translation requirements given above, the Java Virtual Machine and its `class` file format support these changes. Any other valid binary format, such as a compressed or encrypted representation that is mapped back into `class` files by a class loader under the above requirements, will necessarily support these changes as well.

13.2 What Binary Compatibility Is and Is Not

A change to a type is *binary compatible with* (equivalently, does not *break binary compatibility* with) pre-existing binaries if pre-existing binaries that previously linked without error will continue to link without error.

Binaries are compiled to rely on the accessible members and constructors of other classes and interfaces. To preserve binary compatibility, a class or interface should treat its accessible members and constructors, their existence and behavior, as a *contract* with its users.

The Java programming language is designed to prevent additions to contracts and accidental name collisions from breaking binary compatibility. Specifically, addition of more methods overloading a particular method name does not break compatibility with pre-existing binaries. The method signature that the pre-existing binary will use for method lookup is chosen by the method overload resolution algorithm at compile time (§15.12.2).

> If the Java programming language had been designed so that the particular method to be executed was chosen at run time, then such an ambiguity might be detected at run time. Such a rule would imply that adding an additional overloaded method so as to make ambiguity possible at a call site could break compatibility with an unknown number of pre-existing binaries. See §13.4.23 for more discussion.

Binary compatibility is not the same as source compatibility. In particular, the example in §13.4.6 shows that a set of compatible binaries can be produced from sources that will not compile all together. This example is typical: a new declaration is added, changing the meaning of a name in an unchanged part of the source code, while the pre-existing binary for that unchanged part of the source code retains the fully-qualified, previous meaning of the name. Producing a consistent set of source code requires providing a qualified name or field access expression corresponding to the previous meaning.

13.3   Evolution of Packages

A new top level class or interface type may be added to a package without breaking compatibility with pre-existing binaries, provided the new type does not reuse a name previously given to an unrelated type.

If a new type reuses a name previously given to an unrelated type, then a conflict may result, since binaries for both types could not be loaded by the same class loader.

Changes in top level class and interface types that are not `public` and that are not a superclass or superinterface, respectively, of a `public` type, affect only types within the package in which they are declared. Such types may be deleted or otherwise changed, even if incompatibilities are otherwise described here, provided that the affected binaries of that package are updated together.

13.4   Evolution of Classes

This section describes the effects of changes to the declaration of a class and its members and constructors on pre-existing binaries.

13.4.1   `abstract` Classes

If a class that was not declared `abstract` is changed to be declared `abstract`, then pre-existing binaries that attempt to create new instances of that class will throw either an `InstantiationError` at link time, or (if a reflective method is used) an `InstantiationException` at run time; such a change is therefore not recommended for widely distributed classes.

Changing a class that is declared `abstract` to no longer be declared `abstract` does not break compatibility with pre-existing binaries.

13.4.2   `final` Classes

If a class that was not declared `final` is changed to be declared `final`, then a `VerifyError` is thrown if a binary of a pre-existing subclass of this class is loaded, because `final` classes can have no subclasses; such a change is not recommended for widely distributed classes.

Changing a class that is declared `final` to no longer be declared `final` does not break compatibility with pre-existing binaries.

13.4.3 `public` **Classes**

Changing a class that is not declared `public` to be declared `public` does not break compatibility with pre-existing binaries.

If a class that was declared `public` is changed to not be declared `public`, then an `IllegalAccessError` is thrown if a pre-existing binary is linked that needs but no longer has access to the class type; such a change is not recommended for widely distributed classes.

13.4.4 **Superclasses and Superinterfaces**

A `ClassCircularityError` is thrown at load time if a class would be a superclass of itself. Changes to the class hierarchy that could result in such a circularity when newly compiled binaries are loaded with pre-existing binaries are not recommended for widely distributed classes.

Changing the direct superclass or the set of direct superinterfaces of a class type will not break compatibility with pre-existing binaries, provided that the total set of superclasses or superinterfaces, respectively, of the class type loses no members.

If a change to the direct superclass or the set of direct superinterfaces results in any class or interface no longer being a superclass or superinterface, respectively, then linkage errors may result if pre-existing binaries are loaded with the binary of the modified class. Such changes are not recommended for widely distributed classes.

Example 13.4.4-1. Changing A Superclass

Suppose that the following test program:

```
class Hyper { char h = 'h'; }
class Super extends Hyper { char s = 's'; }
class Test extends Super {
    public static void printH(Hyper h) {
        System.out.println(h.h);
    }
    public static void main(String[] args) {
        printH(new Super());
    }
}
```

is compiled and executed, producing the output:

```
h
```

Suppose that a new version of class `Super` is then compiled:

```
class Super { char s = 's'; }
```

This version of class `Super` is not a subclass of `Hyper`. If we then run the existing binaries of `Hyper` and `Test` with the new version of `Super`, then a `VerifyError` is thrown at link time. The verifier objects because the result of `new Super()` cannot be passed as an argument in place of a formal parameter of type `Hyper`, because `Super` is not a subclass of `Hyper`.

It is instructive to consider what might happen without the verification step: the program might run and print:

```
s
```

This demonstrates that without the verifier, the Java type system could be defeated by linking inconsistent binary files, even though each was produced by a correct Java compiler.

The lesson is that an implementation that lacks a verifier or fails to use it will not maintain type safety and is, therefore, not a valid implementation.

The requirement that alternatives in a multi-`catch` clause (§14.20) not be subclasses or superclasses of each other is only a source restriction. Assuming the following client code is legal:

```
try {
    throwAorB();
} catch(ExceptionA | ExceptionB e) {
    ...
}
```

where `ExceptionA` and `ExceptionB` do not have a subclass/superclass relationship when the client is compiled, it is binary compatible with respect to the client for `ExceptionA` and `ExceptionB` to have such a relationship when the client is executed.

This is analogous to other situations where a class transformation that is binary compatible for a client might not be source compatible for the same client.

13.4.5 Class Type Parameters

Adding or removing a type parameter of a class does not, in itself, have any implications for binary compatibility.

If such a type parameter is used in the type of a field or method, that may have the normal implications of changing the aforementioned type.

Renaming a type parameter of a class has no effect with respect to pre-existing binaries.

Changing the first bound of a type parameter of a class may change the erasure (§4.6) of any member that uses that type parameter in its own type, and this may affect binary compatibility. The change of such a bound is analogous to the change of the first bound of a type parameter of a method or constructor (§13.4.13).

Changing any other bound has no effect on binary compatibility.

13.4.6   Class Body and Member Declarations

No incompatibility with pre-existing binaries is caused by adding an instance (respectively `static`) member that has the same name and accessibility (for fields), or same name and accessibility and signature and return type (for methods), as an instance (respectively `static`) member of a superclass or subclass. No error occurs even if the set of classes being linked would encounter a compile-time error.

Deleting a class member or constructor that is not declared `private` may cause a linkage error if the member or constructor is used by a pre-existing binary.

Example 13.4.6-1. Changing A Class Body

```
class Hyper {
    void hello() { System.out.println("hello from Hyper"); }
}
class Super extends Hyper {
    void hello() { System.out.println("hello from Super"); }
}
class Test {
    public static void main(String[] args) {
        new Super().hello();
    }
}
```

This program produces the output:

```
hello from Super
```

Suppose that a new version of class `Super` is produced:

```
class Super extends Hyper {}
```

Then, recompiling `Super` and executing this new binary with the original binaries for `Test` and `Hyper` produces the output:

```
hello from Hyper
```

as expected.

The `super` keyword can be used to access a method declared in a superclass, bypassing any methods declared in the current class. The expression `super`.*Identifier* is resolved, at compile time, to a method m in the superclass s. If the method m is an instance method, then the method which is invoked at run time is the method with the same signature as m that is a member of the direct superclass of the class containing the expression involving `super`.

Example 13.4.6-2. Changing A Superclass

```
class Hyper {
    void hello() { System.out.println("hello from Hyper"); }
}
class Super extends Hyper { }
class Test extends Super {
    public static void main(String[] args) {
        new Test().hello();
    }
    void hello() {
        super.hello();
    }
}
```

This program produces the output:

```
hello from Hyper
```

Suppose that a new version of class `Super` is produced:

```
class Super extends Hyper {
    void hello() { System.out.println("hello from Super"); }
}
```

Then, if `Super` and `Hyper` are recompiled but not `Test`, then running the new binaries with the existing binary of `Test` produces the output:

```
hello from Super
```

as you might expect.

13.4.7   Access to Members and Constructors

Changing the declared access of a member or constructor to permit less access may break compatibility with pre-existing binaries, causing a linkage error to be thrown when these binaries are resolved. Less access is permitted if the access modifier is changed from default access to `private` access; from `protected` access to default or `private` access; or from `public` access to `protected`, default, or `private` access. Changing a member or constructor to permit less access is therefore not recommended for widely distributed classes.

Perhaps surprisingly, the binary format is defined so that changing a member or constructor to be more accessible does not cause a linkage error when a subclass (already) defines a method to have less access.

Example 13.4.7-1. Changing Accessibility

If the package `points` defines the class `Point`:

```
package points;
public class Point {
    public int x, y;
    protected void print() {
        System.out.println("(" + x + "," + y + ")");
    }
}
```

used by the program:

```
class Test extends points.Point {
    public static void main(String[] args) {
        Test t = new Test();
        t.print();
    }
    protected void print() {
        System.out.println("Test");
    }
}
```

then these classes compile and `Test` executes to produce the output:

```
Test
```

If the method `print` in class `Point` is changed to be `public`, and then only the `Point` class is recompiled, and then executed with the previously existing binary for `Test`, then no linkage error occurs. This happens even though it is improper, at compile time, for a `public` method to be overridden by a `protected` method (as shown by the fact that the class `Test` could not be recompiled using this new `Point` class unless `print` in `Test` were changed to be `public`.)

Allowing superclasses to change `protected` methods to be `public` without breaking binaries of pre-existing subclasses helps make binaries less fragile. The alternative, where such a change would cause a linkage error, would create additional binary incompatibilities.

13.4.8 Field Declarations

Widely distributed programs should not expose any fields to their clients. Apart from the binary compatibility issues discussed below, this is generally good software engineering practice. Adding a field to a class may break compatibility with pre-existing binaries that are not recompiled.

Assume a reference to a field f with qualifying type T. Assume further that f is in fact an instance (respectively `static`) field declared in a superclass of T, S, and that the type of f is X.

If a new field of type X with the same name as f is added to a subclass of S that is a superclass of T or T itself, then a linkage error may occur. Such a linkage error will occur only if, in addition to the above, either one of the following conditions hold:

• The new field is less accessible than the old one.

• The new field is a `static` (respectively instance) field.

In particular, no linkage error will occur in the case where a class could no longer be recompiled because a field access previously referenced a field of a superclass with an incompatible type. The previously compiled class with such a reference will continue to reference the field declared in a superclass.

> **Example 13.4.8-1. Adding A Field Declaration**
>
> ```
> class Hyper { String h = "hyper"; }
> class Super extends Hyper { String s = "super"; }
> class Test {
>     public static void main(String[] args) {
>         System.out.println(new Super().h);
>     }
> }
> ```
>
> This program produces the output:
>
> ```
> hyper
> ```
>
> Suppose a new version of class `Super` is produced:
>
> ```
> class Super extends Hyper {
>     String s = "super";
>     int h = 0;
> }
> ```
>
> Then, recompiling `Hyper` and `Super`, and executing the resulting new binaries with the old binary of `Test` produces the output:
>
> ```
> hyper
> ```

The field h of `Hyper` is output by the original binary of `Test`. While this may seem surprising at first, it serves to reduce the number of incompatibilities that occur at run time. (In an ideal world, all source files that needed recompilation would be recompiled whenever any one of them changed, eliminating such surprises. But such a mass recompilation is often impractical or impossible, especially in the Internet. And, as was previously noted, such recompilation would sometimes require further changes to the source code.)

As another example, if the program:

```
class Hyper { String h = "Hyper"; }
class Super extends Hyper { }
class Test extends Super {
    public static void main(String[] args) {
        String s = new Test().h;
        System.out.println(s);
    }
}
```

is compiled and executed, it produces the output:

```
Hyper
```

Suppose that a new version of class `Super` is then compiled:

```
class Super extends Hyper { char h = 'h'; }
```

If the resulting binary is used with the existing binaries for `Hyper` and `Test`, then the output is still:

```
Hyper
```

even though compiling the source for these binaries:

```
class Hyper { String h = "Hyper"; }
class Super extends Hyper { char h = 'h'; }
class Test extends Super {
    public static void main(String[] args) {
        String s = new Test().h;
        System.out.println(s);
    }
}
```

would result in a compile-time error, because the h in the source code for `main` would now be construed as referring to the `char` field declared in `Super`, and a `char` value can't be assigned to a `String`.

Deleting a field from a class will break compatibility with any pre-existing binaries that reference this field, and a `NoSuchFieldError` will be thrown when such a reference from a pre-existing binary is linked. Only `private` fields may be safely deleted from a widely distributed class.

For purposes of binary compatibility, adding or removing a field f whose type involves type variables (§4.4) or parameterized types (§4.5) is equivalent to the addition (respectively, removal) of a field of the same name whose type is the erasure (§4.6) of the type of f.

13.4.9   `final` **Fields and Constants**

If a field that was not declared `final` is changed to be declared `final`, then it can break compatibility with pre-existing binaries that attempt to assign new values to the field.

> **Example 13.4.9-1. Changing A Variable To Be** `final`
>
> ```
> class Super { static char s; }
> class Test extends Super {
>     public static void main(String[] args) {
>         s = 'a';
>         System.out.println(s);
>     }
> }
> ```
>
> This program produces the output:
>
> ```
> a
> ```
>
> Suppose that a new version of class `Super` is produced:
>
> ```
> class Super { static final char s = 'b'; }
> ```
>
> If `Super` is recompiled but not `Test`, then running the new binary with the existing binary of `Test` results in a `IllegalAccessError`.

Deleting the keyword `final` or changing the value to which a field is initialized does not break compatibility with existing binaries.

If a field is a constant variable (§4.12.4), then deleting the keyword `final` or changing its value will not break compatibility with pre-existing binaries by causing them not to run, but they will not see any new value for the usage of the field unless they are recompiled. This is true even if the usage itself is not a compile-time constant expression (§15.28).

This result is a side-effect of the decision to support conditional compilation, as discussed at the end of §14.21.

Example 13.4.9-2. Conditional Compilation

If the example:

```
class Flags { static final boolean debug = true; }
class Test {
    public static void main(String[] args) {
        if (Flags.debug)
            System.out.println("debug is true");
    }
}
```

is compiled and executed, it produces the output:

```
debug is true
```

Suppose that a new version of class `Flags` is produced:

```
class Flags { static final boolean debug = false; }
```

If `Flags` is recompiled but not `Test`, then running the new binary with the existing binary of `Test` produces the output:

```
debug is true
```

because the value of `debug` was a compile-time constant expression, and could have been used in compiling `Test` without making a reference to the class `Flags`.

This behavior would not change if `Flags` were changed to be an interface, as in the modified example:

```
interface Flags { boolean debug = true; }
class Test {
    public static void main(String[] args) {
        if (Flags.debug)
            System.out.println("debug is true");
    }
}
```

The best way to avoid problems with "inconstant constants" in widely-distributed code is to declare as compile-time constants only values which truly are unlikely ever to change. Other than for true mathematical constants, we recommend that source code make very sparing use of class variables that are declared `static` and `final`. If the read-only nature of `final` is required, a better choice is to declare a `private static` variable and a suitable accessor method to get its value.

Thus we recommend:

```
private static int N;
```

```
public static int getN() { return N; }
```

rather than:

```
public static final int N = ...;
```

There is no problem with:

```
public static int N = ...;
```

if N need not be read-only. We also recommend, as a general rule, that only truly constant values be declared in interfaces.

We note, but do not recommend, that if a field of primitive type of an interface may change, its value may be expressed idiomatically as in:

```
interface Flags {
    boolean debug = new Boolean(true).booleanValue();
}
```

ensuring that this value is not a constant. Similar idioms exist for the other primitive types.

One other thing to note is that static final fields that have constant values (whether of primitive or String type) must never appear to have the default initial value for their type (§4.12.5). This means that all such fields appear to be initialized first during class initialization (§8.3.2.1, §9.3.1, §12.4.2).

13.4.10   static **Fields**

If a field that is not declared private was not declared static and is changed to be declared static, or vice versa, then a linkage error, specifically an IncompatibleClassChangeError, will result if the field is used by a pre-existing binary which expected a field of the other kind. Such changes are not recommended in code that has been widely distributed.

13.4.11   transient **Fields**

Adding or deleting a transient modifier of a field does not break compatibility with pre-existing binaries.

13.4.12   **Method and Constructor Declarations**

Adding a method or constructor declaration to a class will not break compatibility with any pre-existing binaries, even in the case where a type could no longer be recompiled because an invocation previously referenced a method or constructor of a superclass with an incompatible type. The previously compiled class with such a reference will continue to reference the method or constructor declared in a superclass.

Assume a reference to a method m with qualifying type T. Assume further that m is in fact an instance (respectively `static`) method declared in a superclass of T, S.

If a new method of type X with the same signature and return type as m is added to a subclass of S that is a superclass of T or T itself, then a linkage error may occur. Such a linkage error will occur only if, in addition to the above, either one of the following conditions hold:

- The new method is less accessible than the old one.

- The new method is a `static` (respectively instance) method.

Deleting a method or constructor from a class may break compatibility with any pre-existing binary that referenced this method or constructor; a `NoSuchMethodError` may be thrown when such a reference from a pre-existing binary is linked. Such an error will occur only if no method with a matching signature and return type is declared in a superclass.

If the source code for a non-inner class contains no declared constructors, the Java compiler automatically supplies a default constructor with no parameters (§8.8.9). Adding one or more constructor declarations to the source code of such a class will prevent this default constructor from being supplied automatically, effectively deleting a constructor, unless one of the new constructors also has no parameters, thus replacing the default constructor. The automatically supplied constructor with no parameters is given the same access modifier as the class of its declaration, so any replacement should have as much or more access if compatibility with pre-existing binaries is to be preserved.

13.4.13 Method and Constructor Type Parameters

Adding or removing a type parameter of a method or constructor does not, in itself, have any implications for binary compatibility.

If such a type parameter is used in the type of the method or constructor, that may have the normal implications of changing the aforementioned type.

Renaming a type parameter of a method or constructor has no effect with respect to pre-existing binaries.

Changing the first bound of a type parameter of a method or constructor may change the erasure (§4.6) of any member that uses that type parameter in its own type, and this may affect binary compatibility. Specifically:

- If the type parameter is used as the type of a field, the effect is as if the field was removed and a field with the same name, whose type is the new erasure of the type variable, was added.

- If the type parameter is used as the type of any formal parameter of a method, but not as the return type, the effect is as if that method were removed, and replaced with a new method that is identical except for the types of the aforementioned formal parameters, which now have the new erasure of the type parameter as their type.

- If the type parameter is used as a return type of a method, but not as the type of any formal parameter of the method, the effect is as if that method were removed, and replaced with a new method that is identical except for the return type, which is now the new erasure of the type parameter.

- If the type parameter is used as a return type of a method and as the type of one or more formal parameters of the method, the effect is as if that method were removed, and replaced with a new method that is identical except for the return type, which is now the new erasure of the type parameter, and except for the types of the aforementioned formal parameters, which now have the new erasure of the type parameter as their types.

Changing any other bound has no effect on binary compatibility.

13.4.14   Method and Constructor Formal Parameters

Changing the name of a formal parameter of a method or constructor does not impact pre-existing binaries.

Changing the name of a method, or the type of a formal parameter to a method or constructor, or adding a parameter to or deleting a parameter from a method or constructor declaration creates a method or constructor with a new signature, and has the combined effect of deleting the method or constructor with the old signature and adding a method or constructor with the new signature (§13.4.12).

Changing the type of the last formal parameter of a method from $T[]$ to a variable arity parameter (§8.4.1) of type T (i.e. to $T...$), and vice versa, does not impact pre-existing binaries.

For purposes of binary compatibility, adding or removing a method or constructor m whose signature involves type variables (§4.4) or parameterized types (§4.5) is equivalent to the addition (respectively, removal) of an otherwise equivalent method whose signature is the erasure (§4.6) of the signature of *m*.

13.4.15   Method Result Type

Changing the result type of a method, or replacing a result type with `void`, or replacing `void` with a result type, has the combined effect of deleting the old method and adding a new method with the new result type or newly `void` result (see §13.4.12).

For purposes of binary compatibility, adding or removing a method or constructor *m* whose return type involves type variables (§4.4) or parameterized types (§4.5) is equivalent to the addition (respectively, removal) of the an otherwise equivalent method whose return type is the erasure (§4.6) of the return type of *m*.

13.4.16   `abstract` **Methods**

Changing a method that is declared `abstract` to no longer be declared `abstract` does not break compatibility with pre-existing binaries.

Changing a method that is not declared `abstract` to be declared `abstract` will break compatibility with pre-existing binaries that previously invoked the method, causing an `AbstractMethodError`.

> **Example 13.4.16-1. Changing A Method To Be** `abstract`
>
> ```
> class Super { void out() { System.out.println("Out"); } }
> class Test extends Super {
>     public static void main(String[] args) {
>         Test t = new Test();
>         System.out.println("Way ");
>         t.out();
>     }
> }
> ```
>
> This program produces the output:
>
> ```
> Way
> Out
> ```
>
> Suppose that a new version of class `Super` is produced:
>
> ```
> abstract class Super {
>     abstract void out();
> }
> ```

If `Super` is recompiled but not `Test`, then running the new binary with the existing binary of `Test` results in an `AbstractMethodError`, because class `Test` has no implementation of the method `out`, and is therefore is (or should be) `abstract`.

13.4.17   `final` **Methods**

Changing a method that is declared `final` to no longer be declared `final` does not break compatibility with pre-existing binaries.

Changing an instance method that is not declared `final` to be declared `final` may break compatibility with existing binaries that depend on the ability to override the method.

Example 13.4.17-1. Changing A Method To Be `final`

```
class Super { void out() { System.out.println("out"); } }
class Test extends Super {
    public static void main(String[] args) {
        Test t = new Test();
        t.out();
    }
    void out() { super.out(); }
}
```

This program produces the output:

```
out
```

Suppose that a new version of class `Super` is produced:

```
class Super { final void out() { System.out.println("!"); } }
```

If `Super` is recompiled but not `Test`, then running the new binary with the existing binary of `Test` results in a `VerifyError` because the class `Test` improperly tries to override the instance method `out`.

Changing a class (`static`) method that is not declared `final` to be declared `final` does not break compatibility with existing binaries, because the method could not have been overridden.

13.4.18   `native` **Methods**

Adding or deleting a `native` modifier of a method does not break compatibility with pre-existing binaries.

The impact of changes to types on pre-existing `native` methods that are not recompiled is beyond the scope of this specification and should be provided with the description of an implementation. Implementations are encouraged, but not required, to implement `native` methods in a way that limits such impact.

13.4.19 `static` **Methods**

If a method that is not declared `private` is also declared `static` (that is, a class method) and is changed to not be declared `static` (that is, to an instance method), or vice versa, then compatibility with pre-existing binaries may be broken, resulting in a linkage time error, namely an `IncompatibleClassChangeError`, if these methods are used by the pre-existing binaries. Such changes are not recommended in code that has been widely distributed.

13.4.20 `synchronized` **Methods**

Adding or deleting a `synchronized` modifier of a method does not break compatibility with pre-existing binaries.

13.4.21 **Method and Constructor Throws**

Changes to the `throws` clause of methods or constructors do not break compatibility with pre-existing binaries; these clauses are checked only at compile time.

13.4.22 **Method and Constructor Body**

Changes to the body of a method or constructor do not break compatibility with pre-existing binaries.

The keyword `final` on a method does not mean that the method can be safely inlined; it means only that the method cannot be overridden. It is still possible that a new version of that method will be provided at link-time. Furthermore, the structure of the original program must be preserved for purposes of reflection.

Therefore, we note that a Java compiler cannot expand a method inline at compile time. In general we suggest that implementations use late-bound (run-time) code generation and optimization.

13.4.23 **Method and Constructor Overloading**

Adding new methods or constructors that overload existing methods or constructors does not break compatibility with pre-existing binaries. The signature to be used for each invocation was determined when these existing binaries were compiled;

therefore newly added methods or constructors will not be used, even if their signatures are both applicable and more specific than the signature originally chosen.

While adding a new overloaded method or constructor may cause a compile-time error the next time a class or interface is compiled because there is no method or constructor that is most specific (§15.12.2.5), no such error occurs when a program is executed, because no overload resolution is done at execution time.

Example 13.4.23-1. Adding An Overloaded Method

```
class Super {
    static void out(float f) {
        System.out.println("float");
    }
}
class Test {
    public static void main(String[] args) {
        Super.out(2);
    }
}
```

This program produces the output:

```
float
```

Suppose that a new version of class Super is produced:

```
class Super {
    static void out(float f) { System.out.println("float"); }
    static void out(int i)   { System.out.println("int");   }
}
```

If Super is recompiled but not Test, then running the new binary with the existing binary of Test still produces the output:

```
float
```

However, if Test is then recompiled, using this new Super, the output is then:

```
int
```

as might have been naively expected in the previous case.

13.4.24   Method Overriding

If an instance method is added to a subclass and it overrides a method in a superclass, then the subclass method will be found by method invocations in pre-existing binaries, and these binaries are not impacted.

If a class method is added to a class, then this method will not be found unless the qualifying type of the reference is the subclass type.

13.4.25   Static Initializers

Adding, deleting, or changing a static initializer (§8.7) of a class does not impact pre-existing binaries.

13.4.26   Evolution of Enums

Adding or reordering constants in an enum type will not break compatibility with pre-existing binaries.

If a pre-existing binary attempts to access an enum constant that no longer exists, the client will fail at run time with a `NoSuchFieldError`. Therefore such a change is not recommended for widely distributed enums.

In all other respects, the binary compatibility rules for enums are identical to those for classes.

13.5   Evolution of Interfaces

This section describes the impact of changes to the declaration of an interface and its members on pre-existing binaries.

13.5.1   `public` Interfaces

Changing an interface that is not declared `public` to be declared `public` does not break compatibility with pre-existing binaries.

If an interface that is declared `public` is changed to not be declared `public`, then an `IllegalAccessError` is thrown if a pre-existing binary is linked that needs but no longer has access to the interface type, so such a change is not recommended for widely distributed interfaces.

13.5.2   Superinterfaces

Changes to the interface hierarchy cause errors in the same way that changes to the class hierarchy do, as described in §13.4.4. In particular, changes that result in any previous superinterface of a class no longer being a superinterface can break compatibility with pre-existing binaries, resulting in a `VerifyError`.

13.5.3   Interface Members

Adding a method to an interface does not break compatibility with pre-existing binaries.

A field added to a superinterface of `c` may hide a field inherited from a superclass of `c`. If the original reference was to an instance field, an `IncompatibleClassChangeError` will result. If the original reference was an assignment, an `IllegalAccessError` will result.

Deleting a member from an interface may cause linkage errors in pre-existing binaries.

Example 13.5.3-1. Deleting An Interface Member

```
interface I { void hello(); }
class Test implements I {
    public static void main(String[] args) {
        I anI = new Test();
        anI.hello();
    }
    public void hello() { System.out.println("hello"); }
}
```

This program produces the output:

```
hello
```

Suppose that a new version of interface `I` is compiled:

```
interface I {}
```

If `I` is recompiled but not `Test`, then running the new binary with the existing binary for `Test` will result in a `NoSuchMethodError`.

13.5.4   Interface Type Parameters

The effects of changes to the type parameters of an interface are the same as those of analogous changes to the type parameters of a class.

13.5.5   Field Declarations

The considerations for changing field declarations in interfaces are the same as those for `static final` fields in classes, as described in §13.4.8 and §13.4.9.

13.5.6   `abstract` **Methods**

The considerations for changing `abstract` method declarations in interfaces are the same as those for `abstract` methods in classes, as described in §13.4.14, §13.4.15, §13.4.21, and §13.4.23.

13.5.7   Evolution of Annotation Types

Annotation types behave exactly like any other interface. Adding or removing an element from an annotation type is analogous to adding or removing a method. There are important considerations governing other changes to annotation types, but these have no effect on the linkage of binaries by the Java Virtual Machine. Rather, such changes affect the behavior of reflective APIs that manipulate annotations. The documentation of these APIs specifies their behavior when various changes are made to the underlying annotation types.

Adding or removing annotations has no effect on the correct linkage of the binary representations of programs in the Java programming language.

CHAPTER 14

Blocks and Statements

THE sequence of execution of a program is controlled by *statements*, which are executed for their effect and do not have values.

Some statements *contain* other statements as part of their structure; such other statements are substatements of the statement. We say that statement *s immediately contains* statement *u* if there is no statement *T* different from *s* and *u* such that *s* contains *T* and *T* contains *u*. In the same manner, some statements contain expressions (§15) as part of their structure.

The first section of this chapter discusses the distinction between normal and abrupt completion of statements (§14.1). Most of the remaining sections explain the various kinds of statements, describing in detail both their normal behavior and any special treatment of abrupt completion.

Blocks are explained first (§14.2), followed by local class declarations (§14.3) and local variable declaration statements (§14.4).

Next a grammatical maneuver that sidesteps the familiar "dangling else" problem (§14.5) is explained.

The last section (§14.21) of this chapter addresses the requirement that every statement be *reachable* in a certain technical sense.

14.1   Normal and Abrupt Completion of Statements

Every statement has a normal mode of execution in which certain computational steps are carried out. The following sections describe the normal mode of execution for each kind of statement.

If all the steps are carried out as described, with no indication of abrupt completion, the statement is said to *complete normally*. However, certain events may prevent a statement from completing normally:

- The `break` (§14.15), `continue` (§14.16), and `return` (§14.17) statements cause a transfer of control that may prevent normal completion of statements that contain them.

- Evaluation of certain expressions may throw exceptions from the Java Virtual Machine (§15.6). An explicit `throw` (§14.18) statement also results in an exception. An exception causes a transfer of control that may prevent normal completion of statements.

If such an event occurs, then execution of one or more statements may be terminated before all steps of their normal mode of execution have completed; such statements are said to *complete abruptly*.

An abrupt completion always has an associated *reason*, which is one of the following:

- A `break` with no label

- A `break` with a given label

- A `continue` with no label

- A `continue` with a given label

- A `return` with no value

- A `return` with a given value

- A `throw` with a given value, including exceptions thrown by the Java Virtual Machine

The terms "complete normally" and "complete abruptly" also apply to the evaluation of expressions (§15.6). The only reason an expression can complete abruptly is that an exception is thrown, because of either a `throw` with a given value (§14.18) or a run-time exception or error (§11, §15.6).

If a statement evaluates an expression, abrupt completion of the expression always causes the immediate abrupt completion of the statement, with the same reason. All succeeding steps in the normal mode of execution are not performed.

Unless otherwise specified in this chapter, abrupt completion of a substatement causes the immediate abrupt completion of the statement itself, with the same reason, and all succeeding steps in the normal mode of execution of the statement are not performed.

Unless otherwise specified, a statement completes normally if all expressions it evaluates and all substatements it executes complete normally.

14.2 Blocks

A *block* is a sequence of statements, local class declarations, and local variable declaration statements within braces.

> *Block:*
>   { *BlockStatements*$_{opt}$ }
>
> *BlockStatements:*
>   *BlockStatement*
>   *BlockStatements BlockStatement*
>
> *BlockStatement:*
>   *LocalVariableDeclarationStatement*
>   *ClassDeclaration*
>   *Statement*

A block is executed by executing each of the local variable declaration statements and other statements in order from first to last (left to right). If all of these block statements complete normally, then the block completes normally. If any of these block statements complete abruptly for any reason, then the block completes abruptly for the same reason.

14.3 Local Class Declarations

A *local class* is a nested class (§8) that is not a member of any class and that has a name (§6.2, §6.7).

All local classes are inner classes (§8.1.3).

Every local class declaration statement is immediately contained by a block (§14.2). Local class declaration statements may be intermixed freely with other kinds of statements in the block.

It is a compile-time error if a local class declaration contains any of the access modifiers `public`, `protected`, or `private` (§6.6), or the modifier `static` (§8.1.1).

The scope and shadowing of a local class declaration is specified in §6.3 and §6.4.

Example 14.3-1. Local Class Declarations

Here is an example that illustrates several aspects of the rules given above:

```
class Global {
    class Cyclic {}

    void foo() {
        new Cyclic(); // create a Global.Cyclic
        class Cyclic extends Cyclic {} // circular definition

        {
            class Local {}
            {
                class Local {} // compile-time error
            }
            class Local {} // compile-time error
            class AnotherLocal {
                void bar() {
                    class Local {} // ok
                }
            }
        }
        class Local {} // ok, not in scope of prior Local
    }
}
```

The first statement of method `foo` creates an instance of the member class `Global.Cyclic` rather than an instance of the local class `Cyclic`, because the local class declaration is not yet in scope.

The fact that the scope of a local class encompasses its own declaration (not only its body) means that the definition of the local class `Cyclic` is indeed cyclic because it extends itself rather than `Global.Cyclic`. Consequently, the declaration of the local class `Cyclic` will be rejected at compile time.

Since local class names cannot be redeclared within the same method (or constructor or initializer, as the case may be), the second and third declarations of `Local` result in compile-time errors. However, `Local` can be redeclared in the context of another, more deeply nested, class such as `AnotherLocal`.

The fourth and last declaration of `Local` is legal, since it occurs outside the scope of any prior declaration of `Local`.

14.4 Local Variable Declaration Statements

A *local variable declaration statement* declares one or more local variable names.

> *LocalVariableDeclarationStatement:*
>   *LocalVariableDeclaration* ;

> *LocalVariableDeclaration:*
>   *VariableModifiers$_{opt}$ Type VariableDeclarators*

The following are repeated from §8.4.1 and §8.3 to make the presentation here clearer:

> *VariableModifiers:*
>   *VariableModifier*
>   *VariableModifiers VariableModifier*

> *VariableModifier: one of*
>   *Annotation* `final`

> *VariableDeclarators:*
>   *VariableDeclarator*
>   *VariableDeclarators , VariableDeclarator*

> *VariableDeclarator:*
>   *VariableDeclaratorId*
>   *VariableDeclaratorId = VariableInitializer*

> *VariableDeclaratorId:*
>   *Identifier*
>   *VariableDeclaratorId* `[]`

> *VariableInitializer:*
>   *Expression*
>   *ArrayInitializer*

Every local variable declaration statement is immediately contained by a block. Local variable declaration statements may be intermixed freely with other kinds of statements in the block.

A local variable declaration can also appear in the header of a `for` statement (§14.14). In this case it is executed in the same manner as if it were part of a local variable declaration statement.

14.4.1   Local Variable Declarators and Types

Each *declarator* in a local variable declaration declares one local variable, whose name is the *Identifier* that appears in the declarator.

If the optional keyword `final` appears at the start of the declarator, the variable being declared is a final variable (§4.12.4).

If an annotation `a` (§9.7) on a local variable declaration corresponds to an annotation type `T`, and `T` has a (meta-)annotation `m` that corresponds to `java.lang.annotation.Target`, then `m` must have an element whose value is `java.lang.annotation.ElementType.LOCAL_VARIABLE`, or a compile-time error occurs.

The declared type of a local variable is denoted by the *Type* that appears in the local variable declaration, followed by any bracket pairs that follow the *Identifier* in the declarator.

A local variable of type `float` always contains a value that is an element of the float value set (§4.2.3); similarly, a local variable of type `double` always contains a value that is an element of the double value set. It is not permitted for a local variable of type `float` to contain an element of the float-extended-exponent value set that is not also an element of the float value set, nor for a local variable of type `double` to contain an element of the double-extended-exponent value set that is not also an element of the double value set.

The scope and shadowing of a local variable is specified in §6.3 and §6.4.

14.4.2   Execution of Local Variable Declarations

A local variable declaration statement is an executable statement. Every time it is executed, the declarators are processed in order from left to right. If a declarator has an initialization expression, the expression is evaluated and its value is assigned to the variable.

> If a declarator does not have an initialization expression, then every reference to the variable must be preceded by execution of an assignment to the variable, or a compile-time error occurs by the rules of §16.

Each initialization (except the first) is executed only if evaluation of the preceding initialization expression completes normally.

Execution of the local variable declaration completes normally only if evaluation of the last initialization expression completes normally.

If the local variable declaration contains no initialization expressions, then executing it always completes normally.

14.5 Statements

There are many kinds of statements in the Java programming language. Most correspond to statements in the C and C++ languages, but some are unique.

As in C and C++, the `if` statement of the Java programming language suffers from the so-called "dangling `else` problem," illustrated by this misleadingly formatted example:

```
if (door.isOpen())
    if (resident.isVisible())
        resident.greet("Hello!");
else door.bell.ring();  // A "dangling else"
```

The problem is that both the outer `if` statement and the inner `if` statement might conceivably own the `else` clause. In this example, one might surmise that the programmer intended the `else` clause to belong to the outer `if` statement.

The Java programming language, like C and C++ and many programming languages before them, arbitrarily decrees that an `else` clause belongs to the innermost `if` to which it might possibly belong. This rule is captured by the following grammar:

Statement:
   StatementWithoutTrailingSubstatement
   LabeledStatement
   IfThenStatement
   IfThenElseStatement
   WhileStatement
   ForStatement

StatementWithoutTrailingSubstatement:
   Block
   EmptyStatement
   ExpressionStatement
   AssertStatement
   SwitchStatement
   DoStatement
   BreakStatement
   ContinueStatement
   ReturnStatement
   SynchronizedStatement
   ThrowStatement
   TryStatement

StatementNoShortIf:
   StatementWithoutTrailingSubstatement
   LabeledStatementNoShortIf
   IfThenElseStatementNoShortIf
   WhileStatementNoShortIf
   ForStatementNoShortIf

The following are repeated from §14.9 to make the presentation here clearer:

IfThenStatement:
   `if (` *Expression* `)` *Statement*

IfThenElseStatement:
   `if (` *Expression* `)` *StatementNoShortIf* `else` *Statement*

IfThenElseStatementNoShortIf:
   `if (` *Expression* `)` *StatementNoShortIf* `else` *StatementNoShortIf*

Statements are thus grammatically divided into two categories: those that might end in an `if` statement that has no `else` clause (a "short `if` statement") and those that definitely do not.

Only statements that definitely do not end in a short `if` statement may appear as an immediate substatement before the keyword `else` in an `if` statement that does have an `else` clause.

This simple rule prevents the "dangling `else`" problem. The execution behavior of a statement with the "no short `if`" restriction is identical to the execution behavior of the same kind of statement without the "no short `if`" restriction; the distinction is drawn purely to resolve the syntactic difficulty.

14.6   The Empty Statement

An empty statement does nothing.

> *EmptyStatement:*
>   *;*

Execution of an empty statement always completes normally.

14.7   Labeled Statements

Statements may have *label* prefixes.

> *LabeledStatement:*
>   *Identifier* : *Statement*

> *LabeledStatementNoShortIf:*
>   *Identifier* : *StatementNoShortIf*

The *Identifier* is declared to be the label of the immediately contained *Statement*.

Unlike C and C++, the Java programming language has no `goto` statement; identifier statement labels are used with `break` (§14.15) or `continue` (§14.16) statements appearing anywhere within the labeled statement.

The scope of a label of a labeled statement is the immediately contained *Statement*.

It is a compile-time error if the name of a label of a labeled statement (§14.7) is used within the scope of the label as a label of another labeled statement.

There is no restriction against using the same identifier as a label and as the name of a package, class, interface, method, field, parameter, or local variable. Use of an identifier to label a statement does not obscure (§6.4.2) a package, class, interface, method, field, parameter, or local variable with the same name. Use of an identifier as a class, interface, method, field, local variable or as the parameter of an exception handler (§14.20) does not obscure a statement label with the same name.

A labeled statement is executed by executing the immediately contained *Statement*.

If the statement is labeled by an *Identifier* and the contained *Statement* completes abruptly because of a `break` with the same *Identifier*, then the labeled statement completes normally. In all other cases of abrupt completion of the *Statement*, the labeled statement completes abruptly for the same reason.

14.8   Expression Statements

Certain kinds of expressions may be used as statements by following them with semicolons.

ExpressionStatement:
  StatementExpression ;

StatementExpression:
  Assignment
  PreIncrementExpression
  PreDecrementExpression
  PostIncrementExpression
  PostDecrementExpression
  MethodInvocation
  ClassInstanceCreationExpression

An *expression statement* is executed by evaluating the expression; if the expression has a value, the value is discarded.

Execution of the expression statement completes normally if and only if evaluation of the expression completes normally.

Unlike C and C++, the Java programming language allows only certain forms of expressions to be used as expression statements. Note that the Java programming language does not allow a "cast to `void`" - `void` is not a type - so the traditional C trick of writing an expression statement such as:

```
(void)... ;   // incorrect!
```

does not work. On the other hand, the Java programming language allows all the most useful kinds of expressions in expressions statements, and it does not require a method invocation used as an expression statement to invoke a `void` method, so such a trick is almost never needed. If a trick is needed, either an assignment statement (§15.26) or a local variable declaration statement (§14.4) can be used instead.

14.9   The `if` Statement

The `if` statement allows conditional execution of a statement or a conditional choice of two statements, executing one or the other but not both.

> *IfThenStatement:*
>   if (*Expression*) *Statement*

> *IfThenElseStatement:*
>   if (*Expression*) *StatementNoShortIf* else *Statement*

> *IfThenElseStatementNoShortIf:*
>   if (*Expression*) *StatementNoShortIf* else *StatementNoShortIf*

The *Expression* must have type `boolean` or `Boolean`, or a compile-time error occurs.

14.9.1   The `if-then` Statement

An `if-then` statement is executed by first evaluating the *Expression*. If the result is of type `Boolean`, it is subject to unboxing conversion (§5.1.8).

If evaluation of the *Expression* or the subsequent unboxing conversion (if any) completes abruptly for some reason, the `if-then` statement completes abruptly for the same reason.

Otherwise, execution continues by making a choice based on the resulting value:

- If the value is `true`, then the contained *Statement* is executed; the `if-then` statement completes normally if and only if execution of the *Statement* completes normally.

- If the value is `false`, no further action is taken and the `if-then` statement completes normally.

14.9.2   The `if-then-else` Statement

An `if-then-else` statement is executed by first evaluating the *Expression*. If the result is of type `Boolean`, it is subject to unboxing conversion (§5.1.8).

If evaluation of the *Expression* or the subsequent unboxing conversion (if any) completes abruptly for some reason, then the `if-then-else` statement completes abruptly for the same reason.

Otherwise, execution continues by making a choice based on the resulting value:

- If the value is `true`, then the first contained *Statement* (the one before the `else` keyword) is executed; the `if-then-else` statement completes normally if and only if execution of that statement completes normally.

- If the value is `false`, then the second contained *Statement* (the one after the `else` keyword) is executed; the `if-then-else` statement completes normally if and only if execution of that statement completes normally.

14.10   The `assert` Statement

An *assertion* is an `assert` statement containing a boolean expression. An assertion is either *enabled* or *disabled*. If the assertion is enabled, execution of the assertion causes evaluation of the boolean expression and an error is reported if the expression evaluates to `false`. If the assertion is disabled, execution of the assertion has no effect whatsoever.

> *AssertStatement:*
>   `assert` *Expression1* `;`
>   `assert` *Expression1* `:` *Expression2* `;`

It is a compile-time error if *Expression1* does not have type `boolean` or `Boolean`.

In the second form of the `assert` statement, it is a compile-time error if *Expression2* is `void` (§15.1).

An `assert` statement that is executed after its class has completed initialization is enabled if and only if the host system has determined that the top level class that lexically contains the `assert` statement enables assertions.

Whether or not a top level class enables assertions is determined no later than the earliest of the initialization of the top level class and the initialization of any class nested in the top level class, and cannot be changed after it has been determined.

An assert statement that is executed before its class has completed initialization is enabled.

> This rule is motivated by a case that demands special treatment. Recall that the assertion status of a class is set no later than the time it is initialized. It is possible, though generally not desirable, to execute methods or constructors prior to initialization. This can happen when a class hierarchy contains a circularity in its static initialization, as in the following example:

```
public class Foo {
    public static void main(String[] args) {
        Baz.testAsserts();
        // Will execute after Baz is initialized.
    }
}
class Bar {
    static {
        Baz.testAsserts();
        // Will execute before Baz is initialized!
    }
}
class Baz extends Bar {
    static void testAsserts() {
        boolean enabled = false;
        assert  enabled = true;
        System.out.println("Asserts " +
        (enabled ? "enabled" : "disabled"));
    }
}
```

> Invoking Baz.testAsserts() causes Baz to be initialized. Before this can happen, Bar must be initialized. Bar's static initializer again invokes Baz.testAsserts(). Because initialization of Baz is already in progress by the current thread, the second invocation executes immediately, though Baz is not initialized (§12.4.2).

> Because of the rule above, if the program above is executed without enabling assertions, it must print:

```
Asserts enabled
Asserts disabled
```

A disabled assert statement does nothing. In particular, neither *Expression1* nor *Expression2* (if it is present) are evaluated. Execution of a disabled assert statement always completes normally.

An enabled `assert` statement is executed by first evaluating *Expression1*. If the result is of type `Boolean`, it is subject to unboxing conversion (§5.1.8).

If evaluation of *Expression1* or the subsequent unboxing conversion (if any) completes abruptly for some reason, the `assert` statement completes abruptly for the same reason.

Otherwise, execution continues by making a choice based on the value of *Expression1*:

- If the value is `true`, no further action is taken and the `assert` statement completes normally.

- If the value is `false`, the execution behavior depends on whether *Expression2* is present:

  - If *Expression2* is present, it is evaluated.

    - If the evaluation completes abruptly for some reason, the `assert` statement completes abruptly for the same reason.

    - If the evaluation completes normally, an `AssertionError` instance whose "detail message" is the resulting value of *Expression2* is created.

      - If the instance creation completes abruptly for some reason, the `assert` statement completes abruptly for the same reason.

      - If the instance creation completes normally, the `assert` statement completes abruptly by throwing the newly created `AssertionError` object.

  - If *Expression2* is not present, an `AssertionError` instance with no "detail message" is created.

    - If the instance creation completes abruptly for some reason, the assert statement completes abruptly for the same reason.

    - If the instance creation completes normally, the assert statement completes abruptly by throwing the newly created `AssertionError` object.

For example, after unmarshalling all of the arguments from a data buffer, a programmer might assert that the number of bytes of data remaining in the buffer is zero. By verifying that the boolean expression is indeed `true`, the system corroborates the programmer's knowledge of the program and increases one's confidence that the program is free of bugs.

Typically, assertion-checking is enabled during program development and testing, and disabled for deployment, to improve performance.

Because assertions may be disabled, programs must not assume that the expressions contained in assertions will be evaluated. Thus, these boolean expressions should generally be free of side effects.

Evaluating such a boolean expression should not affect any state that is visible after the evaluation is complete. It is not illegal for a boolean expression contained in an assertion to have a side effect, but it is generally inappropriate, as it could cause program behavior to vary depending on whether assertions were enabled or disabled.

Along similar lines, assertions should not be used for argument-checking in `public` methods. Argument-checking is typically part of the contract of a method, and this contract must be upheld whether assertions are enabled or disabled.

Another problem with using assertions for argument checking is that erroneous arguments should result in an appropriate run-time exception (such as `IllegalArgumentException`, `ArrayIndexOutOfBoundsException`, or `NullPointerException`). An assertion failure will not throw an appropriate exception. Again, it is not illegal to use assertions for argument checking on `public` methods, but it is generally inappropriate. It is intended that `AssertionError` never be caught, but it is possible to do so, thus the rules for `try` statements should treat assertions appearing in a `try` block similarly to the current treatment of `throw` statements.

14.11 The `switch` **Statement**

The `switch` statement transfers control to one of several statements depending on the value of an expression.

SwitchStatement:
   `switch` (*Expression*) *SwitchBlock*

SwitchBlock:
   { *SwitchBlockStatementGroups*$_{opt}$ *SwitchLabels*$_{opt}$ }

SwitchBlockStatementGroups:
   SwitchBlockStatementGroup
   SwitchBlockStatementGroups SwitchBlockStatementGroup

SwitchBlockStatementGroup:
   SwitchLabels BlockStatements

SwitchLabels:
   SwitchLabel
   SwitchLabels SwitchLabel

SwitchLabel:
   `case` *ConstantExpression* :
   `case` *EnumConstantName* :
   `default` :

EnumConstantName:
   Identifier

The type of the *Expression* must be `char`, `byte`, `short`, `int`, `Character`, `Byte`, `Short`, `Integer`, `String`, or an enum type (§8.9), or a compile-time error occurs.

The body of a `switch` statement is known as a *switch block*.

Any statement immediately contained by the switch block may be labeled with one or more *switch labels*, which are `case` or `default` labels.

These labels are said to be *associated* with the `switch` statement, as are the values of the constant expressions (§15.28) or enum constants (§8.9.1) in the `case` labels.

All of the following must be true, or a compile-time error occurs:

- Every `case` constant expression associated with a `switch` statement must be assignable (§5.2) to the type of the `switch` *Expression*.

- No two of the `case` constant expressions associated with a `switch` statement may have the same value.

- No switch label is `null`.

- At most one `default` label may be associated with the same `switch` statement.

   The prohibition against using `null` as a switch label prevents one from writing code that can never be executed. If the `switch` expression is of a reference type, that is, `String` or a boxed primitive type or an enum type, then a run-time error will occur if the expression evaluates to `null` at run time. In the judgment of the designers of the Java programming language, this is a better outcome than silently skipping the entire `switch` statement or choosing to execute the statements (if any) after the `default` label (if any).

   A Java compiler is encouraged (but not required) to provide a warning if a `switch` on an enum-valued expression lacks a `default` label and lacks `case` labels for one or more of the enum type's constants. (Such a statement will silently do nothing if the expression evaluates to one of the missing constants.)

   In C and C++ the body of a `switch` statement can be a statement and statements with `case` labels do not have to be immediately contained by that statement. Consider the simple loop:

   ```
   for (i = 0; i < n; ++i) foo();
   ```

   where `n` is known to be positive. A trick known as *Duff's device* can be used in C or C++ to unroll the loop, but this is not valid code in the Java programming language:

   ```
   int q = (n+7)/8;
   switch (n%8) {
       case 0: do { foo();     // Great C hack, Tom,
       case 7:      foo();     // but it's not valid here.
       case 6:      foo();
       case 5:      foo();
       case 4:      foo();
       case 3:      foo();
       case 2:      foo();
       case 1:      foo();
               } while (--q > 0);
   }
   ```

   Fortunately, this trick does not seem to be widely known or used. Moreover, it is less needed nowadays; this sort of code transformation is properly in the province of state-of-the-art optimizing compilers.

When the `switch` statement is executed, first the *Expression* is evaluated. If the *Expression* evaluates to `null`, a `NullPointerException` is thrown and the entire `switch` statement completes abruptly for that reason. Otherwise, if the result is of a reference type, it is subject to unboxing conversion (§5.1.8).

If evaluation of the *Expression* or the subsequent unboxing conversion (if any) completes abruptly for some reason, the `switch` statement completes abruptly for the same reason.

Otherwise, execution continues by comparing the value of the *Expression* with each `case` constant, and there is a choice:

- If one of the `case` constants is equal to the value of the expression, then we say that the `case` *matches*, and all statements after the matching `case` label in the `switch` block, if any, are executed in sequence.

  If all these statements complete normally, or if there are no statements after the matching `case` label, then the entire `switch` statement completes normally.

- If no `case` matches but there is a `default` label, then all statements after the matching `default` label in the `switch` block, if any, are executed in sequence.

  If all these statements complete normally, or if there are no statements after the `default` label, then the entire `switch` statement completes normally.

- If no `case` matches and there is no `default` label, then no further action is taken and the `switch` statement completes normally.

If any statement immediately contained by the *Block* body of the `switch` statement completes abruptly, it is handled as follows:

- If execution of the *Statement* completes abruptly because of a `break` with no label, no further action is taken and the `switch` statement completes normally.

- If execution of the *Statement* completes abruptly for any other reason, the `switch` statement completes abruptly for the same reason.

> The case of abrupt completion because of a `break` with a label is handled by the general rule for labeled statements (§14.7).

Example 14.11-1. Fall-Through in the `switch` Statement

As in C and C++, execution of statements in a `switch` block "falls through labels."

For example, the program:

```
class TooMany {
    static void howMany(int k) {
        switch (k) {
            case 1: System.out.print("one ");
            case 2: System.out.print("too ");
            case 3: System.out.println("many");
        }
    }
    public static void main(String[] args) {
        howMany(3);
        howMany(2);
        howMany(1);
    }
```

                }

contains a `switch` block in which the code for each `case` falls through into the code for the next `case`. As a result, the program prints:

```
many
too many
one too many
```

If code is not to fall through `case` to `case` in this manner, then `break` statements should be used, as in this example:

```
class TwoMany {
    static void howMany(int k) {
        switch (k) {
            case 1: System.out.println("one");
                    break;  // exit the switch
            case 2: System.out.println("two");
                    break;  // exit the switch
            case 3: System.out.println("many");
                    break;  // not needed, but good style
        }
    }
    public static void main(String[] args) {
        howMany(1);
        howMany(2);
        howMany(3);
    }
}
```

This program prints:

```
one
two
many
```

14.12   The while Statement

The `while` statement executes an *Expression* and a *Statement* repeatedly until the value of the *Expression* is `false`.

WhileStatement:
  while (*Expression*) *Statement*

WhileStatementNoShortIf:
  while (*Expression*) *StatementNoShortIf*

The *Expression* must have type `boolean` or `Boolean`, or a compile-time error occurs.

A `while` statement is executed by first evaluating the *Expression*. If the result is of type `Boolean`, it is subject to unboxing conversion (§5.1.8).

If evaluation of the *Expression* or the subsequent unboxing conversion (if any) completes abruptly for some reason, the `while` statement completes abruptly for the same reason.

Otherwise, execution continues by making a choice based on the resulting value:

- If the value is `true`, then the contained *Statement* is executed. Then there is a choice:

  - If execution of the *Statement* completes normally, then the entire `while` statement is executed again, beginning by re-evaluating the *Expression*.

  - If execution of the *Statement* completes abruptly, see §14.12.1.

- If the (possibly unboxed) value of the *Expression* is `false`, no further action is taken and the `while` statement completes normally.

    If the (possibly unboxed) value of the *Expression* is `false` the first time it is evaluated, then the *Statement* is not executed.

14.12.1   Abrupt Completion of `while` Statement

Abrupt completion of the contained *Statement* is handled in the following manner:

- If execution of the *Statement* completes abruptly because of a `break` with no label, no further action is taken and the `while` statement completes normally.

- If execution of the *Statement* completes abruptly because of a `continue` with no label, then the entire `while` statement is executed again.

- If execution of the *Statement* completes abruptly because of a `continue` with label `L`, then there is a choice:

  - If the `while` statement has label `L`, then the entire `while` statement is executed again.

  - If the `while` statement does not have label `L`, the `while` statement completes abruptly because of a `continue` with label `L`.

- If execution of the *Statement* completes abruptly for any other reason, the `while` statement completes abruptly for the same reason.

The case of abrupt completion because of a `break` with a label is handled by the general rule for labeled statements (§14.7).

14.13   The do **Statement**

The do statement executes a *Statement* and an *Expression* repeatedly until the value of the *Expression* is `false`.

> *DoStatement:*
>   do *Statement* `while` (*Expression*) ;

The *Expression* must have type `boolean` or `Boolean`, or a compile-time error occurs.

A do statement is executed by first executing the *Statement*. Then there is a choice:

- If execution of the *Statement* completes normally, then the *Expression* is evaluated. If the result is of type `Boolean`, it is subject to unboxing conversion (§5.1.8).

  If evaluation of the *Expression* or the subsequent unboxing conversion (if any) completes abruptly for some reason, the do statement completes abruptly for the same reason.

  Otherwise, there is a choice based on the resulting value:

  - If the value is `true`, then the entire do statement is executed again.

  - If the value is `false`, no further action is taken and the do statement completes normally.

- If execution of the *Statement* completes abruptly, see §14.13.1.

  Executing a do statement always executes the contained *Statement* at least once.

14.13.1   **Abrupt Completion of** do **Statement**

Abrupt completion of the contained *Statement* is handled in the following manner:

- If execution of the *Statement* completes abruptly because of a `break` with no label, then no further action is taken and the do statement completes normally.

- If execution of the *Statement* completes abruptly because of a `continue` with no label, then the *Expression* is evaluated. Then there is a choice based on the resulting value:

  - If the value is `true`, then the entire `do` statement is executed again.

  - If the value is `false`, no further action is taken and the `do` statement completes normally.

- If execution of the *Statement* completes abruptly because of a `continue` with label `L`, then there is a choice:

  - If the `do` statement has label `L`, then the *Expression* is evaluated. Then there is a choice:

    - If the value of the *Expression* is `true`, then the entire `do` statement is executed again.

    - If the value of the *Expression* is `false`, no further action is taken and the `do` statement completes normally.

  - If the `do` statement does not have label `L`, the `do` statement completes abruptly because of a `continue` with label `L`.

- If execution of the *Statement* completes abruptly for any other reason, the `do` statement completes abruptly for the same reason.

> The case of abrupt completion because of a `break` with a label is handled by the general rule for labeled statements (§14.7).

Example 14.13-1. The `do` Statement

The following code is one possible implementation of the `toHexString` method of class `Integer`:

```
public static String toHexString(int i) {
    StringBuffer buf = new StringBuffer(8);
    do {
        buf.append(Character.forDigit(i & 0xF, 16));
        i >>>= 4;
    } while (i != 0);
    return buf.reverse().toString();
}
```

Because at least one digit must be generated, the `do` statement is an appropriate control structure.

14.14   The for **Statement**

The for statement has two forms:

- The basic for statement.

- The enhanced for statement

> *ForStatement:*
>   *BasicForStatement*
>   *EnhancedForStatement*

14.14.1   The basic for **Statement**

The basic for statement executes some initialization code, then executes an *Expression*, a *Statement*, and some update code repeatedly until the value of the *Expression* is false.

> *BasicForStatement:*
>   for (*ForInit$_{opt}$* ; *Expression$_{opt}$* ; *ForUpdate$_{opt}$*) *Statement*

> *ForStatementNoShortIf:*
>   for (*ForInit$_{opt}$* ; *Expression$_{opt}$* ; *ForUpdate$_{opt}$*) *StatementNoShortIf*

> *ForInit:*
>   *StatementExpressionList*
>   *LocalVariableDeclaration*

> *ForUpdate:*
>   *StatementExpressionList*

> *StatementExpressionList:*
>   *StatementExpression*
>   *StatementExpressionList* , *StatementExpression*

The *Expression* must have type boolean or Boolean, or a compile-time error occurs.

The scope and shadowing of a local variable declared in the *ForInit* part of a basic for statement is specified in §6.3 and §6.4.

14.14.1.1   *Initialization of* `for` *Statement*

A `for` statement is executed by first executing the *ForInit* code:

- If the *ForInit* code is a list of statement expressions (§14.8), the expressions are evaluated in sequence from left to right; their values, if any, are discarded.

  If evaluation of any expression completes abruptly for some reason, the `for` statement completes abruptly for the same reason; any *ForInit* statement expressions to the right of the one that completed abruptly are not evaluated.

- If the *ForInit* code is a local variable declaration, it is executed as if it were a local variable declaration statement (§14.4) appearing in a block.

  If execution of the local variable declaration completes abruptly for any reason, the `for` statement completes abruptly for the same reason.

- If the *ForInit* part is not present, no action is taken.

14.14.1.2   *Iteration of* `for` *Statement*

Next, a `for` iteration step is performed, as follows:

- If the *Expression* is present, it is evaluated. If the result is of type `Boolean`, it is subject to unboxing conversion (§5.1.8).

  If evaluation of the *Expression* or the subsequent unboxing conversion (if any) completes abruptly, the `for` statement completes abruptly for the same reason.

  > Otherwise, there is then a choice based on the presence or absence of the *Expression* and the resulting value if the *Expression* is present; see next bullet.

- If the *Expression* is not present, or it is present and the value resulting from its evaluation (including any possible unboxing) is `true`, then the contained *Statement* is executed. Then there is a choice:

  - If execution of the *Statement* completes normally, then the following two steps are performed in sequence:

    1. First, if the *ForUpdate* part is present, the expressions are evaluated in sequence from left to right; their values, if any, are discarded. If evaluation of any expression completes abruptly for some reason, the `for` statement completes abruptly for the same reason; any *ForUpdate* statement expressions to the right of the one that completed abruptly are not evaluated.

       If the *ForUpdate* part is not present, no action is taken.

2.   Second, another `for` iteration step is performed.

- If execution of the *Statement* completes abruptly, see §14.14.1.3.

- If the *Expression* is present and the value resulting from its evaluation (including any possible unboxing) is `false`, no further action is taken and the `for` statement completes normally.

> If the (possibly unboxed) value of the *Expression* is `false` the first time it is evaluated, then the *Statement* is not executed.

If the *Expression* is not present, then the only way a `for` statement can complete normally is by use of a `break` statement.

14.14.1.3   *Abrupt Completion of* for *Statement*

Abrupt completion of the contained *Statement* is handled in the following manner:

- If execution of the *Statement* completes abruptly because of a `break` with no label, no further action is taken and the `for` statement completes normally.

- If execution of the *Statement* completes abruptly because of a `continue` with no label, then the following two steps are performed in sequence:

1.   First, if the *ForUpdate* part is present, the expressions are evaluated in sequence from left to right; their values, if any, are discarded.

   If the *ForUpdate* part is not present, no action is taken.

2.   Second, another `for` iteration step is performed.

- If execution of the *Statement* completes abruptly because of a `continue` with label *L*, then there is a choice:

- If the `for` statement has label *L*, then the following two steps are performed in sequence:

1.   First, if the *ForUpdate* part is present, the expressions are evaluated in sequence from left to right; their values, if any, are discarded.

   If the *ForUpdate* is not present, no action is taken.

2.   Second, another `for` iteration step is performed.

- If the `for` statement does not have label *L*, the `for` statement completes abruptly because of a `continue` with label *L*.

- If execution of the *Statement* completes abruptly for any other reason, the `for` statement completes abruptly for the same reason.

Note that the case of abrupt completion because of a `break` with a label is handled by the general rule for labeled statements (§14.7).

14.14.2   The enhanced `for` statement

The enhanced `for` statement has the form:

EnhancedForStatement:

   for (*FormalParameter* : *Expression*) *Statement*

The following is repeated from §8.4.1 and §8.3 to make the presentation here clearer:

FormalParameter:
  VariableModifiers$_{opt}$ Type VariableDeclaratorId

VariableDeclaratorId:
  Identifier
  VariableDeclaratorId []

The type of the *Expression* must be `Iterable` or an array type (§10.1), or a compile-time error occurs.

The scope and shadowing of a local variable declared in the *FormalParameter* part of an enhanced `for` statement is specified in §6.3 and §6.4.

The meaning of the enhanced `for` statement is given by translation into a basic `for` statement, as follows:

- If the type of *Expression* is a subtype of `Iterable`, then the translation is as follows.

  If the type of *Expression* is a subtype of `Iterable<X>` for some type argument *X*, then let *I* be the type `java.util.Iterator<X>`; otherwise, let *I* be the raw type `java.util.Iterator`.

  The enhanced `for` statement is equivalent to a basic `for` statement of the form:

  ```
  for (I #i = Expression.iterator(); #i.hasNext(); ) {
      VariableModifiersopt TargetType Identifier =
          (TargetType) #i.next();
      Statement
  }
  ```

`#i` is an automatically generated identifier that is distinct from any other identifiers (automatically generated or otherwise) that are in scope (§6.3) at the point where the enhanced `for` statement occurs.

If *Type* (in the *FormalParameter* production) is a reference type, then *TargetType* is *Type*; otherwise, *TargetType* is the upper bound of the capture conversion of the type argument of `I`, or `Object` if `I` is raw.

```
List<? extends Integer> l = ...
for (float i : l) ...
```

will be translated to:

```
for (Iterator<Integer> #i = l.iterator(); #i.hasNext(); ) {
    float #i0 = (Integer)#i.next();
    ...
```

- Otherwise, the *Expression* necessarily has an array type, $T[]$.

Let $L_1 ... L_m$ be the (possibly empty) sequence of labels immediately preceding the enhanced `for` statement.

The enhanced `for` statement is equivalent to a basic `for` statement of the form:

```
T[] #a = Expression;
L₁: L₂: ... Lₘ:
for (int #i = 0; #i < #a.length; #i++) {
    VariableModifiersₒₚₜ TargetType Identifier = #a[#i];
    Statement
}
```

`#a` and `#i` are automatically generated identifiers that are distinct from any other identifiers (automatically generated or otherwise) that are in scope at the point where the enhanced `for` statement occurs.

TargetType is the type of the loop variable as denoted by the *Type* that appears in the *FormalParameter* followed by any bracket pairs that follow the *Identifier* in the *FormalParameter* (§10.2).

Example 14.14-1. Enhanced-`for` And Arrays

The following program, which calculates the sum of an integer array, shows how enhanced `for` works for arrays:

```
int sum(int[] a) {
    int sum = 0;
    for (int i : a) sum += i;
    return sum;
}
```

Example 14.14-2. Enhanced-`for` And Unboxing Conversion

The following program combines the enhanced `for` statement with auto-unboxing to translate a histogram into a frequency table:

```
Map<String, Integer> histogram = ...;
double total = 0;
for (int i : histogram.values())
    total += i;
for (Map.Entry<String, Integer> e : histogram.entrySet())
    System.out.println(e.getKey() + " " + e.getValue() / total);
}
```

14.15   The `break` Statement

A `break` statement transfers control out of an enclosing statement.

> *BreakStatement:*
>   `break` *Identifier*_{opt} ;

A `break` statement with no label attempts to transfer control to the innermost enclosing `switch`, `while`, `do`, or `for` statement of the immediately enclosing method or initializer; this statement, which is called the *break target*, then immediately completes normally.

To be precise, a `break` statement with no label always completes abruptly, the reason being a `break` with no label.

If no `switch`, `while`, `do`, or `for` statement in the immediately enclosing method, constructor, or initializer contains the `break` statement, a compile-time error occurs.

A `break` statement with label *Identifier* attempts to transfer control to the enclosing labeled statement (§14.7) that has the same *Identifier* as its label; this statement, which is called the *break target*, then immediately completes normally. In this case, the break target need not be a `switch`, `while`, `do`, or `for` statement.

To be precise, a `break` statement with label *Identifier* always completes abruptly, the reason being a `break` with label *Identifier*.

A `break` statement must refer to a label within the immediately enclosing method, constructor, or initializer. There are no non-local jumps. If no labeled statement with *Identifier* as its label in the immediately enclosing method, constructor, or initializer contains the `break` statement, a compile-time error occurs.

It can be seen, then, that a `break` statement always completes abruptly.

The preceding descriptions say "attempts to transfer control" rather than just "transfers control" because if there are any try statements (§14.20) within the break target whose try blocks or catch clauses contain the break statement, then any finally clauses of those try statements are executed, in order, innermost to outermost, before control is transferred to the break target. Abrupt completion of a finally clause can disrupt the transfer of control initiated by a break statement.

Example 14.15-1. The break Statement

In the following example, a mathematical graph is represented by an array of arrays. A graph consists of a set of nodes and a set of edges; each edge is an arrow that points from some node to some other node, or from a node to itself. In this example it is assumed that there are no redundant edges; that is, for any two nodes P and Q, where Q may be the same as P, there is at most one edge from P to Q.

Nodes are represented by integers, and there is an edge from node i to node edges[i] [j] for every i and j for which the array reference edges[i][j] does not throw an ArrayIndexOutOfBoundsException.

The task of the method loseEdges, given integers i and j, is to construct a new graph by copying a given graph but omitting the edge from node i to node j, if any, and the edge from node j to node i, if any:

```
class Graph {
    int edges[][];
    public Graph(int[][] edges) { this.edges = edges; }

    public Graph loseEdges(int i, int j) {
        int n = edges.length;
        int[][] newedges = new int[n][];
        for (int k = 0; k < n; ++k) {
edgelist:
{
            int z;
search:
{
            if (k == i) {
                for (z = 0; z < edges[k].length; ++z) {
                    if (edges[k][z] == j) break search;
                }
            } else if (k == j) {
                for (z = 0; z < edges[k].length; ++z) {
                    if (edges[k][z] == i) break search;
                }
            }

            // No edge to be deleted; share this list.
            newedges[k] = edges[k];
            break edgelist;
} //search

            // Copy the list, omitting the edge at position z.
```

```
                    int m = edges[k].length - 1;
                    int ne[] = new int[m];
                    System.arraycopy(edges[k], 0, ne, 0, z);
                    System.arraycopy(edges[k], z+1, ne, z, m-z);
                    newedges[k] = ne;
    } //edgelist
            }
            return new Graph(newedges);
        }
    }
```

Note the use of two statement labels, edgelist and search, and the use of break statements. This allows the code that copies a list, omitting one edge, to be shared between two separate tests, the test for an edge from node i to node j, and the test for an edge from node j to node i.

14.16   The continue Statement

A continue statement may occur only in a while, do, or for statement; statements of these three kinds are called *iteration statements*. Control passes to the loop-continuation point of an iteration statement.

> *ContinueStatement:*
>   continue *Identifier$_{opt}$* ;

A continue statement with no label attempts to transfer control to the innermost enclosing while, do, or for statement of the immediately enclosing method, constructor, or initializer; this statement, which is called the *continue target*, then immediately ends the current iteration and begins a new one.

To be precise, such a continue statement always completes abruptly, the reason being a continue with no label.

If no while, do, or for statement of the immediately enclosing method, constructor, or initializer contains the continue statement, a compile-time error occurs.

A continue statement with label *Identifier* attempts to transfer control to the enclosing labeled statement (§14.7) that has the same *Identifier* as its label; that statement, which is called the *continue target*, then immediately ends the current iteration and begins a new one.

To be precise, a continue statement with label *Identifier* always completes abruptly, the reason being a continue with label *Identifier*.

The continue target must be a while, do, or for statement, or a compile-time error occurs.

A continue statement must refer to a label within the immediately enclosing method, constructor, or initializer. There are no non-local jumps. If no labeled statement with *Identifier* as its label in the immediately enclosing method, constructor, or initializer contains the continue statement, a compile-time error occurs.

It can be seen, then, that a continue statement always completes abruptly.

See the descriptions of the while statement (§14.12), do statement (§14.13), and for statement (§14.14) for a discussion of the handling of abrupt termination because of continue.

The preceding descriptions say "attempts to transfer control" rather than just "transfers control" because if there are any try statements (§14.20) within the continue target whose try blocks or catch clauses contain the continue statement, then any finally clauses of those try statements are executed, in order, innermost to outermost, before control is transferred to the continue target. Abrupt completion of a finally clause can disrupt the transfer of control initiated by a continue statement.

Example 14.16-1. The continue **Statement**

In the Graph class in §14.15, one of the break statements is used to finish execution of the entire body of the outermost for loop. This break can be replaced by a continue if the for loop itself is labeled:

```
class Graph {
    int edges[][];
    public Graph(int[][] edges) { this.edges = edges; }

    public Graph loseEdges(int i, int j) {
        int n = edges.length;
        int[][] newedges = new int[n][];
    edgelists:
        for (int k = 0; k < n; ++k) {
            int z;
    search:
        {
            if (k == i) {
                for (z = 0; z < edges[k].length; ++z) {
                    if (edges[k][z] == j) break search;
                }
            } else if (k == j) {
                for (z = 0; z < edges[k].length; ++z) {
                    if (edges[k][z] == i) break search;
                }
            }

            // No edge to be deleted; share this list.
            newedges[k] = edges[k];
            continue edgelists;
```

```
        } //search

                // Copy the list, omitting the edge at position z.
                int m = edges[k].length - 1;
                int ne[] = new int[m];
                System.arraycopy(edges[k], 0, ne, 0, z);
                System.arraycopy(edges[k], z+1, ne, z, m-z);
                newedges[k] = ne;
            } //edgelists
            return new Graph(newedges);
        }
    }
```

Which to use, if either, is largely a matter of programming style.

14.17 The `return` **Statement**

A `return` statement returns control to the invoker of a method (§8.4, §15.12) or constructor (§8.8, §15.9).

> *ReturnStatement:*
>   `return` *Expression$_{opt}$* ;

A `return` statement is *contained* in the innermost constructor, method, or initializer whose body encloses the `return` statement.

It is a compile-time error if a `return` statement is contained in an instance initializer or a static initializer (§8.6, §8.7).

A `return` statement with no *Expression* must be contained in a method that is declared, using the keyword `void`, not to return any value (§8.4), or in a constructor (§8.8), or a compile-time error occurs.

A `return` statement with no *Expression* attempts to transfer control to the invoker of the method or constructor that contains it. To be precise, a `return` statement with no *Expression* always completes abruptly, the reason being a return with no value.

A `return` statement with an *Expression* must be contained in a method declaration that is declared to return a value (§8.4), or a compile-time error occurs.

The *Expression* must denote a variable or value of some type T, or a compile-time error occurs.

The type T must be assignable (§5.2) to the declared result type of the method, or a compile-time error occurs.

A return statement with an *Expression* attempts to transfer control to the invoker of the method that contains it; the value of the *Expression* becomes the value of the method invocation. More precisely, execution of such a return statement first evaluates the *Expression*. If the evaluation of the *Expression* completes abruptly for some reason, then the return statement completes abruptly for that reason. If evaluation of the *Expression* completes normally, producing a value *v*, then the return statement completes abruptly, the reason being a return with value *v*.

If the expression is of type float and is not FP-strict (§15.4), then the value may be an element of either the float value set or the float-extended-exponent value set (§4.2.3). If the expression is of type double and is not FP-strict, then the value may be an element of either the double value set or the double-extended-exponent value set.

> It can be seen, then, that a return statement always completes abruptly.

> The preceding descriptions say "attempts to transfer control" rather than just "transfers control" because if there are any try statements (§14.20) within the method or constructor whose try blocks or catch clauses contain the return statement, then any finally clauses of those try statements will be executed, in order, innermost to outermost, before control is transferred to the invoker of the method or constructor. Abrupt completion of a finally clause can disrupt the transfer of control initiated by a return statement.

14.18   The throw **Statement**

A throw statement causes an exception (§11) to be thrown. The result is an immediate transfer of control (§11.3) that may exit multiple statements and multiple constructor, instance initializer, static initializer and field initializer evaluations, and method invocations until a try statement (§14.20) is found that catches the thrown value. If no such try statement is found, then execution of the thread (§17) that executed the throw is terminated (§11.3) after invocation of the uncaughtException method for the thread group to which the thread belongs.

> *ThrowStatement:*
>   throw *Expression* ;

The *Expression* in a throw statement must denote either 1) a variable or value of a reference type which is assignable (§5.2) to the type Throwable, or 2) the null reference, or a compile-time error occurs.

> The reference type of the *Expression* will always be a class type (since no interface types are assignable to Throwable) which is not parameterized (since a subclass of Throwable cannot be generic (§8.1.2)).

At least one of the following three conditions must be true, or a compile-time error occurs:

- The type of the *Expression* is an unchecked exception class (§11.1.1) or the null type (§4.1).

- The `throw` statement is contained in the `try` block of a `try` statement (§14.20) and it is not the case that the `try` statement can throw an exception of the type of the *Expression*. (In this case we say the thrown value is *caught* by the `try` statement.)

- The `throw` statement is contained in a method or constructor declaration and the type of the *Expression* is assignable (§5.2) to at least one type listed in the `throws` clause (§8.4.6, §8.8.5) of the declaration.

The exception types that a `throw` statement can throw are specified in §11.2.2.

A `throw` statement first evaluates the *Expression*. Then:

- If evaluation of the *Expression* completes abruptly for some reason, then the `throw` completes abruptly for that reason.

- If evaluation of the *Expression* completes normally, producing a non-`null` value *v*, then the `throw` statement completes abruptly, the reason being a `throw` with value *v*.

- If evaluation of the *Expression* completes normally, producing a `null` value, then an instance *v'* of class `NullPointerException` is created and thrown instead of `null`. The `throw` statement then completes abruptly, the reason being a `throw` with value *v'*.

> It can be seen, then, that a `throw` statement always completes abruptly.

If there are any enclosing `try` statements (§14.20) whose `try` blocks contain the `throw` statement, then any `finally` clauses of those `try` statements are executed as control is transferred outward, until the thrown value is caught. Note that abrupt completion of a `finally` clause can disrupt the transfer of control initiated by a `throw` statement.

If a `throw` statement is contained in a method declaration, but its value is not caught by some `try` statement that contains it, then the invocation of the method completes abruptly because of the `throw`.

If a `throw` statement is contained in a constructor declaration, but its value is not caught by some `try` statement that contains it, then the class instance creation expression that invoked the constructor will complete abruptly because of the throw (§15.9.4).

If a throw statement is contained in a static initializer (§8.7), then a compile-time check (§11.2.3) ensures that either its value is always an unchecked exception or its value is always caught by some try statement that contains it. If at run time, despite this check, the value is not caught by some try statement that contains the throw statement, then the value is rethrown if it is an instance of class Error or one of its subclasses; otherwise, it is wrapped in an ExceptionInInitializerError object, which is then thrown (§12.4.2).

If a throw statement is contained in an instance initializer (§8.6), then a compile-time check (§11.2.3) ensures that either its value is always an unchecked exception or its value is always caught by some try statement that contains it, or the type of the thrown exception (or one of its superclasses) occurs in the throws clause of every constructor of the class.

> By convention, user-declared throwable types should usually be declared to be subclasses of class Exception, which is a subclass of class Throwable (§11.1.1).

14.19 The synchronized **Statement**

A synchronized statement acquires a mutual-exclusion lock (§17.1) on behalf of the executing thread, executes a block, then releases the lock. While the executing thread owns the lock, no other thread may acquire the lock.

> *SynchronizedStatement:*
>   synchronized (*Expression*) *Block*

The type of *Expression* must be a reference type, or a compile-time error occurs.

A synchronized statement is executed by first evaluating the *Expression*. Then:

- If evaluation of the *Expression* completes abruptly for some reason, then the synchronized statement completes abruptly for the same reason.

- Otherwise, if the value of the *Expression* is null, a NullPointerException is thrown.

- Otherwise, let the non-null value of the *Expression* be *v*. The executing thread locks the monitor associated with *v*. Then the *Block* is executed, and then there is a choice:

- If execution of the *Block* completes normally, then the monitor is unlocked and the `synchronized` statement completes normally.

- If execution of the *Block* completes abruptly for any reason, then the monitor is unlocked and the `synchronized` statement completes abruptly for the same reason.

The locks acquired by `synchronized` statements are the same as the locks that are acquired implicitly by `synchronized` methods (§8.4.3.6). A single thread may acquire a lock more than once.

Acquiring the lock associated with an object does not in itself prevent other threads from accessing fields of the object or invoking un-`synchronized` methods on the object. Other threads can also use `synchronized` methods or the `synchronized` statement in a conventional manner to achieve mutual exclusion.

Example 14.19-1. The `synchronized` **Statement**

```
class Test {
    public static void main(String[] args) {
        Test t = new Test();
        synchronized(t) {
            synchronized(t) {
                System.out.println("made it!");
            }
        }
    }
}
```

This program produces the output:

```
made it!
```

Note that this program would deadlock if a single thread were not permitted to lock a monitor more than once.

14.20   The `try` statement

A `try` statement executes a block. If a value is thrown and the `try` statement has one or more `catch` clauses that can catch it, then control will be transferred to the first such `catch` clause. If the `try` statement has a `finally` clause, then another block of code is executed, no matter whether the `try` block completes normally or abruptly, and no matter whether a `catch` clause is first given control.

TryStatement:
   try *Block Catches*
   try *Block Catches_{opt} Finally*
   TryWithResourcesStatement

Catches:
   CatchClause
   Catches CatchClause

CatchClause:
   catch (*CatchFormalParameter*) *Block*

CatchFormalParameter:
   VariableModifiers$_{opt}$ CatchType VariableDeclaratorId

CatchType:
   ClassType
   ClassType | *CatchType*

Finally:
   finally *Block*

The *Block* immediately after the keyword try is called the try *block* of the try statement.

The *Block* immediately after the keyword finally is called the finally *block* of the try statement.

A try statement may have catch clauses, also called *exception handlers*.

A catch clause has exactly one parameter, which is called an *exception parameter*.

The scope and shadowing of an exception parameter is specified in §6.3 and §6.4.

An exception parameter may denote its type as either a single class type or a union of two or more class types (called *alternatives*). The alternatives of a union are syntactically separated by |.

A catch clause whose exception parameter is denoted as a single class type is called a *uni-*catch *clause.*

A catch clause whose exception parameter is denoted as a union of types is called a *multi-*catch *clause.*

Each class type used in the denotation of the type of an exception parameter must be the class `Throwable` or a subclass of `Throwable`, or a compile-time error occurs.

It is a compile-time error if a type variable is used in the denotation of the type of an exception parameter.

It is a compile-time error if a union of types contains two alternatives D_i and D_j ($i \neq j$) where D_i is a subtype of D_j (§4.10.2).

The declared type of an exception parameter that denotes its type with a single class type is that class type.

The declared type of an exception parameter that denotes its type as a union with alternatives $D_1 \mid D_2 \mid \ldots \mid D_n$ is $lub(D_1, D_2, \ldots, D_n)$ (§15.12.2.7).

An exception parameter of a multi-`catch` clause is implicitly declared `final` if it is not explicitly declared `final`.

It is a compile-time error if an exception parameter that is implicitly or explicitly declared `final` is assigned to within the body of the `catch` clause.

In a uni-`catch` clause, an exception parameter that is not declared `final` (implicitly or explicitly) is considered *effectively final* if it never occurs within its scope as the left-hand operand of an assignment operator (§15.26).

> An implicitly final exception parameter is `final` by virtue of its declaration, while an effectively final exception parameter is (as it were) `final` by virtue of how it is used. An exception parameter of a multi-`catch` clause is implicitly final, so will never occur as the left-hand operand of an assignment operator, but it is *not* considered effectively final.

> If an exception parameter is effectively final (in a uni-`catch` clause) or implicitly final (in a multi-`catch` clause), then adding an explicit `final` modifier to its declaration will not introduce any compile-time errors. However, if the exception parameter *of a uni-*`catch` *clause* is explicitly declared `final`, then removing the `final` modifier may introduce compile-time errors. This is because the exception parameter, while still effectively final, can no longer be referenced by, for example, local classes. On the other hand, if there are no compile-time errors, it is possible to further change the program so that the exception parameter is re-assigned and no longer effectively final.

The exception types that a `try` statement can throw are specified in §11.2.2.

The relationship of the exceptions thrown by the `try` block of a `try` statement and caught by the `catch` clauses (if any) of the `try` statement is specified in §11.2.3.

Exception handlers are considered in left-to-right order: the earliest possible `catch` clause accepts the exception, receiving as its argument the thrown exception object, as specified in §11.3.

A multi-catch clause can be thought of as a sequence of uni-catch clauses. That is, a catch clause whose exception parameter type is denoted as a union $D_1 | D_2 | ... | D_n$ is equivalent to a sequence of n catch clauses whose exception parameters have class types $D_1, D_2, ..., D_n$, respectively. For example, the following code:

```
try {
    ... throws ReflectiveOperationException ...
}
catch (ClassNotFoundException | IllegalAccessException ex) {
    ... body ...
}
```

is semantically equivalent to the following code:

```
try {
    ... throws ReflectiveOperationException ...
} catch (final ClassNotFoundException ex1) {
    ... body ...
} catch (final IllegalAccessException ex2) {
    ... body ...
}
```

whereby the multi-catch clause with two alternatives has been translated into two separate catch clauses, one for each alternative. A Java compiler is neither required nor recommended to compile a multi-catch clause by duplicating code in this manner, since it is possible to represent the multi-catch clause in a class file without duplication.

A finally clause ensures that the finally block is executed after the try block and any catch block that might be executed, no matter how control leaves the try block or catch block. Handling of the finally block is rather complex, so the two cases of a try statement with and without a finally block are described separately (§14.20.1, §14.20.2).

A try statement is permitted to omit catch clauses and a finally clause if it is a try-*with-resources* statement (§14.20.3).

14.20.1   Execution of try-catch

A try statement without a finally block is executed by first executing the try block. Then there is a choice:

- If execution of the try block completes normally, then no further action is taken and the try statement completes normally.

- If execution of the try block completes abruptly because of a throw of a value V, then there is a choice:

- If the run-time type of v is assignment compatible with (§5.2) a catchable exception class of any `catch` clause of the `try` statement, then the first (leftmost) such `catch` clause is selected. The value v is assigned to the parameter of the selected `catch` clause, and the *Block* of that `catch` clause is executed, and then there is a choice:

  - If that block completes normally, then the `try` statement completes normally.

  - If that block completes abruptly for any reason, then the `try` statement completes abruptly for the same reason.

- If the run-time type of v is not assignment compatible with a catchable exception class of any `catch` clause of the `try` statement, then the `try` statement completes abruptly because of a `throw` of the value v.

- If execution of the `try` block completes abruptly for any other reason, then the `try` statement completes abruptly for the same reason.

Example 14.20.1-1. Catching An Exception

```
class BlewIt extends Exception {
    BlewIt() { }
    BlewIt(String s) { super(s); }
}
class Test {
    static void blowUp() throws BlewIt { throw new BlewIt(); }

    public static void main(String[] args) {
        try {
            blowUp();
        } catch (RuntimeException r) {
            System.out.println("Caught RuntimeException");
        } catch (BlewIt b) {
            System.out.println("Caught BlewIt");
        }
    }
}
```

Here, the exception `BlewIt` is thrown by the method `blowUp`. The try-catch statement in the body of `main` has two `catch` clauses. The run-time type of the exception is `BlewIt` which is not assignable to a variable of type `RuntimeException`, but is assignable to a variable of type `BlewIt`, so the output of the example is:

```
Caught BlewIt
```

14.20.2   Execution of `try-finally` and `try-catch-finally`

A `try` statement with a `finally` block is executed by first executing the `try` block. Then there is a choice:

- If execution of the `try` block completes normally, then the `finally` block is executed, and then there is a choice:

  - If the `finally` block completes normally, then the `try` statement completes normally.

  - If the `finally` block completes abruptly for reason *s*, then the `try` statement completes abruptly for reason *s*.

- If execution of the `try` block completes abruptly because of a `throw` of a value *V*, then there is a choice:

  - If the run-time type of *V* is assignment compatible with a catchable exception class of any `catch` clause of the `try` statement, then the first (leftmost) such `catch` clause is selected. The value *V* is assigned to the parameter of the selected `catch` clause, and the *Block* of that `catch` clause is executed. Then there is a choice:

    - If the `catch` block completes normally, then the `finally` block is executed. Then there is a choice:

      - If the `finally` block completes normally, then the `try` statement completes normally.

      - If the `finally` block completes abruptly for any reason, then the `try` statement completes abruptly for the same reason.

    - If the `catch` block completes abruptly for reason *R*, then the `finally` block is executed. Then there is a choice:

      - If the `finally` block completes normally, then the `try` statement completes abruptly for reason *R*.

      - If the `finally` block completes abruptly for reason *s*, then the `try` statement completes abruptly for reason *s* (and reason *R* is discarded).

  - If the run-time type of *V* is not assignment compatible with a catchable exception class of any `catch` clause of the `try` statement, then the `finally` block is executed. Then there is a choice:

    - If the `finally` block completes normally, then the `try` statement completes abruptly because of a `throw` of the value *V*.

    - If the `finally` block completes abruptly for reason *s*, then the `try` statement completes abruptly for reason *s* (and the `throw` of value *V* is discarded and forgotten).

- If execution of the `try` block completes abruptly for any other reason R, then the `finally` block is executed, and then there is a choice:

  - If the `finally` block completes normally, then the `try` statement completes abruptly for reason R.

  - If the `finally` block completes abruptly for reason S, then the `try` statement completes abruptly for reason S (and reason R is discarded).

Example 14.20.2-1. Handling An Uncaught Exception With `finally`

```
class BlewIt extends Exception {
    BlewIt() { }
    BlewIt(String s) { super(s); }
}
class Test {
    static void blowUp() throws BlewIt {
        throw new NullPointerException();
    }
    public static void main(String[] args) {
        try {
            blowUp();
        } catch (BlewIt b) {
            System.out.println("Caught BlewIt");
        } finally {
            System.out.println("Uncaught Exception");
        }
    }
}
```

This program produces the output:

```
Uncaught Exception
Exception in thread "main" java.lang.NullPointerException
        at Test.blowUp(Test.java:7)
        at Test.main(Test.java:11)
```

The `NullPointerException` (which is a kind of `RuntimeException`) that is thrown by method `blowUp` is not caught by the `try` statement in `main`, because a `NullPointerException` is not assignable to a variable of type `BlewIt`. This causes the `finally` clause to execute, after which the thread executing `main`, which is the only thread of the test program, terminates because of an uncaught exception, which typically results in printing the exception name and a simple backtrace. However, a backtrace is not required by this specification.

The problem with mandating a backtrace is that an exception can be created at one point in the program and thrown at a later one. It is prohibitively expensive to store a stack trace in an exception unless it is actually thrown (in which case the trace may be generated while unwinding the stack). Hence we do not mandate a back trace in every exception.

14.20.3 `try`-**with-resources**

A `try`-with-resources statement is parameterized with variables (known as *resources*) that are initialized before execution of the `try` block and closed automatically, in the reverse order from which they were initialized, after execution of the `try` block. `catch` clauses and a `finally` clause are often unnecessary when resources are closed automatically.

> *TryWithResourcesStatement:*
>   `try` *ResourceSpecification Block Catches$_{opt}$ Finally$_{opt}$*

> *ResourceSpecification:*
>   (*Resources* ; $_{opt}$)

> *Resources:*
>   *Resource*
>   *Resource* ; *Resources*

> *Resource:*
>   *VariableModifiers$_{opt}$ Type VariableDeclaratorId* = *Expression*

A *ResourceSpecification* declares one or more local variables with initializer expressions to act as *resources* for the `try` statement.

A resource declared in a *ResourceSpecification* is implicitly declared `final` (§4.12.4) if it is not explicitly declared `final`.

The type of a variable declared in a *ResourceSpecification* must be a subtype of `AutoCloseable`, or a compile-time error occurs.

The scope and shadowing of a variable declared in a *ResourceSpecification* is specified in §6.3 and §6.4.

It is a compile-time error for a *ResourceSpecification* to declare two variables with the same name.

Resources are initialized in left-to-right order. If a resource fails to initialize (that is, its initializer expression throws an exception), then all resources initialized so far by the `try`-with-resources statement are closed. If all resources initialize successfully, the `try` block executes as normal and then all non-null resources of the `try`-with-resources statement are closed.

Resources are closed in the reverse order from that in which they were initialized. A resource is closed only if it initialized to a non-null value. An exception from the closing of one resource does not prevent the closing of other resources. Such an exception is *suppressed* if an exception was thrown previously by an initializer, the `try` block, or the closing of a resource.

A `try`-with-resources statement with a *ResourceSpecification* clause that declares multiple resources is treated as if it were multiple `try`-with-resources statements, each of which has a *ResourceSpecification* clause that declares a single *Resource*. When a `try`-with-resources statement with *n Resources* ($n > 1$) is translated, the result is a `try`-with-resources statement with *n-1 Resources*. After *n* such translations, there are *n* nested `try`-`catch`-`finally` statements, and the overall translation is complete.

14.20.3.1 *Basic* `try`-*with-resources*

A `try`-with-resources statement with no `catch` clauses or `finally` clause is called a *basic* `try`-with-resources statement.

The meaning of a basic `try`-with-resources statement:

```
try (VariableModifiersopt R Identifier = Expression ...)
    Block
```

is given by the following translation to a local variable declaration and a `try`-`catch`-`finally` statement:

```
{
    final VariableModifiers_minus_final R Identifier = Expression;
    Throwable #primaryExc = null;

    try ResourceSpecification_tail
        Block
    catch (Throwable #t) {
        #primaryExc = #t;
        throw #t;
    } finally {
        if (Identifier != null) {
            if (#primaryExc != null) {
                try {
                    Identifier.close();
                } catch (Throwable #suppressedExc) {
                    #primaryExc.addSuppressed(#suppressedExc);
                }
            } else {
                Identifier.close();
            }
        }
    }
}
```

VariableModifiers$_{opt}$*_minus_final* is defined as *VariableModifiers*$_{opt}$ without `final`, if present.

`#t`, `#primaryExc`, and `#suppressedExc` are automatically generated identifiers that are distinct from any other identifiers (automatically generated or otherwise) that are in scope at the point where the `try`-with-resources statement occurs.

If the *ResourceSpecification* declares one resource, then *ResourceSpecification_tail* is empty (and the `try-catch-finally` statement is not itself a `try`-with-resources statement).

If the *ResourceSpecification* declares $n > 1$ resources, then *ResourceSpecification_tail* consists of the 2nd, 3rd, ..., n'th resources declared in *ResourceSpecification*, in the same order (and the `try-catch-finally` statement is itself a `try`-with-resources statement).

Reachability and definite assignment rules for the basic `try`-with-resources statement are implicitly specified by the translation above.

In a basic `try`-with-resources statement that manages a single resource:

- If the initialization of the resource completes abruptly because of a `throw` of a value v, then the `try`-with-resources statement completes abruptly because of a `throw` of the value v.

- If the initialization of the resource completes normally, and the `try` block completes abruptly because of a `throw` of a value v, then:

  - If the automatic closing of the resource completes normally, then the `try`-with-resources statement completes abruptly because of a `throw` of the value v.

  - If the automatic closing of the resource completes abruptly because of a `throw` of a value $v2$, then the `try`-with-resources statement completes abruptly because of a `throw` of value v with $v2$ added to the suppressed exception list of v.

- If the initialization of the resource completes normally, and the `try` block completes normally, and the automatic closing of the resource completes abruptly because of a `throw` of a value v, then the `try`-with-resources statement completes abruptly because of a `throw` of the value v.

In a basic `try`-with-resources statement that manages multiple resources:

- If the initialization of a resource completes abruptly because of a `throw` of a value v, then:

- If the automatic closings of all successfully initialized resources (possibly zero) complete normally, then the `try`-with-resources statement completes abruptly because of a `throw` of the value V.

- If the automatic closings of all successfully initialized resources (possibly zero) complete abruptly because of `throw`s of values $V1...Vn$, then the `try`-with-resources statement completes abruptly because of a `throw` of the value V with any remaining values $V1...Vn$ added to the suppressed exception list of V.

- If the initialization of all resources completes normally, and the `try` block completes abruptly because of a `throw` of a value V, then:

  - If the automatic closings of all initialized resources complete normally, then the `try`-with-resources statement completes abruptly because of a `throw` of the value V.

  - If the automatic closings of one or more initialized resources complete abruptly because of `throw`s of values $V1...Vn$, then the `try`-with-resources statement completes abruptly because of a `throw` of the value V with any remaining values $V1...Vn$ added to the suppressed exception list of V.

- If the initialization of every resource completes normally, and the `try` block completes normally, then:

  - If one automatic closing of an initialized resource completes abruptly because of a `throw` of value V, and all other automatic closings of initialized resources complete normally, then the `try`-with-resources statement completes abruptly because of a `throw` of the value V.

  - If more than one automatic closing of an initialized resource completes abruptly because of `throw`s of values $V1...Vn$, then the `try`-with-resources statement completes abruptly because of a `throw` of the value $V1$ with any remaining values $V2...Vn$ added to the suppressed exception list of $V1$ (where $V1$ is the exception from the rightmost resource failing to close and Vn is the exception from the leftmost resource failing to close).

14.20.3.2 Extended `try`-with-resources

A `try`-with-resources statement with at least one `catch` clause and/or a `finally` clause is called an *extended* `try`-with-resources statement.

The meaning of an extended `try`-with-resources statement:

```
try ResourceSpecification
    Block
Catches_opt
Finally_opt
```

is given by the following translation to a basic `try`-with-resources statement (§14.20.3.1) nested inside a `try-catch` or `try-finally` or `try-catch-finally` statement:

```
try {
    try ResourceSpecification
        Block
}
Catches_opt
Finally_opt
```

The effect of the translation is to put the *ResourceSpecification* "inside" the `try` statement. This allows a `catch` clause of an extended `try`-with-resources statement to catch an exception due to the automatic initialization or closing of any resource.

Furthermore, all resources will have been closed (or attempted to be closed) by the time the `finally` block is executed, in keeping with the intent of the `finally` keyword.

14.21   Unreachable Statements

It is a compile-time error if a statement cannot be executed because it is *unreachable*.

> This section is devoted to a precise explanation of the word "reachable." The idea is that there must be some possible execution path from the beginning of the constructor, method, instance initializer, or static initializer that contains the statement to the statement itself. The analysis takes into account the structure of statements. Except for the special treatment of `while`, `do`, and `for` statements whose condition expression has the constant value `true`, the values of expressions are not taken into account in the flow analysis.
>
> For example, a Java compiler will accept the code:
>
> ```
> {
>     int n = 5;
>     while (n > 7) k = 2;
> }
> ```
>
> even though the value of `n` is known at compile time and in principle it can be known at compile time that the assignment to `k` can never be executed.

The rules in this section define two technical terms:

- whether a statement is *reachable*

- whether a statement *can complete normally*

The definitions here allow a statement to complete normally only if it is reachable.

To shorten the description of the rules, the customary abbreviation "iff" is used to mean "if and only if."

A reachable `break` statement *exits a statement* if, within the break target, either there are no `try` statements whose `try` blocks contain the `break` statement, or there are `try` statements whose `try` blocks contain the `break` statement and all `finally` clauses of those `try` statements can complete normally.

> This definition is based on the logic around "attempts to transfer control" in §14.15.

A `continue` statement *continues a* do *statement* if, within the `do` statement, either there are no `try` statements whose `try` blocks contain the `continue` statement, or there are `try` statements whose `try` blocks contain the `continue` statement and all `finally` clauses of those `try` statements can complete normally.

The rules are as follows:

- The block that is the body of a constructor, method, instance initializer, or static initializer is reachable.

- An empty block that is not a switch block can complete normally iff it is reachable.

  A non-empty block that is not a switch block can complete normally iff the last statement in it can complete normally.

  The first statement in a non-empty block that is not a switch block is reachable iff the block is reachable.

  Every other statement *s* in a non-empty block that is not a switch block is reachable iff the statement preceding *s* can complete normally.

- A local class declaration statement can complete normally iff it is reachable.

- A local variable declaration statement can complete normally iff it is reachable.

- An empty statement can complete normally iff it is reachable.

- A labeled statement can complete normally if at least one of the following is true:

  • The contained statement can complete normally.

- There is a reachable `break` statement that exits the labeled statement.

The contained statement is reachable iff the labeled statement is reachable.

- An expression statement can complete normally iff it is reachable.

- The `if` statement, whether or not it has an `else` part, is handled in an unusual manner. For this reason, it is discussed separately at the end of this section.

- An `assert` statement can complete normally iff it is reachable.

- A `switch` statement can complete normally iff at least one of the following is true:

  - The switch block is empty or contains only switch labels.

  - The last statement in the switch block can complete normally.

  - There is at least one switch label after the last switch block statement group.

  - The switch block does not contain a `default` label.

  - There is a reachable `break` statement that exits the `switch` statement.

- A switch block is reachable iff its `switch` statement is reachable.

- A statement in a switch block is reachable iff its `switch` statement is reachable and at least one of the following is true:

  - It bears a `case` or `default` label.

  - There is a statement preceding it in the switch block and that preceding statement can complete normally.

- A `while` statement can complete normally iff at least one of the following is true:

  - The `while` statement is reachable and the condition expression is not a constant expression (§15.28) with value `true`.

  - There is a reachable `break` statement that exits the `while` statement.

The contained statement is reachable iff the `while` statement is reachable and the condition expression is not a constant expression whose value is `false`.

- A `do` statement can complete normally iff at least one of the following is true:

  - The contained statement can complete normally and the condition expression is not a constant expression (§15.28) with value `true`.

  - The `do` statement contains a reachable `continue` statement with no label, and the `do` statement is the innermost `while`, `do`, or `for` statement that contains that continue statement, and the continue statement continues that do statement, and the condition expression is not a constant expression with value true.

- The do statement contains a reachable continue statement with a label L, and the do statement has label L, and the continue statement continues that do statement, and the condition expression is not a constant expression with value true.

- There is a reachable break statement that exits the do statement.

The contained statement is reachable iff the do statement is reachable.

- A basic for statement can complete normally iff at least one of the following is true:

  - The for statement is reachable, there is a condition expression, and the condition expression is not a constant expression (§15.28) with value true.

  - There is a reachable break statement that exits the for statement.

The contained statement is reachable iff the for statement is reachable and the condition expression is not a constant expression whose value is false.

- An enhanced for statement can complete normally iff it is reachable.

- A break, continue, return, or throw statement cannot complete normally.

- A synchronized statement can complete normally iff the contained statement can complete normally.

The contained statement is reachable iff the synchronized statement is reachable.

- A try statement can complete normally iff both of the following are true:

  - The try block can complete normally or any catch block can complete normally.

  - If the try statement has a finally block, then the finally block can complete normally.

- The try block is reachable iff the try statement is reachable.

- A catch block C is reachable iff both of the following are true:

  - Either the type of C's parameter is an unchecked exception type or Throwable; or some expression or throw statement in the try block is reachable and can throw a checked exception whose type is assignable to the parameter of the catch clause C.

An expression is reachable iff the innermost statement containing it is reachable.

See §15.6 for normal and abrupt completion of expressions.

- There is no earlier `catch` block *A* in the `try` statement such that the type of *C*'s parameter is the same as or a subclass of the type of *A*'s parameter.

- The *Block* of a `catch` block is reachable iff the `catch` block is reachable.

- If a `finally` block is present, it is reachable iff the `try` statement is reachable.

One *might expect* the `if` statement to be handled in the following manner:

- An `if-then` statement can complete normally iff at least one of the following is true:
  - The `if-then` statement is reachable and the condition expression is not a constant expression whose value is `true`.
  - The `then`-statement can complete normally.

  The `then`-statement is reachable iff the `if-then` statement is reachable and the condition expression is not a constant expression whose value is `false`.

- An `if-then-else` statement can complete normally iff the `then`-statement can complete normally or the `else`-statement can complete normally.

  The `then`-statement is reachable iff the `if-then-else` statement is reachable and the condition expression is not a constant expression whose value is `false`.

  The `else`-statement is reachable iff the `if-then-else` statement is reachable and the condition expression is not a constant expression whose value is `true`.

This approach would be consistent with the treatment of other control structures. However, in order to allow the if statement to be used conveniently for "conditional compilation" purposes, the actual rules differ.

The rules for the `if` statement are as follows:

- An `if-then` statement can complete normally iff it is reachable.

  The `then`-statement is reachable iff the `if-then` statement is reachable.

- An `if-then-else` statement can complete normally iff the `then`-statement can complete normally or the `else`-statement can complete normally.

  The `then`-statement is reachable iff the `if-then-else` statement is reachable.

  The `else`-statement is reachable iff the `if-then-else` statement is reachable.

As an example, the following statement results in a compile-time error:

```
while (false) { x=3; }
```

because the statement x=3; is not reachable; but the superficially similar case:

```
if (false) { x=3; }
```

does not result in a compile-time error. An optimizing compiler may realize that the statement x=3; will never be executed and may choose to omit the code for that statement from the generated class file, but the statement x=3; is not regarded as "unreachable" in the technical sense specified here.

The rationale for this differing treatment is to allow programmers to define "flag variables" such as:

```
static final boolean DEBUG = false;
```

and then write code such as:

```
if (DEBUG) { x=3; }
```

The idea is that it should be possible to change the value of DEBUG from false to true or from true to false and then compile the code correctly with no other changes to the program text.

This ability to "conditionally compile" has a significant impact on, and relationship to, binary compatibility (§13). If a set of classes that use such a "flag" variable are compiled and conditional code is omitted, it does not suffice later to distribute just a new version of the class or interface that contains the definition of the flag. A change to the value of a flag is, therefore, not binary compatible with pre-existing binaries (§13.4.9). (There are other reasons for such incompatibility as well, such as the use of constants in case labels in switch statements; see §13.4.9.)

CHAPTER 15

Expressions

MUCH of the work in a program is done by evaluating *expressions*, either for their side effects, such as assignments to variables, or for their values, which can be used as arguments or operands in larger expressions, or to affect the execution sequence in statements, or both.

This chapter specifies the meanings of expressions and the rules for their evaluation.

15.1 Evaluation, Denotation, and Result

When an expression in a program is *evaluated* (*executed*), the result denotes one of three things:

- A variable (§4.12) (in C, this would be called an *lvalue*)

- A value (§4.2, §4.3)

- Nothing (the expression is said to be void)

Evaluation of an expression can also produce side effects, because expressions may contain embedded assignments, increment operators, decrement operators, and method invocations.

An expression denotes nothing if and only if it is a method invocation (§15.12) that invokes a method that does not return a value, that is, a method declared void (§8.4). Such an expression can be used only as an expression statement (§14.8), because every other context in which an expression can appear requires the expression to denote something. An expression statement that is a method invocation may also invoke a method that produces a result; in this case the value returned by the method is quietly discarded.

Value set conversion (§5.1.13) is applied to the result of every expression that produces a value.

Each expression occurs in either:

- The declaration of some (class or interface) type that is being declared: in a field initializer, in a static initializer, in an instance initializer, in a constructor declaration, in an annotation, or in the code for a method.

- An annotation (§9.7) of a package or of a top level type declaration.

15.2   Variables as Values

If an expression denotes a variable, and a value is required for use in further evaluation, then the value of that variable is used. In this context, if the expression denotes a variable or a value, we may speak simply of the *value* of the expression.

If the value of a variable of type `float` or `double` is used in this manner, then value set conversion (§5.1.13) is applied to the value of the variable.

15.3   Type of an Expression

If an expression denotes a variable or a value, then the expression has a type known at compile time. The rules for determining the type of an expression are explained separately below for each kind of expression.

The value of an expression is assignment compatible (§5.2) with the type of the expression, unless heap pollution (§4.12.2) occurs.

Likewise, the value stored in a variable is always compatible with the type of the variable, unless heap pollution occurs.

In other words, the value of an expression whose type is T is always suitable for assignment to a variable of type T.

Note that an expression whose type is a class type F that is declared `final` is guaranteed to have a value that is either a null reference or an object whose class is F itself, because `final` types have no subclasses.

15.4   FP-strict Expressions

If the type of an expression is `float` or `double`, then there is a question as to what value set (§4.2.3) the value of the expression is drawn from. This is governed by the rules of value set conversion (§5.1.13); these rules in turn depend on whether or not the expression is *FP-strict*.

Every compile-time constant expression (§15.28) is FP-strict.

If an expression is not a compile-time constant expression, then consider all the class declarations, interface declarations, and method declarations that contain the expression. If *any* such declaration bears the `strictfp` modifier (§8.1.1.3, §8.4.3.5, §9.1.1.2), then the expression is FP-strict.

If a class, interface, or method, x, is declared `strictfp`, then x and any class, interface, method, constructor, instance initializer, static initializer or variable initializer within x is said to be *FP-strict*.

> Note that an annotation (§9.7) element value (§9.6) is always FP-strict, because it is always a compile-time constant expression.

It follows that an expression is not FP-strict if and only if it is not a compile-time constant expression *and* it does not appear within any declaration that has the `strictfp` modifier.

Within an FP-strict expression, all intermediate values must be elements of the float value set or the double value set, implying that the results of all FP-strict expressions must be those predicted by IEEE 754 arithmetic on operands represented using single and double formats.

Within an expression that is not FP-strict, some leeway is granted for an implementation to use an extended exponent range to represent intermediate results; the net effect, roughly speaking, is that a calculation might produce "the correct answer" in situations where exclusive use of the float value set or double value set might result in overflow or underflow.

15.5   Expressions and Run-Time Checks

If the type of an expression is a primitive type, then the value of the expression is of that same primitive type.

If the type of an expression is a reference type, then the class of the referenced object, or even whether the value is a reference to an object rather than `null`, is not necessarily known at compile time. There are a few places in the Java programming language where the actual class of a referenced object affects program execution in a manner that cannot be deduced from the type of the expression. They are as follows:

- Method invocation (§15.12). The particular method used for an invocation `o.m(...)` is chosen based on the methods that are part of the class or interface that is the type of `o`. For instance methods, the class of the object referenced by the run-time value of `o` participates because a subclass may override a specific method already declared in a parent class so that this overriding method is invoked. (The overriding method may or may not choose to further invoke the original overridden `m` method.)

- The `instanceof` operator (§15.20.2). An expression whose type is a reference type may be tested using `instanceof` to find out whether the class of the object referenced by the run-time value of the expression is assignment compatible (§5.2) with some other reference type.

- Casting (§5.5, §15.16). The class of the object referenced by the run-time value of the operand expression might not be compatible with the type specified by the cast. For reference types, this may require a run-time check that throws an exception if the class of the referenced object, as determined at run time, is not assignment compatible (§5.2) with the target type.

- Assignment to an array component of reference type (§10.5, §15.13, §15.26.1). The type-checking rules allow the array type `S[]` to be treated as a subtype of `T[]` if `S` is a subtype of `T`, but this requires a run-time check for assignment to an array component, similar to the check performed for a cast.

- Exception handling (§14.20). An exception is caught by a `catch` clause only if the class of the thrown exception object is an `instanceof` the type of the formal parameter of the `catch` clause.

Situations where the class of an object is not statically known may lead to run-time type errors.

In addition, there are situations where the statically known type may not be accurate at run time. Such situations can arise in a program that gives rise to compile-time unchecked warnings. Such warnings are given in response to operations that cannot be statically guaranteed to be safe, and cannot immediately be subjected to dynamic checking because they involve non-reifiable (§4.7) types. As a result, dynamic checks later in the course of program execution may detect inconsistencies and result in run-time type errors.

A run-time type error can occur only in these situations:

- In a cast, when the actual class of the object referenced by the value of the operand expression is not compatible with the target type specified by the cast operator (§5.5, §15.16); in this case a `ClassCastException` is thrown.

- In an automatically generated cast introduced to ensure the validity of an operation on a non-reifiable type (§4.7).

- In an assignment to an array component of reference type, when the actual class of the object referenced by the value to be assigned is not compatible with the actual run-time component type of the array (§10.5, §15.13, §15.26.1); in this case an `ArrayStoreException` is thrown.

- When an exception is not caught by any `catch` clause of a `try` statement (§14.20); in this case the thread of control that encountered the exception first attempts to invoke an uncaught exception handler (§11.3) and then terminates.

15.6 Normal and Abrupt Completion of Evaluation

Every expression has a normal mode of evaluation in which certain computational steps are carried out. The following sections describe the normal mode of evaluation for each kind of expression.

If all the steps are carried out without an exception being thrown, the expression is said to *complete normally*.

If, however, evaluation of an expression throws an exception, then the expression is said to *complete abruptly*. An abrupt completion always has an associated reason, which is always a `throw` with a given value.

Run-time exceptions are thrown by the predefined operators as follows:

- A class instance creation expression (§15.9), array creation expression (§15.10), array initializer expression (§10.6), or string concatenation operator expression (§15.18.1) throws an `OutOfMemoryError` if there is insufficient memory available.

- An array creation expression (§15.10) throws a `NegativeArraySizeException` if the value of any dimension expression is less than zero.

- A field access expression (§15.11) throws a `NullPointerException` if the value of the object reference expression is `null`.

- A method invocation expression (§15.12) that invokes an instance method throws a `NullPointerException` if the target reference is `null`.

- An array access expression (§15.13) throws a `NullPointerException` if the value of the array reference expression is `null`.

- An array access expression (§15.13) throws an `ArrayIndexOutOfBoundsException` if the value of the array index expression is negative or greater than or equal to the `length` of the array.

- A cast expression (§15.16) throws a `ClassCastException` if a cast is found to be impermissible at run time.

- An integer division (§15.17.2) or integer remainder (§15.17.3) operator throws an `ArithmeticException` if the value of the right-hand operand expression is zero.

- An assignment to an array component of reference type (§15.26.1), a method invocation expression (§15.12), or a prefix or postfix increment (§15.14.2, §15.15.1) or decrement operator (§15.14.3, §15.15.2) may all throw an `OutOfMemoryError` as a result of boxing conversion (§5.1.7).

- An assignment to an array component of reference type (§15.26.1) throws an `ArrayStoreException` when the value to be assigned is not compatible with the component type of the array (§10.5).

A method invocation expression can also result in an exception being thrown if an exception occurs that causes execution of the method body to complete abruptly.

A class instance creation expression can also result in an exception being thrown if an exception occurs that causes execution of the constructor to complete abruptly.

Various linkage and virtual machine errors may also occur during the evaluation of an expression. By their nature, such errors are difficult to predict and difficult to handle.

If an exception occurs, then evaluation of one or more expressions may be terminated before all steps of their normal mode of evaluation are complete; such expressions are said to complete abruptly.

If evaluation of an expression requires evaluation of a subexpression, then abrupt completion of the subexpression always causes the immediate abrupt completion of the expression itself, with the same reason, and all succeeding steps in the normal mode of evaluation are not performed.

The terms "complete normally" and "complete abruptly" are also applied to the execution of statements (§14.1). A statement may complete abruptly for a variety of reasons, not just because an exception is thrown.

15.7 Evaluation Order

The Java programming language guarantees that the operands of operators appear to be evaluated in a specific *evaluation order*, namely, from left to right.

> It is recommended that code not rely crucially on this specification. Code is usually clearer when each expression contains at most one side effect, as its outermost operation, and when code does not depend on exactly which exception arises as a consequence of the left-to-right evaluation of expressions.

15.7.1 Evaluate Left-Hand Operand First

The left-hand operand of a binary operator appears to be fully evaluated before any part of the right-hand operand is evaluated.

If the operator is a compound-assignment operator (§15.26.2), then evaluation of the left-hand operand includes both remembering the variable that the left-hand operand denotes and fetching and saving that variable's value for use in the implied binary operation.

If evaluation of the left-hand operand of a binary operator completes abruptly, no part of the right-hand operand appears to have been evaluated.

Example 15.7.1-1. Left-Hand Operand Is Evaluated First

In the following program, the * operator has a left-hand operand that contains an assignment to a variable and a right-hand operand that contains a reference to the same variable. The value produced by the reference will reflect the fact that the assignment occurred first.

```
class Test1 {
    public static void main(String[] args) {
        int i = 2;
        int j = (i=3) * i;
        System.out.println(j);
    }
}
```

This program produces the output:

9

It is not permitted for evaluation of the ∗ operator to produce 6 instead of 9.

Example 15.7.1-2. Implicit Left-Hand Operand In Operator Of Compound Assigment

In the following program, the two assignment statements both fetch and remember the value of the left-hand operand, which is 9, before the right-hand operand of the addition operator is evaluated, at which point the variable is set to 3.

```
class Test2 {
    public static void main(String[] args) {
        int a = 9;
        a += (a = 3);  // first example
        System.out.println(a);
        int b = 9;
        b = b + (b = 3);  // second example
        System.out.println(b);
    }
}
```

This program produces the output:

```
12
12
```

It is not permitted for either assignment (compound for a, simple for b) to produce the result 6.

See also the example in §15.26.2.

Example 15.7.1-3. Abrupt Completion of Evaluation of the Left-Hand Operand

```
class Test3 {
    public static void main(String[] args) {
        int j = 1;
        try {
            int i = forgetIt() / (j = 2);
        } catch (Exception e) {
            System.out.println(e);
            System.out.println("Now j = " + j);
        }
    }
    static int forgetIt() throws Exception {
        throw new Exception("I'm outta here!");
    }
}
```

This program produces the output:

```
java.lang.Exception: I'm outta here!
Now j = 1
```

That is, the left-hand operand `forgetIt()` of the operator `/` throws an exception before the right-hand operand is evaluated and its embedded assignment of 2 to `j` occurs.

15.7.2 Evaluate Operands before Operation

The Java programming language guarantees that every operand of an operator (except the conditional operators `&&`, `||`, and `? :`) appears to be fully evaluated before any part of the operation itself is performed.

If the binary operator is an integer division `/` (§15.17.2) or integer remainder `%` (§15.17.3), then its execution may raise an `ArithmeticException`, but this exception is thrown only after both operands of the binary operator have been evaluated and only if these evaluations completed normally.

Example 15.7.2-1. Evaluation of Operands Before Operation

```
class Test {
    public static void main(String[] args) {
        int divisor = 0;
        try {
            int i = 1 / (divisor * loseBig());
        } catch (Exception e) {
            System.out.println(e);
        }
    }
    static int loseBig() throws Exception {
        throw new Exception("Shuffle off to Buffalo!");
    }
}
```

This program produces the output:

```
java.lang.Exception: Shuffle off to Buffalo!
```

and not:

```
java.lang.ArithmeticException: / by zero
```

since no part of the division operation, including signaling of a divide-by-zero exception, may appear to occur before the invocation of `loseBig` completes, even though the implementation may be able to detect or infer that the division operation would certainly result in a divide-by-zero exception.

15.7.3 Evaluation Respects Parentheses and Precedence

The Java programming language respects the order of evaluation indicated explicitly by parentheses and implicitly by operator precedence.

An implementation of the Java programming language may not take advantage of algebraic identities such as the associative law to rewrite expressions into a more convenient computational order unless it can be proven that the replacement expression is equivalent in value and in its observable side effects, even in the presence of multiple threads of execution (using the thread execution model in §17), for all possible computational values that might be involved.

In the case of floating-point calculations, this rule applies also for infinity and not-a-number (NaN) values.

For example, `!(x<y)` may not be rewritten as `x>=y`, because these expressions have different values if either x or y is NaN or both are NaN.

Specifically, floating-point calculations that appear to be mathematically associative are unlikely to be computationally associative. Such computations must not be naively reordered.

For example, it is not correct for a Java compiler to rewrite `4.0*x*0.5` as `2.0*x`; while roundoff happens not to be an issue here, there are large values of x for which the first expression produces infinity (because of overflow) but the second expression produces a finite result.

So, for example, the test program:

```
strictfp class Test {
    public static void main(String[] args) {
        double d = 8e+307;
        System.out.println(4.0 * d * 0.5);
        System.out.println(2.0 * d);
    }
}
```

prints:

```
Infinity
1.6e+308
```

because the first expression overflows and the second does not.

In contrast, integer addition and multiplication *are* provably associative in the Java programming language.

For example `a+b+c`, where `a`, `b`, and `c` are local variables (this simplifying assumption avoids issues involving multiple threads and `volatile` variables), will always produce the same answer whether evaluated as `(a+b)+c` or `a+(b+c)`; if the expression `b+c` occurs nearby in the code, a smart Java compiler may be able to use this common subexpression.

15.7.4   Argument Lists are Evaluated Left-to-Right

In a method or constructor invocation or class instance creation expression, argument expressions may appear within the parentheses, separated by commas. Each argument expression appears to be fully evaluated before any part of any argument expression to its right.

If evaluation of an argument expression completes abruptly, no part of any argument expression to its right appears to have been evaluated.

Example 15.7.4-1. Evaluation Order At Method Invocation

```
class Test1 {
    public static void main(String[] args) {
        String s = "going, ";
        print3(s, s, s = "gone");
    }
    static void print3(String a, String b, String c) {
        System.out.println(a + b + c);
    }
}
```

This program produces the output:

```
going, going, gone
```

because the assignment of the string "gone" to s occurs after the first two arguments to print3 have been evaluated.

Example 15.7.4-2. Abrupt Completion of Argument Expression

```
class Test2 {
    static int id;
    public static void main(String[] args) {
        try {
            test(id = 1, oops(), id = 3);
        } catch (Exception e) {
            System.out.println(e + ", id=" + id);
        }
    }
    static int test(int a, int b, int c) {
        return a + b + c;
    }
    static int oops() throws Exception {
        throw new Exception("oops");
    }
}
```

This program produces the output:

```
java.lang.Exception: oops, id=1
```

because the assignment of 3 to id is not executed.

15.7.5   Evaluation Order for Other Expressions

The order of evaluation for some expressions is not completely covered by these general rules, because these expressions may raise exceptional conditions at times that must be specified. See the detailed explanations of evaluation order for the following kinds of expressions:

- class instance creation expressions (§15.9.4)

- array creation expressions (§15.10.1)

- method invocation expressions (§15.12.4)

- array access expressions (§15.13.1)

- assignments involving array components (§15.26)

15.8   Primary Expressions

Primary expressions include most of the simplest kinds of expressions, from which all others are constructed: literals, class literals, field accesses, method invocations, and array accesses. A parenthesized expression is also treated syntactically as a primary expression.

Primary:
  PrimaryNoNewArray
  ArrayCreationExpression

PrimaryNoNewArray:
  Literal
  Type . class
  void . class
  this
  ClassName . this
  (*Expression*)
  ClassInstanceCreationExpression
  FieldAccess
  MethodInvocation
  ArrayAccess

This part of the grammar of the Java programming language is unusual, in two ways. First, one might expect simple names, such as names of local variables and method parameters, to be primary expressions. For technical reasons, names are grouped together with primary expressions a little later when postfix expressions are introduced (§15.14).

The technical reasons have to do with allowing left-to-right parsing of Java programs with only one-token lookahead. Consider the expressions `(z[3])` and `(z[])`. The first is a parenthesized array access (§15.13) and the second is the start of a cast (§15.16). At the point that the look-ahead symbol is `[`, a left-to-right parse will have reduced the `z` to the nonterminal *Name*. In the context of a cast we prefer not to have to reduce the name to a *Primary*, but if *Name* were one of the alternatives for *Primary*, then we could not tell whether to do the reduction (that is, we could not determine whether the current situation would turn out to be a parenthesized array access or a cast) without looking ahead two tokens, to the token following the `[`. The Java grammar presented here avoids the problem by keeping *Name* and *Primary* separate and allowing either in certain other syntax rules (those for *MethodInvocation*, *ArrayAccess*, *PostfixExpression*, but not for *FieldAccess*, because this uses an identifier directly). This strategy effectively defers the question of whether a *Name* should be treated as a *Primary* until more context can be examined.

The second unusual feature avoids a potential grammatical ambiguity in the expression `"new int[3][3]"` which in Java always means a single creation of a multidimensional array, but which, without appropriate grammatical finesse, might also be interpreted as meaning the same as `"(new int[3])[3]"`.

This ambiguity is eliminated by splitting the expected definition of *Primary* into *Primary* and *PrimaryNoNewArray*. (This may be compared to the splitting of *Statement* into *Statement* and *StatementNoShortIf* (§14.5) to avoid the "dangling else" problem.)

15.8.1   Lexical Literals

A literal (§3.10) denotes a fixed, unchanging value.

The following production from §3.10 is repeated here for convenience:

Literal:
   IntegerLiteral
   FloatingPointLiteral
   BooleanLiteral
   CharacterLiteral
   StringLiteral
   NullLiteral

The type of a literal is determined as follows:

- The type of an integer literal (§3.10.1) that ends with L or l is `long` (§4.2.1).

  The type of any other integer literal is `int` (§4.2.1).

- The type of a floating-point literal (§3.10.2) that ends with F or f is float and its value must be an element of the float value set (§4.2.3).

  The type of any other floating-point literal is double and its value must be an element of the double value set (§4.2.3).

- The type of a boolean literal (§3.10.3) is boolean (§4.2.5).

- The type of a character literal (§3.10.4) is char (§4.2.1).

- The type of a string literal (§3.10.5) is String (§4.3.3).

- The type of the null literal null (§3.10.7) is the null type (§4.1); its value is the null reference.

Evaluation of a lexical literal always completes normally.

15.8.2   Class Literals

A *class literal* is an expression consisting of the name of a class, interface, array, or primitive type, or the pseudo-type void, followed by a '.' and the token class.

The type of C.class, where C is the name of a class, interface, or array type (§4.3), is Class<C>.

The type of p.class, where p is the name of a primitive type (§4.2), is Class<B>, where B is the type of an expression of type p after boxing conversion (§5.1.7).

The type of void.class (§8.4.5) is Class<Void>.

It is a compile-time error if the named type is a type variable (§4.4) or a parameterized type (§4.5) or an array whose element type is a type variable or parameterized type.

It is a compile-time error if the named type does not denote a type that is accessible (§6.6) and in scope (§6.3) at the point where the class literal appears.

A class literal evaluates to the Class object for the named type (or for void) as defined by the defining class loader (§12.2) of the class of the current instance.

15.8.3   this

The keyword this may be used only in the body of an instance method, instance initializer, or constructor, or in the initializer of an instance variable of a class. If it appears anywhere else, a compile-time error occurs.

When used as a primary expression, the keyword this denotes a value that is a reference to the object for which the instance method was invoked (§15.12), or to the object being constructed.

The type of this is the class *c* within which the keyword this occurs.

At run time, the class of the actual object referred to may be the class *c* or any subclass of *c*.

The keyword this is also used in a special explicit constructor invocation statement, which can appear at the beginning of a constructor body (§8.8.7).

Example 15.8.3-1. The this **Expression**

```
class IntVector {
    int[] v;
    boolean equals(IntVector other) {
        if (this == other)
            return true;
        if (v.length != other.v.length)
            return false;
        for (int i = 0; i < v.length; i++) {
            if (v[i] != other.v[i]) return false;
        }
        return true;
    }
}
```

Here, the class IntVector implements a method equals, which compares two vectors. If the other vector is the same vector object as the one for which the equals method was invoked, then the check can skip the length and value comparisons. The equals method implements this check by comparing the reference to the other object to this.

15.8.4   Qualified this

Any lexically enclosing instance (§8.1.3) can be referred to by explicitly qualifying the keyword this.

Let *c* be the class denoted by *ClassName*. Let *n* be an integer such that *c* is the *n*'th lexically enclosing class of the class in which the qualified this expression appears.

The value of an expression of the form *ClassName*.this is the *n*'th lexically enclosing instance of this.

The type of the expression is *c*.

It is a compile-time error if the current class is not an inner class of class *c* or *c* itself.

15.8.5   Parenthesized Expressions

A parenthesized expression is a primary expression whose type is the type of the contained expression and whose value at run time is the value of the contained expression. If the contained expression denotes a variable then the parenthesized expression also denotes that variable.

The use of parentheses affects only the *order* of evaluation, except for a corner case whereby `(-2147483648)` and `(-9223372036854775808L)` are legal but `-(2147483648)` and `-(9223372036854775808L)` are illegal.

> This is because the decimal literals `2147483648` and `9223372036854775808L` are allowed only as an operand of the unary minus operator (§3.10.1).

In particular, the presence or absence of parentheses around an expression does not (except for the case noted above) affect in any way:

- the choice of value set (§4.2.3) for the value of an expression of type `float` or `double`.

- whether a variable is definitely assigned, definitely assigned when `true`, definitely assigned when `false`, definitely unassigned, definitely unassigned when `true`, or definitely unassigned when `false` (§16).

15.9   Class Instance Creation Expressions

A class instance creation expression is used to create new objects that are instances of classes.

> *ClassInstanceCreationExpression:*
>   `new` *TypeArguments$_{opt}$ TypeDeclSpecifier TypeArgumentsOrDiamond$_{opt}$*
>   (*ArgumentList$_{opt}$*) *ClassBody$_{opt}$*
>   *Primary* . `new` *TypeArguments$_{opt}$ Identifier TypeArgumentsOrDiamond$_{opt}$*
>   (*ArgumentList$_{opt}$*) *ClassBody$_{opt}$*
>
> *TypeArgumentsOrDiamond:*
>   *TypeArguments*
>   <>
>
> *ArgumentList:*
>   *Expression*
>   *ArgumentList* , *Expression*

A class instance creation expression specifies a class to be instantiated, possibly followed by type arguments (§4.5.1) or a *diamond* ("<>") if the class being instantiated is generic (§8.1.2), followed by (a possibly empty) list of actual value arguments to the constructor.

If the type argument list to the class is empty — the diamond form "<>" — the type arguments of the class are inferred. It is legal, though strongly discouraged as a matter of style, to have white space between the "<" and ">" of a diamond.

If the constructor is generic (§8.8.4), the type arguments to the constructor may similarly either be inferred or passed explicitly. If passed explicitly, the type arguments to the constructor immediately follow the keyword `new`.

It is a compile-time error if a class instance creation expression provides a constructor type argument list but uses "<>" in place of a class type argument list.

> This rule is introduced because inference of a generic class's type arguments may influence the constraints on a generic constructor's type arguments.

It is a compile-time error if any of the type arguments used in a class instance creation expression are wildcard type arguments (§4.5.1).

The exception types that a class instance creation expression can throw are specified in §11.2.1.

Class instance creation expressions have two forms:

- *Unqualified class instance creation expressions* begin with the keyword `new`.

  An unqualified class instance creation expression may be used to create an instance of a class, regardless of whether the class is a top level (§7.6), member (§8.5, §9.5), local (§14.3) or anonymous class (§15.9.5).

- *Qualified class instance creation expressions* begin with a *Primary*.

  A qualified class instance creation expression enables the creation of instances of inner member classes and their anonymous subclasses.

Both unqualified and qualified class instance creation expressions may optionally end with a class body. Such a class instance creation expression declares an *anonymous class* (§15.9.5) and creates an instance of it.

It is a compile-time error if a class instance creation expression declares an anonymous class using the "<>" form for the class's type arguments.

We say that a class is *instantiated* when an instance of the class is created by a class instance creation expression. Class instantiation involves determining what class is to be instantiated, what the enclosing instances (if any) of the newly created instance are, what constructor should be invoked to create the new instance, and what arguments should be passed to that constructor.

15.9.1 Determining the Class being Instantiated

If the class instance creation expression ends in a class body, then the class being instantiated is an anonymous class. Then:

- If the class instance creation expression is an unqualified class instance creation expression, then *TypeDeclSpecifier TypeArgumentsOrDiamond$_{opt}$* must denote a type, T (§4.3, §4.5), or a compile-time error occurs.

  It is a compile-time error if the class or interface named by T is not accessible (§6.6) or if T is an enum type (§8.9).

  If T denotes a class, then an anonymous direct subclass of the class named by T is declared. It is a compile-time error if the class denoted by T is a `final` class.

  If T denotes an interface, then an anonymous direct subclass of `Object` that implements the interface named by T is declared.

  In either case, the body of the subclass is the *ClassBody* given in the class instance creation expression.

  The class being instantiated is the anonymous subclass.

- Otherwise, the class instance creation expression is a qualified class instance creation expression.

  It is a compile-time error if the *Identifier* after the `new` token is not the simple name (§6.2) of an accessible (§6.6) non-`final` inner class (§8.1.3) that is a member of the compile-time type of the *Primary*.

  It is a compile-time error if the name is ambiguous (§8.5) or denotes an enum type.

  When *TypeArguments* are provided after the name, it is a compile-time error if the type arguments, when applied to the named class, do not denote a well-formed parameterized type (§4.5).

  Let T be the type named by the *Identifier* and any type arguments. An anonymous direct subclass of the class named by T is declared. The body of the subclass is the *ClassBody* given in the class instance creation expression.

  The class being instantiated is the anonymous subclass.

If a class instance creation expression does not declare an anonymous class, then:

- If the class instance creation expression is an unqualified class instance creation expression, then the *TypeDeclSpecifier* must denote a class that is accessible (§6.6) and is not an enum type and not `abstract`, or a compile-time error occurs.

  When *TypeArguments* are provided after the class name, it is a compile-time error if the type arguments, when applied to the class, do not denote a well-formed parameterized type (§4.5).

  When "<>" is used to elide type arguments after the class name, it is a compile-time error if the class is not generic.

  The class being instantiated is the class denoted by the *TypeDeclSpecifier*.

- Otherwise, the class instance creation expression is a qualified class instance creation expression.

  It is a compile-time error if the *Identifier* after the `new` token is not the simple name (§6.2) of an accessible (§6.6) non-`abstract` inner class (§8.1.3) *c* that is a member of the compile-time type of the *Primary*.

  It is a compile-time error if the name is ambiguous (§8.5) or denotes an enum type (§8.9).

  When *TypeArguments* are provided after the name, it is a compile-time error if the type arguments, when applied to *c*, do not denote a well-formed parameterized type (§4.5).

  When "<>" is used to elide type arguments after the name, it is a compile-time error if *c* is not generic.

  The class being instantiated is *c*.

The type of the class instance creation expression is the class type being instantiated, as defined above.

15.9.2 Determining Enclosing Instances

Let *c* be the class being instantiated, and let *i* be the instance being created. If *c* is an inner class then *i* may have an immediately enclosing instance. The immediately enclosing instance of *i* (§8.1.3) is determined as follows.

If *c* is an anonymous class, then:

- If the class instance creation expression occurs in a static context (§8.1.3), then *i* has no immediately enclosing instance.

- Otherwise, the immediately enclosing instance of *i* is `this`.

If c is a local class (§14.3), then let o be the innermost lexically enclosing class of c. Let n be an integer such that o is the n'th lexically enclosing class of the class in which the class instance creation expression appears. Then:

- If c occurs in a static context, then i has no immediately enclosing instance.

- Otherwise, if the class instance creation expression occurs in a static context, then a compile-time error occurs.

- Otherwise, the immediately enclosing instance of i is the n'th lexically enclosing instance of `this` (§8.1.3).

Otherwise, c is an inner member class (§8.5), and then:

- If the class instance creation expression is an unqualified class instance creation expression, then:

  - If the class instance creation expression occurs in a static context, then a compile-time error occurs.

  - Otherwise, if c is a member of an enclosing class then let o be the innermost lexically enclosing class of which c is a member, and let n be an integer such that o is the n'th lexically enclosing class of the class in which the class instance creation expression appears.

    The immediately enclosing instance of i is the n'th lexically enclosing instance of `this`.

  - Otherwise, a compile-time error occurs.

- Otherwise, the class instance creation expression is a qualified class instance creation expression.

  The immediately enclosing instance of i is the object that is the value of the *Primary* expression.

In addition, if c is an anonymous class, and the direct superclass of c, s, is an inner class, then i may have an immediately enclosing instance with respect to s. It is determined as follows.

If s is a local class (§14.3), then let o be the innermost lexically enclosing class of s. Let n be an integer such that o is the n'th lexically enclosing class of the class in which the class instance creation expression appears. Then:

- If s occurs within a static context, then i has no immediately enclosing instance with respect to s.

- Otherwise, if the class instance creation expression occurs in a static context, then a compile-time error occurs.

- Otherwise, the immediately enclosing instance of i with respect to s is the n'th lexically enclosing instance of `this`.

Otherwise, s is an inner member class (§8.5), and then:

- If the class instance creation expression is an unqualified class instance creation expression, then:

  - If the class instance creation expression occurs in a static context, then a compile-time error occurs.

  - Otherwise, if s is a member of an enclosing class, then let o be the innermost lexically enclosing class of which s is a member, and let n be an integer such that o is the n'th lexically enclosing class of the class in which the class instance creation expression appears.

    The immediately enclosing instance of i with respect to s is the n'th lexically enclosing instance of `this`.

  - Otherwise, a compile-time error occurs.

- Otherwise, the class instance creation expression is a qualified class instance creation expression.

  The immediately enclosing instance of i with respect to s is the object that is the value of the *Primary* expression.

15.9.3   Choosing the Constructor and its Arguments

Let c be the class being instantiated. To create an instance of c, i, a constructor of c is chosen at compile time by the following rules.

First, the actual arguments to the constructor invocation are determined:

- If c is an anonymous class, and the direct superclass of c, s, is an inner class, then:

  - If s is a local class and s occurs in a static context, then the arguments in the argument list, if any, are the arguments to the constructor, in the order they appear in the expression.

  - Otherwise, the immediately enclosing instance of i with respect to s is the first argument to the constructor, followed by the arguments in the argument list of the class instance creation expression, if any, in the order they appear in the expression.

- Otherwise the arguments in the argument list, if any, are the arguments to the constructor, in the order they appear in the expression.

Second, a constructor of C and corresponding result type and `throws` clause are determined:

- If the class instance creation expression uses "<>" to elide class type arguments, a list of methods $m_1...m_n$ is defined for the purpose of overload resolution and type argument inference.

  Let $c_1...c_n$ be the constructors of class C. Let `#m` be an automatically generated name that is distinct from all constructor and method names in C. For all j ($1 \leq j \leq n$), m_j is defined in terms of c_j as follows:

  - A substitution θ_j is first defined to instantiate the types in c_j.

    Let $F_1...F_p$ be the type parameters of C, and let $G_1...G_q$ be the type parameters (if any) of c_j. Let $X_1...X_p$ and $Y_1...Y_q$ be type variables with distinct names that are not in scope in the body of C.

    θ_j is $[F_1:=X_1, \ldots, F_p:=X_p, G_1:=Y_1, \ldots, G_q:=Y_q]$.

  - The modifiers of m_j are those of c_j.

  - The type parameters of m_j are $X_1...X_p,Y_1...Y_q$. The bound of each parameter, if any, is θ_j applied to the corresponding parameter bound in C or c_j.

  - The return type of m_j is θ_j applied to $C<F_1,...,F_p>$.

  - The name of m_j is `#m`.

  - The (possibly empty) list of argument types of m_j is θ_j applied to the argument types of c_j.

  - The (possibly empty) list of thrown types of m_j is θ_j applied to the thrown types of c_j.

  - The body of m_j is irrelevant.

  To choose a constructor, we temporarily consider $m_1...m_n$ to be members of C. Then one of $m_1...m_n$ is selected, as determined by the class instance creation's argument expressions, using the process described in §15.12.2.

  It is a compile-time error if there is no unique most-specific method that is both applicable and accessible.

  Otherwise, where m_j is the selected method, c_j is the chosen constructor. The result type and `throws` clause of c_j are the same as the return type and `throws` clause determined for m_j (§15.12.2.6).

- Otherwise, the class instance creation expression does not use "<>" to elide class type arguments.

Let T be the type denoted by c followed by any class type arguments in the expression. The process described in §15.12.2, modified to handle constructors, is used to select one of the constructors of T and determine its `throws` clause.

As in method invocations, it is a compile-time error if there is no unique most-specific constructor that is both applicable and accessible.

Otherwise, the result type is T.

Finally, the type of the class instance creation expression is the result type of the chosen constructor, as defined above.

Note that the type of the class instance creation expression may be an anonymous class type, in which case the constructor being invoked is an anonymous constructor (§15.9.5.1).

15.9.4   Run-Time Evaluation of Class Instance Creation Expressions

At run time, evaluation of a class instance creation expression is as follows.

First, if the class instance creation expression is a qualified class instance creation expression, the qualifying primary expression is evaluated. If the qualifying expression evaluates to `null`, a `NullPointerException` is raised, and the class instance creation expression completes abruptly. If the qualifying expression completes abruptly, the class instance creation expression completes abruptly for the same reason.

Next, space is allocated for the new class instance. If there is insufficient space to allocate the object, evaluation of the class instance creation expression completes abruptly by throwing an `OutOfMemoryError`.

The new object contains new instances of all the fields declared in the specified class type and all its superclasses. As each new field instance is created, it is initialized to its default value (§4.12.5).

Next, the actual arguments to the constructor are evaluated, left-to-right. If any of the argument evaluations completes abruptly, any argument expressions to its right are not evaluated, and the class instance creation expression completes abruptly for the same reason.

Next, the selected constructor of the specified class type is invoked. This results in invoking at least one constructor for each superclass of the class type. This process can be directed by explicit constructor invocation statements (§8.8) and is described in detail in §12.5.

The value of a class instance creation expression is a reference to the newly created object of the specified class. Every time the expression is evaluated, a fresh object is created.

Example 15.9.4-1. Evaluation Order and Out-Of-Memory Detection

If evaluation of a class instance creation expression finds there is insufficient memory to perform the creation operation, then an `OutOfMemoryError` is thrown. This check occurs before any argument expressions are evaluated.

So, for example, the test program:

```
class List {
    int value;
    List next;
    static List head = new List(0);
    List(int n) { value = n; next = head; head = this; }
}
class Test {
    public static void main(String[] args) {
        int id = 0, oldid = 0;
        try {
            for (;;) {
                ++id;
                new List(oldid = id);
            }
        } catch (Error e) {
            List.head = null;
            System.out.println(e.getClass() + ", " + (oldid==id));
        }
    }
}
```

prints:

```
class java.lang.OutOfMemoryError, false
```

because the out-of-memory condition is detected before the argument expression `oldid = id` is evaluated.

Compare this to the treatment of array creation expressions (§15.10), for which the out-of-memory condition is detected after evaluation of the dimension expressions (§15.10.1).

15.9.5   Anonymous Class Declarations

An anonymous class declaration is automatically derived from a class instance creation expression by the Java compiler.

An anonymous class is never `abstract` (§8.1.1.1).

An anonymous class is always implicitly `final` (§8.1.1.2).

An anonymous class is always an inner class (§8.1.3); it is never `static` (§8.1.1, §8.5.1).

15.9.5.1 *Anonymous Constructors*

An anonymous class cannot have an explicitly declared constructor. Instead, a Java compiler must automatically provide an anonymous constructor for the anonymous class. The form of the anonymous constructor of an anonymous class c with direct superclass s is as follows:

- If s is not an inner class, or if s is a local class that occurs in a static context, then the anonymous constructor has one formal parameter for each actual argument to the class instance creation expression in which c is declared.

  The actual arguments to the class instance creation expression are used to determine a constructor cs of s, using the same rules as for method invocations (§15.12).

  The type of each formal parameter of the anonymous constructor must be identical to the corresponding formal parameter of cs.

  The body of the constructor consists of an explicit constructor invocation (§8.8.7.1) of the form `super(...)`, where the actual arguments are the formal parameters of the constructor, in the order they were declared.

- Otherwise, the first formal parameter of the constructor of c represents the value of the immediately enclosing instance of i with respect to s. The type of this parameter is the class type that immediately encloses the declaration of s.

  The constructor has an additional formal parameter for each actual argument to the class instance creation expression that declared the anonymous class. The n'th formal parameter e corresponds to the $n\text{-}1$'th actual argument.

  The actual arguments to the class instance creation expression are used to determine a constructor cs of s, using the same rules as for method invocations (§15.12).

  The type of each formal parameter of the anonymous constructor must be identical to the corresponding formal parameter of cs.

  The body of the constructor consists of an explicit constructor invocation (§8.8.7.1) of the form `o.super(...)`, where `o` is the first formal parameter of the constructor, and the actual arguments are the subsequent formal parameters of the constructor, in the order they were declared.

In all cases, the `throws` clause of an anonymous constructor must list all the checked exceptions thrown by the explicit superclass constructor invocation statement contained within the anonymous constructor, and all checked exceptions thrown by any instance initializers or instance variable initializers of the anonymous class.

Note that it is possible for the signature of the anonymous constructor to refer to an inaccessible type (for example, if such a type occurred in the signature of the superclass constructor *cs*). This does not, in itself, cause any errors at either compile-time or run-time.

15.10   Array Creation Expressions

An array creation expression is used to create new arrays (§10).

> *ArrayCreationExpression:*
>   `new` *PrimitiveType DimExprs Dims$_{opt}$*
>   `new` *ClassOrInterfaceType DimExprs Dims$_{opt}$*
>   `new` *PrimitiveType Dims ArrayInitializer*
>   `new` *ClassOrInterfaceType Dims ArrayInitializer*
>
> *DimExprs:*
>   *DimExpr*
>   *DimExprs DimExpr*
>
> *DimExpr:*
>   [*Expression*]
>
> *Dims:*
>   [ ]
>   *Dims* [ ]

An array creation expression creates an object that is a new array whose elements are of the type specified by the *PrimitiveType* or *ClassOrInterfaceType*.

It is a compile-time error if the *ClassOrInterfaceType* does not denote a reifiable type (§4.7). Otherwise, the *ClassOrInterfaceType* may name any named reference type, even an `abstract` class type (§8.1.1.1) or an interface type (§9).

> The rules above imply that the element type in an array creation expression cannot be a parameterized type, other than an unbounded wildcard.

The type of each dimension expression within a *DimExpr* must be a type that is convertible (§5.1.8) to an integral type, or a compile-time error occurs.

Each dimension expression undergoes unary numeric promotion (§5.6.1). The promoted type must be `int`, or a compile-time error occurs.

The type of the array creation expression is an array type that can denoted by a copy of the array creation expression from which the `new` keyword and every *DimExpr* expression and array initializer have been deleted.

> For example, the type of the creation expression:
>
> ```
> new double[3][3][]
> ```
>
> is:
>
> ```
> double[][][]
> ```

15.10.1 Run-Time Evaluation of Array Creation Expressions

At run time, evaluation of an array creation expression behaves as follows:

- If there are no dimension expressions, then there must be an array initializer.

  A newly allocated array will be initialized with the values provided by the array initializer as described in §10.6.

  The value of the array initializer becomes the value of the array creation expression.

- Otherwise, there is no array initializer, and:

  - First, the dimension expressions are evaluated, left-to-right. If any of the expression evaluations completes abruptly, the expressions to the right of it are not evaluated.

  - Next, the values of the dimension expressions are checked. If the value of any *DimExpr* expression is less than zero, then a `NegativeArraySizeException` is thrown.

  - Next, space is allocated for the new array. If there is insufficient space to allocate the array, evaluation of the array creation expression completes abruptly by throwing an `OutOfMemoryError`.

  - Then, if a single *DimExpr* appears, a one-dimensional array is created of the specified length, and each component of the array is initialized to its default value (§4.12.5).

- Otherwise, if *n DimExpr* expressions appear, then array creation effectively executes a set of nested loops of depth *n*-1 to create the implied arrays of arrays.

A multidimensional array need not have arrays of the same length at each level.

Example 15.10.1-1. Array Creation Evaluation

In an array creation expression with one or more dimension expressions, each dimension expression is fully evaluated before any part of any dimension expression to its right. Thus:

```
class Test1 {
    public static void main(String[] args) {
        int i = 4;
        int ia[][] = new int[i][i=3];
        System.out.println(
            "[" + ia.length + "," + ia[0].length + "]");
    }
}
```

prints:

```
[4,3]
```

because the first dimension is calculated as 4 before the second dimension expression sets i to 3.

If evaluation of a dimension expression completes abruptly, no part of any dimension expression to its right will appear to have been evaluated. Thus:

```
class Test2 {
    public static void main(String[] args) {
        int[][] a = { { 00, 01 }, { 10, 11 } };
        int i = 99;
        try {
            a[val()][i = 1]++;
        } catch (Exception e) {
            System.out.println(e + ", i=" + i);
        }
    }
    static int val() throws Exception {
        throw new Exception("unimplemented");
    }
}
```

prints:

```
java.lang.Exception: unimplemented, i=99
```

because the embedded assignment that sets i to 1 is never executed.

Example 15.10.1-2. Multi-Dimensional Array Creation

The declaration:

```
float[][] matrix = new float[3][3];
```

is equivalent in behavior to:

```
float[][] matrix = new float[3][];
for (int d = 0; d < matrix.length; d++)
    matrix[d] = new float[3];
```

and:

```
Age[][][][][] Aquarius = new Age[6][10][8][12][];
```

is equivalent to:

```
Age[][][][][] Aquarius = new Age[6][][][][];
for (int d1 = 0; d1 < Aquarius.length; d1++) {
    Aquarius[d1] = new Age[10][][][];
    for (int d2 = 0; d2 < Aquarius[d1].length; d2++) {
        Aquarius[d1][d2] = new Age[8][][];
        for (int d3 = 0; d3 < Aquarius[d1][d2].length; d3++) {
            Aquarius[d1][d2][d3] = new Age[12][];
        }
    }
}
```

with *d*, *d1*, *d2*, and *d3* replaced by names that are not already locally declared. Thus, a single new expression actually creates one array of length 6, 6 arrays of length 10, 6x10 = 60 arrays of length 8, and 6x10x8 = 480 arrays of length 12. This example leaves the fifth dimension, which would be arrays containing the actual array elements (references to Age objects), initialized only to null references. These arrays can be filled in later by other code, such as:

```
Age[] Hair = { new Age("quartz"), new Age("topaz") };
Aquarius[1][9][6][9] = Hair;
```

A triangular matrix may be created by:

```
float triang[][] = new float[100][];
for (int i = 0; i < triang.length; i++)
    triang[i] = new float[i+1];
```

If evaluation of an array creation expression finds there is insufficient memory to perform the creation operation, then an OutOfMemoryError is thrown. If the array creation expression does not have an array initializer, then this check occurs only after evaluation of all dimension expressions has completed normally. If the array creation expression does have an array initializer, then an `OutOfMemoryError` can occur when an object of reference type is allocated during evaluation of a variable initializer expression, or when space is allocated for an array to hold the values of a (possibly nested) array initializer.

Example 15.10.1-3. `OutOfMemoryError` **and Dimension Expression Evaluation**

```
class Test3 {
    public static void main(String[] args) {
        int len = 0, oldlen = 0;
        Object[] a = new Object[0];
        try {
            for (;;) {
                ++len;
                Object[] temp = new Object[oldlen = len];
                temp[0] = a;
                a = temp;
            }
        } catch (Error e) {
            System.out.println(e + ", " + (oldlen==len));
        }
    }
}
```

This program produces the output:

```
java.lang.OutOfMemoryError, true
```

because the out-of-memory condition is detected after the dimension expression `oldlen = len` is evaluated.

Compare this to class instance creation expressions (§15.9), which detect the out-of-memory condition before evaluating argument expressions (§15.9.4).

15.11   Field Access Expressions

A field access expression may access a field of an object or array, a reference to which is the value of either an expression or the special keyword `super`.

FieldAccess:
   Primary . *Identifier*
   `super` . *Identifier*
   ClassName . `super` . *Identifier*

The meaning of a field access expression is determined using the same rules as for qualified names (§6.5.6.2), but limited by the fact that an expression cannot denote a package, class type, or interface type.

It is also possible to refer to a field of the current instance or current class by using a simple name (§6.5.6.1).

15.11.1 Field Access Using a Primary

The type of the *Primary* must be a reference type T, or a compile-time error occurs.

The meaning of the field access expression is determined as follows:

- If the identifier names several accessible (§6.6) member fields in type T, then the field access is ambiguous and a compile-time error occurs.

- If the identifier does not name an accessible member field in type T, then the field access is undefined and a compile-time error occurs.

- Otherwise, the identifier names a single accessible member field in type T, and the type of the field access expression is the type of the member field after capture conversion (§5.1.10).

At run time, the result of the field access expression is computed as follows: (assuming that the program is correct with respect to definite assignment analysis, i.e. every blank `final` variable is definitely assigned before access)

- If the field is `static`:

  - The *Primary* expression is evaluated, and the result is discarded. If evaluation of the *Primary* expression completes abruptly, the field access expression completes abruptly for the same reason.

  - If the field is a non-blank `final` field, then the result is the value of the specified class variable in the class or interface that is the type of the *Primary* expression.

  - If the field is not `final`, or is a blank `final` and the field access occurs in a constructor, then the result is a variable, namely, the specified class variable in the class that is the type of the *Primary* expression.

- If the field is not `static`:

  - The *Primary* expression is evaluated. If evaluation of the *Primary* expression completes abruptly, the field access expression completes abruptly for the same reason.

- If the value of the *Primary* is `null`, then a `NullPointerException` is thrown.

- If the field is a non-blank `final`, then the result is the value of the named member field in type `T` found in the object referenced by the value of the *Primary*.

- If the field is not `final`, or is a blank `final` and the field access occurs in a constructor, then the result is a variable, namely the named member field in type `T` found in the object referenced by the value of the *Primary*.

Note that only the type of the *Primary* expression, not the class of the actual object referred to at run time, is used in determining which field to use.

Example 15.11.1-1. Static Binding for Field Access

```
class S            { int x = 0; }
class T extends S { int x = 1; }
class Test1 {
    public static void main(String[] args) {
        T t = new T();
        System.out.println("t.x=" + t.x + when("t", t));
        S s = new S();
        System.out.println("s.x=" + s.x + when("s", s));
        s = t;
        System.out.println("s.x=" + s.x + when("s", s));
    }
    static String when(String name, Object t) {
        return " when " + name + " holds a "
                        + t.getClass() + " at run time.";
    }
}
```

This program produces the output:

```
t.x=1 when t holds a class T at run time.
s.x=0 when s holds a class S at run time.
s.x=0 when s holds a class T at run time.
```

The last line shows that, indeed, the field that is accessed does not depend on the runtime class of the referenced object; even if s holds a reference to an object of class T, the expression s.x refers to the x field of class S, because the type of the expression s is S. Objects of class T contain two fields named x, one for class T and one for its superclass S.

This lack of dynamic lookup for field accesses allows programs to be run efficiently with straightforward implementations. The power of late binding and overriding is available, but only when instance methods are used. Consider the same example using instance methods to access the fields:

```
class S            { int x = 0; int z() { return x; } }
class T extends S { int x = 1; int z() { return x; } }
```

```
class Test2 {
    public static void main(String[] args) {
        T t = new T();
        System.out.println("t.z()=" + t.z() + when("t", t));
        S s = new S();
        System.out.println("s.z()=" + s.z() + when("s", s));
        s = t;
        System.out.println("s.z()=" + s.z() + when("s", s));
    }
    static String when(String name, Object t) {
        return " when " + name + " holds a "
                        + t.getClass() + " at run time.";
    }
}
```

Now the output is:

```
t.z()=1 when t holds a class T at run time.
s.z()=0 when s holds a class S at run time.
s.z()=1 when s holds a class T at run time.
```

The last line shows that, indeed, the method that is accessed *does* depend on the run-time class of the referenced object; when s holds a reference to an object of class T, the expression s.z() refers to the z method of class T, despite the fact that the type of the expression s is S. Method z of class T overrides method z of class S.

Example 15.11.1-2. Receiver Variable Is Irrelevant For static **Field Access**

The following program demonstrates that a null reference may be used to access a class (static) variable without causing an exception:

```
class Test3 {
    static String mountain = "Chocorua";
    static Test3 favorite(){
        System.out.print("Mount ");
        return null;
    }
    public static void main(String[] args) {
        System.out.println(favorite().mountain);
    }
}
```

It compiles, executes, and prints:

```
Mount Chocorua
```

Even though the result of favorite() is null, a NullPointerException is not thrown. That "Mount " is printed demonstrates that the *Primary* expression is indeed fully evaluated at run time, despite the fact that only its type, not its value, is used to determine which field to access (because the field mountain is static).

15.11.2   Accessing Superclass Members using super

The form super.*Identifier* refers to the field named *Identifier* of the current object, but with the current object viewed as an instance of the superclass of the current class.

The form T.super.*Identifier* refers to the field named *Identifier* of the lexically enclosing instance corresponding to T, but with that instance viewed as an instance of the superclass of T.

The forms using the keyword super are valid only in an instance method, instance initializer, or constructor, or in the initializer of an instance variable of a class. If they appear anywhere else, a compile-time error occurs.

> These are exactly the same situations in which the keyword this may be used (§15.8.3).

It is a compile-time error if the forms using the keyword super appear in the declaration of class Object, since Object has no superclass.

If a field access expression super.*name* appears within class C, and the immediate superclass of C is class S, then super.*name* is treated exactly as if it had been the expression this.*name* *in the body of class* S. Thus it can access the field *name* that is visible in class S, even if that field is hidden by a declaration of a field *name* in class C.

If a field access expression T.super.*name* appears within class C, and the immediate superclass of the class denoted by T is a class whose fully qualified name is S, then T.super.*name* is treated exactly as if it had been the expression this.*name* *in the body of class* S. Thus it can access the field *name* that is visible in class S, even if that field is hidden by a declaration of a field *name* in class T.

It is a compile-time error if the current class is not an inner class of class T or T itself.

Example 15.11.2-1. The super Expression

```
interface I              { int x = 0; }
class T1 implements I { int x = 1; }
class T2 extends T1    { int x = 2; }
class T3 extends T2 {
    int x = 3;
    void test() {
        System.out.println("x=\t\t"           + x);
        System.out.println("super.x=\t\t"     + super.x);
        System.out.println("((T2)this).x=\t"  + ((T2)this).x);
        System.out.println("((T1)this).x=\t"  + ((T1)this).x);
        System.out.println("((I)this).x=\t"   + ((I)this).x);
    }
}
```

```
class Test {
    public static void main(String[] args) {
        new T3().test();
    }
}
```

This program produces the output:

```
x=              3
super.x=        2
((T2)this).x=   2
((T1)this).x=   1
((I)this).x=    0
```

Within class T3, the expression super.x is treated as if it were:

```
((T2)this).x
```

Note that super.x is not specified in terms of a cast, due to difficulties around access to protected members of the superclass.

15.12   Method Invocation Expressions

A method invocation expression is used to invoke a class or instance method.

> *MethodInvocation:*
>   *MethodName* (*ArgumentList$_{opt}$*)
>   *Primary . NonWildTypeArguments$_{opt}$ Identifier* (*ArgumentList$_{opt}$*)
>   super . *NonWildTypeArguments$_{opt}$ Identifier* (*ArgumentList$_{opt}$*)
>   *ClassName .* super *. NonWildTypeArguments$_{opt}$ Identifier* (*ArgumentList$_{opt}$*)
>   *TypeName . NonWildTypeArguments Identifier* (*ArgumentList$_{opt}$*)

The definition of *ArgumentList* from §15.9 is repeated here for convenience:

> *ArgumentList:*
>   *Expression*
>   *ArgumentList , Expression*

Resolving a method name at compile time is more complicated than resolving a field name because of the possibility of method overloading. Invoking a method at run time is also more complicated than accessing a field because of the possibility of instance method overriding.

Determining the method that will be invoked by a method invocation expression involves several steps. The following three sections describe the compile-time processing of a method invocation; the determination of the type of the method invocation expression is described in §15.12.3.

15.12.1   Compile-Time Step 1: Determine Class or Interface to Search

The first step in processing a method invocation at compile time is to figure out the name of the method to be invoked and which class or interface to check for definitions of methods of that name. There are several cases to consider, depending on the form that precedes the left parenthesis, as follows.

- If the form is *MethodName*, then there are three subcases:

  - If it is a simple name, that is, just an *Identifier*, then the name of the method is the *Identifier*.

    If the *Identifier* appears within the scope (§6.3) of a visible method declaration with that name, then:

    ❖ If there is an enclosing type declaration of which that method is a member, let T be the innermost such type declaration. The class or interface to search is T.

    ❖ Otherwise, the visible method declaration may be in scope due to one or more single-static-import (§7.5.3) or static-import-on-demand (§7.5.4) declarations. There is no class or interface to search, as the method to be invoked is determined later (§15.12.2).

  - If it is a qualified name of the form *TypeName* . *Identifier*, then the name of the method is the *Identifier* and the class to search is the one named by the *TypeName*.

    If *TypeName* is the name of an interface rather than a class, then a compile-time error occurs, because this form can invoke only `static` methods and interfaces have no `static` methods.

  - In all other cases, the qualified name has the form *FieldName* . *Identifier*.

    The name of the method is the *Identifier* and the class or interface to search is the declared type T of the field named by the *FieldName*, if T is a class or interface type, or the upper bound of T if T is a type variable.

- If the form is *Primary* . *NonWildTypeArguments$_{opt}$ Identifier*, then the name of the method is the *Identifier*.

Let T be the type of the *Primary* expression. The class or interface to be searched is T if T is a class or interface type, or the upper bound of T if T is a type variable.

It is a compile-time error if T is not a reference type.

- If the form is `super` . *NonWildTypeArguments$_{opt}$ Identifier*, then the name of the method is the *Identifier* and the class to be searched is the superclass of the class whose declaration contains the method invocation.

Let T be the type declaration immediately enclosing the method invocation. It is a compile-time error if T is the class `Object` or T is an interface.

- If the form is *ClassName* . `super` . *NonWildTypeArguments$_{opt}$ Identifier*, then the name of the method is the *Identifier* and the class to be searched is the superclass of the class C denoted by *ClassName*.

It is a compile-time error if C is not a lexically enclosing class of the current class.

It is a compile-time error if C is the class `Object`.

Let T be the type declaration immediately enclosing the method invocation. It is a compile-time error if T is the class `Object` or T is an interface.

- If the form is *TypeName* . *NonWildTypeArguments Identifier*, then the name of the method is the *Identifier* and the class to be searched is the class C denoted by *TypeName*.

If *TypeName* is the name of an interface rather than a class, then a compile-time error occurs, because this form can invoke only `static` methods and interfaces have no `static` methods.

15.12.2   Compile-Time Step 2: Determine Method Signature

The second step searches the type determined in the previous step for member methods. This step uses the name of the method and the types of the argument expressions to locate methods that are both *accessible* and *applicable*, that is, declarations that can be correctly invoked on the given arguments.

There may be more than one such method, in which case the *most specific* one is chosen. The descriptor (signature plus return type) of the most specific method is one used at run time to perform the method dispatch.

A method is *applicable* if it is either applicable by subtyping (§15.12.2.2), applicable by method invocation conversion (§15.12.2.3), or it is an applicable variable arity method (§15.12.2.4).

The process of determining applicability begins by determining the potentially applicable methods (§15.12.2.1).

The remainder of the process is split into three phases, to ensure compatibility with versions of the Java programming language prior to Java SE 5.0. The phases are:

1. The first phase (§15.12.2.2) performs overload resolution without permitting boxing or unboxing conversion, or the use of variable arity method invocation. If no applicable method is found during this phase then processing continues to the second phase.

   > This guarantees that any calls that were valid in the Java programming language before Java SE 5.0 are not considered ambiguous as the result of the introduction of variable arity methods, implicit boxing and/or unboxing. However, the declaration of a variable arity method (§8.4.1) can change the method chosen for a given method method invocation expression, because a variable arity method is treated as a fixed arity method in the first phase. For example, declaring m(Object...) in a class which already declares m(Object) causes m(Object) to no longer be chosen for some invocation expressions (such as m(null)), as m(Object[]) is more specific.

2. The second phase (§15.12.2.3) performs overload resolution while allowing boxing and unboxing, but still precludes the use of variable arity method invocation. If no applicable method is found during this phase then processing continues to the third phase.

   > This ensures that a method is never chosen through variable arity method invocation if it is applicable through fixed arity method invocation.

3. The third phase (§15.12.2.4) allows overloading to be combined with variable arity methods, boxing, and unboxing.

Deciding whether a method is applicable will, in the case of generic methods (§8.4.4), require that type arguments be determined. Type arguments may be passed explicitly or implicitly. If they are passed implicitly, they must be inferred (§15.12.2.7) from the types of the argument expressions.

If several applicable methods have been identified during one of the three phases of applicability testing, then the most specific one is chosen, as specified in section §15.12.2.5.

Example 15.12.2-1. Method Applicability

```
class Doubler {
        static int two()       { return two(1); }
    private static int two(int i) { return 2*i;     }
}
class Test extends Doubler {
    static long two(long j) { return j+j; }
```

```
        public static void main(String[] args) {
            System.out.println(two(3));
            System.out.println(Doubler.two(3)); // compile-time error
        }
    }
```

For the method invocation two(1) within class Doubler, there are two accessible methods named two, but only the second one is applicable, and so that is the one invoked at run time.

For the method invocation two(3) within class Test, there are two applicable methods, but only the one in class Test is accessible, and so that is the one to be invoked at run time (the argument 3 is converted to type long).

For the method invocation Doubler.two(3), the class Doubler, not class Test, is searched for methods named two; the only applicable method is not accessible, and so this method invocation causes a compile-time error.

Another example is:

```
    class ColoredPoint {
        int x, y;
        byte color;
        void setColor(byte color) { this.color = color; }
    }
    class Test {
        public static void main(String[] args) {
            ColoredPoint cp = new ColoredPoint();
            byte color = 37;
            cp.setColor(color);
            cp.setColor(37);   // compile-time error
        }
    }
```

Here, a compile-time error occurs for the second invocation of setColor, because no applicable method can be found at compile time. The type of the literal 37 is int, and int cannot be converted to byte by method invocation conversion. Assignment conversion, which is used in the initialization of the variable color, performs an implicit conversion of the constant from type int to byte, which is permitted because the value 37 is small enough to be represented in type byte; but such a conversion is not allowed for method invocation conversion.

If the method setColor had, however, been declared to take an int instead of a byte, then both method invocations would be correct; the first invocation would be allowed because method invocation conversion does permit a widening conversion from byte to int. However, a narrowing cast would then be required in the body of setColor:

```
    void setColor(int color) { this.color = (byte)color; }
```

Here is an example of overloading ambiguity. Consider the program:

```
    class Point { int x, y; }
```

```
class ColoredPoint extends Point { int color; }
class Test {
    static void test(ColoredPoint p, Point q) {
        System.out.println("(ColoredPoint, Point)");
    }
    static void test(Point p, ColoredPoint q) {
        System.out.println("(Point, ColoredPoint)");
    }
    public static void main(String[] args) {
        ColoredPoint cp = new ColoredPoint();
        test(cp, cp);  // compile-time error
    }
}
```

This example produces an error at compile time. The problem is that there are two declarations of test that are applicable and accessible, and neither is more specific than the other. Therefore, the method invocation is ambiguous.

If a third definition of test were added:

```
static void test(ColoredPoint p, ColoredPoint q) {
    System.out.println("(ColoredPoint, ColoredPoint)");
}
```

then it would be more specific than the other two, and the method invocation would no longer be ambiguous.

Example 15.12.2-2. Return Type Not Considered During Method Selection

```
class Point { int x, y; }
class ColoredPoint extends Point { int color; }
class Test {
    static int test(ColoredPoint p) {
        return p.color;
    }
    static String test(Point p) {
        return "Point";
    }
    public static void main(String[] args) {
        ColoredPoint cp = new ColoredPoint();
        String s = test(cp);  // compile-time error
    }
}
```

Here, the most specific declaration of method test is the one taking a parameter of type ColoredPoint. Because the result type of the method is int, a compile-time error occurs because an int cannot be converted to a String by assignment conversion. This example shows that the result types of methods do not participate in resolving overloaded methods, so that the second test method, which returns a String, is not chosen, even though it has a result type that would allow the example program to compile without error.

Example 15.12.2-3. Choosing The Most Specific Method

The most specific method is chosen at compile time; its descriptor determines what method is actually executed at run time. If a new method is added to a class, then source code that was compiled with the old definition of the class might not use the new method, even if a recompilation would cause this method to be chosen.

So, for example, consider two compilation units, one for class `Point`:

```
package points;
public class Point {
    public int x, y;
    public Point(int x, int y) { this.x = x; this.y = y; }
    public String toString() { return toString(""); }
    public String toString(String s) {
        return "(" + x + "," + y + s + ")";
    }
}
```

and one for class `ColoredPoint`:

```
package points;
public class ColoredPoint extends Point {
    public static final int
        RED = 0, GREEN = 1, BLUE = 2;
    public static String[] COLORS =
        { "red", "green", "blue" };

    public byte color;
    public ColoredPoint(int x, int y, int color) {
        super(x, y);
        this.color = (byte)color;
    }

    /** Copy all relevant fields of the argument into
        this ColoredPoint object. */
    public void adopt(Point p) { x = p.x; y = p.y; }

    public String toString() {
        String s = "," + COLORS[color];
        return super.toString(s);
    }
}
```

Now consider a third compilation unit that uses `ColoredPoint`:

```
import points.*;
class Test {
    public static void main(String[] args) {
        ColoredPoint cp =
            new ColoredPoint(6, 6, ColoredPoint.RED);
```

```
            ColoredPoint cp2 =
                new ColoredPoint(3, 3, ColoredPoint.GREEN);
            cp.adopt(cp2);
            System.out.println("cp: " + cp);
        }
    }
```

The output is:

```
    cp: (3,3,red)
```

The programmer who coded class `Test` has expected to see the word `green`, because the actual argument, a `ColoredPoint`, has a `color` field, and `color` would seem to be a "relevant field". (Of course, the documentation for the package `points` ought to have been much more precise!)

Notice, by the way, that the most specific method (indeed, the only applicable method) for the method invocation of `adopt` has a signature that indicates a method of one parameter, and the parameter is of type `Point`. This signature becomes part of the binary representation of class `Test` produced by the Java compiler and is used by the method invocation at run time.

Suppose the programmer reported this software error and the maintainer of the `points` package decided, after due deliberation, to correct it by adding a method to class `ColoredPoint`:

```
    public void adopt(ColoredPoint p) {
        adopt((Point)p);
        color = p.color;
    }
```

If the programmer then runs the old binary file for `Test` with the new binary file for `ColoredPoint`, the output is still:

```
    cp: (3,3,red)
```

because the old binary file for `Test` still has the descriptor "one parameter, whose type is `Point`; void" associated with the method call `cp.adopt(cp2)`. If the source code for `Test` is recompiled, the Java compiler will then discover that there are now two applicable `adopt` methods, and that the signature for the more specific one is "one parameter, whose type is `ColoredPoint`; void"; running the program will then produce the desired output:

```
    cp: (3,3,green)
```

With forethought about such problems, the maintainer of the `points` package could fix the `ColoredPoint` class to work with both newly compiled and old code, by adding defensive code to the old `adopt` method for the sake of old code that still invokes it on `ColoredPoint` arguments:

```
    public void adopt(Point p) {
        if (p instanceof ColoredPoint)
```

```
        color = ((ColoredPoint)p).color;
    x = p.x; y = p.y;
  }
```

Ideally, source code should be recompiled whenever code that it depends on is changed. However, in an environment where different classes are maintained by different organizations, this is not always feasible. Defensive programming with careful attention to the problems of class evolution can make upgraded code much more robust. See §13 for a detailed discussion of binary compatibility and type evolution.

15.12.2.1 *Identify Potentially Applicable Methods*

The class or interface determined by compile-time step 1 (§15.12.1) is searched for all member methods that are potentially applicable to this method invocation; members inherited from superclasses and superinterfaces are included in this search.

In addition, if the method invocation has, before the left parenthesis, a *MethodName* of the form *Identifier*, then the search process also examines all member methods that are (a) imported by single-static-import declarations (§7.5.3) and static-import-on-demand declarations (§7.5.4) within the compilation unit (§7.3) within which the method invocation occurs, and (b) not shadowed (§6.4.1) at the place where the method invocation appears, to determine if they are potentially applicable.

A member method is *potentially applicable* to a method invocation if and only if all of the following are true:

- The name of the member is identical to the name of the method in the method invocation.

- The member is accessible (§6.6) to the class or interface in which the method invocation appears.

  > Whether a member method is accessible at a method invocation depends on the access modifier (public, none, protected, or private) in the member's declaration and on where the method invocation appears.

- If the member is a variable arity method with arity n, the arity of the method invocation is greater or equal to $n-1$.

- If the member is a fixed arity method with arity n, the arity of the method invocation is equal to n.

- If the method invocation includes explicit type arguments, and the member is a generic method, then the number of type arguments is equal to the number of type parameters of the method.

This clause implies that a non-generic method may be potentially applicable to an invocation that supplies explicit type arguments. Indeed, it may turn out to be applicable. In such a case, the type arguments will simply be ignored.

This rule stems from issues of compatibility and principles of substitutability. Since interfaces or superclasses may be generified independently of their subtypes, we may override a generic method with a non-generic one. However, the overriding (non-generic) method must be applicable to calls to the generic method, including calls that explicitly pass type arguments. Otherwise the subtype would not be substitutable for its generified supertype.

If the search does not yield at least one method that is potentially applicable, then a compile-time error occurs.

15.12.2.2   *Phase 1: Identify Matching Arity Methods Applicable by Subtyping*

Let m be a potentially applicable method (§15.12.2.1), let e_1, ..., e_n be the actual argument expressions of the method invocation, and let A_i be the type of e_i ($1 \leq i \leq n$). Then:

- If m is a generic method, then let $F_1 \ldots F_n$ be the types of the formal parameters of m, and let $R_1 \ldots R_p$ ($p \geq 1$) be the type parameters of m, and let B_1 be the declared bound of R_1 ($1 \leq l \leq p$). Then:

  - If the method invocation does not provide explicit type arguments, then let $U_1 \ldots U_p$ be the type arguments inferred (§15.12.2.7) for this invocation of m, using a set of initial constraints consisting of the constraints $A_i \ll F_i$ ($1 \leq i \leq n$) for each actual argument expression e_i whose type is a reference type.

  - Otherwise, let $U_1 \ldots U_p$ be the explicit type arguments given in the method invocation.

  Then let $S_i = F_i[R_1=U_1,\ldots,R_p=U_p]$ ($1 \leq i \leq n$) be the types inferred for the formal parameters of m.

- Otherwise, let $S_1 \ldots S_n$ be the types of the formal parameters of m.

The method m is *applicable by subtyping* if and only if both of the following conditions hold:

- For $1 \leq i \leq n$, either:

  - $A_i <: S_i$ (§4.10), or

  - A_i is convertible to some type C_i by unchecked conversion (§5.1.9), and $C_i <: S_i$.

- If m is a generic method as described above, then $U_l <: B_l[R_1=U_1,...,R_p=U_p]$ ($1 \leq l \leq p$).

If no method applicable by subtyping is found, the search for applicable methods continues with phase 2 (§15.12.2.3).

Otherwise, the most specific method (§15.12.2.5) is chosen among the methods that are applicable by subtyping.

15.12.2.3   *Phase 2: Identify Matching Arity Methods Applicable by Method Invocation Conversion*

Let m be a potentially applicable method (§15.12.2.1), let e_1, ..., e_n be the actual argument expressions of the method invocation, and let A_i be the type of e_i ($1 \leq i \leq n$). Then:

- If m is a generic method, then let $F_1 ... F_n$ be the types of the formal parameters of m, and let $R_1 ... R_p$ ($p \geq 1$) be the type parameters of m, and let B_l be the declared bound of R_l ($1 \leq l \leq p$). Then:

  - If the method invocation does not provide explicit type arguments, then let $U_1 ... U_p$ be the type arguments inferred (§15.12.2.7) for this invocation of m, using a set of initial constraints consisting of the constraints $A_i << F_i$ ($1 \leq i \leq n$).

  - Otherwise, let $U_1 ... U_p$ be the explicit type arguments given in the method invocation.

  Then let $S_i = F_i[R_1=U_1,...,R_p=U_p]$ ($1 \leq i \leq n$) be the types inferred for the formal parameters of m.

- Otherwise, let $S_1 ... S_n$ be the types of the formal parameters of m.

The method m is *applicable by method invocation conversion* if and only if both of the following conditions hold:

- For $1 \leq i \leq n$, the type of e_i, A_i, can be converted by method invocation conversion (§5.3) to S_i.

- If m is a generic method as described above, then $U_l <: B_l[R_1=U_1,...,R_p=U_p]$ ($1 \leq l \leq p$).

If no method applicable by method invocation conversion is found, the search for applicable methods continues with phase 3 (§15.12.2.4).

Otherwise, the most specific method (§15.12.2.5) is chosen among the methods that are applicable by method invocation conversion.

15.12.2.4   *Phase 3: Identify Applicable Variable Arity Methods*

Let m be a potentially applicable method (§15.12.2.1) with variable arity, let e_1, ..., e_k be the actual argument expressions of the method invocation, and let A_i be the type of e_i ($1 \leq i \leq k$). Then:

- If m is a generic method, then let F_1 ... F_n ($1 \leq n \leq k+1$) be the types of the formal parameters of m, where $F_n = T[\,]$ for some type T, and let R_1 ... R_p ($p \geq 1$) be the type parameters of m, and let B_l be the declared bound of R_l ($1 \leq l \leq p$). Then:

  - If the method invocation does not provide explicit type arguments then let U_1 ... U_p be the type arguments inferred (§15.12.2.7) for this invocation of m, using a set of initial constraints consisting of the constraints $A_i \ll F_i$ ($1 \leq i < n$) and the constraints $A_j \ll T$ ($n \leq j \leq k$).

  - Otherwise let U_1 ... U_p be the explicit type arguments given in the method invocation.

  Then let $S_i = F_i[R_1 = U_1, ..., R_p = U_p]$ ($1 \leq i \leq n$) be the types inferred for the formal parameters of m.

- Otherwise, let S_1 ... S_n (where $n \leq k+1$) be the types of the formal parameters of m.

The method m is an *applicable variable-arity method* if and only if all of the following conditions hold:

- For $1 \leq i < n$, the type of e_i, A_i, can be converted by method invocation conversion to S_i.

- If $k \geq n$, then for $n \leq i \leq k$, the type of e_i, A_i, can be converted by method invocation conversion to the component type of S_n.

- If $k\ {!=}\ n$, or if $k = n$ and A_n cannot be converted by method invocation conversion to $S_n[\,]$, then the type which is the erasure (§4.6) of S_n is accessible at the point of invocation.

- If m is a generic method as described above, then $U_l <: B_l[R_1 = U_1..., R_p = U_p]$ ($1 \leq l \leq p$).

If no applicable variable arity method is found, a compile-time error occurs.

Otherwise, the most specific method (§15.12.2.5) is chosen among the applicable variable-arity methods.

15.12.2.5   *Choosing the Most Specific Method*

If more than one member method is both accessible and applicable to a method invocation, it is necessary to choose one to provide the descriptor for the run-time method dispatch. The Java programming language uses the rule that the *most specific* method is chosen.

The informal intuition is that one method is more specific than another if any invocation handled by the first method could be passed on to the other one without a compile-time type error.

One fixed-arity member method named m is *more specific* than another member method of the same name and arity if all of the following conditions hold:

- The declared types of the parameters of the first member method are $T_1, ..., T_n$.

- The declared types of the parameters of the other method are $U_1, ..., U_n$.

- If the second method is generic, then let $R_1 ... R_p$ ($p \geq 1$) be its type parameters, let B_l be the declared bound of R_l ($1 \leq l \leq p$), let $A_1 ... A_p$ be the type arguments inferred (§15.12.2.7) for this invocation under the initial constraints $T_i << U_i$ ($1 \leq i \leq n$), and let $S_i = U_i[R_1 = A_1,...,R_p = A_p]$ ($1 \leq i \leq n$).

  Otherwise, let $S_i = U_i$ ($1 \leq i \leq n$).

- For all j from 1 to n, $T_j <: S_j$.

- If the second method is a generic method as described above, then $A_l <: B_l[R_1 = A_1,...,R_p = A_p]$ ($1 \leq l \leq p$).

One variable arity member method named m is *more specific* than another variable arity member method of the same name if either:

1. One member method has n parameters and the other has k parameters, where $n \geq k$, and:

   - The types of the parameters of the first member method are $T_1, ..., T_{n-1}, T_n[\,]$.

   - The types of the parameters of the other method are $U_1, ..., U_{k-1}, U_k[\,]$.

   - If the second method is generic then let $R_1 ... R_p$ ($p \geq 1$) be its type parameters, let B_l be the declared bound of R_l ($1 \leq l \leq p$), let $A_1 ... A_p$ be the type arguments inferred (§15.12.2.7) for this invocation under the initial constraints $T_i << U_i$ ($1 \leq i \leq k-1$) and $T_i << U_k$ ($k \leq i \leq n$), and let $S_i = U_i[R_1 = A_1,...,R_p = A_p]$ ($1 \leq i \leq k$).

     Otherwise, let $S_i = U_i$ ($1 \leq i \leq k$).

   - For all j from 1 to $k-1$, $T_j <: S_j$, and,

   - For all j from k to n, $T_j <: S_k$, and,

   - If the second method is a generic method as described above, then $A_l <: B_l[R_1 = A_1,...,R_p = A_p]$ ($1 \leq l \leq p$).

2. One member method has k parameters and the other has n parameters, where $n \geq k$, and:

- The types of the parameters of the first method are $U_1, ..., U_{k-1}, U_k[\,]$.

- The types of the parameters of the other method are $T_1, ..., T_{n-1}, T_n[\,]$.

- If the second method is generic, then let $R_1 ... R_p$ $(p \geq 1)$ be its type parameters, let B_l be the declared bound of R_l $(1 \leq l \leq p)$, let $A_1 ... A_p$ be the type arguments inferred (§15.12.2.7) for this invocation under the initial constraints $U_i << T_i$ $(1 \leq i \leq k-1)$ and $U_k << T_i$ $(k \leq i \leq n)$, and let $S_i = T_i[R_1=A_1,...,R_p=A_p]$ $(1 \leq i \leq n)$.

  Otherwise, let $S_i = T_i$ $(1 \leq i \leq n)$.

- For all j from 1 to k-1, $U_j <: S_j$, and,

- For all j from k to n, $U_k <: S_j$, and,

- If the second method is a generic method as described above, then $A_l <: B_l[R_1=A_1,...,R_p=A_p]$ $(1 \leq l \leq p)$.

The above conditions are the only circumstances under which one method may be more specific than another.

A method m_1 is *strictly more specific* than another method m_2 if and only if m_1 is more specific than m_2 and m_2 is not more specific than m_1.

A method is said to be *maximally specific* for a method invocation if it is accessible and applicable and there is no other method that is applicable and accessible that is strictly more specific.

If there is exactly one maximally specific method, then that method is in fact the *most specific method*; it is necessarily more specific than any other accessible method that is applicable. It is then subjected to some further compile-time checks as described in §15.12.3.

It is possible that no method is the most specific, because there are two or more methods that are maximally specific. In this case:

- If all the maximally specific methods have override-equivalent (§8.4.2) signatures, then:

  - If exactly one of the maximally specific methods is not declared `abstract`, it is the most specific method.

  - Otherwise, if all the maximally specific methods are declared `abstract`, and the signatures of all of the maximally specific methods have the same erasure (§4.6), then the most specific method is chosen arbitrarily among the subset of the maximally specific methods that have the most specific return type.

However, the most specific method is considered to throw a checked exception if and only if that exception or its erasure is declared in the `throws` clauses of each of the maximally specific methods.

- Otherwise, we say that the method invocation is *ambiguous*, and a compile-time error occurs.

15.12.2.6   *Method Result and Throws Types*

The result type of the chosen method is determined as follows:

- If the chosen method is declared with a return type of `void`, then the result is `void`.

- Otherwise, if unchecked conversion was necessary for the method to be applicable, then the result type is the erasure (§4.6) of the method's declared return type.

- Otherwise, if the chosen method is generic, then for $1 \leq i \leq n$, let F_i be the formal type parameters of the method, let A_i be the actual type arguments inferred for the method invocation, and let R be the return type of the chosen method.

  The result type is obtained by applying capture conversion (§5.1.10) to $R[F_1=A_1,...,F_n=A_n]$.

- Otherwise, the result type is obtained by applying capture conversion (§5.1.10) to the return type of the chosen method .

The exception types of the `throws` clause of the chosen method are determined as follows:

- If unchecked conversion was necessary for the method to be applicable, then the `throws` clause is composed of the erasure (§4.6) of the types in the method's declared `throws` clause.

- Otherwise, if the method being invoked is generic, then for $1 \leq i \leq n$, let F_i be the type parameters of the method, let A_i be the type arguments inferred for the method invocation, and let E_j $(1 \leq j \leq m)$ be the exception types declared in the `throws` clause of the method being invoked.

  The `throws` clause consists of the types $E_j[F_1=A_1,...,F_n=A_n]$.

- Otherwise, the type of the `throws` clause is the type given in the method declaration.

The exception types that a method invocation expression can throw are specified in §11.2.1.

15.12.2.7 *Inferring Type Arguments Based on Actual Arguments*

In this section, we describe the process of inferring type arguments for method and constructor invocations. This process is invoked as a subroutine when testing for method (or constructor) applicability (§15.12.2.2, §15.12.2.3, §15.12.2.4).

> The process of type inference is inherently complex. Therefore, it is useful to give an informal overview of the process before delving into the detailed specification.
>
> Inference begins with an initial set of constraints. Generally, the constraints require that the statically known types of the actual arguments are acceptable given the declared formal parameter types. We discuss the meaning of "acceptable" below.
>
> Given these initial constraints, one may derive a set of supertype and/or equality constraints on the type parameters of the method or constructor.
>
> Next, one must try and find a solution that satisfies the constraints on the type parameters. As a first approximation, if a type parameter is constrained by an equality constraint, then that constraint gives its solution. Bear in mind that the constraint may equate one type parameter with another, and only when the entire set of constraints on all type variables is resolved will we have a solution.
>
> A supertype constraint $T :> X$ implies that the solution is one of supertypes of X. Given several such constraints on T, we can intersect the sets of supertypes implied by each of the constraints, since the type parameter must be a member of all of them. We can then choose the most specific type that is in the intersection.
>
> Computing the intersection is more complicated than one might first realize. Given that a type parameter is constrained to be a supertype of two distinct invocations of a generic type, say `List<Object>` and `List<String>`, the naive intersection operation might yield `Object`. However, a more sophisticated analysis yields a set containing `List<?>`. Similarly, if a type parameter T is constrained to be a supertype of two unrelated interfaces I and J, we might infer T must be `Object`, or we might obtain a tighter bound of I & J. These issues are discussed in more detail later in this section.

We use the following notational conventions in this section:

- Type expressions are represented using the letters A, F, U, V, and W. The letter A is only used to denote the type of an actual argument, and F is only used to denote the type of a formal parameter.

- Type parameters are represented using the letters S and T

- Arguments to parameterized types are represented using the letters X and Y.

- Generic type declarations are represented using the letters G and H.

Inference begins with a set of initial constraints of the form $A \ll F$, $A = F$, or $A \gg F$, where $U \ll V$ indicates that type U is convertible to type V by method invocation conversion (§5.3), and $U >> V$ indicates that type V is convertible to type U by method invocation conversion.

In a simpler world, the constraints could be of the form $A <: F$ - simply requiring that the actual argument types be subtypes of the formal ones. However, reality is more involved. As discussed earlier, method applicability testing consists of up to three phases; this is required for compatibility reasons. Each phase imposes slightly different constraints. If a method is applicable by subtyping (§15.12.2.2), the constraints are indeed subtyping constraints. If a method is applicable by method invocation conversion (§15.12.2.3), the constraints imply that the actual type is convertible to the formal type by method invocation conversion. The situation is similar for the third phase (§15.12.2.4), but the exact form of the constraints differ due to the variable arity.

It is worth noting that a constraint of the form $A = F$ is never part of the initial constraints. However, it can arise as the algorithm recurses. We see this occur in the running example below, when the constraint $A << F$ relates two parameterized types, as in $G<V> << G<U>$.

A constraint of the form $A >> F$ also arises when the algorithm recurses, due to the contravariant subtyping rules associated with lower-bounded wildcards (those of the form $G<?$ super $X>$).

It might be tempting to consider $A >> F$ as being the same as $F << A$, but the problem of inference is not symmetric. We need to remember which participant in the relation includes a type to be inferred.

These constraints are then reduced to a set of simpler constraints of the forms $T :> X$, $T = X$, or $T <: X$, where T is a type parameter of the method. This reduction is achieved by the procedure given below.

It may be that the initial constraints are unsatisfiable; we say that inference is *overconstrained*. In that case, we do not necessarily derive unsatisfiable constraints on the type parameters. Instead, we may infer type arguments for the invocation, but once we substitute the type arguments for the type parameters, the applicability test may fail because the actual argument types are not acceptable given the substituted formal parameter types.

An alternative strategy would be to have type inference itself fail in such cases. A Java compiler may choose to do so, provided the effect is equivalent to that specified here.

Given a constraint of the form $A << F$, $A = F$, or $A >> F$:

If F does not involve a type parameter T_j then no constraint is implied on T_j.

Otherwise, F involves a type parameter T_j, and there are four cases to consider.

1. If A is the type of `null`, no constraint is implied on T_j.

2. Otherwise, if the constraint has the form $A \ll F$:

- If A is a primitive type, then A is converted to a reference type U via boxing conversion and this algorithm is applied recursively to the constraint $U \ll F$.

- Otherwise, if $F = T_j$, then the constraint $T_j :> A$ is implied.

- If $F = U[]$, where the type U involves T_j, then if A is an array type $V[]$, or a type variable with an upper bound that is an array type $V[]$, where V is a reference type, this algorithm is applied recursively to the constraint $V \ll U$.

  > This follows from the covariant subtype relation among array types. The constraint $A \ll F$ in this case means that $A \ll U[]$. A is therefore necessarily an array type $V[]$, or a type variable whose upper bound is an array type $V[]$ - otherwise the relation $A \ll U[]$ could never hold true. It follows that $V[] \ll U[]$. Since array subtyping is covariant, it must be the case that $V \ll U$.

- If F has the form $G<..., Y_{k-1}, U, Y_{k+1}, ...>$, where U is a type expression that involves T_j, then if A has a supertype of the form $G<..., X_{k-1}, V, X_{k+1}, ...>$ where V is a type expression, this algorithm is applied recursively to the constraint $V = U$.

  > For simplicity, assume that G takes a single type argument. If the method invocation being examined is to be applicable, it must be the case that A is a subtype of some invocation of G. Otherwise, $A \ll F$ would never be true.

  > In other words, $A \ll F$, where $F = G<U>$, implies that $A \ll G<V>$ for some V. Now, since U is a type expression (and therefore, U is not a wildcard type argument), it must be the case that $U = V$, by the non-variance of ordinary parameterized type invocations.

  > The formulation above merely generalizes this reasoning to generics with an arbitrary number of type arguments.

- If F has the form $G<..., Y_{k-1}, ?\text{ extends }U, Y_{k+1}, ...>$, where U involves T_j, then if A has a supertype that is one of:

  - $G<..., X_{k-1}, V, X_{k+1}, ...>$, where V is a type expression. Then this algorithm is applied recursively to the constraint $V \ll U$.

    > Again, let's keep things as simple as possible, and consider only the case where G has a single type argument.

    > $A \ll F$ in this case means $A \ll G<?\text{ extends }U>$. As above, it must be the case that A is a subtype of some invocation of G. However, A may now be a subtype of either $G<V>$, or $G<?\text{ extends }V>$, or $G<?\text{ super }V>$. We examine these cases in turn. The first variation is described (generalized to multiple arguments) by the sub-bullet directly above. We therefore have $A = G<V> \ll G<?\text{ extends }U>$. The rules of subtyping for wildcards imply that $V \ll U$.

  - $G<..., X_{k-1}, ?\text{ extends }V, X_{k+1}, ...>$. Then this algorithm is applied recursively to the constraint $V \ll U$.

Extending the analysis above, we have $A = G$`<? extends` V`>` $<<$ G`<? extends` U`>`. The rules of subtyping for wildcards again imply that $V << U$.

- Otherwise, no constraint is implied on T_j.

  Here, we have $A = G$`<? super` V`>` $<<$ G`<? extends` U`>`. In general, we cannot conclude anything in this case. However, it is not necessarily an error. It may be that U will eventually be inferred to be `Object`, in which case the call may indeed be valid. Therefore, we simply refrain from placing any constraint on U.

- If F has the form G`<...,` Y_{k-1}`, ? super` U`,` Y_{k+1}`, ...>`, where U involves T_j, then if A has a supertype that is one of:

  - G`<...,` X_{k-1}`,` V`,` X_{k+1}`, ...>`. Then this algorithm is applied recursively to the constraint $V >> U$.

    As usual, we consider only the case where G has a single type argument.

    $A << F$ in this case means $A << G$`<? super` U`>`. As above, it must be the case that A is a subtype of some invocation of G. A may now be a subtype of either G`<`V`>`, or G`<? extends` V`>`, or G`<? super` V`>`. We examine these cases in turn. The first variation is described (generalized to multiple arguments) by the sub-bullet directly above. We therefore have $A = G$`<`V`>` $<<$ G`<? super` U`>`. The rules of subtyping for wildcards imply that $V >> U$.

  - G`<...,` X_{k-1}`, ? super` V`,` X_{k+1}`, ...>`. Then this algorithm is applied recursively to the constraint $V >> U$.

    We have $A = G$`<? super` V`>` $<<$ G`<? super` U`>`. The rules of subtyping for lower-bounded wildcards again imply that $V >> U$.

  - Otherwise, no constraint is implied on T_j.

    Here, we have $A = G$`<? extends` V`>` $<<$ G`<? super` U`>`. In general, we cannot conclude anything in this case. However, it is not necessarily an error. It may be that U will eventually be inferred to the null type, in which case the call may indeed be valid. Therefore, we simply refrain from placing any constraint on U.

- Otherwise, no constraint is implied on T_j.

3. Otherwise, if the constraint has the form $A = F$:

- If $F = T_j$, then the constraint $T_j = A$ is implied.

- If $F = U[\ ]$ where the type U involves T_j, then if A is an array type $V[\ ]$, or a type variable with an upper bound that is an array type $V[\ ]$, where V is a reference type, this algorithm is applied recursively to the constraint $V = U$.

  If the array types $U[\ ]$ and $V[\ ]$ are the same, their component types must be the same.

- If F has the form $G<..., Y_{k-1}, U, Y_{k+1}, ...>$, where U is type expression that involves T_j, then if A is of the form $G<..., X_{k-1}, V, X_{k+1},...>$ where V is a type expression, this algorithm is applied recursively to the constraint $V = U$.

- If F has the form $G<..., Y_{k-1}, ?$ extends $U, Y_{k+1}, ...>$, where U involves T_j, then if A is one of:

  - $G<..., X_{k-1}, ?$ extends $V, X_{k+1}, ...>$. Then this algorithm is applied recursively to the constraint $V = U$.

  - Otherwise, no constraint is implied on T_j.

- If F has the form $G<..., Y_{k-1}, ?$ super $U, Y_{k+1} ,...>$, where U involves T_j, then if A is one of:

  - $G<..., X_{k-1}, ?$ super $V, X_{k+1}, ...>$. Then this algorithm is applied recursively to the constraint $V = U$.

  - Otherwise, no constraint is implied on T_j.

- Otherwise, no constraint is implied on T_j.

4. Otherwise, if the constraint has the form $A \gg F$:

- If $F = T_j$, then the constraint $T_j <: A$ is implied.

  > We do not make use of such constraints in the main body of the inference algorithm. However, they are used in §15.12.2.8.

- If $F = U[]$, where the type U involves T_j, then if A is an array type $V[]$, or a type variable with an upper bound that is an array type $V[]$, where V is a reference type, this algorithm is applied recursively to the constraint $V \gg U$. Otherwise, no constraint is implied on T_j.

  > This follows from the covariant subtype relation among array types. The constraint $A \gg F$ in this case means that $A \gg U[]$. A is therefore necessarily an array type $V[]$, or a type variable whose upper bound is an array type $V[]$ - otherwise the relation $A \gg U[]$ could never hold true. It follows that $V[] \gg U[]$. Since array subtyping is covariant, it must be the case that $V \gg U$.

- If F has the form $G<..., Y_{k-1}, U, Y_{k+1}, ...>$, where U is a type expression that involves T_j, then:

  - If A is an instance of a non-generic type, then no constraint is implied on T_j.

    > In this case (once again restricting the analysis to the unary case), we have the constraint $A \gg F = G<U>$. A must be a supertype of the generic type G. However, since A is not a parameterized type, it cannot depend upon the type argument U in any way. It is a supertype of $G<X>$ for every X that is a valid type argument to G. No meaningful constraint on U can be derived from A.

  - If A is an invocation of a generic type declaration H, where H is either G or superclass or superinterface of G, then:

    - If $H \neq G$, then let $S_1, ..., S_n$ be the type parameters of G, and let $H<U_1, ..., U_l>$ be the unique invocation of H that is a supertype of $G<S_1, ..., S_n>$, and let $V = H<U_1, ..., U_l>[S_k=U]$. Then, if $V :> F$ this algorithm is applied recursively to the constraint $A \gg V$.

      > Our goal here is to simplify the relationship between A and F. We aim to recursively invoke the algorithm on a simpler case, where the type argument is known to be an invocation of the same generic type declaration as the formal.
      >
      > Let's consider the case where both H and G have only a single type argument. Since we have the constraint $A = H<X> \gg F = G<U>$, where H is distinct from G, it must be the case that H is some proper superclass or superinterface of G. There must be a (non-wildcard) invocation of H that is a supertype of $F = G<U>$. Call this invocation V.
      >
      > If we replace F by V in the constraint, we will have accomplished the goal of relating two invocations of the same generic (as it happens, H).

How do we compute V? The declaration of G must introduce a type parameter S, and there must be some (non-wildcard) invocation of H, $H<U_1>$, that is a supertype of $G<S>$. Substituting the type expression U for S will then yield a (non-wildcard) invocation of H, $H<U_1>[S=U]$, that is a supertype of $G<U>$. For example, in the simplest instance, U_1 might be S, in which case we have $G<S> <: H<S>$, and $G<U>$ $<: H<U> = H<S>[S=U] = V$.

It may be the case that $H<U_1>$ is independent of S - that is, S does not occur in U_1 at all. However, the substitution described above is still valid - in this situation, $V = H<U_1>[S=U] = H<U_1>$. Furthermore, in this circumstance, $G<T> <: H<U_1>$ for any T, and in particular $G<U> <: H<U_1> = V$.

Regardless of whether U_1 depends on S, we have determined the type V, the invocation of H that is a supertype of $G<U>$. We can now invoke the algorithm recursively on the constraint $H<X> = A \gg V = H<U_1>[S=U]$. We will then be able to relate the type arguments of both invocations of H and extract the relevant constraints from them.

❖ Otherwise, if A is of the form $G<..., X_{k-1}, W, X_{k+1}, ...>$, where W is a type expression, this algorithm is applied recursively to the constraint $W = U$.

We have $A = G<W> \gg F = G<U>$ for some type expression W. Since W is a type expression (and not a wildcard type argument), it must be the case that $W = U$, by the invariance of parameterized types.

❖ Otherwise, if A is of the form $G<..., X_{k-1},$? extends $W, X_{k+1}, ...>$, this algorithm is applied recursively to the constraint $W \gg U$.

We have $A = G<?$ extends $W> \gg F = G<U>$ for some type expression W. It must be the case that $W \gg U$, by the subtyping rules for wildcard types.

❖ Otherwise, if A is of the form $G<..., X_{k-1},$? super $W, X_{k+1}, ...>$, this algorithm is applied recursively to the constraint $W \ll U$.

We have $A = G<?$ super $W> \gg F = G<U>$ for some type expression W. It must be the case that $W \ll U$, by the subtyping rules for wildcard types.

❖ Otherwise, no constraint is implied on T_j.

• If F has the form $G<..., Y_{k-1},$? extends $U, Y_{k+1}, ...>$, where U is a type expression that involves T_j, then:

  • If A is an instance of a non-generic type, then no constraint is implied on T_j.

    Once again restricting the analysis to the unary case, we have the constraint $A \gg F = G<?$ extends $U>$. A must be a supertype of the generic type G. However, since A is not a parameterized type, it cannot depend upon U in any way. It is a supertype of the type $G<?$ extends $X>$ for every X such that ? extends X is a valid type argument to G. No meaningful constraint on U can be derived from A.

- If A is an invocation of a generic type declaration H, where H is either G or superclass or superinterface of G, then:

  ❖ If $H \neq G$, then let $S_1, ..., S_n$ be the type parameters of G, and let $H<U_1, ..., U_l>$ be the unique invocation of H that is a supertype of $G<S_1, ..., S_n>$, and let V $= H<?$ extends $U_1, ..., ?$ extends $U_l>[S_k=U]$. Then this algorithm is applied recursively to the constraint $A >> V$.

    > Our goal here is once more to simplify the relationship between A and F, and recursively invoke the algorithm on a simpler case, where the type argument is known to be an invocation of the same generic type as the formal.

    > Assume both H and G have only a single type argument. Since we have the constraint $A = H<X> >> F = G<?$ extends $U>$, where H is distinct from G, it must be the case that H is some proper superclass or superinterface of G. There must be an invocation of $H<Y>$, such that $H<X> >> H<Y>$, that we can use instead of $F = G<?$ extends $U>$.

    > How do we compute $H<Y>$? As before, note that the declaration of G must introduce a type parameter S, and there must be some (non-wildcard) invocation of H, $H<U_1>$, that is a supertype of $G<S>$. However, substituting $?$ extends U for S is not generally valid. To see this, assume $U_1 = T[]$.

    > Instead, we produce an invocation of H, $H<?$ extends $U_1>[S=U]$. In the simplest instance, U_1 might be S, in which case we have $G<S> <: H<S>$, and $G<?$ extends $U> <: H<?$ extends $U> = H<?$ extends $S>[S=U] = V$.

  ❖ Otherwise, if A is of the form $G<..., X_{k-1}, ?$ extends $W, X_{k+1}, ...>$, this algorithm is applied recursively to the constraint $W >> U$.

    > We have $A = G<?$ extends $W> >> F = G<?$ extends $U>$ for some type expression W. By the subtyping rules for wildcards it must be the case that $W >> U$.

  ❖ Otherwise, no constraint is implied on T_j.

- If F has the form $G<..., Y_{k-1}, ?$ super $U, Y_{k+1}, ...>$, where U is a type expression that involves T_j, then A is either:

  - If A is an instance of a non-generic type, then no constraint is implied on T_j.

    > Restricting the analysis to the unary case, we have the constraint $A >> F = G<?$ super $U>$. A must be a supertype of the generic type G. However, since A is not a parameterized type, it cannot depend upon U in any way. It is a supertype of the type $G<?$ super $X>$ for every X such that $?$ super X is a valid type argument to G. No meaningful constraint on U can be derived from A.

  - If A is an invocation of a generic type declaration H, where H is either G or superclass or superinterface of G, then:

❖ If $H \neq G$, then let $S_1, ..., S_n$ be the type parameters of G, and let H<$U_1, ..., U_l$> be the unique invocation of H that is a supertype of G<$S_1, ..., S_n$>, and let $V = H$<? super $U_1, ..., $? super U_l> $[S_k=U]$. Then this algorithm is applied recursively to the constraint $A >> V$.

> The treatment here is analogous to the case where $A = G$<? extends U>. Here our example would produce an invocation H<? super U_1> $[S=U]$.

❖ Otherwise, if A is of the form G<..., X_{k-1}, ? super W, ..., X_{k+1}, ...>, this algorithm is applied recursively to the constraint $W << U$.

> We have $A = G$<? super W> $>> F = G$<? super U> for some type expression W. It must be the case that $W << U$, by the subtyping rules for wildcard types.

❖ Otherwise, no constraint is implied on T_j.

This concludes the process of determining constraints on the type parameters of a method.

Note that this process does not impose any constraints on the type parameters based on their declared bounds. Once type arguments are inferred, they will be tested against the declared bounds of the type parameters as part of applicability testing.

Note also that type inference does not affect soundness in any way. If the types inferred are nonsensical, the invocation will yield a type error. The type inference algorithm should be viewed as a heuristic, designed to perform well in practice. If it fails to infer the desired result, explicit type paramneters may be used instead.

Next, for each type variable T_j $(1 \le j \le n)$, the implied equality constraints are resolved as follows.

For each implied equality constraint $T_j = U$ or $U = T_j$:

- If U is not one of the type parameters of the method, then U is the type inferred for T_j. Then all remaining constraints involving T_j are rewritten such that T_j is replaced with U. There are necessarily no further equality constraints involving T_j, and processing continues with the next type parameter, if any.

- Otherwise, if U is T_j, then this constraint carries no information and may be discarded.

- Otherwise, the constraint is of the form $T_j = T_k$ for $j \ne k$. Then all constraints involving T_j are rewritten such that T_j is replaced with T_k, and processing continues with the next type variable.

Then, for each remaining type variable T_j, the constraints $T_j :> U$ are considered. Given that these constraints are $T_j :> U_1 \ldots T_j :> U_k$, the type of T_j is inferred as lub($U_1 \ldots U_k$), computed as follows:

For a type U, we write ST(U) for the set of supertypes of U, and define the erased supertype set of U:

EST(U) = { v | w in ST(U) and $v = |w|$ } where $|w|$ is the erasure (§4.6) of w.

> The reason for computing the set of erased supertypes is to deal with situations where a type variable is constrained to be a supertype of several distinct invocations of a generic type declaration.

> For example, if $T :>$ List<String> and $T :>$ List<Object>, simply intersecting the sets ST(List<String>) = { List<String>, Collection<String>, Object } and ST(List<Object>) = { List<Object>, Collection<Object>, Object } would yield a set { Object }, and we would have lost track of the fact that T can safely be assumed to be a List.

> In contrast, intersecting EST(List<String>) = { List, Collection, Object } and EST(List<Object>) = { List, Collection, Object } yields { List, Collection, Object }, which we will eventually enable us to infer $T =$ List<?> as described below.

The erased candidate set for type parameter T_j, EC, is the intersection of all the sets EST(U) for each U in $U_1 \ldots U_k$.

The minimal erased candidate set for T_j is:

MEC = { v | v in EC, and for all $w \ne v$ in EC, it is not the case that $w <: v$ }

> Because we are seeking to infer more precise types, we wish to filter out any candidates that are supertypes of other candidates. This is what computing MEC accomplishes.

In our running example, we had EC = { List, Collection, Object }, and now MEC = { List }.

The next step will be to recover type arguments for the inferred types themselves.

For any element G of MEC that is a generic type declaration, define the relevant invocations of G, Inv(G), to be:

$$\text{Inv}(G) = \{ v \mid 1 \leq i \leq k: v \text{ in } \text{ST}(U_i), v = G<...> \}$$

In our running example, the only generic element of MEC is List, and Inv(List) = { List<String>, List<Object> }. We now will seek to find a type argument for List that contains (§4.5.1) both String and Object.

This is done by means of the *least containing invocation* (lci) operation defined below. The first line defines lci() on a set, such as Inv(List), as an operation on a list of the elements of the set. The next line defines the operation on such lists, as a pairwise reduction on the elements of the list. The third line is the definition of lci() on pairs of parameterized types, which in turn relies on the notion of *least containing type argument* (lcta).

lcta() is defined for all six possible cases. Then CandidateInvocation(G) defines the most specific invocation of the generic type G that contains all the invocations of G that are known to be supertypes of T_j. This will be our candidate invocation of G in the bound we infer for T_j.

Define CandidateInvocation(G) = lci(Inv(G)), where lci, the least containing invocation, is defined:

- $\text{lci}(S) = \text{lci}(e_1, ..., e_n)$ where e_i $(1 \leq i \leq n)$ in S

- $\text{lci}(e_1, ..., e_n) = \text{lci}(\text{lci}(e_1, e_2), e_3, ..., e_n)$

- $\text{lci}(G<X_1, ..., X_n>, G<Y_1, ..., Y_n>) = G<\text{lcta}(X_1, Y_1), ..., \text{lcta}(X_n, Y_n)>$

- $\text{lci}(G<X_1, ..., X_n>) = G<\text{lcta}(X_1), ..., \text{lcta}(X_n)>$

where lcta() is the least containing type argument function defined (assuming U and V are type expressions) as:

- $\text{lcta}(U, V) = U$ if $U = V$, otherwise ? extends $\text{lub}(U, V)$

- $\text{lcta}(U, \text{? extends } V) = $? extends $\text{lub}(U, V)$

- $\text{lcta}(U, \text{? super } V) = $? super $\text{glb}(U, V)$

- $\text{lcta}(\text{? extends } U, \text{? extends } V) = $? extends $\text{lub}(U, V)$

- $\text{lcta}(\text{? extends } U, \text{? super } V) = U$ if $U = V$, otherwise ?

- $\text{lcta}(\text{? super } U, \text{? super } V) = $? super $\text{glb}(U, V)$

- lcta(U) = ? if U's upper bound is `Object`, otherwise ? extends lub(U,`Object`)

where glb() is as defined in §5.1.10.

> Finally, we define a bound for T_j based on on all the elements of the minimal erased candidate set of its supertypes. If any of these elements are generic, we use the CandidateInvocation() function to recover the type argument information.

Define Candidate(W) = CandidateInvocation(W) if W is generic, W otherwise.

The inferred type for T_j, lub(U_1 ... U_k), is Candidate(W_1) & ... & Candidate(W_r), where W_i ($1 \leq i \leq r$) are the elements of MEC.

It is possible that the process above yields an infinite type. This is permissible, and a Java compiler must recognize such situations and represent them appropriately using cyclic data structures.

> The possibility of an infinite type stems from the recursive calls to lub(). Readers familiar with recursive types should note that an infinite type is not the same as a recursive type.

15.12.2.8   *Inferring Unresolved Type Arguments*

If any of the method's type arguments were not inferred from the types of the actual arguments, they are now inferred as follows.

- If the method result occurs in a context where it will be subject to assignment conversion (§5.2) to a type S, then let R be the declared result type of the method, and let $R' = R[T_1=B(T_1) ... T_n=B(T_n)]$, where $B(T_i)$ is the type inferred for T_i in the previous section or T_i if no type was inferred.

If S is a reference type, then let S' be S. Otherwise, if S is a primitive type, then let S' be the result of applying boxing conversion (§5.1.7) to S.

Then, a set of initial constraints consisting of:

- the constraint $S' >> R'$, provided R is not `void`; and

- additional constraints $B_i[T_1=B(T_1) ... T_n=B(T_n)] >> T_i$, where B_i is the declared bound of T_i,

- additional constraints $B(T_i) << B_i[T_1=B(T_1) ... T_n=B(T_n)]$, where B_i is the declared bound of T_i,

- for any constraint of the form $V >> T_i$ generated in §15.12.2.7: a constraint $V[T_1=B(T_1) ... T_n=B(T_n)] >> T_i$.

- for any constraint of the form $T_i = V$ generated in §15.12.2.7: a constraint $T_i = V[T_1=B(T_1) ... T_n=B(T_n)]$.

is created and used to infer constraints on the type arguments using the algorithm of §15.12.2.7.

Any equality constraints are resolved, and then, for each remaining constraint of the form $T_i <: U_k$, the argument T_i is inferred to be glb(U_1, ..., U_k) (§5.1.10).

If T_i appears as a type argument in any U_k, then T_i is inferred to be a type variable x whose upper bound is the parameterized type given by glb($U_1[T_i=X]$, ..., $U_k[T_i=X]$) and whose lower bound is the null type.

Any remaining type variable T that has not yet been inferred is then inferred to have type `Object`. If a previously inferred type variable P uses T, then P is inferred to be $P[T=\text{Object}]$.

- Otherwise, the unresolved type arguments are inferred by invoking the procedure described in this section under the assumption that the method result was assigned to a variable of type `Object`.

15.12.3   Compile-Time Step 3: Is the Chosen Method Appropriate?

If there is a most specific method declaration for a method invocation, it is called the *compile-time declaration* for the method invocation.

If the method invocation has, before the left parenthesis, a *MethodName* of the form *Identifier*, and the compile-time declaration is an instance method, then:

- If the method invocation occurs in a static context (§8.1.3), then a compile-time error occurs.

   The reason is that a method invocation of this form cannot be used to invoke an instance method in places where `this` (§15.8.3) is not defined.

- Otherwise, let c be the innermost enclosing class of which the compile-time declaration is a member.

   If the invocation is not directly enclosed by c or an inner class of c, then a compile-time error occurs.

If the method invocation has, before the left parenthesis, a *MethodName* of the form *TypeName . Identifier*, or if the method invocation, before the left parenthesis, has the form *TypeName . NonWildTypeArguments Identifier*, then the compile-time declaration must be `static`, or a compile-time error occurs.

   The reason is that a method invocation of this form does not specify a reference to an object that can serve as this within the instance method.

If the method invocation has, before the left parenthesis, the form `super` . *NonWildTypeArguments*$_{opt}$ *Identifier*, then:

- If the compile-time declaration is `abstract`, a compile-time error occurs.

- If the method invocation occurs in a static context, a compile-time error occurs.

If the method invocation has, before the left parenthesis, the form *ClassName* . `super` . *NonWildTypeArguments*$_{opt}$ *Identifier*, then:

- If the compile-time declaration is `abstract`, a compile-time error occurs.

- If the method invocation occurs in a static context, a compile-time error occurs.

- Otherwise, let *c* be the class denoted by *ClassName*.

  If the invocation is not directly enclosed by *c* or an inner class of *c*, then a compile-time error occurs.

If the compile-time declaration is `void`, then the method invocation must be a top level expression (that is, the *Expression* in an expression statement (§14.8) or in the *ForInit* or *ForUpdate* part of a `for` statement (§14.14)), or a compile-time error occurs.

> The reason is that such a method invocation produces no value and so must be used only in a situation where a value is not needed.

A method is *signature polymorphic* if and only if all of the following conditions hold:

- It is declared in the `java.lang.invoke.MethodHandle` class.

- It takes a single variable arity parameter (§8.4.1) whose declared type is `Object[]`.

- It has a return type of `Object`.

- It is `native`.

> In Java SE 7, the only signature polymorphic methods are the `invoke` and `invokeExact` methods of the class `java.lang.invoke.MethodHandle`.

If the compile-time declaration for the method invocation is *not* a signature polymorphic method, then the types of its parameters are the types of its formal parameters, and the result type is its chosen result type.

Otherwise, if the compile-time declaration for the method invocation is a signature polymorphic method, then:

- The types of its parameters are the static types of the actual argument expressions.

  An argument expression which is the null literal null (§3.10.7) is treated as having the static type Void.

- The result type is determined as follows:

  - If the method invocation expression is an expression statement, the method is void.

  - Otherwise, if the method invocation expression is the operand of a cast expression (§15.16), the return type is the erasure (§4.6) of the type of the cast expression.

  - Otherwise, the return type is the method's declared return type, Object.

The following compile-time information is then associated with the method invocation for use at run time:

- The name of the method.

- The qualifying type of the method invocation (§13.1).

- The number of parameters and the types of the parameters, in order.

- The result type, or void.

- The invocation mode, computed as follows:

  - If the compile-time declaration has the static modifier, then the invocation mode is static.

  - Otherwise, if the compile-time declaration has the private modifier, then the invocation mode is nonvirtual.

  - Otherwise, if the part of the method invocation before the left parenthesis is of the form super . *Identifier* or of the form *ClassName* . super . *Identifier*, then the invocation mode is super.

  - Otherwise, if the compile-time declaration is in an interface, then the invocation mode is interface.

  - Otherwise, the invocation mode is virtual.

If the compile-time declaration for the method invocation is not void, then the type of the method invocation expression is the result type specified in the compile-time declaration.

15.12.4 Run-Time Evaluation of Method Invocation

At run time, method invocation requires five steps. First, a *target reference* may be computed. Second, the argument expressions are evaluated. Third, the accessibility of the method to be invoked is checked. Fourth, the actual code for the method to be executed is located. Fifth, a new activation frame is created, synchronization is performed if necessary, and control is transferred to the method code.

15.12.4.1 *Compute Target Reference (If Necessary)*

There are several cases to consider, depending on which of the five productions for *MethodInvocation* (§15.12) is involved:

1. If the first production for MethodInvocation, which includes a *MethodName*, is involved, then there are three subcases:

    - If the *MethodName* is a simple name, that is, just an *Identifier*, then there are two subcases:

        • If the invocation mode is `static`, then there is no target reference.

        • Otherwise, let *T* be the enclosing type declaration of which the method is a member, and let *n* be an integer such that *T* is the *n*'th lexically enclosing type declaration (§8.1.3) of the class whose declaration immediately contains the method invocation. Then the target reference is the *n*'th lexically enclosing instance (§8.1.3) of `this`.

          It is a compile-time error if the *n*'th lexically enclosing instance (§8.1.3) of `this` does not exist.

    - If the *MethodName* is a qualified name of the form *TypeName* . *Identifier*, then there is no target reference.

    - If the *MethodName* is a qualified name of the form *FieldName* . *Identifier*, then there are two subcases:

        • If the invocation mode is `static`, then there is no target reference. The expression *FieldName* is evaluated, but the result is then discarded.

        • Otherwise, the target reference is the value of the expression *FieldName*.

2. If the second production for *MethodInvocation*, which includes a *Primary*, is involved, then there are two subcases:

    - If the invocation mode is `static`, then there is no target reference. The expression *Primary* is evaluated, but the result is then discarded.

- Otherwise, the expression *Primary* is evaluated and the result is used as the target reference.

In either case, if the evaluation of the *Primary* expression completes abruptly, then no part of any argument expression appears to have been evaluated, and the method invocation completes abruptly for the same reason.

3. If the third production for *MethodInvocation*, which includes the keyword super, is involved, then the target reference is the value of this.

4. If the fourth production for *MethodInvocation*, *ClassName* . super, is involved, then the target reference is the value of *ClassName*.this.

5. If the fifth production for *MethodInvocation*, beginning with *TypeName* . *NonWildTypeArguments*, is involved, then there is no target reference.

Example 15.12.4.1-1. Target References and static **Methods**

When a target reference is computed and then discarded because the invocation mode is static, the reference is not examined to see whether it is null:

```
class Test1 {
    static void mountain() {
        System.out.println("Monadnock");
    }
    static Test1 favorite(){
        System.out.print("Mount ");
        return null;
    }
    public static void main(String[] args) {
        favorite().mountain();
    }
}
```

which prints:

```
Mount Monadnock
```

Here favorite() returns null, yet no NullPointerException is thrown.

Example 15.12.4.1-2. Evaluation Order During Method Invocation

As part of an instance method invocation (§15.12), there is an expression that denotes the object to be invoked. This expression appears to be fully evaluated before any part of any argument expression to the method invocation is evaluated.

So, for example, in:

```
class Test2 {
```

```
public static void main(String[] args) {
    String s = "one";
    if (s.startsWith(s = "two"))
        System.out.println("oops");
}
}
```

the occurrence of s before ".startsWith" is evaluated first, before the argument expression s = "two". Therefore, a reference to the string "one" is remembered as the target reference before the local variable s is changed to refer to the string "two". As a result, the startsWith method is invoked for target object "one" with argument "two", so the result of the invocation is false, as the string "one" does not start with "two". It follows that the test program does not print "oops".

15.12.4.2 *Evaluate Arguments*

The process of evaluating the argument list differs, depending on whether the method being invoked is a fixed arity method or a variable arity method (§8.4.1).

If the method being invoked is a variable arity method m, it necessarily has $n > 0$ formal parameters. The final formal parameter of m necessarily has type $T[]$ for some T, and m is necessarily being invoked with $k \geq 0$ actual argument expressions.

If m is being invoked with $k \neq n$ actual argument expressions, or, if m is being invoked with $k = n$ actual argument expressions and the type of the k'th argument expression is not assignment compatible with $T[]$, then the argument list ($e_1, ..., e_{n-1}, e_n, ..., e_k$) is evaluated as if it were written as ($e_1, ..., e_{n-1}, \text{new } |T[]| \{ e_n, ..., e_k \}$), where $|T[]|$ denotes the erasure (§4.6) of $T[]$.

> The preceding paragraphs are crafted to handle the interaction of parameterized types and array types that occurs in a Java Virtual Machine with erased generics. Namely, if the element type T of the variable array parameter is non-reifiable, e.g. List<String>, then special care must be taken with the array creation expression (§15.10) because the created array's element type must be reifiable. By erasing the array type of the final expression in the argument list, we are guaranteed to obtain a reifiable element type. Then, since the array creation expression appears in a method invocation context, an unchecked conversion (§5.1.9) is possible from the array type with reifiable element type to an array type with non-reifiable element type, specifically that of the variable arity parameter. A Java compiler is required by §5.1.9 to give a compile-time unchecked warning at this conversion. Oracle's reference implementation of a Java compiler identifies the unchecked warning here as a more informative *unchecked generic array creation*.

The argument expressions (possibly rewritten as described above) are now evaluated to yield *argument values*. Each argument value corresponds to exactly one of the method's n formal parameters.

The argument expressions, if any, are evaluated in order, from left to right. If the evaluation of any argument expression completes abruptly, then no part of any argument expression to its right appears to have been evaluated, and the method invocation completes abruptly for the same reason. The result of evaluating the *j*'th argument expression is the *j*'th argument value, for $1 \leq j \leq n$. Evaluation then continues, using the argument values, as described below.

15.12.4.3   *Check Accessibility of Type and Method*

Let *C* be the class containing the method invocation, and let *T* be the qualifying type of the method invocation (§13.1), and let *m* be the name of the method as determined at compile time (§15.12.3).

An implementation of the Java programming language must ensure, as part of linkage, that the method *m* still exists in the type *T*. If this is not true, then a `NoSuchMethodError` (which is a subclass of `IncompatibleClassChangeError`) occurs.

If the invocation mode is `interface`, then the implementation must also check that the target reference type still implements the specified interface. If the target reference type does not still implement the interface, then an `IncompatibleClassChangeError` occurs.

The implementation must also ensure, during linkage, that the type *T* and the method *m* are accessible:

- For the type *T*:

  - If *T* is in the same package as *C*, then *T* is accessible.

  - If *T* is in a different package than *C*, and *T* is `public`, then *T* is accessible.

  - If *T* is in a different package than *C*, and *T* is `protected`, then *T* is accessible if and only if *C* is a subclass of *T*.

- For the method *m*:

  - If *m* is `public`, then *m* is accessible. (All members of interfaces are `public` (§9.2).)

  - If *m* is `protected`, then *m* is accessible if and only if either *T* is in the same package as *C*, or *C* is *T* or a subclass of *T*.

  - If *m* has default (package) access, then *m* is accessible if and only if *T* is in the same package as *C*.

  - If *m* is `private`, then *m* is accessible if and only if *C* is *T*, or *C* encloses *T*, or *T* encloses *C*, or *T* and *C* are both enclosed by a third class.

If either *T* or *m* is not accessible, then an `IllegalAccessError` occurs (§12.3).

15.12.4.4 *Locate Method to Invoke*

The strategy for method lookup depends on the invocation mode.

If the invocation mode is `static`, no target reference is needed and overriding is not allowed. Method *m* of class *T* is the one to be invoked.

Otherwise, an instance method is to be invoked and there is a target reference. If the target reference is `null`, a `NullPointerException` is thrown at this point. Otherwise, the target reference is said to refer to a *target object* and will be used as the value of the keyword `this` in the invoked method. The other four possibilities for the invocation mode are then considered.

If the invocation mode is `nonvirtual`, overriding is not allowed. Method *m* of class *T* is the one to be invoked.

Otherwise, if the invocation mode is `virtual`, and *T* and *m* jointly indicate a signature polymorphic method (§15.12.3), then the target object is an instance of `java.lang.invoke.MethodHandle`. The method handle encapsulates a *type* which is matched against the information associated with the method invocation at compile time (§15.12.3). Details of this matching are given in *The Java Virtual Machine Specification, Java SE 7 Edition* and the Java SE platform API. If matching succeeds, the *target method* encapsulated by the method handle is directly and immediately invoked, *and the procedure in §15.12.4.5 is not executed.*

Otherwise, the invocation mode is `interface`, `virtual`, or `super`, and overriding may occur. A *dynamic method lookup* is used. The dynamic lookup process starts from a class *S*, determined as follows:

- If the invocation mode is `interface` or `virtual`, then *S* is initially the actual run-time class *R* of the target object.

    > This is true even if the target object is an array instance. (Note that for invocation mode `interface`, *R* necessarily implements *T*; for invocation mode `virtual`, *R* is necessarily either *T* or a subclass of *T*.)

- If the invocation mode is `super`, then *S* is initially the qualifying type (§13.1) of the method invocation.

The dynamic method lookup uses the following procedure to search class *S*, and then the superclasses of class *S*, as necessary, for method *m*.

Let *X* be the compile-time type of the target reference of the method invocation. Then:

1. If class *S* contains a declaration for a non-`abstract` method named *m* with the same descriptor (same number of parameters, the same parameter types, and the

same return type) required by the method invocation as determined at compile time (§15.12.3), then:

- If the invocation mode is `super` or `interface`, then this is the method to be invoked, and the procedure terminates.

- If the invocation mode is `virtual`, and the declaration in *s* overrides (§8.4.8.1) *x.m*, then the method declared in *s* is the method to be invoked, and the procedure terminates.

- If the invocation mode is `virtual`, and the declaration in *s* does not override *x.m*, and moreover *x.m* is declared `abstract`, then an `AbstractMethodError` is thrown.

2. Otherwise, if *s* has a superclass, this same lookup procedure is performed recursively using the direct superclass of *s* in place of *s*; the method to be invoked is the result of the recursive invocation of this lookup procedure.

The above procedure (if it terminates without error) will find a non-`abstract`, accessible method to invoke, provided that all classes and interfaces in the program have been consistently compiled. However, if this is not the case, then various errors may occur. The specification of the behavior of a Java Virtual Machine under these circumstances is given by *The Java Virtual Machine Specification, Java SE 7 Edition*.

We note that the dynamic lookup process, while described here explicitly, will often be implemented implicitly, for example as a side-effect of the construction and use of per-class method dispatch tables, or the construction of other per-class structures used for efficient dispatch.

Example 15.12.4.4-1. Overriding and Method Invocation

```
class Point {
    final int EDGE = 20;
    int x, y;
    void move(int dx, int dy) {
        x += dx; y += dy;
        if (Math.abs(x) >= EDGE || Math.abs(y) >= EDGE)
            clear();
    }
    void clear() {
        System.out.println("\tPoint clear");
        x = 0; y = 0;
    }
}
class ColoredPoint extends Point {
    int color;
    void clear() {
        System.out.println("\tColoredPoint clear");
```

```
        super.clear();
        color = 0;
    }
}
```

Here, the subclass `ColoredPoint` extends the `clear` abstraction defined by its superclass `Point`. It does so by overriding the `clear` method with its own method, which invokes the `clear` method of its superclass, using the form `super.clear()`.

This method is then invoked whenever the target object for an invocation of `clear` is a `ColoredPoint`. Even the method `move` in `Point` invokes the `clear` method of class `ColoredPoint` when the class of `this` is `ColoredPoint`, as shown by the output of this test program:

```
class Test1 {
    public static void main(String[] args) {
        Point p = new Point();
        System.out.println("p.move(20,20):");
        p.move(20, 20);

        ColoredPoint cp = new ColoredPoint();
        System.out.println("cp.move(20,20):");
        cp.move(20, 20);

        p = new ColoredPoint();
        System.out.println("p.move(20,20), p colored:");
        p.move(20, 20);
    }
}
```

which is:

```
p.move(20,20):
        Point clear
cp.move(20,20):
        ColoredPoint clear
        Point clear
p.move(20,20), p colored:
        ColoredPoint clear
        Point clear
```

Overriding is sometimes called "late-bound self-reference"; in this example it means that the reference to `clear` in the body of `Point.move` (which is really syntactic shorthand for `this.clear`) invokes a method chosen "late" (at run time, based on the run-time class of the object referenced by `this`) rather than a method chosen "early" (at compile time, based only on the type of `this`). This provides the programmer a powerful way of extending abstractions and is a key idea in object-oriented programming.

Example 15.12.4.4-2. Method Invocation Using `super`

An overridden instance method of a superclass may be accessed by using the keyword `super` to access the members of the immediate superclass, bypassing any overriding declaration in the class that contains the method invocation.

When accessing an instance variable, `super` means the same as a cast of `this` (§15.11.2), but this equivalence does not hold true for method invocation. This is demonstrated by the example:

```
class T1 {
    String s() { return "1"; }
}
class T2 extends T1 {
    String s() { return "2"; }
}
class T3 extends T2 {
    String s() { return "3"; }
    void test() {
        System.out.println("s()=\t\t"        + s());
        System.out.println("super.s()=\t"     + super.s());
        System.out.println("((T2)this).s()=\t" + ((T2)this).s());
        System.out.println("((T1)this).s()=\t" + ((T1)this).s());
    }
}
class Test2 {
    public static void main(String[] args) {
        T3 t3 = new T3();
        t3.test();
    }
}
```

which produces the output:

```
s()=                3
super.s()=          2
((T2)this).s()= 3
((T1)this).s()= 3
```

The casts to types `T1` and `T2` do not change the method that is invoked, because the instance method to be invoked is chosen according to the run-time class of the object referred to by `this`. A cast does not change the class of an object; it only checks that the class is compatible with the specified type.

15.12.4.5   *Create Frame, Synchronize, Transfer Control*

A method *m* in some class *s* has been identified as the one to be invoked.

Now a new *activation frame* is created, containing the target reference (if any) and the argument values (if any), as well as enough space for the local variables and stack for the method to be invoked and any other bookkeeping information that may be required by the implementation (stack pointer, program counter, reference to previous activation frame, and the like). If there is not sufficient memory available to create such an activation frame, a `StackOverflowError` is thrown.

The newly created activation frame becomes the current activation frame. The effect of this is to assign the argument values to corresponding freshly created parameter variables of the method, and to make the target reference available as `this`, if there is a target reference. Before each argument value is assigned to its corresponding parameter variable, it is subjected to method invocation conversion (§5.3), which includes any required value set conversion (§5.1.13).

If the erasure (§4.6) of the type of the method being invoked differs in its signature from the erasure of the type of the compile-time declaration for the method invocation (§15.12.3), then if any of the argument values is an object which is not an instance of a subclass or subinterface of the erasure of the corresponding formal parameter type in the compile-time declaration for the method invocation, then a `ClassCastException` is thrown.

If the method *m* is a `native` method but the necessary native, implementation-dependent binary code has not been loaded or otherwise cannot be dynamically linked, then an `UnsatisfiedLinkError` is thrown.

If the method *m* is not `synchronized`, control is transferred to the body of the method *m* to be invoked.

If the method *m* is `synchronized`, then an object must be locked before the transfer of control. No further progress can be made until the current thread can obtain the lock. If there is a target reference, then the target object must be locked; otherwise the `Class` object for class *s*, the class of the method *m*, must be locked. Control is then transferred to the body of the method *m* to be invoked. The object is automatically unlocked when execution of the body of the method has completed, whether normally or abruptly. The locking and unlocking behavior is exactly as if the body of the method were embedded in a `synchronized` statement (§14.19).

Example 15.12.4.5-1. Invoked Method Signature Has Different Erasure Than Compile-Time Method Signature

Consider the declarations:

```
abstract class C<T> {
    abstract T id(T x);
}
class D extends C<String> {
    String id(String x) { return x; }
}
```

Now, given an invocation:

```
C c = new D();
c.id(new Object());  // fails with a ClassCastException
```

The erasure of the actual method being invoked, `D.id()`, differs in its signature from that of the compile-time method declaration, `C.id()`. The former takes an argument of type `String` while the latter takes an argument of type `Object`. The invocation fails with a `ClassCastException` before the body of the method is executed.

Such situations can only arise if the program gives rise to a compile-time unchecked warning (§4.8, §5.1.9, §5.5.2, §8.4.1, §8.4.8.3, §8.4.8.4, §9.4.1.2, §15.12.4.2).

Implementations can enforce these semantics by creating *bridge methods*. In the above example, the following bridge method would be created in class `D`:

```
Object id(Object x) { return id((String) x); }
```

This is the method that would actually be invoked by the Java Virtual Machine in response to the call `c.id(new Object())` shown above, and it will execute the cast and fail, as required.

15.13   Array Access Expressions

An array access expression refers to a variable that is a component of an array.

> *ArrayAccess:*
>   *ExpressionName* [*Expression*]
>   *PrimaryNoNewArray* [*Expression*]

An array access expression contains two subexpressions, the *array reference expression* (before the left bracket) and the *index expression* (within the brackets).

> Note that the array reference expression may be a name or any primary expression that is not an array creation expression (§15.10).

The type of the array reference expression must be an array type (call it $T[]$, an array whose components are of type T), or a compile-time error occurs.

The index expression undergoes unary numeric promotion (§5.6.1). The promoted type must be `int`, or a compile-time error occurs.

The type of the array access expression is the result of applying capture conversion (§5.1.10) to T.

The result of an array access expression is a variable of type T, namely the variable within the array selected by the value of the index expression.

This resulting variable, which is a component of the array, is never considered `final`, even if the array reference expression denoted a `final` variable.

15.13.1   Run-Time Evaluation of Array Access

An array access expression is evaluated using the following procedure:

- First, the array reference expression is evaluated. If this evaluation completes abruptly, then the array access completes abruptly for the same reason and the index expression is not evaluated.

- Otherwise, the index expression is evaluated. If this evaluation completes abruptly, then the array access completes abruptly for the same reason.

- Otherwise, if the value of the array reference expression is `null`, then a `NullPointerException` is thrown.

- Otherwise, the value of the array reference expression indeed refers to an array. If the value of the index expression is less than zero, or greater than or equal to the array's `length`, then an `ArrayIndexOutOfBoundsException` is thrown.

- Otherwise, the result of the array access is the variable of type T, within the array, selected by the value of the index expression.

Example 15.13-1. Array Reference Is Evaluated First

In an array access, the expression to the left of the brackets appears to be fully evaluated before any part of the expression within the brackets is evaluated. For example, in the (admittedly monstrous) expression `a[(a=b)[3]]`, the expression `a` is fully evaluated before the expression `(a=b)[3]`; this means that the original value of `a` is fetched and remembered while the expression `(a=b)[3]` is evaluated. This array referenced by the original value of `a` is then subscripted by a value that is element 3 of another array (possibly the same array) that was referenced by `b` and is now also referenced by `a`.

Thus, the program:

```
class Test1 {
    public static void main(String[] args) {
        int[] a = { 11, 12, 13, 14 };
        int[] b = { 0, 1, 2, 3 };
        System.out.println(a[(a=b)[3]]);
    }
}
```

prints:

14

because the monstrous expression's value is equivalent to a[b[3]] or a[3] or 14.

Example 15.13-2. Abrupt Completion of Array Reference Evaluation

If evaluation of the expression to the left of the brackets completes abruptly, no part of the expression within the brackets will appear to have been evaluated. Thus, the program:

```
class Test2 {
    public static void main(String[] args) {
        int index = 1;
        try {
            skedaddle()[index=2]++;
        } catch (Exception e) {
            System.out.println(e + ", index=" + index);
        }
    }
    static int[] skedaddle() throws Exception {
        throw new Exception("Ciao");
    }
}
```

prints:

```
java.lang.Exception: Ciao, index=1
```

because the embedded assignment of 2 to index never occurs.

Example 15.13-3. null Array Reference

If the array reference expression produces null instead of a reference to an array, then a NullPointerException is thrown at run time, but only after all parts of the array access expression have been evaluated and only if these evaluations completed normally. Thus, the program:

```
class Test3 {
    public static void main(String[] args) {
        int index = 1;
        try {
            nada()[index=2]++;
        } catch (Exception e) {
            System.out.println(e + ", index=" + index);
        }
    }
    static int[] nada() { return null; }
}
```

prints:

```
java.lang.NullPointerException, index=2
```

because the embedded assignment of 2 to `index` occurs before the check for a `null` array reference expression. As a related example, the program:

```
class Test4 {
    public static void main(String[] args) {
        int[] a = null;
        try {
            int i = a[vamoose()];
            System.out.println(i);
        } catch (Exception e) {
            System.out.println(e);
        }
    }
    static int vamoose() throws Exception {
        throw new Exception("Twenty-three skidoo!");
    }
}
```

always prints:

```
java.lang.Exception: Twenty-three skidoo!
```

A `NullPointerException` never occurs, because the index expression must be completely evaluated before any part of the array access occurs, and that includes the check as to whether the value of the array reference expression is `null`.

15.14 Postfix Expressions

Postfix expressions include uses of the postfix ++ and -- operators. Names are not considered to be primary expressions (§15.8), but are handled separately in the grammar to avoid certain ambiguities. They become interchangeable only here, at the level of precedence of postfix expressions.

> *PostfixExpression:*
>   *Primary*
>   *ExpressionName*
>   *PostIncrementExpression*
>   *PostDecrementExpression*

15.14.1 Expression Names

The rules for evaluating expression names are given in §6.5.6.

15.14.2   Postfix Increment Operator ++

A postfix expression followed by a ++ operator is a postfix increment expression.

> *PostIncrementExpression:*
>   *PostfixExpression* ++

The result of the postfix expression must be a variable of a type that is convertible (§5.1.8) to a numeric type, or a compile-time error occurs.

The type of the postfix increment expression is the type of the variable. The result of the postfix increment expression is not a variable, but a value.

At run time, if evaluation of the operand expression completes abruptly, then the postfix increment expression completes abruptly for the same reason and no incrementation occurs. Otherwise, the value 1 is added to the value of the variable and the sum is stored back into the variable. Before the addition, binary numeric promotion (§5.6.2) is performed on the value 1 and the value of the variable. If necessary, the sum is narrowed by a narrowing primitive conversion (§5.1.3) and/ or subjected to boxing conversion (§5.1.7) to the type of the variable before it is stored. The value of the postfix increment expression is the value of the variable *before* the new value is stored.

> Note that the binary numeric promotion mentioned above may include unboxing conversion (§5.1.8) and value set conversion (§5.1.13). If necessary, value set conversion is applied to the sum prior to its being stored in the variable.

A variable that is declared `final` cannot be incremented because when an access of such a `final` variable is used as an expression, the result is a value, not a variable. Thus, it cannot be used as the operand of a postfix increment operator.

15.14.3   Postfix Decrement Operator --

A postfix expression followed by a -- operator is a postfix decrement expression.

> *PostDecrementExpression:*
>   *PostfixExpression* --

The result of the postfix expression must be a variable of a type that is convertible (§5.1.8) to a numeric type, or a compile-time error occurs.

The type of the postfix decrement expression is the type of the variable. The result of the postfix decrement expression is not a variable, but a value.

At run time, if evaluation of the operand expression completes abruptly, then the postfix decrement expression completes abruptly for the same reason and no decrementation occurs. Otherwise, the value 1 is subtracted from the value of the variable and the difference is stored back into the variable. Before the subtraction, binary numeric promotion (§5.6.2) is performed on the value 1 and the value of the variable. If necessary, the difference is narrowed by a narrowing primitive conversion (§5.1.3) and/or subjected to boxing conversion (§5.1.7) to the type of the variable before it is stored. The value of the postfix decrement expression is the value of the variable *before* the new value is stored.

> Note that the binary numeric promotion mentioned above may include unboxing conversion (§5.1.8) and value set conversion (§5.1.13). If necessary, value set conversion is applied to the difference prior to its being stored in the variable.

A variable that is declared `final` cannot be decremented because when an access of such a `final` variable is used as an expression, the result is a value, not a variable. Thus, it cannot be used as the operand of a postfix decrement operator.

15.15   Unary Operators

The operators +, -, ++, --, ~, !, and the cast operator (§15.16) are called the *unary operators*.

UnaryExpression:
  PreIncrementExpression
  PreDecrementExpression
  + *UnaryExpression*
  – *UnaryExpression*
  UnaryExpressionNotPlusMinus

PreIncrementExpression:
  ++ *UnaryExpression*

PreDecrementExpression:
  –– *UnaryExpression*

UnaryExpressionNotPlusMinus:
  PostfixExpression
  ~ *UnaryExpression*
  ! *UnaryExpression*
  CastExpression

Expressions with unary operators group right-to-left, so that `-~x` means the same as `-(~x)`.

15.15.1   Prefix Increment Operator ++

A unary expression preceded by a `++` operator is a prefix increment expression.

The result of the unary expression must be a variable of a type that is convertible (§5.1.8) to a numeric type, or a compile-time error occurs.

The type of the prefix increment expression is the type of the variable. The result of the prefix increment expression is not a variable, but a value.

At run time, if evaluation of the operand expression completes abruptly, then the prefix increment expression completes abruptly for the same reason and no incrementation occurs. Otherwise, the value `1` is added to the value of the variable and the sum is stored back into the variable. Before the addition, binary numeric promotion (§5.6.2) is performed on the value `1` and the value of the variable. If necessary, the sum is narrowed by a narrowing primitive conversion (§5.1.3) and/ or subjected to boxing conversion (§5.1.7) to the type of the variable before it is stored. The value of the prefix increment expression is the value of the variable *after* the new value is stored.

Note that the binary numeric promotion mentioned above may include unboxing conversion (§5.1.8) and value set conversion (§5.1.13). If necessary, value set conversion is applied to the sum prior to its being stored in the variable.

A variable that is declared `final` cannot be incremented because when an access of such a `final` variable is used as an expression, the result is a value, not a variable. Thus, it cannot be used as the operand of a prefix increment operator.

15.15.2 Prefix Decrement Operator `--`

A unary expression preceded by a `--` operator is a prefix decrement expression.

The result of the unary expression must be a variable of a type that is convertible (§5.1.8) to a numeric type, or a compile-time error occurs.

The type of the prefix decrement expression is the type of the variable. The result of the prefix decrement expression is not a variable, but a value.

At run time, if evaluation of the operand expression completes abruptly, then the prefix decrement expression completes abruptly for the same reason and no decrementation occurs. Otherwise, the value 1 is subtracted from the value of the variable and the difference is stored back into the variable. Before the subtraction, binary numeric promotion (§5.6.2) is performed on the value 1 and the value of the variable. If necessary, the difference is narrowed by a narrowing primitive conversion (§5.1.3) and/or subjected to boxing conversion (§5.1.7) to the type of the variable before it is stored. The value of the prefix decrement expression is the value of the variable *after* the new value is stored.

Note that the binary numeric promotion mentioned above may include unboxing conversion (§5.1.8) and value set conversion (§5.1.13). If necessary, format conversion is applied to the difference prior to its being stored in the variable.

A variable that is declared `final` cannot be decremented because when an access of such a `final` variable is used as an expression, the result is a value, not a variable. Thus, it cannot be used as the operand of a prefix decrement operator.

15.15.3 Unary Plus Operator `+`

The type of the operand expression of the unary + operator must be a type that is convertible (§5.1.8) to a primitive numeric type, or a compile-time error occurs.

Unary numeric promotion (§5.6.1) is performed on the operand. The type of the unary plus expression is the promoted type of the operand. The result of the unary plus expression is not a variable, but a value, even if the result of the operand expression is a variable.

At run time, the value of the unary plus expression is the promoted value of the operand.

15.15.4 Unary Minus Operator –

The type of the operand expression of the unary – operator must be a type that is convertible (§5.1.8) to a primitive numeric type, or a compile-time error occurs.

Unary numeric promotion (§5.6.1) is performed on the operand.

The type of the unary minus expression is the promoted type of the operand.

Note that unary numeric promotion performs value set conversion (§5.1.13). Whatever value set the promoted operand value is drawn from, the unary negation operation is carried out and the result is drawn from that same value set. That result is then subject to further value set conversion.

At run time, the value of the unary minus expression is the arithmetic negation of the promoted value of the operand.

For integer values, negation is the same as subtraction from zero. The Java programming language uses two's-complement representation for integers, and the range of two's-complement values is not symmetric, so negation of the maximum negative `int` or `long` results in that same maximum negative number. Overflow occurs in this case, but no exception is thrown. For all integer values `x`, `-x` equals `(~x)+1`.

For floating-point values, negation is *not* the same as subtraction from zero, because if `x` is `+0.0`, then `0.0-x` is `+0.0`, but `-x` is `-0.0`. Unary minus merely inverts the sign of a floating-point number. Special cases of interest:

• If the operand is NaN, the result is NaN. (Recall that NaN has no sign (§4.2.3).)

• If the operand is an infinity, the result is the infinity of opposite sign.

• If the operand is a zero, the result is the zero of opposite sign.

15.15.5 Bitwise Complement Operator ~

The type of the operand expression of the unary ~ operator must be a type that is convertible (§5.1.8) to a primitive integral type, or a compile-time error occurs.

Unary numeric promotion (§5.6.1) is performed on the operand. The type of the unary bitwise complement expression is the promoted type of the operand.

At run time, the value of the unary bitwise complement expression is the bitwise complement of the promoted value of the operand. In all cases, ~x equals `(-x)-1`.

15.15.6 Logical Complement Operator !

The type of the operand expression of the unary `!` operator must be `boolean` or `Boolean`, or a compile-time error occurs.

The type of the unary logical complement expression is `boolean`.

At run time, the operand is subject to unboxing conversion (§5.1.8) if necessary. The value of the unary logical complement expression is `true` if the (possibly converted) operand value is `false`, and `false` if the (possibly converted) operand value is `true`.

15.16 Cast Expressions

A cast expression converts, at run time, a value of one numeric type to a similar value of another numeric type; or confirms, at compile time, that the type of an expression is `boolean`; or checks, at run time, that a reference value refers to an object whose class is compatible with a specified reference type.

The parentheses and the type they contain are sometimes called the *cast operator*.

CastExpression:
  (*PrimitiveType*) *UnaryExpression*
  (*ReferenceType*) *UnaryExpressionNotPlusMinus*

See §15.15 for a discussion of the distinction between *UnaryExpression* and *UnaryExpressionNotPlusMinus*.

The type of a cast expression is the result of applying capture conversion (§5.1.10) to the type whose name appears within the parentheses.

The result of a cast expression is not a variable, but a value, even if the result of the operand expression is a variable.

A cast operator has no effect on the choice of value set (§4.2.3) for a value of type `float` or type `double`. Consequently, a cast to type `float` within an expression that is not FP-strict (§15.4) does not necessarily cause its value to be converted to an element of the float value set, and a cast to type `double` within an expression that is not FP-strict does not necessarily cause its value to be converted to an element of the double value set.

It is a compile-time error if the compile-time type of the operand may never be cast to the type specified by the cast operator according to the rules of casting conversion (§5.5).

> Some casts result in an error at compile time. Some casts can be proven, at compile time, always to be correct at run time. For example, it is always correct to convert a value of a class type to the type of its superclass; such a cast should require no special action at run time. Finally, some casts cannot be proven to be either always correct or always incorrect at compile time. Such casts require a test at run time. See §5.5 for details.

Otherwise, at run time, the operand value is converted (if necessary) by casting conversion to the type specified by the cast operator.

A `ClassCastException` is thrown if a cast is found at run time to be impermissible.

15.17 Multiplicative Operators

The operators `*`, `/`, and `%` are called the *multiplicative operators*.

> *MultiplicativeExpression:*
>   *UnaryExpression*
>   *MultiplicativeExpression * UnaryExpression*
>   *MultiplicativeExpression / UnaryExpression*
>   *MultiplicativeExpression % UnaryExpression*

The multiplicative operators have the same precedence and are syntactically left-associative (they group left-to-right).

The type of each of the operands of a multiplicative operator must be a type that is convertible (§5.1.8) to a primitive numeric type, or a compile-time error occurs.

Binary numeric promotion is performed on the operands (§5.6.2).

> Note that binary numeric promotion performs value set conversion (§5.1.13) and may perform unboxing conversion (§5.1.8).

The type of a multiplicative expression is the promoted type of its operands.

If the promoted type is `int` or `long`, then integer arithmetic is performed.

If the promoted type is `float` or `double`, then floating-point arithmetic is performed.

15.17.1 Multiplication Operator *

The binary * operator performs multiplication, producing the product of its operands.

Multiplication is a commutative operation if the operand expressions have no side effects.

Integer multiplication is associative when the operands are all of the same type.

Floating-point multiplication is not associative.

If an integer multiplication overflows, then the result is the low-order bits of the mathematical product as represented in some sufficiently large two's-complement format. As a result, if overflow occurs, then the sign of the result may not be the same as the sign of the mathematical product of the two operand values.

The result of a floating-point multiplication is determined by the rules of IEEE 754 arithmetic:

- If either operand is NaN, the result is NaN.

- If the result is not NaN, the sign of the result is positive if both operands have the same sign, and negative if the operands have different signs.

- Multiplication of an infinity by a zero results in NaN.

- Multiplication of an infinity by a finite value results in a signed infinity. The sign is determined by the rule stated above.

- In the remaining cases, where neither an infinity nor NaN is involved, the exact mathematical product is computed. A floating-point value set is then chosen:

  - If the multiplication expression is FP-strict (§15.4):

    - If the type of the multiplication expression is `float`, then the float value set must be chosen.

    - If the type of the multiplication expression is `double`, then the double value set must be chosen.

  - If the multiplication expression is not FP-strict:

    - If the type of the multiplication expression is `float`, then either the float value set or the float-extended-exponent value set may be chosen, at the whim of the implementation.

501

❖ If the type of the multiplication expression is `double`, then either the double value set or the double-extended-exponent value set may be chosen, at the whim of the implementation.

Next, a value must be chosen from the chosen value set to represent the product.

If the magnitude of the product is too large to represent, we say the operation overflows; the result is then an infinity of appropriate sign.

Otherwise, the product is rounded to the nearest value in the chosen value set using IEEE 754 round-to-nearest mode. The Java programming language requires support of gradual underflow as defined by IEEE 754 (§4.2.4).

Despite the fact that overflow, underflow, or loss of information may occur, evaluation of a multiplication operator * never throws a run-time exception.

15.17.2   Division Operator /

The binary / operator performs division, producing the quotient of its operands. The left-hand operand is the *dividend* and the right-hand operand is the *divisor*.

Integer division rounds toward 0. That is, the quotient produced for operands n and d that are integers after binary numeric promotion (§5.6.2) is an integer value q whose magnitude is as large as possible while satisfying $|d \cdot q| \leq |n|$. Moreover, q is positive when $|n| \geq |d|$ and n and d have the same sign, but q is negative when $|n| \geq |d|$ and n and d have opposite signs.

There is one special case that does not satisfy this rule: if the dividend is the negative integer of largest possible magnitude for its type, and the divisor is -1, then integer overflow occurs and the result is equal to the dividend. Despite the overflow, no exception is thrown in this case. On the other hand, if the value of the divisor in an integer division is 0, then an `ArithmeticException` is thrown.

The result of a floating-point division is determined by the rules of IEEE 754 arithmetic:

• If either operand is NaN, the result is NaN.

• If the result is not NaN, the sign of the result is positive if both operands have the same sign, and negative if the operands have different signs.

• Division of an infinity by an infinity results in NaN.

• Division of an infinity by a finite value results in a signed infinity. The sign is determined by the rule stated above.

- Division of a finite value by an infinity results in a signed zero. The sign is determined by the rule stated above.

- Division of a zero by a zero results in NaN; division of zero by any other finite value results in a signed zero. The sign is determined by the rule stated above.

- Division of a nonzero finite value by a zero results in a signed infinity. The sign is determined by the rule stated above.

- In the remaining cases, where neither an infinity nor NaN is involved, the exact mathematical quotient is computed. A floating-point value set is then chosen:

  - If the division expression is FP-strict (§15.4):

    - If the type of the division expression is `float`, then the float value set must be chosen.

    - If the type of the division expression is `double`, then the double value set must be chosen.

  - If the division expression is not FP-strict:

    - If the type of the division expression is `float`, then either the float value set or the float-extended-exponent value set may be chosen, at the whim of the implementation.

    - If the type of the division expression is `double`, then either the double value set or the double-extended-exponent value set may be chosen, at the whim of the implementation.

  Next, a value must be chosen from the chosen value set to represent the quotient.

  If the magnitude of the quotient is too large to represent, we say the operation overflows; the result is then an infinity of appropriate sign.

  Otherwise, the quotient is rounded to the nearest value in the chosen value set using IEEE 754 round-to-nearest mode. The Java programming language requires support of gradual underflow as defined by IEEE 754 (§4.2.4).

Despite the fact that overflow, underflow, division by zero, or loss of information may occur, evaluation of a floating-point division operator / never throws a run-time exception.

15.17.3 Remainder Operator %

The binary % operator is said to yield the remainder of its operands from an implied division; the left-hand operand is the *dividend* and the right-hand operand is the *divisor*.

In C and C++, the remainder operator accepts only integral operands, but in the Java programming language, it also accepts floating-point operands.

The remainder operation for operands that are integers after binary numeric promotion (§5.6.2) produces a result value such that `(a/b)*b+(a%b)` is equal to `a`.

This identity holds even in the special case that the dividend is the negative integer of largest possible magnitude for its type and the divisor is `-1` (the remainder is `0`).

It follows from this rule that the result of the remainder operation can be negative only if the dividend is negative, and can be positive only if the dividend is positive. Moreover, the magnitude of the result is always less than the magnitude of the divisor.

If the value of the divisor for an integer remainder operator is `0`, then an `ArithmeticException` is thrown.

Example 15.17.3-1. Integer Remainder Operator

```
class Test1 {
    public static void main(String[] args) {
        int a = 5%3;   // 2
        int b = 5/3;   // 1
        System.out.println("5%3 produces " + a +
                        " (note that 5/3 produces " + b + ")");

        int c = 5%(-3);   // 2
        int d = 5/(-3);   // -1
        System.out.println("5%(-3) produces " + c +
                        " (note that 5/(-3) produces " + d + ")");

        int e = (-5)%3;   // -2
        int f = (-5)/3;   // -1
        System.out.println("(-5)%3 produces " + e +
                        " (note that (-5)/3 produces " + f + ")");

        int g = (-5)%(-3);   // -2
        int h = (-5)/(-3);   // 1
        System.out.println("(-5)%(-3) produces " + g +
                        " (note that (-5)/(-3) produces " + h + ")");
    }
}
```

This program produces the output:

```
5%3 produces 2 (note that 5/3 produces 1)
5%(-3) produces 2 (note that 5/(-3) produces -1)
(-5)%3 produces -2 (note that (-5)/3 produces -1)
(-5)%(-3) produces -2 (note that (-5)/(-3) produces 1)
```

The result of a floating-point remainder operation as computed by the % operator is *not* the same as that produced by the remainder operation defined by IEEE 754. The IEEE 754 remainder operation computes the remainder from a rounding division, not a truncating division, and so its behavior is *not* analogous to that of the usual integer remainder operator. Instead, the Java programming language defines % on floating-point operations to behave in a manner analogous to that of the integer remainder operator; this may be compared with the C library function fmod. The IEEE 754 remainder operation may be computed by the library routine Math.IEEEremainder.

The result of a floating-point remainder operation is determined by the rules of IEEE 754 arithmetic:

- If either operand is NaN, the result is NaN.

- If the result is not NaN, the sign of the result equals the sign of the dividend.

- If the dividend is an infinity, or the divisor is a zero, or both, the result is NaN.

- If the dividend is finite and the divisor is an infinity, the result equals the dividend.

- If the dividend is a zero and the divisor is finite, the result equals the dividend.

- In the remaining cases, where neither an infinity, nor a zero, nor NaN is involved, the floating-point remainder r from the division of a dividend n by a divisor d is defined by the mathematical relation $r = n - (d \cdot q)$ where q is an integer that is negative only if n/d is negative and positive only if n/d is positive, and whose magnitude is as large as possible without exceeding the magnitude of the true mathematical quotient of n and d.

Evaluation of a floating-point remainder operator % never throws a run-time exception, even if the right-hand operand is zero. Overflow, underflow, or loss of precision cannot occur.

Example 15.17.3-2. Floating-Point Remainder Operator

```
class Test2 {
    public static void main(String[] args) {
        double a = 5.0%3.0;    // 2.0
        System.out.println("5.0%3.0 produces " + a);

        double b = 5.0%(-3.0);  // 2.0
        System.out.println("5.0%(-3.0) produces " + b);

        double c = (-5.0)%3.0;  // -2.0
        System.out.println("(-5.0)%3.0 produces " + c);

        double d = (-5.0)%(-3.0);  // -2.0
```

```
                    System.out.println("(-5.0)%(-3.0) produces " + d);
            }
        }
```

This program produces the output:

```
    5.0%3.0 produces 2.0
    5.0%(-3.0) produces 2.0
    (-5.0)%3.0 produces -2.0
    (-5.0)%(-3.0) produces -2.0
```

15.18   Additive Operators

The operators + and – are called the *additive operators*.

> *AdditiveExpression:*
>   *MultiplicativeExpression*
>   *AdditiveExpression + MultiplicativeExpression*
>   *AdditiveExpression – MultiplicativeExpression*

The additive operators have the same precedence and are syntactically left-associative (they group left-to-right).

If the type of either operand of a + operator is String, then the operation is string concatenation.

Otherwise, the type of each of the operands of the + operator must be a type that is convertible (§5.1.8) to a primitive numeric type, or a compile-time error occurs.

In every case, the type of each of the operands of the binary – operator must be a type that is convertible (§5.1.8) to a primitive numeric type, or a compile-time error occurs.

15.18.1   String Concatenation Operator +

If only one operand expression is of type String, then string conversion (§5.1.11) is performed on the other operand to produce a string at run time.

The result of string concatenation is a reference to a String object that is the concatenation of the two operand strings. The characters of the left-hand operand precede the characters of the right-hand operand in the newly created string.

The String object is newly created (§12.5) unless the expression is a compile-time constant expression (§15.28).

An implementation may choose to perform conversion and concatenation in one step to avoid creating and then discarding an intermediate String object. To increase the performance of repeated string concatenation, a Java compiler may use the StringBuffer class or a similar technique to reduce the number of intermediate String objects that are created by evaluation of an expression.

For primitive types, an implementation may also optimize away the creation of a wrapper object by converting directly from a primitive type to a string.

Example 15.18.1-1. String Concatenation

The example expression:

```
"The square root of 2 is " + Math.sqrt(2)
```

produces the result:

```
"The square root of 2 is 1.4142135623730952"
```

The + operator is syntactically left-associative, no matter whether it is determined by type analysis to represent string concatenation or numeric addition. In some cases care is required to get the desired result. For example, the expression:

```
a + b + c
```

is always regarded as meaning:

```
(a + b) + c
```

Therefore the result of the expression:

```
1 + 2 + " fiddlers"
```

is:

```
"3 fiddlers"
```

but the result of:

```
"fiddlers " + 1 + 2
```

is:

```
"fiddlers 12"
```

Example 15.18.1-2. String Concatenation and Conditionals

In this jocular little example:

```
class Bottles {
   static void printSong(Object stuff, int n) {
      String plural = (n == 1) ? "" : "s";
loop: while (true) {
         System.out.println(n + " bottle" + plural
               + " of " + stuff + " on the wall,");
         System.out.println(n + " bottle" + plural
               + " of " + stuff + ";");
         System.out.println("You take one down "
               + "and pass it around:");
         --n;
         plural = (n == 1) ? "" : "s";
         if (n == 0)
            break loop;
         System.out.println(n + " bottle" + plural
               + " of " + stuff + " on the wall!");
         System.out.println();
      }
      System.out.println("No bottles of " +
               stuff + " on the wall!");
   }

   public static void main(String[] args) {
      printSong("slime", 3);
   }
}
```

the method `printSong` will print a version of a children's song. Popular values for `stuff` include "pop" and "beer"; the most popular value for n is `100`. Here is the output that results from running the program:

```
3 bottles of slime on the wall,
3 bottles of slime;
You take one down and pass it around:
2 bottles of slime on the wall!

2 bottles of slime on the wall,
2 bottles of slime;
You take one down and pass it around:
1 bottle of slime on the wall!

1 bottle of slime on the wall,
1 bottle of slime;
You take one down and pass it around:
No bottles of slime on the wall!
```

In the code, note the careful conditional generation of the singular "bottle" when appropriate rather than the plural "bottles"; note also how the string concatenation operator was used to break the long constant string:

```
"You take one down and pass it around:"
```

into two pieces to avoid an inconveniently long line in the source code.

15.18.2   Additive Operators (+ and –) for Numeric Types

The binary + operator performs addition when applied to two operands of numeric type, producing the sum of the operands.

The binary – operator performs subtraction, producing the difference of two numeric operands.

Binary numeric promotion is performed on the operands (§5.6.2).

> Note that binary numeric promotion performs value set conversion (§5.1.13) and may perform unboxing conversion (§5.1.8).

The type of an additive expression on numeric operands is the promoted type of its operands.

If this promoted type is `int` or `long`, then integer arithmetic is performed.

If this promoted type is `float` or `double`, then floating-point arithmetic is performed.

Addition is a commutative operation if the operand expressions have no side effects.

Integer addition is associative when the operands are all of the same type.

Floating-point addition is not associative.

If an integer addition overflows, then the result is the low-order bits of the mathematical sum as represented in some sufficiently large two's-complement format. If overflow occurs, then the sign of the result is not the same as the sign of the mathematical sum of the two operand values.

The result of a floating-point addition is determined using the following rules of IEEE 754 arithmetic:

• If either operand is NaN, the result is NaN.

• The sum of two infinities of opposite sign is NaN.

• The sum of two infinities of the same sign is the infinity of that sign.

• The sum of an infinity and a finite value is equal to the infinite operand.

• The sum of two zeros of opposite sign is positive zero.

• The sum of two zeros of the same sign is the zero of that sign.

- The sum of a zero and a nonzero finite value is equal to the nonzero operand.

- The sum of two nonzero finite values of the same magnitude and opposite sign is positive zero.

- In the remaining cases, where neither an infinity, nor a zero, nor NaN is involved, and the operands have the same sign or have different magnitudes, the exact mathematical sum is computed. A floating-point value set is then chosen:

  - If the addition expression is FP-strict (§15.4):

    - If the type of the addition expression is `float`, then the float value set must be chosen.

    - If the type of the addition expression is `double`, then the double value set must be chosen.

  - If the addition expression is not FP-strict:

    - If the type of the addition expression is `float`, then either the float value set or the float-extended-exponent value set may be chosen, at the whim of the implementation.

    - If the type of the addition expression is `double`, then either the double value set or the double-extended-exponent value set may be chosen, at the whim of the implementation.

  Next, a value must be chosen from the chosen value set to represent the sum.

  If the magnitude of the sum is too large to represent, we say the operation overflows; the result is then an infinity of appropriate sign.

  Otherwise, the sum is rounded to the nearest value in the chosen value set using IEEE 754 round-to-nearest mode. The Java programming language requires support of gradual underflow as defined by IEEE 754 (§4.2.4).

The binary - operator performs subtraction when applied to two operands of numeric type, producing the difference of its operands; the left-hand operand is the *minuend* and the right-hand operand is the *subtrahend*.

For both integer and floating-point subtraction, it is always the case that `a-b` produces the same result as `a+(-b)`.

Note that, for integer values, subtraction from zero is the same as negation. However, for floating-point operands, subtraction from zero is *not* the same as negation, because if x is `+0.0`, then `0.0-x` is `+0.0`, but `-x` is `-0.0`.

Despite the fact that overflow, underflow, or loss of information may occur, evaluation of a numeric additive operator never throws a run-time exception.

15.19   Shift Operators

The operators << (left shift), >> (signed right shift), and >>> (unsigned right shift) are called the *shift operators*. The left-hand operand of a shift operator is the value to be shifted; the right-hand operand specifies the shift distance.

> *ShiftExpression:*
>   *AdditiveExpression*
>   *ShiftExpression* << *AdditiveExpression*
>   *ShiftExpression* >> *AdditiveExpression*
>   *ShiftExpression* >>> *AdditiveExpression*

The shift operators are syntactically left-associative (they group left-to-right).

Unary numeric promotion (§5.6.1) is performed on each operand separately. (Binary numeric promotion (§5.6.2) is *not* performed on the operands.)

It is a compile-time error if the type of each of the operands of a shift operator, after unary numeric promotion, is not a primitive integral type.

The type of the shift expression is the promoted type of the left-hand operand.

If the promoted type of the left-hand operand is int, only the five lowest-order bits of the right-hand operand are used as the shift distance. It is as if the right-hand operand were subjected to a bitwise logical AND operator & (§15.22.1) with the mask value 0x1f (0b11111). The shift distance actually used is therefore always in the range 0 to 31, inclusive.

If the promoted type of the left-hand operand is long, then only the six lowest-order bits of the right-hand operand are used as the shift distance. It is as if the right-hand operand were subjected to a bitwise logical AND operator & (§15.22.1) with the mask value 0x3f (0b111111). The shift distance actually used is therefore always in the range 0 to 63, inclusive.

At run time, shift operations are performed on the two's-complement integer representation of the value of the left operand.

The value of $n << s$ is n left-shifted s bit positions; this is equivalent (even if overflow occurs) to multiplication by two to the power s.

The value of $n >> s$ is n right-shifted s bit positions with sign-extension. The resulting value is $\lfloor n \ / \ 2^s \rfloor$. For non-negative values of n, this is equivalent to truncating integer division, as computed by the integer division operator /, by two to the power s.

The value of $n >>> s$ is n right-shifted s bit positions with zero-extension, where:

- If n is positive, then the result is the same as that of $n >> s$.
- If n is negative and the type of the left-hand operand is `int`, then the result is equal to that of the expression $(n >> s) + (2 << \mathtt{\sim}s)$.
- If n is negative and the type of the left-hand operand is `long`, then the result is equal to that of the expression $(n >> s) + (2L << \mathtt{\sim}s)$.

> The added term $(2 << \mathtt{\sim}s)$ or $(2L << \mathtt{\sim}s)$ cancels out the propagated sign bit.

> Note that, because of the implicit masking of the right-hand operand of a shift operator, $\mathtt{\sim}s$ as a shift distance is equivalent to $31-s$ when shifting an `int` value and to $63-s$ when shifting a `long` value.

15.20 Relational Operators

The numerical comparison operators <, >, <=, and >=, and the `instanceof` operator, are called the *relational operators*.

> *RelationalExpression:*
>   *ShiftExpression*
>   *RelationalExpression* < *ShiftExpression*
>   *RelationalExpression* > *ShiftExpression*
>   *RelationalExpression* <= *ShiftExpression*
>   *RelationalExpression* >= *ShiftExpression*
>   *RelationalExpression* `instanceof` *ReferenceType*

The relational operators are syntactically left-associative (they group left-to-right).

> However, this fact is not useful. For example, a<b<c parses as (a<b)<c, which is always a compile-time error, because the type of a<b is always `boolean` and < is not an operator on `boolean` values.

The type of a relational expression is always `boolean`.

15.20.1 Numerical Comparison Operators <, <=, >, and >=

The type of each of the operands of a numerical comparison operator must be a type that is convertible (§5.1.8) to a primitive numeric type, or a compile-time error occurs.

Binary numeric promotion is performed on the operands (§5.6.2).

Note that binary numeric promotion performs value set conversion (§5.1.13) and may perform unboxing conversion (§5.1.8).

If the promoted type of the operands is `int` or `long`, then signed integer comparison is performed.

If the promoted type is `float` or `double`, then floating-point comparison is performed.

Comparison is carried out accurately on floating-point values, no matter what value sets their representing values were drawn from.

The result of a floating-point comparison, as determined by the specification of the IEEE 754 standard, is:

- If either operand is NaN, then the result is false.

- All values other than NaN are ordered, with negative infinity less than all finite values, and positive infinity greater than all finite values.

- Positive zero and negative zero are considered equal.

    For example, `-0.0<0.0` is `false`, but `-0.0<=0.0` is `true`.

    Note, however, that the methods `Math.min` and `Math.max` treat negative zero as being strictly smaller than positive zero.

Subject to these considerations for floating-point numbers, the following rules then hold for integer operands or for floating-point operands other than NaN:

- The value produced by the < operator is `true` if the value of the left-hand operand is less than the value of the right-hand operand, and otherwise is `false`.

- The value produced by the <= operator is `true` if the value of the left-hand operand is less than or equal to the value of the right-hand operand, and otherwise is `false`.

- The value produced by the > operator is `true` if the value of the left-hand operand is greater than the value of the right-hand operand, and otherwise is `false`.

- The value produced by the >= operator is `true` if the value of the left-hand operand is greater than or equal to the value of the right-hand operand, and otherwise is `false`.

15.20.2   Type Comparison Operator `instanceof`

The type of the *RelationalExpression* operand of the `instanceof` operator must be a reference type or the null type; otherwise, a compile-time error occurs.

It is a compile-time error if the *ReferenceType* mentioned after the `instanceof` operator does not denote a reference type that is reifiable (§4.7).

If a cast of the *RelationalExpression* to the *ReferenceType* would be rejected as a compile-time error, then the `instanceof` relational expression likewise produces a compile-time error. In such a situation, the result of the `instanceof` expression could never be true.

At run time, the result of the `instanceof` operator is `true` if the value of the *RelationalExpression* is not `null` and the reference could be cast (§15.16) to the *ReferenceType* without raising a `ClassCastException`. Otherwise the result is `false`.

Example 15.20.2-1. The `instanceof` Operator

```
class Point   { int x, y; }
class Element { int atomicNumber; }
class Test {
    public static void main(String[] args) {
        Point   p = new Point();
        Element e = new Element();
        if (e instanceof Point) {  // compile-time error
            System.out.println("I get your point!");
            p = (Point)e;  // compile-time error
        }
    }
}
```

This program results in two compile-time errors. The cast `(Point)e` is incorrect because no instance of `Element` or any of its possible subclasses (none are shown here) could possibly be an instance of any subclass of `Point`. The `instanceof` expression is incorrect for exactly the same reason. If, on the other hand, the class `Point` were a subclass of `Element` (an admittedly strange notion in this example):

```
class Point extends Element { int x, y; }
```

then the cast would be possible, though it would require a run-time check, and the `instanceof` expression would then be sensible and valid. The cast `(Point)e` would never raise an exception because it would not be executed if the value of `e` could not correctly be cast to type `Point`.

15.21   Equality Operators

The operators `==` (equal to) and `!=` (not equal to) are called the *equality operators*.

EqualityExpression:
  RelationalExpression
  EqualityExpression == *RelationalExpression*
  EqualityExpression != *RelationalExpression*

The equality operators are syntactically left-associative (they group left-to-right)

> However, this fact is essentially never useful. For example, a==b==c parses as (a==b)==c. The result type of a==b is always boolean, and c must therefore be of type boolean or a compile-time error occurs. Thus, a==b==c does not test to see whether a, b, and c are all equal.

The equality operators are commutative if the operand expressions have no side effects.

The equality operators are analogous to the relational operators except for their lower precedence. Thus, a<b==c<d is true whenever a<b and c<d have the same truth value.

The equality operators may be used to compare two operands that are convertible (§5.1.8) to numeric type, or two operands of type boolean or Boolean, or two operands that are each of either reference type or the null type. All other cases result in a compile-time error.

The type of an equality expression is always boolean.

In all cases, a!=b produces the same result as !(a==b).

15.21.1   Numerical Equality Operators == and !=

If the operands of an equality operator are both of numeric type, or one is of numeric type and the other is convertible (§5.1.8) to numeric type, binary numeric promotion is performed on the operands (§5.6.2).

> Note that binary numeric promotion performs value set conversion (§5.1.13) and may perform unboxing conversion (§5.1.8).

If the promoted type of the operands is int or long, then an integer equality test is performed.

If the promoted type is float or double, then a floating-point equality test is performed.

Comparison is carried out accurately on floating-point values, no matter what value sets their representing values were drawn from.

Floating-point equality testing is performed in accordance with the rules of the IEEE 754 standard:

- If either operand is NaN, then the result of `==` is `false` but the result of `!=` is `true`.

  Indeed, the test `x!=x` is `true` if and only if the value of `x` is NaN.

  > The methods `Float.isNaN` and `Double.isNaN` may also be used to test whether a value is NaN.

- Positive zero and negative zero are considered equal.

  > For example, `-0.0==0.0` is `true`.

- Otherwise, two distinct floating-point values are considered unequal by the equality operators.

  In particular, there is one value representing positive infinity and one value representing negative infinity; each compares equal only to itself, and each compares unequal to all other values.

Subject to these considerations for floating-point numbers, the following rules then hold for integer operands or for floating-point operands other than NaN:

- The value produced by the `==` operator is `true` if the value of the left-hand operand is equal to the value of the right-hand operand; otherwise, the result is `false`.

- The value produced by the `!=` operator is `true` if the value of the left-hand operand is not equal to the value of the right-hand operand; otherwise, the result is `false`.

15.21.2   Boolean Equality Operators `==` and `!=`

If the operands of an equality operator are both of type `boolean`, or if one operand is of type `boolean` and the other is of type `Boolean`, then the operation is boolean equality.

The boolean equality operators are associative.

If one of the operands is of type `Boolean`, it is subjected to unboxing conversion (§5.1.8).

The result of `==` is `true` if the operands (after any required unboxing conversion) are both `true` or both `false`; otherwise, the result is `false`.

The result of `!=` is `false` if the operands are both `true` or both `false`; otherwise, the result is `true`.

Thus != behaves the same as ^ (§15.22.2) when applied to boolean operands.

15.21.3   Reference Equality Operators == and !=

If the operands of an equality operator are both of either reference type or the null type, then the operation is object equality.

It is a compile-time error if it is impossible to convert the type of either operand to the type of the other by a casting conversion (§5.5). The run-time values of the two operands would necessarily be unequal.

At run time, the result of == is true if the operand values are both null or both refer to the same object or array; otherwise, the result is false.

The result of != is false if the operand values are both null or both refer to the same object or array; otherwise, the result is true.

While == may be used to compare references of type String, such an equality test determines whether or not the two operands refer to the same String object. The result is false if the operands are distinct String objects, even if they contain the same sequence of characters (§3.10.5). The contents of two strings s and t can be tested for equality by the method invocation s.equals(t).

15.22   Bitwise and Logical Operators

The *bitwise operators* and *logical operators* include the AND operator &, exclusive OR operator ^, and inclusive OR operator |.

> *AndExpression:*
>   *EqualityExpression*
>   *AndExpression* & *EqualityExpression*
>
> *ExclusiveOrExpression:*
>   *AndExpression*
>   *ExclusiveOrExpression* ^ *AndExpression*
>
> *InclusiveOrExpression:*
>   *ExclusiveOrExpression*
>   *InclusiveOrExpression* | *ExclusiveOrExpression*

These operators have different precedence, with & having the highest precedence and | the lowest precedence.

Each of these operators is syntactically left-associative (each groups left-to-right).

Each operator is commutative if the operand expressions have no side effects.

Each operator is associative.

The bitwise and logical operators may be used to compare two operands of numeric type or two operands of type `boolean`. All other cases result in a compile-time error.

15.22.1   Integer Bitwise Operators `&`, `^`, and `|`

When both operands of an operator `&`, `^`, or `|` are of a type that is convertible (§5.1.8) to a primitive integral type, binary numeric promotion is first performed on the operands (§5.6.2).

The type of the bitwise operator expression is the promoted type of the operands.

For `&`, the result value is the bitwise AND of the operand values.

For `^`, the result value is the bitwise exclusive OR of the operand values.

For `|`, the result value is the bitwise inclusive OR of the operand values.

For example, the result of the expression:

```
0xff00 & 0xf0f0
```

is:

```
0xf000
```

The result of the expression:

```
0xff00 ^ 0xf0f0
```

is:

```
0x0ff0
```

The result of the expression:

```
0xff00 | 0xf0f0
```

is:

```
0xfff0
```

15.22.2   Boolean Logical Operators &, ^, and |

When both operands of a &, ^, or | operator are of type `boolean` or `Boolean`, then the type of the bitwise operator expression is `boolean`. In all cases, the operands are subject to unboxing conversion (§5.1.8) as necessary.

For &, the result value is `true` if both operand values are `true`; otherwise, the result is `false`.

For ^, the result value is `true` if the operand values are different; otherwise, the result is `false`.

For |, the result value is `false` if both operand values are `false`; otherwise, the result is `true`.

15.23   Conditional-And Operator &&

The conditional-and operator && is like & (§15.22.2), but evaluates its right-hand operand only if the value of its left-hand operand is `true`.

> *ConditionalAndExpression:*
>   *InclusiveOrExpression*
>   *ConditionalAndExpression* && *InclusiveOrExpression*

The conditional-and operator is syntactically left-associative (it groups left-to-right).

The conditional-and operator is fully associative with respect to both side effects and result value. That is, for any expressions *a*, *b*, and *c*, evaluation of the expression `((`*a*`) && (`*b*`)) && (`*c*`)` produces the same result, with the same side effects occurring in the same order, as evaluation of the expression `(`*a*`) && ((`*b*`) && (`*c*`))`.

Each operand of the conditional-and operator must be of type `boolean` or `Boolean`, or a compile-time error occurs.

The type of a conditional-and expression is always `boolean`.

At run time, the left-hand operand expression is evaluated first; if the result has type `Boolean`, it is subjected to unboxing conversion (§5.1.8).

If the resulting value is `false`, the value of the conditional-and expression is `false` and the right-hand operand expression is not evaluated.

If the value of the left-hand operand is `true`, then the right-hand expression is evaluated; if the result has type `Boolean`, it is subjected to unboxing conversion (§5.1.8). The resulting value becomes the value of the conditional-and expression.

Thus, `&&` computes the same result as `&` on `boolean` operands. It differs only in that the right-hand operand expression is evaluated conditionally rather than always.

15.24   Conditional-Or Operator `||`

The conditional-or operator `||` operator is like `|` (§15.22.2), but evaluates its right-hand operand only if the value of its left-hand operand is `false`.

> *ConditionalOrExpression:*
>   *ConditionalAndExpression*
>   *ConditionalOrExpression* `||` *ConditionalAndExpression*

The conditional-or operator is syntactically left-associative (it groups left-to-right).

The conditional-or operator is fully associative with respect to both side effects and result value. That is, for any expressions *a*, *b*, and *c*, evaluation of the expression `((`*a*`) || (`*b*`)) || (`*c*`)` produces the same result, with the same side effects occurring in the same order, as evaluation of the expression `(`*a*`) || ((`*b*`) || (`*c*`))`.

Each operand of the conditional-or operator must be of type `boolean` or `Boolean`, or a compile-time error occurs.

The type of a conditional-or expression is always `boolean`.

At run time, the left-hand operand expression is evaluated first; if the result has type `Boolean`, it is subjected to unboxing conversion (§5.1.8).

If the resulting value is `true`, the value of the conditional-or expression is `true` and the right-hand operand expression is not evaluated.

If the value of the left-hand operand is `false`, then the right-hand expression is evaluated; if the result has type `Boolean`, it is subjected to unboxing conversion (§5.1.8). The resulting value becomes the value of the conditional-or expression.

Thus, `||` compures the same result as `|` on `boolean` or `Boolean` operands. It differs only in that the right-hand operand expression is evaluated conditionally rather than always.

15.25   Conditional Operator ? :

The conditional operator ? : uses the boolean value of one expression to decide which of two other expressions should be evaluated.

> *ConditionalExpression:*
>   *ConditionalOrExpression*
>   *ConditionalOrExpression* ? *Expression* : *ConditionalExpression*

The conditional operator is syntactically right-associative (it groups right-to-left). Thus, a?b:c?d:e?f:g means the same as a?b:(c?d:(e?f:g)).

The conditional operator has three operand expressions. ? appears between the first and second expressions, and : appears between the second and third expressions.

The first expression must be of type boolean or Boolean, or a compile-time error occurs.

It is a compile-time error for either the second or the third operand expression to be an invocation of a void method.

> In fact, by the grammar of expression statements (§14.8), it is not permitted for a conditional expression to appear in any context where an invocation of a void method could appear.

The type of a conditional expression is determined as follows:

- If the second and third operands have the same type (which may be the null type), then that is the type of the conditional expression.

- If one of the second and third operands is of primitive type T, and the type of the other is the result of applying boxing conversion (§5.1.7) to T, then the type of the conditional expression is T.

- If one of the second and third operands is of the null type and the type of the other is a reference type, then the type of the conditional expression is that reference type.

- Otherwise, if the second and third operands have types that are convertible (§5.1.8) to numeric types, then there are several cases:

  - If one of the operands is of type byte or Byte and the other is of type short or Short, then the type of the conditional expression is short.

  - If one of the operands is of type T where T is byte, short, or char, and the other operand is a constant expression (§15.28) of type int whose value is representable in type T, then the type of the conditional expression is T.

- If one of the operands is of type T, where T is `Byte`, `Short`, or `Character`, and the other operand is a constant expression (§15.28) of type `int` whose value is representable in the type U which is the result of applying unboxing conversion to T, then the type of the conditional expression is U.

- Otherwise, binary numeric promotion (§5.6.2) is applied to the operand types, and the type of the conditional expression is the promoted type of the second and third operands.

   > Note that binary numeric promotion performs value set conversion (§5.1.13) and may perform unboxing conversion (§5.1.8).

- Otherwise, the second and third operands are of types S_1 and S_2 respectively. Let T_1 be the type that results from applying boxing conversion to S_1, and let T_2 be the type that results from applying boxing conversion to S_2.

   The type of the conditional expression is the result of applying capture conversion (§5.1.10) to lub(T_1, T_2) (§15.12.2.7).

At run time, the first operand expression of the conditional expression is evaluated first. If necessary, unboxing conversion is performed on the result.

The resulting `boolean` value is then used to choose either the second or the third operand expression:

- If the value of the first operand is `true`, then the second operand expression is chosen.

- If the value of the first operand is `false`, then the third operand expression is chosen.

The chosen operand expression is then evaluated and the resulting value is converted to the type of the conditional expression as determined by the rules stated above.

This conversion may include boxing (§5.1.7) or unboxing (§5.1.8) conversion.

The operand expression not chosen is not evaluated for that particular evaluation of the conditional expression.

15.26   Assignment Operators

There are 12 *assignment operators*; all are syntactically right-associative (they group right-to-left). Thus, a=b=c means a=(b=c), which assigns the value of c to b and then assigns the value of b to a.

> *AssignmentExpression:*
>   *ConditionalExpression*
>   *Assignment*

> *Assignment:*
>   *LeftHandSide AssignmentOperator AssignmentExpression*

> *LeftHandSide:*
>   *ExpressionName*
>   *FieldAccess*
>   *ArrayAccess*

> *AssignmentOperator: one of*
>   = *= /= %= += -= <<= >>= >>>= &= ^= |=

The result of the first operand of an assignment operator must be a variable, or a compile-time error occurs.

This operand may be a named variable, such as a local variable or a field of the current object or class, or it may be a computed variable, as can result from a field access (§15.11) or an array access (§15.13).

The type of the assignment expression is the type of the variable after capture conversion (§5.1.10).

At run time, the result of the assignment expression is the value of the variable after the assignment has occurred. The result of an assignment expression is not itself a variable.

A variable that is declared final cannot be assigned to (unless it is definitely unassigned (§16)), because when an access of such a final variable is used as an expression, the result is a value, not a variable, and so it cannot be used as the first operand of an assignment operator.

15.26.1   Simple Assignment Operator =

A compile-time error occurs if the type of the right-hand operand cannot be converted to the type of the variable by assignment conversion (§5.2).

At run time, the expression is evaluated in one of three ways.

If the left-hand operand expression is a field access expression (§15.11) `e.f`, possibly enclosed in one or more pairs of parentheses, then:

- First, the expression `e` is evaluated. If evaluation of `e` completes abruptly, the assignment expression completes abruptly for the same reason.

- Next, the right hand operand is evaluated. If evaluation of the right hand expression completes abruptly, the assignment expression completes abruptly for the same reason.

- Then, if the field denoted by `e.f` is not `static` and the result of the evaluation of `e` above is `null`, then a `NullPointerException` is thrown.

- Otherwise, the variable denoted by `e.f` is assigned the value of the right hand operand as computed above.

If the left-hand operand is an array access expression (§15.13), possibly enclosed in one or more pairs of parentheses, then:

- First, the array reference subexpression of the left-hand operand array access expression is evaluated. If this evaluation completes abruptly, then the assignment expression completes abruptly for the same reason; the index subexpression (of the left-hand operand array access expression) and the right-hand operand are not evaluated and no assignment occurs.

- Otherwise, the index subexpression of the left-hand operand array access expression is evaluated. If this evaluation completes abruptly, then the assignment expression completes abruptly for the same reason and the right-hand operand is not evaluated and no assignment occurs.

- Otherwise, the right-hand operand is evaluated. If this evaluation completes abruptly, then the assignment expression completes abruptly for the same reason and no assignment occurs.

- Otherwise, if the value of the array reference subexpression is `null`, then no assignment occurs and a `NullPointerException` is thrown.

- Otherwise, the value of the array reference subexpression indeed refers to an array. If the value of the index subexpression is less than zero, or greater than or equal to the `length` of the array, then no assignment occurs and an `ArrayIndexOutOfBoundsException` is thrown.

- Otherwise, the value of the index subexpression is used to select a component of the array referred to by the value of the array reference subexpression.

This component is a variable; call its type *SC*. Also, let *TC* be the type of the left-hand operand of the assignment operator as determined at compile time. Then there are two possibilities:

- If *TC* is a primitive type, then *SC* is necessarily the same as *TC*.

  The value of the right-hand operand is converted to the type of the selected array component, is subjected to value set conversion (§5.1.13) to the appropriate standard value set (not an extended-exponent value set), and the result of the conversion is stored into the array component.

- If *TC* is a reference type, then *SC* may not be the same as *TC*, but rather a type that extends or implements *TC*.

  Let *RC* be the class of the object referred to by the value of the right-hand operand at run time.

  A Java compiler may be able to prove at compile time that the array component will be of type *TC* exactly (for example, *TC* might be `final`). But if a Java compiler cannot prove at compile time that the array component will be of type *TC* exactly, then a check must be performed at run time to ensure that the class *RC* is assignment compatible (§5.2) with the actual type *SC* of the array component.

  > This check is similar to a narrowing cast (§5.5, §15.16), except that if the check fails, an `ArrayStoreException` is thrown rather than a `ClassCastException`.

  If class *RC* is not assignable to type *SC*, then no assignment occurs and an `ArrayStoreException` is thrown.

  Otherwise, the reference value of the right-hand operand is stored into the selected array component.

Otherwise, three steps are required:

- First, the left-hand operand is evaluated to produce a variable. If this evaluation completes abruptly, then the assignment expression completes abruptly for the same reason; the right-hand operand is not evaluated and no assignment occurs.

- Otherwise, the right-hand operand is evaluated. If this evaluation completes abruptly, then the assignment expression completes abruptly for the same reason and no assignment occurs.

- Otherwise, the value of the right-hand operand is converted to the type of the left-hand variable, is subjected to value set conversion (§5.1.13) to the appropriate standard value set (not an extended-exponent value set), and the result of the conversion is stored into the variable.

Example 15.26.1-1. Simple Assignment To An Array Component

```
class ArrayReferenceThrow extends RuntimeException { }
class IndexThrow          extends RuntimeException { }
class RightHandSideThrow  extends RuntimeException { }

class IllustrateSimpleArrayAssignment {
    static Object[] objects = { new Object(), new Object() };
    static Thread[] threads = { new Thread(), new Thread() };

    static Object[] arrayThrow() {
        throw new ArrayReferenceThrow();
    }
    static int indexThrow() {
        throw new IndexThrow();
    }
    static Thread rightThrow() {
        throw new RightHandSideThrow();
    }
    static String name(Object q) {
        String sq = q.getClass().getName();
        int k = sq.lastIndexOf('.');
        return (k < 0) ? sq : sq.substring(k+1);
    }

    static void testFour(Object[] x, int j, Object y) {
        String sx = x == null ? "null" : name(x[0]) + "s";
        String sy = name(y);
        System.out.println();
        try {
            System.out.print(sx + "[throw]=throw => ");
            x[indexThrow()] = rightThrow();
            System.out.println("Okay!");
        } catch (Throwable e) { System.out.println(name(e)); }
        try {
            System.out.print(sx + "[throw]=" + sy + " => ");
            x[indexThrow()] = y;
            System.out.println("Okay!");
        } catch (Throwable e) { System.out.println(name(e)); }
        try {
            System.out.print(sx + "[" + j + "]=throw => ");
            x[j] = rightThrow();
            System.out.println("Okay!");
```

```
            } catch (Throwable e) { System.out.println(name(e)); }
            try {
                System.out.print(sx + "[" + j + "]=" + sy + " => ");
                x[j] = y;
                System.out.println("Okay!");
            } catch (Throwable e) { System.out.println(name(e)); }
        }

    public static void main(String[] args) {
        try {
            System.out.print("throw[throw]=throw => ");
            arrayThrow()[indexThrow()] = rightThrow();
            System.out.println("Okay!");
        } catch (Throwable e) { System.out.println(name(e)); }
        try {
            System.out.print("throw[throw]=Thread => ");
            arrayThrow()[indexThrow()] = new Thread();
            System.out.println("Okay!");
        } catch (Throwable e) { System.out.println(name(e)); }
        try {
            System.out.print("throw[1]=throw => ");
            arrayThrow()[1] = rightThrow();
            System.out.println("Okay!");
        } catch (Throwable e) { System.out.println(name(e)); }
        try {
            System.out.print("throw[1]=Thread => ");
            arrayThrow()[1] = new Thread();
            System.out.println("Okay!");
        } catch (Throwable e) { System.out.println(name(e)); }

        testFour(null, 1, new StringBuffer());
        testFour(null, 9, new Thread());
        testFour(objects, 1, new StringBuffer());
        testFour(objects, 1, new Thread());
        testFour(objects, 9, new StringBuffer());
        testFour(objects, 9, new Thread());
        testFour(threads, 1, new StringBuffer());
        testFour(threads, 1, new Thread());
        testFour(threads, 9, new StringBuffer());
        testFour(threads, 9, new Thread());
    }
}
```

This program produces the output:

```
throw[throw]=throw => ArrayReferenceThrow
throw[throw]=Thread => ArrayReferenceThrow
throw[1]=throw => ArrayReferenceThrow
throw[1]=Thread => ArrayReferenceThrow

null[throw]=throw => IndexThrow
null[throw]=StringBuffer => IndexThrow
null[1]=throw => RightHandSideThrow
null[1]=StringBuffer => NullPointerException

null[throw]=throw => IndexThrow
null[throw]=Thread => IndexThrow
null[9]=throw => RightHandSideThrow
null[9]=Thread => NullPointerException

Objects[throw]=throw => IndexThrow
Objects[throw]=StringBuffer => IndexThrow
Objects[1]=throw => RightHandSideThrow
Objects[1]=StringBuffer => Okay!

Objects[throw]=throw => IndexThrow
Objects[throw]=Thread => IndexThrow
Objects[1]=throw => RightHandSideThrow
Objects[1]=Thread => Okay!

Objects[throw]=throw => IndexThrow
Objects[throw]=StringBuffer => IndexThrow
Objects[9]=throw => RightHandSideThrow
Objects[9]=StringBuffer => ArrayIndexOutOfBoundsException

Objects[throw]=throw => IndexThrow
Objects[throw]=Thread => IndexThrow
Objects[9]=throw => RightHandSideThrow
Objects[9]=Thread => ArrayIndexOutOfBoundsException

Threads[throw]=throw => IndexThrow
Threads[throw]=StringBuffer => IndexThrow
Threads[1]=throw => RightHandSideThrow
Threads[1]=StringBuffer => ArrayStoreException

Threads[throw]=throw => IndexThrow
Threads[throw]=Thread => IndexThrow
Threads[1]=throw => RightHandSideThrow
Threads[1]=Thread => Okay!

Threads[throw]=throw => IndexThrow
Threads[throw]=StringBuffer => IndexThrow
Threads[9]=throw => RightHandSideThrow
Threads[9]=StringBuffer => ArrayIndexOutOfBoundsException

Threads[throw]=throw => IndexThrow
Threads[throw]=Thread => IndexThrow
Threads[9]=throw => RightHandSideThrow
Threads[9]=Thread => ArrayIndexOutOfBoundsException
```

The most interesting case of the lot is thirteenth from the end:

```
Threads[1]=StringBuffer => ArrayStoreException
```

which indicates that the attempt to store a reference to a `StringBuffer` into an array whose components are of type `Thread` throws an `ArrayStoreException`. The code is type-correct at compile time: the assignment has a left-hand side of type `Object[]` and a right-hand side of type `Object`. At run time, the first actual argument to method `testFour` is a reference to an instance of "array of `Thread`" and the third actual argument is a reference to an instance of class `StringBuffer`.

15.26.2 Compound Assignment Operators

A compound assignment expression of the form *E1* *op=* *E2* is equivalent to *E1* *= (T) ((E1) op (E2))*, where *T* is the type of *E1*, except that *E1* is evaluated only once.

For example, the following code is correct:

```
short x = 3;
x += 4.6;
```

and results in x having the value 7 because it is equivalent to:

```
short x = 3;
x = (short)(x + 4.6);
```

At run time, the expression is evaluated in one of two ways.

If the left-hand operand expression is not an array access expression, then:

- First, the left-hand operand is evaluated to produce a variable. If this evaluation completes abruptly, then the assignment expression completes abruptly for the same reason; the right-hand operand is not evaluated and no assignment occurs.

- Otherwise, the value of the left-hand operand is saved and then the right-hand operand is evaluated. If this evaluation completes abruptly, then the assignment expression completes abruptly for the same reason and no assignment occurs.

- Otherwise, the saved value of the left-hand variable and the value of the right-hand operand are used to perform the binary operation indicated by the compound assignment operator. If this operation completes abruptly, then the assignment expression completes abruptly for the same reason and no assignment occurs.

- Otherwise, the result of the binary operation is converted to the type of the left-hand variable, subjected to value set conversion (§5.1.13) to the appropriate standard value set (not an extended-exponent value set), and the result of the conversion is stored into the variable.

If the left-hand operand expression is an array access expression (§15.13), then:

- First, the array reference subexpression of the left-hand operand array access expression is evaluated. If this evaluation completes abruptly, then the assignment expression completes abruptly for the same reason; the index subexpression (of the left-hand operand array access expression) and the right-hand operand are not evaluated and no assignment occurs.

- Otherwise, the index subexpression of the left-hand operand array access expression is evaluated. If this evaluation completes abruptly, then the assignment expression completes abruptly for the same reason and the right-hand operand is not evaluated and no assignment occurs.

- Otherwise, if the value of the array reference subexpression is `null`, then no assignment occurs and a `NullPointerException` is thrown.

- Otherwise, the value of the array reference subexpression indeed refers to an array. If the value of the index subexpression is less than zero, or greater than or equal to the `length` of the array, then no assignment occurs and an `ArrayIndexOutOfBoundsException` is thrown.

- Otherwise, the value of the index subexpression is used to select a component of the array referred to by the value of the array reference subexpression. The value of this component is saved and then the right-hand operand is evaluated. If this evaluation completes abruptly, then the assignment expression completes abruptly for the same reason and no assignment occurs.

  > For a simple assignment operator, the evaluation of the right-hand operand occurs before the checks of the array reference subexpression and the index subexpression, but for a compound assignment operator, the evaluation of the right-hand operand occurs after these checks.

- Otherwise, consider the array component selected in the previous step, whose value was saved. This component is a variable; call its type S. Also, let T be the type of the left-hand operand of the assignment operator as determined at compile time.

  - If T is a primitive type, then S is necessarily the same as T.

    The saved value of the array component and the value of the right-hand operand are used to perform the binary operation indicated by the compound assignment operator.

If this operation completes abruptly (the only possibility is an integer division by zero - see §15.17.2), then the assignment expression completes abruptly for the same reason and no assignment occurs.

Otherwise, the result of the binary operation is converted to the type of the selected array component, subjected to value set conversion (§5.1.13) to the appropriate standard value set (not an extended-exponent value set), and the result of the conversion is stored into the array component.

* If T is a reference type, then it must be `String`. Because class `String` is a `final` class, S must also be `String`.

> Therefore the run-time check that is sometimes required for the simple assignment operator is never required for a compound assignment operator.

The saved value of the array component and the value of the right-hand operand are used to perform the binary operation (string concatenation) indicated by the compound assignment operator (which is necessarily +=). If this operation completes abruptly, then the assignment expression completes abruptly for the same reason and no assignment occurs.

Otherwise, the `String` result of the binary operation is stored into the array component.

Example 15.26.2-1. Compound Assignment To An Array Component

```
class ArrayReferenceThrow extends RuntimeException { }
class IndexThrow         extends RuntimeException { }
class RightHandSideThrow extends RuntimeException { }

class IllustrateCompoundArrayAssignment {
    static String[] strings = { "Simon", "Garfunkel" };
    static double[] doubles = { Math.E, Math.PI };

    static String[] stringsThrow() {
        throw new ArrayReferenceThrow();
    }
    static double[] doublesThrow() {
        throw new ArrayReferenceThrow();
    }
    static int indexThrow() {
        throw new IndexThrow();
    }
    static String stringThrow() {
        throw new RightHandSideThrow();
    }
    static double doubleThrow() {
        throw new RightHandSideThrow();
    }
```

```
static String name(Object q) {
    String sq = q.getClass().getName();
    int k = sq.lastIndexOf('.');
    return (k < 0) ? sq : sq.substring(k+1);
}

static void testEight(String[] x, double[] z, int j) {
    String sx = (x == null) ? "null" : "Strings";
    String sz = (z == null) ? "null" : "doubles";
    System.out.println();
    try {
        System.out.print(sx + "[throw]+=throw => ");
        x[indexThrow()] += stringThrow();
        System.out.println("Okay!");
    } catch (Throwable e) { System.out.println(name(e)); }
    try {
        System.out.print(sz + "[throw]+=throw => ");
        z[indexThrow()] += doubleThrow();
        System.out.println("Okay!");
    } catch (Throwable e) { System.out.println(name(e)); }
    try {
        System.out.print(sx + "[throw]+=\"heh\" => ");
        x[indexThrow()] += "heh";
        System.out.println("Okay!");
    } catch (Throwable e) { System.out.println(name(e)); }
    try {
        System.out.print(sz + "[throw]+=12345 => ");
        z[indexThrow()] += 12345;
        System.out.println("Okay!");
    } catch (Throwable e) { System.out.println(name(e)); }
    try {
        System.out.print(sx + "[" + j + "]+=throw => ");
        x[j] += stringThrow();
        System.out.println("Okay!");
    } catch (Throwable e) { System.out.println(name(e)); }
    try {
        System.out.print(sz + "[" + j + "]+=throw => ");
        z[j] += doubleThrow();
        System.out.println("Okay!");
    } catch (Throwable e) { System.out.println(name(e)); }
    try {
        System.out.print(sx + "[" + j + "]+=\"heh\" => ");
        x[j] += "heh";
        System.out.println("Okay!");
    } catch (Throwable e) { System.out.println(name(e)); }
    try {
        System.out.print(sz + "[" + j + "]+=12345 => ");
        z[j] += 12345;
        System.out.println("Okay!");
    } catch (Throwable e) { System.out.println(name(e)); }
}

public static void main(String[] args) {
```

```
            try {
                System.out.print("throw[throw]+=throw => ");
                stringsThrow()[indexThrow()] += stringThrow();
                System.out.println("Okay!");
            } catch (Throwable e) { System.out.println(name(e)); }
            try {
                System.out.print("throw[throw]+=throw => ");
                doublesThrow()[indexThrow()] += doubleThrow();
                System.out.println("Okay!");
            } catch (Throwable e) { System.out.println(name(e)); }
            try {
                System.out.print("throw[throw]+=\"heh\" => ");
                stringsThrow()[indexThrow()] += "heh";
                System.out.println("Okay!");
            } catch (Throwable e) { System.out.println(name(e)); }
            try {
                System.out.print("throw[throw]+=12345 => ");
                doublesThrow()[indexThrow()] += 12345;
                System.out.println("Okay!");
            } catch (Throwable e) { System.out.println(name(e)); }
            try {
                System.out.print("throw[1]+=throw => ");
                stringsThrow()[1] += stringThrow();
                System.out.println("Okay!");
            } catch (Throwable e) { System.out.println(name(e)); }
            try {
                System.out.print("throw[1]+=throw => ");
                doublesThrow()[1] += doubleThrow();
                System.out.println("Okay!");
            } catch (Throwable e) { System.out.println(name(e)); }
            try {
                System.out.print("throw[1]+=\"heh\" => ");
                stringsThrow()[1] += "heh";
                System.out.println("Okay!");
            } catch (Throwable e) { System.out.println(name(e)); }
            try {
                System.out.print("throw[1]+=12345 => ");
                doublesThrow()[1] += 12345;
                System.out.println("Okay!");
            } catch (Throwable e) { System.out.println(name(e)); }
            testEight(null, null, 1);
            testEight(null, null, 9);
            testEight(strings, doubles, 1);
            testEight(strings, doubles, 9);
        }
    }
```

This program produces the output:

```
throw[throw]+=throw => ArrayReferenceThrow
throw[throw]+=throw => ArrayReferenceThrow
throw[throw]+="heh" => ArrayReferenceThrow
throw[throw]+=12345 => ArrayReferenceThrow
throw[1]+=throw => ArrayReferenceThrow
throw[1]+=throw => ArrayReferenceThrow
throw[1]+="heh" => ArrayReferenceThrow
throw[1]+=12345 => ArrayReferenceThrow

null[throw]+=throw => IndexThrow
null[throw]+=throw => IndexThrow
null[throw]+="heh" => IndexThrow
null[throw]+=12345 => IndexThrow
null[1]+=throw => NullPointerException
null[1]+=throw => NullPointerException
null[1]+="heh" => NullPointerException
null[1]+=12345 => NullPointerException

null[throw]+=throw => IndexThrow
null[throw]+=throw => IndexThrow
null[throw]+="heh" => IndexThrow
null[throw]+=12345 => IndexThrow
null[9]+=throw => NullPointerException
null[9]+=throw => NullPointerException
null[9]+="heh" => NullPointerException
null[9]+=12345 => NullPointerException

Strings[throw]+=throw => IndexThrow
doubles[throw]+=throw => IndexThrow
Strings[throw]+="heh" => IndexThrow
doubles[throw]+=12345 => IndexThrow
Strings[1]+=throw => RightHandSideThrow
doubles[1]+=throw => RightHandSideThrow
Strings[1]+="heh" => Okay!
doubles[1]+=12345 => Okay!

Strings[throw]+=throw => IndexThrow
doubles[throw]+=throw => IndexThrow
Strings[throw]+="heh" => IndexThrow
doubles[throw]+=12345 => IndexThrow
Strings[9]+=throw => ArrayIndexOutOfBoundsException
doubles[9]+=throw => ArrayIndexOutOfBoundsException
Strings[9]+="heh" => ArrayIndexOutOfBoundsException
doubles[9]+=12345 => ArrayIndexOutOfBoundsException
```

The most interesting cases of the lot are eleventh and twelfth from the end:

```
Strings[1]+=throw => RightHandSideThrow
doubles[1]+=throw => RightHandSideThrow
```

They are the cases where a right-hand side that throws an exception actually gets to throw the exception; moreover, they are the only such cases in the lot. This demonstrates that the evaluation of the right-hand operand indeed occurs after the checks for a null array reference value and an out-of-bounds index value.

Example 15.26.2-2. Value Of Left-Hand Side Of Compound Assignment Is Saved Before Evaluation Of Right-Hand Side

```
class Test {
    public static void main(String[] args) {
        int k = 1;
        int[] a = { 1 };
        k += (k = 4) * (k + 2);
        a[0] += (a[0] = 4) * (a[0] + 2);
        System.out.println("k==" + k + " and a[0]==" + a[0]);
    }
}
```

This program produces the output:

```
k==25 and a[0]==25
```

The value 1 of k is saved by the compound assignment operator += before its right-hand operand (k = 4) * (k + 2) is evaluated. Evaluation of this right-hand operand then assigns 4 to k, calculates the value 6 for k + 2, and then multiplies 4 by 6 to get 24. This is added to the saved value 1 to get 25, which is then stored into k by the += operator. An identical analysis applies to the case that uses a[0].

In short, the statements:

```
k += (k = 4) * (k + 2);
a[0] += (a[0] = 4) * (a[0] + 2);
```

behave in exactly the same manner as the statements:

```
k = k + (k = 4) * (k + 2);
a[0] = a[0] + (a[0] = 4) * (a[0] + 2);
```

15.27 Expression

An *Expression* is any assignment expression:

Expression:
  AssignmentExpression

Unlike C and C++, the Java programming language has no comma operator.

15.28   Constant Expressions

> *ConstantExpression:*
>   *Expression*

A compile-time *constant expression* is an expression denoting a value of primitive type or a `String` that does not complete abruptly and is composed using only the following:

- Literals of primitive type and literals of type `String` (§3.10.1, §3.10.2, §3.10.3, §3.10.4, §3.10.5)

- Casts to primitive types and casts to type `String` (§15.16)

- The unary operators +, -, ~, and ! (but not ++ or --) (§15.15.3, §15.15.4, §15.15.5, §15.15.6)

- The multiplicative operators *, /, and % (§15.17)

- The additive operators + and - (§15.18)

- The shift operators <<, >>, and >>> (§15.19)

- The relational operators <, <=, >, and >= (but not `instanceof`) (§15.20)

- The equality operators == and != (§15.21)

- The bitwise and logical operators &, ^, and | (§15.22)

- The conditional-and operator && and the conditional-or operator || (§15.23, §15.24)

- The ternary conditional operator ? : (§15.25)

- Parenthesized expressions (§15.8.5) whose contained expression is a constant expression.

- Simple names (§6.5.6.1) that refer to constant variables (§4.12.4).

- Qualified names (§6.5.6.2) of the form *TypeName* . *Identifier* that refer to constant variables (§4.12.4).

Compile-time constant expressions of type `String` are always "interned" so as to share unique instances, using the method `String.intern`.

A compile-time constant expression is always treated as FP-strict (§15.4), even if it occurs in a context where a non-constant expression would not be considered to be FP-strict.

Compile-time constant expressions are used in `case` labels in `switch` statements (§14.11) and have a special significance for assignment conversion (§5.2) and initialization of a class or interface (§12.4.2). They may also govern the ability of a `while`, `do`, or `for` statement to complete normally (§14.21), and the type of a conditional operator ? : with numeric operands.

Example 15.28-1. Constant Expressions

```
true
(short)(1*2*3*4*5*6)
Integer.MAX_VALUE / 2
2.0 * Math.PI
"The integer " + Long.MAX_VALUE + " is mighty big."
```

CHAPTER 16

Definite Assignment

$\mathbf{E}$ACH local variable (§14.4) and every blank `final` field (§4.12.4, §8.3.1.2) must have a *definitely assigned* value when any access of its value occurs.

An access to its value consists of the simple name of the variable (or, for a field, the simple name of the field qualified by `this`) occurring anywhere in an expression except as the left-hand operand of the simple assignment operator = (§15.26.1).

For every access of a local variable or blank `final` field *x*, *x* must be definitely assigned before the access, or a compile-time error occurs.

Similarly, every blank `final` variable must be assigned at most once; it must be *definitely unassigned* when an assignment to it occurs.

Such an assignment is defined to occur if and only if either the simple name of the variable (or, for a field, its simple name qualified by `this`) occurs on the left hand side of an assignment operator.

For every assignment to a blank `final` variable, the variable must be definitely unassigned before the assignment, or a compile-time error occurs.

The remainder of this chapter is devoted to a precise explanation of the words "definitely assigned before" and "definitely unassigned before".

The idea behind definite assignment is that an assignment to the local variable or blank `final` field must occur on every possible execution path to the access. Similarly, the idea behind definite unassignment is that no other assignment to the blank `final` variable is permitted to occur on any possible execution path to an assignment.

The analysis takes into account the structure of statements and expressions; it also provides a special treatment of the expression operators !, &&, ||, and ? :, and of boolean-valued constant expressions.

Except for the special treatment of the conditional boolean operators `&&`, `||`, and `? :` and of boolean-valued constant expressions, the values of expressions are not taken into account in the flow analysis.

Example 16-1. Definite Assignment Considers Structure of Statements and Expressions

A Java compiler recognizes that `k` is definitely assigned before its access (as an argument of a method invocation) in the code:

```
{
    int k;
    if (v > 0 && (k = System.in.read()) >= 0)
        System.out.println(k);
}
```

because the access occurs only if the value of the expression:

```
v > 0 && (k = System.in.read()) >= 0
```

is `true`, and the value can be `true` only if the assignment to `k` is executed (more properly, evaluated).

Similarly, a Java compiler will recognize that in the code:

```
{
    int k;
    while (true) {
        k = n;
        if (k >= 5) break;
        n = 6;
    }
    System.out.println(k);
}
```

the variable `k` is definitely assigned by the `while` statement because the condition expression `true` never has the value `false`, so only the `break` statement can cause the `while` statement to complete normally, and `k` is definitely assigned before the `break` statement.

On the other hand, the code:

```
{
    int k;
    while (n < 4) {
        k = n;
        if (k >= 5) break;
        n = 6;
    }
    System.out.println(k);    /* k is not "definitely assigned"
                                 before this statement */
}
```

```
    }
```

must be rejected by a Java compiler, because in this case the `while` statement is not guaranteed to execute its body as far as the rules of definite assignment are concerned.

Example 16-2. Definite Assignment Does Not Consider Values of Expressions

A Java compiler must produce a compile-time error for the code:

```
    {
        int k;
        int n = 5;
        if (n > 2)
            k = 3;
        System.out.println(k);  /* k is not "definitely assigned"
                                     before this statement */
    }
```

even though the value of n is known at compile time, and in principle it can be known at compile time that the assignment to k will always be executed (more properly, evaluated). A Java compiler must operate according to the rules laid out in this section. The rules recognize only constant expressions; in this example, the expression n > 2 is not a constant expression as defined in §15.28.

As another example, a Java compiler will accept the code:

```
    void flow(boolean flag) {
        int k;
        if (flag)
            k = 3;
        else
            k = 4;
        System.out.println(k);
    }
```

as far as definite assignment of k is concerned, because the rules outlined in this section allow it to tell that k is assigned no matter whether the flag is true or false. But the rules do not accept the variation:

```
    void flow(boolean flag) {
        int k;
        if (flag)
            k = 3;
        if (!flag)
            k = 4;
        System.out.println(k);  /* k is not "definitely assigned"
                                     before this statement */
    }
```

and so compiling this program must cause a compile-time error to occur.

Example 16-3. Definite Unassignment

A Java compiler will accept the code:

```
void unflow(boolean flag) {
    final int k;
    if (flag) {
        k = 3;
        System.out.println(k);
    }
    else {
        k = 4;
        System.out.println(k);
    }
}
```

as far as definite unassignment of k is concerned, because the rules outlined in this section allow it to tell that k is assigned at most once (indeed, exactly once) no matter whether the flag is true or false. But the rules do not accept the variation:

```
void unflow(boolean flag) {
    final int k;
    if (flag) {
        k = 3;
        System.out.println(k);
    }
    if (!flag) {
        k = 4;
        System.out.println(k);   /* k is not "definitely unassigned"
                                        before this statement */
    }
}
```

and so compiling this program must cause a compile-time error to occur.

In order to precisely specify all the cases of definite assignment, the rules in this section define several technical terms:

- whether a variable is *definitely assigned before* a statement or expression;

- whether a variable is *definitely unassigned before* a statement or expression;

- whether a variable is *definitely assigned after* a statement or expression; and

- whether a variable is *definitely unassigned after* a statement or expression.

For boolean-valued expressions, the last two are refined into four cases:

- whether a variable is *definitely assigned after* the expression *when true*;

- whether a variable is *definitely unassigned after* the expression *when true*;

- whether a variable is *definitely assigned after* the expression *when false*; and

- whether a variable is *definitely unassigned* after the expression *when false*.

Here, *when true* and *when false* refer to the value of the expression.

> For example, the local variable `k` is definitely assigned a value after evaluation of the expression:
>
> ```
> a && ((k=m) > 5)
> ```
>
> when the expression is `true` but not when the expression is `false` (because if `a` is false, then the assignment to `k` is not necessarily executed (more properly, evaluated)).

The phrase "*v* is definitely assigned after *x*" (where *v* is a local variable and *x* is a statement or expression) means "*v* is definitely assigned after *x* if *x* completes normally". If *x* completes abruptly, the assignment need not have occurred, and the rules stated here take this into account.

> A peculiar consequence of this definition is that "*v* is definitely assigned after `break;`" is always true! Because a `break` statement never completes normally, it is vacuously true that *v* has been assigned a value if the `break` statement completes normally.

The statement "*v* is definitely unassigned after *x*" (where *v* is a variable and *x* is a statement or expression) means "*v* is definitely unassigned after *x* if *x* completes normally".

> An even more peculiar consequence of this definition is that "*v* is definitely unassigned after `break;`" is always true! Because a `break` statement never completes normally, it is vacuously true that *v* has not been assigned a value if the `break` statement completes normally. (For that matter, it is also vacuously true that the moon is made of green cheese if the `break` statement completes normally.)

In all, there are four possibilities for a variable *v* after a statement or expression has been executed:

- *v* is definitely assigned and is not definitely unassigned.

  (The flow analysis rules prove that an assignment to *v* has occurred.)

- *v* is definitely unassigned and is not definitely assigned.

  (The flow analysis rules prove that an assignment to *v* has not occurred.)

- *v* is not definitely assigned and is not definitely unassigned.

  (The rules cannot prove whether or not an assignment to *v* has occurred.)

- *v* is definitely assigned and is definitely unassigned.

(It is impossible for the statement or expression to complete normally.)

To shorten the rules, the customary abbreviation "iff" is used to mean "if and only if". We also use an abbreviation convention: if a rule contains one or more occurrences of "[un]assigned" then it stands for two rules, one with every occurrence of "[un]assigned" replaced by "definitely assigned" and one with every occurrence of "[un]assigned" replaced by "definitely unassigned".

For example:

- V is [un]assigned after an empty statement iff it is [un]assigned before the empty statement.

should be understood to stand for two rules:

- V is definitely assigned after an empty statement iff it is definitely assigned before the empty statement.

- V is definitely unassigned after an empty statement iff it is definitely unassigned before the empty statement.

Throughout the rest of this chapter, we will, unless explicitly stated otherwise, write V to represent a local variable or a blank `final` field (for rules of definite assignment) or a blank `final` variable (for rules of definite unassignment). Likewise, we will use a, b, c, and e to represent expressions, and S and T to represent statements. We will use the phrase "a is V" to mean that a is either the simple name of the variable V, or V's simple name qualified by `this` (ignoring parentheses). We will use the phrase "a is not V" to mean the negation of "a is V".

The definite unassignment analysis of loop statements raises a special problem. Consider the statement `while (e) s`. In order to determine whether V is definitely unassigned within some subexpression of e, we need to determine whether V is definitely unassigned before e. One might argue, by analogy with the rule for definite assignment (§16.2.10), that V is definitely unassigned before e iff it is definitely unassigned before the `while` statement. However, such a rule is inadequate for our purposes. If e evaluates to `true`, the statement S will be executed. Later, if V is assigned by S, then in the following iteration(s) V will have already been assigned when e is evaluated. Under the rule suggested above, it would be possible to assign V multiple times, which is exactly what we have sought to avoid by introducing these rules.

A revised rule would be: "V is definitely unassigned before e iff it is definitely unassigned before the `while` statement and definitely unassigned after S". However, when we formulate the rule for S, we find: "V is definitely unassigned before S iff it is definitely unassigned after e when true". This leads to a circularity. In effect, V is definitely unassigned *before* the loop condition e only if it is unassigned *after* the loop as a whole!

We break this vicious circle using a hypothetical analysis of the loop condition and body. For example, if we assume that V is definitely unassigned before e (regardless of whether V

really is definitely unassigned before *e*), and can then prove that *v* was definitely unassigned after *e* then we know that *e* does not assign *v*. This is stated more formally as:

Assuming *v* is definitely unassigned before *e*, *v* is definitely unassigned after *e*.

Variations on the above analysis are used to define well founded definite unassignment rules for all loop statements in the Java programming language.

16.1   Definite Assignment and Expressions

16.1.1   Boolean Constant Expressions

- *v* is [un]assigned after any constant expression (§15.28) whose value is `true` when false.

- *v* is [un]assigned after any constant expression whose value is `false` when true.

- *v* is [un]assigned after any constant expression whose value is `true` when true iff *v* is [un]assigned before the constant expression.

- *v* is [un]assigned after any constant expression whose value is `false` when false iff *v* is [un]assigned before the constant expression.

- *v* is [un]assigned after a boolean-valued constant expression *e* iff *v* is [un]assigned after *e* when true and *v* is [un]assigned after *e* when false.

    This is equivalent to saying that *v* is [un]assigned after *e* iff *v* is [un]assigned before *e*.

Because a constant expression whose value is `true` never has the value `false`, and a constant expression whose value is `false` never has the value `true`, the first two rules are vacuously satisfied. They are helpful in analyzing expressions involving the operators `&&` (§16.1.2), `||` (§16.1.3), `!` (§16.1.4), and `?  :` (§16.1.5).

16.1.2   Conditional-And Operator `&&`

- *v* is [un]assigned after *a* `&&` *b* (§15.23) when true iff *v* is [un]assigned after *b* when true.

- *v* is [un]assigned after *a* `&&` *b* when false iff *v* is [un]assigned after *a* when false and *v* is [un]assigned after *b* when false.

- *v* is [un]assigned before *a* iff *v* is [un]assigned before *a* `&&` *b*.

- *v* is [un]assigned before *b* iff *v* is [un]assigned after *a* when true.

- v is [un]assigned after *a* && *b* iff v is [un]assigned after *a* && *b* when true and v is [un]assigned after *a* && *b* when false.

16.1.3   Conditional-Or Operator ||

- v is [un]assigned after *a* || *b* (§15.24) when true iff v is [un]assigned after *a* when true and v is [un]assigned after *b* when true.

- v is [un]assigned after *a* || *b* when false iff v is [un]assigned after *b* when false.

- v is [un]assigned before *a* iff v is [un]assigned before *a* || *b*.

- v is [un]assigned before *b* iff v is [un]assigned after *a* when false.

- v is [un]assigned after *a* || *b* iff v is [un]assigned after *a* || *b* when true and v is [un]assigned after *a* || *b* when false.

16.1.4   Logical Complement Operator !

- v is [un]assigned after ! *a* (§15.15.6) when true iff v is [un]assigned after *a* when false.

- v is [un]assigned after ! *a* when false iff v is [un]assigned after *a* when true.

- v is [un]assigned before *a* iff v is [un]assigned before ! *a*.

- v is [un]assigned after ! *a* iff v is [un]assigned after ! *a* when true and v is [un]assigned after ! *a* when false.

  This is equivalent to saying that v is [un]assigned after ! *a* iff v is [un]assigned after *a*.

16.1.5   Conditional Operator ? :

Suppose that *b* and *c* are boolean-valued expressions.

- v is [un]assigned after *a* ? *b* : *c* (§15.25) when true iff v is [un]assigned after *b* when true and v is [un]assigned after *c* when true.

- v is [un]assigned after *a* ? *b* : *c* when false iff v is [un]assigned after *b* when false and v is [un]assigned after *c* when false.

- v is [un]assigned before *a* iff v is [un]assigned before *a* ? *b* : *c*.

- v is [un]assigned before *b* iff v is [un]assigned after *a* when true.

- v is [un]assigned before *c* iff v is [un]assigned after *a* when false.

- *v* is [un]assigned after *a* ? *b* : *c* iff *v* is [un]assigned after *a* ? *b* : *c* when true and *v* is [un]assigned after *a* ? *b* : *c* when false.

16.1.6   Conditional Operator ? :

Suppose that *b* and *c* are expressions that are not boolean-valued.

- *v* is [un]assigned after *a* ? *b* : *c* (§15.25) iff *v* is [un]assigned after *b* and *v* is [un]assigned after *c*.
- *v* is [un]assigned before *a* iff *v* is [un]assigned before *a* ? *b* : *c*.
- *v* is [un]assigned before *b* iff *v* is [un]assigned after *a* when true.
- *v* is [un]assigned before *c* iff *v* is [un]assigned after *a* when false.

16.1.7   Other Expressions of Type `boolean`

Suppose that *e* is an expression of type `boolean` and is not a boolean constant expression, logical complement expression ! *a*, conditional-and expression *a* && *b*, conditional-or expression *a* || *b*, or conditional expression *a* ? *b* : *c*.

- *v* is [un]assigned after *e* when true iff *v* is [un]assigned after *e*.
- *v* is [un]assigned after *e* when false iff *v* is [un]assigned after *e*.

16.1.8   Assignment Expressions

Consider an assignment expression *a* - *b*, *a* += *b*, *a* -= *b*, *a* *= *b*, *a* /= *b*, *a* %= *b*, *a* <<= *b*, *a* >>= *b*, *a* >>>= *b*, *a* &= *b*, *a* |= *b*, or *a* ^= *b* (§15.26).

- *v* is definitely assigned after the assignment expression iff either:
  - *a* is *v*, or
  - *v* is definitely assigned after *b*.
- *v* is definitely unassigned after the assignment expression iff *a* is not *v* and *v* is definitely unassigned after *b*.
- *v* is [un]assigned before *a* iff *v* is [un]assigned before the assignment expression.
- *v* is [un]assigned before *b* iff *v* is [un]assigned after *a*.

  Note that if *a* is *v* and *v* is not definitely assigned before a compound assignment such as *a* &= *b*, then a compile-time error will necessarily occur. The first rule for definite assignment stated above includes the disjunct "*a* is *v*" even for compound assignment expressions, not just simple assignments, so that *v* will be considered to have been definitely assigned at later points in the code. Including the disjunct "*a* is *v*" does not affect the binary decision as to whether a program is acceptable or will result in a compile-time error, but it affects how many different points in the code may be regarded as erroneous, and so in practice it can improve the quality of error reporting. A similar remark applies to the inclusion of the conjunct "*a* is not *v*" in the first rule for definite unassignment stated above.

16.1.9   Operators ++ and --

- *v* is definitely assigned after ++a (§15.15.1), --a (§15.15.2), a++ (§15.14.2), or a-- (§15.14.3) iff either *a* is *v* or *v* is definitely assigned after the operand expression.

- *v* is definitely unassigned after ++a, --a, a++, or a-- iff *a* is not *v* and *v* is definitely unassigned after the operand expression.

- *v* is [un]assigned before *a* iff *v* is [un]assigned before ++a, --a, a++, or a--.

16.1.10   Other Expressions

If an expression is not a boolean constant expression, and is not a preincrement expression ++a, predecrement expression --a, postincrement expression a++, postdecrement expression a--, logical complement expression !a, conditional-and expression a && b, conditional-or expression a || b, conditional expression a ? b : c, or assignment expression, then the following rules apply:

- If the expression has no subexpressions, *v* is [un]assigned after the expression iff *v* is [un]assigned before the expression.

  This case applies to literals, names, this (both qualified and unqualified), unqualified class instance creation expressions with no arguments, initialized array creation expressions whose initializers contain no expressions, unqualified superclass field access expressions, named method invocations with no arguments, and unqualified superclass method invocations with no arguments.

- If the expression has subexpressions, *v* is [un]assigned after the expression iff *v* is [un]assigned after its rightmost immediate subexpression.

  There is a piece of subtle reasoning behind the assertion that a variable *v* can be known to be definitely unassigned after a method invocation. Taken by itself, at face value and without qualification, such an assertion is not always true, because an invoked method can perform assignments. But it must be remembered that, for the purposes of the Java programming language, the concept of definite unassignment is applied only to blank final variables. If *v* is a blank final local variable, then only the method to which its declaration belongs can perform assignments to *v*. If *v* is a blank final field, then only a constructor or an initializer for the class containing the declaration for *v* can perform assignments to *v*; no method can perform assignments to *v*. Finally, explicit constructor invocations (§8.8.7.1) are handled specially (§16.9); although they are syntactically similar to expression statements containing method invocations, they are not expression statements and therefore the rules of this section do not apply to explicit constructor invocations.

For any immediate subexpression y of an expression x, v is [un]assigned before y iff one of the following situations is true:

- y is the leftmost immediate subexpression of x and v is [un]assigned before x.

- y is the right-hand operand of a binary operator and v is [un]assigned after the left-hand operand.

- x is an array access, y is the subexpression within the brackets, and v is [un]assigned after the subexpression before the brackets.

- x is a primary method invocation expression, y is the first argument expression in the method invocation expression, and v is [un]assigned after the primary expression that computes the target object.

- x is a method invocation expression or a class instance creation expression; y is an argument expression, but not the first; and v is [un]assigned after the argument expression to the left of y.

- x is a qualified class instance creation expression, y is the first argument expression in the class instance creation expression, and v is [un]assigned after the primary expression that computes the qualifying object.

- x is an array instance creation expression; y is a dimension expression, but not the first; and v is [un]assigned after the dimension expression to the left of y.

- x is an array instance creation expression initialized via an array initializer; y is the array initializer in x; and v is [un]assigned after the dimension expression to the left of y.

16.2   Definite Assignment and Statements

16.2.1   Empty Statements

- v is [un]assigned after an empty statement (§14.6) iff it is [un]assigned before the empty statement.

16.2.2   Blocks

- A blank `final` member field v is definitely assigned (and moreover is not definitely unassigned) before the block (§14.2) that is the body of any method in the scope of v and before the declaration of any class declared within the scope of v.

- A local variable v is definitely unassigned (and moreover is not definitely assigned) before the block that is the body of the constructor, method, instance initializer or static initializer that declares v.

- Let c be a class declared within the scope of v. Then v is definitely assigned before the block that is the body of any constructor, method, instance initializer, or static initializer declared in c iff v is definitely assigned before the declaration of c.

  > Note that there are no rules that would allow us to conclude that v is definitely unassigned before the block that is the body of any constructor, method, instance initializer, or static initializer declared in c. We can informally conclude that v is not definitely unassigned before the block that is the body of any constructor, method, instance initializer, or static initializer declared in c, but there is no need for such a rule to be stated explicitly.

- v is [un]assigned after an empty block iff v is [un]assigned before the empty block.

- v is [un]assigned after a non-empty block iff v is [un]assigned after the last statement in the block.

- v is [un]assigned before the first statement of the block iff v is [un]assigned before the block.

- v is [un]assigned before any other statement s of the block iff v is [un]assigned after the statement immediately preceding s in the block.

We say that v is definitely unassigned everywhere in a block B iff:

- v is definitely unassigned before B.

- v is definitely assigned after e in every assignment expression $V = e$, $V \mathrel{+}= e$, $V \mathrel{-}= e$, $V \mathrel{*}= e$, $V \mathrel{/}= e$, $V \mathrel{\%}= e$, $V \mathrel{<<}= e$, $V \mathrel{>>}= e$, $V \mathrel{>>>}= e$, $V \mathrel{\&}= e$, $V \mathrel{|}= e$, or $V \mathrel{\hat{}}= e$ that occurs in B.

- v is definitely assigned before every expression $++V$, $--V$, $V++$, or $V--$. that occurs in B.

  > These conditions are counterintuitive and require some explanation. Consider a simple assignment $V = e$. If V is definitely assigned after e, then either:
  >
  > - The assignment occurs in dead code, and V is vacuously definitely assigned. In this case, the assignment will not actually take place, and we can assume that V is not being assigned by the assignment expression. Or:
  >
  >   - V was already assigned by an earlier expression prior to e. In this case the current assignment will cause a compile-time error.

So, we can conclude that if the conditions are met by a program that causes no compile time error, then any assignments to V in B will not actually take place at run time.

16.2.3   Local Class Declaration Statements

- V is [un]assigned after a local class declaration statement (§14.3) iff V is [un]assigned before the local class declaration statement.

16.2.4   Local Variable Declaration Statements

- V is [un]assigned after a local variable declaration statement (§14.4) that contains no variable initializers iff V is [un]assigned before the local variable declaration statement.

- V is definitely assigned after a local variable declaration statement that contains at least one variable initializer iff either V is definitely assigned after the last variable initializer in the local variable declaration statement or the last variable initializer in the declaration is in the declarator that declares V.

- V is definitely unassigned after a local variable declaration statement that contains at least one variable initializer iff V is definitely unassigned after the last variable initializer in the local variable declaration statement and the last variable initializer in the declaration is not in the declarator that declares V.

- V is [un]assigned before the first variable initializer in a local variable declaration statement iff V is [un]assigned before the local variable declaration statement.

- V is definitely assigned before any variable initializer e other than the first one in the local variable declaration statement iff either V is definitely assigned after the variable initializer to the left of e or the initializer expression to the left of e is in the declarator that declares V.

- V is definitely unassigned before any variable initializer e other than the first one in the local variable declaration statement iff V is definitely unassigned after the variable initializer to the left of e and the initializer expression to the left of e is not in the declarator that declares V.

16.2.5   Labeled Statements

- V is [un]assigned after a labeled statement $L : S$ (where L is a label) (§14.7) iff V is [un]assigned after S and V is [un]assigned before every `break` statement that may exit the labeled statement $L : S$.

- V is [un]assigned before S iff V is [un]assigned before $L : S$.

16.2.6   Expression Statements

- v is [un]assigned after an expression statement e; (§14.8) iff it is [un]assigned after e.

- v is [un]assigned before e iff it is [un]assigned before e; .

16.2.7   `if` Statements

The following rules apply to a statement `if (e)` S (§14.9.1) :

- v is [un]assigned after `if (e)` S iff v is [un]assigned after S and v is [un]assigned after e when false.

- v is [un]assigned before e iff v is [un]assigned before `if (e)` S.

- v is [un]assigned before S iff v is [un]assigned after e when true.

The following rules apply to a statement `if (e)` S `else` T (§14.9.2) :

- v is [un]assigned after `if (e)` S `else` T iff v is [un]assigned after S and v is [un]assigned after T.

- v is [un]assigned before e iff v is [un]assigned before `if (e)` S `else` T.

- v is [un]assigned before S iff v is [un]assigned after e when true.

- v is [un]assigned before T iff v is [un]assigned after e when false.

16.2.8   `assert` Statements

The following rules apply both to a statement `assert` e_1 and to a statement `assert` e_1 : e_2 (§14.10) :

- v is [un]assigned before e_1 iff v is [un]assigned before the `assert` statement.

- v is definitely assigned after the `assert` statement iff v is definitely assigned before the `assert` statement.

- v is definitely unassigned after the `assert` statement iff v is definitely unassigned before the `assert` statement and v is definitely unassigned after e_1 when true.

The following rule applies to a statement `assert` e_1 : e_2 :

- v is [un]assigned before e_2 iff v is [un]assigned after e_1 when false.

16.2.9 `switch` **Statements**

- v is [un]assigned after a `switch` statement (§14.11) iff all of the following are true:

  - Either there is a `default` label in the switch block or v is [un]assigned after the switch expression.

  - Either there are no switch labels in the switch block that do not begin a block-statement-group (that is, there are no switch labels immediately before the "}" that ends the switch block) or v is [un]assigned after the switch expression.

  - Either the switch block contains no block-statement-groups or v is [un]assigned after the last block-statement of the last block-statement-group.

  - v is [un]assigned before every `break` statement that may exit the `switch` statement.

- v is [un]assigned before the switch expression iff v is [un]assigned before the `switch` statement.

If a switch block contains at least one block-statement-group, then the following rules also apply:

- v is [un]assigned before the first block-statement of the first block-statement-group in the switch block iff v is [un]assigned after the switch expression.

- v is [un]assigned before the first block-statement of any block-statement-group other than the first iff v is [un]assigned after the switch expression and v is [un]assigned after the preceding block-statement.

16.2.10 `while` **Statements**

- v is [un]assigned after `while (e) s` (§14.12) iff v is [un]assigned after e when false and v is [un]assigned before every `break` statement for which the `while` statement is the break target.

- v is definitely assigned before e iff v is definitely assigned before the `while` statement.

- v is definitely unassigned before e iff all of the following conditions hold:

  - v is definitely unassigned before the `while` statement.

  - Assuming v is definitely unassigned before e, v is definitely unassigned after s.

  - Assuming v is definitely unassigned before e, v is definitely unassigned before every `continue` statement for which the `while` statement is the continue target.

- *v* is [un]assigned before *s* iff *v* is [un]assigned after *e* when true.

16.2.11   do **Statements**

- *v* is [un]assigned after do *S* while (e); (§14.13) iff *v* is [un]assigned after *e* when false and *v* is [un]assigned before every break statement for which the do statement is the break target.

- *v* is definitely assigned before *s* iff *v* is definitely assigned before the do statement.

- *v* is definitely unassigned before *s* iff all of the following conditions hold:

  - *v* is definitely unassigned before the do statement.

  - Assuming *v* is definitely unassigned before *s*, *v* is definitely unassigned after *e* when true.

- *v* is [un]assigned before *e* iff *v* is [un]assigned after *s* and *v* is [un]assigned before every continue statement for which the do statement is the continue target.

16.2.12   for **Statements**

The rules herein cover the basic for statement (§14.14.1). Since the enhanced for (§14.14.2) statement is defined by translation to a basic for statement, no special rules need to be provided for it.

- *v* is [un]assigned after a for statement iff both of the following are true:

  - Either a condition expression is not present or *v* is [un]assigned after the condition expression when false.

  - *v* is [un]assigned before every break statement for which the for statement is the break target.

- *v* is [un]assigned before the initialization part of the for statement iff *v* is [un]assigned before the for statement.

- *v* is definitely assigned before the condition part of the for statement iff *v* is definitely assigned after the initialization part of the for statement.

- *v* is definitely unassigned before the condition part of the for statement iff all of the following conditions hold:

  - *v* is definitely unassigned after the initialization part of the for statement.

- Assuming v is definitely unassigned before the condition part of the `for` statement, v is definitely unassigned after the contained statement.

- Assuming v is definitely unassigned before the contained statement, v is definitely unassigned before every `continue` statement for which the `for` statement is the continue target.

- v is [un]assigned before the contained statement iff either of the following is true:

  - A condition expression is present and v is [un]assigned after the condition expression when true.

  - No condition expression is present and v is [un]assigned after the initialization part of the `for` statement.

- v is [un]assigned before the incrementation part of the `for` statement iff v is [un]assigned after the contained statement and v is [un]assigned before every `continue` statement for which the `for` statement is the continue target.

16.2.12.1 *Initialization Part of* `for` *Statement*

- If the initialization part of the `for` statement is a local variable declaration statement, the rules of §16.2.4 apply.

- Otherwise, if the initialization part is empty, then v is [un]assigned after the initialization part iff v is [un]assigned before the initialization part.

- Otherwise, three rules apply:

  - v is [un]assigned after the initialization part iff v is [un]assigned after the last expression statement in the initialization part.

  - v is [un]assigned before the first expression statement in the initialization part iff v is [un]assigned before the initialization part.

  - v is [un]assigned before an expression statement s other than the first in the initialization part iff v is [un]assigned after the expression statement immediately preceding s.

16.2.12.2 *Incrementation Part of* `for` *Statement*

- If the incrementation part of the `for` statement is empty, then v is [un]assigned after the incrementation part iff v is [un]assigned before the incrementation part.

- Otherwise, three rules apply:

- *v* is [un]assigned after the incrementation part iff *v* is [un]assigned after the last expression statement in the incrementation part.

- *v* is [un]assigned before the first expression statement in the incrementation part iff *v* is [un]assigned before the incrementation part.

- *v* is [un]assigned before an expression statement *s* other than the first in the incrementation part iff *v* is [un]assigned after the expression statement immediately preceding *s*.

16.2.13   break, continue, return, **and** throw **Statements**

- By convention, we say that *v* is [un]assigned after any break, continue, return, or throw statement (§14.15, §14.16, §14.17, §14.18).

  > The notion that a variable is "[un]assigned after" a statement or expression really means "is [un]assigned after the statement or expression completes normally". Because a break, continue, return, or throw statement never completes normally, it vacuously satisfies this notion.

- In a return statement with an expression *e* or a throw statement with an expression *e*, *v* is [un]assigned before *e* iff *v* is [un]assigned before the return or throw statement.

16.2.14   synchronized **Statements**

- *v* is [un]assigned after synchronized (e) *S* (§14.19) iff *v* is [un]assigned after *S*.

- *v* is [un]assigned before *e* iff *v* is [un]assigned before the statement synchronized (e) *S*.

- *v* is [un]assigned before *S* iff *v* is [un]assigned after *e*.

16.2.15   try **Statements**

These rules apply to every try statement (§14.20), whether or not it has a finally block:

- *v* is [un]assigned before the try block iff *v* is [un]assigned before the try statement.

- *v* is definitely assigned before a catch block iff *v* is definitely assigned before the try block.

- *v* is definitely unassigned before a `catch` block iff all of the following conditions hold:

  - *v* is definitely unassigned after the `try` block.

  - *v* is definitely unassigned before every `return` statement that belongs to the `try` block.

  - *v* is definitely unassigned after *e* in every statement of the form `throw e` that belongs to the `try` block.

  - *v* is definitely unassigned after every `assert` statement that occurs in the `try` block.

  - *v* is definitely unassigned before every `break` statement that belongs to the `try` block and whose break target contains (or is) the `try` statement.

  - *v* is definitely unassigned before every `continue` statement that belongs to the `try` block and whose continue target contains the `try` statement.

If a `try` statement does not have a `finally` block, then this rule also applies:

- *v* is [un]assigned after the `try` statement iff *v* is [un]assigned after the `try` block and *v* is [un]assigned after every `catch` block in the `try` statement.

If a `try` statement does have a `finally` block, then these rules also apply:

- *v* is definitely assigned after the `try` statement iff at least one of the following is true:

  - *v* is definitely assigned after the `try` block and *v* is definitely assigned after every `catch` block in the `try` statement.

  - *v* is definitely assigned after the `finally` block.

  - *v* is definitely unassigned after a `try` statement iff *v* is definitely unassigned after the `finally` block.

- *v* is definitely assigned before the `finally` block iff *v* is definitely assigned before the `try` statement.

- *v* is definitely unassigned before the `finally` block iff all of the following conditions hold:

  - *v* is definitely unassigned after the `try` block.

  - *v* is definitely unassigned before every `return` statement that belongs to the `try` block.

- *v* is definitely unassigned after *e* in every statement of the form `throw e` that belongs to the `try` block.

- *v* is definitely unassigned after every `assert` statement that occurs in the `try` block.

- *v* is definitely unassigned before every `break` statement that belongs to the `try` block and whose break target contains (or is) the `try` statement.

- *v* is definitely unassigned before every `continue` statement that belongs to the `try` block and whose continue target contains the `try` statement.

- *v* is definitely unassigned after every `catch` block of the `try` statement.

16.3   Definite Assignment and Parameters

- A formal parameter *v* of a method or constructor (§8.4.1, §8.8.1) is definitely assigned (and moreover is not definitely unassigned) before the body of the method or constructor.

- An exception parameter *v* of a `catch` clause (§14.20) is definitely assigned (and moreover is not definitely unassigned) before the body of the `catch` clause.

16.4   Definite Assignment and Array Initializers

- *v* is [un]assigned after an empty array initializer (§10.6) iff *v* is [un]assigned before the empty array initializer.

- *v* is [un]assigned after a non-empty array initializer iff *v* is [un]assigned after the last variable initializer in the array initializer.

- *v* is [un]assigned before the first variable initializer of the array initializer iff *v* is [un]assigned before the array initializer.

- *v* is [un]assigned before any other variable initializer *e* of the array initializer iff *v* is [un]assigned after the variable initializer to the left of *e* in the array initializer.

16.5 Definite Assignment and Enum Constants

The rules determining when a variable is definitely assigned or definitely unassigned before an enum constant (§8.9.1) are given in §16.8.

> This is because an enum constant is essentially a `static final` field (§8.3.1.1, §8.3.1.2) that is initialized with a class instance creation expression (§15.9).

- v is definitely assigned before the declaration of a class body of an enum constant with no arguments that is declared within the scope of v iff v is definitely assigned before the enum constant.

- v is definitely assigned before the declaration of a class body of an enum constant with arguments that is declared within the scope of v iff v is definitely assigned after the last argument expression of the enum constant

The definite assignment/unassignment status of any construct within the class body of an enum constant is governed by the usual rules for classes.

- v is [un]assigned before the first argument to an enum constant iff it is [un]assigned before the enum constant.

- v is [un]assigned before y (an argument of an enum constant, but not the first) iff v is [un]assigned after the argument to the left of y.

16.6 Definite Assignment and Anonymous Classes

- v is definitely assigned before an anonymous class declaration (§15.9.5) that is declared within the scope of v iff v is definitely assigned after the class instance creation expression that declares the anonymous class.

> It should be clear that if an anonymous class is implicitly defined by an enum constant, the rules of §16.5 apply.

16.7 Definite Assignment and Member Types

Let c be a class, and let v be a blank `final` member field of c. Then:

- v is definitely assigned (and moreover, not definitely unassigned) before the declaration of any member type (§8.5, §9.5) of c.

Let c be a class declared within the scope of v. Then:

- v is definitely assigned before a member type declaration of c iff v is definitely assigned before the declaration of c.

16.8   Definite Assignment and Static Initializers

Let c be a class declared within the scope of v. Then:

- v is definitely assigned before an enum constant (§8.9.1) or static variable initializer (§8.3.2.1) of c iff v is definitely assigned before the declaration of c.

  > Note that there are no rules that would allow us to conclude that v is definitely unassigned before a static variable initializer or enum constant. We can informally conclude that v is not definitely unassigned before any static variable initializer of c, but there is no need for such a rule to be stated explicitly.

Let c be a class, and let v be a blank `static final` member field of c, declared in c. Then:

- v is definitely unassigned (and moreover is not definitely assigned) before the leftmost enum constant, static initializer (§8.7), or static variable initializer of c.

- v is [un]assigned before an enum constant, static initializer, or static variable initializer of c other than the leftmost iff v is [un]assigned after the preceding enum constant, static initializer, or static variable initializer of c.

Let c be a class, and let v be a blank `static final` member field of c, declared in a superclass of c. Then:

- v is definitely assigned (and moreover is not definitely unassigned) before every enum constant of c.

- v is definitely assigned (and moreover is not definitely unassigned) before the block that is the body of a static initializer of c.

- v is definitely assigned (and moreover is not definitely unassigned) before every static variable initializer of c.

16.9   Definite Assignment, Constructors, and Instance Initializers

Let c be a class declared within the scope of v. Then:

- v is definitely assigned before an instance variable initializer (§8.3.2.2) of c iff v is definitely assigned before the declaration of c.

  > Note that there are no rules that would allow us to conclude that v is definitely unassigned before an instance variable initializer. We can informally conclude that v is not definitely unassigned before any instance variable initializer of c, but there is no need for such a rule to be stated explicitly.

Let c be a class, and let v be a blank `final` non-`static` member field of c, declared in c. Then:

- v is definitely unassigned (and moreover is not definitely assigned) before the leftmost instance initializer (§8.6) or instance variable initializer of c.

- v is [un]assigned before an instance initializer or instance variable initializer of c other than the leftmost iff v is [un]assigned after the preceding instance initializer or instance variable initializer of c.

The following rules hold within the constructors (§8.8.7) of class c:

- v is definitely assigned (and moreover is not definitely unassigned) after an alternate constructor invocation (§8.8.7.1).

- v is definitely unassigned (and moreover is not definitely assigned) before an explicit or implicit superclass constructor invocation (§8.8.7.1).

- If c has no instance initializers or instance variable initializers, then v is not definitely assigned (and moreover is definitely unassigned) after an explicit or implicit superclass constructor invocation.

- If c has at least one instance initializer or instance variable initializer then v is [un]assigned after an explicit or implicit superclass constructor invocation iff v is [un]assigned after the rightmost instance initializer or instance variable initializer of c.

Let c be a class, and let v be a blank `final` member field of c, declared in a superclass of c. Then:

- v is definitely assigned (and moreover is not definitely unassigned) before the block that is the body of a constructor or instance initializer of c.

- v is definitely assigned (and moreover is not definitely unassigned) before every instance variable initializer of c.

CHAPTER 17

Threads and Locks

WHILE most of the discussion in the preceding chapters is concerned only with the behavior of code as executed a single statement or expression at a time, that is, by a single *thread*, the Java Virtual Machine can support many threads of execution at once. These threads independently execute code that operates on values and objects residing in a shared main memory. Threads may be supported by having many hardware processors, by time-slicing a single hardware processor, or by time-slicing many hardware processors.

Threads are represented by the `Thread` class. The only way for a user to create a thread is to create an object of this class; each thread is associated with such an object. A thread will start when the `start()` method is invoked on the corresponding `Thread` object.

The behavior of threads, particularly when not correctly synchronized, can be confusing and counterintuitive. This chapter describes the semantics of multithreaded programs; it includes rules for which values may be seen by a read of shared memory that is updated by multiple threads. As the specification is similar to the *memory models* for different hardware architectures, these semantics are known as the *Java programming language memory model*. When no confusion can arise, we will simply refer to these rules as "the memory model".

These semantics do not prescribe how a multithreaded program should be executed. Rather, they describe the behaviors that multithreaded programs are allowed to exhibit. Any execution strategy that generates only allowed behaviors is an acceptable execution strategy.

17.1   Synchronization

The Java programming language provides multiple mechanisms for communicating between threads. The most basic of these methods is *synchronization*, which is implemented using *monitors*. Each object in Java is associated with a monitor, which a thread can *lock* or *unlock*. Only one thread at a time may hold a lock on a monitor. Any other threads attempting to lock that monitor are blocked until they can obtain a lock on that monitor. A thread *t* may lock a particular monitor multiple times; each unlock reverses the effect of one lock operation.

The `synchronized` statement (§14.19) computes a reference to an object; it then attempts to perform a lock action on that object's monitor and does not proceed further until the lock action has successfully completed. After the lock action has been performed, the body of the `synchronized` statement is executed. If execution of the body is ever completed, either normally or abruptly, an unlock action is automatically performed on that same monitor.

A `synchronized` method (§8.4.3.6) automatically performs a lock action when it is invoked; its body is not executed until the lock action has successfully completed. If the method is an instance method, it locks the monitor associated with the instance for which it was invoked (that is, the object that will be known as `this` during execution of the body of the method). If the method is `static`, it locks the monitor associated with the `Class` object that represents the class in which the method is defined. If execution of the method's body is ever completed, either normally or abruptly, an unlock action is automatically performed on that same monitor.

The Java programming language neither prevents nor requires detection of deadlock conditions. Programs where threads hold (directly or indirectly) locks on multiple objects should use conventional techniques for deadlock avoidance, creating higher-level locking primitives that do not deadlock, if necessary.

Other mechanisms, such as reads and writes of `volatile` variables and the use of classes in the `java.util.concurrent` package, provide alternative ways of synchronization.

17.2   Wait Sets and Notification

Every object, in addition to having an associated monitor, has an associated *wait set*. A wait set is a set of threads.

When an object is first created, its wait set is empty. Elementary actions that add threads to and remove threads from wait sets are atomic. Wait sets are manipulated solely through the methods `Object.wait`, `Object.notify`, and `Object.notifyAll`.

Wait set manipulations can also be affected by the interruption status of a thread, and by the `Thread` class's methods dealing with interruption. Additionally, the `Thread` class's methods for sleeping and joining other threads have properties derived from those of wait and notification actions.

17.2.1 Wait

Wait actions occur upon invocation of `wait()`, or the timed forms `wait(long millisecs)` and `wait(long millisecs, int nanosecs)`.

> A call of `wait(long millisecs)` with a parameter of zero, or a call of `wait(long millisecs, int nanosecs)` with two zero parameters, is equivalent to an invocation of `wait()`.

A thread *returns normally* from a wait if it returns without throwing an `InterruptedException`.

Let thread *t* be the thread executing the `wait` method on object *m*, and let *n* be the number of lock actions by *t* on *m* that have not been matched by unlock actions. One of the following actions occurs:

- If *n* is zero (i.e., thread *t* does not already possess the lock for target *m*), then an `IllegalMonitorStateException` is thrown.

- If this is a timed wait and the `nanosecs` argument is not in the range of `0-999999` or the `millisecs` argument is negative, then an `IllegalArgumentException` is thrown.

- If thread *t* is interrupted, then an `InterruptedException` is thrown and *t*'s interruption status is set to false.

- Otherwise, the following sequence occurs:

  1. Thread *t* is added to the wait set of object *m*, and performs *n* unlock actions on *m*.

  2. Thread *t* does not execute any further instructions until it has been removed from *m*'s wait set. The thread may be removed from the wait set due to any one of the following actions, and will resume sometime afterward:

- A `notify` action being performed on *m* in which *t* is selected for removal from the wait set.

- A `notifyAll` action being performed on *m*.

- An `interrupt` action being performed on *t*.

- If this is a timed wait, an internal action removing *t* from *m*'s wait set that occurs after at least `millisecs` milliseconds plus `nanosecs` nanoseconds elapse since the beginning of this wait action.

- An internal action by the implementation. Implementations are permitted, although not encouraged, to perform "spurious wake-ups", that is, to remove threads from wait sets and thus enable resumption without explicit instructions to do so.

    > Notice that this provision necessitates the Java coding practice of using `wait` only within loops that terminate only when some logical condition that the thread is waiting for holds.

Each thread must determine an order over the events that could cause it to be removed from a wait set. That order does not have to be consistent with other orderings, but the thread must behave as though those events occurred in that order.

For example, if a thread *t* is in the wait set for *m*, and then both an interrupt of *t* and a notification of *m* occur, there must be an order over these events. If the interrupt is deemed to have occurred first, then *t* will eventually return from `wait` by throwing `InterruptedException`, and some other thread in the wait set for *m* (if any exist at the time of the notification) must receive the notification. If the notification is deemed to have occurred first, then *t* will eventually return normally from `wait` with an interrupt still pending.

3. Thread *t* performs *n* lock actions on *m*.

4. If thread *t* was removed from *m*'s wait set in step 2 due to an interrupt, then *t*'s interruption status is set to false and the `wait` method throws `InterruptedException`.

17.2.2 Notification

Notification actions occur upon invocation of methods `notify` and `notifyAll`.

Let thread *t* be the thread executing either of these methods on object *m*, and let *n* be the number of lock actions by *t* on *m* that have not been matched by unlock actions. One of the following actions occurs:

- If *n* is zero, then an `IllegalMonitorStateException` is thrown.

  This is the case where thread *t* does not already possess the lock for target *m*.

- If *n* is greater than zero and this is a `notify` action, then if *m*'s wait set is not empty, a thread *u* that is a member of *m*'s current wait set is selected and removed from the wait set.

  There is no guarantee about which thread in the wait set is selected. This removal from the wait set enables *u*'s resumption in a wait action. Notice, however, that *u*'s lock actions upon resumption cannot succeed until some time after *t* fully unlocks the monitor for *m*.

- If *n* is greater than zero and this is a `notifyAll` action, then all threads are removed from *m*'s wait set, and thus resume.

  Notice, however, that only one of them at a time will lock the monitor required during the resumption of wait.

17.2.3 Interruptions

Interruption actions occur upon invocation of `Thread.interrupt`, as well as methods defined to invoke it in turn, such as `ThreadGroup.interrupt`.

Let *t* be the thread invoking `u.interrupt`, for some thread *u*, where *t* and *u* may be the same. This action causes *u*'s interruption status to be set to true.

Additionally, if there exists some object *m* whose wait set contains *u*, then *u* is removed from *m*'s wait set. This enables *u* to resume in a wait action, in which case this wait will, after re-locking *m*'s monitor, throw `InterruptedException`.

Invocations of `Thread.isInterrupted` can determine a thread's interruption status. The `static` method `Thread.interrupted` may be invoked by a thread to observe and clear its own interruption status.

17.2.4 Interactions of Waits, Notification, and Interruption

The above specifications allow us to determine several properties having to do with the interaction of waits, notification, and interruption.

If a thread is both notified and interrupted while waiting, it may either:

- return normally from `wait`, while still having a pending interrupt (in other words, a call to `Thread.interrupted` would return true)

- return from `wait` by throwing an `InterruptedException`

The thread may not reset its interrupt status and return normally from the call to `wait`.

Similarly, notifications cannot be lost due to interrupts. Assume that a set *s* of threads is in the wait set of an object *m*, and another thread performs a `notify` on *m*. Then either:

- at least one thread in *s* must return normally from `wait`, or

- all of the threads in *s* must exit `wait` by throwing `InterruptedException`

Note that if a thread is both interrupted and woken via `notify`, and that thread returns from `wait` by throwing an `InterruptedException`, then some other thread in the wait set must be notified.

17.3   Sleep and Yield

`Thread.sleep` causes the currently executing thread to sleep (temporarily cease execution) for the specified duration, subject to the precision and accuracy of system timers and schedulers. The thread does not lose ownership of any monitors, and resumption of execution will depend on scheduling and the availability of processors on which to execute the thread.

It is important to note that neither `Thread.sleep` nor `Thread.yield` have any synchronization semantics. In particular, the compiler does not have to flush writes cached in registers out to shared memory before a call to `Thread.sleep` or `Thread.yield`, nor does the compiler have to reload values cached in registers after a call to `Thread.sleep` or `Thread.yield`.

> For example, in the following (broken) code fragment, assume that `this.done` is a non-volatile `boolean` field:

```
while (!this.done)
    Thread.sleep(1000);
```

> The compiler is free to read the field `this.done` just once, and reuse the cached value in each execution of the loop. This would mean that the loop would never terminate, even if another thread changed the value of `this.done`.

17.4 Memory Model

A *memory model* describes, given a program and an execution trace of that program, whether the execution trace is a legal execution of the program. The Java programming language memory model works by examining each read in an execution trace and checking that the write observed by that read is valid according to certain rules.

The memory model describes possible behaviors of a program. An implementation is free to produce any code it likes, as long as all resulting executions of a program produce a result that can be predicted by the memory model.

This provides a great deal of freedom for the implementor to perform a myriad of code transformations, including the reordering of actions and removal of unnecessary synchronization.

Example 17.4-1. Incorrectly Synchronized Programs May Exhibit Surprising Behavior

The semantics of the Java programming language allow compilers and microprocessors to perform optimizations that can interact with incorrectly synchronized code in ways that can produce behaviors that seem paradoxical. Here are some examples of how incorrectly synchronized programs may exhibit surprising behaviors.

Consider, for example, the example program traces shown in Table 17.1. This program uses local variables r1 and r2 and shared variables A and B. Initially, A == B == 0.

Table 17.1. Surprising results caused by statement reordering - original code

Thread 1	Thread 2
1: r2 = A;	3: r1 = B;
2: B = 1;	4: A = 2;

It may appear that the result r2 == 2 and r1 == 1 is impossible. Intuitively, either instruction 1 or instruction 3 should come first in an execution. If instruction 1 comes first, it should not be able to see the write at instruction 4. If instruction 3 comes first, it should not be able to see the write at instruction 2.

If some execution exhibited this behavior, then we would know that instruction 4 came before instruction 1, which came before instruction 2, which came before instruction 3, which came before instruction 4. This is, on the face of it, absurd.

However, compilers are allowed to reorder the instructions in either thread, when this does not affect the execution of that thread in isolation. If instruction 1 is reordered with instruction 2, as shown in the trace in Table 17.2, then it is easy to see how the result r2 == 2 and r1 == 1 might occur.

Table 17.2. Surprising results caused by statement reordering - valid compiler transformation

Thread 1	Thread 2
B = 1;	r1 = B;
r2 = A;	A = 2;

To some programmers, this behavior may seem "broken". However, it should be noted that this code is improperly synchronized:

- there is a write in one thread,
- a read of the same variable by another thread,
- and the write and read are not ordered by synchronization.

This situation is an example of a *data race* (§17.4.5). When code contains a data race, counterintuitive results are often possible.

Several mechanisms can produce the reordering in Table 17.2. A Just-In-Time compiler in a Java Virtual Machine implementation may rearrange code, or the processor. In addition, the memory hierarchy of the architecture on which a Java Virtual Machine implementation is run may make it appear as if code is being reordered. In this chapter, we shall refer to anything that can reorder code as a *compiler*.

Another example of surprising results can be seen in Table 17.3. Initially, p == q and p.x == 0. This program is also incorrectly synchronized; it writes to shared memory without enforcing any ordering between those writes.

Table 17.3. Surprising results caused by forward substitution

Thread 1	Thread 2
r1 = p;	r6 = p;
r2 = r1.x;	r6.x = 3;
r3 = q;	
r4 = r3.x;	
r5 = r1.x;	

One common compiler optimization involves having the value read for r2 reused for r5: they arc both reads of r1.x with no intervening write. This situation is shown in Table 17.4.

Table 17.4. Surprising results caused by forward substitution

Thread 1	Thread 2
r1 = p;	r6 = p;
r2 = r1.x;	r6.x = 3;
r3 = q;	
r4 = r3.x;	
r5 = r2;	

Now consider the case where the assignment to r6.x in Thread 2 happens between the first read of r1.x and the read of r3.x in Thread 1. If the compiler decides to reuse the value of r2 for the r5, then r2 and r5 will have the value 0, and r4 will have the value 3. From the perspective of the programmer, the value stored at p.x has changed from 0 to 3 and then changed back.

The memory model determines what values can be read at every point in the program. The actions of each thread in isolation must behave as governed by the semantics of that thread, with the exception that the values seen by each read are determined by the memory model. When we refer to this, we say that the program obeys *intra-thread semantics*. Intra-thread semantics are the semantics for single-threaded programs, and allow the complete prediction of the behavior of a thread based on the values seen by read actions within the thread. To determine if the actions of thread *t* in an execution are legal, we simply evaluate the implementation of thread *t* as it would be performed in a single-threaded context, as defined in the rest of this specification.

Each time the evaluation of thread *t* generates an inter-thread action, it must match the inter-thread action *a* of *t* that comes next in program order. If *a* is a read, then further evaluation of *t* uses the value seen by *a* as determined by the memory model.

This section provides the specification of the Java programming language memory model except for issues dealing with final fields, which are described in §17.5.

> The memory model specified herein is not fundamentally based in the object-oriented nature of the Java programming language. For conciseness and simplicity in our examples, we often exhibit code fragments without class or method definitions, or explicit dereferencing. Most examples consist of two or more threads containing statements with access to local variables, shared global variables, or instance fields of an object. We typically use variables names such as *r1* or *r2* to indicate variables local to a method or thread. Such variables are not accessible by other threads.

17.4.1   Shared Variables

Memory that can be shared between threads is called *shared memory* or *heap memory*.

All instance fields, `static` fields, and array elements are stored in heap memory. In this chapter, we use the term *variable* to refer to both fields and array elements.

Local variables (§14.4), formal method parameters (§8.4.1), and exception handler parameters (§14.20) are never shared between threads and are unaffected by the memory model.

Two accesses to (reads of or writes to) the same variable are said to be *conflicting* if at least one of the accesses is a write.

17.4.2   Actions

An *inter-thread action* is an action performed by one thread that can be detected or directly influenced by another thread. There are several kinds of inter-thread action that a program may perform:

- *Read* (normal, or non-volatile). Reading a variable.

- *Write* (normal, or non-volatile). Writing a variable.

- *Synchronization actions*, which are:

  - *Volatile read*. A volatile read of a variable.

  - *Volatile write*. A volatile write of a variable.

  - *Lock*. Locking a monitor

  - *Unlock*. Unlocking a monitor.

  - The (synthetic) first and last action of a thread.

  - Actions that start a thread or detect that a thread has terminated (§17.4.4).

- *External Actions*. An external action is an action that may be observable outside of an execution, and has a result based on an environment external to the execution.

- *Thread divergence actions* (§17.4.9). A thread divergence action is only performed by a thread that is in an infinite loop in which no memory, synchronization, or external actions are performed. If a thread performs a thread divergence action, it will be followed by an infinite number of thread divergence actions.

Thread divergence actions are introduced to model how a thread may cause all other threads to stall and fail to make progress.

This specification is only concerned with inter-thread actions. We do not need to concern ourselves with intra-thread actions (e.g., adding two local variables and storing the result in a third local variable). As previously mentioned, all threads need to obey the correct intra-thread semantics for Java programs. We will usually refere to inter-thread actions more succinctly as simply *actions*.

An action a is described by a tuple $< t, k, v, u >$, comprising:

- t - the thread performing the action

- k - the kind of action

- v - the variable or monitor involved in the action.

  For lock actions, v is the monitor being locked; for unlock actions, v is the monitor being unlocked.

  If the action is a (volatile or non-volatile) read, v is the variable being read.

  If the action is a (volatile or non-volatile) write, v is the variable being written.

- u - an arbitrary unique identifier for the action

An external action tuple contains an additional component, which contains the results of the external action as perceived by the thread performing the action. This may be information as to the success or failure of the action, and any values read by the action.

Parameters to the external action (e.g., which bytes are written to which socket) are not part of the external action tuple. These parameters are set up by other actions within the thread and can be determined by examining the intra-thread semantics. They are not explicitly discussed in the memory model.

In non-terminating executions, not all external actions are observable. Non-terminating executions and observable actions are discussed in §17.4.9.

17.4.3 Programs and Program Order

Among all the inter-thread actions performed by each thread t, the *program order* of t is a total order that reflects the order in which these actions would be performed according to the intra-thread semantics of t.

A set of actions is *sequentially consistent* if all actions occur in a total order (the execution order) that is consistent with program order, and furthermore, each read *r* of a variable *v* sees the value written by the write *w* to *v* such that:

- *w* comes before *r* in the execution order, and

- there is no other write *w'* such that *w* comes before *w'* and *w'* comes before *r* in the execution order.

Sequential consistency is a very strong guarantee that is made about visibility and ordering in an execution of a program. Within a sequentially consistent execution, there is a total order over all individual actions (such as reads and writes) which is consistent with the order of the program, and each individual action is atomic and is immediately visible to every thread.

If a program has no data races, then all executions of the program will appear to be sequentially consistent.

Sequential consistency and/or freedom from data races still allows errors arising from groups of operations that need to be perceived atomically and are not.

> If we were to use sequential consistency as our memory model, many of the compiler and processor optimizations that we have discussed would be illegal. For example, in the trace in Table 17.3, as soon as the write of 3 to p.x occurred, subsequent reads of that location would be required to see that value.

17.4.4   Synchronization Order

Every execution has a *synchronization order*. A synchronization order is a total order over all of the synchronization actions of an execution. For each thread *t*, the synchronization order of the synchronization actions (§17.4.2) in *t* is consistent with the program order (§17.4.3) of *t*.

Synchronization actions induce the *synchronized-with* relation on actions, defined as follows:

- An unlock action on monitor *m synchronizes-with* all subsequent lock actions on *m* (where "subsequent" is defined according to the synchronization order).

- A write to a volatile variable *v* (§8.3.1.4) *synchronizes-with* all subsequent reads of *v* by any thread (where "subsequent" is defined according to the synchronization order).

- An action that starts a thread *synchronizes-with* the first action in the thread it starts.

- The write of the default value (zero, `false`, or `null`) to each variable *synchronizes-with* the first action in every thread.

  > Although it may seem a little strange to write a default value to a variable before the object containing the variable is allocated, conceptually every object is created at the start of the program with its default initialized values.

- The final action in a thread *T1 synchronizes-with* any action in another thread *T2* that detects that *T1* has terminated.

  > *T2* may accomplish this by calling *T1*.isAlive() or *T1*.join().

- If thread *T1* interrupts thread *T2*, the interrupt by *T1 synchronizes-with* any point where any other thread (including *T2*) determines that *T2* has been interrupted (by having an `InterruptedException` thrown or by invoking `Thread.interrupted` or `Thread.isInterrupted`).

The source of a *synchronizes-with* edge is called a *release*, and the destination is called an *acquire*.

17.4.5 Happens-before Order

Two actions can be ordered by a *happens-before* relationship. If one action *happens-before* another, then the first is visible to and ordered before the second.

If we have two actions *x* and *y*, we write *hb(x, y)* to indicate that *x happens-before y*.

- If *x* and *y* are actions of the same thread and *x* comes before *y* in program order, then *hb(x, y)*.

- There is a *happens-before* edge from the end of a constructor of an object to the start of a finalizer (§12.6) for that object.

- If an action *x synchronizes-with* a following action *y*, then we also have *hb(x, y)*.

- If *hb(x, y)* and *hb(y, z)*, then *hb(x, z)*.

The `wait` methods of class `Object` (§17.2.1) have lock and unlock actions associated with them; their *happens-before* relationships are defined by these associated actions.

It should be noted that the presence of a *happens-before* relationship between two actions does not necessarily imply that they have to take place in that order in an implementation. If the reordering produces results consistent with a legal execution, it is not illegal.

For example, the write of a default value to every field of an object constructed by a thread need not happen before the beginning of that thread, as long as no read ever observes that fact.

More specifically, if two actions share a *happens-before* relationship, they do not necessarily have to appear to have happened in that order to any code with which they do not share a *happens-before* relationship. Writes in one thread that are in a data race with reads in another thread may, for example, appear to occur out of order to those reads.

The *happens-before* relation defines when data races take place.

A set of synchronization edges, *S*, is *sufficient* if it is the minimal set such that the transitive closure of *S* with the program order determines all of the *happens-before* edges in the execution. This set is unique.

It follows from the above definitions that:

- An unlock on a monitor *happens-before* every subsequent lock on that monitor.

- A write to a `volatile` field (§8.3.1.4) *happens-before* every subsequent read of that field.

- A call to `start()` on a thread *happens-before* any actions in the started thread.

- All actions in a thread *happen-before* any other thread successfully returns from a `join()` on that thread.

- The default initialization of any object *happens-before* any other actions (other than default-writes) of a program.

When a program contains two conflicting accesses (§17.4.1) that are not ordered by a happens-before relationship, it is said to contain a *data race*.

The semantics of operations other than inter-thread actions, such as reads of array lengths (§10.7), executions of checked casts (§5.5, §15.16), and invocations of virtual methods (§15.12), are not directly affected by data races.

Therefore, a data race cannot cause incorrect behavior such as returning the wrong length for an array.

A program is *correctly synchronized* if and only if all sequentially consistent executions are free of data races.

If a program is correctly synchronized, then all executions of the program will appear to be sequentially consistent (§17.4.3).

This is an extremely strong guarantee for programmers. Programmers do not need to reason about reorderings to determine that their code contains data races. Therefore they do not need to reason about reorderings when determining whether their code is correctly synchronized. Once the determination that the code is correctly synchronized is made, the programmer does not need to worry that reorderings will affect his or her code.

A program must be correctly synchronized to avoid the kinds of counterintuitive behaviors that can be observed when code is reordered. The use of correct synchronization does not ensure that the overall behavior of a program is correct. However, its use does allow a programmer to reason about the possible behaviors of a program in a simple way; the behavior of a correctly synchronized program is much less dependent on possible reorderings. Without correct synchronization, very strange, confusing and counterintuitive behaviors are possible.

We say that a read r of a variable v is allowed to observe a write w to v if, in the *happens-before* partial order of the execution trace:

- r is not ordered before w (i.e., it is not the case that $hb(r, w)$), and

- there is no intervening write w' to v (i.e. no write w' to v such that $hb(w, w')$ and $hb(w', r)$).

Informally, a read r is allowed to see the result of a write w if there is no *happens-before* ordering to prevent that read.

A set of actions A is *happens-before consistent* if for all reads r in A, where $W(r)$ is the write action seen by r, it is not the case that either $hb(r, W(r))$ or that there exists a write w in A such that $w.v = r.v$ and $hb(W(r), w)$ and $hb(w, r)$.

In a *happens-before consistent* set of actions, each read sees a write that it is allowed to see by the *happens-before* ordering.

Example 17.4.5-1. Happens-before Consistency

For the trace in Table 17.5, initially `A == B == 0`. The trace can observe `r2 == 0` and `r1 == 0` and still be *happens-before consistent*, since there are execution orders that allow each read to see the appropriate write.

Table 17.5. Behavior allowed by happens-before consistency, but not sequential consistency.

Thread 1	Thread 2
B = 1;	A = 2;
r2 = A;	r1 = B;

Since there is no synchronization, each read can see either the write of the initial value or the write by the other thread. An execution order that displays this behavior is:

```
1: B = 1;
3: A = 2;
2: r2 = A;  // sees initial write of 0
4: r1 = B;  // sees initial write of 0
```

Another execution order that is happens-before consistent is:

```
1: r2 = A;  // sees write of A = 2
3: r1 = B;  // sees write of B = 1
2: B = 1;
4: A = 2;
```

In this execution, the reads see writes that occur later in the execution order. This may seem counterintuitive, but is allowed by *happens-before* consistency. Allowing reads to see later writes can sometimes produce unacceptable behaviors.

17.4.6   Executions

An execution E is described by a tuple $< P, A, po, so, W, V, sw, hb >$, comprising:

- P - a program

- A - a set of actions

- po - program order, which for each thread t, is a total order over all actions performed by t in A

- so - synchronization order, which is a total order over all synchronization actions in A

- W - a write-seen function, which for each read r in A, gives $W(r)$, the write action seen by r in E.

- V - a value-written function, which for each write w in A, gives $V(w)$, the value written by w in E.

- sw - synchronizes-with, a partial order over synchronization actions

- hb - happens-before, a partial order over actions

Note that the synchronizes-with and happens-before elements are uniquely determined by the other components of an execution and the rules for well-formed executions (§17.4.7).

An execution is *happens-before consistent* if its set of actions is *happens-before consistent* (§17.4.5).

17.4.7 Well-Formed Executions

We only consider well-formed executions. An execution $E = <P, A, po, so, W, V, sw, hb>$ is well formed if the following conditions are true:

1. Each read sees a write to the same variable in the execution.

    All reads and writes of volatile variables are volatile actions. For all reads r in A, we have $W(r)$ in A and $W(r).v = r.v$. The variable $r.v$ is volatile if and only if r is a volatile read, and the variable $w.v$ is volatile if and only if w is a volatile write.

2. The happens-before order is a partial order.

    The happens-before order is given by the transitive closure of synchronizes-with edges and program order. It must be a valid partial order: reflexive, transitive and antisymmetric.

3. The execution obeys intra-thread consistency.

    For each thread t, the actions performed by t in A are the same as would be generated by that thread in program-order in isolation, with each write w writing the value $V(w)$, given that each read r sees the value $V(W(r))$. Values seen by each read are determined by the memory model. The program order given must reflect the program order in which the actions would be performed according to the intra-thread semantics of P.

4. The execution is *happens-before consistent* (§17.4.6).

5. The execution obeys synchronization-order consistency.

    For all volatile reads r in A, it is not the case that either $so(r, W(r))$ or that there exists a write w in A such that $w.v = r.v$ and $so(W(r), w)$ and $so(w, r)$.

17.4.8 Executions and Causality Requirements

We use $f|_d$ to denote the function given by restricting the domain of f to d. For all x in d, $f|_d(x) = f(x)$, and for all x not in d, $f|_d(x)$ is undefined.

We use $p|_d$ to represent the restriction of the partial order p to the elements in d. For all x,y in d, $p(x,y)$ if and only if $p|_d(x,y)$. If either x or y are not in d, then it is not the case that $p|_d(x,y)$.

A well-formed execution $E = <P, A, po, so, W, V, sw, hb>$ is validated by *committing* actions from A. If all of the actions in A can be committed, then the execution satisfies the causality requirements of the Java programming language memory model.

Starting with the empty set as C_0, we perform a sequence of steps where we take actions from the set of actions A and add them to a set of committed actions C_i to get a new set of committed actions C_{i+1}. To demonstrate that this is reasonable, for each C_i we need to demonstrate an execution E containing C_i that meets certain conditions.

Formally, an execution E *satisfies the causality requirements of the Java programming language memory model* if and only if there exist:

- Sets of actions C_0, C_1, ... such that:

  - C_0 is the empty set

  - C_i is a proper subset of C_{i+1}

  - $A = \cup (C_0, C_1, ...)$

  If A is finite, then the sequence C_0, C_1, ... will be finite, ending in a set $C_n = A$.

  If A is infinite, then the sequence C_0, C_1, ... may be infinite, and it must be the case that the union of all elements of this infinite sequence is equal to A.

- Well-formed executions E_1, ..., where $E_i = <P, A_i, po_i, so_i, W_i, V_i, sw_i, hb_i>$.

Given these sets of actions C_0, ... and executions E_1, ... , every action in C_i must be one of the actions in E_i. All actions in C_i must share the same relative happens-before order and synchronization order in both E_i and E. Formally:

1. C_i is a subset of A_i

2. $hb_i|_{C_i} = hb|_{C_i}$

3. $so_i|_{C_i} = so|_{C_i}$

The values written by the writes in C_i must be the same in both E_i and E. Only the reads in C_{i-1} need to see the same writes in E_i as in E. Formally:

4. $V_i|_{C_i} = V|_{C_i}$

5. $W_i|_{C_{i-1}} = W|_{C_{i-1}}$

All reads in E_i that are not in C_{i-1} must see writes that happen-before them. Each read r in $C_i - C_{i-1}$ must see writes in C_{i-1} in both E_i and E, but may see a different write in E_i from the one it sees in E. Formally:

6. For any read r in $A_i - C_{i-1}$, we have $hb_i(W_i(r), r)$

7. For any read r in $(C_i - C_{i-1})$, we have $W_i(r)$ in C_{i-1} and $W(r)$ in C_{i-1}

Given a set of sufficient synchronizes-with edges for E_i, if there is a release-acquire pair that happens-before (§17.4.5) an action you are committing, then that pair must be present in all E_j, where $j \geq i$. Formally:

8. Let ssw_i be the sw_i edges that are also in the transitive reduction of hb_i but not in *po*. We call ssw_i the *sufficient synchronizes-with edges for* E_i. If $ssw_i(x, y)$ and $hb_i(y, z)$ and z in C_i, then $sw_j(x, y)$ for all $j \geq i$.

   If an action y is committed, all external actions that happen-before y are also committed.

9. If y is in C_i, x is an external action and $hb_i(x, y)$, then x in C_i.

Example 17.4.8-1. Happens-before Consistency Is Not Sufficient

Happens-before consistency is a necessary, but not sufficient, set of constraints. Merely enforcing happens-before consistency would allow for unacceptable behaviors - those that violate the requirements we have established for programs. For example, happens-before consistency allows values to appear "out of thin air". This can be seen by a detailed examination of the trace in Table 17.6.

Table 17.6. Happens-before consistency is not sufficient

Thread 1	Thread 2
`r1 = x;`	`r2 = y;`
`if (r1 != 0) y = 1;`	`if (r2 != 0) x = 1;`

The code shown in Table 17.6 is correctly synchronized. This may seem surprising, since it does not perform any synchronization actions. Remember, however, that a program is correctly synchronized if, when it is executed in a sequentially consistent manner, there are no data races. If this code is executed in a sequentially consistent way, each action will occur in program order, and neither of the writes will occur. Since no writes occur, there can be no data races: the program is correctly synchronized.

Since this program is correctly synchronized, the only behaviors we can allow are sequentially consistent behaviors. However, there is an execution of this program that is happens-before consistent, but not sequentially consistent:

```
r1 = x;  // sees write of x = 1
y = 1;
r2 = y;  // sees write of y = 1
x = 1;
```

This result is happens-before consistent: there is no happens-before relationship that prevents it from occurring. However, it is clearly not acceptable: there is no sequentially consistent execution that would result in this behavior. The fact that we allow a read to see a write that comes later in the execution order can sometimes thus result in unacceptable behaviors.

Although allowing reads to see writes that come later in the execution order is sometimes undesirable, it is also sometimes necessary. As we saw above, the trace in Table 17.5 requires some reads to see writes that occur later in the execution order. Since the reads come first in each thread, the very first action in the execution order must be a read. If that read cannot see a write that occurs later, then it cannot see any value other than the initial value for the variable it reads. This is clearly not reflective of all behaviors.

We refer to the issue of when reads can see future writes as *causality*, because of issues that arise in cases like the one found in Table 17.6. In that case, the reads cause the writes to occur, and the writes cause the reads to occur. There is no "first cause" for the actions. Our memory model therefore needs a consistent way of determining which reads can see writes early.

Examples such as the one found in Table 17.6 demonstrate that the specification must be careful when stating whether a read can see a write that occurs later in the execution (bearing in mind that if a read sees a write that occurs later in the execution, it represents the fact that the write is actually performed carly).

The memory model takes as input a given execution, and a program, and determines whether that execution is a legal execution of the program. It does this by gradually building a set of "committed" actions that reflect which actions were executed by the program. Usually, the next action to be committed will reflect the next action that can be performed by a sequentially consistent execution. However, to reflect reads that need to see later writes, we allow some actions to be committed earlier than other actions that happen-before them.

Obviously, some actions may be committed early and some may not. If, for example, one of the writes in Table 17.6 were committed before the read of that variable, the read could see the write, and the "out-of-thin-air" result could occur. Informally, we allow an action to be committed early if we know that the action can occur without assuming some data race occurs. In Table 17.6, we cannot perform either write early, because the writes cannot occur unless the reads see the result of a data race.

17.4.9   Observable Behavior and Nonterminating Executions

For programs that always terminate in some bounded finite period of time, their behavior can be understood (informally) simply in terms of their allowable executions. For programs that can fail to terminate in a bounded amount of time, more subtle issues arise.

The observable behavior of a program is defined by the finite sets of external actions that the program may perform. A program that, for example, simply prints "Hello" forever is described by a set of behaviors that for any non-negative integer *i*, includes the behavior of printing "Hello" *i* times.

Termination is not explicitly modeled as a behavior, but a program can easily be extended to generate an additional external action *executionTermination* that occurs when all threads have terminated.

We also define a special *hang* action. If behavior is described by a set of external actions including a *hang* action, it indicates a behavior where after the external actions are observed, the program can run for an unbounded amount of time without performing any additional external actions or terminating. Programs can hang if all threads are blocked or if the program can perform an unbounded number of actions without performing any external actions.

A thread can be blocked in a variety of circumstances, such as when it is attempting to acquire a lock or perform an external action (such as a read) that depends on external data.

An execution may result in a thread being blocked indefinitely and the execution's not terminating. In such cases, the actions generated by the blocked thread must consist of all actions generated by that thread up to and including the action that caused the thread to be blocked, and no actions that would be generated by the thread after that action.

To reason about observable behaviors, we need to talk about sets of observable actions.

If O is a set of observable actions for an execution E, then set O must be a subset of E's actions, A, and must contain only a finite number of actions, even if A contains an infinite number of actions. Furthermore, if an action y is in O, and either $hb(x, y)$ or $so(x, y)$, then x is in O.

Note that a set of observable actions are not restricted to external actions. Rather, only external actions that are in a set of observable actions are deemed to be observable external actions.

A behavior B is an allowable behavior of a program P if and only if B is a finite set of external actions and either:

- There exists an execution E of P, and a set O of observable actions for E, and B is the set of external actions in O (If any threads in E end in a blocked state and O contains all actions in E, then B may also contain a *hang* action); or

- There exists a set O of actions such that B consists of a *hang* action plus all the external actions in O and for all $k \geq |O|$, there exists an execution E of P with actions A, and there exists a set of actions O' such that:

  - Both O and O' are subsets of A that fulfill the requirements for sets of observable actions.

  - $O \subseteq O' \subseteq A$

  - $|O'| \geq k$

• *O' - O* contains no external actions

> Note that a behavior *B* does not describe the order in which the external actions in *B* are observed, but other (internal) constraints on how the external actions are generated and performed may impose such constraints.

17.5 `final` Field Semantics

Fields declared final are initialized once, but never changed under normal circumstances. The detailed semantics of `final` fields are somewhat different from those of normal fields. In particular, compilers have a great deal of freedom to move reads of `final` fields across synchronization barriers and calls to arbitrary or unknown methods. Correspondingly, compilers are allowed to keep the value of a `final` field cached in a register and not reload it from memory in situations where a non-`final` field would have to be reloaded.

`final` fields also allow programmers to implement thread-safe immutable objects without synchronization. A thread-safe immutable object is seen as immutable by all threads, even if a data race is used to pass references to the immutable object between threads. This can provide safety guarantees against misuse of an immutable class by incorrect or malicious code. `final` fields must be used correctly to provide a guarantee of immutability.

An object is considered to be *completely initialized* when its constructor finishes. A thread that can only see a reference to an object after that object has been completely initialized is guaranteed to see the correctly initialized values for that object's `final` fields.

The usage model for `final` fields is a simple one: Set the `final` fields for an object in that object's constructor; and do not write a reference to the object being constructed in a place where another thread can see it before the object's constructor is finished. If this is followed, then when the object is seen by another thread, that thread will always see the correctly constructed version of that object's `final` fields. It will also see versions of any object or array referenced by those `final` fields that are at least as up-to-date as the `final` fields are.

Example 17.5-1. `final` **Fields In The Java Memory Model**

The program below illustrates how `final` fields compare to normal fields.

```
class FinalFieldExample {
    final int x;
    int y;
```

```
        static FinalFieldExample f;

        public FinalFieldExample() {
            x = 3;
            y = 4;
        }

        static void writer() {
            f = new FinalFieldExample();
        }

        static void reader() {
            if (f != null) {
                int i = f.x;   // guaranteed to see 3
                int j = f.y;   // could see 0
            }
        }
    }
```

The class `FinalFieldExample` has a `final int` field `x` and a non-`final int` field `y`. One thread might execute the method `writer` and another might execute the method `reader`.

Because the `writer` method writes `f` *after* the object's constructor finishes, the `reader` method will be guaranteed to see the properly initialized value for `f.x`: it will read the value 3. However, `f.y` is not `final`; the `reader` method is therefore not guaranteed to see the value 4 for it.

Example 17.5-2. `final` **Fields For Security**

`final` fields are designed to allow for necessary security guarantees. Consider the following program. One thread (which we shall refer to as thread 1) executes:

```
Global.s = "/tmp/usr".substring(4);
```

while another thread (thread 2) executes

```
String myS = Global.s;
if (myS.equals("/tmp")) System.out.println(myS);
```

`String` objects are intended to be immutable and string operations do not perform synchronization. While the `String` implementation does not have any data races, other code could have data races involving the use of `String` objects, and the memory model makes weak guarantees for programs that have data races. In particular, if the fields of the `String` class were not `final`, then it would be possible (although unlikely) that thread 2 could initially see the default value of 0 for the offset of the string object, allowing it to compare as equal to `"/tmp"`. A later operation on the `String` object might see the correct offset of 4, so that the `String` object is perceived as being `"/usr"`. Many security features of the Java programming language depend upon `String` objects being perceived as truly immutable, even if malicious code is using data races to pass `String` references between threads.

17.5.1   Semantics of `final` Fields

Let *o* be an object, and *c* be a constructor for *o* in which a `final` field *f* is written. A *freeze* action on `final` field *f* of *o* takes place when *c* exits, either normally or abruptly.

Note that if one constructor invokes another constructor, and the invoked constructor sets a `final` field, the freeze for the `final` field takes place at the end of the invoked constructor.

For each execution, the behavior of reads is influenced by two additional partial orders, the dereference chain *dereferences()* and the memory chain *mc()*, which are considered to be part of the execution (and thus, fixed for any particular execution). These partial orders must satisfy the following constraints (which need not have a unique solution):

- Dereference Chain: If an action *a* is a read or write of a field or element of an object *o* by a thread *t* that did not initialize *o*, then there must exist some read *r* by thread *t* that sees the address of *o* such that *r dereferences(r, a)*.

- Memory Chain: There are several constraints on the memory chain ordering:

  - If *r* is a read that sees a write *w*, then it must be the case that *mc(w, r)*.

  - If *r* and *a* are actions such that *dereferences(r, a)*, then it must be the case that *mc(r, a)*.

  - If *w* is a write of the address of an object *o* by a thread *t* that did not initialize *o*, then there must exist some read *r* by thread *t* that sees the address of *o* such that *mc(r, w)*.

Given a write *w*, a freeze *f*, an action *a* (that is not a read of a `final` field), a read *r₁* of the `final` field frozen by *f*, and a read *r₂* such that *hb(w, f)*, *hb(f, a)*, *mc(a, r₁)*, and *dereferences(r₁, r₂)*, then when determining which values can be seen by *r₂*, we consider *hb(w, r₂)*. (This *happens-before* ordering does not transitively close with other *happens-before* orderings.)

Note that the *dereferences* order is reflexive, and *r₁* can be the same as *r₂*.

For reads of `final` fields, the only writes that are deemed to come before the read of the `final` field are the ones derived through the `final` field semantics.

17.5.2   Reading `final` Fields During Construction

A read of a `final` field of an object within the thread that constructs that object is ordered with respect to the initialization of that field within the constructor by the usual *happens-before* rules. If the read occurs after the field is set in the constructor, it sees the value the final field is assigned, otherwise it sees the default value.

17.5.3 Subsequent Modification of final Fields

In some cases, such as deserialization, the system will need to change the final fields of an object after construction. final fields can be changed via reflection and other implementation-dependent means. The only pattern in which this has reasonable semantics is one in which an object is constructed and then the final fields of the object are updated. The object should not be made visible to other threads, nor should the final fields be read, until all updates to the final fields of the object are complete. Freezes of a final field occur both at the end of the constructor in which the final field is set, and immediately after each modification of a final field via reflection or other special mechanism.

Even then, there are a number of complications. If a final field is initialized to a compile-time constant expression (§15.28) in the field declaration, changes to the final field may not be observed, since uses of that final field are replaced at compile time with the value of the constant expression.

Another problem is that the specification allows aggressive optimization of final fields. Within a thread, it is permissible to reorder reads of a final field with those modifications of a final field that do not take place in the constructor.

Example 17.5.3-1. Aggressive Optimization of final Fields

```
class A {
    final int x;
    A() {
        x = 1;
    }

    int f() {
        return d(this,this);
    }

    int d(A a1, A a2) {
        int i = a1.x;
        g(a1);
        int j = a2.x;
        return j - i;
    }

    static void g(A a) {
        // uses reflection to change a.x to 2
    }
}
```

In the d method, the compiler is allowed to reorder the reads of x and the call to g freely. Thus, new A().f() could return –1, 0, or 1.

An implementation may provide a way to execute a block of code in a final-*field-safe context*. If an object is constructed within a final-field-safe context, the reads of a final field of that object will not be reordered with modifications of that final field that occur within that final-field-safe context.

A final-field-safe context has additional protections. If a thread has seen an incorrectly published reference to an object that allows the thread to see the default value of a final field, and then, within a final-field-safe context, reads a properly published reference to the object, it will be guaranteed to see the correct value of the final field. In the formalism, code executed within a final-field-safe context is treated as a separate thread (for the purposes of final field semantics only).

In an implementation, a compiler should not move an access to a final field into or out of a final-field-safe context (although it can be moved around the execution of such a context, so long as the object is not constructed within that context).

> One place where use of a final-field-safe context would be appropriate is in an executor or thread pool. By executing each Runnable in a separate final-field-safe context, the executor could guarantee that incorrect access by one Runnable to a object *o* will not remove final field guarantees for other Runnables handled by the same executor.

17.5.4   Write-protected Fields

Normally, a field that is final and static may not be modified. However, System.in, System.out, and System.err are static final fields that, for legacy reasons, must be allowed to be changed by the methods System.setIn, System.setOut, and System.setErr. We refer to these fields as being *write-protected* to distinguish them from ordinary final fields.

The compiler needs to treat these fields differently from other final fields. For example, a read of an ordinary final field is "immune" to synchronization: the barrier involved in a lock or volatile read does not have to affect what value is read from a final field. Since the value of write-protected fields may be seen to change, synchronization events should have an effect on them. Therefore, the semantics dictate that these fields be treated as normal fields that cannot be changed by user code, unless that user code is in the System class.

17.6 Word Tearing

One consideration for implementations of the Java Virtual Machine is that every field and array element is considered distinct; updates to one field or element must not interact with reads or updates of any other field or element. In particular, two threads that update adjacent elements of a byte array separately must not interfere or interact and do not need synchronization to ensure sequential consistency.

Some processors do not provide the ability to write to a single byte. It would be illegal to implement byte array updates on such a processor by simply reading an entire word, updating the appropriate byte, and then writing the entire word back to memory. This problem is sometimes known as *word tearing*, and on processors that cannot easily update a single byte in isolation some other approach will be required.

Example 17.6-1. Detection of Word Tearing

The following program is a test case to detect word tearing:

```
public class WordTearing extends Thread {
    static final int LENGTH = 8;
    static final int ITERS  = 1000000;
    static byte[] counts    = new byte[LENGTH];
    static Thread[] threads = new Thread[LENGTH];

    final int id;
    WordTearing(int i) {
        id = i;
    }

    public void run() {
        byte v = 0;
        for (int i = 0; i < ITERS; i++) {
            byte v2 = counts[id];
            if (v != v2) {
                System.err.println("Word-Tearing found: " +
                            "counts[" + id + "] = "+ v2 +
                            ", should be " + v);
                return;
            }
            v++;
            counts[id] = v;
        }
    }

    public static void main(String[] args) {
        for (int i = 0; i < LENGTH; ++i)
            (threads[i] = new WordTearing(i)).start();
    }
}
```

This makes the point that bytes must not be overwritten by writes to adjacent bytes.

17.7 Non-atomic Treatment of double and long

For the purposes of the Java programming language memory model, a single write to a non-volatile long or double value is treated as two separate writes: one to each 32-bit half. This can result in a situation where a thread sees the first 32 bits of a 64-bit value from one write, and the second 32 bits from another write.

Writes and reads of volatile long and double values are always atomic.

Writes to and reads of references are always atomic, regardless of whether they are implemented as 32-bit or 64-bit values.

> Some implementations may find it convenient to divide a single write action on a 64-bit long or double value into two write actions on adjacent 32-bit values. For efficiency's sake, this behavior is implementation-specific; an implementation of the Java Virtual Machine is free to perform writes to long and double values atomically or in two parts.
>
> Implementations of the Java Virtual Machine are encouraged to avoid splitting 64-bit values where possible. Programmers are encouraged to declare shared 64-bit values as volatile or synchronize their programs correctly to avoid possible complications.

CHAPTER **18**

Syntax

THIS chapter presents a grammar for the Java programming language.

The grammar presented piecemeal in the preceding chapters (§2.3) is much better for exposition, but it is not well suited as a basis for a parser. The grammar presented in this chapter is the basis for the reference implementation. Note that it is not an LL(1) grammar, though in many cases it minimizes the necessary look ahead.

The grammar below uses the following BNF-style conventions:

- *[x]* denotes zero or one occurrences of *x*.

- *{x}* denotes zero or more occurrences of *x*.

- *(x | y)* means one of either *x* or *y*.

Identifier:
  IDENTIFIER

QualifiedIdentifier:
  Identifier { . Identifier }

QualifiedIdentifierList:
  QualifiedIdentifier { , QualifiedIdentifier }

CompilationUnit:
  [[Annotations] package *QualifiedIdentifier ;]*
                {ImportDeclaration} {TypeDeclaration}

ImportDeclaration:
  import *[*static*] Identifier { . Identifier } [. *] ;*

TypeDeclaration:
  ClassOrInterfaceDeclaration
  ;

ClassOrInterfaceDeclaration:
  {Modifier} (ClassDeclaration | InterfaceDeclaration)

ClassDeclaration:
  NormalClassDeclaration
  EnumDeclaration

InterfaceDeclaration:
  NormalInterfaceDeclaration
  AnnotationTypeDeclaration

NormalClassDeclaration:
  class *Identifier [TypeParameters]*
                *[*extends *Type] [*implements *TypeList] ClassBody*

EnumDeclaration:
  enum *Identifier [*implements *TypeList] EnumBody*

NormalInterfaceDeclaration:
  interface *Identifier [TypeParameters] [*extends *TypeList] InterfaceBody*

AnnotationTypeDeclaration:
  @ interface *Identifier AnnotationTypeBody*

Type:
  BasicType {[]*}*
  ReferenceType {[]*}*

BasicType:
  byte
  short
  char
  int
  long
  float
  double
  boolean

ReferenceType:
  Identifier [TypeArguments] { . Identifier [TypeArguments] }

TypeArguments:
  < TypeArgument { , TypeArgument } >

TypeArgument:
  ReferenceType
  *? [(*extends | super*) ReferenceType]*

NonWildcardTypeArguments:
  < TypeList >

TypeList:
  ReferenceType { , ReferenceType }

TypeArgumentsOrDiamond:
  < >
  TypeArguments

NonWildcardTypeArgumentsOrDiamond:
  < >
  NonWildcardTypeArguments

TypeParameters:
  < TypeParameter { , TypeParameter } >

TypeParameter:
  *Identifier [*extends *Bound]*

Bound:
  ReferenceType { & *ReferenceType }*

Modifier:
   Annotation
   `public`
   `protected`
   `private`
   `static`
   `abstract`
   `final`
   `native`
   `synchronized`
   `transient`
   `volatile`
   `strictfp`

Annotations:
   Annotation {Annotation}

Annotation:
   @ *QualifiedIdentifier [⟨ [AnnotationElement] ⟩]*

AnnotationElement:
   ElementValuePairs
   ElementValue

ElementValuePairs:
   ElementValuePair { , ElementValuePair }

ElementValuePair:
   Identifier = ElementValue

ElementValue:
   Annotation
   Expression1
   ElementValueArrayInitializer

ElementValueArrayInitializer:
   { *[ElementValues] [,]* }

ElementValues:
   ElementValue { , ElementValue }

ClassBody:
  { { *ClassBodyDeclaration* } }

ClassBodyDeclaration:
  ;
  {*Modifier*} *MemberDecl*
  [static] *Block*

MemberDecl:
  MethodOrFieldDecl
  void *Identifier VoidMethodDeclaratorRest*
  Identifier ConstructorDeclaratorRest
  GenericMethodOrConstructorDecl
  ClassDeclaration
  InterfaceDeclaration

MethodOrFieldDecl:
  Type Identifier MethodOrFieldRest

MethodOrFieldRest:
  FieldDeclaratorsRest ;
  MethodDeclaratorRest

FieldDeclaratorsRest:
  VariableDeclaratorRest { , *VariableDeclarator* }

MethodDeclaratorRest:
  FormalParameters {[]} [throws *QualifiedIdentifierList*] (*Block* | ;)

VoidMethodDeclaratorRest:
  FormalParameters [throws *QualifiedIdentifierList*] (*Block* | ;)

ConstructorDeclaratorRest:
  FormalParameters [throws *QualifiedIdentifierList*] *Block*

GenericMethodOrConstructorDecl:
  TypeParameters GenericMethodOrConstructorRest

GenericMethodOrConstructorRest:
  (*Type* | void) *Identifier MethodDeclaratorRest*
  Identifier ConstructorDeclaratorRest

InterfaceBody:
   { { InterfaceBodyDeclaration } }

InterfaceBodyDeclaration:
   ;
   {Modifier} InterfaceMemberDecl

InterfaceMemberDecl:
   InterfaceMethodOrFieldDecl
   void *Identifier VoidInterfaceMethodDeclaratorRest*
   InterfaceGenericMethodDecl
   ClassDeclaration
   InterfaceDeclaration

InterfaceMethodOrFieldDecl:
   Type Identifier InterfaceMethodOrFieldRest

InterfaceMethodOrFieldRest:
   ConstantDeclaratorsRest ;
   InterfaceMethodDeclaratorRest

ConstantDeclaratorsRest:
   ConstantDeclaratorRest { , ConstantDeclarator }

ConstantDeclaratorRest:
   {[]*} = VariableInitializer*

ConstantDeclarator:
   Identifier ConstantDeclaratorRest

InterfaceMethodDeclaratorRest:
   FormalParameters {[]*} [*throws *QualifiedIdentifierList] ;*

VoidInterfaceMethodDeclaratorRest:
   *FormalParameters [*throws *QualifiedIdentifierList] ;*

InterfaceGenericMethodDecl:
   TypeParameters (Type | void*) Identifier InterfaceMethodDeclaratorRest*

FormalParameters:
  (*[FormalParameterDecls]*)

FormalParameterDecls:
  {VariableModifier} Type FormalParameterDeclsRest

VariableModifier:
  `final`
  Annotation

FormalParameterDeclsRest:
  VariableDeclaratorId [, FormalParameterDecls]
  ... VariableDeclaratorId

VariableDeclaratorId:
  Identifier {`[]`*}*

VariableDeclarators:
  VariableDeclarator { , VariableDeclarator }

VariableDeclarator:
  Identifier VariableDeclaratorRest

VariableDeclaratorRest:
  {`[]`*} [= VariableInitializer]*

VariableInitializer:
  ArrayInitializer
  Expression

ArrayInitializer:
  { *[VariableInitializer { , VariableInitializer } [,]]* }

Block:
  { *BlockStatements* }

BlockStatements:
  { *BlockStatement* }

BlockStatement:
  LocalVariableDeclarationStatement
  ClassOrInterfaceDeclaration
  [Identifier :] Statement

LocalVariableDeclarationStatement:
  { *VariableModifier* } *Type VariableDeclarators* ;

Statement:
  Block

  ;

  Identifier : Statement
  StatementExpression ;
  if *ParExpression Statement* [else *Statement*]
  assert *Expression [: Expression]* ;
  switch *ParExpression* { *SwitchBlockStatementGroups* }
  while *ParExpression Statement*
  do *Statement* while *ParExpression* ;
  for (*ForControl*) *Statement*
  break *[Identifier]* ;
  continue *[Identifier]* ;
  return *[Expression]* ;
  throw *Expression* ;
  synchronized *ParExpression Block*
  try *Block (Catches | [Catches] Finally)*
  try *ResourceSpecification Block [Catches] [Finally]*

StatementExpression:
  Expression

Catches:
  CatchClause { CatchClause }

CatchClause:
  `catch` (*{VariableModifier} CatchType Identifier*) *Block*

CatchType:
  QualifiedIdentifier { | QualifiedIdentifier }

Finally:
  `finally` *Block*

ResourceSpecification:
  (*Resources [;]*)

Resources:
  Resource { ; Resource }

Resource:
  {VariableModifier} ReferenceType VariableDeclaratorId = Expression

SwitchBlockStatementGroups:
  { SwitchBlockStatementGroup }

SwitchBlockStatementGroup:
  SwitchLabels BlockStatements

SwitchLabels:
  SwitchLabel { SwitchLabel }

SwitchLabel:
  `case` *Expression* :
  `case` *EnumConstantName* :
  `default` :

EnumConstantName:
  Identifier

ForControl:
  ForVarControl
  ForInit ; [Expression] ; [ForUpdate]

ForVarControl:
  {VariableModifier} Type VariableDeclaratorId ForVarControlRest

ForVarControlRest:
  ForVariableDeclaratorsRest ; [Expression] ; [ForUpdate]
  : Expression

ForVariableDeclaratorsRest:
  [= VariableInitializer] { , VariableDeclarator }

ForInit:
ForUpdate:
  StatementExpression { , StatementExpression }

Expression:
   Expression1 [AssignmentOperator Expression1]

AssignmentOperator:
   =
   +=
   -=
   *=
   /=
   &=
   |=
   ^=
   %=
   <<=
   >>=
   >>>=

Expression1:
   Expression2 [Expression1Rest]

Expression1Rest:
   ? *Expression* : *Expression1*

Expression2:
   Expression3 [Expression2Rest]

Expression2Rest:
   { *InfixOp Expression3* }
   instanceof *Type*

InfixOp:
   | |
   & &
   |
   ^
   &
   ==
   ! =
   <
   >
   <=
   >=
   <<
   >>
   >>>
   +
   –
   *
   /
   %

Expression3:
  PrefixOp Expression3
  ⟨ *(Expression | Type)* ⟩ *Expression3*
  Primary { Selector } { PostfixOp }

PrefixOp:
   ++
   – –
   !
   ~
   +
   –

PostfixOp:
   ++
   – –

Primary:
  Literal
  ParExpression
  `this` *[Arguments]*
  `super` *SuperSuffix*
  `new` *Creator*
  NonWildcardTypeArguments (ExplicitGenericInvocationSuffix | `this` *Arguments)*
  Identifier { . Identifier } [IdentifierSuffix]
  BasicType {`[]`*} .* `class`
  `void . class`

Literal:
  IntegerLiteral
  FloatingPointLiteral
  CharacterLiteral
  StringLiteral
  BooleanLiteral
  NullLiteral

ParExpression:
  (*Expression*)

Arguments:
  (*[Expression { , Expression }]*)

SuperSuffix:
  Arguments
  . Identifier [Arguments]

ExplicitGenericInvocationSuffix:
  `super` *SuperSuffix*
  Identifier Arguments

Creator:
　NonWildcardTypeArguments CreatedName ClassCreatorRest
　CreatedName (ClassCreatorRest | ArrayCreatorRest)

CreatedName:
　Identifier [TypeArgumentsOrDiamond] { . Identifier [TypeArgumentsOrDiamond] }

ClassCreatorRest:
　Arguments [ClassBody]

ArrayCreatorRest:
　[(] {[]} ArrayInitializer | Expression] {[Expression]} {[]})

IdentifierSuffix:
　[({[]} . class | Expression)]
　Arguments
　*. (*class *| ExplicitGenericInvocation |* this *|* super *Arguments |*
　　　　　　new [NonWildcardTypeArguments] InnerCreator)

ExplicitGenericInvocation:
　NonWildcardTypeArguments ExplicitGenericInvocationSuffix

InnerCreator:
　Identifier [NonWildcardTypeArgumentsOrDiamond] ClassCreatorRest

Selector:
　. Identifier [Arguments]
　. ExplicitGenericInvocation
　. this
　. super *SuperSuffix*
　. new *[NonWildcardTypeArguments] InnerCreator*
　[Expression]

EnumBody:
  { *[EnumConstants] [,] [EnumBodyDeclarations]* }

EnumConstants:
  EnumConstant
  EnumConstants , EnumConstant

EnumConstant:
  [Annotations] Identifier [Arguments] [ClassBody]

EnumBodyDeclarations:
  ; *{ClassBodyDeclaration}*

AnnotationTypeBody:
  { *[AnnotationTypeElementDeclarations]* }

AnnotationTypeElementDeclarations:
  AnnotationTypeElementDeclaration
  AnnotationTypeElementDeclarations AnnotationTypeElementDeclaration

AnnotationTypeElementDeclaration:
  {Modifier} AnnotationTypeElementRest

AnnotationTypeElementRest:
  Type Identifier AnnotationMethodOrConstantRest ;
  ClassDeclaration
  InterfaceDeclaration
  EnumDeclaration
  AnnotationTypeDeclaration

AnnotationMethodOrConstantRest:
  AnnotationMethodRest
  ConstantDeclaratorsRest

AnnotationMethodRest:
  ( ) *[[]] [*default *ElementValue]*

Index

M

binary numeric promotion, 119

constant expressions, 536

floating-point operations, 48

integer operations, 43

N

name classification

access control, 152

named packages, 168

annotations, 285

names, 121

names and identifiers, 127

determining the class being instantiated, 434, 435

import declarations, 170

local class declarations, 367

named packages, 168

shadowing and obscuring, 133

narrowing primitive conversion, 90

casting conversion, 108

floating-point operations, 49

narrowing primitive conversion, 91

postfix decrement operator --, 495

postfix increment operator ++, 494

prefix decrement operator --, 497

prefix increment operator ++, 496

widening and narrowing primitive conversion, 93

narrowing reference conversion, 93

casting conversion, 109

native methods, 224, 358

new keyword

abstract classes, 182

constructor declarations, 244, 244

constructor overloading, 251

creation of new class instances, 327

exception analysis of expressions, 308

form of a binary, 341

initial values of variables, 81, 81

instance initializers, 243

kinds of variables, 79

method invocation conversion, 106

names and identifiers, 128

normal and abrupt completion of evaluation, 421

objects, 54, 54

return statement, 396

run-time handling of an exception, 312

String conversion, 99

syntactic classification of a name according to context, 142, 142, 142

types, classes, and interfaces, 82

non-atomic treatment of double and long, 590

normal and abrupt completion of evaluation, 421

causes of Exceptions, 305

normal and abrupt completion of statements, 366, 366

run-time handling of an exception, 312

normal and abrupt completion of statements, 365

method body, 229

normal and abrupt completion of evaluation, 423

run-time handling of an exception, 312

normal annotations, 286

notation, 6

notification, 566

null literal, 39

compile-time step 3: is the chosen method appropriate?, 480

identifiers, 24

kinds of types and values, 42

lexical literals, 430

numeric promotions, 117

S

Appendix A. Limited License Grant

Specification: JSR-000901 Java® Language Specification ("Specification")
Version: 7
Status: Final Release
Release: July 2011

Copyright © 1997, 2013, Oracle America, Inc. and/or its affiliates. All rights reserved.
500 Oracle Parkway, Redwood City, California 94065, U.S.A.

LIMITED LICENSE GRANTS

1. License for Evaluation Purposes. Oracle hereby grants you a fully-paid, non-exclusive, non-transferable, worldwide, limited license (without the right to sublicense), under Oracle's applicable intellectual property rights to view, download, use and reproduce the Specification only for the purpose of internal evaluation. This includes (i) developing applications intended to run on an implementation of the Specification, provided that such applications do not themselves implement any portion(s) of the Specification, and (ii) discussing the Specification with any third party; and (iii) excerpting brief portions of the Specification in oral or written communications which discuss the Specification provided that such excerpts do not in the aggregate constitute a significant portion of the Specification.

2. License for the Distribution of Compliant Implementations. Oracle also grants you a perpetual, non-exclusive, non-transferable, worldwide, fully paid-up, royalty free, limited license (without the right to sublicense) under any applicable copyrights or, subject to the provisions of subsection 4 below, patent rights it may have covering the Specification to create and/or distribute an Independent Implementation of the Specification that: (a) fully implements the Specification including all its required interfaces and functionality; (b) does not modify, subset, superset or otherwise extend the Licensor Name Space, or include any public or protected packages, classes, Java interfaces, fields or methods within the Licensor Name Space other than those required/authorized by the Specification or Specifications being implemented; and (c) passes the Technology Compatibility Kit (including satisfying the requirements of the applicable TCK Users Guide) for such Specification ("Compliant Implementation"). In addition, the foregoing license is expressly conditioned on your not acting outside its scope. No license

is granted hereunder for any other purpose (including, for example, modifying the Specification, other than to the extent of your fair use rights, or distributing the Specification to third parties). Also, no right, title, or interest in or to any trademarks, service marks, or trade names of Oracle or Oracle's licensors is granted hereunder. Java, and Java-related logos, marks and names are trademarks or registered trademarks of Oracle in the U.S. and other countries.

3. Pass-through Conditions. You need not include limitations (a)-(c) from the previous paragraph or any other particular "pass through" requirements in any license You grant concerning the use of your Independent Implementation or products derived from it. However, except with respect to Independent Implementations (and products derived from them) that satisfy limitations (a)-(c) from the previous paragraph, You may neither: (a) grant or otherwise pass through to your licensees any licenses under Oracle's applicable intellectual property rights; nor (b) authorize your licensees to make any claims concerning their implementation's compliance with the Specification in question.

4. Reciprocity Concerning Patent Licenses.

a. With respect to any patent claims covered by the license granted under subparagraph 2 above that would be infringed by all technically feasible implementations of the Specification, such license is conditioned upon your offering on fair, reasonable and non-discriminatory terms, to any party seeking it from You, a perpetual, non-exclusive, non-transferable, worldwide license under Your patent rights which are or would be infringed by all technically feasible implementations of the Specification to develop, distribute and use a Compliant Implementation.

b. With respect to any patent claims owned by Oracle and covered by the license granted under subparagraph 2, whether or not their infringement can be avoided in a technically feasible manner when implementing the Specification, such license shall terminate with respect to such claims if You initiate a claim against Oracle that it has, in the course of performing its responsibilities as the Specification Lead, induced any other entity to infringe Your patent rights.

c. Also with respect to any patent claims owned by Oracle and covered by the license granted under subparagraph 2 above, where the infringement of such claims can be avoided in a technically feasible manner when implementing the Specification such license, with respect to such claims, shall terminate if You initiate a claim against Oracle that its making, having made, using, offering to sell, selling or importing a Compliant Implementation infringes Your patent rights.

5. Definitions. For the purposes of this Agreement: "Independent Implementation" shall mean an implementation of the Specification that neither derives from any

of Oracle's source code or binary code materials nor, except with an appropriate and separate license from Oracle, includes any of Oracle's source code or binary code materials; "Licensor Name Space" shall mean the public class or interface declarations whose names begin with "java", "javax", "com.sun" or their equivalents in any subsequent naming convention adopted by Oracle through the Java Community Process, or any recognized successors or replacements thereof; and "Technology Compatibility Kit" or "TCK" shall mean the test suite and accompanying TCK User's Guide provided by Oracle which corresponds to the Specification and that was available either (i) from Oracle 120 days before the first release of Your Independent Implementation that allows its use for commercial purposes, or (ii) more recently than 120 days from such release but against which You elect to test Your implementation of the Specification.

This Agreement will terminate immediately without notice from Oracle if you breach the Agreement or act outside the scope of the licenses granted above.

DISCLAIMER OF WARRANTIES

THE SPECIFICATION IS PROVIDED "AS IS". ORACLE MAKES NO REPRESENTATIONS OR WARRANTIES, EITHER EXPRESS OR IMPLIED, INCLUDING BUT NOT LIMITED TO, WARRANTIES OF MERCHANTABILITY, FITNESS FOR A PARTICULAR PURPOSE, NON-INFRINGEMENT (INCLUDING AS A CONSEQUENCE OF ANY PRACTICE OR IMPLEMENTATION OF THE SPECIFICATION), OR THAT THE CONTENTS OF THE SPECIFICATION ARE SUITABLE FOR ANY PURPOSE. This document does not represent any commitment to release or implement any portion of the Specification in any product. In addition, the Specification could include technical inaccuracies or typographical errors.

LIMITATION OF LIABILITY

TO THE EXTENT NOT PROHIBITED BY LAW, IN NO EVENT WILL ORACLE OR ITS LICENSORS BE LIABLE FOR ANY DAMAGES, INCLUDING WITHOUT LIMITATION, LOST REVENUE, PROFITS OR DATA, OR FOR SPECIAL, INDIRECT, CONSEQUENTIAL, INCIDENTAL OR PUNITIVE DAMAGES, HOWEVER CAUSED AND REGARDLESS OF THE THEORY OF LIABILITY, ARISING OUT OF OR RELATED IN ANY WAY TO YOUR HAVING, IMPLEMENTING OR OTHERWISE USING THE SPECIFICATION, EVEN IF ORACLE AND/OR ITS LICENSORS HAVE BEEN ADVISED OF THE POSSIBILITY OF SUCH DAMAGES.

You will indemnify, hold harmless, and defend Oracle and its licensors from any claims arising or resulting from: (i) your use of the Specification; (ii) the use or distribution of your Java application, applet and/or implementation; and/or (iii) any claims that later versions or releases of any Specification furnished to you are incompatible with the Specification provided to you under this license.

RESTRICTED RIGHTS LEGEND

U.S. Government: If this Specification is being acquired by or on behalf of the U.S. Government or by a U.S. Government prime contractor or subcontractor (at any tier), then the Government's rights in the Software and accompanying documentation shall be only as set forth in this license; this is in accordance with 48 C.F.R. 227.7201 through 227.7202-4 (for Department of Defense (DoD) acquisitions) and with 48 C.F.R. 2.101 and 12.212 (for non-DoD acquisitions).

REPORT

If you provide Oracle with any comments or suggestions concerning the Specification ("Feedback"), you hereby: (i) agree that such Feedback is provided on a non-proprietary and non-confidential basis, and (ii) grant Oracle a perpetual, non-exclusive, worldwide, fully paid-up, irrevocable license, with the right to sublicense through multiple levels of sublicensees, to incorporate, disclose, and use without limitation the Feedback for any purpose.

GENERAL TERMS

Any action related to this Agreement will be governed by California law and controlling U.S. federal law. The U.N. Convention for the International Sale of Goods and the choice of law rules of any jurisdiction will not apply.

The Specification is subject to U.S. export control laws and may be subject to export or import regulations in other countries. Licensee agrees to comply strictly with all such laws and regulations and acknowledges that it has the responsibility to obtain such licenses to export, re-export or import as may be required after delivery to Licensee.

This Agreement is the parties' entire agreement relating to its subject matter. It supersedes all prior or contemporaneous oral or written communications, proposals, conditions, representations and warranties and prevails over any conflicting or additional terms of any quote, order, acknowledgment, or other communication between the parties relating to its subject matter during the term of this Agreement. No modification to this Agreement will be binding, unless in writing and signed by an authorized representative of each party.